Research Methods in
Psychology

This book is dedicated to Dr Lynne Millward, 1962–2012

4th Edition

Research Methods in
Psychology

Edited by

Glynis M. Breakwell, Jonathan A. Smith and Daniel B. Wright

Los Angeles | London | New Delhi
Singapore | Washington DC

Los Angeles | London | New Delhi
Singapore | Washington DC

SAGE Publications Ltd
1 Oliver's Yard
55 City Road
London EC1Y 1SP

SAGE Publications Inc.
2455 Teller Road
Thousand Oaks, California 91320

SAGE Publications India Pvt Ltd
B 1/I 1 Mohan Cooperative Industrial Area
Mathura RoadA
New Delhi 110 044

SAGE Publications Asia-Pacific Pte Ltd
3 Church Street
#10-04 Samsung Hub
Singapore 049483

Editor: Michael Carmichael
Development editor: Robin Lupton
Editorial assistant: Alana Clogan
Production editor: Katherine Haw
Copyeditor: Cenveo Publisher Services
Proofreader: Cenveo Publisher Services
Marketing manager: Michael Ainsley
Cover design: Wendy Scott
Typeset by: Cenveo Publisher Services
Printed by: Ashford Colour Press Ltd,
    Gosport, Hants

FSC
www.fsc.org
MIX
Paper from
responsible sources
FSC® C011748

First published 2012

Library of Congress Control Number: 2012930912

British Library Cataloguing in Publication data

A catalogue record for this book is available from
the British Library

ISBN 978-0-85702-263-9
ISBN 978-0-85702-264-6 (pbk)

Contents

List of Contributors

Dame Glynis M. Breakwell has been a Professor of Psychology for over 20 years and is currently the Vice Chancellor of the University of Bath. Her research focuses upon identity process theory and social representations, leadership in complex organisations, and the psychology of risk management, perception and communication. She has published more than 20 books, several of which are on research methods. She is an adviser to government and private sector companies on the use of psychological methods and theories.

Marianna E. Carlucci received her PhD in psychology from Florida International University. She is an Assistant Professor at Loyola University Maryland in Baltimore. Her main research area is in eyewitness memory.

Adrian Coyle is a senior lecturer and the Course Director for the MSc in social psychology in the School of Psychology at the University of Surrey. His research and publications have addressed a range of topics, principally psychological issues in religion and spirituality, identity, bereavement and sexuality. The vast majority of his research is qualitative, employing a range of methods. With Evanthia Lyons, he was editor of *Analysing Qualitative Data in Psychology*.

Rudi Dallos is Professor and Director of Clinical Psychology at Plymouth University. His clinical work specialises in family therapy which includes live and recorded observation of family dynamics. His research interests include explorations of family dynamics in relation to eating disorders and self-harm and attachment dynamics. Recent publications include *An Introduction to Family Therapy*, *Reflective Practice in Psychotherapy* and *Counselling* and *Research Methods in Counselling and Psychotherapy*.

Virginia Eatough is a lecturer in the Department of Psychological Sciences at Birkbeck University of London where she teaches qualitative research methods and critical analysis. Her primary research focus is the study of emotion and emotional experience from a phenomenological psychology perspective. In particular she is interested in the role of feelings in our emotional life. Primarily, she uses hermeneutic–phenomenological approaches, such as interpretative phenomenological analysis (IPA), as well as techniques that emphasise accessing the tacit pre-reflective dimensions of experience, such as focusing and meditation. Other related and ongoing research interests include adult crying, alexithymia, living with chronic progressive illness such as Parkinson's disease, and developing the relationship between phenomenological methods and neuroscience.

Chris Fife-Schaw is a Professor and former Head of Psychology at the University of Surrey. His research has included studies of perceptions of food-related hazards, young people's responses to AIDS/HIV, public responses to genetic technologies and risk perception and communication of water-borne hazards. He lectures in social psychology, research methods and structural equation modelling, and his research interests are in risk perception, models of behavioural regulation and developing alternative measures of attitudes that do not involve questionnaires.

Karen Henwood is a Professor in the School of Social Sciences at Cardiff University. She has long-standing research interests in qualitative research methodologies and methods in the social sciences and psychology. Her 1992 article (with Nick Pidgeon) in the *British Journal of Psychology* 'Qualitative research and psychological theorising' was followed by many co-authored book chapters on grounded theory. Most recently she has written about qualitative longitudinal/temporal research methods for the APA *Handbook of Qualitative Methods in Psychology*. She has published findings from a number of large-scale, qualitative and mixed methods projects, and works mainly in interdisciplinary fields of inquiry (gender, risk, environment).

Graham Hole is a senior lecturer in the School of Psychology at the University of Sussex. He has a wide experience of using different methodologies in psychological research, having started his career performing observational studies of animal behaviour before shifting to using psychophysical techniques to investigate low-level visual perception. His current research interests centre around using experimental methods to investigate two different areas of cognitive psychology: 'pure' research on face recognition, and 'applied' research on perception and attention in relation to car driving. He has written 50 scientific papers and three books, including *How to Design and Report Experiments*, co-authored with Andy Field.

Kamala London is an Associate Professor of Psychology at the University of Toledo. Her research examines how we can tailor forensic proceedings to best suit children's developing abilities. She teaches undergraduate and graduate courses on statistics and developmental psychology. She has served as an expert witness in about 20 states across the United States, at Fort Knox for the US Military and also in New Zealand. She has presented her research at dozens of national and international conferences, invited talks and in various publications. She has written over 25 publications, including two co-authored award-winning statistics textbooks. Her work has been cited by the United States Supreme Court.

Katherine McGuire is a doctoral student in the psychology department at the University of Toledo. She teaches undergraduate courses in statistics and psychology. Her main interests include memory development in children, adolescents and young adults with an emphasis on psychology and the law.

Jeremy Miles is a behavioural scientist working at the RAND Corporation, and is Professor of Quantitative Methods at the Pardee-RAND Graduate school. He is author of over 100 journal articles and several books, including *Applying Regression and Correlation* (with Mark Shevlin) and *Discovering Statistics Using SAS* (with Andy Field). He is associate editor of the *British Journal of Mathematical and Statistical Psychology* and statistical advisor to the editorial board of both the *British Journal of Health Psychology* and the *British Journal of Clinical Psychology*.

Lynne Millward was an Occupational and Social Psychologist who practised applied psychology in the work and organisational domain for 20 years. Her research was oriented primarily towards informing organisational strategy and policy on issues such as equal opportunities, merger, diversity, recruitment, retention, training and development, appraisal, stress management and change management. This work was funded by a range of bodies and organisations, including the Economic and Social Research Council, the Ministry of Defence, QinetiQ, the National Health Service and the National Audit Office. She was author or co-author of three books: *Understanding Occupational and Organizational Psychology, Organizational Research Methods, and Basic Evaluation Methods: Analysing Performance, Practice and Procedure*. At the time of her death in 2012, Lynne was Reader in the School of Psychology at the University of Surrey where she fulfilled the role of Undergraduate Course Director.

Nick Pidgeon is Professor of Applied Psychology at Cardiff University. He has research interests in people's perception of risk and its communication with particular applications to public policy decision making, environmental issues (such as biotechnology, nuclear power and climate change) and industrial safety. He has authored (jointly with Karen Henwood) a number of methodological papers on grounded theory for psychologists.

John Rust is Professor of Psychometrics and Director of the Psychometrics Centre at the University of Cambridge. He is author of *Modern Psychometrics*, now in its third edition, as well as several psychometric tests and UK standardisation projects. His recent work focuses on the development of Concerto, an open source system for the administration of adaptive tests online.

Jonathan A. Smith is Professor of Psychology at Birkbeck University of London. His main interests lie in the application of qualitative methods in psychology. He has edited a number of books in this area. He has also developed a particular qualitative approach, interpretative phenomenological analysis, and employed it in a wide range of research projects in psychology.

Patrick Sturgis is Professor of Research Methodology and Director of the ESRC National Centre for Research Methods. He has a BA in Psychology from the University of Liverpool and a Master of Science and PhD in Social Psychology from the London School of Economics. His research interests are in the areas of survey methodology, statistical modelling, public opinion and political behaviour, public understanding of science and technology, social capital, and social mobility. He is Principal Investigator of the Wellcome Monitor Study and President of the European Survey Research Association (ESRA).

Daniella K. Villalba is a graduate student at Florida International University. Her research interests centre around the interaction between psychology and the law. Her main research focus is eyewitness memory. Specifically, she is interested in the underlying factors that lead witnesses to become overconfident in lineup identifications and in finding ways to prevent overconfidence. She is also interested in examining investigative interviewing techniques that can help witnesses provide more detailed and accurate accounts of the witnessed event. Finally, she is interested in examining the circumstances in which memory conformity is more likely to occur.

Daniel B. Wright is a Professor of Legal Psychology at Florida International University. His interests are in human memory (particularly eyewitness reliability) and methodology (particularly statistics). He received the 2009 Psychonomics Society award for methodology.

What This Book Does: Key features and additional resources

Our primary aim in all four editions of this book has been to provide clear and practical guidance to the major research methods used in psychology. The book has broad methodological coverage and is written by people whom we consider to be experts in using a particular approach. We believe both quantitative and qualitative methods have an important contribution to make to psychology and therefore we give extensive coverage of both.

It is gratifying to hear that our aims have been realized; we've received some wonderful feedback over the years that the book is very accessible to students. Therefore this edition retains all the qualities that have become tried and trusted. However, in order to make the book even more comprehensive, this fourth edition includes a number of new chapters offering much more extensive coverage of statistics and there are additional new chapters on content analysis and writing up your research. In order to make the book accessible and engaging, the book and its companion website incorporate a range of user-friendly features.

Key features in every chapter of the book include:

1. Opening chapter aims and introductions
2. Key terms for each chapter. In addition definitions for each term are available in the glossary at the back of the book
3. A range of text boxes with multiple functions, these include:
   - Outlines of key psychological studies
   - Summaries of concepts, statistical formulae and methodological debates presented in an interesting and engaging manner

- Examples of process of analysis
- Presentations of similarities/differences in contrasting approaches to doing psychological research

4. Suggested further readings at the end of every chapter

5. Exercises and discussion questions for each chapter to help students reflect on and test what they have learned

About the Companion Website

Additional online resources to help support your learning are available at http://www.sagepub.co.uk/breakwell4e

For Lecturers:

- **Testbank questions** for selected chapters providing a time saving question bank, which can be used to prompt in-class discussion, for assignments or exams. The quantitative chapters are supported by 20 multiple-choice questions and the qualitative chapters by 3 short-answer questions.
- **PowerPoint Slides** containing the key figures and tables from the book can be quickly and easily adapted to support your lecturers.
- **VLE Cartridge** allowing lecturers to quickly upload these additional materials to virtual learning environments.

For Students:

- **Short-answer and multiple-choice questions** from selected chapters (subdivided as for the lecturer testbank) allowing you to test your understanding.
- **Flashcards** of items in glossary for each chapter to provide a quick and engaging way to revise these for exams.

Part 1

Introduction

1

Research Questions and Planning Research

Glynis M. Breakwell, Daniel B. Wright and Jonathan A. Smith

CONTENTS

1.1 WHAT IS THIS BOOK FOR?

This book is designed to be a fairly comprehensive introduction to the research methods used in psychology. It is aimed at students who may be learning about these methods for the first time – either as undergraduates or postgraduates. However, it can also act as a source for experienced researchers who simply want to refresh and update their appreciation of particular methods.

This is the fourth edition of the book and it is very different from the earlier ones. Unlike earlier editions, it integrates explanations and illustrations of the statistics that can be used in research designs. It is more focused on presenting a step-by-step description of the methods and assumes no prior exposure to the methods. It is consequently much more usable by first and second year undergraduates. It is written by an international team of contributors who are attuned to the demands of a variety of different educational courses – in both North America and in Europe.

1.2 HOW IS THE BOOK ORGANISED?

The book covers the most common approaches in both quantitative and qualitative methods. It is broken into two main sections. The first deals with quantitative methods, including the most popular statistical techniques that are used. The second deals with qualitative methods. Each section has its own introduction explaining the distinctive natures of the two approaches to doing research. Therefore, this chapter is brief and deals with the more general issues that need to be considered when conducting research.

1.3 AIMS OF THE CHAPTER

This chapter covers the general issues that you should consider when:

- choosing a research question;
- choosing a research method;
- planning the research;
- executing the research.

Exercises are provided that allow you to test your understanding of these issues.

1.4 CHOOSING A RESEARCH QUESTION

Irrespective of the research method used, research is essentially the process of collecting information and then interpreting it. In addition, researchers increasingly regard communicating their findings as part of the research task. The nature of the information collected will be determined by the research question that you ask. What is a 'research question'? Well, first, it needs to be distinguished from a research topic.

People choose their research topics for all sorts of reasons – such as personal interest or curiosity, professional necessity associated with doing a particular job or solving a specific practical problem or a desire to explore a theory. However, selecting and pursuing a research topic is not always a simple matter. What initially seems like an interesting and important issue may be difficult to address for a variety of reasons. These difficulties normally boil down to two groups:

- the conceptual obstacles – for example, the topic is so multi-faceted and complex that it is difficult to know where to start collecting your information;

- the practical obstacles – for example, you do not have the resources (i.e. the time, money or expertise) to collect the information you need, or you cannot get access to the information you need (i.e. permissions are not forthcoming or the technology that would allow the information to be collected is not available for one reason or another).

These two types of obstacle mean that researchers have to refine their research topic and be very selective in the issues that they will choose to address. Refinement and selection typically involve stripping away some layers of the research topic and concentrating on a particular element of it. This process of stripping away should result in a very precise 'research question' that can be addressed in practice.

Box 1.1 describes a classic example of the way a research question can be addressed in a manageable way in practice. The 'Bobo doll' experiment illustrated that children would copy behaviour that they observed if the person exhibiting the behaviour was rewarded for it. It also showed that the effect occurred even when the person was observed on video. This was subsequently tied to arguments about the impact of violence portrayed on TV or in films upon the development of aggressive behaviour in children. It is however important to remember that the original 'Bobo doll' experiments were not designed to address the research question, 'Does watching violence on TV lead to the audience acting in a more violent way in their everyday lives?' The experiments were never designed to test the effect of anything that closely resembled the sort of violence seen on TV and they

Box 1.1 Stripping the research question down to basics

'Why are people aggressive?' This is a question that has been asked through the ages of human civilization. Recently, aggression has been seen as just a specific form of social behaviour which is acquired and maintained in the same way as any other social behaviour. This would suggest that we 'learn' aggression. We 'learn' when our aggression is rewarded or punished and, according to learning theory, this will shape whether and when we will act aggressively. Also, we observe others and learn when, where and with whom we should be aggressive by watching what others do and how they are treated.

The important research question is: Do we learn our aggressive behaviour from other people? This is a very big question. Too big to address unless it can be refined – stripped down to a core that allows us to test a specific assertion. Bandura, Ross and Ross (1961, 1963) did just that in a series of experiments that are regarded as classics (the 'Bobo doll' studies). In the experiments, some children observed an adult playing with some toys: he stormed into the room and hit a doll (the Bobo doll) with a large rubber hammer, and then kicked and shouted at it. Other children saw the adult playing quietly with the toys. In another phase of the experiment, the man was either seen to be rewarded by the experimenter or not. The children then had a chance to play with the same toys. They were more likely to imitate the man's behaviour when he had been rewarded for it. This occurred whether they had seen the man on a video or in the flesh. Further, the effect was found irrespective of whether the person watched was real or a comic character.

These experiments stripped the big research question down to a manageable and specific question: Do children emulate the aggression exhibited by a model that they have observed if the model has been rewarded for being aggressive and they are subsequently placed in the same context as that model? The answer to this question becomes part of the answer to the bigger question.

did not assess any effects of behaviour in natural settings. Extrapolation from the experiments to the impact of TV violence would be unjustified. Bandura and his colleagues in generating their 'stripped down research question' could provide one example, from a closely controlled situation, of the way social modelling of behaviour occurs. In doing so, they provided a platform for other researchers to start to examine further how social modelling affects aggression, but it is important not to lose track of the limitations of what can actually be asserted on the basis of a single experiment.

One way to develop a manageable research question is to list all of the aspects of the research topic that interest you and then to focus in on the aspect that you regard as most crucial. This can be thought about as a process of mapping the relationships between different aspects of the topic and then serially focusing down upon the details of one aspect. It is then possible to map the elements within that one aspect. The greatest problem with most initial research proposals we read is that they try to tackle too much. Rome was not built in a day, and to address all aspects of most interesting research questions requires multiple teams of researchers using a variety of methods. What is important is that your research is done well enough to be part of this multi-pronged attack! Box 1.2 gives an outline of mapping a research topic.

Mapping of this sort is useful because you have to sort out what you think are the key elements in the topic that you want to explore. Exercise 1, at the end of this chapter, presents you with a mapping task. You might want to try it now.

The mapping exercise will also provide you with basis for conducting a systematic literature search of the research that has been done on the research question in the past. If you start with too broad a research topic, conducting a literature search can be a nightmare – the volume of material is too great and a lot of it will in reality be irrelevant to your prime concerns and interests. It is useful to do the mapping

Box 1.2 Mapping a research topic

Let us start with the broad research topic:

Does the way you speak affect the way other people treat you?

Mapping would ensure that the research examines each element of the question to define its meaning. So, what is meant by 'the way you speak'? Is it the content of what you say? Is it the emotional tone? Is it your accent? Is it your dialect? Is it non-verbal accompaniments of speech (like gestures)? Or is it the vocal but not verbal elements of your speech (such as speed of delivery)? Similarly, what is meant by 'affect'? Is it direct or indirect influence? Is it immediate or slow to emerge? Is it short or long term? Is it consistent or occasional? Is it accidental or deliberate? And so on. Who are the 'other people'? Is it a specific group or type of person? What is their relationship with you? Finally, what is meant by 'treat you'? Is it the way these people react to you personally and directly at the time of the interaction or is it the way they deal with you subsequently? Is it what they say and do or is it what they think? The mapping would also query whether the context of the interaction was important to the effect of your speech upon the other person. It would look to outline likely contextual effects.

So the initial broad research topic might be specifically mapped as:

If you speak in a way that is stereotypically regarded as characteristic of people from a disadvantaged background during an interview you will be less likely to get a job offer than if you displayed standard speech patterns.

Box 1.2 (Continued)

Equally, it could be specifically mapped as:

> If you speak with your own local accent in a family social gathering you will be regarded by family members as more trustworthy.

There are many other specific mappings that could be produced. You might like to see how many you can generate. The important thing to remember when you do the mapping is that you want to arrive at a question that is specific enough for you to be able to collect information that will allow you to answer the question. After you have the specific question, you will still need to generate an operational definition of each of the elements of the question. This is a different sort of mapping. An operational definition of an element is a statement of how that element will be assessed (or measured) within the research. So, for instance, in respect of the second research question above, how would you assess whether family members regarded the speaker as more trustworthy? It could be operationalised in terms of the willingness of family members to follow instructions or advice you give. It could be measured using simple ratings by family members. The important thing here is that you should be clear about the operational definitions of each element in the research question. There are usually several ways to operationalise a concept. You should try to be clear on why you choose the one that you do. Most significant psychological constructs (like intelligence or personality) can be operationalised in many ways, and often the one you choose will be driven by the theory that you find most useful.

exercise even if you are already aware of literature in an area because the specific refined research question may alert you to new literatures.

The literature search is usually a very important element in conducting research. Once you have your first version of a precise research question, it makes sense to conduct the literature search. The literature search should tell you whether the work you are thinking of doing has already been done. It should tell you what methods other people have used to address the question or similar questions. It should tell you what other people have found. It should tell you how they have interpreted their findings. It should tell you whether there is consensus or disagreement in findings and in their interpretation. It should tell you the key researchers in the area in which you are interested. It will tell you where this type of research is usually published, so you know where you might expect to publish your work when the time comes. It will show you the expectations that other researchers have about the details that need to be provided about the information collection and analysis in studies on this research area. Some sort of literature search is almost always an integral part of doing excellent research. Different researchers have different views on how comprehensive the search should be – for some it should be as complete as possible, for others it is more like a sampling exercise – helping the researcher to see the type of work that has been done. Once you have done the search, you should be able to further refine your research question. You will be able to elaborate it or simplify it as a result of knowing what other researchers have discovered and concluded. There is now no excuse for failure to conduct a literature search with the availability of electronic databases internationally.

This chapter does not examine how theory can often be the source used for developing a clear research question. In previous editions of this book (Breakwell & Rose, 2006) the role of theory was described in the introductory chapters. In this edition, the editors have decided that the role of theory construction and testing should be considered in the individual chapters where methods are described so that the diversity of approaches to the role of theory can be better understood (see also Jaccard & Jacoby, 2010).

1.5 CHOOSING A RESEARCH METHOD

Most research topics can be addressed by most research methods – at some level and to some degree. The research methods that you choose to use for any specific research question will depend to some extent upon your own theoretical and methodological preferences. However, often the nature of the research question implicates a particular research method as the most suitable one for that study. In choosing a method you might consider a series of questions:

- Is the method compatible with the theoretical assumptions built into your research question?

- Will the method allow you to collect the key information you need to address the research question?

- Will the method allow you to draw inferences from the information collected that are justifiable in the face of critical review?

- Do you have the time, resources and expertise to apply the method properly?

- If you use it, will the other researchers that work in the area listen to your conclusions?

1.6 PLANNING THE RESEARCH

Having chosen your research question and having chosen your method, you still have to plan the research. This entails working through in detail the sequence of activities that go to make up the research study. Usually the activities fall into clusters:

- Designing the study – specifying what information you need and how you will collect it, from whom, and when and where.

- Preparing materials (including for instance, questionnaires, laboratory space, interview schedules).

- Identifying participants for the study and then contacting and gaining their agreement to be involved (including timetabling information collection from them).

- Ensuring that what you intend to do is ethical (see more on this below).

- Collection of information.

- Collation and recording of information.

- Analysis of information – always decide on your analytical approach before you collect the information. The analytical approach will affect the number of participants you need and the structure of the information that you have to collect.

- Reporting of analysis and dissemination of conclusions (including feedback to participants if relevant).

You should identify what you need to achieve in each of these areas of activity and gain a realistic idea of how long it will take and what resources (e.g. help from other people or financial support) it will need.

An important part of preparing the main information collection is the piloting of the research. Piloting is necessary irrespective of the method you use. Basically, piloting entails checking out whether the techniques that you are using to collect information are actually doing what you think they are doing. It involves running the information collection process with a small number of participants to see if there are unanticipated difficulties. In such pilots, the participants are often asked to give their feedback on how they reacted to what happened to them and this is used to improve the study. Sometimes, pilot studies can prevent a lot of wasted time and effort. The information collected from the pilot study should not be included in the data collected from the main study. The pilot is really a trial of the way the study is designed and is being executed, so material from it should not be indiscriminately mixed with information collected subsequently in the full study.

Following the pilot work, it may be necessary to refine the means of collecting information or change the definition of the participant group (or even tweak your research question). For instance, you may pilot an interview schedule with a group of children and find that it works well with 11-year-olds but not with any less than 8 years of age. You then have to decide whether to change the interview schedule or stick with only having participants over the age of 8. If you change the interview schedule, you may consider it necessary to do another pilot study to check that the new schedule actually did work with the younger age groups.

Once the piloting has been completed, the overall plan for the conduct of the research can be outlined. Having the plan, and sticking to it as far as possible, is a useful discipline. Of course, plans often change as you get into a study and things do not quite pan out as you expected. Consciously adjusting the plan as things change is important. Revisit the plan and update it. Do not allow circumstances to make you lose track of what you should be doing.

1.7 EXECUTING THE RESEARCH

Putting the research design into practice should simply require diligence if the earlier planning has been comprehensive. However, there are some generic pointers to take into account when executing a research plan:

- Do not bite off more than you can chew – be realistic about what you are able to do. If in doubt, get a more experienced researcher to check your plan to see whether it is practicable.

- Before embarking on the information collection, ask yourself, 'Have I ignored something important?' This is the time to be self-critical. Everyone makes errors, so it pays to check what you are missing. If you have the slightest doubt about the viability of what you are going to do, stop and think it through again.

- Check what you are going to do against what other people have done before – if you are doing it differently, do you know why and what it will mean for the information you collect?

- Know exactly what you have done and make sure you are able to describe it in detail so that another researcher could do the same things subsequently. Good record keeping is essential. Having the habit of recording what you do and think in the course of research is tremendously useful, especially if you want to go back to a study some time later to develop it further or simply to re-do it.

When designing or executing a piece of research it is imperative that you comply with ethical standards that have been developed in psychology. Internationally, professional associations of psychologists have evolved regulations that indicate where the boundaries of ethical research practice lie. The specifics are changing over time and any researcher should consult the code of ethics that applies in their own area of practice. For example, the reference list gives the American Psychological Association and the British Psychological Society websites that contain their codes of ethics. The essential ingredients of these ethical codes can be summarised as:

- Never put participants at risk either physically or mentally – avoid any harm.

- Wherever possible, participants should be fully informed of the purpose and content of the research so that they can give their informed consent to their participation.

- Intentional deception of participants should be avoided if at all possible and particularly where participants are likely to object once they are told they have been deceived. Where possible, alternatives to deception should be adopted.

- Participants should be fully aware that they can withdraw from the study at any point in it and can refuse to have information that they have given used subsequently. It should be stressed that they can do this without penalty.

- Naturalistic observation of participants in everyday settings creates specific ethical issues. Gaining informed consent may not be possible. Participants are not aware they are in the study so they cannot withdraw from it. This means that the researcher must be scrupulous in protecting the privacy and the well-being of those who are observed.

- Information collected should be kept confidential unless prior authorisation is given by the participant. The anonymity of participants should be assured unless otherwise agreed with them.

- Participants should be 'debriefed' at the end of a study (i.e. they should be told what the researcher was trying to discover and why any manipulation of the participants was done).

- The ethics of a study also extend to the way information is used once it is analysed. The researcher must be alert to the potential ancillary uses to which information or results may be put. If you think in advance that there is a strong possibility that a third party might use the information you have collected to harm a person, then it is likely to be unethical to proceed.

Most researchers will find that their research designs if they involve human participants will have to be vetted and accepted by an ethical committee (either in

> ## Box 1.3 A check list of questions to ask yourself before starting your research project
>
> 1. Do you have a coherent research question?
> 2. Will the design and methodology chosen enable you to address that research question?
> 3. Have you had training in the analytic technique you intend to use?
> 4. Is the study feasible in the time you have available?
> 5. Have you constructed a set of deadlines for each stage of the project?
> 6. Has your supervisor approved the project design?
> 7. Have you read some of the literature relevant to your study area?
> 8. Is your planned sample size sufficient for the type of analysis you intend to perform?
> 9. Do you have access to enough participants to reach your required sample size, having factored in non-uptake?
> 10. Do you have access to any equipment you may need?
> 11. Have you made arrangements for where the study will take place?
> 12. Have you completed any necessary ethics approval procedures?
> 13. Have you arranged for participants to give informed consent?
> 14. Have you conducted a pilot study?

the organisation to which they are attached or in the organisation responsible for the participants). Ethical vetting can be time-consuming and should not be treated lightly. In executing a research plan, gaining ethical approval can be a significant hurdle.

Box 1.3 provides a checklist of things to consider when designing research. This chapter has not considered one key element in executing research – the report of your work and its findings. The process of reporting is covered in the final chapter of this book.

1.8 CONCLUSION

Conducting research effectively is all about knowing very specifically what you want to ask and collecting the appropriate information to provide an answer. Much of the rest of this book focuses upon the methods that allow you to collect appropriate information. In learning about those methods, it is valuable to bear in mind that, no matter how proficient you become in applying a method, if you cannot articulate your research question clearly, you will be wasting a lot of effort.

1.9 **EXERCISES**

1 If the big research topic is: 'How do leaders gain power?', how would you analyse each part of the question to come up with a research question that was specific enough to allow you to answer it? Describe each of the elements in the question that you consider. Once you have finished, ask another student whether you have missed any important issue.

2 Pair up with another student. Each of you has to design a study for a research question that your partner sets. Once you both have your designs, spend some time mutually critiquing them. Find two strengths and two weaknesses in each design. Try to rectify the weaknesses.

3 Choose any empirical article published in a psychology journal. Identify what its prime research question was. Consider what other design could be used to examine the same question, or think about how changing the design or approach would affect the ability to answer the research question. Discuss with other students on your course whether your design is effective.

Part 2

Quantitative Research: Data Collection and Analysis

2

Introduction to Quantitative Research

Chris Fife-Schaw

CONTENTS

AIMS OF THIS CHAPTER

This chapter is about the idea of quantification as used in psychological studies and it explains why psychologists might want to use numbers to test hypotheses and develop theories. It covers some of the basic ideas surrounding hypothesis testing and describes the traditional categories of measurement used in psychological science. This traditional categorisation system is important for understanding how to conduct good research but is also key to making decisions about how to analyse the data generated by a study. The chapter also briefly describes some of the challenges to this orthodox view.

KEY TERMS

approximate value
continuous variables
discrete variables
exhaustiveness
falsifiability
hypothetico-deductive method
measurement

mutual exclusivity
population
real limits
replication
sample
type I error
type II error

2.1 INTRODUCTION

Many of the nineteenth and early twentieth century pioneers of psychology thought that psychological phenomena were in principle no different from any other phenomena in the natural world and that they therefore ought to be open to scientific study in ways similar to those used by biologists and physicists. Sigmund Freud, probably the most famous psychologist of them all, was convinced that by systematically observing his patients, much like a biologist observes plants and animals, he could generate scientific theories about why people do what they do. Although Freud's theories have subsequently been criticised for not being good scientific theories – more on what a 'good scientific theory' is later – he nonetheless felt that following the principles of scientific investigation used in other disciplines would be the best way forward, and this would certainly be better than sitting around speculating on people's behaviour.

Deciding on what counts as 'science' and what is 'scientific' is not quite as straightforward as it might first seem and there is a vast literature on the philosophy of science which attempts to pin these things down. For the early psychologists the model of good science was physics, where careful and ostensibly objective observations were made which allowed physicists to produce theories which in turn led to predictions or hypotheses which could be tested by making observations in the future. If these observations produced data consistent with the hypotheses we would be more inclined to believe the theories that generated the hypotheses in the first place. If many different sets of observations and experiments produced data consistent with a theory we would conclude, by a process of induction that the theory is probably true and applies both now and in the future. A classic example would be the relationship between the orbits of the moon and the earth and the size and timing of the tides in the oceans. Once scientists were able to predict the orbits of the earth and the moon and measure tidal heights accurately they observed the correlation between the phase of the moon and the size of the tide, and they were able to induce 'laws' linking the tides to the phases of the moon which allowed them to produce tide tables that have helped save countless thousands of lives since.

While this seems a much more reasonable way to establish knowledge than wise men (for historically it was usually men with women's views being largely ignored) speculating on the nature of life, the universe and everything it has its problems as a model of good science. Perhaps the most fundamental is that induction works on the basis that what has happened in the past – that is, when we were making our observations – will happen in the future and there will no be exceptions. The particular observations we make in our studies lead us to general 'laws' or theories. Sir Karl Popper (1963) introduced a very important idea – falsifiability – which points out that a single counter example to a theory can render a theory either totally wrong or in need of serious modification. The classic example used is that of the naturalist who is studying swans and notices that in a lake all the swans are white. From this a proposition is induced that all swans are white and as the naturalist continues to travel and continues to see white swans this firms up the belief in the proposition which is gradually edging towards the status of a 'true' theory. If, however, the naturalist went to a lake and saw a single black swan then the proposition 'all swans are white' can no longer be true and has thus been falsified.

For Popper the thing that distinguishes scientific theories from non-scientific ones is that scientific theories produce propositions or hypotheses that are at least in principle falsifiable. If they are stated in such a way that any observation would be consistent with the theory (a charge that was levelled at many of Freud's theories) then the theory cannot make useful predictions and thus should not be treated as scientific. If I came up with a theory that said that people who were punished harshly when they were children might commit violent crimes when they are teenagers this would be essentially unfalsifiable. If I find a violent teenage criminal who was not harshly punished that would not challenge my theory, and neither would finding adults who had never committed violent crimes as teenagers who had nonetheless been punished harshly as kids. If I recast the theory to say that harshly punished children become violent teenagers this would become potentially falsifiable, as the finding of single harshly punished person who had gone through their teenage years non-violently would falsify the theory. This is almost certainly not a true hypothesis and you might ask whether this requirement for potential falsifiability severely limits the possibility of asking interesting questions. It can in certain circumstances, but in this example it would be perfectly reasonable to rephrase the theory to predict that early harsh punishment increases the likelihood of later teenage violent criminality. Here there is a possibility of falsification since if the proportion of violent teenagers is higher among the less harshly punished the proposition will have been falsified.

A second problem with induction is that in practice scientists rarely start their work with no prior expectations about what it is that they are hoping to find out. Popper calls these expectations 'conjectures' and the argument is that scientists do not really sit around waiting to observe relationships between just any sets of phenomena; they go out intentionally to study something and have some implicit theories (conjectures) that guide what questions they ask and how they will make their observations. In my punishment example I presumably looked at this because I had a hunch that harsh parents produced violent teenagers. In setting out to study this I would have to decide on what counted as harsh punishment in childhood and I would have to decide which crimes counted as violent ones and collect observations accordingly. Deciding on what counts as harsh punishment involves me in making a range of quite subjective and historically time-bound judgements. In the eighteenth century, for instance, children could expect to be physically chastised by a whole range of adults pretty much as a matter of course, and even adults could be subjected to floggings by their betters for what we would now regard as relatively minor transgressions; harshness is therefore a relative concept. The point here is simply that the process of induction rarely if ever proceeds without there being some element of subjective input from the scientist; it is not the entirely neutral and objective process that early psychologists hoped for.

Popper's requirement that theories produce hypotheses that are potentially falsifiable is still regarded by many as the mark of a good scientific theory, but it is focused on proving theories wrong rather than on knowing when we are right or how to choose between two competing theories that try to explain the same thing. The most common approach used in psychology today is to combine inductive processes acknowledging the potentially subjective aspects of this in what has come to be known as the hypothetico-deductive method. In the hypothetico-deductive method predictions or hypotheses are formally stated and subjected to some form of empirical test. Often this will be in the form of an experiment (Chapter 3), a quasi-experiment (Chapter 4) or it could be in an observational study (Chapter 14). The precise technique used is not important but what is important is that deductions are made about the theory that generated the hypothesis based on the results of this test. If the study data are consistent with the hypothesis (the predictions) this is good news for the theory. If they are not then this casts doubt on the theory.

The hypothetico-deductive method is in fact really a process since no single test of a hypothesis would usually be enough to establish whether a theory is true or totally false. Various different studies are conducted and if the body of evidence in favour of the theory builds up over time it is more likely that we will believe that it is worth keeping. If the various studies produce negative or mixed results for the theory we will probably want to reject it or at least revise it. We then need to come up with a new/revised theory – possibly by induction, possibly by intuition – and develop new tests of the hypotheses generated by this new or revised theory. Thus the process is an iterative one and the hope is that, provided the quality of the research is high, we will gradually end up with theories that seem to survive all fair attempts to falsify them (see Figure 2.1). Thus repeating studies – replication – is a valuable scientific activity even if it may not seem as exciting as conducting a completely new study. We never get to a point, however, where we know for certain that our theory is definitely true and will be so for all time and in all circumstances, but the weight of evidence supporting it will lead us to *act as if* to all intents and purposes it is true.

There are critics of the hypothetico-deductive approach and of falsification. Strict falsificationists would expect scientists to abandon theories in the face of *any* theoretically inconsistent observations and the evidence is that quite often they do not. For example, had early hydrographers abandoned their tide tables the first time that their tidal height predictions were wrong marine navigation would be a much more hazardous activity than it is now. The basic premise of tidal theory, that the phase of the moon determines the height of the water over the seabed, is regarded as

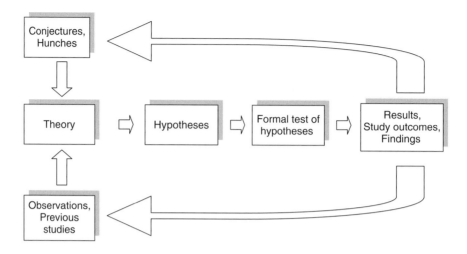

Figure 2.1   The cycle of induction and deduction in the hypothetico-deductive approach

essentially correct, but tidal height is also influenced by other things like atmospheric pressure – when there is high pressure the sea is squashed onto the seabed – which was not recognised initially. It would have been a big mistake to reject the 'phase of the moon causes the tides' theory outright on the basis of this theory-inconsistent evidence. The theory just needed modification. So, while the possibility of falsification is always desirable we need to be wary of rejecting theories outright too early – they may be partially correct.

2.2 STATISTICAL INFERENCE AND HYPOTHESIS TESTING

Whenever we run an empirical study like an experiment or an observational study we will almost always be studying a sample of people (or animals, or dyads or whatever the focus of the study is) rather than observing all members of the population. For my theory predicting that early harsh punishment increases the likelihood of later teenage violent criminality I will not be able to study all teenagers from the UK, let alone the rest of the world, so I will inevitably have to draw on a sample of teenagers and hope to make valid inferences about all teenagers based on my findings from this sample. I will nonetheless want to draw conclusions about all teenagers and not just the ones I have studied so I will have to find some way of saying how confident I am in my inference that what I find in my particular sample of teenagers – whether my hypothesis should be rejected or retained – should be applied to the population of all teenagers.

Box 2.1 On confusing terminology in statistics books: populations and samples

In the section on statistical inference I referred to getting samples from populations and wrote about this in the sense of you getting a sample of people from the relevant population and getting them to participate in your study. This is what most people understand when taking samples of things and most of us are aware of the idea of samples of members of the public being asked questions in polls in order to gauge 'public opinion'. In many statistics books you will see the terms 'sample' and 'population' used in a somewhat more precise way. Strictly speaking, inferential statistical tests make inferences about a population of *scores* on some variables from the sample of *scores* on these variables. The sample of people you have in your study generates a sample of scores on the variables of interest and they might produce a different set of scores had you tested them on another day. This may seem like a very subtle point, and for many purposes it makes no difference to what you will do, but there are occasions when the same sample of *people* will generate multiple *samples of scores*, so be aware of this distinction.

One way to improve my confidence is to make sure that my sample of teenagers is very large for, as we find out in Chapter 9, the closer in size the sample is to the size of the population, the more confidence we can have in any conclusions we draw from the sample data. However, increasing the size of the sample is both costly, eventually prohibitively so, and after a point the added confidence brought about by increasing the sample size ever further is not that great – how much more confident will I be if I study 1.1 million teenagers than if I study just one million? To get over this problem statistical inference tests have been developed that allow us estimate how confident we can be in accepting or rejecting a hypothesis.

The classical statistical inference tests proceed by identifying two kinds of hypothesis relating to a study – the null hypothesis and the alternative hypothesis. The null hypothesis is what the inference tests actually test and this appears slightly odd at first sight. The null hypothesis in an experiment is the statement that the independent variable (the thing we manipulate in the experiment – see Chapter 3) has *no effect* at all on the dependent variable (the thing that the independent variable is supposed to influence) *in the population*. In a correlational study the null hypothesis would normally be that two variables are not associated, or correlated, with one another *in the population*. In my punishment study the null hypothesis is that there is no difference in the likelihood of criminality between harshly and less harshly punished teenagers *in the population*. It is sometimes casually referred to as the 'no effect' hypothesis. Note that what happens in the *sample* is not what we are really interested in. The null hypothesis is usually referred to as H_0.

The alternative hypothesis is our 'hunch' hypothesis: that the independent variable does indeed affect the dependent variable *in the population* or that two variables are correlated with one another *in the population* – that harshly punished children are more likely to become criminal teenagers *in the population*. However, this is only one hypothesis in a range of possible alternative explanations about what is actually going on in our studies and we cannot treat our preferred alternative hypothesis as absolutely true even if we reject the null hypothesis. In an experiment, for example, it may be that some third, unmeasured variable affects both our independent and dependent variables but we were simply unaware of it. The alternative hypothesis is referred to as H_1.

It is easier to show that a hypothesis is false than it is to show that a hypothesis is true. As we saw from the work of Popper on falsifiability there is a philosophical argument that says that we can only ever prove that something is not true: we can never show that something is absolutely true. It is for this reason that inference tests focus on testing the null hypothesis. If we can show that the 'no effect' null hypothesis is not true then there is something going on and an alternative hypothesis, hopefully our preferred hypothesis, may be a more accurate reflection of reality. We never end up saying that our preferred hypothesis is true, however, as it has not been tested directly.

Statistical inference tests will tell us how confident we can be that we have made the right decision when we make our judgement about the null hypothesis. If you think about it, there are two kinds of mistake or error we could commit when we make this decision.

A type I error would have occurred if you rejected a true null hypothesis. This is where you conclude that the independent variable did affect the dependent variable when, in fact, it did not. This can happen when, by chance, you allocate people who were already high scorers to one condition in your experiment and low scorers to another. When you measure scores on the dependent variable, the difference between the conditions is due to the fact that the people were different before you started, *not* because the independent variable had any effect. In terms of correlational analyses, type I errors occur when you say that the two variables were related to one another when, in fact, they were not.

Most common statistical tests give you an estimate of the probability of having made a type I error. They do this by using information about the size of relationships between the observations you have made, the size of the sample and the design of your study. If the probability of having made a type I error is high then you should not throw away the null hypothesis just yet. If the probability is very low (conventionally less than 0.05, a 1 in 20 chance) then it is probably safe to reject the null hypothesis, in which case some other alternative hypothesis must be true, quite possibly your preferred alternative hypothesis but not necessarily so.

The probability of making a type I error will never be exactly zero; that is, there is no chance of being wrong about rejecting the null hypothesis, since your data will have come from a sample and you do not know whether there are exceptional cases that you are unaware of in the unsampled part of the population.

A type II error occurs when you fail to reject a false null hypothesis. You conclude that the independent variable has no influence on the dependent variable when it actually does. This happens sometimes because the size of the treatment effect is very small and hard to notice in your sample. It can also happen when you get the opposite of the example given for type I errors. Here, by chance, you allocate people who were already high scorers on the dependent variable to the treatment condition that actually lowers scores and vice versa. The effect of the experiment is to level up the two groups so that there is now no difference between treatment groups on the scores and you accept the null hypothesis of 'no differences' between groups. In fact, the independent variable had a big effect but your sampling obscured this. With correlational designs, type II errors have occurred when you conclude that there is no relationship between your two variables when, in fact, there is. If you publish such 'non-findings', then it may discourage people from investigating a potentially important effect in the future.

Estimates of the likelihood of having made these errors allow us to have varying degrees of confidence in making inferences about what is happening in the population from what is happening in our samples. To estimate these probabilities we obviously need to have our measurements in the form of numbers, and it is partly because of the need to get good estimates of the confidence we can have in making inferences that so much effort has been devoted to developing good numerical measures of the variables we are interested in. Chapter 9 deals with statistical inference and hypothesis testing in much more detail, but in the next section we look at ways in which measurements are conceived.

2.3 QUANTIFICATION AND LEVELS OF MEASUREMENT

It is often incorrectly assumed that 'proper' scientific studies have to involve numbers in some way or another. This is partly a function of the need to quantify our confidence about inferences we make from sample-generated findings (the probabilities of making type I and type II errors) but as you will see from Part 3 of this book it is perfectly possible to advance knowledge and develop useful theories without recourse to numbers. While there are many aspects of the research process that do not involve measurement using numbers and, indeed, some fields of enquiry where explicit measurement is avoided altogether, the majority of current research studies in psychology do involve it in some form.

Measurement here is defined as the assigning of numbers to objects, events or observations according to some set of rules. Sometimes these numbers will be used just to indicate that an observation belongs to a certain category or has a certain quality; at other times these numbers will mean that the observation has more of some property than an observation that is given a lower number. These observations could be generated directly by the research participants (e.g. people's ratings of certain stimuli) or by the researcher by, for example, observing the participants' behaviours in different situations. For many studies, whether a research hypothesis stands or falls will depend on how well the key concepts have been measured, independently of whether or not it is a worthy hypothesis. It is also the case that before we can construct grand psychological theories we must first be able to measure and describe things in these theories validly and with reasonable accuracy (Cattell, 1981).

In much of psychology we have to measure psychological properties indirectly because we have no direct access to the mental constructs we want to measure. It is a straightforward matter to measure length and we can do this fairly directly by offering up our measuring instrument (e.g. a ruler or tape measure) to the object we want to measure. However, in the case of IQ, for example, we can only infer levels of intelligence from tests that ask people to solve problems of varying difficulty. We assume that people who solve more of the more-difficult problems are more intelligent than people who get them wrong, but we cannot yet see intelligence in any more direct way than this. The existence of something called intelligence is itself a hypothesis and the debate about what IQ tests *actually* measure has often been a heated one. While few people would argue about what a ruler measures, the quantities measured by many psychological measurement instruments are more open to debate and much more obviously depend on the theoretical perspective of the researcher than is perhaps the case in the physical sciences.

This does not mean that psychological measurements are arbitrary or of little value. A great deal of effort has been expended in establishing the reliability and validity of psychological measures over the last century. There are now libraries of well-validated tests for all sorts of psychological phenomena which can be used very effectively as long as the manuals are used appropriately. Chapter 7 outlines the principles involved in test construction and development commonly used in psychology.

While many established tests exist, psychologists are often confronted by the need to create their own measures to deal with the specific problems they have. This may be because nobody has yet developed a test for the particular kinds of phenomena they are interested in. It may be that they are measuring something which has not been measured before or, perhaps, that the existing tests are too cumbersome for their purposes. In these cases more attention has to be paid to the precise meaning and nature of the new measures.

It goes without saying that the goal is always to measure things as well as possible but there are often trade-offs that have to be made. Measurements that demand lots of time and effort from participants may induce fatigue and boredom that may simply introduce unwanted 'noise' into the measurements. On the other hand, measurements that are very simple and quick to make can be crude and inaccurate. Ultimately judgements have to be made as to whether the measurements are 'good enough' for their stated purposes.

2.4 **CLASSIFYING MEASUREMENTS**

Whether you use a ready made measure or create your own, you will need to know what class of measurement you have used, as how you classify a measurement will have an impact on the kinds of numerical analyses you can perform on the data later on. S.S. Stevens (1946) proposed that all measurements can be classified as being of one of four types. This system has become dominant within psychology and no methods textbook would be complete without describing it. There are, however, other important alternative conceptualisations of measurement such as those of Luce *et al.* (1990) and Adams (1966) and objections to the way psychologists think (or rather, do not think) about their measures (see Box 2.2). Stevens' classification remains the best known but it is only one way of thinking about measurement.

2.4.1 **Nominal/categorical measurements**

Nominal or categorical measurements (variables) reflect qualitative differences rather than quantitative ones. Common examples include categories like yes/no, present/absent, pass/fail, male/female or Conservative/Liberal/Labour. When setting up a categorical measurement system the only requirements are those of mutual exclusivity and exhaustiveness. Mutual exclusivity means that each

---

Box 2.2 Are we deluding ourselves about our measures? A word of caution

The beginning of this century has seen a challenge to the orthodoxy on measurement presented in this book coming most notably from Joel Michell (e.g. Michell, 2000). Michell's arguments are highly detailed philosophical ones and it is difficult to represent them fairly in a short space; however, a key idea in his work is that in the rush to appear to be 'hard' scientists like physicists, psychologists have failed to consider some fundamental questions about what they are assuming when they attempt to measure psychological attributes. When coming up with a quantitative measure of some attribute psychologists are assuming that the attribute concerned has a quantitative structure, yet this is rarely, if ever, tested even though Michell argues that this is in principle an empirical question that is open to investigation. When trying to measure job satisfaction, say, psychologists rarely stop and ask the question, 'Is job satisfaction really a quantitative attribute?' – it is already assumed to be quantitative and indeed it is necessary to assume this if the quantitative test scores are to have any sensible meaning. The focus usually moves directly on to how satisfaction test scores are quantitatively related to other variables even though the quantitative nature of satisfaction was never actually established. Satisfaction could be a categorical state for instance – people could be

---

Box 2.2 (Continued)

either satisfied or not and there might be no sense in which someone who has been satisfied can become even more satisfied. A crude example might be that you could be 'satisfied' (in the sense of being satiated) after having a very big meal but having another big meal would not make you any more satisfied. Also, it is far from proven that dissatisfaction is the dimensional opposite of satisfaction.

The existence of a test that produces numbers does not establish that the attribute being 'measured' is really quantitative and a lot of bogus 'science' may be built on flawed measurement assumptions. Although Michell speculates about why psychologists and psychometricians have not bothered with establishing that given attributes are quantitative, doing this is not a simple matter. Conjoint measurement theory (e.g. Luce and Tukey, 1964) offers one of the few ways to address this at the moment and Michell (2000) gives a nice illustrative example. Other methods have proven illusive yet the need for them is clear – we should not be attempting to present psychology as a rigorous science that measures quantitative things if we cannot establish that the things we want to measure are actually quantitative in the first place.

---

observation (person, case, score) cannot fall into more than one category; somebody cannot, for example, both pass and fail a test at the same time. Exhaustiveness simply means that the category system should have enough categories for all the observations. For example, when asking people about handedness, a category system of left-handed and right-handed would not be exhaustive since some people might say they were ambidextrous.

A key feature of categorical measurements is that there is no *necessary* sense in which one category has more or less of a particular quality: they are simply different. Males are different from females (at least at some biological level) and northerners come from the north and southerners do not. Sometimes, however, this will seem like an odd assumption. Surely 'passing' something is better than 'failing', for example? Well, yes, in certain cases this would be so, but this would depend on what your *a priori* theory about the measure was. If you believed that 'passing' was more valuable and reflected more positively on somebody (that they were more intelligent, paid more attention, etc.) then that is a matter for you as a researcher; the use of a pass/fail category system itself does not inherently contain any notion of greater or lesser value.

To allow us to use computers to help with analyses, we commonly assign numbers to observations in each category. For instance we might assign (code) a value of 1 for males and 2 for females. The important point is that although females have a numerically larger number there is no suggestion that being female is somehow better or has more value. Again, this can cause confusion, especially as computers deal only with numbers and not their meanings. You could, for instance, ask the computer to calculate the mean sex of your participants and it might come up with a figure like 1.54; clearly this is pretty uninformative.

Although the categories of a categorical variable do not necessarily have any value associated with them, this does not mean that they cannot reflect some underlying dimension in some circumstances if this is what you want to do. As an example, you might classify people you are observing in the street as 'young' or 'old' because you do not want to approach them to ask their ages directly. While this is likely to be an extremely rough and ready classification, this system implies an underlying continuous dimension of age even though we place people in only two categories.

The criteria for categorical measurement do not rule out the possibility of having a category of 'uncategorisable'. If you did have such a category you would satisfy both the mutual exclusivity and exhaustiveness criteria, but if there were a lot of 'uncategorisable' observations then the value of the categorisation system might be questionable. How useful is it to have a variable on which the majority of observations are 'uncategorisable'? This can only truly be answered with reference to the research question.

2.4.2 Ordinal level measures

This is the next level of measurement in terms of complexity. As before, the assumptions of mutual exclusivity and exhaustiveness apply and cases are still assigned to categories. The big difference is that now the categories themselves can be rank ordered with reference to some external criteria such that being in one category can be regarded as having more or less of some underlying quantity than being in another category. A lecturer might want to rank order their students in terms of general ability at statistics. They could put each student into one of five categories: excellent, good, average, poor, diabolical. Clare might fall into the 'excellent' category and Jane into the 'good' category. Clare is better at statistics than Jane, but what we do not know is just how much better Clare is than Jane. The rankings reflect more or less of something but not *how much* more or less.

Most psychological test scores should strictly be regarded as ordinal measures. For instance, one of the subscales of the well-known NEO PI-R personality test (Costa & McCrae, 1992) is designed to measure extroversion. Like other extroversion measures this one allows us to infer levels of extroversion from responses to items about self-reported behaviours and preferences, it does not measure extroversion in any direct sense. Years of validation studies have shown how high scorers will tend to behave in a more extroverted manner in the future, but all the test can do is rank order people in terms of extroversion. If two people differ by three points on the scale we cannot say *how much* more extroverted the higher scoring person is, just that they are more extroverted. Here the scale intervals do not map directly on to some psychological reality in the way that the length of a stick can be measured in centimetres using a ruler. The fundamental unit of measurement is not known.

Since many mental constructs within psychology cannot be observed directly, most measures tend to be ordinal. Attitudes, intentions, opinions, personality characteristics, psychological wellbeing, depression, and so on, are all constructs which are thought to vary in degree between individuals but tend only to allow indirect ordinal measurements. This conclusion is a point of contention for many researchers, since one of the implications of assuming these measures to be ordinal is that some parametric statistical tests should not be used with them. Indeed even the humble mean is not used appropriately with ordinal measures (the median is a more appropriate measure of central tendency). This sits uneasily with what you will see when you read academic journal articles, where you will regularly find means and parametric statistics applied to ordinal measures. We will deal with this issue later in this chapter (see also Chapter 9).

2.4.3 Interval level measures

Like an ordinal scale, the numbers associated with an interval measure reflect more or less of some underlying dimension. The key distinction is that with interval level measures, numerically equal distances on the scale reflect equal differences in the underlying dimension. For example, the 2°C difference in temperature between 38°C and 40°C is the same as the 2°C difference between 5°C and 7°C.

As we will see later, many psychologists are prepared to assume that scores on psychological tests can be treated as interval level measures so that they can carry out more sophisticated analyses on their data. A well-known example of this practice is the use of IQ test scores. In order to treat scores as interval level measures, the assumption is made that the 5-point difference in IQ between someone who scores 75 and someone who gets 80 means the same difference in intelligence as the difference between someone who score 155 and someone who scores 160.

2.4.4 Ratio scale measures

These differ from interval level measures only in that they have a potential absolute zero value. Good examples of ratio scales are length, time and number of correct answers on a test. It is possible to have zero (no) length, for something to take no time, or for someone to get no answers correct on a test. An important corollary of having an absolute zero is that, for example, someone who gets four questions right has got twice as many questions right as someone who got only two right.

The ratio of scores to one another now carries some sensible meaning which was not the case for the interval scale.

The difference between interval and ratio scales is easiest to explain with an example. Say we measure reaction times to dangers presented to people in a driving simulator. This could be measured in seconds and would be a ratio scale measurement, as 0 seconds is a possible (if a little unlikely) score and someone who takes 2 seconds is taking twice as long to react as someone who takes 1 second.

If, on average, people take 800 milliseconds (0.8 of a second) to react we could just look at the *difference* between the observed reaction time and this average level of performance. In this case the level of measurement is on an interval scale. Our first person scores 1200 ms (i.e. takes 1200 ms longer than the average of 800 ms) and the second person scores 200 ms (i.e. takes 200 ms more than the average). However, the first person did not take six times longer (1200 ms divided by 200 ms) than the second. They did take 1000 ms longer, so the *interval* remains meaningful but the ratio element does not.

True psychological ratio scale measures are quite rare, though there is often confusion about this when it comes to taking scores from scales made up of individual problem items in ability tests. We might measure the number of simple arithmetic problems that people can get right, for instance. We test people on 50 items and simply count the number that are correct. The number that are correct is a ratio scale measure since four right is twice as many as two right, and it is possible to get none right at all (absolute zero). As long as we consider our measure to be *only* an indication of the number correct there is no problem and we can treat them as ratio scale measures.

If, however, we were to treat the scores as reflecting ability at arithmetic then the measure would become an ordinal one. A score of zero might not reflect absolutely no ability at all, as the problems might have been so difficult that only those with above average ability would be able to get any of them right. It would also be a mistake to assume that all the items were equally difficult. Twenty of the questions might be easy and these might be answered correctly by most people. Getting one of these correct and adding one point to your score would be fairly easy. The remaining items may be much more difficult and earning another point by getting one of these correct might require much more ability. In other words, the requirement that equal intervals between scores reflect equal differences in ability is not met and we should strictly speaking treat the scores as an ordinal measure of ability. Even when doing this we are assuming that ability is a quantitative entity though we will not have established this directly (see Box 2.2).

As will hopefully have become clear, there is a hierarchical distinction between the types of measurement described in this section. Nominal measures give information on whether two objects are the same or different, ordinal measures add information concerning more or less of a quantity, interval measures add information on the distance between objects and ratio scale measures add the absolute zero standard.

2.5 DISCRETE VERSUS CONTINUOUS VARIABLES

Many types of measurement result in indices that consist of indivisible categories. If someone scores 13 on our 50-item arithmetic test, they might have scored 14 on a better day but they could never have scored 13½. The score 13½ was not possible as the individual questions can be marked only correct or incorrect. Measures like this are called discrete variables since they can have only discrete, whole number values.

Some variables like height and time are referred to as continuous variables since they could be divided into ever smaller units of measure. We could measure height in metres, then centimetres, then millimetres, then micrometres, then nanometres and so on until we got to the point where our measuring instrument could not make any finer discrimination. There are an infinite number of possible values that fall between any two observed values. Continuous variables can be divided up into an infinite number of fractional parts. Ultimately it is the accuracy of our measuring instrument that puts limits on the measurement of continuous variables. If our ruler can only measure accurately to the nearest millimetre we must settle for that degree of precision.

When measuring a continuous variable you end up recording a single figure but this really represents an interval on the measurement scale rather than a single value. It is therefore always an approximate value. If we time someone doing a task to the nearest second, say it takes them 20 seconds, we are really saying that the time taken lies somewhere in the interval between 19.5 and 20.5 seconds. Had it actually taken them 19.4 seconds we would have rounded the time to 19 seconds, not 20 seconds (note: when rounding a number that ends with a numeral 5, round to the nearest even number). Similarly, an elapsed time of 20.6 seconds would have been rounded to 21 seconds. This is shown in Figure 2.2.

In this example we are deliberately recording times only to the nearest second but, in principle, the choice of any measurement tool carries with it a limit to the degree of accuracy that can be achieved and thus the rounding process will have to happen even if we are unaware of it. We will still be reporting a time that corresponds to an interval and not a discrete value. If our stopwatch could record times to the nearest 100th of a second, say, and we recorded a time of 20.12 seconds, this would still mean we were saying that the time taken lies somewhere in the

Figure 2.2　Real limits on a continuous variable

interval between 20.115 and 20.125 seconds. These boundary values are referred to as real limits.

It is always desirable to use the most accurate measure practicable. Any calculations done using approximate values necessarily include that approximation in the final result. If you use two or more approximate values in a calculation the scope for misleading results increases dramatically. So it is always preferable to use approximate measures associated with the smallest intervals possible so as to minimise this problem. Although our variables might be theoretically continuous, like time and length, the act of measurement always reduces the measure to a discrete one.

2.6 MEASUREMENT ERRORS

The goal of all researchers should be to minimise measurement errors. Put formally, these are the discrepancies between the observed value of your measurement and the 'true' value. There is a simple formula to illustrate this:

observed score = true score + error

The 'error' term may be positive or negative. Obviously it would be nice to have the error term as small as possible. If you were measuring people's heights with a ruler marked off in inches then you could probably only measure accurately to within half an inch. Having a ruler marked off in millimetres would give rise to much more accurate measurement and finer distinctions between individuals could be made (see the previous section). In a similar way, psychological measures should strive to make as fine a set of distinctions between people as possible. Assuming your measure is valid, it makes sense to have more points on your measurement scale rather than fewer.

This holds true only so long as you believe the individual points on the scale carry the same meaning for all participants. When it comes to ratio scale and interval level measures, such as time, this is not a problem. You could measure time to the nearest millionth of a second, though you might find the timing equipment a bit expensive. For most psychological research, timing to the nearest millisecond is accurate enough. Things get much more difficult when you have ordinal measures, and problems crop up when you try to label individual responses on your ordinal scale. For example, say you have an attitude statement about a political issue and you would like people to tell you how much they agree or disagree with it. You could provide a five-point scale as follows:

1   strongly agree
2   agree
3   neither agree or disagree
4   disagree
5   strongly disagree

Most respondents would know what they were required to do with such a response scale. While you could not be certain that all those who 'agreed' had agreed to the same extent, you would probably feel reasonably happy that they did not intend to tell you they had very strong views on the topic. Similarly it is probably safe to assume that they are not entirely equivocal about the issue either.

If you gave this question to several hundred people in a survey, however, you would find that so many people had the same score on the item that it did not discriminate very much between people. In this situation you might want to increase the number of response options available. A seven-point scale could be used and it would be reasonably easy to label the response options. You might even think a nine-point scale was appropriate, though labelling all the points might prove more of a challenge. Indeed you could simply label the end- and mid-points, leaving the rest unlabelled.

Why not opt for a 29-point scale instead? This would give even greater discrimination, surely? The answer, unfortunately, is no. People would now have trouble working out where they should indicate their response on the scale. Should it be the 18th or the 19th point or even the 20th? Such a response format increases the scope for confusion and will introduce, rather than reduce, measurement error. There is also the problem that we still do not know that all people responding at point 19 agree to the same extent. Multi-point ordinal scales can introduce an unfortunate illusion of precision.

2.7 CHOICES OVER LEVELS OF MEASUREMENT

In the previous and very traditional section I have implicitly suggested that ratio and interval level measurement is to be preferred over ordinal or categorical measures. The reason for this is that in most cases a good ratio scale measure will contain more information about the thing being measured than a good ordinal measure. You would probably rather have temperature reported in degrees Celsius than on a scale of very cold, cold, neither warm nor cold, warm, hot, very hot. You should always strive for greater accuracy of measurement where possible.

Naturally some kinds of variable are always going to be categorical (e.g. gender) and some are always going to be ordinal (e.g. most scaled psychological measures). In these cases you should not regard your measures as somehow inferior. Whilst it would be nice to think that ultimately we will have much more direct measures of attitudes and personalities, for example, these are not likely for the foreseeable future.

There are some common practices which should be discouraged, however. The most notorious of these is the collapsing of ordinal measures into categorical ones. It is quite common to see researchers take an attitude item with a seven-point agree/disagree response format and collapse the data into a simple three-point scale of agree/uncertain/disagree. This practice degrades the measurement by removing the extremity information. There are three kinds of motive for collapsing data in this way. One is the desire to use simpler statistical procedures; a second is to make graphs and tables clearer; and the third is that you might not believe that your seven-point measure is very accurate or valid. With the ready availability of comprehensive statistics books and computer programs the first problem is easily overcome. While clarifying graphs and tables is an admirable aim it would be desirable to collapse the scores only for this purpose and to conduct statistical analyses on the un-collapsed data. The third justification is also a 'justification' for not using the measure at all! If you doubt the validity or accuracy of a measure then you should think twice about using it in the first place.

2.8 THE RELATIONSHIP BETWEEN LEVEL OF MEASUREMENT AND STATISTICS

Most statistics textbooks present readers with 'decision trees' which help you select the correct statistical test to use providing you know the answers to a number of simple questions about your data and research design. These are very useful, and some are provided in Chapter 9.

These decision trees ask about the level of measurement for your data as well as the nature of the distribution of scores on the measure that you expect in the population from which your sample scores were drawn. The topic of distributions of scores is dealt with in Chapter 9 but the level of measurement issue is relevant here, particularly at the boundary between ordinal and interval level measures.

The attraction of parametric tests, ones that assume something about the distribution of scores in the population (e.g. the *t*-test, ANOVA), is that there are many more of them than non-parametric tests. They often allow you to ask interesting questions about your data that are not easily answered without using such parametric procedures. To say that your measure is 'only' ordinal, rather than interval level, usually rules out many of these useful procedures. Two views have developed over the appropriateness of treating ordinal measures as interval ones. Those interested in reading more on this debate should see Henkel (1975), Labovitz (1975), Townsend and Ashby (1984), Stine (1989) and Davison and Sharma (1990), among many others.

One view states that, most of the time, providing the quality of an ordinal measure is good, you will arrive at the same conclusions using parametric techniques as you would have using more appropriate non-parametric tests (assuming there was one available). It is argued that while most psychological measures are technically ordinal measures, some of the better measures lie in a region somewhere between ordinal and interval level measurement (see Minium *et al.*, 1993).

Take a simple example of a seven-point response scale for an attitude item. At one level this allows you to rank order people relative to their agreement with the statement. It is also likely that a two-point difference in scores for two individuals reflects more of a difference than if they had only differed by one point. The possibility that you might be able to rank order the magnitude of *differences*, while not implying interval level measurement, suggests that the measure contains more information than merely how to rank order the respondents. The argument then runs that it would be wasteful to throw away this additional useful information and so unnecessarily limit the possibility of revealing greater theoretical insights by using more elaborate parametric statistical procedures.

The more traditional and strict view (e.g. Henkel, 1975; Stine, 1989) says that using sophisticated techniques designed for one level of measurement on data of a less sophisticated level simply results in nonsense. Computer outputs will provide you with sensible-looking figures but these will still be nonsense and should not be used to draw inferences about anything. This line of argument also rejects the claim that using parametric tests with ordinal data will lead to the same conclusion *most of the time* on the grounds that you will have no way of knowing when you have stumbled across an exception to this 'rule'.

The debate on this issue continues. The safest solution, advocated by Blalock (1988), is to conduct analyses on ordinal measures using both parametric and non-parametric techniques where possible. Then, where both procedures lead you to the same substantive conclusion, when reporting parametric test results, you will at least know that you are not misleading anyone. You should be guided more by the non-parametric procedures if the conclusions are contradictory. What would be unacceptable would be to select the statistical procedure that leads to results that support your hypothesis. It is important to be consistent in reporting findings, so you must decide that either your data meet the assumptions for parametric procedures or that they do not.

Ultimately, whether this issue matters depends on the seriousness of making a mistake and who the audience for this research is likely to be. Research on a drug or an intervention that may change people's lives demands the most strict and conservative approach to the analysis. On the other hand, if your research topic is more esoteric and your audience is restricted to researchers in a field that has regularly used (abused?) parametric techniques on ordinal data, then you may find it difficult to get a hearing if you do not report findings in the accepted way.

2.9 CONCLUSION

This chapter has described the main issues surrounding levels of measurement and quantification in psychology as well as briefly looking at the logic behind quantitative hypothesis testing. In time, the research community may come to an alternative system of measurement classifications (cf. the debate discussed above). However, the Stevens system described here remains the dominant one in psychology for the time being. Chapter 9 takes this a step further by looking at the principles of statistical inference in more detail.

2.10 EXERCISES

1 Take three psychological research questions that you are interested in. Can you formulate hypotheses relating to each question that could be tested in a study? What kinds of results would falsify these hypotheses?
2 Think of a psychological variable that you are interested in. Can you create a nominal, ordinal, interval and ratio-scale version of it? If not, why is this?

2.11 DISCUSSION QUESTIONS

1 Should psychologists abandon attempts to mimic the 'hard' sciences? If they did, what would be the implications?
2 Is it going to be possible to find 'laws' of psychology in the same way as we have laws of physics?
3 Are there constructs in psychology which cannot in principle be measured by an instrument on one of Stevens' four measurement levels? Why is this?

2.12 FURTHER READING

All good statistics textbooks explain Stevens' classification system and the relationship levels of measurement and statistics, though few books will go much beyond what has been presented here and in Chapter 9. Many of the key papers on the debate about measurement and statistics have appeared in the *Psychological Bulletin* and are likely to continue to appear in that journal. Chalmers' (1999) *What is this thing called science? An assessment of the nature and status of science and its methods*, 3rd edition, is a classic textbook on the philosophy of science and although it is oriented towards the physical sciences it still gives a good introduction to the philosophy of science.

3
Experimental Design

Graham Hole

CONTENTS

AIMS OF THIS CHAPTER

After reading this chapter, you should have a better understanding of the following:

1 the advantages and disadvantages of the experimental method, with respect to the scientific study of behaviour;
2 why confounding variables can cause problems for the interpretation of research findings, and how they can be overcome;
3 commonly used types of experimental design, together with their advantages and disadvantages;
4 the relative merits of between-groups and within-subjects designs;
5 the nature of 'time', 'group' and 'reactivity' threats to validity, and how they can be tackled.

KEY TERMS

between-groups design
between-subjects design
blind testing
cohort effects confounding
  variables
counter-balancing
cross-sectional design
dependent variable (DV)
differential attrition
differential mortality
double-blind testing
ecological validity
evaluation apprehension
experiment
experimenter effects
external validity
Hawthorne effect
independent variable (IV)
internal validity
John Henry effect
Latin Squares design

longitudinal design
matched-pairs design
mixed design
multifactorial design
operational definition
order effects
placebo effect
post-test only/control group
  design
power
pre-test/post-test control group
  design
Pygmalion effect
randomisation
reactivity
regression towards the mean
reliability
repeated measures design
Solomon four-group design
validity
within-subjects design

3.1 **INTRODUCTION**

This chapter will begin by explaining why the experimental method is so popular among psychologists, and then go on to discuss the methodological issues involved in designing good experiments. Different types of experimental design will be described, together with their advantages and disadvantages. 'Validity' (the extent to which the experiment has measured what you intended it to measure) is an important consideration in designing an experiment. This chapter will outline various threats to validity and show how a well-designed experiment can overcome most of them. It ends with three pieces of useful advice that should be kept in mind when designing *any* study, experimental or otherwise.

3.2 **THE ADVANTAGES OF THE EXPERIMENTAL METHOD**

The experimental method is just a systematic way of acquiring knowledge, but it has played a pivotal role in helping us to understand the physical world. Although its origins can be traced back to medieval Islamic times, it was not until the birth of experimental psychology in the late nineteenth century that people realised it could be used to understand our psychological world too.

The reason why experimental methods are so useful is that they enable us to determine causal relationships between variables. ('Variables' are simply things that can vary, such as 'age', 'gender', 'neuroticism', 'political affiliation', 'sleepiness', 'deodorant preference', and so on). An important aspect of science is the description of phenomena, but we only understand them fully when we can explain why they occur – that is, when we have identified their causes. What does it really mean to say that one thing 'causes' another? Without getting into deep philosophical discussions, it implies that the relationship between two variables has the following properties:

(a) change in variable A is associated with change in variable B;
(b) change in variable A reliably precedes change in variable B;
(c) without change in A, change in B does not occur (though this is only true if A is the sole cause of B).

To give a concrete example, suppose I was interested in finding out whether emotional stress (variable A) affected people's memory for events (variable B). One way to tackle this might be to find eyewitnesses to various crimes and measure their reported level of stress as well as the completeness of their memory for the crime. This might reveal that stress and memory were somehow related, so that stressed individuals recalled more events than unstressed people.[1] Positive correlations (see Chapter 11) between variables like this are often misinterpreted as showing that the two variables have a causal relationship, but in fact correlations are usually difficult to interpret. It might be that stress affects memory, but it is also possible that memory affects stress – perhaps the people who remembered more showed higher stress levels because their superior memories enabled the events to affect them more deeply. There might even be a third factor (or set of factors) that gave rise to both the differences in stress level and the differences in memory: perhaps highly neurotic individuals are both more highly stressed and have better memories for events, so that there is actually no direct relationship between stress levels and memory at all.

In short, correlation is no proof of causality. To demonstrate that stress levels *cause* memory changes, I have to do more than just show that changes in one variable are associated with changes in the other. I also have to satisfy the other two conditions outlined above: I need to show that changes in stress level precede the memory changes, and not the other way round, because in our universe consequences normally follow their antecedents. I also have to show that *without* the changes in stress level, the memory changes do not occur. To demonstrate the latter point is particularly problematic in psychology, because many phenomena have more than one cause. Memory for events is affected by many different factors, so pinning down the role of stress is tricky.

This is where the experimental method comes in. It is based on one of a number of techniques for investigating causation that were outlined by the philosopher J.S. Mill (1882). Mill suggested that the best way to identify a causal relationship between two variables was to look at the effects produced by two situations that were identical except in one respect. If the phenomenon of interest occurred in one of these situations but not the other, then the difference between them must be the cause of the phenomenon. Mill called this 'the Method of Difference', and it is the basis of modern experimental methods.

While acknowledging the usefulness of both experimental and observational techniques as methods for investigating nature, Mill pointed out two additional advantages of the experimental method. First, in an experiment, it is often possible to produce many more variations of circumstances than can occur under natural conditions; we can 'add to nature's experiments a multitude of experiments of our own' (1882, p. 274). Thus we could generate events that varied in their level of

---

1   In practice, the relationship between stress and eyewitness memory is complicated, with some studies showing that stress enhances recall and others showing the opposite. See Deffenbacher *et al.* (2004) for a review of this literature, and a theory to explain these conflicting findings.

stressfulness and measure their effects, rather than looking for naturally occurring variations in stressfulness. Second, the experimental method enables us to produce events to order, rather than waiting for them to occur naturally, and allows us to control the circumstances in which they occur. Mill was thinking of electricity when he made these points – and of the advantages of generating electricity in a lab as opposed to waiting for lightning storms to occur – but they apply with equal force to behaviour.

3.3 THE BASIC PRINCIPLES OF THE EXPERIMENTAL METHOD

To translate the Method of Difference into an experiment, we have to carry out the following steps. We need to formulate a specific, testable question or *hypothesis*, such as, 'Does stress impair memory for events?' To answer it, we manipulate one variable (the independent variable, or IV), and measure the effects of these manipulations on another variable (the dependent variable, or DV), while keeping all other variables as constant as possible. In terms of our example, stress level is our IV and recall performance is our DV. We want to manipulate stress level, and measure the effects of this on recall performance. One way to do this would be to take two groups of participants who were initially similar, and then measure their recall performance after one of the groups had been exposed to a stressful event and the other had not. If the *only* consistent difference between the groups is the stressful event; it follows that any subsequent difference between the groups in memory performance is probably attributable to this – we have shown that being exposed to a stressful event causes changes in memory performance (see Figure 3.1).

3.4 THE PERIL OF CONFOUNDING VARIABLES

In designing an experiment, the tricky bit is to ensure that the independent variable is the *only* thing that varies systematically between the groups. If anything else varies consistently as well, then the results become uninterpretable: the changes in the dependent variable might be occurring because of our manipulations of the independent variable, or because of changes in other variables, or both. Variables that have unwanted influences on our experimental results are called confounding variables. For example, if we were looking at the effects of stress on memory, we would need to make sure that our two groups of participants were as similar as possible in every respect except one – the fact that one of the groups received a stressful experience. If the two groups also differed consistently in, say, initial anxiety level, then any differences between the groups in recall performance could occur for all sorts of reasons. It might be that recall was affected solely by stress, solely by

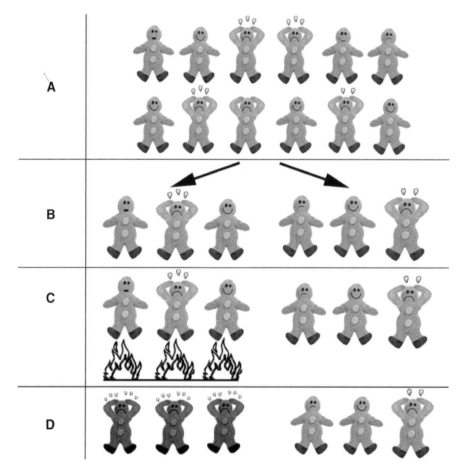

Figure 3.1 A satisfactory experimental design. A, A population of gingerbread people, varying in anxiety level. B, Two random samples from the population, who are initially similar (in this instance they do not differ *systematically* in terms of anxiety level, or any other variables for that matter). C, The experimental group (left) get a stressful treatment (cooking) that the control group (right) do not. D, The two groups' anxiety levels are measured. The experimental group are more anxious than the control group. We can be sure that this difference is due to our experimental manipulation (cooking) because this was the *only* systematic difference between the two groups

anxiety, or by some interaction between stress and anxiety levels – we would have no way of knowing which of these possibilities was true, and the experiment would have been a waste of time for all concerned (see Figure 3.2). Confounding variables like this, which differ systematically with respect to our experimental manipulations, need to be avoided at all costs.

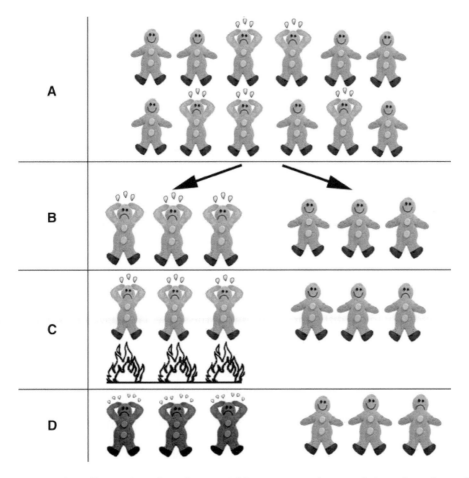

Figure 3.2   The effects of confounding variables. A, A population of gingerbread people, varying in anxiety level. B, Two samples from the population who differ systematically in their pre-existing level of anxiety. C, The experimental group (left) get a stressful treatment (cooking) that the control group (right) do not. D, The two groups' anxiety levels are measured. The experimental group are more anxious than the control group. We cannot tell whether this difference is due to our experimental manipulation (cooking) because this was not the only systematic difference between the two groups – they differed in pre-existing anxiety level too

In attempting to avoid confounding variables, we also need to take care that our manipulation of the independent variable is affecting only the variable that we are interested in, and not other ones as well. For example, if we administer a stressful experience to one of our two groups, this might well affect not just their stress levels, but also influence them in other ways too: they might also become more angry, resentful, unhappy, and so on.

3.5 **ELIMINATING CONFOUNDING VARIABLES**

The effects of many confounding variables can be minimised by careful attention to how the experiment is conducted. For example, in our hypothetical experiment, we could make sure that everyone, regardless of group, was tested under very similar conditions as far as heating, lighting, ventilation and noise levels were concerned. We could greatly reduce any variations in how the experimenter behaved towards the participants by conducting the experiment in as standardised a fashion as possible (perhaps by giving each participant a sheet of written instructions or by presenting the instructions to them on a computer screen).

It is more difficult to deal with confounding variables that stem from the participants themselves: people spontaneously vary in all sorts of ways that might affect their performance in an experiment. We do not want a situation in which all of the people in one group are more intelligent, or more motivated, or more anxious than those in the other group. If this happens, we are back in the situation of not being able to disentangle the effects of the independent variable from those of other co-varying factors. To avoid this problem, a standard technique is to allocate participants *randomly* to the different conditions of the study. This does not eliminate the variations between participants, but it does spread them across the different conditions of the study. This ensures that they are unlikely to vary systematically in concert with the manipulations of the IV. Individual differences between participants will still add 'noise' (variability) to the data, but at least they will not produce *systematic* differences between the conditions.

Random allocation of participants to conditions is so important as a means to avoid systematic confounds, that it is a defining attribute of the experimental method. (Experiments in which randomisation is not possible are called *quasi-experiments*: see Chapter 4.) Randomisation should apply not just to the allocation of participants to conditions, but also to the way in which the experimenter conducts the study. For example, it is a bad idea to test all of the participants in one condition before testing all of the participants in another condition, because this runs the risk of introducing systematic confounds into the study. The experimenters' demeanour might change over time, as they become more practised and/or bored at running the study, and this might affect the way the participants behave. Another possibility is that different kinds of participants might sign up for morning or afternoon sessions, or on different days.

J.S. Mill's 'Method of Difference' stipulates that two conditions should be identical except for one thing (the experimenter's manipulation of the independent variable). He was thinking in terms of the physical sciences, where this consistency is easier to attain. In practice, at least until we perfect human cloning,[2] Mill's ideal will

---

2 One option is to use naturally occurring 'clones', namely monozygotic (identical) twins. Because they are derived from a single fertilised egg, identical twins have the same genes. Usually, they are also

be unachievable with human beings because they show so much natural variation. However, randomisation enables us to ensure that our conditions have no *consistent* differences between them (in terms of the characteristics of the participants or in terms of how we behave towards them) except for our manipulation of the IV. This is good enough for the experimental method to be able to detect causal relationships between variables in the field of human behaviour.

3.6 REDUCING 'NOISE' IN THE DATA

Randomisation is an effective way of neutralising confounding variables by making them unsystematic in their effects. However, as mentioned above, randomisation does not *remove* the effects of potential confounding variables altogether; it merely makes their effects unsystematic with respect to those of the independent variable. It is still highly desirable to try to eliminate their effects wherever possible, because this will increase our chances of detecting any results from our manipulations of the independent variable. You can think of a participant's response in an experiment as being a measurement that is actually comprised of their 'true' score plus 'error' or 'noise' produced by the effects of other variables, just as it is conceptualised in the chapter on psychometrics (Chapter 7). We generally want to know if, on average, the true scores of one group are different from those of the other group. In practice, we cannot separate out the true scores and errors; all we have is the overall score for each participant. Therefore we end up comparing the 'true scores plus error' for one group, to the 'true scores plus error' for the other group. If the difference between the true scores is large relative to the amount of random 'noise', then the effects of the errors will not matter – we will still be able to detect that our manipulations of the independent variable have had differing effects on the two groups. However, if the effects of the independent variable on participants' scores are small compared to the effects of the error, then we might well be unable to detect any difference between our two groups even though it does exist.

Therefore, good experimental design aims to reduce the amount of variation introduced into the results by factors other than the independent variable, in order to maximise the chances of detecting effects of the independent variable. While it is vital to avoid systematically varying confounding variables, it is also highly desirable to avoid randomly varying ones. In both cases, the solution is the same: ensure

reared in the same environment. As a result, they are closely matched in many respects. Twin research has a long history in psychology, and has been useful in attempts to disentangle genetic and environmental factors in disorders such as schizophrenia and autism (e.g. Ronald *et al.*, 2005). However, since only 4 in 1000 births produce monozygotic twins, for most experiments the use of twins isn't very feasible as a routine way of producing matched experimental groups!

that everything is as similar as possible across the different conditions in a study, except for your manipulations of the independent variable. Later in this chapter, alternative designs are discussed which can enable us to take some of this error into account.

3.7 OPERATIONAL DEFINITIONS OF INDEPENDENT AND DEPENDENT VARIABLES

Another way to reduce 'noise' in your data is to have precise definitions for all of the variables concerned. Our initially fairly vague idea, that stress might affect memory, needs to be turned into something which is precise and testable. In our example, we would need unambiguous definitions of both 'stress' and 'memory performance'. They need to be unambiguous so that we can measure them properly. The measure of memory performance would need to be quantitative so that we can assess the size of any difference between the groups in as objective a way as possible (normally by using a statistical test of some kind). Sometimes variables are fairly clear-cut and their definitions need no clarification (e.g. if you were looking at 'sex differences', you probably would not need to define what was meant by male and female). However, many concepts in psychology are rather vague and an **operational definition** is required – we define things like 'impulsivity', 'anxiety' and 'intelligence' in terms of how we measure them. Other workers may not agree with our definitions, but at least everyone is clear about what the definition is.

3.8 BETWEEN-GROUPS VERSUS WITHIN-SUBJECTS DESIGNS

Yet another way in which 'noise' can be reduced in experiments is by using a within-subjects design. So far we have only discussed between-groups designs (also known as between-subjects designs), in which each participant is in only one of the conditions in the experiment. In within-subjects designs (also known as repeated-measures designs) each participant is in more than one condition. There are advantages and disadvantages to both types of design, and which type is chosen will depend on the particular study.

Within-subjects designs have a number of advantages over between-groups designs. First, they have a big practical advantage, because they reduce the number of participants that are needed. This saves time (because trying to find participants is often one of the most tedious aspects of running a study) and money (if you are paying people to participate in your study). Within-subjects designs have a statistical advantage too, because they are generally more sensitive to the experimenter's manipulations than are between-groups designs. In a between-groups design, participants in one group receive a different treatment from the experimenter than participants in the other group, but the two groups also differ in many other respects. As mentioned earlier, good experimental design will ensure that the two groups do not *systematically* differ in these other factors, but even so these factors will add 'noise' to the data. This 'noise' is greatly reduced in an experiment that uses a within-subjects design. The same people are participating in all conditions, and so the principal difference between the conditions is the one introduced by the experimenter. This makes the data less noisy, so any effects of the manipulations of the independent variable are more likely to be detectable. This is especially advantageous when studying phenomena that show considerable variation between individuals.

The advantages of within-subjects designs mean that, wherever possible, they should be used in preference to between-groups designs. However between-groups designs are useful in two situations. First, there are many circumstances in which it is impossible to use a within-subjects design. For example, if you want to look at questions involving variables such as personality or gender, which are inherently fixed attributes of a person, you have no option but to use different groups of people and hence a between-groups design. Second, a big disadvantage of within-subjects designs is that they are susceptible to order effects: participation in one condition can produce changes in the participants that then affect their performance in other conditions. For example, participants might become more practised at the experimental task, or more bored or fatigued. If everyone participates in the conditions in the same order, these effects will become systematically confounding variables, and it will be impossible to know whether any differences between the conditions are due to your manipulations of the independent variable, or due to increased practice, boredom, and so on. For this reason, within-subjects designs generally try to take account of order effects by using counter-balancing.

3.9 COUNTER-BALANCING

Sometimes an experimental manipulation has effects on the participants that are irreversible. For example, Sieverding *et al.* (2010) recently published a study on the effects of social influences on health-related behaviour. A group of men who were told that cancer screening was popular were more likely to say that they would go for screening themselves, than were a similar group who were told that asking for cancer screening was a relatively uncommon behaviour. Clearly it would be impossible to use a within-subjects design in circumstances like this: you couldn't test a participant in one or another condition and then ask them to forget what you had just told them, so that they could be tested in the other condition!

However, if the effects of a manipulation are temporary, order effects can be minimised by means of counter-balancing: half of the participants perform the conditions in one order, and the other half perform them in the opposite order. (It is important to randomly allocate participants to one order or the other, so that there are no consistent differences between those who experience one order and those who experience the other.) Note that counter-balancing does not remove order effects, but merely allows you to detect them. It is therefore preferable to the alternative solution of merely using a different random order of conditions for each participant. With counter-balancing, 'order of testing' becomes an independent variable in its own right, and it can be incorporated into the statistical analysis of the data.

One problem with counter-balancing is that it can get quite complicated with more complex experimental designs in which you have more than two conditions. With two conditions, you need two orders (AB and BA). With three conditions, you need six different orders (ABC, ACB, BCA, BAC, CAB, CBA), while with four conditions you need 24! Not only does it get complicated to work out the orders with large numbers of conditions, but you would also need a large number of participants (one group for each possible order). Experiments which use a large number of conditions in a repeated-measures design are sometimes referred to as Latin Squares designs, because the different orders can be arranged in a grid such that each row represents a unique sequence.

There is also the problem that counter-balancing assumes that the order effects are symmetrical, in the sense that carry-over effects from condition A to condition B are similar to those from condition B to condition A. Suppose we are interested in the effects of two doses of a drug. We opt for a within-subjects design, so that all of the participants are tested after taking both doses of the drug. Half of them take the low dose first and the high dose second, while the other half take the doses in the opposite order. If the testing sessions are close together in time, and the effects of the higher dose take longer to wear off than the effects of the lower dose, we could end up with a situation in which counter-balancing fails to ensure that the two orders are comparable. Although those who take the low dose first are fully recovered before they take the high dose, those who take the high dose first are still affected by the drug when they come to take the low dose. The solution in a situation like this is to lengthen the time interval between the two sessions. However, in general if there is any doubt about the symmetry of order effects, it is usually better to use a between-subjects design instead.

3.10 MATCHED PAIRS DESIGN

This is a special version of the between-groups design, in which participants are paired up on the basis of variables that might have an effect on the dependent variable. So they might be matched on age, IQ, personality measures, and so on. (As mentioned earlier, using monozygotic twins would be the ideal way to do this, although seldom feasible in practice.) Once this is done, the members of each pair are then randomly allocated to one or the other of the experiment's conditions. The advantage of this method is that it can reduce the amount of 'noise' in the data produced by extraneous variables, because they end up affecting both groups equally. The problem is that you do not necessarily know if participants have been matched on the most relevant variables as far as your research question is concerned. For example, in a study investigating the effects of high or low social anxiety on emotion perception, it might be worth matching the participants in the social anxiety groups on other personality measures (such as depression) but it would be pointless to do so on variables that are quite unrelated to social anxiety or emotion perception, such as the participants' heights.

3.11 **RELIABILITY AND VALIDITY**

A good experiment produces results which are reliable, valid and worth knowing (see also Chapter 7 on psychometrics). 'Reliability' simply means that the results are reproducible – that they are consistent. A basic tenet of science is that data are open to scrutiny and that experimental results are potentially replicable. That is, other scientists, who are perhaps sceptical of my claims, should be able to repeat my study and get similar results.

Replication is an important part of the experimental method, and it actually occurs in two distinct ways. Earlier, I said that my basic experiment would compare two groups of participants. But why use groups? Why not just take two individuals, stress one but not the other, and then compare their recall performance? It comes back to the problem of systematic confounding variables again: if we used only two people, they would differ in many ways, and we would not be able to tell whether the differences between them in recall performance were due to stress or some other factor (e.g. the stressed person might have had a better memory than the unstressed person to begin with). By using lots of participants in each group, we are effectively performing lots of replications of the procedure within the same study. By randomly allocating participants to the different conditions, we stand a good chance of ensuring that any differences between the participants will not co-vary systematically with group membership. For example, it might well be that some of the participants have inherently better memories than others, but by allocating them randomly to the experimental and control groups, we are unlikely to end up with a situation in which all of the people with good memories are in one group or the other. (As we shall see, there are experimental designs that enable us to go beyond merely *assuming* that randomisation has achieved this end.)

The other way in which we can check reliability is by repeating the experiment. In practice, most psychologists perform an experiment, publish the results in a scientific paper (together with a clear description of how it was carried out) and then leave it to other researchers to try to replicate it. But the important thing is that an experiment should be potentially replicable.

'Validity' means that the results are measuring what we think they are measuring, and not something else. This is quite a separate issue from reliability. Results can be highly reliable but not valid. For example, shoe size is a highly reliable measure, at least among adults. My shoe size is the same today as it was ten years ago, and I would be highly surprised if it was different in ten years' time. However, shoe size is not a valid measure of anxiety; anxious people do not have smaller or larger feet than non-anxious people. In this case it is fairly obvious that my measure is not valid, but in many cases things are not so clear-cut.

Here is a real-world example where validity issues intrude into the interpretation of experimental results. 'Weapon focus' is an interesting phenomenon in research on eyewitness behaviour. Research suggests that if a weapon is visible onlookers will pay attention to it, at the expense of encoding information about other aspects of the scene. This has been investigated by experiments in which two groups see videos of a staged event which differ in one crucial factor: the presence or absence of a weapon. On a subsequent memory test, people in the 'weapon' group recall less information from the video than do people in the 'control' group who see a non-threatening object instead. This kind of study has been replicated on a number of occasions, albeit with variable results (see the review in Steblay, 1992). However, while the result of this manipulation is reasonably reliable, the *interpretation* of it is less clear-cut. Pickel (1998) found a similar effect on recall performance when the 'criminal' in her study wielded a raw (but Salmonella-free) chicken as opposed to a gun. This calls into question the validity of the 'weapon focus' effect as originally conceived. The original researchers assumed that they were manipulating the participants' stress level by using a gun or a knife, but instead they may have been manipulating novelty – weapons are unusual and therefore attention-grabbing. Hope and Wright (2007) subsequently showed that notwithstanding Pickel's findings, the threatening nature of weapons does seem to have a role to play in the weapon focus effect. However, the point for the present discussion is that experiments can be methodologically rigorous, and can produce reliable results, without those results necessarily being a valid measure of what the researchers thought they were measuring.

There are different types of validity that need to be considered when designing a study. Internal validity refers to the extent to which we can be sure that the changes that we observe in our measurements have actually been produced by our manipulations, rather than by other factors. This is a measure of how well our experiment was designed and executed. External validity (or ecological validity) refers to the extent to which the results have any real-world relevance.

An example might make this distinction clearer. There are now many well-designed and carefully conducted experiments that have used driving simulators to investigate the effects on drivers' performance of using a mobile phone. Most of these experiments compare how well people drive in a simulator when they are undistracted, to how well they can drive while concurrently performing some task via a mobile phone. Normal conversation is very variable, so most experimenters try to keep the mobile phone task as constant between participants as possible, by making them do tasks like mental arithmetic or logical reasoning exercises. Such experiments have high internal validity: we can be fairly certain that any observed impairments in driving performance are directly attributable to the distracting task, because the participants in the different conditions are tested under exactly the same conditions except for the presence or absence of the 'mobile phone' task. We can be less certain of these experiments' external validity however. First, driving in a simulator is not the same as real driving – for one thing, participants know that they cannot be killed or injured in a simulator. Second, the mobile phone tasks are often rather artificial. It might be that in everyday life, mobile phone conversations are less distracting to drivers because normal conversation is less mentally demanding than doing mental arithmetic, and because it is self-paced rather than involving answering questions at a rate dictated by an experimenter.[3] This example illustrates a dilemma often faced by experimenters: increased control over internal validity may come at the cost of some loss of external validity.

3.12 FACTORS AFFECTING RELIABILITY

3.12.1 Sample size

To maximise reliability, you should ensure you use enough participants in your study. In general, the more participants you can test, the better: many psychology experiments use too small a sample size and thus suffer from a lack of power (the ability to detect an experimental effect if one exists). There is no simple answer to the question of how many participants need to be used: it depends on the inherent variability present in the phenomenon being investigated. If your manipulations of the independent variable are likely to have a large effect on the participants, and the members of each group respond in a similar way (i.e. there is little variability in performance within each group), then you will probably need to test fewer people than if your manipulations produce small and variable effects on participants.

There are various formulae for calculating how many participants you would need in order to detect an effect of a given size. The StatPages.net website (http://statpages.org) contains links to some excellent programs that will perform 'power

---

3 In the interests of road safety, I am playing devil's advocate here. There is good evidence from a variety of sources – 'real world' driving experiments and accident statistics, as well as simulator studies involving more natural conversations – to suggest that using a mobile phone while driving is dangerously distracting for drivers (regardless of whether it's hand-held or hands-free: see Hole (2007) for a review of the evidence). Don't do it!

analysis' for you. However, their disadvantage is that they generally require the user to have some prior knowledge of the degree of natural variability in the phenomenon being investigated, and that is rarely available in practice. Looking at previous research on a topic can often give you some idea of what would constitute an adequate number of participants for an experiment on that topic.

3.12.2 The stability of the phenomenon being investigated

Some phenomena are inherently more reliable than others. For example, trait anxiety is a personality characteristic and, as such, measurements of it are likely to be more reliable than measurements of state anxiety (which is more affected by events).

3.13 FACTORS AFFECTING VALIDITY

The validity of an experiment's results can be affected by all sorts of factors. We have already dealt at length with systematic confounding variables, which are fatal to validity. Campbell and Stanley (1966) produced a catalogue of possible 'threats' to validity. They can be grouped into three broad categories: 'time threats', where effects produced by the passage of time contaminate the experiment's results; 'group threats', due to problems in how participants are allocated to experimental conditions; and 'reactivity threats', arising from participants' reactivity to the experimental situation. When designing a study, it is worth thinking about these, to see if any of them might cause you problems.

3.13.1 Time threats

The passage of time can affect the validity of a study's results in various ways. These are particularly likely to cause problems for developmental studies, but could affect any study that took place over a prolonged period of time.

History

Participants can have experiences that are unrelated to your experiment, but which affect their performance. I was once involved in a study that was trying to see if children's memory for events was enhanced by presenting information both visually and auditorily as opposed to just auditorily. We presented children with either a complete recording of a TV programme called 'Noah and Nelly' or just the soundtrack, and then measured their memory for the events that occurred in it. Unfortunately this coincided with some of the children being told the biblical story of Noah at school, so they confused him with the TV character. As a result, we obtained messy and ultimately unusable data.

Maturation

Maturational changes are a particular problem in developmental studies. Sometimes changes due to growth and development can be confused with changes due to the experimenter's manipulations. For example, suppose you were interested in examining the effects of a programme to help children learn to read. You test children's reading ability at two different ages, before and after your training programme, and find their reading has improved. You might be tempted to attribute this improvement to your intervention, but it might have occurred anyway, as a consequence of the children's normal cognitive development over time.

Repeated testing

Sometimes participants' behaviour might change as a consequence of repeated testing. For example, suppose you wanted to see if play with educational toys improved children's intelligence. You could do this by giving the children a number of play sessions, and measuring their IQ at various points during the study. An apparent improvement in IQ might be erroneously attributed to the play experiences, when really it is wholly or partially due to the fact that the children have become practised at doing IQ tests. Obviously it would be silly to use exactly the same test each time, because people might well remember the answers they had given before. However, with many tests improvement can occur because people become more adept at using certain strategies to tackle the general types of items that appear in the tests.

Instrument change

In the physical sciences, it is good practice to periodically calibrate any measuring tools. Otherwise they can go out of adjustment and produce changes that might be mistaken for real changes in the property being measured. Similar things can happen in psychology, and these include not just changes in any equipment being used, but also changes in the way the experimenter conducts the study. At the start of a study, an experimenter might be more hesitant and less polished in dealing with participants; towards the end, the experimenter might be more brusque, bored or slick. These changes in the experimenter's demeanour might affect the participants' responses in all sorts of ways: participants might respond by being more cautious or less enthusiastic about performing well.

Experimenters can guard against these kinds of effects in two ways. First, automating the experimental procedure as much as possible can help to minimise any effects of the experimenter's demeanour. Instructions should be standardised as much as possible (something which is easy if the study is administered by computer, but which can also be achieved by giving the participants instructions on a sheet of paper rather than orally). Second, the experimenter can ensure that any changes in the way in which they run the study do not produce *systematic* differences between groups of participants. For example, it is not a good idea to test all of the participants in one condition and then move on to the next. It's better to test them in a random order (any effects produced by changes in the experimenter's behaviour will then be distributed randomly across the different experimental conditions), rather than systematically co-varying together with changes to the independent variable.

3.13.2 **Group threats**

Initial non-equivalence of groups

Ideally, the groups in an experiment should differ only in terms of the independent variable being manipulated by the experimenter: there should be no other systematic differences between the groups. For many research topics, this will be impossible to achieve in practice. For example, if you are interested in sex differences, you cannot randomly allocate participants to being male or female. As a result, the groups will differ in many respects, because males and females do not just differ biologically but have different life experiences as well. The same is true if you wanted to look at the effects of age: older and younger people differ in many ways other than just in terms of chronological age. Cohort effects like these can complicate the interpretation of any differences found between the groups, because you cannot be certain that the differences are solely due to the variable that you are interested in (e.g. chromosomal sex or chronological age).

Strictly speaking, experiments involving 'subject variables' such as age and gender are not true experiments, because the experimenter cannot randomly assign participants to the different conditions of the study: they are really *quasi-experiments* (see Chapter 4). This is not to say that such experiments are useless; you just have to be aware of their limitations. In the case of sex and age differences, in particular, it is easy to slip into the trap of thinking that observed differences are solely attributable to the biologically based differences between the groups (chromosomal sex and chronological age), whereas the reality is that any observed differences are a mishmash of biological and experiential (cultural and historical) factors.

Selection–maturation interaction

Problems can arise if participants differ in both the experimenter's manipulations and maturational factors. For example, suppose you were interested in the effects of children's gender on how well they attended to sex education information, and you found that your group of boys (with an average age of 11) remembered the information better than the girls (who had an average age of 9). Because these groups differed in age as well as gender, it is possible that these variables interacted to produce your observed results. The observed difference might have arisen, at least in part, because many of the boys had reached puberty, and hence had become very interested in girls, so that they perceived sex education information as being relevant to them. In contrast, perhaps many of the girls were still prepubescent and hence not so interested in boys or information about sex education. What you have really measured in this case is not the effects on memory of gender, but the effects of an interaction between gender and perceived relevance of information to the participant, produced by the maturational difference between the groups.

Regression towards the mean

If someone scores particularly poorly on a test, the chances are that they are likely to do better the next time they are tested. Similarly, if they do really well, they are likely to perform worse on a subsequent occasion. Following an extreme score, the next score is likely to be more average, a tendency called regression towards the mean. Suppose you are interested in the effects of a remedial reading programme for dyslexic children. You select a large group of children. An initial measurement of their reading ability produces a mixture of scores and you give the reading programme to the children with very low scores. You administer your programme, and a second reading test shows that their reading performance has improved. Therefore, you conclude that your programme has been effective in improving dyslexic children's reading ability. This is not a valid conclusion because regression towards the mean could be affecting the scores on the second test.

Regression towards the mean is often a problem in applied research. Frequently, governments introduce road safety legislation in response to high accident rates. The next year, the accident rates are lower, and the government claims the credit for the reduction. In fact, the government's action may have had nothing at all to do with the drop in accidents: the accident rate might well have decreased the following year anyway, due to regression towards the mean. (A sceptic might argue that regression towards the mean is the main way in which many types of alternative medicine work: I go to the osteoreflexochirocrystallopyramidologist when my backache is particularly bad, and the next day I feel a bit better – but I probably would have done so anyway, because when something is really bad it is more likely to get a bit better than to get even worse.)

Differential mortality

This sounds a bit extreme, but it merely refers to problems of interpretation that arise if participants are more likely to drop out of one group than another. It is also known as *differential attrition*. Suppose we want to compare two methods of treating spider phobia: repeatedly talking about spiders in a calm, relaxed setting, versus repeated episodes of 'flooding' (we place the patient in a cage and drop dozens of spiders on them). We start with 20 patients in each condition. At the end of the study, we find that there are only a few people left in the 'flooding' group: the rest have decided to quit the experiment. However, the few that are left no longer have a spider phobia – compared to the relaxation group, they are much improved. Can we conclude that our treatment has worked? Unfortunately, we cannot. There may be important differences between the participants that remain in the study and those that dropped out, and these may have had an important influence on the outcome of the treatment. For example, the ones that remain in the 'flooding' condition may have been less phobic to begin with, or more motivated to overcome their phobia. In contrast, because the relaxation treatment is less gruelling, everyone has remained, including those who are highly phobic. Because of differential mortality, we cannot tell how much of any observed difference between our groups is due to our manipulations, and how much of it comes from systematic differences between the participants that remain and those that dropped out.

3.13.3 Participant reactivity threats

As a cognitive psychologist who is interested in comparatively 'low-level' visual perception, I sometimes wish that participants consisted merely of an eyeball connected to a finger (well, preferably that they consisted of just the eyeball, but the finger would be necessary so that they could make a response). Unfortunately, humans are a bit more complicated than this: the experiment is a social situation, and participants come to experiments with all sorts of preconceptions and expectations about what is likely to happen, and how they should behave. These are highly likely to affect their behaviour.

A notorious example of this is the 'Hawthorne effect'. Between 1924 and 1932, researchers set out to find out the effects of factors such as illumination levels and shift duration on workers' productivity at the Hawthorne factory near Chicago. They ended up discovering that pretty much any change increased productivity, including a return to the original working conditions – the workers seem to have responded to the increased interest in them by working harder. Experimenter effects (and in particular the Hawthorne effect) have become somewhat exaggerated by psychology textbooks, but they do have some basis in fact. Draper (2009), in a discussion of the facts behind the myths, concludes that the Hawthorne effect was actually produced by the operation of a number of factors. However, as he points out, it is important in demonstrating the dangers of trying to treat participants as if they are merely 'material systems'.

Evaluation apprehension

Evaluation apprehension refers to the fact that participants may feel anxious about being evaluated by the experimenter, and hence respond differently from how they would if they were not in an experimental situation. Participants often treat the experiment as a personal test of their abilities: consequently they may try to present themselves in the best light to the experimenter, and may be anxious to be seen to be 'doing well'. Participants may try to work out what the experiment is about and behave so as to help the experimenter by producing the 'right' results. In the jargon, they respond to the 'demand characteristics' of the experimental situation, and this can seriously distort their responses.

Experimenter effects

There is ample research suggesting that an experimenter's expectations and beliefs can affect the behaviour of their participants, sometimes biasing them to respond in ways that are in line with the experimenter's hypotheses (e.g. Rosenthal, 1966). In an educational setting, this is known as the Pygmalion effect. Rosenthal and Jacobson (1992) led schoolteachers to believe that some of their pupils would develop much faster than the rest (although in fact these children had been selected purely randomly). To some extent, the 'gifted' children's performance improved in accordance with the expectations that had been instilled in the teachers.

Control group's awareness of its status

This can be a problem in applied research. Suppose you are an occupational psychologist who is interested in comparing the effects of environmental factors on office workers' productivity. The experimental group gets moved to a nice airy office with pot plants, carpets and a coffee machine, while the control group remains in the dark, dingy windowless office that they have always had. If people are aware that they are in a control group, they might feel that they are missing out on the benefits that are being obtained by the experimental group. This could lead to resentment, so that the control group perform more poorly than they might otherwise have done. Alternatively it might lead to increased competitiveness, so that they actually perform better than they would otherwise have done (the so-called John Henry effect).

  Sometimes it is possible to circumvent these problems by promising everyone the experimental treatment but at different times. This way, you have an experimental group and a control group, and then the control group go on to receive the experimental treatment subsequently.

Blind and double-blind procedures

One way to avoid reactivity threats is to use blind or double-blind procedures in order to carry out a study. In a blind (or single-blind) procedure, the participants do not know which condition of the study they have been allocated to. This approach is commonplace in medical research. For example, in a drug study, one group might be given a drug while the other receives a 'placebo' which looks and tastes similar but lacks the drug's active ingredients. The use of a 'blind' procedure like this ensures that the participants' behaviour cannot be affected by their awareness of which treatment they have been assigned to.

This is important, because not only can the experimenter's expectations affect the study's outcome, as mentioned earlier, but so too can the expectations of the participants themselves. This is shown nicely by a recent study on acupuncture, by Bausell *et al.* (2005). They examined the effects of acupuncture on the severity of pain following dental surgery. Acupuncture actually proved to be no better than a placebo (a sham acupuncture treatment) in reducing the pain: both were equally ineffective. However, at the end of the study Bausell *et al.* also asked the patients which treatment they *thought* they had received. Those who *believed* they had received acupuncture rated their pain as less severe than those who *believed* they had been in the placebo group (regardless of which group the participants had actually been assigned to). This raises the possibility that any analgesic effects of acupuncture are produced by the patients' expectations about the treatment's efficacy, rather than by the treatment itself. More generally, it highlights the importance of taking account of how participants' expectations and beliefs might affect an experiment's results.

An even better strategy for coping with reactivity threats is to run the experiment under 'double-blind' conditions. In this arrangement, not only are the participants unaware of which condition they are in, but so too is the experimenter who administers the treatments to them. The advantage of the double-blind procedure is that there is no scope for the participants' behaviour to be affected by the experimenter effects mentioned earlier. For example, suppose you wanted to study the effects of small amounts of alcohol on cognitive functioning. It is well established that in circumstances like these, the expectations of the experimenter and the participants can sometimes influence the results (see Testa *et al.*, 2006, for a review). Consequently, it would be advisable to run the study under double-blind condiions. One group of participants could drink orange juice laced with vodka (which is fairly tasteless on its own), and another group could drink pure orange juice (perhaps with just a small amount of alcohol smeared on the glass, so that these participants couldn't tell that they were drinking only juice). The drinks could be prepared by one experimenter and then administered to the participants by a second experimenter who has no idea which of the drinks contain alcohol. This second experimenter could also test the participants. In this way, the effects of alcohol could be measured, uncontaminated by any effects of the expectations of the participants or the experimenters.

A disadvantage of the 'double blind' procedure is that it takes extra time and effort to run the study, because the experimenter who allocates participants to groups needs an assistant to actually test them. Also, of course, there are many psychology studies in which it would be impossible to use 'blind' or 'double-blind' techniques; for example, if you were investigating age, gender or ethnic differences, it would be fairly obvious who was in which group.

3.14 TYPES OF EXPERIMENTAL DESIGN

Many of the threats to validity can be overcome by careful attention to experimental design. This section outlines some commonly used experimental designs, and examines their advantages and disadvantages.

3.14.1 'Post-test only/control group' design

This is the simplest form of experiment that we can do, and the one we have discussed so far when talking about 'experiments'. We have two groups: an 'experimental' group that receive some form of treatment, and a 'control' group that do not. We allocate participants randomly to one group or the other, so that the only systematic difference between them is the one that we have produced. We then compare their performance after the experimental group have received their treatment. If the two groups now differ, we can conclude that the difference has arisen because of what we did to the experimental group (see Figure 3.3). The disadvantage of this design is that we are assuming that random allocation of participants to the two groups will ensure that any observed differences are not due to pre-existing group differences. However, we have no way of knowing for certain that this assumption is actually correct. Occasionally random allocation can produce very non-random-looking effects, precisely because it is random!

3.14.2 'Pre-test/post-test control group' design

This is similar to the previous design, except that we give everyone a pre-test to ensure that the two groups are initially comparable before the treatment is administered to the experimental group (see Figure 3.4). The disadvantage of this design is that the pre-test might in itself affect the participants' subsequent behaviour. If so, we might end up measuring not just the effect of our experimental manipulation, but the effect of this in interaction with the effects of the pre-test. For example, suppose we were interested in the effects of music on mood. We could randomly allocate participants to one of two conditions: listening to happy music or listening to sad music. To ensure that we do not have a disproportionate number of depressed people in one group or the other (i.e. that our randomisation procedure was effective at eliminating systematic differences between the groups), we could give all the participants a questionnaire to measure their mood before they listen to the music. This could reassure us that the two groups were indeed initially comparable in terms of their mood, but it would also have the disadvantage of possibly alerting them to the fact that their mood was a variable of interest to the experimenter. This in turn might affect the way in which they responded to the music.

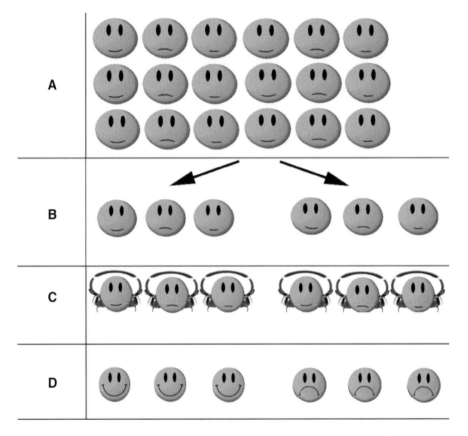

Figure 3.3   The 'post-test only/control group' design. A, A population of people, varying randomly in mood. B, Two random samples from the population; random selection means the samples *probably* do not differ systematically in mood. C, The two groups are given different treatments to induce a mood, either happy music (left) or sad music (right). D, The two groups are measured on a mood test. One group are happy, while the other group are sad. We can be reasonably sure that this difference is due to our experimental manipulation (mood induction by music) because this was probably the only systematic difference between the two groups. However, the lack of any pre-test means that we do not know this for certain

3.14.3 Solomon four-group design

This design is an improvement over the previous one because it can show whether pre-testing has in itself affected participants' behaviour. It requires at least four groups: two are experimental groups and two are control groups (see Figure 3.5). One of the experimental groups and one of the control groups receive a pre-test.

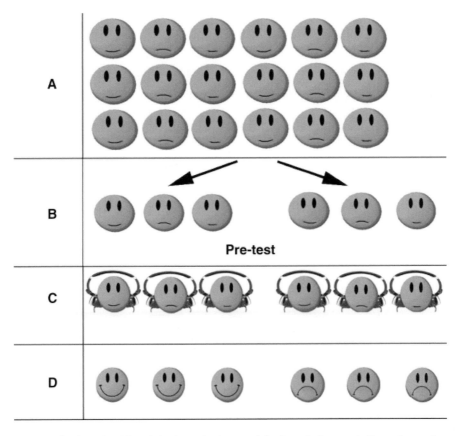

Figure 3.4 The 'pre-test/post-test control group' design. A, A population of people, varying randomly in mood. B, Two random samples from this population who initially do not differ systematically in mood, as established by a pre-test. C, The two groups are given different treatments to induce a mood, either happy music (left) or sad music (right). D, The two groups are measured on a mood test. One group are happy, while the other group are sad. We can be sure that this difference is due to our experimental manipulation (mood induction by music) because this was the only systematic difference between the two groups, *and* the pre-test reassures us that they were comparable in mood before the experiment took place

The other two groups do not. By comparing the two experimental groups to each other, and the two control groups to each other, it is possible to see if pre-testing has had any effects. By comparing the experimental groups to the control groups, it is possible to see if the experimental treatment has had any effects. This is a powerful design. Sadly it is not often used in practice, primarily because of its expense (it requires double the number of participants compared to the 'pre-test/post-test control group' design).

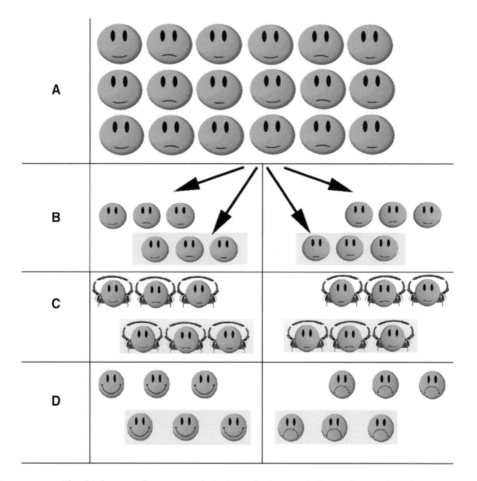

Figure 3.5 The 'Solomon four-group' design. A, A population of people who vary randomly in mood. B, Four random samples from this population who initially do not differ systematically in mood; for the two shaded groups, this is *confirmed* by a pre-test; for the two unshaded groups, it is *assumed* that random allocation has ensured this. C, Two pairs of groups are given different treatments to induce a mood, either happy music (left) or sad music (right); each pair contains one pre-tested group, and one group that was not pre-tested. D, The four groups are measured on a mood test. The two groups on the left are both happy, while the two groups on the left are both sad. We can be sure that this difference is due to our experimental manipulation (mood induction by music). In this case, we find no difference between the two happy groups, and no difference between the two sad groups. This allows us to be confident that in this case, pre-testing for mood had no systematic effects on performance

3.15 **EXPERIMENTAL DESIGNS AND THREATS TO VALIDITY**

Even the most basic experimental design (the 'post-test only/control group' design) can cope well with many of Campbell and Stanley's threats to internal validity. The control group provides a baseline against which to assess the changes produced by the experimenter's manipulations of the independent variable. Because the control group is identical to the experimental group in all respects except for the IV manipulations, history and maturation threats should affect the two groups in similar ways. These factors could complicate the interpretation of the results and affect their external validity, but at least you could be reasonably sure that any *systematic* difference between the groups arose from your manipulations.

Instrument change should affect all groups equally, if the experimenter takes care to run participants from different groups in a random order. Regression towards the mean should not be a problem as long as the control and experimental groups are similar in terms of their initial performance. The pre-test/post-test design and the Solomon four-group design both have the additional advantage that they enable you to measure the extent to which regression towards the mean has occurred, rather than simply control for its influence on the results as in the simpler post-test only design. Experimental designs do not cope well with the effects of differential mortality, however: this can seriously distort the conclusions from a study, especially if the participants have all dropped out of the study for similar reasons. It then becomes difficult to know to what extent the results are due to the experimenter's manipulations, rather than to some interaction between this and the characteristics of the participants.

Experimenter effects, in the sense of the experimenter unconsciously influencing the participants' behaviour, can be prevented by using a double-blind administration procedure (although sadly this is extremely rare in most areas of psychological research). Even if this ideal is not attained, experimenter effects can often be reduced by using standardised procedures for the administration of instructions to participants. Many experiments can be presented entirely via a computer, so one way to reduce experimenter effects is to seat the participant in front of the computer, start the experiment and then leave the room until they have finished.[4]

---

4 At the end of the nineteenth century, the rise of Darwinism provoked a great deal of interest in animal intelligence. The psychologist Otto Pfungst (1911) investigated 'Clever Hans', a horse who could apparently solve complex arithmetic problems by tapping out the answer with his hoof. Pfungst found that Clever Hans had learnt to respond to subtle non-verbal cues from his audience, who leant forwards slightly in anticipation as the number of taps approached the correct answer. Similar effects can happen in the laboratory, with the experimenter quite unconsciously affecting participants' responses. If you are watching a participant as they make the 'wrong' responses in your experiment, it is all too easy to frown or sigh as a result, and hence possibly bias that person's subsequent responses!

The other reactivity threats – especially evaluation apprehension – are difficult to eliminate with any of these designs. In fact, reactivity effects are an inherent problem with the experimental method. They are likely to be more serious for some areas of research than for others; for example, one might expect them to be worse for researchers investigating social behaviour or personality than for researchers studying cognition. However, even cognitive research is bedevilled by the problem that participants often treat the experiment as a test of their abilities, and consequently adopt whatever strategies they can find to maximise their performance. One possible solution to the problem of reactivity is to design the study so that participants either have no way of knowing what the experiment is about (as in the 'single-blind' procedure described earlier), or so that they are actively deceived about the aims of the study. Many experiments use the former technique, which places the participants in a somewhat strange position: they agree to take part in a study while in a state of ignorance about its purpose but on the understanding that all will be revealed to them afterwards! A second method, using deceit, may be unavoidable in certain circumstances, but is generally to be avoided. First, strictly speaking, it is unethical. It contravenes one of the basic principles of research, that participants should give their informed consent to taking part. On more practical grounds, it fosters a distrust of psychologists by participants, so that even when a study is actually no more than it seems, participants are looking for hidden agendas.

3.16 MORE ADVANCED EXPERIMENTAL DESIGNS

Up to now we have considered fairly straightforward experimental designs based on the idea of comparing an experimental group to a control group. These are fine for many purposes, but real-life phenomena are often complicated and hence require more sophisticated experiments to do them justice.

The simplest extension of the basic experiment is to add more groups or conditions. Instead of looking at the effects of the presence or absence of an independent variable, we could look at different states (or 'levels') of it. For example, some people believe that the food colourant tartrazine (E102) causes hyperactivity in children. We could run an experiment that straightforwardly tested this hypothesis by giving one group of children food containing a certain amount of tartrazine and another group of children food that did not. However, how much tartrazine do we give our experimental group? It becomes a fairly arbitrary decision. If we give them too little, we might not find any effect, and if we give them too much, we might produce hyperactivity but at the expense of ecological validity. ('Yes, tartrazine did make the children run around on the ceiling, but in real life they are unlikely to eat a bucketful of it as in the present experiment.')

By testing a number of groups, each of whom consumed a different amount of tartrazine, we could find out a lot more about its effects than if we simply compared a 'no tartrazine' group to a single group that had consumed some arbitrary amount of it. Comparing two groups can tell us that an independent variable has 'an effect' on the dependent variable, but it does not tell us much about the *nature* of that effect. In this case, a comparison of two groups could tell us that tartrazine does produce hyperactivity, but little more than that. Perhaps the more tartrazine a child consumes, the more hyperactive they become, in a progressive, dose-dependent manner; or maybe tartrazine has an 'all-or-nothing' effect, so that no discernible effects occur until a certain amount is consumed, beyond which the child becomes manic and it does not matter how much more is consumed. Questions like these can be answered by including more groups in the experiment.

In this instance the different levels of the independent variable correspond to different values of a *quantitative* independent variable – they are all varying amounts on the same dimension (the amount of tartrazine). It's equally possible to have a number of groups that correspond to different levels of a *qualitative* (or *categorical*) independent variable, where the different levels are different in kind from each other. For example, we might be interested in the effects of a range of different food additives on hyperactivity. Unlike 'tartrazine level', 'type of additive' is not something that can be placed on a numerical scale, but it's equally valid to use it as an independent variable.

3.17 LONGITUDINAL VERSUS CROSS-SECTIONAL DESIGNS

These designs are a special case of the between-groups/within-subjects dichotomy, often used in developmental research. In a longitudinal design, you test the same participants at different ages. In a cross-sectional design, you test a different group of participants for each age that you are interested in. The two types of design have the same advantages and disadvantages as within-subjects and between-groups designs, respectively. Longitudinal designs are prone to carry-over effects due to repeated testing, and events that occur during the course of the study may affect the participants' behaviour. They also take a long time to run, which in some cases may make them unfeasible (e.g. if you were interested in the development of a phenomenon from infancy to old age, you would have to be pretty patient to use a longitudinal design!).

Cross-sectional designs are quicker to run, but they are prone to cohort effects: the participants do not just differ in age, but also in life experiences. A good example of this is the effect of age on driving performance. Elderly drivers' accident rates are somewhat higher than those of middle-aged drivers (though still much lower than those of the under-25s). Most of the explanations for this focus on age-related cognitive decline. However, elderly drivers also learned to drive under very different conditions than younger drivers: the driving test was easier, and there was less traffic on the roads. Perhaps elderly drivers have always been poor drivers, and were never as good as current-day middle-aged drivers, even when they were middle-aged themselves. It is hard to know whether the differences between middle-aged and elderly drivers are due to differences in chronological age or differences in life experiences because in practice the two are inextricably intertwined.

3.18 MULTIFACTORIAL DESIGNS

So far, we have only considered experiments in which a single independent variable is manipulated. However the experimental method can also be applied to situations in which we look at the effects of more than one independent variable at a time, within one and the same study. Instead of simply asking, 'Does tartrazine cause hyperactivity', we can ask more complicated questions, such as, 'Does tartrazine cause hyperactivity, and does the size of this effect depend on the age of the child?' This is an example of a multifactorial design. Now we have two independent variables in our study (tartrazine consumption, and age of child) which would enable us to detect any *interaction* between these two variables. An interaction occurs when the effects of one of the independent variables differ depending on the state of the other independent variable. For example, if tartrazine produces hyperactivity, but this effect is most pronounced in younger children, then we have an interaction between tartrazine consumption and age: the effects of tartrazine cannot be considered in isolation because they depend on the child's age.

A design for an experiment like this might be as follows. We could test three different age groups: 5-, 7- and 9-year-olds. Half of the children in each age group would eat food containing tartrazine, and the rest would eat similar food that did not contain the additive. This would give us six groups of participants to test.

As with the simpler experimental designs, it would be vital to allocate participants randomly to the different conditions. If this was a cross-sectional design, then obviously it would not be possible to allocate children randomly to one of the three age groups. However, within each age group, we would definitely allocate children randomly to the 'tartrazine' and 'no tartrazine' conditions.

You could include even more variables into the study; for example, we might also want to see if the effects of tartrazine varied by gender. We would now have twelve groups (six groups as before, consisting solely of boys; and another six groups of girls experiencing the same conditions). I would not recommend going beyond three independent variables in a single experiment because interpreting the statistical output from such a complex design is often extremely difficult, due to all the complex interactions between the independent variables that can occur.

3.19 **MIXED DESIGNS**

Multifactorial designs can be wholly between-groups (so that you have a separate group of participants for each permutation of your independent variables), wholly within-subjects, or a 'mixed' design that uses both between-groups and within-subjects measures in the same study. For example, suppose you were interested in sex differences in the effects of alcohol on coordination. You could examine this by using a mixed design. Sex differences would have to be a between-groups variable, but alcohol consumption could be a repeated-measures variable: each person could be tested twice, once while drunk and once while sober. Again, to avoid possible order effects, the alcohol consumption conditions would have to be counter-balanced, so that half of the males and half of the females would be tested in one order and the remainder in the opposite order (see Figure 3.6).

3.20 **MULTIPLE DEPENDENT VARIABLES**

So far I have discussed experimental designs which involve the experimenter manipulating one or more independent variables, and measuring the effects of these manipulations on a single dependent variable. However, you can have more than one dependent variable in a study if you wish. In some areas of research it is quite routine to take more than one measure of participants' behaviour. This is particu-larly useful in clinical neuropsychological research, where taking measures of both accuracy and response times can provide a more complete picture of brain-damaged patients' cognitive abilities than would be obtained if only accuracy were considered. For example, some popular neuropsychological tests of face-processing abilities, such as the Benton Face Recognition Test, can underestimate the extent of patients' face-processing deficits because they allow unlimited time for patients to make their decisions. When response time is taken into account as well as response accuracy, the true extent of these patients' impairment is revealed (Duchaine & Weidenfeld, 2003).

3.21 **CONCLUSION**

In designing a study, you should always think about the following three issues.

First, is an experimental approach the most appropriate for the question that I want to answer? As mentioned earlier, the experimental method is a very powerful one, but it may not always be the best one to use. Experiments are often intrusive, and they tend to lack ecological validity. The chief disadvantage of the experimental method is that participants are usually aware that they are in an experiment, and

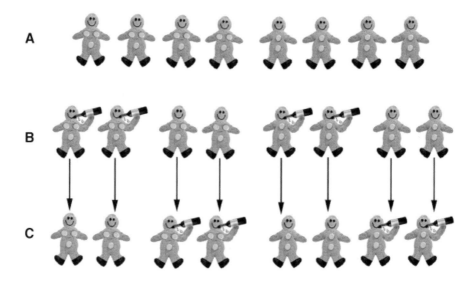

Figure 3.6 An example of a mixed design for investigating the effects of alcohol and gender on coordination. A, A population of men and women, from which two random samples of men and women are taken (they represent the independent-measures IV of 'gender' in this study) – in case you are unfamiliar with gingerbread anatomy, men have two buttons, and women have three. B, To study the effects of the repeated-measures IV, 'alcohol consumption', we test everyone twice, but counterbalance the order of testing; first we test half of the men and half of the women after drinking alcohol, the remaining men and women are tested while sober. C, Everyone is then tested a second time – now the people who were tested while drunk the first time are tested while sober, and the people who were sober the first time are tested while drunk

so may change their behaviour in some way. As a consequence, psychology experiments are often better at discovering what people *can* do, rather than finding out how they behave normally. Sometimes a correlational method or a qualitative approach will be preferable. In practice, many issues are best addressed by attacking them with a variety of different methods, a process of 'converging operations'.

As mentioned earlier, the experiment is a social situation, and participants are not passive recipients of treatments doled out by the experimenter. Therefore, if you decide to use an experimental approach, spend some time thinking about how participants will construe your experimental setup. What will they make of your task, and how will they try to tackle it? Are there any obvious strategies that they could use, that might render the results invalid? After you have tested participants, you should always 'debrief' them: you should explain to them what the aim of the study is, and reassure them that their performance was satisfactory so that they leave in a contented state of mind. The debriefing is a good opportunity to find out from participants what they thought the experiment was about (which is especially useful if you withhold the purpose of the study from the participants until they have finished it), and how they thought they tackled the task.

Second, how am I going to analyse the data that I obtain? *Never* design an experiment without thinking about what data are going to be collected and how they are going to be analysed statistically. If you design a study without thinking about the subsequent data analysis, you run the risk of ending up with data that cannot be analysed, or at best can only be analysed in comparatively crude ways. As a general strategy, whenever possible it is better to design your study so that you end up with one or more scores for each participant rather than participants merely falling into categories. This is because scores permit the use of much more powerful statistical tests than do 'head counts'. But whatever you decide to do, it is much better to think about these issues at the outset, as an integral part of designing the study, rather than afterwards.

Third, do not be too ambitious with your research questions. As Isaac Newton once said:

> To explain all nature is too difficult a task for any one man or even for any one age. 'Tis much better to do a little with certainty, and leave the rest for others that come after you, than to explain all things.
>
> Newton (1704), cited in Westfall (1983)

In other words, it is much better to answer a small question well, than a big question badly. It is somewhat ironic that this advice came from someone who tackled huge topics such as universal laws of gravitation and the nature of light, but it is still good advice. Students often want to include lots of different variables in one and the same study, and modern statistical packages encourage this by making complex multifactorial analyses comparatively easy to perform. However, this usually leads to designs that are over-complex, difficult to interpret, and which lack sufficient statistical power to answer the questions being posed. It is better to aim for simple, straightforward experimental designs that can potentially produce clear answers to specific questions.

3.22 EXERCISES

1 Try investigating experimenter effects for yourself. Construct a list of 20 'concrete' words (like 'scissors', 'doughnut' and 'cement') and twenty 'abstract' words (like 'optimism', 'integrity' and 'disdain'),

randomly intermixed. (Can you think of possible problems that might arise in constructing this word list?) Find 20 participants. For each participant, show them the list for one minute and then ask them to write down as many of the words as they can remember. For half of the participants, before they try to recall the words, nonchalantly say 'previous research suggests that people find it easier to remember the abstract words than the concrete ones'. Tell the remaining participants that 'previous research suggests that people find it easier to remember the concrete words than the abstract ones'. See how many abstract words, and how many concrete words, are recalled by the two groups.

2   Look through some newspapers (or their online versions) to find a couple of articles that report the results of some scientific research. The popular tabloids will be best for this exercise, as they tend to report studies in the most simplistic and sensationalist way. Look at the conclusions drawn by the article, and decide whether they are justified by the research that was actually done. Consider all of the methodological issues described in this chapter, and see how many could potentially apply to your selected articles.

3.23 DISCUSSION QUESTIONS

1   The sports clothing company 'Hadadash' are interested in measuring the effectiveness of their new design of running shoe. They take two groups of amateur athletes, one group from a local gym and the other from a local running club. The gym members get the new shoes and the running club members use their existing shoes. The average 100 metre time for the 'new shoe' group is one second faster than for the 'old shoe' group. Hadadash therefore decide to provide the shoes to the British marathon team, in a bid to improve their chances of success in the next Olympics. What are the possible problems with this study that would lead you to question Hadadash's decision?

2   Imagine that you are Otto Pfungst, faced with the horse, 'Clever Hans'. How would you design a study to test whether or not 'Clever Hans' really could solve arithmetic problems?

3   A psychologist is interested in how gender affects how four-year-olds' play with toys. Design a study to investigate this issue. What would constitute valid measures in this situation? Identify some possible threats to validity that need to be taken into account in interpreting the results.

3.24 **FURTHER READING**

Field and Hole (2003) contains lots of useful information on experimental design and related issues, such as how to write up your study. Harris (2008) is a good alternative to Field and Hole (though not nearly as funny). Robson (2011) is a great resource for anyone thinking of doing 'applied' research of any kind. Shadish *et al.* (2002) is in many respects an update on Campbell and Stanley's (1963) classic work on experimental and quasi-experimental designs.

4

Quasi-experimental Designs

Chris Fife-Schaw

CONTENTS

AIMS OF THIS CHAPTER

This chapter deals with experiments where, for a variety of reasons, you do not have full control over the allocation of participants to experimental conditions as is required in true experiments. Three common quasi-experimental designs are described; the non-equivalent control group design, the time series design and the time series with non-equivalent control group design.

KEY TERMS

compensatory rivalry
contamination effects
external validity
history effects
instrumentation effects
internal validity
interrupted time series

maturational effects
multiple time series design
regression to the mean
sample selection bias
selection/maturation interaction
subject or participant mortality
testing effects

4.1 **INTRODUCTION**

In Chapter 3 the basics of classical experimental designs were discussed. The value of doing experiments is that they offer the most clear-cut route to testing hypotheses about causes and effects. The experimenter has control over the relevant independent variables and allocates participants to conditions at random in an attempt to make sure that they know exactly what is responsible for the changes they observe.

This is to be contrasted with observational and correlational approaches, where we might be able to show that two variables appear to be related to one another but it is difficult to determine whether there is a causal relationship between the variables (where one 'causes' the other) or some third variable is responsible for the observed relationship. Although this may seem less than satisfactory – after all, we usually want to be able to say what causes what – correlational studies are often the best we can hope for in many real-world situations. Practical considerations may limit the amount of control we can expect to have in such situations, so we have to be careful whenever we try to interpret relationships between variables.

In between correlational and experimental approaches lie two other kinds of study: the pre-experiment and the quasi-experiment. Pre-experiments are best thought of as studies that are done simply to get an initial feel for what is going on in a particular situation prior to conducting a more rigorous investigation; this is probably best illustrated by an example.

4.2 **PRE-EXPERIMENTS**

I once attended a rapid-reading course in an attempt to increase the speed with which I could get through paperwork. The university was happy to supply this kind of training as it would help the staff perform better and this should, in turn, help the university to be more efficient. A consultant was hired to do the training. In line with the current political concern to evaluate everything, the consultant felt obliged to conduct an experiment to see if the training had actually worked. Before the training started we were given a report to read and we were asked to time our reading of it and answer some factual questions about the report's content. Having done this, the training went ahead and at the end of the day we were tested on our reading speed again. So that the times and test scores could be readily compared we read the same text and answered the same questions as before. Needless to say reading speed had increased dramatically (four times quicker in my case) and accuracy was very high. The consultant, with evident satisfaction, declared the day a success. Of course the problem here is that we do not really know if the training had any effect on reading speed at all. Whether we have been able to accurately detect the effect of the training is referred to as the internal validity of the experiment.

There are several problems with this evaluation which challenge its internal validity even though at first sight it looks like a reasonable thing to have done. First, the test materials were the same on both occasions and since we had seen them only about seven hours previously there is a strong possibility that we were remembering the content rather than displaying skills learned in the interim. Thus the improvements may have been reflecting memory for the material rather than any real increased reading speed. You do not need to be a psychologist to know that it is easier to read something quickly if you already know what it is about. The same applies to the 'test' questions. Such threats to the experiment's internal validity are called testing effects. In all sorts of studies, repeatedly exposing participants to the test materials is likely to make them familiar with them and less anxious about what they have to do. Such effects tend to inflate post-test scores. In fairness, were the consultant to have used a different report and different test questions, it would have been even more difficult to know what any differences in reading speed could be attributed to. The second text might have been naturally easier to read or, possibly, more difficult.

A second problem concerns what are called maturational effects. Merely having the time to concentrate on reading speed even without experiencing the training may have led to improvements. As none of those tested had been allowed to spend the day thinking about rapid reading without also being exposed to the training, we do not really know whether the training itself had an effect.

Another problem concerns sample selection bias. All those present felt that they had a reading speed problem and, at least at the start of the day, were motivated to improve. You had to volunteer for the course and there was no external pressure on people to attend. Having put a day aside to improve reading skills, not trying hard to improve would have been somewhat perverse. This factor, in conjunction with the potential maturational effects noted above, may have served to increase scores on the retest. Again, we cannot really say how effective the training was, and even if it was effective here, it might be somewhat less useful when people are not so keen to be trained. This latter point refers to the external validity of the study: just how generalisable are the findings? If training works, does it only work for very committed people?

It should be noted that all of these problems concern the experiment (as a pre-experiment) and do not say anything about the virtues of the course. It may have worked very well or it may not. Whichever is the case, this study shed very little light on the issue. This is obviously not an ideal way to demonstrate that the training package increased reading speed.

Other common forms of pre-experiment are often found in news stories where some sort of intervention has to be evaluated. An example would be to see if peer teaching improved computing skills by comparing children's exam performances in schools that had adopted peer teaching with ones that had maintained traditional teacher-led methods. At one level this looks like a reasonable comparison between treatment groups – one group that gets peer teaching and one that does not. Clearly a true controlled experiment is not possible as it would be ethically and politically unacceptable to randomly allocate children to schools and thus to the 'treatment' conditions.

There are numerous problems in interpreting any differences that are observed between the groups. First, there is the question of whether the schools are comparable. Perhaps the schools that adopt peer teaching simply have more able or more socially advantaged children in them in the first place. Those children from better off backgrounds may be expected to have newer and better computers at home and be more computer literate, for instance. There is also a possibility that some event, such as a cutback in funds for computer maintenance, may occur in one school and not in another. Such a sudden change in one of the groups is known as a history effect and may lead to a difference between the groups which is not attributable to the treatment (here peer teaching) but is due to something else. While pre-experiments may seem so flawed as to be pointless, they do serve a purpose of highlighting problems that need to be addressed when the resources become available to do something more impressive and rigorous.

4.3 QUASI-EXPERIMENTS

Many of the problems discussed in relation to pre-experiments reduce the degree of certainty you can have that the 'treatment' actually caused the observed differences in the dependent variable of interest (i.e. the study's internal validity). Because of this, it is rare to see pre-experiments in academic journals. However, many of the research questions that we would like to answer simply cannot be answered by resorting to true experiments. This is usually because either we cannot randomly allocate participants to treatment conditions for practical reasons or it would be unethical to do so (e.g. if it would mean withholding treatment from someone who needs it). In the computer skills example above, for instance, we could not randomly allocate children to the schools.

Quasi-experiments should not be seen, however, as always inferior to true experiments. Sometimes quasi-experiments are the next logical step in a long research process where laboratory-based experimental findings need to be tested in practical situations to see if the findings are really useful. Laboratory-based experiments often reveal intriguing insights, yet the practical importance, or substantive significance, of these can only be assessed quasi-experimentally. Laboratory studies may have shown that under certain highly controlled conditions, peer teaching improves computer test scores, but the 'real' issue is whether peer teaching is generally a good thing for children in their schools. This is a question about the external validity of the laboratory-based studies.

Three classical quasi-experimental designs exist which attempt to overcome the threats to internal validity discussed above. What is presented below is a summary of the three prototypical designs; many variations of these are possible (see Cook & Campbell, 1979).

4.4 NON-EQUIVALENT CONTROL GROUP DESIGNS

As we saw in the example of the computer skills, the two groups (as defined by which school they attended) may not have been comparable. The intervention of peer teaching (the treatment) may have had an effect on test scores but we cannot be sure that the peer teaching group was not already better at computing, prior to the inception of the new programme. The non-equivalent control group design (NECG) overcomes this by requiring a pre-test of computing skill as well as a post-test. The pre-test allows us to have some idea of how similar the control and treatment group were before the intervention.

Figure 4.1 shows some possible outcomes from a simple NECG design. In graph A the control group starts off scoring less than the treatment group, reflecting the non-equivalence of the two groups; finding a control group with exactly equivalent scores in a quasi-experimental design is difficult. Both groups improve after the intervention but the treatment group has clearly improved more than the control group. This is quite a realistic picture to find in studies of educational interventions like the computer skills study. We would expect the control group to improve a bit as, after all, they are still being taught and are still maturing. If the treatment had an effect, then scores should have improved more than might have been expected if the intervention had not taken place. Graph B shows what might have happened if the treatment had no effect. Scores in both groups change about the same amount.

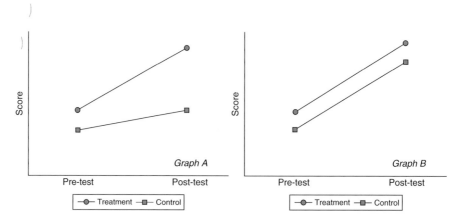

Figure 4.1   Non-equivalent control group designs

The graphs in Figure 4.1 are prototypical and reflect improvements over time. It is, of course, possible for all sorts of patterns to be found. Non-equivalent controls may outscore the treatment group at the pre-test; they may even be equal. Perhaps a treatment serves to allow the treatment group to 'catch up' with the controls. The treatment might decrease scores. There are many possibilities. In all cases you are looking for an interaction between treatment condition (treatment vs. control) and time of measurement (pre-test vs. post-test). You would obviously test for such an interaction statistically (see Chapter 10), but by plotting graphs like these you should observe lines of differing gradients; parallel lines usually indicate no treatment effect (but see later).

4.4.1 Problems with NECG designs

Almost by definition, NECG designs suffer from potential sample selection biases. In studies of 'alternative' therapeutic interventions in particular, there is often a problem that those who get a new treatment had actually sought it out, perhaps because traditional treatments had not worked for them. Such people may be highly motivated to see the new treatment succeed and might have ideological objections to existing treatments. There is also the possibility that those offering the therapy may, consciously or unconsciously, select people they believe would benefit from it or who they think will comply with the treatment regimen. Those who are thought likely to be 'difficult' cases, or for whom the disease may have progressed too far, might not be selected and may even end up appearing in the control group.

Clearly it would be unethical to refuse a new treatment to those who want it or to force those content with existing treatments to receive a new but still untested treatment. However, where possible, you should attempt to have control over, or at least full knowledge of, how the samples are selected. Be aware that those whose efforts are being evaluated will have a vested interest in the outcome of your study.

Even though we have pre-test measures by which we can compare samples, this does not guarantee that the two groups were truly equivalent before the treatment started. If one group was more able or 'brighter', maturation may proceed at a faster rate in that group than the other. We might expect, for instance, that children's computer skills improve with age (maturation) and that more able children learn these skills more quickly and easily. Were the treatment group to contain proportionately more high ability children, group differences may arise out of these differential rates of maturation rather than exposure to the peer teaching method. This is referred to as a selection–maturation interaction. As the pre-test is usually only used to compare groups on the dependent variable, such a problem may remain undetected. One obvious solution would be to measure variables that might conceivably lead to differential maturation rates at the pre-test (e.g. IQ), though this also increases demands on participants.

Statistical regression to the mean is another phenomenon which may influence interpretation of the data. Regression towards the mean is reflected in very high pre-test scorers scoring lower at post-test and very low pre-test scorers scoring higher at post-test. If we are studying people who score at the extremes on the dependent variable we may mistake changes at post-test for this regression to the mean. Why this happens is a little difficult to grasp at first but depends on the fact that our test measures will inevitably contain some errors (see Chapter 7). Cook and Campbell (1979) use an everyday example which is fairly easy to understand; the following is an embellished version of their example.

If we have an ability test like an exam we might do worse than our 'true' ability because we were distracted by other students, we were extremely badly hung over (more so than usual) and we had revised topics which did not come up on the paper. We know that if we took an exam for the same subject again we might expect to do better next time, more accurately reflecting our ability. This is because we would expect these sources of error (failures to record our true ability) to be less likely to *all* co-occur next time around. Similarly, if we were very lucky, the exam might only contain questions on the topics we had revised and we might be fortunate enough to sit the exam on the only day of the year when we were not hung over and everybody behaved themselves in the exam hall. This time we might get a mark that somewhat overstated our true ability in the subject. However, we probably would not expect to be so lucky if we took a similar exam again without further revision.

Across a sample of people, those with mid-range scores are likely to be about equally influenced by these errors (inflating and reducing scores) so they would cancel out on average, leading to no systematic bias in our experiment. People at the extremes, however, are *less likely* to score more extremely on being retested as some of those who had extreme scores at pre-test will have done, because their scores had already been inflated (or reduced) by chance factors or errors unrelated to ability. Since extremely large errors are relatively less likely than moderate size errors, two consecutive large errors in the same direction are very unlikely. This means that post-test scores will tend towards the population's mean score.

For quasi-experiments, this is a particular problem when the treatment group has been selected because of the participants' low scores on the dependent variable (e.g. selecting people with poor computing skills for the peer teaching method). The simplest way to guard against this (though easier said than done) is to ensure that your control group is also drawn from the pool of extreme scorers. The ethics of denying an intervention to children who are particularly bad at computing are clearly an issue here. The problem is also more likely to influence results if your dependent measure has low test–retest reliability. The less reliable the measure (i.e. the more error-prone it is) the more there is likely to be regression to the mean.

Contamination effects occur when, despite your best efforts, the treatment and control groups influence each other in some way. This can often be quite subtle and difficult to detect. In the computer skills study it might happen that a group of keen parents on hearing about the good peer teaching going on at another local school start an after-school club where their children engage in peer teaching around a computer. Thus, although their children are in the control group they may actually be experiencing the treatment, thus leading to potential ambiguity in interpreting the results if the children start to improve to the same levels as the treatment group. Contamination effects are a big problem for studies evaluating health treatments where participants may want to seek additional treatments on top of the one being studied. You might want to evaluate the efficacy of a new cognitive therapy intervention for depression and have a treatment group and a normal drug-treatment control group. Problems arise if those in your normal drug-treatment group also decide to seek a talking therapy from someone else or if your treatment group members even seek out other sources of anti-depressant medication.

Finally, history effects can affect the validity of NECG studies. If some event, in addition to the treatment intervention, occurs between pre-test and post-test in one group only, then it is not clear what any group differences at post-test should be attributed to. For example, an evaluation of a persuasive campaign to promote commuting to work by urban railways in different cities may be invalidated if the 'treatment' city suffers from road travel chaos caused by unanticipated roadworks on the main commuter routes during the period of the study. People may flock to the trains but only because driving to work (their preferred method) was nearly impossible on the test days. You should be aware that all these effects can work to enhance group differences *or* to obscure them.

4.5 TIME SERIES DESIGNS

Time series designs involve having only one sample but taking measurements of the dependent variable on three or more occasions. Such designs are sometimes referred to as interrupted time series designs as the treatment intervention 'interrupts' an otherwise seamless time series of observations. Figure 4.2 gives an illustration of some hypothetical time series data.

As you can see, the main feature that you are looking for when collecting time series data is that the only substantial change in scores coincides with the intervention. The virtue of such a design is that it is relatively less likely that short-term historical events (i.e. history effects) will either (a) co-occur with the treatment and/or (b) have a lasting effect over time. It is also unlikely that small differences pre- and post-intervention will be maintained if the treatment really has no effect. Any maturation effects should be reflected in gradual trends in time series data and not in radical changes occurring at the same time as the intervention.

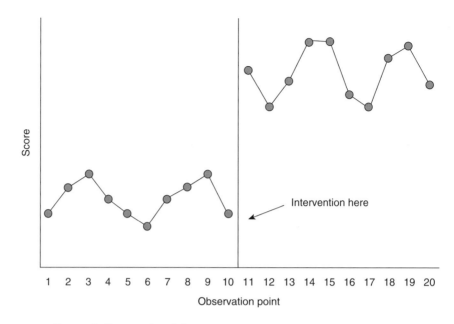

Figure 4.2 Example time series data

For time series studies to work well, multiple data collection/observation points are required. It is difficult to detect trends of any kind with just three observation points so, where possible, opt for as many observation points as is realistic but pay due regard to participant fatigue, boredom and irritation.

4.5.1 Problems with time series designs

Time series studies potentially suffer from the threat of testing effects to their validity. As these studies, by definition, require repeated administration of the same dependent measures, there is a tendency for people to gradually do better as time goes on. This is a separate phenomenon from maturation effects as testing effects arise out of familiarity with the measurement procedures. When presented with a novel test, for instance, we usually do not know what is required and may be anxious about our performance. Repeated exposure to the test and growing familiarity should reduce these anxieties and allow us to perform better. It is also possible that respondents might come to know what they are being asked about and develop more efficient answering strategies, allowing them to respond more quickly. This is especially a problem where measurements are timed.

The net impact of testing effects is that, if the *magnitude* of the treatment effect itself is small, it may get swamped by the testing effects. If the size of the treatment effect is relatively large there will be little problem in determining that the treatment actually had an effect.

Another potential problem concerns instrumentation effects. This refers to changes in the accuracy or reliability of measurements over time. One good example would be the reporting of crimes. Over time the likelihood of reporting (and the police recording) crimes changes as a function of changes in the social representation of the crimes rather than their frequency *per se*. What may have been regarded as common assault in the past may come to be seen as a racially motivated attack in more enlightened times. Similarly, women are now encouraged to report sexual attacks and the social opprobrium that used to follow a claim of rape is now somewhat reduced, though nonetheless still present. What this is really about is a change in the way the measures are taken and their relative accuracy. Studies that involve measures taken by observers are particularly at risk from instrumentation effects as observers learn how to use the coding schedule more efficiently or, more likely (and worse), become fatigued by the schedule and attempt their own reinterpretation of it.

Subject or participant mortality refers to the loss of participants from your study over time. Time series studies, especially those that cover long periods, are prone to participant mortality problems which are usually outside the experimenter's control. Some participants may indeed die during the study, but it is more normal that some will drop out through boredom or a lack of interest or perhaps because they move house. If you do not have a large sample to start with you run the risk that you will have too few people left at the end of the study to enable you to draw any reliable conclusions at all.

Participant mortality would not be such a great problem were it a truly random event. However, reasons for leaving that are related to the nature of the study (e.g. a lack of interest in the research topic or the intrusive nature of the measures) can lead to a situation where the surviving sample becomes progressively more biased in favour of showing that the treatment works. Say you were trying to evaluate the effect of a local waste recycling advertising campaign and had started regular assessments of how much waste people recycled. Even if you started with a fairly representative sample of the population, you might well find that by the time you had started the adverts and were collecting post-intervention observations, only environmentally committed people were still ready and willing to help you with the project. In all likelihood, your estimates of average post-intervention waste recycling behaviour would be considerably higher than the pre-intervention average, but this would be mainly due to sample mortality rather than the effect of the adverts.

Careful mapping of sample survivors' pre- and post-intervention behaviour would overcome this problem, but this is naturally a rather unsatisfactory solution since such a campaign was presumably intended to change the behaviour of the less environmentally committed people who were lost to the study. Needless to say, strenuous efforts have to be made to maintain the sample.

4.6 TIME SERIES WITH NON-EQUIVALENT CONTROL GROUP DESIGNS

Many of the problems associated with time series and NECG designs are neatly overcome by the combination of the two approaches in the time series with non-equivalent control group (TSNECG) design, sometimes also called the multiple time-series design. An extended series of data collection points are used with both the treatment group and the non-equivalent control. The key advantage of the TSNECG design is that you should be able to tell both whether a treatment has an effect compared with a control group and that the effect only occurs at a point after the introduction of the treatment. It helps to rule out many of the individual threats to validity outlined previously.

Figure 4.3 illustrates what we would hope to find if there really was a strong treatment effect. It shows there is variability in scores over time and there appears to be a gradual improvement in scores in the control group, potentially via testing, instrumentation or maturation effects; however, the post-intervention scores for the treatment group are considerably higher than for the controls suggesting that there really was an effect of the treatment intervention.

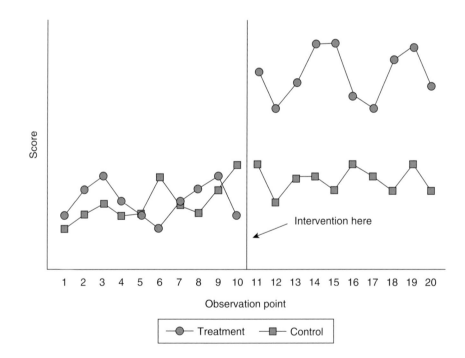

Figure 4.3   Time series with non-equivalent control group

4.6.1 **Problems with TSNECG designs**

The price to be paid for minimising so many threats to validity is all-round increased cost and the need to study many more people. This is not a problem when conducting research on existing archival data but may be a serious problem if you intend to collect fresh data.

Differential sample mortality in the two groups can be a problem. If people who are somewhat apathetic to the study are differentially more likely to be lost from one group than the other, then group differences may be artificially enhanced or constrained. It is also possible with studies that last for some time that the control group will become exposed to, or aware of, the treatment. People in the two groups may mix and discuss the intervention, and control group members may either seek the treatment for themselves or withdraw from the study through becoming aware that they may never be exposed to the treatment or intervention.

Sometimes, merely being aware of the existence of a 'problem' that needs treating may change behaviours of control group members. If control group members come to feel that they are being deliberately disadvantaged in some way they may choose to perform less well when measurements are taken. This may be a serious problem if researchers are heavy-handed and insensitive in the way they interact with people. Alternatively, control group members may compensate for not receiving the treatment by trying harder to perform well. This is called compensatory rivalry and would serve to obscure true treatment effects.

TSNECG designs are not immune to the other threats to validity discussed earlier, especially if the magnitude of the treatment effect is weak and the variability between scores on successive observations is relatively high. In common with the single-case designs (see Box 4.1), detecting a treatment effect is easiest when it is possible to establish a fairly clear-cut stable baseline in both the control group and the treatment group prior to the intervention. As with true experiments, it may be necessary to increase sample sizes substantially in order to provide the necessary statistical power to detect these weak effects.

4.7 **MODIFICATIONS TO THE BASIC DESIGNS**

The basic designs described here are really the tip of the iceberg in terms of possibilities. With NECG designs there is no necessity to have only two treatment conditions (treatment and control). It is possible to have many different levels of the treatment or combinations of treatments in one design. For example, we might extend the computer skills example to include a control (traditional teaching) group, a group that had two periods a week of peer teaching and one that had four per week. In fairness to traditional methods of teaching, we might also divide the control group into one that had two periods per week and one that had four periods of

Box 4.1 Single-case designs

Usually researchers are urged to seek out large samples to increase their confidence in the conclusions they draw from a study but it is perfectly possible to conduct meaningful experiments on single cases. The most common single-case design is the A-B-A design which shares many of the characteristics of the time-series design discussed in this chapter.

The A-B-A design is the best-known single-case experimental design in which the target behaviour or response is clearly specified and measurements are carried out continuously throughout three phases of the experiment: A, B and A again. The first occurrence of Phase A is the baseline phase during which the natural occurrence of the target behaviour or response is monitored; in Phase B the treatment/intervention is introduced. To increase our confidence that the treatment in Phase B is responsible for any changes we see, the treatment is then removed and responses monitored in what amounts to another baseline Phase A. A hypothetical example of an A-B-A design is illustrated in Figure 4.4.

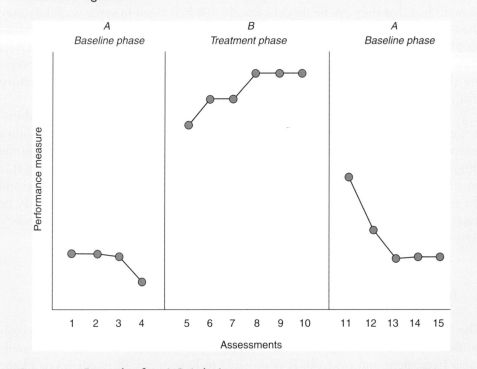

Figure 4.4   Example of an A-B-A design

There is however an important reservation concerning the clinical application of the A-B-A design; this is that it may not be possible to tell whether any behaviour change

Box 4.1 (Continued)

that occurs following onset of the treatment results from the treatment *per se* or from changes that are part of the recovery process that would have happened even without the treatment. This issue is particularly problematic when there is only weak evidence of an experimental effect; that is, only a slight improvement is seen. One way of overcoming this problem is to use a control variable. A control variable would be another aspect of behaviour which would be as susceptible to the effects of recovery as the experimental variable, but is not thought to be something that will be influenced by the treatment. If the effects found following treatment were due to naturally occurring, non-treatment-related recovery then the curves for the treatment and control variables should be parallel.

A-B-A designs are most commonly used in clinical settings where clinicians are interested in finding out whether a treatment intervention will work for a particular patient, usually with a relatively unique combination of problems (treatments for comparatively common conditions are usually tested using true experiments in the form of randomised control trials; see Chapter 3). The A-B-A design presents some fairly obvious ethical problems, as a potentially valuable treatment is systematically being removed from someone who might benefit from it. To deal with this, many variations on the A-B-A design have been suggested such as the A-B-A-B design where the study finishes with a treatment phase which can then be extended beyond the end of the study if the treatment works, but a phase of withdrawal still allows an opportunity for the efficacy of the treatment given in the B phases to be evaluated. There are other variations on the A-B-A-B design; for example, having multiple treatment and baseline phases (A-B-A-B-A-B-A-B) or incorporating another treatment (A-B-A-C-A-B-A-C).

traditional teaching. Clearly, this new design is much more useful to curriculum developers since it not only tells us whether peer teaching is better than traditional methods, but also whether spending more time on computing yields worthwhile increases in skill level. Assuming we had enough schools prepared to help, we could even add a group that gets both traditional and peer teaching for a total of four periods.

Sometimes concerns about testing effects may lead us to believe that post-test measures will be unduly influenced by people having completed the pre-test. An example might be of a knowledge test with a short period between pre- and post-test. In such a situation we might expect people to remember the items, thus inflating the apparent power of any intervention. It is also often the case that merely asking people about some aspect of their lives changes their behaviour in that domain. For instance, merely asking about your waste recycling activities might make you think that you ought to recycle more waste. Somebody showing interest in your behaviour may change it. This is called the Hawthorne effect after the electricity plant in Illinois where the phenomenon was first formally described in studies on attempts to enhance worker performance (Roethlisberger and Dickson, 1939). It is possible to get over both sorts of problem by using separate pre- and post-test samples so that different individuals take the pre- and post-tests. This approach is only sensible if you have a large pool of people from which to draw your samples and you can draw them by some fairly random procedure.

For time series designs and TSNECG designs it is possible to adopt treatment withdrawal designs. These involve intervening with the treatment and then, at a later point, withdrawing it and observing a subsequent fall in scores on the dependent measure. This approach works best when the treatment is not expected to have a lasting effect on the dependent variable and has to be 'maintained' in some sense for the effect to be shown. An example might be to evaluate the effectiveness of camera-based speed checks on stretches of road. Speeds could be monitored surreptitiously for some period before erecting the camera systems then, after a period with the cameras in place, they could be removed to see if speeds gradually increased in their absence. The cameras could be re-erected later to see if speeds fell again.

4.8 CONCLUSION

With all the potential problems associated with each quasi-experimental design, you might be thinking that they are too fraught with difficulties to make them worthwhile. The difficulties, however, are inevitable whenever you forego experimental control in order to do research outside the laboratory. What I hope to have shown you is that there are some rigorous methods available and, while they will not always lead you to unambiguous answers to your research questions, they do at least flag up the likely threats to validity. If you know where potential interpretative problems lie then you can address them and make some estimate of the likely impact these could have had on the results of your study. Quasi-experiments, providing they are conducted with due care, can be the most powerful available means by which to test important hypotheses.

4.9 **EXERCISES**

1   Design your own pre-experiment and think about what you would have to do to make it into a true experiment or a quasi-experiment.
2   Take a look at the week's newspapers and pick out the stories where something has been evaluated – there are usually lots of these in the 'quality' press. For each one, what kind of design was used? If you cannot tell, what information do you need in order to make the judgement? What are the likely threats to the validity of the conclusions that were reached?

4.10 **DISCUSSION QUESTIONS**

1   How far does the lack of control over allocation of participants to experimental conditions undermine the validity of findings of quasi-experiments?
2   Are pre-experiments essentially an unethical waste of participants' time?

4.11 **FURTHER READING**

The classic text in this area is Donald Campbell and Julian Stanley's (1966) *Experimental and quasi-experimental designs for research*. This is a very short book of only 70 pages which had first appeared as a chapter in Gage (1963) and it is the place where quasi-experimental designs were first comprehensively explained. William Shadish, Thomas Cook and Donald Campbell produced a more detailed text called *Experimental and quasi-experimental designs for generalized causal inference* in 2002. This contains discussions of the major designs and a few more, as well as information about the appropriate statistical models to be used with each design. For single-case studies John Todman and Pat Dugard's *Single-case and small-n experimental design* (2001) expands on the examples given here.

5

Surveys and Sampling

Patrick Sturgis

CONTENTS

AIMS OF THIS CHAPTER

This chapter introduces the notion of inference from sample to population by way of random sampling. Key concepts from statistical theory are discussed and some of the main practical sampling strategies reviewed. We then move on to consider some of the factors affecting the precision of survey estimates and the importance of interview mode in determining response rates and data quality.

KEY TERMS

census	response rate
central limit theorem	sample
clustering	sampling distribution
complex sample design	sampling frame
confidence interval	sampling without replacement
disproportionate stratification	simple random sample
epsem	standard error
non-response bias	statistical inference
population	survey mode
precision	systematic random sampling
probability distribution	unbiased estimator
proportionate stratification	weighting
quota sampling	

5.1 INTRODUCTION

This chapter will focus on the use of random sampling for making inferences from samples to populations. Random sampling is dealt with in depth in sociology and political science and, though psychologists conduct surveys less often, psychologists' surveys might benefit from the methodological sophistication found elsewhere in the social sciences. In particular, the chapter focuses on the concept of sampling distributions and how they can be used to draw inferences from samples to populations. We also consider the threat to the validity of inference in the presence of non-response and review some of the primary practical strategies for drawing samples and obtaining data from sampled units.

Conceptually, surveys and sampling techniques are not tied to any particular philosophical viewpoint. Those adopting a hypothetico-deductive approach will be concerned to sample appropriately, as will those taking a more constructivist perspective. Whenever the goal is to make statements about a group of people then, unless you approach all the members of that group, how you draw your sample from that group will determine how much confidence you can have in the generality of your findings.

Similarly, surveys are not tied to any particular data gathering technique. While structured questionnaires are by far the most common form of data collection in surveys, it is perfectly possible to collect qualitative data, or to count, weigh and observe population units within a sample survey. Even experimental investigations can be done using survey techniques, with respondents randomly allocated to treatment and control groups, usually differing in question wording or information provided in the questionnaire. Physiological and other more invasive measures can also be collected in surveys. The Health Survey for England (see www.esds.ac.uk/government/hse/), for instance, collects height, weight, blood pressure and lung function measurements as part of the interview.

5.2 STATISTICAL INFERENCE: FROM SAMPLE TO POPULATION

The underlying motivation of sampling is to make statistical inferences from samples to populations. That is, we wish to use known facts (responses from the sample) to understand unknown facts (responses in the population) (King *et al*. 1996). A population is the universe of objects in the 'real world' in which we are interested. These objects may be individuals, households, organisations, countries or practically anything we can define as belonging to a single taxonomic class. Because populations are often extremely large, or even infinite, it is usually impossible – for cost and practical reasons – to take measurements on every element in the population. For this reason, more often than not, we draw a sample and generalise from the properties of the sample to the broader population. In addition to the cost savings this entails, we are usually able to make more – and more-detailed – observations on each sample element. When we do make observations on every element in the population, we are conducting a population census and the issue of inference is not applicable, as we will know from our data the true score of the population on the variable of interest, measurement error notwithstanding.

Making valid and reliable inferences from a sample to a population is a cornerstone of science and there are many pitfalls that may crop up along the way in our efforts to do this. Because of such difficulties, we often hear researchers attempting to limit the claims they are making for their analyses by saying their results 'apply only to the sample at hand and should be generalised to the broader population with caution'. Such claims should be viewed with scepticism, for we are hardly ever interested in the idiosyncratic characteristics of a particular sample. Furthermore, even when this sort of statement is made, generalisation to a population is usually implicit in the conclusion being drawn.

Fortunately, if a sample is collected properly, it is possible to make valid and reliable generalisations to the broader population within quantifiable bounds of error. To appreciate how this is done, it is first necessary to understand the concept of sampling distributions, as this is the key that allows us to link our specific sample with the broader population.

5.2.1 Sampling distributions

When we talk about distributions, we usually understand this as referring to the distribution of values on a particular variable in our sample or in the broader population. Such distributions are known as probability distributions, as they describe the probability of observing each of the different possible values a variable can take in the sample or population. Probability distributions have different shapes and are named according to the shape they assume. For example, the normal distribution – or bell curve – describes how human samples and populations vary on characteristics such as height or intelligence (see Figure 5.1 for an example of a normal distribution).

The logic of probability distributions, however, can also be applied to statistics. A statistic is just a mathematical transformation or formula applied to a set of numerical data. The distribution of possible values of a statistic in a population is referred to as the sampling distribution of that statistic. The difference between the distribution of a variable (a probability distribution) and the distribution of a statistic (a sampling distribution) can be somewhat confusing. However, it is important to understand this distinction if the rationale of inferential statistics using random sampling is to be properly understood.

When we draw a random sample from a population, it is just one of many samples that might have been drawn using the same design and, therefore, observations made on any one sample are likely to be different from each other and from the 'true value' in the population (although some will be the same). Imagine we were to draw 10,000 (or some other very large number) random samples of 1000 individuals from a population. On each sample we calculate a statistic, say the mean age in years and we then plot the mean age obtained from each sample on a histogram (a histogram is a chart that uses bars to represent the number of times a particular value occurred). This histogram would represent the *sampling distribution* of the mean of age in this population. Do not worry about the practicalities of actually drawing all these samples, as we are only talking about a *hypothetical* set of possible samples that could, in theory, be drawn.

Sampling distributions are useful because they allow us to make statements about how likely it is that the true population value will fall within the margin of error of the estimate we make from the sample we have drawn. This is because the sampling distribution tells us the frequency with which the statistic in our particular sample would be found in the population of all possible samples. But how do we know the sampling distribution of our statistic without drawing a huge number of samples each time we wish to make use of it? Fortunately, we don't need to actually draw all the samples that would be necessary to physically plot sampling distributions because of known mathematical links between the parameters of a random sample and the sampling distribution from which it is taken.

If we draw a sufficiently large random sample, all the information necessary for drawing inferences about the population from which the sample was drawn is contained within the sample data. To understand how this is so, it is important to understand a number of additional, inter-related ideas. The first, and possibly the most important of these, is the concept and properties of the normal distribution.

5.2.2 The normal distribution

The exact shape of the normal distribution is defined by a function which has only two parameters: mean and standard deviation. The standard deviation (s.d.) is a measure of dispersion and can be thought of as a measure of how much, on average, people differ from the sample mean.

A characteristic property of the normal distribution is that 68% of all of its observations fall within a range of 1 standard deviations from the mean, a range of 1.96 standard deviations covers 95% of the scores and 2.58 standard deviations covers 99% of all the observed scores. This has the useful consequence that, when a variable is normally distributed, we are able to tell what proportion of a sample falls within a range of values around the sample mean.

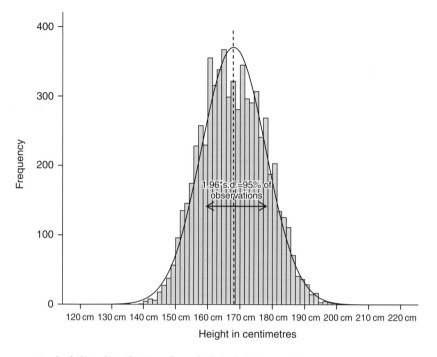

Figure 5.1 Probability distribution for adult height in centimetres

For example, Figure 5.1 shows an example of a normally distributed variable. Let's imagine that this is the distribution of the variable 'height in centimetres' from a randomly drawn sample. We run some descriptive analyses and establish that the mean height in our sample is 168 cm and the standard deviation is 10. If we assume that the data are normally distributed, we know that 95% of sample cases will be within the range of

$$168 \pm (1.96 \times 10) = 168 \pm 19.60$$

which is the range 148.4 to 187.6. Note that had we wanted to talk about a more precisely defined group, say 99% of cases, we would have multiplied the standard deviation by 2.58 rather than 1.96. This is because 2.58 standard deviations covers 99% of the normal distribution. The consequence of this is that the range of values increases to 142.2–193.8. Another way of putting this is that the probability of a given individual in the sample being 187.6 cm or taller (or 184.4 cm or shorter) is 0.05 (or 5%).

So, the normal distribution is useful in that it enables us to make statements about the probability or likelihood of observing particular values. But so far, this only refers to the characteristics of our particular sample. How does this enable us to use the sample data to make statements about the whole population? This is possible because of the following links between the properties of sample statistics and their corresponding sampling distribution:

1   When the distribution of a variable is normal in the population, the sampling distribution of the mean (and many other statistics) is also normal.
2   Even when the distribution of the variable in the population is not normal, central limit theorem tells us that, as sample size increases, the sampling distribution of the mean (and many other statistics) becomes normal.
3   The sample mean (and many other statistics) is an unbiased estimator of the population mean. This means that if we draw repeated random samples (of the same size) from the population and estimate the mean, the mean of these means will itself converge to the population mean when the sample of means is large enough.
4   Although, we usually don't know the standard deviation of the sampling distribution, it turns out that we can use the sample standard deviation as an estimate of it, known as the standard error (s.e.) of the sampling distribution. This is done by dividing the sample standard deviation by the square root of the sample size.

5.2.3 Confidence levels and confident intervals

So, from the above points, we know that so long as the sample is random (more on what this means later) and of sufficient size, we can assume that it provides an unbiased estimate of the true population mean (note that this does not mean it is equal to the true population mean, just that the sample mean is an unbiased estimate of it). We also know that the shape of the sampling distribution is normal and that the sample standard deviation provides us with a very good estimate of the standard deviation (standard error) of this sampling distribution. Armed with this knowledge, we can use exactly the same logic as we did on individual cases in our sample earlier in discussing the properties of normal distributions, but this time referring to the target population.

Rather than saying that 95% of observations in our sample fall within 1.96 standard deviations of the mean, we can say that if we were to draw 100 samples of the same size, we would expect only 5 of them to have means that fall outside our estimate of the mean ±1.96 standard errors. Another (more common) way of saying the same thing is that we are 95% confident that the true population mean falls within the range of the sample mean ±1.96 standard errors.

To illustrate, if we drew a random sample of 1,000 individuals (assuming no non-response or measurement error) and calculated the mean age to be 45 and the standard deviation to be 10, we could say that we are 95% confident that the true population mean age is 45 years plus or minus 0.62 years:

s.e. = s.d./$\sqrt{n}$ (formula for s.e. of mean)
s.e. = 10/$\sqrt{1,000}$ (put in actual values)
s.e. = 10/31.623 = 0.316 (perform calculations)
1.96 × 0.316 = 0.62   (multiply by 1.96 [1.96 s.e.s = 95% of distribution])

This introduces the linked ideas of confidence levels and confidence intervals – for a given level of confidence, say 95%, we specify the interval within which the true population value will fall. Although this discussion has been concerned with the mean, the same logic applies to many other inferential statistics, such as proportions, differences between means and regression coefficients.

It is important to note that this 'magical process' linking sample to population parameters can break down at various points in the research process, predominantly during the sampling and measurement stages. However, if we are confident that our sample has been properly drawn (i.e. randomly and without non-response bias), the sample size is large enough (> about 100) and the characteristic of interest has been validly measured (i.e. without bias or random error), the logic of inference is unassailable. It is this logic that enables us to make very definite statements about the characteristics of populations such as 'people in Britain' (which at the last count approached 60 million) based on samples of only 1,000 individuals.

5.2.4 Factors affecting the precision of estimates

The width of the confidence interval is referred to as the precision of the estimate. The wider the confidence interval, the less precise the estimate and vice versa. From the previous discussion, we can tell that the two factors affecting the precision of our estimates are the variance and sample size. The more variable the thing we are measuring is in the population, the less precise our estimates will be – holding sample size constant.

The larger the size of our sample, the more precise our estimates will be – holding variance constant. However, because the standard error decreases as a function of the square root of the sample size, there are steadily diminishing returns for precision by increasing sample size. Thus increasing sample size (n) from 500 to 1,000 reduces the standard error by 29%, while increasing it from 1,000 to 1,500 reduces the standard error by only 18%. This is why many opinion poll samples have a sample size of around 1,000.

Another factor affecting the precision of estimates is the way in which a random sample is drawn. As we shall see in sections 5.4 and 5.5 there are a number of different ways of drawing random samples and which one we choose influences the reliability of the estimates we make from the sample data.

5.3 **NON-RESPONSE**

The logic of statistical inference using random sampling derives its strength from its mathematical underpinning. If all relevant theoretical assumptions are met, we can have great confidence in the inferences made about the population. In the real world of survey research, however, human populations rarely conform to the assumptions of mathematical laws!

One of the primary areas in which the mathematical assumptions underpinning random sampling are rarely met in practice is that of response rate. The response rate is calculated by dividing the number of achieved interviews by the total sample size. Although this sounds straightforward, in practice, the question of what goes into the numerator and what goes into the denominator of this equation can be difficult to decide and can have a substantial influence on the overall response rate (see Lynn *et al*. 2001). So, if we draw a sample of 1,000 households and a able to conduct interviews with only 650 of these, the response rate would be 650/1,000 = 65%. Conversely, the non-response rate for this survey would be 35%. In practice, there are likely to be some non-residential addresses on a sampling frame of households (in the UK this is usually around 10% for samples drawn from the Postcode Address File) and these ineligible addresses should be omitted from response rate calculation. Non-response occurs for many different reasons but the most common are 'non-contact', when no contact is made with the selected unit (usually a person) for the duration of fieldwork, and 'refusals', when contact is made but the selected unit declines to participate. This type of non-response is referred to as unit non-response, as no information is obtained at all on the non-responding sample unit. A second type of non-response is when a respondent provides an interview but does not complete all the items in the questionnaire. This item non-response might be deliberate, in the case of sensitive questions such as those relating to income or drug use. Alternatively, respondents may omit items inadvertently through haste or as a result of poor questionnaire design.

The basic sampling theory outlined in section 5.2 assumes that responses are obtained to all items from all sampled population units. However, if for various reasons, some sample members fail to provide answers to some or all of the questions, there is a real risk that survey estimates will be biased. That is to say, the survey estimate will be systematically different from the true value in the population. Because the variance of estimators is a function of sample size, non-response also results in less precise population estimates. The latter problem is not particularly serious, however, because we can build an anticipated level of non-response into the survey design and still achieve the required sample size, by drawing a larger initial sample than would be necessary in the event of a 100% response rate.

While a low response rate may indicate the existence of non-response bias, it is important to note that it does not automatically mean that all estimates from that survey will be biased. Bias only arises if non-respondents are different from respondents on the variable in question. So, if a survey measures people's annual income and richer individuals are less likely to respond to the survey than poorer individuals, the estimate of mean income in the population made from this sample will be biased (we would underestimate mean income in the population). However, if the mean income of responders is no different to that of non-responders, the estimate will be unbiased, even with a very low response rate.

By the same token, bias should be thought of as relating to particular variables, not samples as a whole. One estimate from a sample with non-response might be biased, while another estimate from the same survey may exhibit no bias at all. What determines whether an estimate is biased or not is the difference between responders and non-responders on each particular variable. Survey researchers are currently very concerned about non-response bias because response rates around the world have been in decline for the past 20 to 30 years (de Leeuw & Hox, 2001). While it was once common to achieve response rates in the 70–80% range, now such high response rates are much more difficult to achieve. It is not entirely clear why response rates are declining so steadily but key factors are thought to relate to societal and demographic change and the increasing number of requests for survey participation that are received by members of the public.

Fortunately, high and rising rates of non-response can be mitigated by improving interviewer training, the timing of calls at addresses and the general design of surveys. Non-response weighting, a process whereby under-represented groups in the sample can be weighted up to match their composition in the population, can also be used during analysis to remove or reduce bias arising as a result of non-response.

5.4 SAMPLING STRATEGIES

Thus far we have focused on the conceptual foundations of survey sampling. In practical terms, though, how do you go about selecting a sample from a population? This decision will depend on the type of measurements you want to make, the nature of the population being studied, the complexity of your survey design and the resources available.

The first stage in any survey is to define the population from which you want to draw your sample. For example, you might be interested in the effects of youth unemployment on psychological wellbeing and thus need to study samples from the population of employed and unemployed youth. Or, you might have a developmental hypothesis that some cognitive abilities change around the seventh or eighth year, so you might sample from the population of children aged between 5 and 11. Determining the exact population from which you wish to sample is important as you must be clear about the population to which inferences are to be made.

Having an explicit and detailed description of your population is also important, because for most sampling strategies you will need a sampling frame, which is a list of all members of the population. For large-scale surveys of the general population of adults in the UK, the Electoral Register and the Postcode Address File are the most commonly used sampling frames. The Electoral Register is available in libraries and main post offices and lists people eligible to vote. The Electoral Register is used only rarely these days because it does not have anywhere near complete coverage (many people are not on the Electoral Register). Recent legislation also allows people who are registered to vote to be removed from the publicly available register.

The Postcode Address File (PAF) lists all UK addresses to which mail can be sent and is available in computerised form. It has very high coverage of UK addresses (approaching 100%) and is regularly updated. As the PAF is not a list of individuals, but of addresses, contact must first be made with the household and a randomly selected household member interviewed (if the survey is of individuals, rather than households). The PAF contains approximately 13% non-domestic addresses so many of the sampled addresses are considered ineligible for the survey. This proportion of addresses being ineligible needs to be factored into estimates of sample size requirements. Several companies now exist who will draw samples from the PAF and other population frames at a commercial rate.

We now turn to a consideration of the different ways in which samples can be drawn from the sampling frame, once the population has been defined and the list obtained.

5.4.1 Simple random samples

Although it is rarely used in practice for national samples, the simple random sample (SRS) is the yardstick by which other sampling strategies are judged. An SRS gives every unit in the population an equal probability of selection. For this reason, simple random samples are referred to as epsem (for Equal Probability of SElection Method). To draw an SRS, every population unit must be assigned a unique identification number ranging from 1 to N (where N is the total population size). Random numbers between 1 and N are then drawn (using a random number table or other random number generating device) until the required sample size is achieved. If the same number is drawn more than once, it is not selected into the sample multiple times, we simply draw another number until we find one that has not already been selected. This is called sampling without replacement and is the normal practice in survey sampling.

Although the vast majority of survey samples are now drawn using computers, if completed by hand an SRS can be cumbersome and time consuming. An alternative approach – systematic random sampling – can be simpler and more convenient. To draw a systematic random sample, begin by assigning every population unit a unique number in ascending order. Next, calculate the sampling interval, i, which is the ratio of the required sample size (n) to the population total (N): $i = N/n$. A random number between 1 and i is then generated, called the seed number, representing the unique identifier of the first population unit to be included in the sample. Next the sampling interval, i, is summed with the random number between 1 and i and this is taken as the second unit in the sample. The process is continued until the sampling frame has been reached and the desired sample size achieved.

To illustrate, let us assume that you have a sampling frame containing 1,600 names and you want a random sample of 200 to receive your questionnaire. The sampling interval here would be 1,600/200 = 8. The next step is to use random number tables to select a number between 1 and 8 to give the seed number to start with. Say you get a 5. You would select the 5th person on the list, then the 13th (5 + 8), then the 21st (13 + 8) and so on. Strictly speaking, this procedure is not an epsem design, since once the 5th person has been selected the 4th and 6th cases cannot be selected, as the order of the list determines who is now selected. However, for most practical purposes, systematic random sampling can be considered as equivalent to simple random sampling.

SRS techniques are generally impractical when you wish to sample from large and geographically diffuse populations, such as 'adults in the UK'. Interviewers would need to be sent to all corners of the country, at great practical inconvenience and expense. For this reason, simple random sample designs are rarely used in practice for this type of survey. Where sample designs divert from equal probability of selection methods, they are referred to as complex sample designs.

5.4.2 Complex sample designs

The two main ways in which sample designs divert from equal probability of selection methods is in the use of clustering and stratification. Clustering – or multistage selection – is almost always used on national, face-to-face interview surveys, as non-clustered designs are both impractical from the perspective of data collection agencies and prohibitively expensive for funders of research. The basic idea of a clustered design is to select the sample in stages so that individual sample units are clustered into groups of geographical proximity. Consider conducting a survey of secondary school pupils. We might begin by drawing a sample of schools and then randomly selecting pupils within each school. This would make the interviewers' job much easier than if a simple random sample had been used, because each interviewer would need to visit only one or two schools to conduct all their interviews.

For a fixed cost, then, clustering produces more precise population estimates than a simple random sample would. However, for a fixed sample size, clustered designs are subject to larger standard errors. This is because there tends to be greater similarity, on many characteristics, between people who live close by one another than there is between independently selected members of the total population. For instance, size of garden, number of bedrooms and household income are all variables that are intuitively likely to be more similar within a neighbourhood than they are in the country as a whole. When we draw clustered samples, we are therefore likely to obtain samples of households that are more similar to one another on many variables than a simple random sample of households would yield. It is important to take account of this greater similarity between respondents in a clustered sample when calculating standard errors, because they will generally be larger than would be the case for a simple random sample of the same size.

National probability surveys also routinely employ stratification in the selection of sample units. Stratification divides the sample into separate sub-groups and then draws random samples from within each group. These sub-samples are then combined to form the complete issued sample. Strata are created through the cross-classification of variables contained on the sampling frame, which are known or believed to correlate with key survey variables. So long as the latter assumption holds true, stratification will reduce sampling error, relative to an un-stratified sample design of the same size.

Sampling within strata can be either proportionate or disproportionate to population size. In addition to obtaining increases in statistical efficiency, disproportionate stratification is often used to ensure that robust estimates can be made within substantively important strata. For instance, surveys of the population of Great Britain (GB) might disproportionately sample within strata formed by the three countries of Great Britain. 'Over-sampling' within the Wales stratum would enable separate estimates to be produced for people living in Wales, where sample size might be too small under a proportionate stratification. To produce estimates representative of the GB population from such a disproportionate allocation, however, sample units from Wales would need to be down-weighted to their correct population proportion.

Another common feature of national probability sample surveys is the use of post-survey weighting. Weighting is generally applied to correct for unequal selection probabilities and non-response bias. The main purpose of this weighting is to reduce bias in population estimates by up-weighting population sub-groups that are under-represented and down-weighting those that are over-represented in the sample. A less desirable by-product of weighting, however, is that it can, when the variance of the weights is large, result in a loss of precision; that is, standard errors that are larger than they would be for un-weighted estimates.

5.4.3 Complex designs and variance estimation

A net effect of clustering, stratification and weighting, is that the standard errors of these 'complex' sample designs tend to be different (smaller or larger, but usually larger) than those of a simple random sample. The difference in the precision of the estimates produced by a complex design relative to a simple random sample is known as the design effect (*deff*). The design effect is the ratio of the actual variance, under the sampling method used, to the variance calculated under the assumption of simple random sampling. This number will obviously vary for different variables in the survey – some may be heavily influenced by design effects and others less so.

For cluster samples, the main components of *deff* are the intra-class correlation or *rho* (the Greek letter ρ), and the number of units within each cluster. Rho is a statistical estimate of within-cluster homogeneity. It can be thought of as the probability that two units drawn randomly from the same cluster will have the same value on the variable in question, relative to two units drawn at random from the population as a whole. Thus, a rho of 0.10 indicates that two units randomly selected from within the same cluster are 10% more likely to have the same value than are two randomly selected units in the population as a whole. Estimation of rho is beyond the scope of this chapter but it can be easily obtained from commercially available statistical software. The design effect is calculated as follows:

$deff = 1 + \rho\,(n - 1)$, where:

- *deff* is the design effect;
- ρ is the intra-class correlation for the variable in question;
- and *n* is the size of the cluster (an average is taken where clusters differ in size).

From this formula, we can see that the design effect increases as the cluster size (in most instances the number of addresses sampled within a postcode sector) increases, and as ρ (within cluster homogeneity) increases.

A somewhat more readily interpretable derivation of the design effect is the design factor or *deft*, which is simply the square root of *deff*. *Deft* is an inflation factor for the standard errors obtained using a complex survey design. For example, a *deft* value of 2, indicates that the standard errors are twice as large as they would have been had the design been a simple random sample. *Deft* can also be used to obtain the effective sample size, *neff*, which, as the name suggests, gives for a complex survey design, the sample size that would have been required to obtain the same level of precision in a simple random sample.

In order to estimate variance correctly when analysing survey data with a complex design, two main statistical approaches are available: Taylor Series approximation and Balanced Repeated Replication (BRR). An alternative to BRR, based on the jackknife (a computer intensive method which allows the standard error to be calculated), can also be used to take account of these complex design factors (see Skinner *et al.* 1989).

An extended discussion of the properties of these estimators is beyond the scope of this chapter, but see Groves *et al.* (2004) for an accessible treatment. For the substantive analyst, however, the important thing to note is that many popular statistical software packages do not implement these procedures as standard. This means that, for a great many analyses routinely conducted by researchers, these packages produce standard error estimates as if they were taken from a simple random sample, ignoring complex design factors. If there is significant within-cluster homogeneity on particular survey variables, if stratification has been used, or if any form of weighting has been applied during estimation, standard errors will, therefore, be biased.

5.4.4 Quota sampling

Quota sampling attempts to create a representative sample by specifying quotas, or targets, of particular types of people that need to be included to represent the population of interest. As an example, let us assume we know that 50% of the population in a particular age group are female and that 16% of males and 14% of females are left-handed. We want a sample that is representative of both sex and handedness: we decide on a sample size, say 100, and then set quotas. We need 50 males and 50 females. We also need to balance the handedness of respondents appropriately within the sexes, so we set four quotas as follows: 8 left-handed males (16% of 50), 42 right-handed males, 7 left-handed females (14% of 50) and 43 right-handed females.

Once the sample is defined, the researcher approaches people in the relevant age group, confirms their sex and asks them about handedness. People continue to be recruited into the sample until the quotas have been filled. Once we have our seven left-handed females we reject any subsequent left-handed females that come along. If we ask a right-handed male to take part in the survey and he declines, we just keep asking more right-handed men to take part until the quota is filled.

The great advantage of quota sampling is that a sample that looks like the population in terms of key characteristics can be obtained very quickly and cheaply. No population listing is required; only information about the population characteristics with which to define quotas is needed. However, selection biases may serve to render the sample unrepresentative of the target population on variables upon which quotas have not been set. People who are not physically near the sampling point could never enter the sample. The researcher might only approach people who look as if they would be polite and cooperative and, therefore, under-represent rude and un-cooperative people in the sample. People who are not easily classified as male or female just by observation may be excluded by not being approached. If you have multiple levels of controls on the quotas (e.g. male left-handers over 60 with ginger hair) filling some quotas may prove very difficult.

5.5 SURVEY MODE

An important decision which must be made before a sample can be drawn is the mode in which the survey is to be conducted. The mode of a survey relates to the way in which the questionnaire (or other survey instrument) is completed and the degree of interviewer involvement. The primary distinction in terms of mode is between whether the questionnaire is administered by an interviewer, or is completed by the respondent themselves. Whether a survey is interviewer administered or self-completion has a strong bearing on the response rate, the quality and quantity of data that can be obtained and the overall cost of the survey.

Most interviewer administered surveys now use personal computers to enter, store and transmit questionnaire data, which makes fieldwork more efficient and reduces keying and other data entry errors. The 'gold standard' in terms of survey mode is Computer Assisted Personal Interview (CAPI) which generally achieves the highest response rates and obtains the highest quality data but comes at the greatest monetary cost, as it requires an expensive human resource – interviewers. Computer Assisted Telephone Interviewing (CATI) is also common in the UK, as in many other countries. It can achieve reasonably high response rates, though generally considerably lower than in CAPI surveys. The maximum interview length for a CATI survey is also considerably shorter than can be achieved in personal interview surveys. Because all interviews are conducted from a central location, costs are considerably lower than for face-to-face interview surveys. However, the speed with which data can be obtained is significantly faster for CATI than for face-to-face interview modes. On the downside, the introduction of call screening technology, the increase in multiple phone lines in residential properties and the growing prevalence of 'mobile only' individuals has made the job of the telephone researcher increasingly difficult.

Using a self-administration mode significantly reduces costs. However, response rates and the quality of data obtained are generally considerably lower when no interviewer is used. Until recently, postal surveys were practically the sole exemplar of self-administered surveys but the past ten to fifteen years has witnessed a rapid expansion of Internet-based survey research. Conducting surveys on the internet can offer a vast pool of potential respondents at lightning turnaround speeds and at vastly reduced cost, relative to other survey modes.

In addition, of course, the internet is able to harness all the information technology and multimedia functions that are largely absent from phone and face-to-face interactions. There is the realistic possibility, for instance, that 'virtual interviewers' could administer questionnaires to respondents, tailored to each respondent's background and personal preferences, matching 'interviewer' and respondent in terms of race and sex, for example.

Yet, with all the potential benefits of the Internet for survey research there come many potential pitfalls. Although the proportion of online households has increased dramatically in recent years, there remain a significant minority who do not have access to the internet. And these households are very different from the online population in terms of their demographic characteristics, attitudes and beliefs. It is, of course, likely that the 'offline' section of the population will continue to diminish in the years ahead and so the scope for population based survey research on the internet will, in all likelihood, increase. However, even with full population penetration, the lack of sampling frames, or other ways of generating probability samples of internet users means that probabilistic inference of the sort that has been covered in this chapter is difficult and costly.

For now, the very large and increasing number of surveys that are conducted on the internet, for the most part use 'online panels' of respondents who have been recruited from a wide variety of sources and are given some form of monetary incentive to take part in surveys. Because these panels often contain very large numbers of individuals who have provided demographic and other information about themselves, it is possible to draw quota samples which closely match the population on a broad range of characteristics. And, despite the low cost and flexibility of such online panel samples, research has shown that they often exhibit quite substantial biases across a broad range of estimates.

5.6 SMALL SAMPLE ISSUES

In common with lots of textbooks on sampling and survey design I have stressed the desirability of getting a large sample. Generalisations about the population are likely to be more convincing to others when there is a well-drawn large sample. Large samples produce parameter estimates with small standard errors and increase the statistical power of hypothesis tests (see Chapter 9). Studies done with small samples can yield ambiguous non-significant results, as you cannot usually tell whether the result was because the null hypothesis (see Chapter 9) was true or because your sample was too small. You cannot turn this around and conclude that because your sample was small any effect you observe must therefore be 'significant', however tempting this might seem!

The realities of doing psychological research on many topics are such that getting large samples is simply not possible. Much clinical research on patients with specific complaints/disorders cannot obtain large samples as, thankfully, such groups are not large. Research on offenders with particular criminal histories (e.g. child murderers) is usually done on small samples as, again, mercifully, there are not lots of such offenders to study. Given this and the desirability of large samples, is such research therefore a waste of time?

Obviously the answer is 'no'. Insights gained from researching such topics can be very valuable and will often have important practical implications. Indeed, studies on single cases can be particularly useful (see Chapter 4) especially when the single individual is studied intensively. What is needed is a recognition that 'research' does not just mean experiments, big samples and lots of statistics. Some useful illustrative examples of important small sample clinical research can be found in Powell and Adams (1993).

The use of inferential statistics (see Chapter 9) implies that hypotheses are being tested and that studies have been designed as 'fair' tests of these hypotheses. One of these criteria for 'fairness' is that you have a big enough sample to give you sufficient statistical power to make the results of such tests unambiguous. If you know in advance that your sample will be small then you should not place too much emphasis on statistical tests. It might be better to regard your study as exploratory or as contributing to a database that later researchers using meta-analysis (a procedure that combines the results of multiple studies) might merge together with similar studies. This increases the effective sample size, thereby allowing more powerful statistical testing. You should also remember that the magnitude of any differences or correlations you find (the effect sizes) may be of importance separately from their statistical significance.

Studies with small samples may give indications of fruitful avenues for future research. If a phenomenon looks interesting in a small-scale project, funding agencies may be more inclined to put in the resources to allow the collection of data from a larger sample, perhaps by increasing the size of the catchment area or period of time available for data collection. A clinical study, for instance, may have had to be based on clients presenting themselves at a small number of clinics in a relatively short period. Extra resources, made available because of the promise of your initial study, may allow you to go to more clinics over a much longer period, thereby permitting the sampling of much more of the population of interest. Essentially, this is to view small sample work as a kind of pilot study.

5.7 CONCLUSIONS

This brief overview of survey design and sampling should give you some idea of the theory underlying statistical inference from sample to population, the main issues involved in drawing a random sample and some of the main pitfalls of the various kinds of design. The last decade has seen a growth in the number of psychologists involved in large-scale survey investigations and this trend looks likely to continue. Surveys offer the potential to answer a range of research questions that have until now remained in the realm of speculation. Surveys are now more cost effective than ever before and funding agencies are progressively more willing to invest in big surveys than at any time in the past. However, the value of such surveys will continue to depend crucially on good design and attention to the kinds of issues discussed here.

5.8 DISCUSSION QUESTIONS

1 Some people say that samples are only interesting insofar as they represent the population from which they are drawn. What do you think? Might we ever be interested in the characteristics of the sample itself, without making inferences to the population?
2 If you undertake a survey and obtain a low response rate of 30%, does this mean that estimates you make using the data will be biased?
3 Do you think that most surveys will be carried out on the Internet in the future? What are the main barriers to undertaking surveys on the Internet?

5.9 FURTHER READING

Most texts on survey and sampling issues tend to be oriented towards sociologists and other social scientists rather than specifically to psychologists. This should not prevent you reading them, since the issues related to sociological data apply equally to psychological data. Moser and Kalton's (1971) text is widely admired as one of the most detailed yet accessible works on survey design and sampling. The more recent *Survey Methodology* by Groves *et al.* (2004) provides an accessible account of the fundamentals of survey sampling and survey methodology more generally.

6

Questionnaire Design

Chris Fife-Schaw

CONTENTS

AIMS OF THIS CHAPTER

This chapter is about the design and use of questionnaires for psychological research and describes some of the common problems and pitfalls associated with them. It deals with the types of research question that can be addressed with questionnaires and common wording and response formats as well as outlining common problems. It also describes the use of web-based questionnaire surveys.

KEY TERMS

acquiescence bias
back translation
bogus pipeline
categorical responses
closed ended formats: coding
   errors
filter questions

multiple response items
non-attitudes
open-ended formats
ranking scales
rating scales
satisficing

INTRODUCTION

The humble questionnaire is probably the single most common research tool in the social sciences. The main advantages of questionnaires are their apparent simplicity, their versatility and their low cost. For many research topics, questionnaires provide data which are of a good enough quality both to test hypotheses and to make real-world policy suggestions. Where people want to make population parameter estimates (estimates of numerical characteristics of a population like the average number of visits to church per week or the number of people with positive attitudes towards immigrants), the cost advantage of questionnaires over interviews means that many more people can be questioned for a given amount of money than might otherwise be possible. Questionnaires are a relatively well-understood technology and there are numerous guides to designing good questionnaires (e.g. Sudman & Bradburn, 1982; Oppenheim, 1992; Gillham, 2008).

Designing the perfect questionnaire is probably impossible, however. Experience shows that you can rarely design one that all your respondents, let alone your academic peers, are happy with. Similarly it is unlikely that you will finish a questionnaire study without asking yourself the 'why didn't I ask about X?' question. This is not a failing of questionnaire methods themselves so much as an inevitable part of the research process; however, this is not to say that careful questionnaire design can be ignored. There have been too many questionnaires produced over the years containing basic errors that have seriously undermined the value of the data collected. Therefore, you should always try to minimise the number of these errors, and hopefully what follows will flag up the more obvious problems.

The focus here is on self-completion questionnaires, either of the pen-and-paper or web-based variety, though the section on item wording contains some ideas that apply equally to interview schedules. You should read this chapter in conjunction with Chapter 5 on sampling.

WHAT INFORMATION DO YOU WANT?

The very versatility of the questionnaire as a data gathering technique makes it difficult to generalise about its appropriate uses, but it is useful to try to classify common aims since the temptation is often to milk questionnaire data to meet a number of different aims simultaneously while fulfilling none of them particularly well. Being clear about the purpose of your study should help focus the questionnaire design process.

6.2.1 Hypothesis generation

In this mode, questionnaires are useful for asking a large number of people 'what if?', exploratory types of question. The idea is to understand how people respond to certain issues. When attempting to get insights in this way, it is often a good idea to let people to make open-ended responses, unconstrained by your own expectations about what kinds of response are going to be useful to you. This kind of information can also be obtained by unstructured interviews and group discussions but a questionnaire study can give you a feel for the range of likely responses and a rough idea of how common certain responses are.

Sometimes the goal is to see if there is any underlying dimension, or potential causal factor, that influences responses to a set of questionnaire items (in the jargon of these things an item is a single question from the questionnaire) and exploratory data analytic procedures, such as exploratory factor analysis and cluster analysis, are commonly used (see Chapter 12). As there is often no established theory that generates hypotheses about the items, only your hunches and intuitions, such analytic procedures, are best thought of as generating hypotheses about the nature of certain items for future studies.

6.2.2 Test development and validation

A common application of questionnaires is in the realm of test development. This can take many forms. A set of items may be being considered as a potential scale to measure a psychological construct such as, say, depression or agreeableness, where scores on these items might be combined to make a single index of the construct. The aim is to collect responses to the items so that various psychometric procedures can be used to test reliability and/or validity. A set of items supposedly measuring some psychological construct may be administered to groups with known characteristics so as to attempt to assess the validity of the measure. Chapter 7 outlines many of the standard statistical procedures associated with this use of the questionnaire.

6.2.3 Population parameter estimation

Once a range of measures exists, either as published tests or as the result of procedures outlined in Chapter 7, questionnaires can be used to estimate population scores on such tests. For instance, you might want to estimate the levels of psychological wellbeing among police officers. After appropriate sampling, you could use a questionnaire containing the General Health Questionnaire (GHQ; Goldberg, 1972) and treat the resulting scores as an estimate of the 'true' level of psychological wellbeing among police officers. These estimates can then be compared with norms, the responses of other groups who have taken the GHQ in the past.

6.2.4 Hypothesis and model testing

If measures of key constructs already exist then questionnaires can be useful for hypothesis testing purposes. Common examples would include testing causal models (e.g. the Theory of Planned Behaviour) or confirming the hypothesised factor structure underlying responses to a set of pre-existing items. Testing for hypothesised differences between identifiable groups on specified measures is another common application, as is the evaluation of an intervention (e.g. a new teaching programme).

In an ideal world you would keep the above aims – hypothesis testing, test development and hypothesis testing – separate and conduct different studies to deal with each aim in turn. In reality, limited resources are likely to mean that you will need to combine some of these aims within one study. For instance, it is common to specify a new measure (e.g. a set of scaled items) and then attempt hypothesis testing within the same data set. This practice tends to mean that the validity of the measure is not fully established and the interpretation of the data necessarily requires greater caution than would be the case had an established measure been used.

6.3 OPEN VERSUS CLOSED RESPONSE FORMATS

A major distinction lies between open-ended and closed-ended response formats. With open-ended formats respondents are asked to write down their response to a question in any terms that they see fit. When asking about occupations it would be impossible to list all occupations, so you would usually allow respondents to make an open-ended response and write down their occupation. Similarly, you might ask people to give their reasons for domestic waste recycling and allow them to list as many reasons as they felt they had for recycling. Closed-ended formats require the researcher to have a reasonable idea of the likely responses to the items in advance. In the recycling example, they would need to provide a list of likely reasons for recycling and ask respondents to say which of the reasons applied to them.

The advantages of closed-ended formats are that they clarify the response alternatives for the respondent and they reduce the number of ambiguous answers that might be given. Open-ended questions often prompt people into providing lots of responses even if these are often substantively the same. Also, from a clerical point of view, they reduce the number of coding errors in the data set. Coding errors occur when the researcher misinterprets an open-ended response at the stage of turning verbal responses into numbers that can be used for computer analysis. People can answer closed-format items quickly, making responding to you at all more attractive if they are under time pressure.

There are many disadvantages of closed-ended formats but perhaps the two most important are that they can create artificial forced choices and rule out unexpected responses. Your list of reasons for recycling may not include one that is very important for some people. Making up the response categories is often difficult as they must cover the full range of likely responses.

Another problem concerns the shared meanings attached to the words used in the questionnaires. For instance, the term 'tea' is used differently by people from different social strata and different geographical locations in the UK. Most people would recognise 'tea' as a drink, but for some people it is also a light snack in the afternoon and for others a larger meal in the early evening. This is a rather quaint example, but closed-ended response formats assume that people share the same understanding of the items and response categories as does the researcher. There are other biasing effects that occur when using closed-ended formats and these will be discussed later.

While it might seem that there are a lot of problems with closed-ended response formats, the main reason for their popularity lies in the difficulties of analysing open-ended responses. Open-ended responses simply do not lend themselves to easy numerical analysis in the same way that closed response formats do. It is possible to turn such responses into numbers and, of course, it is possible to analyse data without recourse to numbers and statistics at all (see Part 3 of this book), but most questionnaire designers tend towards maximising the number of closed-ended items wherever possible.

To get over the problems with closed-ended items, it is essential that the items you choose to use and the response options you give are ones that potential respondents would use and understand. This means that you need to go out and talk to potential respondents to find out what they think the key questions are and what their responses would be. Running a series of focus groups (see Chapter 17) is often useful for this purpose. Taped interviews or focus groups give useful insights that ought to be drawn on when designing your questionnaire. Having done this it is still important that careful pilot work is done to see if respondents understand your questions and respond appropriately.

6.4 COMMON RESPONSE FORMATS

6.4.1 Categorical response formats

These formats would include those in Figure 6.1. Note that with categorical response formats it is possible to have items where respondents can circle more than one

1) Have you ever attended school in the UK? *(please circle one answer)*	YES	NO
2) Are you male or female? *(please circle one answer)*	MALE	FEMALE
3) If there were a General Election tomorrow which political party would you vote for? *(please circle one answer)*	CONSERVATIVE LIBERAL LABOUR ANOTHER PARTY WOULD NOT VOTE DO NOT KNOW	
4) Which of the following items have you purchased in the last week? *(You may circle more than one item)*	APPLES PEARS ORANGES	

Figure 6.1   Examples of categorical response formats

response, as is the case with question 4 in the figure. Such items are referred to as multiple response items. Care is needed when coding the responses to such items into a computer since, for example, question 4 contains effectively three separate responses: one for whether apples were purchased, one for pears and one for oranges.

6.4.2 Rating scales

Examples of rating scales would include those in Figure 6.2. Here people are asked to circle one of the five alternative responses. It is perfectly possible to present the response options as in Figure 6.3. Having numbered each option people can be asked to write in the number that corresponds to their chosen option in a box next to the question statement, or to tick boxes laid out so that the response options form columns.

6.4.3 Ranking formats

Examples of ranking formats would include those in Figure 6.4.

Please say how much you agree or disagree with the
following statement: (*Please circle one response only*)

The government's transport policy will be
good for the environment in the long term

STRONGLY AGREE

AGREE

UNCERTAIN

DISAGREE

STRONGLY DISAGREE

or

How important is EU expansion to you, personally?

EXTREMELY IMPORTANT

VERY IMPORTANT

MODERATELY IMPORTANT

NOT VERY IMPORTANT

NOT IMPORTANT AT ALL

Figure 6.2   Common rating scale response formats

Alternative A

Using the scale below, please tell us how much you agree or disagree with the
following statements by placing a number in the box provided.

1	2	3	4	5
Strongly Agree	**Agree**	**Neither Agree nor Disagree**	**Disagree**	**Strongly Disagree**

1) The government's transport policy will be good for the environment in the long term ☐

- -

Alternative B

Please tick one box for each question.

	Strongly Agree	Agree	Neither Agree nor Disagree	Disagree	Strongly Disagree
1) The government's transport policy will be good for the environment in the long term	☐	☐	☐	☐	☐

- -

Alternative C

1) The government's transport policy will be good for the environment in the long term
(*Please circle one number only*)

Strongly Agree   1   2   3   4   5   Strongly Disagree

Figure 6.3   Alternative layouts for rating scale responses

Which of the following do you feel are the most important factors to consider when choosing a new car?

Please rank the following in order of importance. Number them so that 1 = most important, 2 = next most important, through to 6 = least important.

Fuel consumption	——
Maximum speed	——
Quick acceleration	——
Having a safety cage/cell	——
Servicing costs	——
Status/prestige	——

Figure 6.4   *An example of a ranking response format*

Box 6.1 Using 'Don't know' and 'No opinion' response options

In a great many questionnaire surveys you will find questions which offer 'Don't know' or 'No opinion' as one of the possible responses. This is usually done, particularly in studies of people's attitudes and opinions, to get over what is called the non-attitude problem. This was first identified in a now classic work by Philip Converse (Converse, 1964) which raised the possibility that when surveyors ask questions in surveys people may make up their responses on the spot so as to provide an answer and to avoid looking stupid. The problem with this, he suggested, was that it was unlikely in such cases that the response really meant anything at all. If you asked people the same question again they might well say something different and the responses were very unlikely to be predictive of any future behaviour (often the main reason why we are interested in people's attitudes in the first place).

To deal with non-attitudes the argument runs that we should give people the option to say that they have no opinion and they can indicate the lack of opinion without feeling inadequate in any way. This should improve the quality of the data and there will be less 'noise' in it to mess up our analyses. For many years this has been the accepted wisdom but in a series of studies by Jon Krosnick and colleagues (Krosnick *et al.*, 2002) this has been seriously challenged. Without going into the details of the quite elegant studies, they conclude that there is very little evidence that offering 'Don't know' or 'No opinion' options improves the quality of the data at all. They show that many respondents will adopt what they call **satisficing** response strategies and will use the 'No opinion' options even when they have a real opinion which they could express. Some of this will be due to a lack of motivation to reflect on their attitudes and some due to time pressures and fatigue among other factors. While they do not go so far as to claim that excluding 'No opinion' options would improve data quality they seriously undermine claims that including them improves data quality at all.

These findings, while not especially helpful in telling you as a questionnaire designer what to do, should at least give you reason to challenge claims from others who want you to include 'No opinion' options that doing so will improve data quality.

6.5 COMMON WORDING PROBLEMS

In this section I have grouped together a range of common wording problems that you should be aware of. Oppenheim (1992) and Sudman and Bradburn (1982) among other texts provide more examples of these types of wording problem.

6.5.1 Vague/ambiguous terminology

If you are vague in the phrasing of your questions you cannot be sure what responses to the items mean. An example would be in the wording of frequency response options for behavioural report items, as in Figure 6.5. Just what does 'frequently' mean here? Every hour? Twice a fortnight? Such a term is sometimes referred to as a vague quantifier. Respondents will try to guess what you mean by 'frequently' but they may not all make the same guess, leading to hidden ambiguity in the data.

Another problem under this heading concerns ill-defined terms. In sexual behaviour research, for instance, researchers were initially keen to ask people if they felt they were sexually promiscuous or not. Unfortunately, research has shown (Spencer *et al*. 1988) that the public are unsure what 'promiscuous' means in terms of absolute numbers of sexual partners – some people believe promiscuity is just a term that applies to people who have had more partners than they have!

6.5.2 Technical terminology

It might seem like a good idea to use technically correct terminology to get over problems of the ambiguity of day-to-day language. For some research topics this may be appropriate but you should pilot your form carefully to be sure that respondents will understand the terms. If appropriate you can give both a technical and a lay explanation for problematic terms in the introduction to the questionnaire. You should always try to use plain English wherever possible.

How often do you clean your teeth?	FREQUENTLY
(please circle one answer)	OFTEN
	INFREQUENTLY
	NEVER

Figure 6.5   Example of vague quantifier response format wording

6.5.3 **Hypothetical questions**

In many research areas you are interested in asking people, 'What would you do if …?' types of question. Questions about hypothetical future situations must appear reasonable to people if their answers are to be meaningful. If you were to ask, say, 'If it appeared that the British National Party could win the next general election would you vote for them?', the meaning of the response depends on accepting the idea that the British National Party might be in a position to win the election. You might think it was (at least potentially), and some people might agree with you, but others might not. Responses from these two groups may not be comparable and there is little you could do about this unless you also asked whether this premise was acceptable first.

6.5.4 **Leading questions**

Questions such as, 'Would you agree that the government's policies on health are unfair?' will suggest to some people that you would like them to agree with you. Similarly, 'Do you agree that Brand Z washes whiter?' might be harder to disagree with than a more neutrally worded item. In such cases you may be indicating something about what would be regarded by some as a 'right' response so these ought to be avoided. One of the big objections to the use of questionnaire surveys for informing policy decisions is that often interest groups (and governments) ask questions in their surveys in such a way that a certain outcomes are made more likely. Those objecting to the conclusions then find it easy to dismiss the survey evidence as simply biased.

6.5.5 **Value judgements**

Item wordings should not contain implicit value judgements. In a similar way to leading questions, you should not express your own views, or those of the research sponsor, in question items. An example of this would be, 'Do you agree that adherents of backward religions should be excluded from holding public office?'

6.5.6 **Context effects**

Context effects are somewhat more subtle effects on responses that are dependent on the nature of the other questions on the form. Take the following question as an example: 'How many pints of beer did you drink last week?' In the context of a survey into British students' lifestyles and leisure activities this seems like a reasonable question and males in particular might give relatively high figures in response. If you had asked the same question in the context of a questionnaire on health behaviours and heart disease, responses might well be lower. You should be aware of the potential impact of surrounding questions on your target item.

Box 6.2 More on question order effects

Schuman and Presser (1996) report a series of studies that highlight just how sensitive respondents can be to the order in which questions are asked. They noticed that the following general question about abortion had been used in two US surveys, one in 1978 the other in 1979. The question asked: 'Do you think it should be possible for a pregnant woman to obtain a legal abortion if she is married and does not want any more children?' In the 1978 survey 40.3% said 'yes' to this question while in 1979 54.9% said 'yes'. This was a major change in public opinion if taken at face value, as it suggested that in 1979 a majority of the US public now supported legalised abortion whereas that was not the case a year before. As you will be expecting, rather than concluding that there was a real change in public opinion, Schuman and Presser took a closer look at the adjacent items in the surveys and decided to run some experiments to see whether another question on abortion in the 1978 survey had influenced subsequent responses to this more general question.

In the experiment they used two questions; the 'general' question above and a more 'specific' one which asked: 'Do you think it should be possible for a pregnant woman to obtain a legal abortion if there is a strong chance of serious defect in the baby?' The questions were presented in the context of a larger survey, with the general question either immediately preceding or following the specific question. The other questions adjacent to these items were about labour relations and not concerned with abortion. The table below presents the percentages agreeing with each item.

Order:		Specific/general					General/specific		
		General item					General item		
		Yes	No				Yes	No	
Specific item	Yes	47.1	36.9	84.0	Specific item	Yes	57.4	25.6	83.0
	No	1.0	15.0	16.0		No	3.3	13.8	17.1
		48.1	51.9	100%			60.7	39.4	100%
				(293)					(305)

The table shows clearly that while the endorsement levels for the specific abortion question remain the same, the question order had a major impact on the numbers agreeing with the general question.

Schuman and Presser (1994) provide a number of possible mechanisms to explain why this effect might occur and there is not space to go into these in detail. However, this example is one of the better-known examples of question order effects – there are many others of varying types – and it is impossible to be sure that subtle order effects are absent from questionnaire surveys. The only real checks are to do experiments like those above, though naturally these are expensive and even these may still leave you uncertain about exactly how many people really agree with the item!

6.5.7 'Double-barrelled' questions

Try to avoid items that involve multiple premises as the meanings of responses are then unclear. Take the example, 'Do you believe the training programme was a good one and effective in teaching you new skills?' If someone disagreed with this item it could be because they thought the programme was generally good but ineffective for them personally, or bad and ineffective, or even effective for them despite being of poor quality. Here it is not clear exactly which premise is being disagreed (or agreed) with. If the question can be broken up into two questions then you should ask the two questions.

6.5.8 Hidden assumptions

Items should not contain hidden assumptions. The most famous example of this sort of problem is contained in the question, 'When did you stop beating your wife?' This assumes you used to beat your wife and, indeed, that you had a wife to beat. The exact origin of this classic question is a matter of debate though strangely Bugs Bunny did pose it to Elmer Fudd in a now withdrawn Warner Brothers cartoon.

6.5.9 Social desirability

While it might seem a source of irritation, people like to present themselves in a positive light when answering questionnaires. If you were asked if you ever gave to charity, for instance, then saying 'no' (assuming this to be the true answer) says something about you that you may not want to convey to the researcher. Many apparently innocuous questions have response options which, if selected, might indicate something negative about the respondent. This leads to potential biases in response patterns which you want to avoid.

Sometimes social desirability phenomena can be quite subtle. For example, Krosnick and Schuman (1988) have shown that people are more prepared to agree 'not to allow' something than to 'forbid' the same thing. Though these responses are logically equivalent the latter one is thought to carry with it undesirable author-itarian overtones, making some people who are actually in favour of forbidding things less likely to tell you that they are.

6.5.10 Sensitive issues

You should be wary of assuming that your respondents find your questions as acceptable as you do. When you are engaged in research on sensitive issues (e.g. death, sex, religion) your questions may cause offence to certain groups. It is good

Box 6.3 Using questionnaires for cross-cultural research

The apparent simplicity of the questionnaire makes it very attractive to researchers who want to collect data in a number of different countries and want to use country or culture as an explanatory variable. Simple examples might include asking whether people in country A are more satisfied with their jobs than people in country B: are people from southern European nations happier than their north European counterparts? The Eurobarometer surveys are the best known of these.

The standard advice when attempting to use a questionnaire in more than one country is to get the questionnaire back-translated. **Back-translation** involves having your questionnaire translated into the target language and then having a separate, independent individual translate the questionnaire back into the original language. The task is to ensure that the original and back-translated versions of the questionnaire are equivalent in meaning. In practice it is rare for the two versions to be absolutely identical but most researchers are prepared to use the translation if the two versions are 'close enough' in meaning.

While this procedure has some rigour, it does not ensure that scores can be meaningfully compared. Many cultures differ in the degree to which filling in questionnaires is a normal everyday occurrence. In some countries questionnaires are only usually encountered when the government or other authority sponsors them. People in these countries are not used to the Western concept of social research and scientific enquiry and will respond as if responding to the government or authority, with all the biases that that might bring with it. More subtly Hui and Triandis (1989) point out that in some cultures expressing moderate positions on questionnaire items is positively valued and in other cultures there is a tendency to say 'yes' or 'agree' with questions whatever they are about – also called an **acquiescence bias**. Clearly data from such countries are not easily compared, as mean scores in the former country will tend towards mid-scale values while the latter country will generate more extreme values *even though* there may be no meaningful differences between the countries on the construct being measured. One solution to this is to attempt standardisation by expressing item scores relative to each individual's average score across items. Another strategy is to avoid using response scales with mid-points and/or to reduce the number of response options on the scale.

Despite these remedial options, achieving cross-cultural equivalence of measures is very difficult and researchers are well advised to attempt to demonstrate the cross-cultural equivalence of their measures (e.g. by using multi-group confirmatory factor analyses – see Chapter 12) before assuming comparisons or contrasts can be legitimately made.

practice to ask about sensitive issues as directly, yet with as much sympathy for your respondents, as possible. Do not try to get at sensitive information indirectly by attempting to deceive respondents. If you cannot ask something directly then you should think about approaching the issue via an alternative method.

6.6 TYPES OF INFORMATION GLEANED FROM QUESTIONNAIRES

Questionnaires can be used to gather a variety of types of information. You can ask about people's background and other factual, demographic information. You can ask about their behaviours, their attitudes or beliefs, their knowledge or their intentions and aspirations. Each type of information is associated with particular difficulties which we will now discuss.

6.6.1 Background and demographic data

Most questionnaires will ask for some information about the respondent's background. Numerous texts deal with how to ask for this demographic information (e.g. Gillham, 2008; http://surveynet.ac.uk/) and it is well worth spending time consulting such resources if in doubt about how to phrase certain items. Although these types of information are readily accessible to the respondents themselves, it is surprising how often people resist giving this information. You should consider some of the following issues.

Age

Do you need to know a person's age exactly? Some people may not want to declare their ages exactly, so it may be appropriate to ask people to indicate their approximate age in a series of age bands (e.g. 18–25, 26–35, 36–50, etc.). How many bands you need will depend on how crucial it is to distinguish between respondents on the basis of age. If you need to know ages more accurately, then you should ask directly, making it clear how accurate you want the answer to be. You can ask for ages in years, or in years and months. It is possible to ask for dates of birth as an alternative. Asking for greater precision runs the risk of some respondents not answering the question at all.

Biological sex

It is good idea to make this a forced-choice, male/female item. If you leave the response category open-ended someone will put something silly in. Although social scientists draw a distinction between biological sex and gender and often wish to classify the respondent's gender, the term 'gender' is not well understood by many people and may serve to confuse them. Unless it is central to your research it is probably easiest to use an item like question 2 in Figure 6.1. A question asking, 'What is your gender?' can also annoy certain sections of society and produce unusable responses.

Ethnicity and nationality

Ethnicity and nationality are two bits of information about respondents that you may want to ask about despite the fact that the very act of asking for this information is heavily laden with political baggage. Many people confuse nationality with ethnicity and, as a researcher, you should be absolutely clear what information you need *and why*. Remember that being 'British' is a statement about nationality not ethnicity. People may reasonably want to know why their ethnicity or nationality is relevant to your study and what use you will make of this information. Research that may reveal important differences between ethnic groups may be regarded as politically suspect by whichever group is likely to come out worst in the survey. If you must ask about nationality and/or ethnicity you should be sure that such information cannot be used to systematically disadvantage any group. Resist the temptation to ask people about their race, since, although people talk about races in everyday life as if they existed, the concept of race has been discredited because it has proven impossible to determine what constitutes a race in practice (see Afkhami *et al.* 2009, for a detailed discussion of ethnicity).

Social class or socio-economic status

Social stratification is a topic on which so much has been written that it is difficult to provide simple guidance on good practice. There are several systems of classification, with most involving defining class on the basis of the nature of the person's occupation. This means obtaining enough information about someone's job to permit accurate classification. A common problem is that if someone says they are an 'engineer' this could mean anything, from someone who repairs TVs through to someone who designs satellites. You need more information such as that provided by the items in Figure 6.6.

When studying women it is difficult to know *whose* social class/status should be assessed. There is a debate (e.g. Dale *et al.* 1985) about how women's social class should be measured, particularly as women's jobs tend to carry a lower occupational status than men's jobs in some classification systems. Basing a woman's social status on her husband's occupation is done but is probably unsound and ignores those who are not married.

```
What is your job called?          _____
What job do you do?               _____
Where do you work?                _____
What does the employer make or do? _____

Is the work full-, or part-time? (Please ring one answer)

                              FULL-TIME
                              PART-TIME (less than 30 hrs a week)
```

Figure 6.6   **Example occupation questions**

Difficulties also occur when trying to classify young people's occupations. Occupations common among people at the beginning of their careers tend to carry low status yet they may still lead to high status careers in later life. Using parental class/status is one possible solution but it is unclear at what age a person's occupation should be regarded as a good indication of their class/status. Classifying students and the unemployed also remains problematic.

When asking about social class/status you should be clear in your mind what it is you really want to know about the respondent. Sociologists have spent decades theorising about what constitutes our social status and even a cursory dip into the literature will make it clear that such concepts as 'class', 'status' and 'advantage' are complex yet very slippery things indeed: psychologists should beware of the temptation to accept measures of 'status' uncritically. For many psychological applications it might be more appropriate to simply ask about factors such as income and educational history, since it may be these variables you are really interested in rather than a stratification based on occupations.

Income

A person's income is perhaps one of the most sensitive issues you can ask about. Requests for exact amounts are often regarded with suspicion, and common practice in market research is to provide income bands (e.g. £0–£5,000 p.a., £5,001–£10,000 p.a., etc.) and ask respondents to select one band only. Respondents need to be assured that their responses will not be handed over to HM Revenue and Customs or any other government agency.

With many factual types of responses it can be useful to ask respondents to tick a box if they do not wish to provide certain bits of information. This helps you distinguish between data that are missing because people did not want to provide some information, and data that are missing because people simply neglected to fill in the form completely. Providing an option not to respond like this may help to make people feel more relaxed about providing other sorts of information. Making people feel they have to answer absolutely everything may make some feel they would rather not respond at all. Obviously, you cannot do this with items that are crucial to your study's design. There is a useful resource outlining alternative ways to ask for social stratification information (including examples) at http://surveynet.ac.uk/.

6.6.2 **Behavioural reports**

By their nature, questions asking about past behaviours assume people can remember these events as well as being willing to tell a researcher about them. Both assumptions need to be considered for each new item you generate. It will come as no surprise that sensitive and socially undesirable behaviours are often misreported if reported at all. Enquiries about sexual activities are thought to produce over-reporting in some groups and under-reporting in others (see Boulton, 1994). Reports of involvement (or not) in illegal practices are also likely to be prone to biases.

It would be a mistake to assume that biases apply just to the under-reporting of private and/or undesirable acts. Sudman and Bradburn (1982) report studies that suggest over-reporting biases apply to socially desirable behaviours too (e.g. charity donations, library use). Given these problems, the best solution in the absence of corroborative data is to introduce additional items elsewhere in the questionnaire to test for consistency in reporting. If someone is going to misrepresent their behaviour to you, then if they are inconsistent at least you have clear grounds to exclude their responses from your analyses.

In some cases it may be possible to make people believe that you will have an alternative way to find out about their behaviour. This tactic is called the bogus pipeline. In a questionnaire study on children's smoking behaviour, Evans *et al.* (1978) took saliva samples at the time of questioning and led the children to believe that the saliva would be used to confirm what they said on the questionnaire. In fact, the cost of saliva testing was too high to permit all the samples to be tested but compared to a control group, the group who thought their behaviours could be monitored reported higher levels of smoking. Where appropriate, this strategy seems likely to improve the quality of behavioural report data, though you should be wary of deliberate attempts to deceive respondents, especially if you will be unable to fully debrief them.

Assessment of the frequency of behaviours done in the past is an area where there has been much research activity (see Gaskell *et al.* 1993a). What is clear is that you should avoid vague response categories (such as 'regularly') as discussed earlier. When asked about very regular, mundane events people may find it easier to estimate how often they have done the act in a given time period, since they are unlikely to remember every time they did the act. When asking about more memorable, major life-events, you can ask for more specific recall.

6.6.3 **Attitudes and opinions**

People's attitudes and opinions are often of great interest but there is debate about how measuring them is best done. The most common procedure is to present a statement and ask people to rate on a scale (usually five or seven points) how much they agree or disagree with the statement (see Figure 6.3). It is possible to use more than five or seven points. You can provide a line with the ends labelled 'strongly agree' and 'strongly disagree' and ask respondents simply to mark their preferred position on this agreement dimension with a cross. This procedure requires the researcher to use a ruler or template on each response to get a usable score for computational purposes.

An alternative to the rating scale is the forced-choice design, where two opposing statements are presented and the respondent must choose to endorse one or the other. This procedure is less common as it does not give information about the extremity of agreement/disagreement. However, five- or seven-point rating scales can suffer from people's over-reliance on the neutral response ('neither agree nor disagree') rather than committing themselves to expressing an opinion (see Box 6.1).

All pen-and-paper attitude measurements make a number of assumptions. The first is that people actually have attitudes towards the issues and that they have ready access to them. The second is that these can be adequately reflected in simple ratings or forced-choice judgements. Sometimes you will see the type of rating scale presented in Figure 6.3 referred to as a Likert scale. This is only technically true if the item has been developed following Likert's standardised procedure and this may not always be the case.

Given these kinds of problems it is common to ask multiple questions about the same attitude object in the hope that greater accuracy will be achieved. Multiple item measures of attitudes allow for the possibility of measuring the internal reliability of the items and thus how much 'error' there is in the measurement of the attitude (see Chapter 7).

6.6.4 **Knowledge**

Quite often it would be useful to assess factual knowledge in a questionnaire survey. Such 'tests' can be carried out but the validity of responses and thus the knowledge scores has to be considered to be in some doubt. Unless you can be present at the time of testing you cannot be certain who answered the test. This could apply to the whole questionnaire, of course, but people may simply ask someone else for help with the difficult questions so that they do not appear ignorant. Tests of this sort can be used reasonably successfully in non-survey settings on populations such as school pupils and employees where you can exert some control over the testing conditions.

6.6.5 **Intentions, expectations and aspirations**

Many social psychological theories are concerned with accounting for intentions, expectations and aspirations which are fairly easily assessed via questionnaires. You should be careful to specify an appropriate time frame for such items, as vague specifications can lead to vague responses. For instance, if you were to ask, 'Do you expect to invest in a savings plan in the future?', people could quite reasonably say, 'Who knows?' A much better form would be to ask, 'As far as you can tell, do you expect to open a savings plan in the next year?'

6.7 **EXISTING SCALES AND MEASURES**

When using established measures it is often tempting to alter the wording of some items to make them sound better or to clarify them a little. It is quite surprising how many published and well-established measures contain wording errors like those outlined in the earlier sections of this chapter. It is also the case that scales developed in other countries can contain culturally specific phrases or assume some familiarity with cultural norms that would be inappropriate for your sample. Should you change item wordings or leave them as they are? It is not possible to answer this with a categorical 'yes' or 'no'. One side of the argument says that any fiddling with item wordings will change the nature of the scale so that it is no longer equivalent to the original. Hence, comparability of scores between your study and existing research is no longer appropriate. You might be tempted to make minor changes in the hope that scale scores will still be comparable but, in the absence of supporting validity data, this cannot be assumed.

The other side of the argument says that it is poor research practice to administer questionnaires that contain phrases or assumptions that your respondents are unlikely to be familiar with. It may alienate them or make them think the items are silly or not serious. As an example, early versions of the Wilson–Patterson Conservatism Scale (Wilson & Patterson, 1968) contained items asking people to endorse (or not) chaperones, pyjama parties and beatniks among other potential indicators of conservative attitudes. At the time (the 1960s) chaperones, pyjama parties and beatniks were topical and made sense in such a questionnaire but today these items would raise eyebrows.

The point about the latter example is that the scale would presumably no longer be particularly valid (indeed Wilson subsequently updated the scale). Even though you might wish to compare current levels of conservatism with those found in the 1960s and 1970s by using an equivalent measure, it is doubtful that such a comparative study would be very informative. You should always consider this potential lack of validity when thinking about using an existing measure that was not validated on the type of sample that you are going to study. You may need to consider attempting to establish validity yourself (e.g. via a criterion groups approach; see Chapter 7).

6.8 QUESTIONNAIRE LAYOUT

This section deals with issues in the presentation of your questionnaire. There is always a trade-off between on the one hand better presentation (and thus, one hopes, better quality data and higher response rate), and on the other, increased cost.

6.8.1 Respondent motivation

Unless you will be present at the administration of the questionnaire, explanatory notes need to be provided. These should spell out the broad aims of the study and why the individual's participation is important. The person must be encouraged to feel that their responses are valued by you and that you will treat them with respect no matter what their responses are. Wherever possible, you should ensure anonymity for respondents. If the research design requires you to be able to identify individual respondents, acknowledge this and state you will ensure confidentiality (and, of course, mean it). If you intend to keep computerised records of responses that could identify respondents, in the UK you (or your organisation) should be registered under the Data Protection Act as a holder of such information. Tell respondents that you are registered.

Promise to give feedback to respondents (which is always good practice), and explain how you will do this. Compliance is likely to be higher if people can find out what happened to their answers and what benefits may have come from the study. Always thank respondents for their help in the introductory notes *and* at the end of the form.

6.8.2 **Case identifiers**

It is good housekeeping practice to be able to identify individual questionnaires (though not necessarily individuals) so that when you find problems with the data later on you can use the computer to tell you which questionnaire the problem is associated with. If you fail to do this with a large survey it will be very difficult to find the right questionnaire and make any valid corrections to the data.

6.8.3 **Length**

There are no rules to guide you on the optimum length for a questionnaire since this depends so much on the topic of the study, the method of distribution (e.g. postal, face-to-face, web) and the anticipated enthusiasm of your respondents. There are some rough guidelines that can be given, however. The problem facing most researchers is how to ask all the questions they want to ask without tiring or boring their respondents to death. How long it takes to answer a questionnaire can only really be assessed via pilot work, and it is worth piloting the form on people who are likely, on *a priori* grounds, to have difficulty with it. Experience would suggest that forms that take more than 45 minutes to complete are only appropriate where the respondent can be assumed to be very highly motivated to help you.

Very short questionnaires (one or two pages) have the virtue of not taxing people unduly, though they may not be taken very seriously either. It would be rare to have a substantive research issue that could be addressed with such a small questionnaire, and some respondents may think the exercise can only be superficial and thus adopt a less than serious attitude towards answering.

6.8.3 Question order

There is a debate about where in a questionnaire to collect information about respondent demographics (age, sex, etc.) – should you collect it at the beginning or the end of a questionnaire? There is a consensus that asking these questions in the middle of the questionnaire is probably not a good idea but little agreement about whether to ask these relatively easy questions at the beginning or the end. This is information that people have ready access to and will have little difficulty in providing. Some argue that if you ask for this information at the beginning then you will definitely have information on your sample's characteristics even if they do not go on to complete the whole of the form. The counter argument is that having easy to answer questions at the end will maximise the chances that people will complete the whole thing – as they tire of your questionnaire they get asked progressively less taxing questions.

It is rare to place extremely sensitive questions right at the beginning of a form. People need time to get accustomed to the types of issues you are interested in, so starting off with your equivalent of 'When did you stop beating your wife?' will not make the respondent feel at ease.

6.8.4 Question density

You may be tempted to cram lots of questions into a small number of pages so that the questionnaire booklet does not look too large and daunting. Generally, this is counterproductive, as squashing lots of items into a small space makes the form look complex and raises the possibility that respondents will get confused and put their responses in the wrong places. Clear, self-evident layout will enhance the possibility of getting valid information from your sample.

6.8.5 Questions that do not apply to everybody

It is often the case that you are forced to use a single form to ask questions and that some of these will not be applicable to some people. For instance, you may not wish to ask unemployed respondents about how many hours they work. If you cannot provide a separate questionnaire for the unemployed, you will need to use filter questions. An example is shown in Figure 6.7.

6.8.6 Typeface and size

Some people will find small, densely packed text difficult to read. Pick a clear font (typeface) and make it reasonably large (12 point or bigger). Use a different font or colour for instructions and bold or italic lettering for filter questions.

```
1) Are you currently unemployed ?          YES
                                           NO

   If you answered 'YES' to question 1, ignore question 2 and carry on with question 3.

2) How many hours did you work last week ? _____ hours

   Everyone should answer question 3

3) Are you male or female?                 MALE
                                           FEMALE
```

Figure 6.7   An example of a filter question

6.8.7 The use of graphics in response options

Most respondents are either oblivious to, or do not need to know that their carefully thought through responses to our questions will be turned into numbers for statistical analysis. Indeed they may not like the idea that their heartfelt agreement with a statement on an issue will most probably be turned into a single number later to be aggregated with a range of other responses in a composite index (see Chapter 10).

Although commonly used, asking people to respond by circling a number on a scale can carry certain threats to the validity of the data. First there will be those who mistakenly assume that bigger is better and misunderstand the nature of the response scale. There will also be some who do not understand numbered scales at all and would not be able to make the conceptual leap to link the numbers with a latent dimension of agreement. There are various ways around this. One is to abandon numbers and use tick boxes laid out in a line that implies the relevant response dimension (most often agree/disagree as in alternative B in Figure 6.3). Another is to use graphics such as 'smiley' faces which can convey happiness/sadness with regard to the questionnaire item. This is a particularly useful approach with children.

6.9 USING THE WEB TO ADMINISTER QUESTIONNAIRES

The appeal of using the worldwide web as a means of getting questionnaires out to large numbers of people quickly is great. Potentially, there are millions of people out there who could answer your questionnaire if only they were aware of it and, with modern on-line survey software such as SurveyMonkey (www.surveymonkey.com/) and FreeOnlineSurveys (www.freeonlinesurveys.com/), the costs of running a survey can be very low indeed. There are savings in time to be had since the web offers the opportunity to contact people quickly and once they have decided to respond their responses are collected electronically and can be immediately down-loaded into statistical software, cutting out the time-consuming data entry phase of paper questionnaires and reducing coding errors. If you want to study particular groups (e.g. people with a particular medical condition or fans of Norwegian Black Metal) you can use the existence of pre-existing web communities to help you get access to samples that would be otherwise quite hard to find using traditional sur-veying techniques. Members of such groups are likely to be committed to their group membership and potentially more enthusiastic about answering questions about something that interests them.

Web-based surveys also offer the potential for introducing new elements not easily incorporated in the traditional pen-and-paper questionnaire survey. For example it is possible to embed short movie or sound clips in the survey so that people can respond to these much more engaging stimuli very shortly after having seen them. Hypertext links can be included, so that if your respondents do not know the meaning of a term they can click on a link to get a definition. It is possible to adapt the pattern of questioning based on the answers people have given to ear-lier questions in the survey. At its most basic level you can prevent people moving on to the next sections in the survey until they have completed the previous sec-tion. This offers the hope that there will be fewer missing responses in the final data set. If some questions will not be relevant to certain groups you can use their previ-ous answers to select which questions they are asked next. The possibilities for online surveys have only begun to be explored.

Online questionnaires are not without their limitations and the most obvious problems are associated with sampling and knowing who is (or is not) answering your questionnaire. Sampling issues and response biases are discussed in Chapter 5 but an obvious limitation for web surveys is that socially disadvantaged parts of the population, those with certain disabilities and those who have chosen not to have a domestic computer will not be included in any surveys. In the absence of lists of all known Internet users it is quite difficult to achieve true probability samples (see Chapter 5), so when you get your data you do not really know whether your sample is representative of any particular population. You can look to see whether the demographic profile of your sample looks like the profile of the target population, which can give you greater confidence about any inferences you make from the data and this may be 'good enough' for some purposes (e.g. looking at relationships between answers within your questionnaire) but less satisfactory for others (e.g. estimating parameters of the population).

6.10 CONCLUSION

This chapter has attempted to alert you to many common problems in question-naire design. The solutions proposed here are intended as guides to good practice

Box 6.4 Some simple do's and don'ts for web-based questionnaire surveys

Do	Do Not
• Begin the questionnaire on the first screen with a question that is simple to answer.	• Let the screen get too cluttered – avoid unnecessary graphics especially moving ones or ones that take a long time to download.
• Give clear guidance on the format of information that you want (e.g. DD/MM/YY for dates).	• Have too many questions on one page – avoid matrices of responses of more than 10–15 rows.
• Use a radio button specifically for 'none-of the above' types of responses.	• Put so much on each page that the user has to do a lot of scrolling to see all the questions – use separate pages.
• Give visual cues for the task in drop-down boxes (e.g. 'select one').	
• Make sure that the size of the boxes you give to allow free-format responses matches the likely amount of information you want from respondents.	• Use lots of different response formats.
• Use checking routines to make sure that the respondent has given you essential information (e.g. their gender if that is a key variable in your study).	• Force people to make responses unless absolutely necessary – this can be irritating and encourage invalid and/or silly responses.
• Give an open-ended field for 'other' responses where respondents might not want to use your pre-coded response options.	• Make the first option visible in drop-down boxes: it may suggest answers and may be misunderstood as an answer when respondents do not choose any answer.
• Use hypertext links that people can click on to see definitions of technical terms, etc.	• Use default filled radio buttons – these may suggest a preferred answer.
• Encrypt the responses to protect the rights and privacy of the respondents.	• Have radio buttons, etc., that are small and require very accurate mouse clicking.

but you should not feel that these are the only possible solutions to these difficulties. Much more inventive use could be made of questionnaires than is currently the case. Guides such as this necessarily deal with common problems but you should not limit yourself to asking about the broad general topics covered here. Breakwell and Canter (1993), for example, illustrate a number of possibilities for alternative questionnaire approaches to the social psychological topic of social representation; such experimentation should be encouraged in other research domains too.

6.11 **EXERCISES**

1   Think of a psychological construct that you would like to measure (e.g. an attitude towards something, a state like happiness or perhaps a trait like agreeableness). See if you can generate ten different questions that you could ask people about this without repeating yourself. Ask five friends to respond to these items without telling them what it is you are trying to measure and see if they can guess what the construct concerned is (pick something that is not too obvious – like attitudes towards Hitler). If they guess correctly ask them which was the best question and which one they thought was the least good question and why. If they get it wrong, ask them what they think was being measured and why.

2   Think of a current controversial political issue and ask two groups of 20 people about their attitude toward the issue. In the manner of Krosnick and Schuman's (1988) study on 'forbidding' versus 'not allowing' things ask one group of people the questions using forceful language and the other group logically equivalent questions but using more passive language. See if this manipulation has an effect on the level of support for the issue.

6.12 **DISCUSSION QUESTIONS**

1   Is it ever possible to find out people's true attitudes towards controversial issues?
2   Should important policies or life-changing decisions be based on data drawn from questionnaire studies?
3   Is it the case that when trying to find out the opinions of large numbers of people there is no real alternative to the questionnaire survey?

6.13 **FURTHER READING**

Fielding *et al.* (2008) *The handbook of online research methods* contains good discussions of the pros and cons of internet surveys. The book also looks at the potential for other kinds of online research, such as studying friendship groups and social networks or conducting online focus groups. It has good coverage of data quality issues.

The Survey Resources Network (http://surveynet.ac.uk/) is a web resource funded by the UK's Economic and Research Council that collects together best practice in questionnaire design and survey methodology and has examples of good and bad ways to ask common questions that researchers need to ask.

Oppenheim's (1992) *Questionnaire design, interviewing and attitude measurement* is still a good and clear introduction to questionnaire design, as is the older Sudman and Bradburn (1982) book *Asking questions: A practical guide to questionnaire design*. Schuman and Presser's (1996) *Questions and answers in attitude surveys: Experiments on question form, writing and context* reports an intriguing series of experimental studies with survey data which highlight the sensitivity of respondents to quite minor wording changes in questionnaire items.

7
Psychometrics

John Rust

CONTENTS

This chapter is about psychometrics; the science of psychological assessment. It will introduce not only the theory and practice of testing, but also the many issues associate with the use of psychological tests in society. Once you understand how ability, achievement, IQ and personality testing works, you will be able to apply the same psychometric principles to other forms of assessment, such as interviews, essays and social surveys.

KEY TERMS

classical test theory (CTT)
computer adaptive testing
  (CAT)
differential item functioning
  (DIF)
item response theory (IRT)

psychometrics
reliability
standardisation
test equivalence
the Flynn effect
validity

7.1 **INTRODUCTION**

Psychometrics is the science of psychological assessment. While assessment itself has been dated back 3,000 years to its origins in China when the Chinese Emperor set up assessment centres for prospective civil servants, its science saw its origins in the late nineteenth century when statisticians began devising tools for the analysis of individual differences. Psychometrics since then has developed in two phases. Phase one, called Classical Test Theory (CTT) began around 1890 when James McKeen Cattell derived the first psychometric tests. Its influence is still with us today and most of the tests currently in use were originally derived under the principles of CTT. Phase two began with the introduction of Item Response Theory (IRT), separately by Georg Rasch and Allan Birnbaum, in the 1960s. IRT models the behaviour of test respondents and test items within a common framework, and with the advance of modelling techniques in statistics it has become the dominant frame of reference for modern psychometric test development and use in the twenty-first century.

Psychometric testing is a fundamental aspect of modern life. We are tested at school to monitor our performance. We are tested at the end of school to provide us with our first academic credentials, a process that will continue throughout our learning life. We have to pass both practical and written tests to obtain our driving licences and to be able to practice our professions. We are tested in order to gain special provision (e.g. for learning difficulties) or to obtain prizes. When we buy on credit or apply for a mortgage we have to fill in forms that are scored in much the same manner. We are tested at work, when we apply for promotion, and when we seek another job. The forms of assessment can also take many forms – interview, examination, multiple-choice, diagnostic, practical, continuous assessment, and so on. But in spite of the wide variety of applications and manifestations, all assessments share a common set of fundamental characteristics – they should be reliable, valid, standardised and free from bias. There are good assessments, and bad assessments, and there is a science of how to maximise the quality of assessment. That science is psychometrics. There is no other aspect of the field of psychology that has such an impact on individuals in their daily lives.

7.2 **TYPES OF PSYCHOMETRIC TEST**

Tests can be divided into two major categories, knowledge-based and person-based. Those based on knowledge look for levels of optimal performance; they assess how much you know or the best you can do in a particular situation and are used to assess ability, aptitude, attainment and achievement. Examples of knowledge-based tests are school and university examinations, intelligence tests and tests of specific abilities. Person-based tests exist to assess your typical performance: how you normally behave. They include personality tests, attitude scales and social surveys as well as tests of mood, motivation, beliefs, interests and clinical symptomology. One major difference between these two types of test is that knowledge-based tests are necessarily hierarchical and cumulative. The development of human knowledge moves in a particular direction from not knowing to knowing. Person-based tests on the other hand carry no such implication. Different personalities and different attitudes are just different, and there is no intrinsic implication that to hold one attitude is necessarily better or worse, or more or less advanced, than the holding of another.

7.3 THE PSYCHOMETRIC PRINCIPLES

The fundamental building blocks of psychometric theory are the four psychometric principles of reliability, validity, standardisation and equivalence. Reliability is based on a theory of measurement called the theory of true scores or latent trait theory. A reliable test will produce the same or a very similar result whoever it is scored by and irrespective of when and the circumstances in which it was taken. Validity is the extent to which an assessment is fit for purpose. Scores on a recruitment test may be reliable, but do those who obtain higher scores actually perform better once selected? Standardisation describes the process whereby a particular person's score is interpreted, either in relation to the performance of others or in relation to what they can do or how they will behave in practice. Equivalence looks for consistency in how a test deals with different social groups; does it assess the same characteristics in each group or is its use unfair to some? The psychometric principles are crucial, both in the development of new tests and in the evaluation of existing ones. They also provide the framework by which different forms of assessment can themselves be assessed, enabling informed decisions to be made about alternative strategies (e.g. interview or psychometric test, or indeed perhaps both).

7.4 INTELLIGENCE TESTING

The archetypal and certainly most controversial psychometric tests are those of intelligence. Intelligence quotient (IQ) testing began in earnest in 1905 when Alfred Binet devised the first tests of general ability for use in educational selection for Parisian schools. Binet's intelligence scales provided a set of standards that were easy and quick to administer, and which effectively discriminated between children who were seen by teachers to be bright and children who were seen as dull, as well as between mentally retarded children in institutions and children in ordinary schools. They rapidly attracted the attention of psychologists elsewhere, and were translated into many languages including English. In 1916, Stanford University produced the definitive English language version that formed the basis for many subsequent revisions. Today the Stanford–Binet Intelligence Scales are in their fifth edition.

A second major impetus for the development of IQ testing was its use for recruitment to the US military during the First World War. The Army alpha and beta tests were subsequently administered to many millions of potential recruits. These tests formed the basis for the Scholastic Aptitude Test (SAT) used then and now for university entrance in the US and for the 11-plus examination for selection to grammar schools in the UK. The underlying rationale for these developments was a desire that access to education should be based on merit rather than privilege. However, the idea that merit consisted of intelligence proved to be exceptionally controversial, as was the ideology behind many of those who advocated IQ testing, a movement that had been particularly influenced by the eugenicist ideas of Sir Francis Galton. Galton believed that intelligence was not only inherited but also represented a step in the evolutionary ladder; some races possessing more of this quality than others. Applied eugenics in the first half of the twentieth century led to the curtailment of travelling rights and liberties of persons with low IQ, to sterilisation programmes and, in some countries, to euthanasia. Arguments about the reasons behind differences in IQ scores between groups continue today. However these differences have been forced into perspective by the Flynn effect, the observation by James Flynn that mean IQ scores for all groups are increasing by on average between 3 and 4 IQ points per decade (Flynn 1984). These changes over time and over generations swamp any differences between groups, and indeed it seems that the Flynn effect may be levelling off for the highest scoring groups, suggesting that one day there may be a level playing field. In 1987 a further paper by Flynn extended his research beyond the USA and found similar results in another 14 countries. Clearly the relationship between genes and environment in terms of how they influence IQ scores must be rather more complex than had originally been thought.

Today, the focus has shifted away from intelligence and towards ability. The former is limited to potential, but much potential is unfulfilled. More usually our life choices lead us down varied paths, towards specialisms that fulfil our interests and ambitions.

Alternative models of intelligence are exemplified by the work of Howard Gardner (1983) and Robert Sternberg (1990). Gardner argues that there are multiple intelligences, each linked with an independent and separate system within the human brain. These are linguistic intelligence, logical–mathematical intelligence, spatial intelligence, musical intelligence, bodily-kinaesthetic intelligence, interpersonal intelligence and intrapersonal intelligence. Many of these correspond with traditional notions that are tested within IQ tests. However, Gardner emphasises the distinctive nature of some of these intelligences and their ability to operate independently of each other. He associates linguistic intelligence, for example, with skills in the use of oral language.

Sternberg, in his triarchic model, suggests three major forms of intelligence – analytic, creative and practical. While analytic intelligence, measured by classical IQ tests, is important, it is not always the most relevant. He gives an apocryphal example of a brilliant mathematician who appeared to have no insight at all into human relationships, to such an extent that when his wife left him unexpectedly he was completely unable to come up with any meaningful explanation. Doubts about the sufficiency of classical notions of intelligence have also been expressed in the business world. High IQ is associated with the ability to solve problems set by others, such as in a test or examination. A successful business entrepreneur, however, needs to ask good questions rather than supply good answers. It is the ability to come up with good questions that characterises the creative form of intelligence. People with practical intelligence are 'streetwise', and they are often the most successful in life. They know the right people, avoid making powerful enemies, and are able to work out the unspoken rules of the game.

Thus, those with analytic intelligence do well on IQ tests, appear 'clever', are able to solve preset problems, learn quickly, appear knowledgeable, are able to automate their expertise and normally pass exams easily. Those with creative intelligence are able to identify new questions, are able to see new possibilities in a situation, can generate new ideas and can 'achieve the impossible'. Those with practical intelligence appear to be 'wise', they want to understand and can stand back and deconstruct a proposal or idea, they will question the reasons for wanting to know and can integrate their knowledge for a deeper purpose.

7.5 NEUROPSYCHOLOGICAL ASSESSMENT

Neuropsychological tests are used in clinical practice to make assessments of patients' comparative levels of cognitive performance. This may happen, for example, when someone has suffered brain damage following a road accident. There have traditionally been two major systems in use, the Halstead–Reitan Batteries (Reitan, 1955), and the Luria–Nebraska Neuropsychological Test Battery (Golden *et al.* 1978).

Both these batteries form an important part of the diagnostic work of neuropsychologists, brain scientists and clinicians. They have been particularly successful in diagnosing brain damage in 18–45 year olds. Difficulties are encountered with children (where the constant presence of developmental change always makes medical diagnosis difficult), and in older people, where the effects of brain damage become confounded with the mental deterioration that is part of the normal aging process.

7.6 PERSONALITY TESTING

The form of personality test with which people are most familiar is the self-report inventory, comprising a series of items to which individuals respond according to how they view themselves. Well known examples are the 16PF, the Myer–Briggs Personality

Indicator (MBTI) and the NEO. While pencil-and-paper versions of personality tests are still in use, most such testing today is carried out by computer or over the Internet. The advantages of self-report inventories are that they are quick and easy to administer, they can be administered to groups, the scoring is objective and the responses are obtained directly from person being assessed. Limitations may be that those assessed may not have good insight about themselves, they may try to present themselves in the best possible light, they may try to present themselves according to what they think is expected or desired, and it is difficult to know whether the questionnaire has been completed with due care and attention.

The results of self-report psychometric personality tests are often reported as a personality profile. Within a profile, not one but many test scores are presented, but in such a way that they can be compared with each other. These are called sub-scales, and there can often be items from as many as 20 sub-scales in one personality test with the items randomly interspersed, the items only being brought together for scoring purposes. Raw sub-scale scores need to be standardised (see section 7.3), and the set of standardised sub-scale scores are then illustrated on a profile sheet (see Figure 7.1.) One of the earliest profile systems developed was the Minnesota Multiphasic Personality Inventory (MMPI), which is still in use today and which provides a good general example of the technique. The MMPI was developed as a broad-spectrum personality test to be used on psychiatric patients, usually

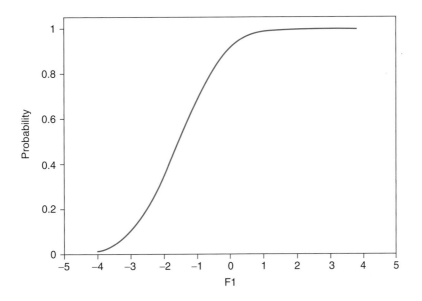

Figure 7.1   An Item Characteristic Curve (ICC) for a single item. F1 on the *x* axis represents the ability dimensions (normally called theta). The *y* axis represents the probability of getting the item right. The further to the right a person's score on the ability dimension, the higher their probability of getting the item right

on admission to psychiatric hospital. It consists of over 400 personality test style items (of the type: 'Are you a nervous person?', 'Do you sometimes hear voices?', 'Are there enemies who are out to get you?', etc.), which form a set of sub-scales within the overall questionnaire. Within the MMPI there are sub-scales of hypochondriasis, depression, hysteria, psychopathy, paranoia, psychoasthenia, schizophrenia, hypomania and masculinity–femininity. These sub-scales are each scored separately, and each is subjected to separate standardisation. An individual's MMPI sub-scale scores are entered as points on a graph, and the points joined to form a profile. On such a profile, areas that are particularly problematic will appear as peaks on the graph, the higher the peak the greater the disturbance. Psychiatrists who see large numbers of such profiles for their patients will soon begin to recognise common patterns, representing well-known conditions, such as paranoid schizophrenia for example. Expert use of MMPI profiles can save a clinician a great deal of time.

Self-report questionnaires are not limited to personality assessment. In the Jackson Vocational Interest Survey (Jackson, 1977), for example, respondents are required to choose between options such as 'Acting in a school play' and 'Teaching children how to write'. The survey produces scales such as job security, dominant leadership and stamina. Another example is Giotto, an ipsative test of integrity for use in occupational settings. Respondents are presented with alternative adjectives, such as 'tolerant' versus 'secure', and asked to select the one that most applies to them. Giotto's scale scores are designed to identify the strongest and weakest aspects of the respondent's character. A major benefit of the ipsative format is to reduce 'faking good' by forcing individuals to choose between options that are similar with respect to social desirability.

7.7 PSYCHOMETRICS AS MEASUREMENT

The basic measurement theory in psychometrics, the theory of true scores, also known as 'latent trait theory' states simply that any score on an item or a test by a respondent can be represented by two component parts: the respondent's true score on whatever the item measures, and some error of measurement. This theory was first formulated by Edgeworth (1888):

> I think it is intelligible to speak of the mean judgment of competent critics as the true judgment; and deviations from that mean as errors. This central figure which is, or may be supposed to be, assigned by the greatest number of equally competent judges, is to be regarded as the true value …, just as the true weight of a body is determined by taking the mean of several discrepant measurements.

In formulaic terns:

$$X = T + E$$

where X symbolises the observed score, T symbolises the true score and E is the error. Of our four psychometric principles, that of reliability is most closely related to true score theory

7.8 RELIABILITY

Reliability is often explained in terms of the measuring process in physics or engineering. When we measure, for example, the length of a table we assume that our measurements are reasonably reliable. In the social sciences on the other hand, unreliability of our measures can be a major problem. We may find that, for example, a pupil gets a score of 73 on a geography test on one occasion, and a score of 68 two weeks later on the same test, and we would probably feel that these figures were as close as we could reasonably expect in a classroom test. Reliabilities are normally calculated using the correlation coefficient (see Chapter 11), whether between two raters or between two occasions. All published tests are required to report details of reliability and of how it was calculated, and whenever a test is constructed and used, information on reliability must be included. Types of reliability include inter-rater, test–retest, parallel forms, split-half and internal consistency.

Inter-rater reliability applies particularly to cases where there is more than one examiner – for example, essay markers or interviewers. Reliability here can be found by correlating any two sets of marks or ratings. Test–retest reliability involves administering the test twice to the same group of respondents, with an interval between the two administrations of, say, one week, and correlating the scores on the two occasions. Test–retest reliability is sometimes referred to as test stability. Although the test–retest method seems straightforward, there are circumstances in which it is inappropriate, as skills, motivation and memory from the first administration will influence the second. For this reason an alternative technique for estimating reliability is the parallel-forms method. Here we have not one version of the test but two, linked in a systematic manner. Tests constructed in this way are said to be parallel. For parallel forms reliability, each person is given both versions of the test to complete, and the reliability is the correlation between the two. A widely used approximation to parallel-forms reliability is split-half reliability, in which a test is split into two in random fashion. For each individual two scores are obtained, one for each half of the test, and these scores are correlated and then adjusted for the change in test length by the use of the Spearman–Brown formula:

$$r_{test} = 2 \times r_{half} / (1 + r_{half})$$

where r_{test} is the reliability of the test, and r_{half} is the correlation obtained between the two halves of the test. Coefficient alpha (Cronbach's alpha) is frequently used in preference to split-half reliability. Cronbach's alpha is a functional average of all possible split-half reliabilities, and so long as all possible split halves are approximately parallel this works well. Two caveats; first, this is not the case if some of the splits divide meaningful areas of the test specification; for example, all arithmetic items in one half, all geometry items in the other. Second, it is possible, serendipitously but counterproductively, to increase alpha by limiting items to narrower and narrower areas of the test specification, thus excluding important aspects of the desired trait.

What counts as a 'good' reliability depends on the circumstances. It is very unusual for an assessment or psychometric test to have a reliability above 0.96; only individual broad spectrum tests of general ability achieve this level. As a rule of thumb, group tests of ability should have reliabilities over 0.8, tests of personality over 0.7, essay marks over 0.6 and interviews over 0.5. Constructs that are more difficult to measure such as creativity, or projective tests such as the Rorscharch inkblot test, rarely have reliabilities greater than 0.3.

7.9 VALIDITY

Just because a test is reliable does not necessarily mean it has validity. Validity only exists within the context of a stated purpose for the test. For example, handwriting analysis may be reliable in that different graphologists usually follow the same rulebook, and hence will interpret the same characteristic (e.g. forward leaning writing) in the same way. But this is a quite separate issue from whether or not those with forward leaning writing actually have the same personality characteristic (being forward-looking, would you believe).

The validity of a test also has many different forms. Face validity concerns the acceptability of the test items, to both test user and respondent, for the operation being carried out. The content validity of a test examines the extent to which the test specification under which the test was constructed reflects the particular purpose for which the test is being developed (see 'constructing your own test'). Content validity has sometimes been described as criterion-related or domain-referenced validity in circumstances where the test designer is using the criterion-referenced framework for skills learning and curriculum evaluation. Predictive validity is the major form of statistical validity, and is employed wherever tests are used to make predictions; for example, the use of a test for recruitment. It is represented as a correlation between the test score itself, and an assessment of the degree of success in the job; for example, as rated by supervisors or, for sales staff, sales figures.

Concurrent validity describes the correlation of a new test with existing tests that purport to measure the same construct. But what counts as the same construct? This is the province of construct validation. Within the theory of true scores, construct validation addresses the question, 'True score on what?', and begins with an attempt to deconstruct the concept in question. Constructs are ideas: intelligent, creative, dyslexic, psychic, psychopath, and so on, that may or may not be useful to explain the behaviour of people in real life. To show that a psychological construct is valid it is necessary to show that it contributes something extra to existing knowledge over and above what is already known, whether this be either an increased ability to predict and control, or simply parsimony, an ability to reduce complexity to an underlying simple structure. Campbell and Fiske (1959) pointed out that construct validity demanded not only that a test correlate with some other measures it resembles, but also that it should not correlate with measures from which it should differ. They designated the first type of correlation 'convergent validity', and the second type 'discriminant validity'. Differential validity is demonstrated by the discrepancy between convergent and discriminant validity.

7.10 **STANDARDISATION**

Simply knowing someone's raw score on a test tells us nothing unless we know something about the test's standardisation characteristics. A person may seem delighted when told that their score on a test is 78 – but the delight will fade if they learn that everyone else who took the test scored over 425. There are two types of standardisation, norm-referenced and criterion-referenced. Criterion-referenced tests tell us what a person with a particular score or higher can or cannot be expected to know or do. Norm-referenced tests tell us how someone's score compares with the score of a sample of others who took the test.

The easiest way to norm-reference a test is simply to place everyone's scores in order and find out the rank order of the person in question. Rank orders can then be presented as percentiles (e.g. X did better than 23% of others who took the test). However a disadvantage of this approach is that it throws away information coming from the actual sizes of the differences between raw scores, something that is lost when data are ranked – it treats the data as ordinal rather than interval (see Chapter 2) .

If the scale is truly interval and it approximates a normal distribution (see Chapter 2) then we can express a person's score in standard deviation units, and a person's score can be presented as a z-score (A z-score is the distance, in standard deviations, that a score is away from the mean). A person may, for example, be 1.00 standard deviations above the mean, or 2.00 or −1.70 (i.e. 1.7 standard deviations below the mean). Such scores are referred to in psychometrics as 'standard scores', and using z-tables they can easily be converted into percentiles and vice versa; for example, a standard score of −1.00 means that a person scores higher than 16% of people in his group. The group in question is called the norm group.

Standard scores on a test normally range between −3.0 and +3.0, and have a mean of zero. This is not a very convenient way to present an individual's score; most people would object if told that their score on a test was −1.3! There is, therefore, a set of conventions that are applied to these standard scores to make them more presentable. The most common of these are the T-score, the stanine and the 'IQ' formats. For T-scores we multiply the z-score by 10 and add 50. Thus a standard score of –1.3 becomes (–1.3 × 10) + 50 = 37 – which is much more respectable. The advantage of this format is that it turns the scores into something that resembles the traditional classroom mark, which normally has a mean of about 50 with most scores lying between 20 and 80. *T*-scores are as easily interpretable as *z*-scores. For example, if someone has a *T*-score of 70, it is immediately clear that they are two standard deviations above the mean, equivalent to a *z*-score of 2, and by working backwards through the *z*-tables we can easily find that such a score is in the top 2.3% of scores on that test.

The stanine technique transforms the standard scores to a scale running from 1 to 9, with a mean of 5 and a standard deviation of 2. This standardisation is widely used, as a set of scores from 1 to 9 (rather like marking out of 10) has much intuitive appeal. There are no negatives and no decimals, which are, by convention, rounded off either downwards or to the nearest whole number. The rather similar sten score is standardisation to a scale running from 1 to 10, with a mean of 5.5 and a standard deviation of 2. The sten and stanine are both widely used in personality testing. Although they seem very similar, there is one important difference. With the stanine the score of 5 represents an average band (ranging before rounding from 4.5 to 5.5, which is one-quarter of a standard deviation below the mean to one-quarter of a standard deviation above the mean). With the sten, on the other hand, there is no average as such. A score of 5 represents the low average band (ranging from 4.5 to 5.5; that is, one-half a standard deviation below the mean to the mean itself), and a score of 6 represents the high average band (ranging from 5.5 to 6.5; that is, from the mean itself to one standard deviation above the mean).

The 'IQ' format originated when the definition of Stanford–Binet IQ scores was changed from one based on the ratio of mental age to chronological age (the original meaning of 'Intelligence Quotient'), to the now widely used standardisation approach. The IQ transformation is based on a mean of 100 and a standard deviation of 15; thus a standard score of –1.3 becomes an IQ score of (–1.3 × 15) + 100 = 80.5 (or 80 when rounded off). An IQ score of 130 (i.e. 100 + (2 × 15)) is two standard deviations above the mean and, as two standard deviations means a *z*-score of 2, we can tell from *z*-tables that such a score or higher would be obtained by less than 2.3% of the population. Some IQ tests use different standard deviations; for example, Cattell uses 16 scale points rather than 15. IQ-style scores are best avoided by psychometricians today. They have become something of a cult, and their extrapolations bear very little relation to normal scientific processes. IQs of 160, for example, often appear as news items in the media, yet 160 would be 4 standard deviations above the mean. As such a high score would occur in the general population only 3 times in 100,000, we would need to have had a normal group of about 1,000,000 individuals to obtain the relevant comparisons. The behaviour of individuals at probability levels of less than 3 in 100,000 is not something that can meaningfully be summarised in an IQ score. The whole conception of a unitary trait of intelligence breaks down at these extremes.

7.11 **BIAS IN TESTING AND ASSESSMENT**

Tests used for selection should be free from bias, whether it be in terms of gender, race, culture, language or any other group difference, and in most countries there is a substantial amount of legislation that protects individuals on this basis. In most cases both direct and indirect discrimination are illegal. Indirect discrimination occurs when, even in the absence of overt discrimination, the chance of obtaining a job or a promotion is dependent on a requirement that is more likely to be met by one group than by another.

Classically there have been three major categories of test bias: item bias, intrinsic test bias and extrinsic test bias. Within modern psychometrics these are referred to as Differential Item Functioning (DIF), measurement invariance and adverse impact respectively. In a wide variety of settings in which instruments of assessment are used, it is necessary ethically, legally, practically and conceptually to reassure users and audiences that the test is fit for purpose and not biased in favour – or against – any particular group. This requires that persons who are at the same location on the underlying trait or attribute measured by the inventory respond to an item in the same way, regardless of any other characteristic they may have.

DIF describes a situation where the bias exists within the individual items of which the test is composed. Linguistic forms of item bias are the most common, especially where idiomatic usage of language is involved. For example, the Standard English rule that two negatives make a positive is not followed among all dialects and traditions of English. As in other languages, double negatives can add emphasis. Applications of DIF analysis range from the identification of potentially biased questions in school examinations and recruitment tests to the identification of possible confounds when interpreting the results of social surveys.

Items that do not have this property of measurement invariance (Holland *et al.* 2007) are said to be biased as a result of differential item functioning (Penfield & Camilli, 2007). The simplest type of DIF analysis in a model-based framework assumes that the items in an instrument perform similarly in their discriminating power with respect to the measurement of the target construct, but that item intercept is shifted in one direction or another in comparison to the reference group (uniform DIF). Here the response function; that is, the curve which relates the level of the construct being measured to the actual level of response to the item, remains parallel for the two groups but does not share the same location. This type of DIF can be detected in a Multiple Indicator Multiple Cause (MIMIC) model where the impact of a grouping characteristic on the item intercept is explored in addition to the impact of the grouping characteristic on the latent factor itself. For examination boards all over the world the development of advanced statistical methods of DIF analysis is a key issue to which substantial resources have been assigned. Borsboom (2006) makes the observation that bias can never be a 'yes' or 'no' matter, as groups will always differ to some degree given a large enough sample size. The important question is what amount of difference is acceptable. While there is plenty of literature emphasising detection of DIF, there is often little insight into explaining it; rather there is a perhaps spurious emphasis on its removal (which is probably impossible). It is prudent to note that with huge sample sizes, such as those achieved in educational testing, it will always be possible to detect DIF at some level when statistical power is so high. This contrasts with legal requirements for tests to be 'bias free'. Clearly, freedom from bias can only be demonstrated to a certain degree; there will always be some level of item bias that should be considered ignorable.

Measurement invariance occurs where differences in the mean score of two groups are due to the characteristics of the test and not to any difference between the groups in the trait or function being measured. Absence of measurement invariance can be due to the test having different reliability for the two groups, or to group differences in the validity of the test (e.g. the same trait being measured in different proportions in the two groups, the measurement of an additional trait in one group, the measurement of unique traits in each group, or the test measuring nothing in common when applied to the two groups). Thus, for example, if a general knowledge test was administered in English to two groups, one of which was fluent in English while the other included people with a wide range of competencies in the English language, then while the test may be measuring general knowledge in one group, it would be highly contaminated by a measure of competency in English in the other group. This form of bias often occurs where a test has been constructed to match the characteristics of successful applicants from one particular group, which may not be so valid when applied to another; deviations in content validity are particularly likely to produce lower test scores in deviating groups. The standard modern psychometric procedure for investigating measurement invariance between groups is Multi Group Confirmatory Factor Analysis.

The remaining form of bias, adverse impact, can still occur even when the effects of DIF and measurement invariance have been eliminated. This is because differences in test scores may continue to reflect genuine differences between groups. In these cases the use of the test, although itself unbiased, still results in disproportionate selection of some groups at the expense of the others. This situation is much more common in practice than either DIF or measurement invariance, and is most often, although not always, the consequence of social deprivation. For example, an immigrant group that lives in a deprived inner city area where the schools are of poor quality is relatively unlikely to generate successes in terms of the academic qualifications of its children. The lack of these qualifications does not necessarily represent any bias in the examination but is more likely due to lack of opportunity. Where the community suffers deprivation for several generations this lack of opportunity can be reflected in a lack of encouragement by parents, and a cycle of deprivation may be established. In most countries policies that lead to adverse impact may be just as illegal as those involving bias in the tests themselves, and there are no simple answers to the problem. There are, however, strategies. In the US, for example, the US Equal Opportunity Commission has issued guidelines for selectors in these situations. They argue that affirmative action programmes should in general de-emphasise race, and emphasise instead the educational level of the parents, the relative educational level of the peer group, the examination level, the quality of schooling and the availability of compensatory facilities. They further recommend job re-specification, the introduction of specific training programmes, and the equalisation of numbers of applications by changing advertising strategies.

7.12 HOW TO CONSTRUCT YOUR OWN PSYCHOMETRIC TEST

The first step in developing a psychometric test is to ask yourself, 'What is it for?' Unless you have a clear and precise answer to this question your test results will not tell you what you want to know. Next, you need to design the test specification. This is a framework for developing the test or questionnaire. A grid structure is generally used with Content Areas along the horizontal axis and Manifestations (ways in which the content areas may become manifest) along the vertical axis. For practical reasons, between four and seven categories are usually employed along each axis. Fewer often results in too narrow a test or questionnaire, and more can be too cumbersome to deal with. A clear purpose will enable you to specify the content of your test. The content areas should cover everything that is relevant to the purpose of the test. The ways in which the content areas may manifest themselves will vary according to the type of test or questionnaire under construction. For example, tests designed to measure educational attainment may use Bloom's taxonomy of educational objectives to tap different forms of knowledge. For tests and questionnaires that are more psychological in nature, behavioural, cognitive and affective manifestations of the content areas may be more appropriate. For personality questionnaires you will need to balance for socially desirable and socially undesirable aspects of the trait, and also for acquiescence. The latter is achieved by allowing half of the items to manifest positively (e.g. 'I am outgoing' in an extraversion scale), and half to manifest negatively (e.g. 'I am shy' in an extraversion scale). The number of cells in your test specification will be the number of content areas multiplied by the number of manifestations. Between 16 and 25 cells (i.e. 4×4, 4×5, 5×4 or 5×5) are generally considered ideal for sufficient breadth while maintaining manageability. Each cell in the test specification represents the interaction of a content area with a manifestation of that content area. By writing items for your test that correspond to each cell of its specification, you will ensure that all aspects that are relevant to its purpose will be covered.

The next step is to write the items. You will need at least two items per cell as the later piloting and item analysis process will eliminate some of them (you should start with at least twice as many candidate items as you aim to have in the final test). For details on types of items and questionnaire design see Chapter 6.

Next follows the pilot study, for which a sample of respondents should be obtained with similar relevant characteristics to those people for whom the test is intended. To collect data, one option is to hand out paper-and-pencil versions in public places such as shopping centres, train and bus stations, airport lounges, doctors' waiting rooms or canteens of large organisations. However, it is much more convenient to use a survey tool on the Internet (many are available as freeware). Contact can be via webpage, email or social network. Remember to obtain the demographic information from the respondents to help with the validation of your questionnaire at a later stage. The number of respondents in the pilot study should be about three times the number of items, but more is better and the minimum number is at least one more than the number of items.

Next, the data from the pilot study needs to be subjected to item analysis. Classical item analysis has concentrated on two statistics, item facility and item discrimination. In a knowledge-based test of optimal performance, item facility is obtained by calculating the ratio of the number of respondents who give the wrong response to the whole number of respondents. If all the respondents are wrong on an item, this statistic will be equal to 1; if nobody gets it wrong, the statistic will be 0 – that is, the easier the item the higher the index. Item discrimination relates the score on each item to the score on the test as a whole. If those who have low scores on the test as a whole are just as likely to get an item right as those with high scores, then it will have zero discrimination. If all those who get it right have a higher score than all those who get it wrong, its discrimination will be 1. For tests of typical performance the statistics are similar. However the 'difficulty' value varies between one and the number of response options (e.g. for strongly disagree = 1, disagree = 2, agree = 3 and strongly agree = 4, the difficulty value will be between 1 and 4). For Classical Test Theory the difficulty value and the item discrimination are easily calculated as the item mean and the item/total-test-score correlation using any statistical software or spreadsheet program. It is recommended that difficulty values for knowledge-based tests should be between 0.2 and 0.8, and discrimination indices should be at least 0.2. However, make sure that you don't trash the test specification in the process. The match of the final choice of items against the original specification is the new test's content validity. Lose its balance at your peril.

7.13 FACTORIAL VALIDITY

So far we have assumed that we have a test that is only measuring one construct. Thus, a test of intelligence should only be measuring intelligence, a test of numeracy only numeracy and a test of extraversion only extraversion. So long as the correlations between the items can be explained by only one underlying factor (see exploratory factor analysis in Chapter 12) then this will be the case, and indeed so long as we have set out to measure only one latent construct, classical item analysis may well achieve our purpose. However, in many situations, particularly personality testing, it is common practice to construct several scales in parallel, each scale mirroring a factor within an exploratory factor analysis. When this is done within Classical Test Theory then various checks and balances between the items can contribute to the neutralisation of confounds such as response bias and DIF. However, with Item Response Theory approaches, to which we now turn, the demands are rather more stringent.

7.14 **ITEM RESPONSE THEORY**

Item Response Theory (IRT) underpins modern psychometrics, and offers many advantages over Classical Test Theory. It began with attempts to relate binary data (right or wrong answers to individual items in ability tests) to an underlying dimension. At the item level, psychometric data are normally nominal, binary or ordinal (see Chapter 2) rather than interval or continuous, while most parametric statistical models are only appropriate for the latter. In item analysis a linear approximation works reasonably well as long as the difficult values of the items lie somewhere between 0.2 and 0.8, but outside these extremes the linear (or straight line) model provides a very poor fit.

IRT saw its origins in a different model of measurement to that propounded by the original theory of true scores, that of Louis Guttman (1944). Guttman suggested that, in circumstances where all the items in a test are measuring the same underlying trait, when items are arranged in order of difficulty, a person's score on a test should be the point along the implicit scale where their response shifts from right answers to wrong answers.

RRRRRRRRRRRWWWWWWWWWW

In practice, of course, this point is rather more imprecise. The following is perhaps rather more likely:

RRRRRRRWRRWWWRWWWWWWWWWW

But with the introduction of the notion of probability it is still possible to suggest an 'ability' somewhere along the line, perhaps at the point where the chance of the person obtaining the right response is 50/50. Georg Rasch was the first to plot such a probabilistic curve, now called an Item Characteristic Curve (ICC) or Item Response Function (see Figure 7.2). This plots the probability of a correct response against the latent ability of the respondent, and will vary for each item. Notably, it is not a

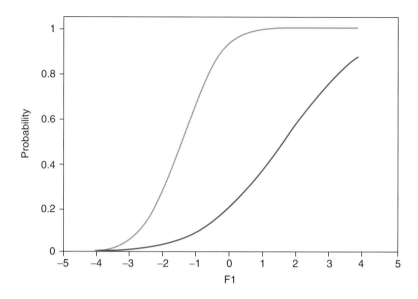

Figure 7.2 Two Item Characteristic Curves (ICCs) for items of different levels of difficulty and discrimination. The light blue item is easier than the dark blue item. For example, a person with ability of −1 has about a 0.75 probability of getting the item right, while the equivalent probability for the dark blue item is less than 0.1. Also, the light blue item has higher discrimination than the dark blue item, which is indicated by its steeper slope

straight line, but takes the shape of an elongated 'S'. Today such lines are known to statisticians as logit, logistic or probit functions (as used, for example, in logistic regression). Rasch, and later Allan Birnbaum, were able to show that the two classical item characteristics of difficulty and discrimination mapped onto these curves by changes of shape and position. An item of increased difficulty was shifted to the right, while an item with higher discrimination had a steeper slope (see Figure 7.2). Thus each item has its own curve, and it will be expected to move in an upward direction from left to right, although the extent to which it does this is a property of the item. The starting point on the left-hand side of the ICC frame represents the probability of a person with very low ability getting the item right. If the ability axis is started at a low enough level this might be expected to be always zero, but this only applies if there is no guessing effect. Thus if a person of very low ability guesses the answer to a multiple choice item with four choices he has a 25% chance of getting the right answer by chance, and the curve for such an item would therefore be expected to begin at the 0.25 probability point of the y axis.

The aim of Item Response Theory is to look at the fundamental algebraic characteristics of these ICC curves and to try to model them in such a way that a set of equations can be extracted that can predict the curve from some basic data.

This modelling is the same as that involved in the more familiar process of obtaining the equation to a straight line. This is, you will remember, based on the equation $y = a + bx$, that if a and b are known then so is the position of the straight line itself within the xy frame. When the ICC is modelled in this way the situation unfortunately turns out to be somewhat more complex, but easily achieved with a computer. There is a general consensus that four variables (parameters) are required to define an ICC. These are one respondent's ability and the three item parameters of difficulty, discrimination and guessing. If the values of the three parameters are known, then it is possible to reconstruct the ICC.

In earlier days the model of the full process was too mathematically complex, time consuming and expensive for computers at the time, and for these reasons attempts were made to simplify the full model by approximating the ICC with a lower number of parameters. The three basic models of IRT which resulted have become known as the one-, two- and three-parameter models, depending on how many of the three needed to describe the ICC are considered. Rasch himself was the main proponent of the one-parameter model (1980) as he was able to show that if it is assumed that any guessing factor is held constant (as is the case if all items are of the same type), and if only items with equal discrimination are accepted, then some of the restrictions of classical psychometrics are loosened. In particular, the model seemed to be able to generate, on computer, a single statistic for each item which enabled that item to be used in a wide variety of different situations, regardless of which other items were included in the test and of the particular respondents involved. This approach showed considerable promise in the calibration of item banks and also for test equating – a field of educational measurement within which scores from candidates who have taken different but similar tests are placed on the same scale.

Other practical advantages of using IRT also became apparent; for example, its ability to assign reliability ('information') at different points of the scale, particularly at particular decision thresholds. Classical Test Theory maintains a standard reliability for the scale as a whole which is not always realistic, particularly towards the extremes. IRT also allows individual estimation of reliability – a reliability of the results for each respondent as well as for the test as a whole.

7.15 CONFIRMATORY FACTOR ANALYSIS

For the gains inherent in an IRT approach to be realised it must first be established that each scale is strictly unidimensional. This unidimensionality can be tested within the framework of Confirmatory Factor Analysis (CFA). Today, CFA routines are regularly included in statistical modelling programs (such as Stata, Mplus, R, etc.) and are readily available for download from the Internet. Model fit statistics within these programs can rapidly tell us which items need changing or deleting in order to achieve our aim. One of the beauties of the IRT approach is that it can easily be illustrated by graphical output from these programs.

The past 20 years have seen the coming together of structural equation modelling approaches within statistics (see Chapter 12) with IRT from psychometrics to form the new field of latent variable modelling. For example, a CFA carried out on binary test data with the loadings (discriminations) held constant has been shown to be an algebraic identity with the Rasch model, making the fit of this model relatively straightforward within standard modelling software. Further developments in modelling are allowing the fit of more complex IRT models, offering solutions to many standard psychometric problems, both pure and applied. Hence, it is now possible to examine the characteristics not just of correct versus incorrect responses, but also of the behaviour of intervening response categories. In a personality test with response options of 'strongly agree', 'agree', 'uncertain', 'disagree' and 'strongly disagree', for example, it is of interest to know which people actually choose from these options. Item analysis using IRT may tell us whether some of these categories are redundant or may suggest how they could be improved. A good introduction to these techniques appears in Embretson and Reise (2000). Further developments enable us to address the consequences of acquiescence bias in personality questionnaires by including not only the hypothesised factors in a confirmatory factor analysis but also the effects of having balanced positive and negative items in these scales. These models also enable us to address important missing data issues, such as the absence of responses in a speeded test (i.e., a test with a strict time limit) to the items towards the end of the test.

7.16 **ADAPTIVE TESTING**

Today, IRT is increasingly recognised as a solution to what has become the holy grail of psychometric testing – adaptivity. Computerisation and the Internet offer the potential to make testing responsive to the behaviour of the candidate, a field known as **Computer Adaptive Testing (CAT)**. If the next items to be presented can be chosen on the basis of responses already given, this would enable dependable results from administration of 50% fewer items (Haladyna & Roid, 1983). In these cases, the entire item bank is held within the computer, and as each item is presented to the respondent on screen and responded to, a calculation is made as to which of the remaining items in the bank should be given next in order to obtain the maximum information. The respondent's score is an ongoing calculation, based on the most likely ability of the subject based on the combined probability generated from responses to all items presented so far. As more items are presented this estimate becomes more accurate and testing is terminated once a pre-designed level of precision is achieved.

A further way in which the use of the computer is being extended is in the generation of expert narrative reports. Where the test is a profile battery, the computer is able to identify extremes, to interpret these in the light of other sub-scale scores, and to make recommendations. Roid (1986) pointed out that there are four major concerns which arise from the use of computers in test interpretation: (i) that it is questionable whether computers are any better than human experts; (ii) that the computerised reports may reach the hands of inexperienced or unqualified people; (iii) that the decision rules may not be public; and (iv) that computerised reports may not be sufficiently validated. The problems are similar to those encountered in the use of computerised expert systems for any decision-making process involving human beings, where thought has to be given to the consequences of a wrong decision that may have to be justified in a court of law.

7.17 EXERCISES

Construct a psychometric test of your own, proceeding through the various stages outlined in this chapter. Then carry out a pilot study and an item analysis of the results. Next obtain its reliability, and consider evidence for its validity.

7.18 DISCUSSION QUESTIONS

1   Lord Kelvin (1824–1907) said, 'If anything exists it must exist in some quantity and can therefore be measured' Was he right?
2   Can intelligence be measured?

7.19 FURTHER READING

Rust and Golombok's (2009) *Modern psychometrics: the science of psychological assessment* is an excellent introduction to the whole field of psychometrics particularly suited for those who do not want detailed mathematics. Brown's (2006) *Confirmatory factor analysis for applied researchers* is a classic book on applying CFA in practice. Urbina's (2004) *Essentials of psychological testing* is the standard psychometric textbook. Flynn's (2009) *What is intelligence? Beyond the Flynn effect* is a 'must read' for all those interested in IQ.

8

Descriptive Statistics: Graphical and Numerical Methods

Marianna E. Carlucci and Daniel B. Wright

CONTENTS

After reading this chapter you will have a better understanding of what descriptive statistics are and why we use them. You will be able to enter your data, graph your data and look for patterns in your data using several graphical procedures.

KEY TERMS

boxplot	histogram
descriptive statistics	inferential statistics
dummy code	mean
exploratory data analysis (EDA)	outlier
five-number summary	standard deviation

8.1 **INTRODUCTION**

Descriptive statistics allow you to organise and to summarise your data set with a few key statistics and graphs. They provide information about your sample; they *describe* your sample. The next chapter, on inferential statistics, takes this information and allows you to *infer* aspects of the population of interest. The initial search for patterns in your data is often called exploratory data analysis, usually abbreviated to EDA (Tukey, 1977).

It is good practice to begin data analysis with descriptive statistics before moving onto more complex inferential analyses. Doing this allows you to get a feel for the data and can also help you to spot data entry mistakes that may hide important results in later analyses. By looking at descriptive statistics you can check for any patterns in the data that may guide later analyses. Another advantage of beginning with descriptive statistics is that inferential statistics make certain assumptions about the data. For example, some tests assume that there are no extremely large or small values. This can be examined with EDA. Statistics is about revealing patterns in data and communicating these patterns to others. Descriptive statistics are the beginning of that conversation.

This chapter is divided into three main sections. The first section describes how to enter the data into a computer. The second section describes how to graph a single variable. The third section describes how to graph two variables simultaneously. Relevant numerical statistics are described when discussing the graphs to which they are most associated. This is different from a lot of literature on descriptive statistics where the primary focus is on numerical statistics and graphs are seen as a useful complement. We believe descriptive statistics should begin with graphs, and numerical statistics should be used to supplement these.

Data sets: Several real and made-up data sets are used in this chapter. Each is described where it is first introduced and is available in a couple of formats on this chapter's webpage (www2.fiu.edu/~dwright/Descript).

8.2 **ENTERING DATA**

Before you can analyse your data you will need to enter them into a program that will allow you to make graphs and to calculate different statistics. There are several popular programs on the market that can help with data analysis. Some of them are free (e.g. R and lots of specialist packages) and some of them require licenses (e.g. SAS, SPSS). Some of them are probably already in your computer (e.g. Excel). SPSS is one of the most popular statistical packages so there is a good chance you will use it. The choice of program to use will probably have been made for you either by your teacher or more likely as department or university policy. If you are in the position to choose your own program, we recommend choosing whichever program the people you work with use (since they can answer questions). Once you have learned one program it is relatively easy to learn new ones.

Once you have your program, the next step is to input the data. For most programs the data are entered as a rectangular table, what mathematicians call a matrix, where along the top are variable names and each participant has one line of data. Suppose you asked a sample of men and women of different ages what their favourite Lindsay Lohan movie is. The data for the first seven people might look like Table 8.1.

You need to decide variable names for the four columns. Variable names should be fairly short (some programs only allow eight characters) and be meaningful enough so that you know what they are. Calling something *variable3* is not descriptive enough. Many programs allow you to write in longer variable descriptions. Here, the first column is a person-identifier. You should always have one of these. If your data are from a pen-and-paper questionnaire this number should be written on the questionnaire. Having an identifier is important also because some procedures in some programs re-order the data. It is worth having a convention for naming identifiers because you will have them in every data file you create. *partno* is good since it is short for participant number. Some programs are case sensitive such that *partno* would not be the same as *Partno,* so be careful.

The second column is gender, a binary variable (see Chapter 2). Most packages would allow you just to keep it like this with the words 'male' and 'female' as values. You would have to tell the program that instead of having numerical data you have string variables (or alphanumeric data). We do not recommend this for many reasons. The most important is that the computer will treat male, mail and

Table 8.1 Example of data input for sample who answered the question "What is your favourite Lindsay Lohan movie?"

1	male	34	Bobby
2	male	44 and three-quarters	Freaky Friday
3	female	67	Bobby
4	male	11	Herbie
5	female	47	Who is Lindsay Lohan?
6	female	44	Fully Loaded
7	female	22	That one about Robert Kennedy's assassination
:	:	:	:

man as different genders and if there is the odd space in the column the computer will get confused. Instead, we recommend using dummy variable coding. This means using a series of 0s and 1s, where 1 means the presence of whatever characteristic and 0 means the absence. Thus, if we called the variable *female* then 1 would mean female and 0 would mean the absence of female (i.e. male). Coding binary variables 0 and 1 is better than 1 and 2 for two reasons. The first is that it is easier for data entry. When data are entered there are almost always errors. What is important is that you have methods to detect these errors. If you use 1 and 2 for your values some of the errors will probably be the other valid value. This means that you will not know it is an error. By coding with 0 and 1, data entry errors are more easily detected. The second reason is that for some statistical procedures, like regression (see Chapter 11), it is easier to interpret the output if you use 0 and 1 coding.

The third column is age. The variable could be called *ageyrs*, for age in years (developmental psychologists often have both an age in years variable and an age in months variable). The numbers in that column can be used for the data, but what should be done with the value for the 44 and three-quarters person? (And people write this!) While this person is closer to 45, you should still write 44 because that value is for people from 44 years and 0 days to 44 years and 364 days.

The final column is the person's favourite Lindsay Lohan movie; people had to choose only one (allowing more than one choice creates both data entry complications and analysis complications). This is a categorical variable with more than two categories so it is not binary. Lindsay has appeared in several films (12 at the time of writing). People could write any of these and might not know the actual film name. The first thing to do is get a piece of paper and assign numbers to each film. The first participant wrote *Bobby* (where Lohan was nominated for a Screen Actors Guild award) and this is assigned 1. The next participant wrote *Freaky Friday*. This is assigned 2. The third participant wrote *Bobby*, so this is a 1. The fourth wrote *Herbie*. There are several *Herbie* films but only one with Ms Lohan, *Herbie: Fully Loaded*. This gets the value 3. Participant number 5 wrote 'Who is Lindsay Lohan?'. After searching through our Lindsay Lohan archives, this does not match any of the star's films. This could be coded as 'Don't know' and assigned a numeric value. Another alternative is to say the data for this person is missing for this variable. In most packages you would assign this a value (choose a value that could not occur; −99 is often used) and then tell the program this value means the data are missing for this person for this variable. Some programs have you write NA for 'Not Available'. Do not just leave the cell empty; this will confuse procedures in some programs. The sixth participant wrote *Fully Loaded*, which gets the value 3. It is important to note that what this person wrote shares no words with what participant 4 wrote. It takes knowledge about the films to know that they are referring to the same film. Similarly, participant 7 described the film *Bobby*, so the analyst would need to know to code this as 1. The data file could now be written as Table 8.2.

Table 8.2 Numerically coded data from sample who answered the question "What is your favourite Lindsay Lohan movie?"

partno	female	ageyrs	LLmovie
1	0	34	1
2	0	44	2
3	1	67	1
4	0	11	3
5	1	47	−99
6	1	44	3
7	1	22	1
:	:	:	:

The variable names are put into a header. If you are entering data for a large project, discuss the variable names and overall layout of the data with a colleague to make sure that the data will be entered correctly. You do not want to have to enter the data more than once. It is also good practice to write a codebook that describes each variable and any extra details of the study.

The next step is actually entering the data into the program. Although data can be transferred between programs (and even entered in Word or Excel and transferred; but this is a pain, do not do this), it is usually best to enter the data into the program that you will use. Data entry is incredibly important (if numbers are entered incorrectly, it can ruin the entire study), but is not exciting. First, some 'do not's'. Do not rush it. Do not work for hours at time (human resources say you should not stare at a computer screen for more than 40 minutes without a break). Do not listen to music (it slows you down – wouldn't you rather finish sooner than listen to Britney?). Some people like doing data entry in pairs; some people find this a distraction. In our experience, paired data entry leads to more errors and is not twice as fast, so we recommend avoiding it.

Now some 'do's'. Do get comfortable and remove distractions. If you are a caffiend, prepare your nervous system. Most keyboards have a 10-key number pad. Try this out. If you are comfortable with it, data entry is easier and more accurate than using the keys at the top of the keyboard. Set a limit for each 40-minute session so that you do not try to do just one more (that one inevitably has errors). Stretch and reward yourself when you finish.

Data entry is not a race. It is not a competition where you want to show people how much data you can enter (none of your supervisors will be impressed with fast data entry because they know that accurate data entry takes time). Data entry is about accuracy and not how quickly it gets done. Check for errors. We discuss some methods for finding data entry errors, but some errors will always go undetected, so the best method is avoidance.

Suppose you wanted to know the sexual behavior patterns of the students at Jersey Shore High School (if you've never been to the Jersey Shore just know that they really like tanning, working out and … tanning). You may ask the students questions about such things as age, gender, onset of certain behaviours, how many sexual partners each student has had, and so on. These may be important variables in your study. You want to know if there are associations among these variables. Entering variables into a data file is where you begin to answer that question. Thus, it is extremely important to limit errors during data entry. Entering the wrong variable or making many mistakes can obscure relationships between your variables or reveal relationships that do not actually exist. Once the data are entered the data file might look like the SPSS data file shown in Figure 8.1.

8.2.1 Checking for rogue data

*Sexual Behavior.sav [DataSet1] - SPSS Statistics Data Editor

File Edit View Data Transform Analyze Graphs Utilities Add-ons Window Help

14:

	High_School	Age	Female	Dates_Total	Oral_Sex	SexualPartners	var
1	1	14	0	40	13	4	
2	2	15	1	40	12	2	
3	1	14	1	50	15	2	
4	2	16	1	12	14	1	
5	3	16	1	20	13	6	
6	1	17	1	25	20	4	
7	4	18	0	37	40	4	
8	2	16	0	38	45	3	
9	3	15	0	40	26	2	
10	2	15	0	45	28	2	
11	4	16	1	32	45	3	
12	1	17	0	20	41	2	
13	3	18	1	21	20	2	
14	2	15	0	25	13	1	
15	4	14	1	27	8	1	
16	1	15	1	28	5	2	
17	2	16	0	12	13	1	
18	3	17	1	10	15	2	
19	4	18	0	14	16	2	
20	2	16	1	15	18	2	
21	3	19	1	38	2	2	

Figure 8.1 Data of students from Jersey Shore High School in SPSS

Data entry errors happen, but their number can be lessened and sometimes rogue data can be identified. Here are a few suggestions to minimise errors and to catch them.

1 Do not think while entering data!

We do memory research and our data are usually whether somebody says they saw some stimulus before or not (sometimes they have, sometimes they have not). It could be tempting to have people enter whether the participant was right or wrong. This would require looking at the participant's response and whether the item was shown and identifying if they are the same. This would require extra thought. Let the computer do this later; just type what the participant wrote.

2 Use codes which will help identify rogue data

The example of coding *female* as 0 and 1 is good because errors can be discovered. You could even do 0 and 6, or something like that, but this could be more difficult to remember and could cause problems for some statistical procedures in some packages. If you code your data as 0 and 1 but find a value of 3, then you know you have a data entry error.

3 Enter at least some of the data twice

Data entry is boring, but is very important. If the data are entered twice, you can compare the files and see if there are differences. If there are differences then at least one of them is in error. This should be done at least for a subset. If errors arise then you can find out if one data entry person is more responsible than the other. Sometimes data-entry people have to be re-trained or 'removed'.

4 Remove invalid values and check unrealistic values

All statistics programs allow you to make a frequency table for each variable. This allows you to see if there are invalid numbers (e.g. 4 for our *female* variable) or unlikely numbers (see below for football players' weights). Sometimes a value will stand out because of values for other variables. For example, somebody saying that they have 0 years of formal education will occur in most surveys and in most surveys there will be people who tick 'doctor' as their occupation, but these values should not co-occur.

5 Stress accuracy over speed

We are repeating ourselves, but it is vital to do data entry slowly and meticulously.

6 Stress accuracy over speed

We are repeating ourselves, but it is vital to do data entry slowly and meticulously.

8.3 GRAPHING DATA FOR SINGLE VARIABLES

One way to describe data is to graph them. Graphing data allows you to look at a visual representation of the patterns (if they exist) in your data. There are several graphs that you can use to get a feel for your data. In this section we will discuss the histogram, the boxplot and a simple bar graph. At each stage we will discuss the numerical statistics which are associated with the graph. Most of this section focuses on histograms.

8.3.1 Histograms

There are many types of histograms. We describe three types: dot histogram, stem and leaf diagram, and the generic histogram (or just histogram). All the histograms show the sample's distribution for a single variable. These require that the variable can be thought of as some relatively continuous measure. The name of the variable is placed horizontally below the x-axis and split into bins. Bins are the critical concept in histograms. They are how you divide the x-axis and methods for deciding how many bins to have and how wide they should be are discussed later. The number of people whose values are in each bin is shown. This is called the frequency. The shape of this graph is referred to as the variable's distribution. We will discuss distributions more at the end of this section.

The dot histogram

A dot histogram is like Milton Bradley's game Connect Four™. Each column is a bin and each individual is a dot (or a disk in the game). The dot for that person is placed in the appropriate bin. If there is already a dot in the bin, it goes on top of the existing dot, like in Connect Four. This is best explained through an example. The roster for the Florida International University (FIU) Panther's American football team (the soccer team would weigh less) provides the weights, in pounds (lbs),[1] of most of the players (2.2 lbs ≈ 1 kg). In ascending order these are:

<u>145</u>, 160, 170, 173, 175, 175, 175, 175, 176, 176, 178, 178, 178, 180, 181, 183, 183, 184, 185, 185, 186, 189, 189, 190, 191, 191, 194, 195, 195, 196, 197, 199, 200, 200, 200, 201, 201, 201, 202, 202, 205, 205, 205, 207, 210, 210, 213, 213,

---

1 Downloaded 20 Aug, 2010 from http://www.fiusports.com/SportSelect.dbml?SPSID=49160&SPID=4780&DB_OEM_ID=11700&Q_SEASON=2010

215, 215, 215, 217, 217, 219, 220, 220, 221, 223, 223, 227, 233, 235, 244, 245, 246, 247, 247, 248, 250, 260, 260, 262, 265, 265, 268, 270, 270, 270, 271, 272, 274, 274, 276, 276, 278, 278, 280, 281, 283, 283, 285, 285, 288, 305, 311, 320, <u>1195</u>

Before doing any graphs or analyses the data should be quickly scanned to look for data entry errors. There is someone listed at 1,195 lbs. While people can weigh this much (Manuel Uribe weighed 1,810 lbs), the rigours of football training would make it unlikely that anyone of this weight could participate. We checked the FIU web page and this was a typing error by one of the authors. The person weighed 195 lbs. The other underlined value is for 145 lbs, quite normal for university students and possible for a place kicker in football, but this was for Paul Crawford, a highly recruited Texan lineman who ESPN listed as 6'8", 230 lbs in his senior year in high school. The current FIU web page lists the freshman at 6'9" and 145 lbs. We are confident enough not to bother the busy coaching staff to check that they meant 245 lbs.

We will use bins of 10 lbs width, because this is a nice round number (more on choice of bin width below). Because the data are sorted (you will have to imagine the 145 is 245 and the 1195 is 195), it is easy to count how many are in each bin.

160s 1
170s 11
180s 10
190s 10
200s 12
210s 10
220s 6
230s 2
240s 7
250s 1
260s 6
270s 11
280s 7
290s 0
300s 1
310s 1
320s 1

The dot histogram is created, essentially, by flipping this list around and adding the appropriate numbers of dots (see Figure 8.2). This can be done in a word processing package. Suppose you wanted to graph how many sexual partners students at Jersey Shore High School had ($n = 100$). You could count up how many sexual partners each student had and then get an average or **mean** (discussed later in the chapter). Suppose the mean was four. This tells you that on average student at Jersey Shore

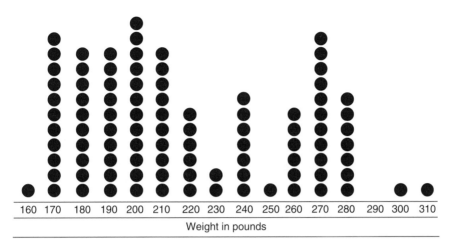

Figure 8.2   A dot histogram of football players' weights. Each dot corresponds to one player

High School has had four sexual partners but it does not give you much more information. By creating a dot histogram you can see outliers (adolescents with many more partners) and other types of information discussed later.

In the US people's weights are usually given in pounds (lbs). In the UK weights are usually measured in stones (14 lbs) and in the rest of Europe in kilograms (2.2 lbs). How does changing the scale affect the shape of the histogram and stems?

Optional extra: Weight in pounds (and stones) is a measure of force (how much your body and the Earth are attracted to each other by gravity); it varies so that Americans weigh less in pounds when they stand on the moon. Kilograms are a measure of mass, which is the same on the Earth and Moon. Thus, our bestselling book, *Lose Weight, Wear a Cool Helmet, and Go to the Moon*, only sold well in America and the UK. Europeans using this method to lose kilograms were disappointed with the results.

Stem-and-leaf diagram

The dots in Figures 8.2 and 8.3 each represent a person. In Figure 8.2 their placement shows how many pounds that person weighs but the dot itself provides no other information. A stem-and-leaf diagram (Tukey, 1977) allows the individual dots to provide information. The stem is usually the first digit or two of the numbers, and the leaves are the final digit. This is best explained by looking at an actual diagram. Figure 8.4 shows a stem-and-leaf diagram for the football players' weights.

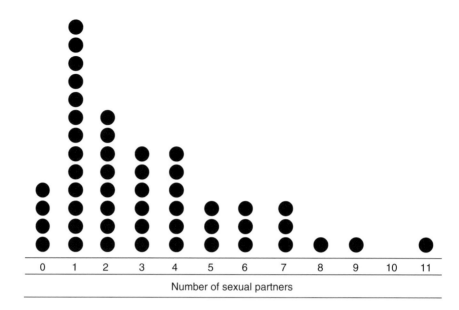

Figure 8.3 A dot histogram of the number of sexual partners. Each dot corresponds to one sexual partner

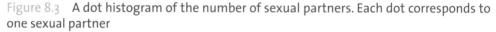

Stem	Leaf
16	0
17	03555566888
18	0133455699
19	0114555679
20	000111225557
21	0033555779
22	001337
23	35
24	4556778
25	0
26	002558
27	00012446688
28	0133558
29	
30	5
31	1

Figure 8.4 A stem-and-leaf diagram for the football players' weights

This can be made in a word processing package or in most statistics packages. This was made in the statistics program R and then we copied and pasted it into the chapter. When copying text from a statistics package into a word processing package it is important to make sure a non-scalable font like Courier is used so that each character takes up the same amount of room.

The stem says which bin from the dot histogram the values are in, but rather than just denoting the person with a dot, a number is placed there. Thus, from the dot histogram we could tell that two of the players weighed in the 230s. From the stem-and-leaf diagram we know one weighs 233 lbs and one weighs 235 lbs.

Make your own stem-and-leaf plot. Ask 20 friends or family members how many CDs they have purchased (digitally or physically) in the past 12 months. Plot the results using a stem-and-leaf plot. Combine your data with a few of your classmates' data and make a stem-and-leaf. Does the group stem-and-leaf look similar to the individual ones?

How accurate do you think people's responses were? How would responses be affected by memory errors and social desirability?

The generic histogram

The dot histogram and stem-and-leaf plot are alternatives to the generic histogram, often called frequency histogram or just histogram. The first step is to decide how many bins to have, how wide they should be and where they should be. This is really important and statisticians have written algorithms that suggest answers to these decisions. These are embedded within the statistics programs that you will use. Box 8.1 describes some of these. These are just suggestions. The computer will not know, for example, that if you have data on ages in months that it may be good to choose bins of 12-months width. The programs that you will use will allow you to control these aspects of making a histogram.

Your choice of bin width and location should be made so that it shows *real* patterns in the data (*real* is in italics, and is the focus of the next chapter) without showing random idiosyncratic fluctuations. From our knowledge of football we expect a histogram should show that there are a large number of people spread out fairly widely around 200 lbs for the non-linemen and a group that are heavier for the linemen (if you know rugby better, think of those not in the scrum and those in the scrum). The methods described in Box 8.1 suggest a bin width of between 20 and 30 lbs. Figure 8.5 shows bin widths of 10, 25 and 50 lbs. The 10 lbs bin width shows a lot more information than is necessary and it may be misleading. For example, it shows a lot of players in the 240s, but few in the 230s or 250s. Is this something *real* in the data that we would expect in other football teams? Probably not, and therefore it is best not to focus on that idiosyncratic aspect of the 2010 FIU Panthers (who beat University of Toledo in the 2010 Little Caesars Bowl). The 25 lbs bin width shows that there appear to be two distinct groups of players. The 50 lbs bin width graph fails to reveal that there appear to be two groups in the data. It shows too little information. Using what you know about the scale, what is suggested by the statisticians' methods and what the different histograms look like should allow

Box 8.1 Rules for suggesting bin width

Beware: The information below is a bit technical.

The program we used to make the histograms in Figure 8.5 was R. It has three built-in procedures for suggesting the bin width: Sturges, Scott and Freedman–Diaconis, as well as letting you decide bin width and location (which we do in Figure 8.5). Sturges published his method in the 1920s and it is implemented in many programs as the default. The approximate bin width is the *range* of the data divided by ($\log_2(n)$ + 1). $\log_2(n)$ is read 'log base 2 of n' where n is the sample size. $\log_2$ means the power that 2 needs to be taken to for it to equal n. In the football example, n = 97. $\log_2(97)$ = 6.6 because $2^{6.6}$ = 97. According to the Sturges rule the bin width should be approximately (320–160)/(6.6 + 1) = 21.05. Methodologists tend not to like this approach as much as the next two.

Scott's rule uses 3.49 times the *standard deviation*, divided by $n^{1/3}$. $n^{1/3}$ means the cube root of n (or $\sqrt[3]{n}$), so the value which multiplied by itself 3 times gives n. Here 4.595 × 4.595 × 4.595 is 97. The standard deviation of the weight variable is 39.58. Thus, Scott's rule yields (3.49 × 39.58)/4.595 = 30.15. The Freedman–Diaconis rule is two times the *inter-quartile range* (IQR) divided by $n^{1/3}$. For the football data this is: 2 × 71/4.595 = 30.90. Matt Wand (1997) has written a lot on bin choice and has produced more complex methods that he argues are better (on the chapter's web page we show how to use one of his methods in R).

All the histogram functions take the values from these rules and then make them 'pretty'. This means they try to use round numbers for the bin width and have them in sensible places (so a bin does not start at 6.47). So, the histogram procedures just use these as suggestions. You should also. Try several bin widths and locations. For assignments/publications, it is rare that the program's defaults (for any graphical procedure) are the best to use.

* Some statistical concepts described here come up later in this chapter and are italicized here, so you might want to return to this box later.

you to choose a good bin width and location of bins. In general expect to try several until you are satisfied. We would use the middle panel, 25 lbs width. Notice also how we labeled the axes. If you ever thought the people who mark your assignments are evil because they reduce marks for things like not using good axis labels, you are right.

The main thing to look out for when making histograms is providing *enough* information without going over or under. That is, if your bins are too large then you will not provide enough information, if your bins are too small then you will provide too much information. Figure 8.6 shows another example, the frequency of dates Jersey Shore High School students go on. Which do you think is the best one?

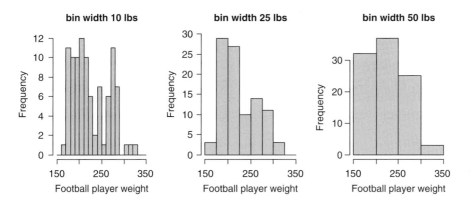

Figure 8.5   Three histograms of football players' weight, each with different bin widths

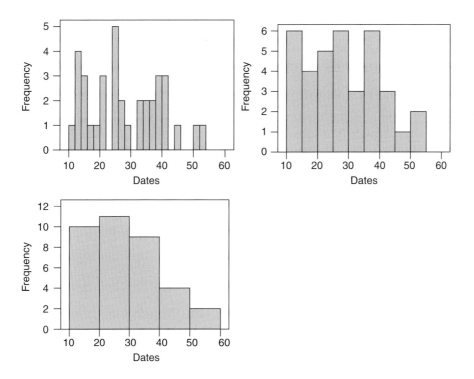

Figure 8.6   Three histograms of amount of dates students from Jersey Shore High School

You may hear the phrase 'true histogram'. We do not like that phrase because the word 'true' conjures up images of an Orwellian council or the diatribes of sidewalk preachers, politicians or talkshow hosts. But, what some people call a true histogram is where the y-axis is re-scaled so that the total area in the shaded regions is 1, and therefore the height of the bar is equal to the proportion in that sample within that bin.

8.3.2 Numerical statistics associated with histograms

Figure 8.5 shows histograms for the football players' weight data. The shape of the bars is often called the variable's distribution. You can imagine drawing a smooth line along the tops of the bars and in fact there is a field of statistics, kernel density estimation, which does this. Mathematical statisticians describe various theoretical distributions. The most discussed of these is the normal curve (or bell-shaped curve or Gaussian curve). It is a symmetric curve around the middle of the data. The normal curve has a complex equation associated with it, but the important aspect of it is that it can be described by two parameters: the mean and the standard deviation. The mean is one of the most common descriptive statistics and is often denoted with a line over the variable's name. If the variable is called x it is $\bar{x}$. It is what sports broadcasters call the average. To find the mean you add up all the scores and divide by the number of scores. In mathematical notation, this is: $\bar{x} = \sum \frac{x_i}{n}$. The capital Greek letter Σ means to add together (or to sum up). The x_i means all the values of that variable (the subscript i tells the reader that x has different values for different people, thus x_1 is the value for the first person, x_2 is the value for the second person, etc.) and n is the sample size. For the footballer weight data the total weight of the team is 21,734 lbs for the 97 people listed, or a mean of 224 lbs.

A second statistic, the standard deviation, defines how spread out the normal distribution is. It is:

$$\sqrt{\frac{(x_i - \bar{x})^2}{n-1}}$$

Calculating this by hand can be tricky (and there is a second equation that makes hand calculation a little easier), but usually you let the computer do it. What is important is what it means. For each individual, the distance between that person's value and the mean is squared. All these squared values are added together, and then the sum is divided by the number of people in the sample minus 1 (some texts say

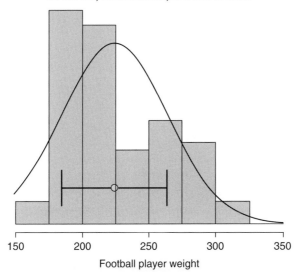

25 lbs bin, normal curve, and s.d. interval

Football player weight

Figure 8.7   Histogram of football players' weight with 25 lbs bin width

to divide by n rather than $n - 1$ here, but the difference is small, and is discussed in Chapter 9). This can be thought of as the mean of the squared deviations and it is called the *variance*. If you take the square root you get the standard deviation. For the football data, s.d. = 39.58 lbs. Figure 8.7 shows these plotted onto the 25 lbs bin histogram for the football players' weight. The mean is a measure of the centre of the data, what the statisticians call the *central tendency*, and the standard deviation is a measure of the spread of the data. Both are in the same units as the original variables. These statistics can be calculated for any interval variable.

Figure 8.7 also shows a curve for the normal distribution, with the same mean and standard deviation as the data, plotted on top of the histogram. It is clear that the distribution does not look that much like the normal curve. The right side seems stretched out because of a few heavy people. There are several ways to measure asymmetry or *skewness* of a distribution and there is some debate among statisticians about the best way to do this (and thus some variability among the computer packages for how to calculate this). For more information, see the chapter's web page. In practice, it is unlikely that you will ever calculate skewness by hand and therefore the computational details are moot. The important concept to remember is that skewness values above 0 usually mean that the tail is pulled to the right and skewness values below 0 have a tail pulled to the left. Distributions that look roughly like the normal distribution have skewness values near 0. The data in Figure 8.8 have skewness. This is called a positive skew. Some statistical tests assume

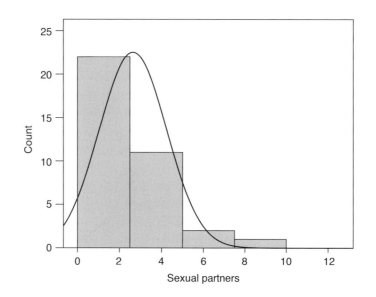

Figure 8.8   Positively skewed distribution of number of sexual partners reported by high school students at Jersey Shore High School

that the data are normally distributed. If the observed skewness value is below −1 or above 1 this means the distribution is different enough from the normal distribution to be of some concern. This will be important later, when you do inferential statistics. Above in Figure 8.8, is the distribution of the sexual partners data from Jersey Shore High School. Notice the positive skew of sexual partners.

8.3.3 Boxplots (or box-and-whisker plot)

Numerical statistics for the boxplot

The boxplot requires calculating some numerical statistics and then graphing these numbers. The statistics are often called the five-number summary. The five numbers are those that divide the sample scores into four approximately equal-sized groups. They are the minimum data point, maximum data point, the middle number (called the median), the number that splits the lowest 25% of the sample from the highest 75% of the sample (Q1) and the number that splits the lowest 75% of the sample from the highest 25% of the sample (Q3). These numbers provide the researcher with a bird's-eye view of the data; a general feeling of the data. Computing these numbers is fairly easy for small to medium sample sizes. However, with large sample sizes it is best to let a computer calculate them. Most programs will calculate these (and the statisticians also disagree about how to do this so the programs often do it in slightly different ways).

The *minimum* is the lowest number in the data set. Going back to the student sexual behaviour data, consider the data from nine of Jersey Shore's finest:

Number of dates: 12, 13, 15, 16, 21, 22, 23, 37 and 40.

You can see that 12 is the minimum or lowest number in the data set. That means that 12 dates is the least number of dates any person from our sample of 9 adolescents from Jersey Shore High School went on. The maximum is the highest number, here 40 dates. The difference between the maximum and the minimum is called the range. Here this is 40 − 12 = 28 dates. Q1 is 15 dates, Q3 is 23 dates and the median is 21. The easiest way to calculate the five-number summary (other than letting a computer do it) is to rank each data point from lowest to highest:

Value	12	13	15	16	21	22	23	37	40
Rank	1	2	3	4	5	6	7	8	9
	Minimum		Q1		Median		Q3		Maximum

> How accurate do you think the teenagers from Jersey High School are at estimating the number of dates they have been on and partners they have had? Is there any reason to suspect that they would not be truthful or accurate?

Using the default settings in R, the five-number summary for the football players' weights is: minimum = 160, Q1 = 191, median = 215, Q3 = 262 and maximum = 320. These are sometimes presented in a table with some additional information.

Table 8.3   Table of five-number summary for the football players' weights

$n = 97$		
215		Units = lbs
191	262	IQR = 71
160	320	range = 160

This tells us that the weight of 50% of the team is between 191 and 262 lbs, and that the median is 215 lbs. The median is a very important statistic. Galton (1907) has a great paper where he discussed people estimating the weight of an ox. He describes how any individual person's estimate is likely to be in error, but that if you take the median of several people it is likely to be closer to the actual value. He describes this as the *vox popoli*, the people's voice.

Making a boxplot

The boxplot is a graph of the five-number summary. It is a visual representation of all the numbers discussed previously. We will describe two versions, one created by the computer (an actual boxplot) and a simplified version that can be drawn easily by hand, called a quartile plot (Tufte, 2001) . Many of the computer packages use slightly different ways of making boxplots (Reese, 2005), but they all produce the same basic diagrams. A rectangular box is drawn from the lower quartile to the upper quartile and a vertical line is placed within the box to denote the median. The whiskers are usually defined as $1.5 \times$ IQR. The IQR for the dating data is Q3 – Q1, so 23 – 15 = 8. The maximum possible lengths of the whiskers would be $1.5 \times 8 = 12$ dates in both directions. Usually, the whiskers are placed at the most extreme observed value within the possible length. Using the football data yields the boxplot shown in Figure 8.9.

Sometimes you may have values that are very extreme. When there are values outside the whiskers they should be shown. Sometimes it is useful to distinguish cases just outside the whiskers from those far outside the whiskers. Tukey (1977) calls points more than 1.5 IQR from the median as *outside* points and those 3.0 IQR from the median as *far outside* points. Figure 8.10 shows the number of sexual partners for 36 high school students sampled in the sexual behavior study at Jersey Shore High School. One of the people, participant #22, is *outside*.

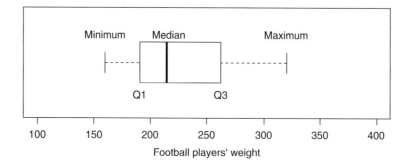

Figure 8.9   Boxplot of football player's weight

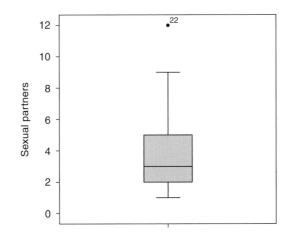

Figure 8.10   Number of sexual partners for students at Jersey Shore High School. The dot at the far top of the graph denotes an outlier

8.3.4 **Single variable barplot**

When you have a categorical variable all the previous graphs are inappropriate. One way to decide if a variable is categorical is to see whether the variable still makes sense if the order of the different values is switched. If the graph still makes sense then the variable is categorical. When you have a single categorical variable a barplot (or bar graph) is an appropriate graphical method. Barplots and histograms sometimes look similar, but they are fundamentally different because the order of the bars can be swapped around.

Consider the following example. Carol Karlsen's (1987) *The Devil in the Shape of a Woman* provides data on many of those accused of witchcraft during the hysteria surrounding witches in colonial New England. The most famous of these were the Salem outbreaks in 1692, but there were others in New England (and in other places, including some still occurring). Nowadays, people can buy shot glasses to glorify these murders. Karlsen (1987) recorded the marital status of those accused (from her table 9): 51 single, 38 widowed, 4 divorced/deserted and 148 married. Marital status is a categorical variable and we will use this variable to illustrate making a barplot.

An appropriate univariate statistic for categorical data is the proportions in each of the categories. A proportion is the number of people in that category divided by the total number of people in the whole sample. The total number of people in the sample, usually labeled n, is: 51 + 38 + 4 + 148 = 241. The proportions for these categories are:

single: 51/241 = 0.21
widowed: 38/241 = 0.16
divorced: 4/241 = 0.02
married: 148/241 = 0.61

The total of all the proportions should add up to 1, so 0.21 + 0.16 + 0.02 + 0.61 = 1.00, although sometimes the sum is slightly different because of rounding, so if you get 1.01 or 0.99 do not worry. The category with the largest proportion is called the *mode*. Here the mode is for married women, and is 0.61. This means the most frequently occurring category of marital status in these accused witches was married.

To make a barplot, these categories are placed below the *x*-axis and either the frequency (the 51, 38, 4 and 148) or the proportions (0.21, 0.16, 0.02 and 0.61) are the heights of the bars. Figure 8.11 shows the barplot. We re-ordered the categories because people begin as single and then need to get married if they are to become divorced or widowed, we placed single on the far left, then married, and then widowed and divorced. Divorces were rarer then than they are now.

It is worth noting that sometimes proportions are written as .61, 0.61 or 61%. The important thing is that you remain consistent within any single assignment so that you do not confuse your readers.

An alternative statistic to proportions is the odds. The observed *odds* of a response are the number of people with that response divided by all the people without that response. Thus, there were 51 single women and in total 241 women, and there-fore 241 − 51 = 190 unmarried women. The odds of being single is 51/190 = 0.27. If the proportion is 0.50, the odds will be 1.00, and if the proportion is greater than

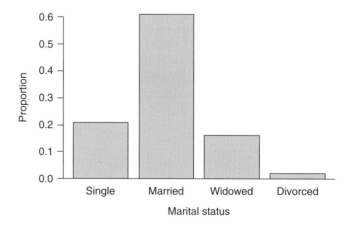

Figure 8.11 **Barplot of the proportion of single, married, widowed and divorced women accused of being witches**

0.50 the odds will be greater than 1.00. The odds of being married in this sample are 1.59. Here are the odds for each category:

single: 51/190 = 0.27   (a proportion of 0.50)
widowed: 38/203 = .19 (equates with an odds of 1.00)
divorced: 4/237 = 0.02
married: 148/93 = 1.59

Although odds may seem a less intuitive statistic than proportions, it has better statistical properties than proportions and therefore more advanced statistics for categorical data tend to build on the odds rather than the proportions.

8.4 GRAPHING TWO VARIABLES

Two variables are graphed together to allow you to look at the relationship between them. We will go through three examples in this section. The first is where there is one categorical variable and one continuous variable. There are several techniques that can be used. We use a barplot but rather than having frequency or proportion on the *y*-axis we use the mean (or median) of the variable. Second, scatter plots are used to show the relationship between two continuous variables. The third is where there are two categorical variables, and is called a clustered barplot.

8.4.1 Barplots for group differences

Barplots can be used when your independent variable is categorical. For example, if you wanted to know what type of music was best for remembering studied information you could recruit 60 people to take part in a study and randomly allocate them into one of three listening conditions: Lindsay Lohan's *Speak*, Lindsay Lohan's *A Little More Personal*, or the British thrash metal band *Fracture Pattern*. Participants listen to one of these while reading a chapter from Huxley's *Doors of Perception* and then are given a 20-item test on the material. You could calculate the mean or the median of number of correct answers for each group. These can be used rather than the frequencies in the single variable barplot. Figure 8.12 shows the mean and the median barplots for some data we created (see the chapter's web page). The mean is more affected by a couple of outliers (a couple of people listening to *Fracture Pattern* did well, but most did very poorly). Using means makes *Fracture Pattern* appear the best for people, whereas, in fact, it works only for a small number of people.

Your barplot would consist of three bars that would show recall for each of the three types of music. On the *y*-axis you would plot the dependent variable, recall

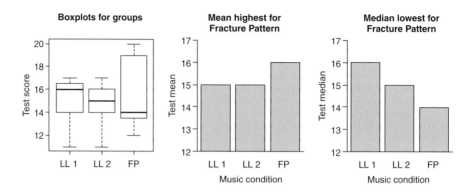

Figure 8.12 Mean and median barplots for music study

during the test. Bar graphs are displayed in both scientific and popular media. When making a bar graph (either by hand or in a statistics package) be sure to pay attention to details that may confuse the desired audience. Using a simple font, concise labels and proper categories will make your data easier to read. Remember, the main goal is to communicate information about the data you have collected, so do not use unnecessary intricacies, designs or effects.

8.4.2 Scatter plots

The scatter plot is incredibly useful when graphing two continuous variables. Often, you want to observe the relationship between two variables that use different scales. An easy way to see if there is any relationship between two dependent measures is to graph them on a scatter plot. To make a scatter plot put the values of one variable along the x-axis and the values of another variable along the y-axis, or vice versa. Each point on the graph represents a pair of values for a single individual. Once all the dots have been plotted you can to draw a straight line through the data. You should practise doing this freehand to get a feel for it.

Scatter plots show the relation between two variables that are each measured on scales. Consider the data for chilis shown in Figure 8.13 (from Wright & London, 2009). On the x-axis is the length of each chili in centimeters and on the y-axis is the heat on a 0 to 10 scale (but one chili gets a 10.5 because it is that HOT). A dot is placed within the graph for each chili. The figure shows that as chilis get longer, they tend to become less hot. It is the small chilis that are the most dangerous. The figure also shows an outlier. This is Nu Mex Big Jim, a chili genetically modified to be big. It is an outlier because it stands out from the rest of the data.

A common statistic for scatter plots is the correlation. It measures how well a straight line would fit through the data. It has a complex equation and is dealt with

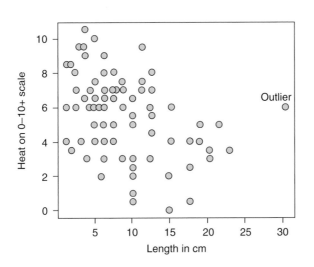

Figure 8.13 Scatter plot of length of each chili (*x*-axis) and heat on a 0 to 10 scale (*y*-axis)

thoroughly in Chapter 11. For now it is important to know that a correlation goes from −1 to +1. Sometimes people will leap into complex statistics like the correlation without looking at the data. In the exercises you are asked to consider some recent data from EDA (not exploratory data analysis, but the Engendered Dolphin Association). There are two variables: 'ocean' is how much the winter low temperature is above the 20-year average for the Atlantic and 'fishstock' is the percentage of fishstock, greater than 2 cm, per cubic kilometre. The correlation is 0.13, which is a little above 0, which suggests ocean locations with higher winter temperatures have larger fish. The data are available on the chapter's web page. One of the exercises asks you to explore if anything is fishy about these data.

8.4.3 **Graphing two categorical variables**

The most common and usually the most useful way to present categorical data is with a table. Tables can convey much precise numerical information. There are many rules for making good tables. While we show how to make graphs for multiple categorical variables, we also recommend you consider using tables to present your data.

Our first example comes from memory research. Carlucci *et al.* (2011) had a confederate (someone working for us) approach pairs of people on South Beach, Florida, and ask one of them what time it was. The confederate walked out of view. A research assistant approached and spoke either with the person with whom the confederate spoke (who we will call the actor) or the bystander. The research assistant asked the person to identify the confederate from a set of six faces. All the faces looked similar to the confederate, but none were him (called a 'target-absent lineup'). So the person who was asked to make the identification had to make an error. The important part of the study came next. The assistant turned to the other person, who was either the actor or the bystander. Carlucci and colleagues were interested in whether this person would conform (go along with the other person) and if so whether the bystander would conform more than the actor. They found 23 of the 93 actors conformed (24.7%; chance was 1/6 = 16.7%) and 37 of the 83 bystanders conformed (44.6%). The study has important implications for eyewitness investigations.

A barplot can be made by placing bars for the frequencies next to each other as in Figure 8.14. The critical choice is which variable to have separated by the clusters (here the level of grayness of the bars) and which to have denoted along the *x*-axis. Here we have put participant's role along the *x*-axis and used different shades of grey to denote whether they conformed or not. There are only four pieces of information in this graph. This means it has a low data-to-ink ratio (Tufte, 1977). Usually, if you have this little information you would describe it in the text or incorporate it into a table.

To get a measure of conformity for bystanders we can take the odds of conforming: 37/46 = 0.804. This means they are more likely not to conform than to conform, but given they are choosing from six faces this is still above chance. The odds for actors conforming was 23/70 = 0.29. The ratio of these can be compared: 0.804/0.329 = 2.44. This means the odds of a bystander conforming are more than twice the size of the odds of an actor conforming. This is called the odds ratio.

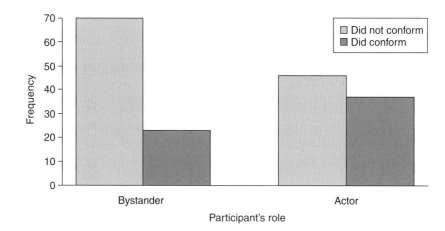

Figure 8.14 **Barplot showing conformity. Participants' role is on the *x*-axis and frequency of conformity is on the *y*-axis**

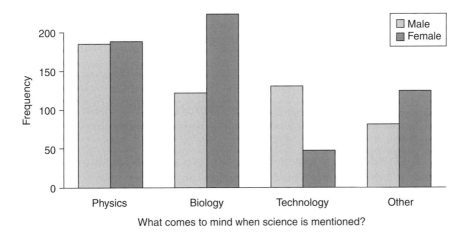

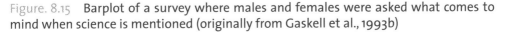

Figure. 8.15 Barplot of a survey where males and females were asked what comes to mind when science is mentioned (originally from Gaskell et al., 1993b)

There are many other descriptive statistics that can be used in this situation (see Wright *et al.* 2009), but the odds ratio is one of the most popular.

Barplots can be used when the variables have several categories. Figure 8.15 shows data originally from Gaskell *et al.* (1993; data from table 8.7 in Wright, 1997) from a survey where males and females were asked what comes to mind when science is mentioned. The figure shows that women are more likely to think of biological science (which includes psychology) and males are more likely to think of technology.

8.5 CONCLUSIONS

The goal of this chapter was to familiarise you with ways to summarise your data. Histograms and boxplots both convey information about single variables. They are univariate (uni, from the Latin *unus* meaning one) procedures. How much of the information that is displayed in a histogram depends on the type of histogram and the bin size. Procedures like the stem-and-leaf diagram display more precise information than the generic histogram. As the width of the bin increases, information is lost. With boxplots most of the information is not presented. It is assumed that the key points of the distribution can be summarised with a small set of numbers and including information on only a few outlying cases. You may use one of these or a combination of these to graph your data and get a feel for any patterns that may be present. Checking for data entry errors and patterns in the data will help guide later analyses.

8.6 EXERCISES AND DISCUSSION QUESTIONS

1   Why is describing your data important?
2   What is the difference between descriptive statistics and inferential statistics? Which should you start with?
3   Using the data you gathered from your 20 friends (their music buying habits) calculate the mean, median and mode. Construct a boxplot. Are there any outliers?
4   Look in your local newspaper and find a bar graph. What information does it summarise? What would you do to make it more informative?
5   What should you keep in mind when choosing histogram bin widths?
6   How should you check for data entry problems? What important guidelines should you keep in mind whenever you are entering data?
7   What are the differences among the different graphs described in this chapter (histogram, stem- and- leaf plot, boxplot, bar plot and scatter plot)? When should each be used?
8   What is a five-number summary?
9   How can you measure how spread out your data are?

8.7 FURTHER READING

Reese (2005) is a short article with illustrations that provides a good overview of how to construct a boxplot. See Reese's other short articles on similar topics, including construction of bar charts. Tufte (2001) gives a great overview of statistical graphics. The second edition provides high-resolution graphics. Tukey (1977) is a ground-breaking text that provides step-by-step guides. Out of print but available at online retailers.

9

Inferential Statistics

Marianna E. Carlucci and Daniel B. Wright

CONTENTS

After reading this chapter you will have a better understanding of what inferential statistics are and when we use them. You should be able to design an experiment and know what kind of statistical test you will need to use to interpret the results of your experiment.

KEY TERMS

alpha level	odds ratio
chi-square	one-way analysis of variance
Cohen's *d*	population
confidence interval	power
correlation	sample
effect size	statistical significance
Mann-Whitney *U* test	*t*-test
matched-pair *t*-test	within-subjects ANOVA

9.1 **INTRODUCTION**

Descriptive statistics were discussed in Chapter 8. They are an important initial step in understanding what your data are like. Descriptive statistics allow you to describe your sample data but do not allow you to make statements about the population of interest. Inferential statistics, however, do allow you to make statements about your population of interest. For example, suppose you ran a study looking at the video game usage of 26 children between the ages of 11 and 16. Calculating the mean would tell you about the 26 children in your study but not about the population of interest, all children in your population aged 11 to 16.

The techniques discussed in this chapter will allow you to infer aspects of the population of interest using sample data. They will also allow you to assess if there are notable differences between groups or relationships between variables in the population. This is important for understanding if manipulations work (that independent variables affect the dependent variables). For example, say you want to test a new drug to see if it is effective in controlling symptoms of obsessive compulsive disorder (OCD). Using inferential statistics will allow you to assess differences between the experimental group (the group that gets the drug) and the control group (the group that does not get the drug). An inferential test between the groups will help you to decide if the drug was effective.

$$\boxed{\text{Population}} \underset{\text{make inferences about}}{\overset{\text{take cases from}}{\rightleftarrows}} \boxed{\text{Sample}}$$

One way to determine if there is a difference between your groups is to look at the sample mean. The sample mean is important because, if you have sampled correctly, then it provides a good estimate for the population mean. The population mean is sometimes denoted with the Greek letter μ ('mu'). It is impossible for us to know what the population mean is because we cannot sample the entire population of interest. For example, pretend we want to know how many obsessive compulsive symptoms those with OCD suffer from. We measure this by looking at the mean number of OCD symptoms displayed by a sample of people with OCD. Let's say the mean number of OCD symptoms in the experimental group is 12. This mean tells you about the sample mean, which you can use to infer the mean of the population of interest. It tells you how many symptoms, on average, a person with OCD suffers from. However, the only way to find the population mean would be to sample every person with OCD. Unfortunately, we do not have the time or resources to sample the entire population of interest in most studies so we use statistics like the sample mean to get an idea about what the population mean may be. Then, we can construct confidence intervals for these sample data to see how precise our estimates are. This is a big step and requires faith in the sampling methods used by the researcher (see Chapter 5).

To calculate a confidence interval of a mean you need to know the number of people in the sample, the sample mean and the sample standard deviation, and decide on what confidence level you want to use. The sample standard deviation describes the spread of your sample or the variability within your data. A small standard deviation tells you that the scores are close together while a large standard deviation tells you that there is more variability in the scores. When calculating a confidence interval you also need to make a couple of assumptions. The main assumption to consider is that the variable is sampled from a population that is normally distributed. Most researchers use a 95% confidence interval, meaning that if the experiment was repeated over and over the true population value would be in the confidence interval 95% of the time. The equation for the 95% confidence interval is:

$$CI_{95\%} = x \pm t_{0.05} \frac{sd}{\sqrt{n}}$$

Suppose we want to construct a 95% confidence interval for the mean weight of FIU football players (see Chapter 8 for the original example). The number of people in the sample is 96, the sample mean is 223 and the sample standard deviation is 38. The corresponding confidence interval for these data is 7.6.

$$CI_{95\%} = 223 \pm 1.98 \frac{38}{\sqrt{96}} = 223 \pm 7.68$$

9.2 STATISTICAL TESTS

Before we begin our discussion on specific statistical tests it is important to understand that different tests are available depending on the assumptions you make about your data. Parametric tests are used when the data conform to certain assumptions. One assumption that many statistical tests make is about the distribution (discussed in Chapter 8) and in particular that it is normally distributed. If this assumption is violated, then alternatives exist which can be used. Some of the most used tests are listed in Table 9.1.

9.2.1 Significance/power

Inferential statistics often rely on whether a particular test is 'statistically significant'. That is, that the probability of your results happening solely due to chance is low. Chapter 2 discussed type I and type II errors; you must assign a criterion to be used when determining if one of these errors has been made. This criterion is known

Table 9.1 List of statistical tests

Test	Assumes normality	Does not assume normality
Two independent groups	Independent measures t-test	Mann–Whitney test
More than two independent groups	ANOVA	Kruskal–Wallis
Repeated measures (2 conditions)	Matched-pair t-test	Wilcoxon test
Repeated measures (>2 conditions)	Repeated measures ANOVA	Friedman's ANOVA
Correlation	Pearson correlation	Spearman correlation

as the alpha level (α), which is conditional on the alternative not being different. Most researchers place the critical value at 0.05. So, if the p value associated with a test statistic is 0.05 or less then the researcher can feel reasonably comfortable in saying that their results are not due to chance.

Another aspect of research you must consider is the concept of power. Power is the ability to detect differences between groups, if a difference exists. Stated a different way, power is the probability of rejecting the null hypothesis when the alternative hypothesis is true. Several things can increase or decrease the power of a statistical test. Power is affected by alpha level such that more conservative alpha levels (0.01, for example) have less power. Power is also affected by sample size such that large sample sizes yield more power. Power is also affected by whether you do a one-tailed or two-tailed test (discussed later). Two-tailed tests are less powerful than one-tailed tests. Power is also affected by the minimum effect size you want to detect. Effect size is the degree to which two variables are associated or related. If you want to detect a small effect you will need more people. Without adequate power your study could yield null effects even when the true effect size is important, which would mean you missed the opportunity to observe an effect. Below we discuss one way of determining power *before* you conduct your experiment. This will save you a headache later if you find you ran your study but did not have enough power to detect differences between your groups.

One way to increase power is to conduct a less conservative test by using a larger alpha level. For example, using alpha (α) = 0.05 instead of alpha (α) = 0.01. This increases the chance of obtaining a statistically significant result (rejecting the null hypothesis) when the null hypothesis is false; that is, it reduces the risk of type II error. However, it increases the risk of obtaining a statistically significant result when the null hypothesis is true. That is, it increases the risk of a type I error.

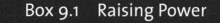

Box 9.1   Raising Power

To raise power:

1 Use reliable measures
2 Increase the sample size
3 Use a powerful research design (e.g. within-subjects design)
4 Increase the alpha level
5 Use a one-tailed test (if appropriate, but we discourage this)

One last note on power: power will be very important when interpreting your results. If your statistical tests yield a non-significant result then one reason for this might be a lack of power (you did not have enough participants, for example). To be safe, it is advised that you conduct a power analysis before carrying out your study so that you know how many participants you need to gather for your particular design. There are many ways to do a power analysis but we like to use the software G*Power (www.psycho.uni-duesseldorf.de/aap/projects/gpower/). G*Power is free and can be downloaded easily. By inputting the type of statistical test you will conduct and a few other parameters (alpha, minimum effect size, etc.) you can get an estimate of how many participants you need to recruit (Faul *et al.* 2007). Their web page includes a tutorial for using the software.

Notice that G*Power prompts you about whether you want to conduct a one-tailed test or a two-tailed test. This pertains to the concept of null hypothesis significance testing (NHST). The null hypothesis is usually 'no difference' between groups. The alternative hypothesis is usually the opposite of whatever the null hypothesis is. Sometimes a researcher predicts the direction of the difference between the groups. So, the alternative hypothesis is that one group will be better than the other. This is an example of a one-tailed test. A one-tailed test is done when your research question or hypothesis is directional. One-tailed tests are associated with increased power. Attractive as that may be, most researchers warn against doing one-tailed tests. Instead you should always conduct a two-tailed test. A two-tailed test may reveal important information that you may miss if you conduct a one-tailed test. For example, a researcher conducting a study on psychological therapies may want to know if a type of therapy is better than no therapy (a one-tailed hypothesis). However, it would also be important for the researcher to discover if the therapy want *worse* than no therapy. This is what Scott Lilienfeld (2007) discussed when he stressed that the first priority in therapeutic interventions should be to 'do no harm'. If a one-tailed test was done then harmful therapies might be administered without knowing that they were actually harmful. For example, Lilienfeld found that some relaxation treatments for panic-prone patients actually induced

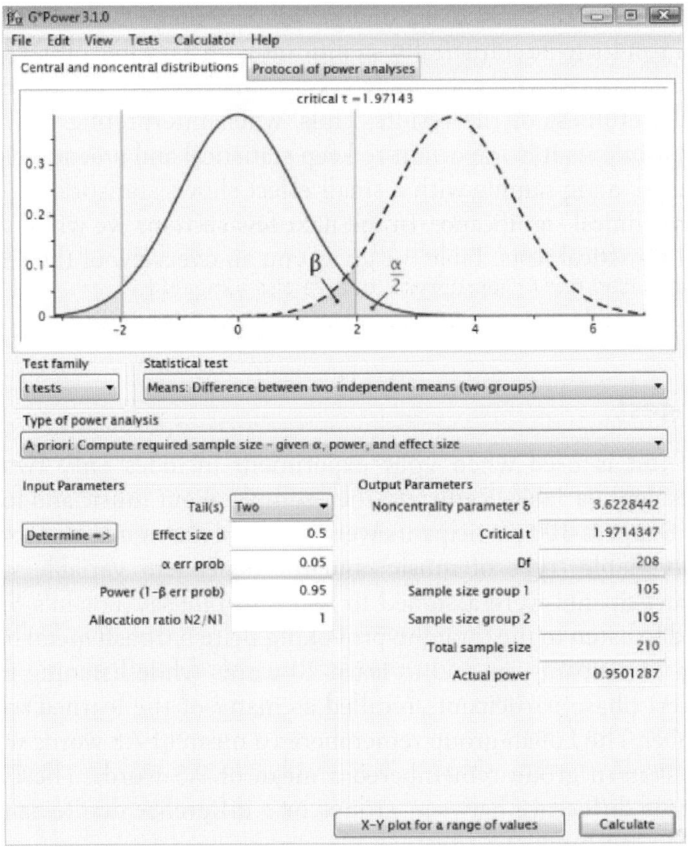

Figure 9.1   Screenshot of G*Power output

panic attacks. The *New England Journal of Medicine* requires that 'except when one-sided tests are required by study design, such as in noninferiority trials, all reported *P* values should be two-sided' (*New England Journal of Medicine* website).

One important distinction is 'statistical significance' and 'practical significance'. You cannot make decisions about your experiment by focusing on the *p* value and nothing else. You need to interpret your results in terms of both statistical significance and practical significance. Suppose you conduct a study and find that a certain anti-epilepsy drug has a higher mean effect in a sample of 500 children. However, the *p* value associated with the test is 0.06. Does this mean that you cannot interpret your results in terms of practical significance? The drug may be able to help many children who suffer from seizures though the statistical significance is just outside of the acceptable range. Conversely, imagine you conduct a study on a new planet and find that humans can live well over 200 years on this new planet due to the properties of the oxygen there. This new planet is many light years away and only a very expensive space ship that can carry one person can make it there. You find your experimental results to be statistically significant with a p value of 0.0001. However, the effect size associated with your study is very small so the p value is not indicative of the actual usefulness of the results. Thus, when interpreting your results and designing experiments it is important to keep statistical and practical significance in mind. In general, a big sample with a small effect shows statistical significance but may not show clinical significance. In the next few sections we will discuss a series of inferential statistical tests. Table 9.1 gives you an overview of the tests described in this chapter.

9.2.2 The *t*-test

The group *t*-test is used when your experiment includes only two levels of a single independent variable. Return to the example about music and learning from section 8.4.1 Suppose 100 participants were randomly assigned to two levels of the independent variable (type of music) and the dependent variable was learning. Fifty-eight participants were assigned to listen to Lindsay Lohan's *Speak* and 42 were assigned to listen to the thought-provoking British thrash metal band Fracture Pattern. Each participant was told to learn 20 words while listening to the music. During the test phase participants recalled as many of the learned words as they could remember. The Lohan group remembered a mean of 7.8 words while those in the Fracture Pattern group remembered a mean of 9.5 words. These means may represent a true difference between groups or a difference due to sampling error. To find out you can conduct a *t*-test.

The *t*-test has certain assumptions that you must satisfy before using it. The first is that the data are independent, meaning that the answers for one participant are not dependent on the answers for another participant. For example, participants did not recall the words together. Assume this is true in our music study. The second is that the distribution of differences must be normally distributed. Assume for now this is true in our music study. We can use the independent samples *t*-test for this experiment. Once a *t*-test is conducted we will get an output that will include the *t* value and the critical value for that test, the p value. You can use a probability table to get the p value associated with a particular t statistic and degrees of freedom, but computer packages can provide more precise p values so it is worth using those. The p value is the probability of observing data as extreme as observed, assuming the null hypothesis is true. Usually, researchers assign the critical value at 0.05, meaning that a p value of 0.05 or less is considered a statistically significant result not likely to be due to chance but rather representing an actual difference between groups. Here, that learning can be influenced by the type of music playing. In this case we could interpret the statistically significant results by saying that listening to the British thrash metal band Fracture Pattern produce different amounts of learning when compared to learning while listening to Lindsay Lohan.

Figure 9.2   'Breadcrumbs' for doing an independent samples *t*-test in SPSS

T-Test

[DataSet1] C: \Users\labuser\Desktop\LL.sav

Group Statistics

	Group	N	Mean	Std. Deviation	Std. Error Mean
WordsRecalled	.00	58	7.8276	2.31	0.3
	1.00	42	9.4524	2.66	0.41

Independent Samples Test

		Levene's Test for Equality of Variances		t-test for Equality of Means							
										95% Confidence Interval of the Difference	
		F	Sig.	t	df	Sig. (2-tailed)	Mean Difference	Std. Error Difference	Lower	Upper
WordsRecalled	Equal variances assumed	2.632	.108	−3.255	98	.002	−1.62	0.5	−2.62	−0.63
	Equal variances not assumed			−3.182	80.679	.002	−1.62	0.51	−2.64	−0.61

Figure 9.3   Output for an independent samples *t*-test in SPSS

To conduct a group *t*-test in SPSS go to *Analyze* then click on *Compare Means* and choose *Independent-Samples t Test* (Figure 9.2). You will be prompted to pick your test variable (in this case, words recalled) and grouping variable (in this case, listening group).

Figure 9.3 shows the SPSS output for an independent samples test. The 'group statistics' box shows you the means for each group. The Lohan group was coded as '0' and the Fracture Pattern group was coded as '1'. The means are 7.8 and 9.5, respectively. Looking at the box below tells you if the difference between the means is statistically significant. The *p* value for the test is 0.002, which is below the critical value 0.05. Thus, we can conclude that the difference between these means is statistically significant.

9.2.3 **Mann–Whitney *U* test**

If your data are not normally distributed then there are alternatives to the *t*-test that you can use. The Mann–Whitney *U* test can be used for assessing whether two independent samples are significantly different from one another. The calculations of a Mann–Whitney *U* test are a bit different from the calculations of a *t*-test. It involves ranking all the data, ignoring which music group the person was in, and then comparing the ranks for the two groups. However, interpreting the output from most statistics programs of a Mann–Whitney *U* test is similar to interpreting the output for a *t*-test.

9.2.4 **Matched-pair *t*-test**

For within-subjects designs you can use a matched-pair *t*-test. You may see it referred to as a paired *t*-test or paired samples *t*-test or dependent *t*-test. The interpretation of this test is identical to the traditional *t*-test. Simply look at the *t* value, and the *p* value associated with the *t* value to determine if a statistical difference between groups exists.

9.2.5 **One-way analysis of variance (ANOVA)**

When your experiment has more than two groups you cannot use a *t*-test. The appropriate statistical test is a between-subjects or one-way analysis of variance (ANOVA). To conduct an ANOVA your data must conform to the assumptions of the test. The assumptions are that the groups are independent (did not answer together), that the distribution is normal, and that the variances of the groups are equal. Levene's test is usually used to determine if group variances are equal formally, it tests whether the variances of the populations from the different samples are equal.

ANOVAs are very popular and are often seen in journal articles. When you read a journal article and see that the researchers have performed an ANOVA then you assume that the data are normally distributed and the groups have similar variances and that there are more than two levels of an independent variable being compared. When looking at the output of an ANOVA you will have to look at the *F* ratio and the *p* value associated with the *F* ratio to determine if differences exist among the experimental groups. If differences do exist then you can move on and determine where these differences lie (which groups are different from one another). There are two types of comparisons but we will concentrate on post-hoc comparisons here.

Pretend you conducted an experiment with three levels of an independent variable. You may feel an ANOVA is too complicated and would rather do a *t*-test but you have more than two groups. You may think to yourself, 'Why can't I just do a series of *t*-tests comparing level 1 with level 2, level 1 with level 3, and level 2 with level 3?'. The problem is that doing multiple two-sample *t*-tests increases your chances of committing a type I error and a type II error.

Going back to the music example. Suppose you also wanted to know the effects of Gangsta Rap on learning so you have participants listen to Ice-T (the original Gangsta Rapper) while studying 20 words. During data analysis your goal is to see if there are any differences among the three groups (Lohan, Fracture Pattern and Ice-T). You may be tempted to do a series of *t*-tests comparing the Lohan group to the Fracture Pattern group then comparing the Lohan group to the Ice-T group, and so on. However, as previously stated, this would increase your chances of making an error. Instead, you would conduct an ANOVA to see if there were any differences between the three listening conditions. Below are the outputs and how to interpret

Oneway

[DataSet1] C:\Users\labuser\Desktop\LL.sav

ANOVA

WordsRecalled

	Sum of Squares	df	Mean Square	F	Sig.
Between Groups	130.774	2	65.387	10.373	.000
Within Groups	939.200	149	6.303		
Total	1069.974	151			

results of an ANOVA. To conduct an ANOVA go to *Analyze,* click *Compare Means* and choose *One-Way ANOVA* (Figure 9.4).

Analyze ⟶ Compare Means ⟶ F$_A$ One-Way ANOVA...

Figure 9.4   'Breadcrumbs' for doing a one-way ANOVA in SPSS

You will be prompted to pick a post hoc comparison to do along with the ANOVA. You can choose from over 20 in SPSS. All of them do the similar things – they allow you to correct for type I errors. Some are more robust than others. Remember, that just knowing that there is a difference between groups does not tell you *where* the differences lie so it is important to do a post-hoc test. There is debate about the relative merits of each post-hoc test. For our listening study we picked Tukey's Honestly Significant Difference (HSD) test which is one of the most popular. The Tukey HSD test is named after John Tukey. The Tukey HSD test conducts pairwise comparisons between all possible mean combinations to detect differences between groups. Figure 9.5 shows a Tukey HSD post-hoc test for the music study. The Lohan group was coded as '0', the Fracture Pattern group was coded as '1' and the Ice-T group was coded as '2'. The output gives you the pairwise comparisons for all groups. The first line shows the comparison between group 0 (Lohan) and group 1 (Fracture Pattern) as a statistically significant difference (at the 0.005 level). This tells you that the mean differences between these groups are significant (Lohan vs. Ice-T). Look at the last line where group 2 (Ice-T) is compared to group 1 (Fracture Pattern). Notice that this difference is not significant, meaning that the mean difference between these groups is not statistically significant.

Eta-squared is another index you can look at when conducting an ANOVA. Eta-squared is a measure of effect size for ANOVAs and is sometimes denoted as η^2. It is provided on SPSS outputs. Eta-squared is the amount of variance accounted for

Post-Hoc Tests

Multiple Comparisons

WordsRecalled
Tukey HSD

(I) Group	(J) Group	Mean Difference (I-J)	Std. Error	Sig.	95% Confidence Interval	
					Lower Bound	Upper Bound
.00	1.00	−1.62479*	.50868	.005	−2.8290	−.4206
	2.00	−2.07626*	.47948	.000	−3.2114	−.9412
1.00	.00	1.62479*	.50868	.005	.4206	2.8290
	2.00	−.45147	.52086	.662	−1.6845	.7816
2.00	.00	2.07626*	.47948	.000	.9412	3.2114
	1.00	.45147	.52086	.662	−.7816	1.6845

*. The mean difference is significant at the 0.05 level.

Figure 9.5   Output for Tukey HSD in SPSS

by the predictor variable (or independent variable). To interpret eta-squared you may use conventions promoted by Cohen (1988) where 0.20 is a small effect, 0.50 is a medium effect and anything over 0.80 is a large effect.

There are many types of ANOVAs you can use depending on how many levels of independent variable you have and how many independent variables you have. Usually, a one-way ANOVA is used for experiments that include two or more independent groups. A factorial ANOVA is used when the experiment includes two independent variables where each has two levels. This is often termed a '2 by 2' experimental design and the appropriate test is the factorial ANOVA and is covered in Chapter 10. Note than when interpreting a factorial ANOVA you must interpret both main effects and interactions. A main effect is when one of the independent variables affects the dependent variable, above and beyond the other independent variables. It alerts you to the fact that the effects on the dependent variable are a result of the mixing of the independent variables (see Jaccard (1998) for an in-depth explanation. If your data do not meet the assumptions of ANOVA then you can use the Kruskal–Wallis non-parametric test.

9.2.6 Within-subjects ANOVA

There is also an ANOVA you can use if you have a within-subjects design. If your participants receive all the levels of the independent variable then a repeated measures ANOVA can be conducted. This is often useful if you want to increase the power of your study. So, you get each participant to listen to Lindsay Lohan's music while studying 20 words. Then, you test those participants on those 20 words. You may now choose to give your participants a 'mental break' before having them study another 20 words while listening to Fracture Pattern. Next, you have partici-pants recall the 20 words they studied while listening to Fracture Pattern. Then they listen to Ice-T while studying another set of 20 words. Because participants listened to all three music conditions this is a within-subjects design and you can use a repeated measures ANOVA to assess differences in learning between the music conditions. Note: the order in which the music is played may make a differ-ence so you will want to check for any order effects or counterbalance the presenta-tion order to your participants.

Friedman's test is the alternative to the repeated measures ANOVA, based on ranking the data, and it is less influenced by outliers. Like many of the alternative procedures presented in this book, it is based on ranking the data. The first step in doing Friedman's test is ranking the values within each case for all the different treatments.

Just like the *t*-test and Mann–Whitney U test, there are alternatives to the ANOVA in the event that your data to not conform to the assumptions of a parametric test. In this case, the appropriate test is the Kruskal–Wallis one-way analysis of variance. It is essentially an extension of the Mann–Whitney U test to be used when you conduct an experiment with two or more groups. It also ranks the data to compute differences among groups.

9.2.7 Chi-square (χ^2)

Sometimes you will want to examine the association between two categorical variables. You may design an experiment where your dependent variable is a dichotomous decision such as 'yes/no' or 'guilty/not guilty', and where your inde-pendent variable is categorical. You could create a clustered bar graph as shown in Chapter 8. The appropriate statistical test is the Chi-square (χ^2) test. The χ^2 test is mainly used to test if there is an association between two variables. For example, if you wanted to look at how gender is associated with guilty/not guilty decisions then the χ^2 would be an appropriate test of whether these two variables are associ-ated. The null hypothesis is that there is no association between the two variables or that the odds ratio is 1. If there is no association, the χ^2 value should be small. If there is an association, this value should be larger. As such, χ^2 is a measure of how badly the model of no association fits the data.

Recall that in Chapter 8 we discussed a study conducted in South Beach, Florida. Carlucci *et al.* (2011) had a confederate approach pairs of people and ask one of them what time it was. The confederate walked out of view. A research assistant approached and spoke either with the person who the confederate spoke with (whom we will call the actor) or the bystander. The research assistant asked the person to identify the confederate from a set of six faces. All the faces looked similar to the confeder-ate, but none were actually him (called a 'target-absent lineup'). So this person had to make an error. What Carlucci *et al.* wanted to know was if there was an association between what the first person said and what the second person said. The most appropriate test for these kind of data is a χ^2 test . A χ^2 test revealed an association between what the first person said and what the second person said, $\chi^2(5) = 71.31$, $p < 0.001$. Using this test statistic Carlucci *et al.* were able to observe memory conformity in their study.

Box 9.2   Interpreting Chi-square

Small χ^2 value: No association detected. Do not reject H_0 (null hypothesis).
Large χ^2 value: An association detected. Reject H_0.

9.3 TYPES OF EFFECT SIZES

In 1999, Leland Wilkinson and the APA Task force on Statistical Inference noted that researchers should 'always present effect sizes for primary outcomes' (p. 599). Effect size tells you about the relationship between two or more variables in a sample. Effect sizes are important because they complement *p* values which provide no more information than 'significant' and 'not significant'. Effect size, on the other hand, provides useful information about how big the effect is. Thus, it relates to the practical applications of a particular finding. Suppose that a researcher finds that a particular drug was effective in reducing insomnia in a sample of 500 people at the *p* < 0.001 level. The researcher might conclude that the drug is effective in reducing insomnia in the population of interest. This would be a hasty conclusion and the researcher should look at other measures to understand the relative impact of the statistical results. This is where researchers can turn to different effect size measures. Effect sizes help researchers estimate the magnitude of relationships among variables. Below we discuss some of the more commonly used effect size measures.

9.3.1 Correlation

A correlation is the association between two variables. Remember that in Chapter 8 we drew a line through a scatterplot. Sometimes the line fits well and sometimes it does not. A correlation statistic measures how close points are to the regression line, what is sometimes referred to as the 'fit' of the regression line. The most often used correlation is *Pearson's product moment correlation*. Pearson described a correlation as ranging from –1 to +1. The sign tells you whether the relationship between the two variables is positive or negative. The number tells you the magnitude of the relationship. For example, pretend we conducted a study looking at alcohol consumption and academic performance. Suppose we wanted to see if there was a correlation between these two variables and found that the correlation was −0.50. In this case we have a negative correlation which tells us that as one variable goes up the other variable goes down. In this case we would probably find that as alcohol consumption goes up, academic performance goes down. One important concept to understand about correlations is that they do not imply that one of the correlated variables directly influences the other. For example, if a researcher found a positive correlation between ice cream sales and crime rates in Central Park they could not conclude that eating ice cream causes an increase in crime because there may be other variables causing this relationship. The sign of the correlation does not tell the entire story. You must look at the magnitude of the correlation. In this case it is 0.50 and very close to 1 so the correlation is strong. This means that the negative relationship between alcohol consumption and academic performance is almost 1, almost perfect, and so we can be somewhat confident that an increase in alcohol consumption is associated with a decrease in academic performance. r is used to denote a correlation. As a very rough rule of thumb, Cohen (1992) describes $r = 0.1$, 0.3 and 0.5, as 'small', 'medium' and 'large'. These labels should not be applied without consideration of what the correlation is of, and should not be interpreted as a measure of importance.

In many cases there is a clear relationship, but it is not linear. Figure 9.6 shows some examples where there are clear relationships, but they are not linear. The correlations may be high, as with panel (d), but clearly a straight line does not describe these data.

9.3.2 Cohen's *d*

Cohen's *d* is another popular measure of the relationship between variables. Cohen's *d* was created by Jacob Cohen and is defined as the difference between two means divided by the standard deviation. It is fairly simple to calculate Cohen's *d* since all the necessary statistics for calculation are provided on most SPSS outputs. Also, there are established conventions that make interpreting Cohen's *d* simple as well. An effect size of 0.2 to 0.3 is said to be a 'small' effect, 0.5 is said to be a 'medium' effect and 0.8 and above is said to be a 'large' effect. There has been some concern that these are arbitrary labels and we agree. As a researcher you should interpret the practical significance of the results using the effect size labels as guides not as rules.

$$d = \frac{\text{mean}_1 - \text{mean}_2}{\sqrt{\dfrac{SD_1^2 + SD_2^2}{2}}}$$

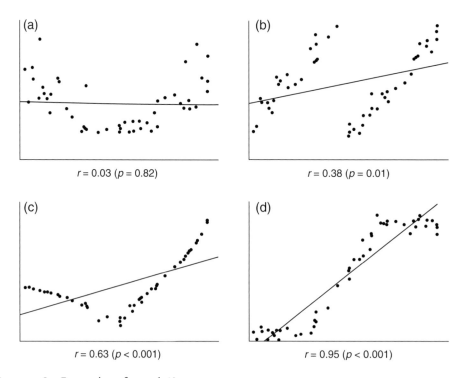

Figure 9.6   **Examples of correlations**

You will need three pieces of information to calculate Cohen's *d*: the mean of group 1, the mean of group 2 and the standard deviation from either group. Note that you may use this calculation if the standard deviations for the groups are homogenous. If the standard deviations for the groups differ then you may use a *pooled standard deviation* instead, which is the square root of the average of the squared standard deviations.

Using the information from the *t*-test example above (Figure 9.7):

Mean 1 is 7.8276
Mean 2 is 9.4524
Standard deviation is 2.66

$$\frac{7.8276 - 9.4524}{2.66} = -0.61$$

The results show that we have between a medium and a large effect, meaning that our results have practical significance.

t-Test

```
[DataSet1] c:\Users\labuser\Desktop\LL.sav
```

Group Statistics

	Group	N	Mean	Std. Deviation	Std. Error Mean
WordsRecalled	.00	58	7.8276	2.31	0.3
	1.00	42	9.4524	2.66	0.41

Using the information from the *t*-test example above:

Mean 1 is 7.8276
Mean 2 is 9.4524
Standard deviation is 2.66

$$\frac{7.8276 - 9.4524}{2.66} = -0.61$$

Figure 9.7   Output for the music study and calculation for Cohen's *d*

Box 9.3

Alpha (α): Probability of making a type I error when H_0 is true.
Power: Probability of rejecting the null hypothesis when the alternative hypothesis is true (that is NOT making a type II error).
Null hypothesis: Often no difference between groups.
Alternative hypothesis: Often difference between groups.

9.3.3 Odds ratio

Finally, if the variables of interest are binary then the odds ratio (OR) is a useful effect size measure. You may have seen odds ratios used in newspaper or magazine articles. For example, one study found that British men are more likely to have a secret bank account than women. The study found that 22% of men admit to hiding money from their wives compared with 11% of women. By using an odds ratio it gives the reader an intuitive sense about how often a phenomenon occurs.

$$(22/78)/(11/89) = 2.28$$

9.4 CONCLUSION

In this chapter we discussed how to go about making inferences about the population of interest when we collect information from a sample. As you read, there are many different types of tests you can use to make inferences. In fact, there are more tests that we simply could not cover in this chapter or even in this book! However, with these tools you will be able to test basic scientific hypotheses. This chapter also discussed important theoretical and practical issues in statistics. Knowing the difference between statistical significance and practical significance is not only important in the behavioral sciences but can also help you make decisions in your own life regarding what products you purchase, how you interpret news stories, etc.

9.5 EXERCISES

1   Conduct your very own music study. Gather 30 of your friends and split them into two groups of 15. Have one group listen to one type of music while studying a group of words and have the other group listen to another type of music while studying a group of words. Record how many words they can recall and enter these in SPSS (or any other statistical package you use). Plot your data to see if you meet the assumptions of most statistical tests (e.g., is it normally distributed?). Then, pick the appropriate statistical test to run. Is there a difference in learning between the two groups? What inferences can you make using the information from your sample? Lets say you had 4 different groups. What statistical test would you conduct in that case?

2   Download G*Power. How many participants do you need to execute an independent samples t-test with power of 0.80? When should you conduct a power analysis?

Using the output from exercise 1 calculate Cohen's d for the data. *Is the effect size small or large?* What conclusions can you draw about music types and learning?

9.6 DISCUSSION QUESTIONS

1   Describe the relationship between the population of interest and a sample.
2   How do researchers make inferences about a population of interest based on a sample?
3   Describe issues associated with sampling. What is random sampling? What is a convenience sample? Which type is most often used in psychological research?
4   What is a confidence interval? Why is it important to provide confidence intervals?
5   Which characteristics of your sample should you consider when picking a statistical test?

6 What does the term 'statistically significant' mean? What does it tell you about your statistic? What are some misconceptions associated with the term?

7 What is 'power'? What conclusions can you make about your data if you do not achieve appropriate levels of power? What can you do to increase power?

8 What is the difference between 'statistical significance' and 'practical significance'?

9 When should you conduct a t-test? When should you conduct an ANOVA? What characteristics of your data should you consider before executing these statistical tests? What happens if you violate an assumption of these statistical tests?

10 Why do ANOVA's require post-hoc comparisons?

11 Pretend you want to understand the association between ice cream consumption and headaches. You gather information from 30 people about their ice cream consumption habits and how often they get headaches. What statistical test of association would you conduct?

12 What is an effect size? Why has the APA encouraged researchers to report effect sizes? What are some effect size indices?

13 What is hypothesis testing? What are its advantages and disadvantages?

14 What is a type I error? What is a type II error? When is each type of error most detrimental?

9.7 FURTHER READING

Power is described in detail, with numerous tables for many different situations, in Cohen (1988). Cohen (1990) is an insightful essay about designing studies and being cautious about about making inferences. Field (2009) describes how to do all the tests described here in SPSS. Jaccard (1998) describes the next steps in making inference (see also chapters 10–12 here). Siegel and Castellan (1988) is a classic text for conducting analysis based on ranks. Wright and London (2009) is an introductory text that covers all of these aspects.

10

Factorial ANOVA

Katherine McGuire and Kamala London

CONTENTS

AIMS OF THIS CHAPTER

This chapter will help you understand:

* when to use factorial ANOVA;
* the necessary calculations to obtain an *F* ratio used in hypothesis testing and the interpretation of this value;
* how to identify and interpret output from SPSS for a factorial analysis;
* how to effectively communicate results from your data in writing;
* various required and supplementary statistical analyses that facilitate better and more complete interpretations of your data.

KEY TERMS

between-groups variance	levels
carry-over effects	main effects
cells	marginal means
degrees of freedom	mean squares
effect sizes	post-hoc analyses
F ratio	simple effects
factors	sums of squares
interactions	within-groups variance

10.1 **INTRODUCTION**

We often want to determine if there is a relationship or difference between two or more populations. We use samples to draw conclusions about populations in order to determine if there is enough evidence to suggest that something that is true for our sample will also be true of the population. In other words, we want to know if our independent variable has reliably affected our dependent variable. Since we never expect samples to be exactly alike, in order to test our hypotheses we not only need to know if a difference exists but also whether any differences we find are due to our independent variable or just due to random variation. An analysis of variance (ANOVA) allows us to evaluate mean differences between two or more populations.

The term analysis of variance describes to us how ANOVA works. Specifically, the ANOVA compares the variability among means between groups to the variability in scores that make up each mean within each group. This leads to two possible sources of variation. Between-groups variance is variability in our means between the groups we are comparing. It is also referred to as treatment variance, since we hope that a majority of this variance is due to our manipulation of the independent variable. Within-groups variance is variability in the scores that make up each of our group means that is due to individual differences or factors that should affect all groups equally. It is also referred to as error variance, not because it is caused by error (though it can be), but because this variance is outside of the experimenter's control and is from a source other than which we are interested in (i.e. our experimental manipulation).

The most basic form of ANOVA, a one-way ANOVA, allows us to explore variations between means when we have one independent variable and two or more groups that we want to compare. However, the psychological phenomena we find interesting enough to examine often occur as a result of interplay between multiple factors. For example, we may want to explore whether expert testimony (present or not present) helps people distinguish forensic interview quality (poor, typical or good). The two independent variables, then, are presence of expert testimony and quality of forensic interview. The dependent measure would be mock jurors' ratings of interview quality.

There are many methods available to you depending on how you organise your data, your research methodology, and so on. A factorial ANOVA provides one method of examining such an association. This design is used when you have two or more independent variables and a dependent variable that is a continuous measure. The independent variables are referred to as factors, hence the name *factorial* ANOVA. You can have several conditions within each independent variable. Conditions within an independent variable are called levels. You can then compare each level of a factor to all levels in other factors. In the expert testimony example above, we have two factors (presence of expert testimony and interview quality). Presence of expert testimony has two levels (either present or not) and interview quality has three levels (poor, typical or good).

10.2 **ASSUMPTIONS**

In order to be confident that you obtain reliable results, there are a few assumptions for factorial ANOVA that are similar to other parametric statistics.

- Normality: the dependent variable is normally distributed within each group.

- Homogeneity of variance: within-group variances are approximately equal for each group.

- Observed scores are independent: knowing one observation does not allow prediction of another observation. In other words, there is no effect of one observation on another.

ANOVA is fairly robust to violations of the first two assumptions, especially when your sample sizes among groups are equal. The final assumption, however, leads to serious consequences when violated unless you are running a within-subjects design. If however, violations of assumptions make it unsafe to proceed with an ANOVA, alternatives are available. These include transforming your data or using an alternative non-parametric test. These alternatives are not discussed in depth in this chapter (for interested readers, see Howell, 2010). Checking assumptions is not something that is usually reported in a manuscript unless serious violations were apparent that caused the researcher to use an alternative method that would require further explanation. It is assumed that the researcher has explored the possibility of assumption violations and has responded appropriately.

10.2.1 **Example**

The weapons focus effect refers to a witness's decreased ability to attend to external stimuli during a crime when a weapon is present. Surrounding details that could be important in an investigation (e.g. perpetrator characteristics) are overridden by an intense focus on the weapon. Suppose you want to examine two potential factors in the effect: weapon type (i.e. a gun or a knife) and weapon position consisting of three different threat levels. You categorise high threat as pointed at someone, medium threat as in a hand but not directed at anyone, and lowest threat as visible but not in the perpetrator's hand. The dependent variable is the number of correctly identified target features (out of 10) of the perpetrator. This type of design would require a 2×3 factorial ANOVA with 2 factors. Factor 1, weapon type, consists of two levels. Factor 2, weapon position, consists of three levels. You can then pair each level of weapon type with that of weapon position. Each level that corresponds to another level is referred to as a cell. We will use this example to demonstrate the remaining concepts in this chapter.

10.3 TYPES OF FACTORIAL ANOVAS

There are three different types of factorial ANOVAs.

10.3.1 Between-subjects design

In a between-subjects design completely different groups of individuals for each condition of the experiment are used. Each participant is assigned to only one level of an independent variable in the experiment. The total number of groups (or cells) needed is determined by multiplying the number of levels in each of the factors. For the weapon focus study example, subjects should be randomly assigned to one of six different conditions (see Table 10.1). Assuming we want at least 30 subjects per cell, then, we would need a total of 180 subjects for the study.

10.3.2 Within-subjects design

Within-subjects designs use the same participants for all levels of the experiment. Using this type of design in our example would mean that each group of participants serving in cell 1 (Gun; High Threat) would serve in the other five cells as well (see Table 10.2). The order of the different conditions would need to be carefully counterbalanced. If they are not, then effects in the study could be due to carry-over effects. For example, if we always expose participants to the gun condition first, they could habituate and when the knife is shown the effect of the weapon could diminish.

Table 10.1 An example between-subjects design using weapon type and weapon position as between-subjects variables

		Weapon position		
		High threat	Medium threat	Lowest threat
Weapon type	Gun	Group$_1$	Group$_2$	Group$_3$
	Knife	Group$_4$	Group$_5$	Group$_6$

Table 10.2   An example within-subjects design using weapon type and weapon position as within-subjects variables

Weapon type		Weapon position		
		High threat	Medium threat	Lowest threat
	Gun	Group$_1$	Group$_1$	Group$_1$
	Knife	Group$_1$	Group$_1$	Group$_1$

Table 10.3   An example mixed design using weapon type as a within-subjects variable and weapon position as a between-subjects variable

Weapon type		Weapon position		
		High threat	Medium threat	Lowest threat
	Gun	Group$_1$	Group$_2$	Group$_3$
	Knife	Group$_1$	Group$_2$	Group$_3$

In other cases, it may be entirely inappropriate to use a within-subjects design. For example, if you are administering new drug choices to your participants to determine effects on depression levels, you could not administer each drug to all your participants. If you found an effect, you would not be able to tell which drug (or combination of drugs) produced the effect.

10.3.3 Mixed design

Mixed designs use a mixture of between- and within-subjects variables for the independent variables. For example, we could treat weapon position as a between-subjects factor and weapon type as a within-subjects variable (see Table 10.3). Again, counterbalancing the order of conditions is critical.

We will focus primarily on the between-subjects design with two factors. More complex designs are possible and will be easier to grasp following an understanding of more basic factorial designs.

10.4 MAIN EFFECTS AND INTERACTIONS

Using factorial ANOVA, you can examine the main effects of two or more individual independent variables. Main effects are the effects each factor has on the dependent variable, alone and in isolation from other independent variables.

You can also detect interactions among variables. An interaction occurs when the effects of one variable change according to the levels of another variable. Interactions can only be detected when the variables are examined in combination.

Main effects and interactions are tested by hypotheses and you can have as many main effects as there are independent variables. We will continue with our example. For our purposes, we have three hypotheses to test: two hypotheses for main effects (one for each of our factors) and one for an interaction. The number of hypotheses you can have for interactions will correspond to the number of all possible combinations of your independent variables.

In order to determine the effect of our factors (weapon type and weapon position) we will measure how well individuals are able to identify 10 target perpetrator characteristics. Table 10.4 contains the raw scores for each of our participants, $N =$ 18. Of course, we would have very low power using such a small sample size, but since we will be performing calculations with our data by hand we will keep observations to a minimum.

Right away we can see that there some numerical differences. When we look at each of the row means we see those in the gun condition (M_{A1}) did worse than those in the knife condition (M_{A2}), regardless of weapon position. When we look at the column means, we see those exposed to the highest level of threat (M_{B1}) did worse than the other two threat levels (M_{B2} or M_{B3}), regardless of weapon type. Looking at marginal means is a good place to start exploring and understanding your data. However, not every participant will respond to our manipulations in exactly the

Table 10.4   Raw scores for $N = 18$ in a 2 (weapon type) × 3 (weapon position) between-subjects design

Weapon type	Weapon position			
	High threat	Medium threat	Lowest threat	
Gun	4	4	5	
	6	4	4	
	4	7	6	$M_{A1} = 4.89$
	$M_1 = 4.67$	$M_2 = 5$	$M_3 = 5$	
Knife	3	5	7	
	4	6	9	
	4	5	8	$M_{A2} = 5.66$
	$M_4 = 3.67$	$M_5 = 5.33$	$M_6 = 8$	
	$M_{B1} = 4.17$	$M_{B2} = 5.17$	$M_{B3} = 6.5$	$G = 5.28$

Table 10.5   ANOVA notation and terminology

Notation	Meaning
Σ	Sum up everything that follows
X_{ijk}	Individual scores that are denoted by their row (i), column (j), and individual place (k). For example $X_{2,3,2}$ would correspond in our example to the second individual in row 2, column 3 (i.e., the subject whose data value is '9')
$A_k, B_k, C_k, \dots$ etc.	Factor levels. In our example, A corresponds to weapon type. Since this factor has two levels, $A1$ is designated as our "gun condition" and $A2$ as our knife condition. Likewise, B corresponds to our factor of weapon position, with 3 possible levels within it
M_i	Means. Means with a single number subscript (e.g., M_1) are numbered based on cells. For example, M_1 corresponds to Factor A, level 1 and Factor B, level 1; M_2 corresponds to Factor A, level 1, and Factor B, level 2, etc. Means with a letter and number subscript (e.g. M_{A2}) are labeled corresponding to factor (A, B, C, etc.,) and the level of that factor
G	The grand mean. This is the mean we get from averaging all the scores in our data
SS	Sums of squares

same way, so variability from each participant and group of participants is expected. In essence, what we want to know is whether more of the variance in the responses is due to individual variation (error variance) or from our experimental manipulation. To investigate this we must calculate the variability from the different sources within our data.

10.5 CALCULATIONS

Statistical notation is necessary to shorten formulas and to convey concepts more simply. Notation also varies between different texts and information sources. Table 10.5 has the basic notation you will need for the calculations; any further notation is explained as introduced.

10.6 THE *F* RATIO

We cannot compare the differences between means directly as we do with other statistical tests (i.e. *t*-tests) because it is not possible to calculate a sample mean difference between more than two samples. Instead, we analyse variance. The overall goal of our calculations is to obtain an F ratio that we can use to test our hypotheses. The F ratio is a measure of variance between our sample means divided by the variance in our sample expected by chance alone.

Variances in ANOVA are called mean squares. The numerator is referred to as $MS_{between}$ and sometimes as MS_{group} or $MS_{treat.}$ The denominator is referred to as MS_{error} and sometimes as $MS_{within.}$ Since the F ratio is computed from two variances it is always a positive number. Since the numerator is our between-subjects variance, we should expect the ratio to be close to 1 if the null hypothesis is supported. This indicates that there is just as much variability due to individual differences as there is from our treatment. If our independent variable(s) really did have an effect, our ratio should be noticeably larger than 1. How much larger? That's what significance testing will tell us.

There are several calculations necessary to obtain our F ratio. A summary table like the one in Table 10.6 helps to organise the results of all our calculations. Statistical software also produces a summary table that breaks down the factorial ANOVA. Though all the terms may not make sense yet, after walking through each calculation you will be able to complete the table.

We can start looking at variability by calculating sums of squares (SS) from different sources within our data. Sums of squares are given their name based on their function, which is to square the deviations that fall about the mean and sum them up. SS is calculated for formulas more basic than factorial ANOVA but may not have been referred to as such. For example, you have calculated SS before when calculating the variance, which is the sum of squares divided by $n - 1$. The same formula is used here, only we will be dividing by degrees of freedom (df). Degrees of freedom are the number of scores we are working with that are free to vary. More specifically, they represent the maximum number of components in a formula that we can vary before our statistic is fully determined. For example, if we have a sample size of 3 and our scores are 2, 3 and 4, then our mean is equal to 3. We can only change the value of two of these scores before the final score is determined to maintain our statistic ($M = 3$).

Table 10.6 ANOVA summary table

Source	SS	df	MS	F	Criteria for decision
Between A					
Between B					
Interaction (A × B)					
Within (error)					
Total					

Conceptual formulas are given below to help demonstrate the underlying logic of calculations. These formulas are used in the examples given. For each formula we discuss in the remainder of this chapter, an example using our own weapon data is included directly below it in a box. Most of the formulas given are intended for use when you have a balanced design (i.e. when each of your conditions have the same sample size). Since this is rarely the case, use of alternative computational formulas is often required (for interested readers, see Howell, 2010).

For factorial ANOVA, there are four formulas for sum of squares to partition off variability.

$$SS_{Total} = \Sigma(X_i - G)^2$$

where X_i = each individual raw score. SS_{Total} gives us our total variability in our data and is calculated by subtracting the grand mean (G) from each individual score, squaring it, and then adding up all the squares.

$$
\begin{aligned}
SS_{Total} &= (4 - 5.28)^2 + (6 - 5.28)^2 + (4 - 5.28)^2 + (4 - 5.28)^2 + (4 - 5.28)^2 \\
&+ (7 - 5.28)^2 + (5 - 5.28)^2 + (4 - 5.28)^2 + (6 - 5.28)^2 + (3 - 5.28)^2 \\
&+ (4 - 5.28)^2 + (4 - 5.28)^2 + (5 - 5.28)^2 + (6 - 5.28)^2 + (5 - 5.28)^2 \\
&+ (7 - 5.28)^2 + (9 - 5.28)^2 + (8 - 5.28)^2 = 45.6112
\end{aligned}
$$

$$SS_{within} = \Sigma (X - M_i)^2$$

where M_i = each cell mean. SS_{within} for a factor is calculated by adding all the sums of squares for cells by using each individual score and subtracting the cell mean that corresponds to that individual.

$$
\begin{aligned}
SS_{within} &= (4 - 4.67)^2 + (6 - 4.67)^2 + (4 - 4.67)^2 + (4 - 5)^2 + (4 - 5)^2 + (7 - 5)^2 \\
&+ (5 - 5)^2 + (4 - 5)^2 + (6 - 5)^2 + (3 - 3.67)^2 + (4 - 3.67)^2 + (4 - 3.67)^2 \\
&+ (5 - 5.33)^2 + (6 - 5.33)^2 + (5 - 5.33)^2 + (7 - 8)^2 + (9 - 8)^2 + (8 - 8)^2 \\
&= 14.001
\end{aligned}
$$

$$SS_{between} = n_i \Sigma(M_{ij} - G)^2$$

where n_i = the number of participants in each level of the factor; M_{ij} = the mean for each level; and G = the grand mean. $SS_{between}$ is calculated for each independent variable by using the mean from each level of an independent variable and subtracting the grand mean for each. This is calculated for each factor and for the interaction as well.

$$
\begin{aligned}
&SS_{between}: \\
&SS_{A(weapon\ type)} = 9[(4.89 - 5.28)^2 + (5.66 - 5.28)^2] = 2.6685 \\
&SS_{B(weapon\ position)} = 6[(4.17 - 5.28)^2 + (5.17 - 5.28)^2 + (6.5 - 5.28)^2] = 16.3956
\end{aligned}
$$

Table 10.7

df	Formula	Our example
df_{Total}	$N - 1$	$18 - 1 = 17$
$df_{between}$ (calculated for each IV)	$k_i - 1$ (where k_i is the number of groups for a factor)	$df_A = 2 - 1 = 1$ $df_B = 3 - 1 = 2$
df_{within}	$N - ab$ (where a is the number of levels in factor A and b is the number of levels in factor B	$18 - (3 \times 2) = 12$
$df_{interaction}$	$(df_A)(df_B)$	$2 \times 1 = 2$

$$SS_{interaction} = SS_{Total} - (\Sigma SS_{between} + SS_{within})$$

$SS_{interaction}$ is calculated simply by adding up all of our $SS_{between}$ values, adding this value to our SS_{within} value, and subtracting the sum of this combined value from our SS_{total}:

$$SS_{A \times B} = 45.6112 - (2.6685 + 16.3956 + 14.001) = 12.5461$$

Now that we have all of the sums of squares we need we can calculate our variances. In order to convert our sums of squares into variances we must first divide each SS by a corresponding df. The result will give us our mean squares, which are the final values we will need to calculate our F ratio. Calculations for each df are listed in Table 10.7.

We will need both the numerator ($MS_{between}$) and the denominator (MS_{within}) of our F ratio. Since we need an F ratio for each of our tests for main effects, we will need an $MS_{between}$ for each of our factors as well as for our interactions. For MS_{within} this value is based on all scores and the mean of all groups. Therefore, the same value is used in all calculations of F ratios. Keep in mind, since values are corrected by df, they are no longer representing the variances in our sample but are instead intended as estimates of the population.

$$MS_{between} = \frac{SS_{between}}{df_{between}}$$

$$MS_{between(A)} = \frac{2.6685}{1} = 2.6685$$

$$MS_{between(B)} = \frac{16.3956}{2} = 8.1978$$

$$= MS_{interaction} = \frac{SS_{interaction}}{df_{interaction}}$$

$$MS_{A \times B} = \frac{12.5461}{2} = 6.2731$$

$$MS_{within} = \frac{SS_{within}}{df_{within}}$$

$$MS_{within} = \frac{14.001}{12} = 1.1668$$

Finally, we have all the information we need to calculate our F ratios.

$$F_{main} = \frac{MS_{between}}{MS_{within}}$$

$$F_A = \frac{2.6685}{1.1668} = 2.287$$

$$F_B = \frac{8.1978}{1.1668} = 7.0259$$

$$F_{interaction} = \frac{MS_{interaction}}{MS_{within}}$$

$$F_{interaction} = \frac{6.2731}{1.1668} = 5.3763$$

10.7 THE *F* DISTRIBUTION AND *F* TABLE

Now that we have our F ratios, what do these values mean? In order to determine the significance of our obtained F values we must compare them to a predetermined criterion. This is where our F distribution becomes useful. We can look at our obtained F to see where it falls on the entire F distribution. See Figure 10.1 for an example of an F distribution.

Our goal is to compare our obtained F to a critical F on the F distribution. The F distribution is an asymmetrical distribution determined by two sources of degrees of freedom (between and within). The shape of the distribution changes with each

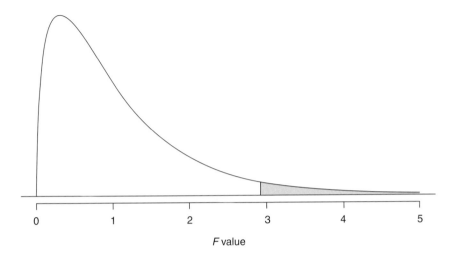

Figure 10.1 *F distribution*

df combination (a smaller *df* leads to a more spread out distribution), leading to a different *F* distribution for every combination. The *x*-axis of the distribution represents a continuous distribution of *F* values, while the *y*-axis represents the probability of obtaining that value (*p* value).

The probability we deem acceptable is determined by alpha. Using this, the distribution tells you how likely it is that you will obtain a given *F* based on chance alone given certain degrees of freedoms. Each value of *F* is associated with a precise *p* value and larger *F* values are associated with smaller *p* values. This is because the farther out toward the tail of the distribution your observation lies, the lower the probability that this value would have occurred by chance alone. In essence, the distribution allows us to put a numerical value to the question: If our null hypothesis is true and there really are no differences between our groups in the population, how likely is it that we would obtain such an *F* as we did in our data? The less likely it is, the more comfortable we are with rejecting the null hypothesis.

The *F* table (Table 10.8) shows the critical *F* (the minimum *F* value we need to reject the null) for both 0.05 and 0.01 probabilities. The degrees of freedom are listed across the top (*df* numerator) and left side (*df* denominator) of the table. Simply locate the point at which your *df* numerator value and *df* denominator value intersect. The first value (printed in bold) is the value when $\alpha = 0.05$, the value directly beneath corresponds to $\alpha = 0.01$. Notice that the *F* critical when $\alpha = 0.05$ is smaller than the *F* critical when $\alpha = 0.01$. This is because, as mentioned, smaller probabilities are associated with larger *F* values. You can then compare your obtained *F* value to the critical *F* found in the table. If your obtained *F* value exceeds your

Table 10.8 The F distribution. The top value in each row is the necessary F value to reject the hypothesis at $p = 0.05$. The second value is for $p = 0.01$.

df	161.45	199.50	215.71	224.58	230.16	233.99	236.77	238.88	240.54	241.88	248.01	251.77	254.19
1	**161.45**	**199.50**	**215.71**	**224.58**	**230.16**	**233.99**	**236.77**	**238.88**	**240.54**	**241.88**	**248.01**	**251.77**	**254.19**
	4052.18	4999.50	5403.35	5624.58	5763.65	5858.99	5928.36	5981.07	6022.47	6055.85	6208.73	6302.52	6362.68
2	**18.51**	**19.00**	**19.16**	**19.25**	**19.30**	**19.33**	**19.35**	**19.37**	**19.38**	**19.40**	**19.45**	**19.48**	**19.49**
	98.50	99.00	99.17	99.25	99.30	99.33	99.36	99.37	99.39	99.40	99.45	99.48	99.50
3	**10.13**	**9.55**	**9.28**	**9.12**	**9.01**	**8.94**	**8.89**	**8.85**	**8.81**	**8.79**	**8.66**	**8.58**	**8.53**
	34.12	30.82	29.46	28.71	28.24	27.91	27.67	27.49	27.35	27.23	26.69	26.35	26.14
4	**7.71**	**6.94**	**6.59**	**6.39**	**6.26**	**6.16**	**6.09**	**6.04**	**6.00**	**5.96**	**5.80**	**5.70**	**5.63**
	21.20	18.00	16.69	15.98	15.52	15.21	14.98	14.80	14.66	14.55	14.02	13.69	13.47
5	**6.61**	**5.79**	**5.41**	**5.19**	**5.05**	**4.95**	**4.88**	**4.82**	**4.77**	**4.74**	**4.56**	**4.44**	**4.37**
	16.26	13.27	12.06	11.39	10.97	10.67	10.46	10.29	10.16	10.05	9.55	9.24	9.03
6	**5.99**	**5.14**	**4.76**	**4.53**	**4.39**	**4.28**	**4.21**	**4.15**	**4.10**	**4.06**	**3.87**	**3.75**	**3.67**
	13.75	10.92	9.78	9.15	8.75	8.47	8.26	8.10	7.98	7.87	7.40	7.09	6.89
7	**5.59**	**4.74**	**4.35**	**4.12**	**3.97**	**3.87**	**3.79**	**3.73**	**3.68**	**3.64**	**3.44**	**3.32**	**3.23**
	12.25	9.55	8.45	7.85	7.46	7.19	6.99	6.84	6.72	6.62	6.16	5.86	5.66
8	**5.32**	**4.46**	**4.07**	**3.84**	**3.69**	**3.58**	**3.50**	**3.44**	**3.39**	**3.35**	**3.15**	**3.02**	**2.93**
	11.26	8.65	7.59	7.01	6.63	6.37	6.18	6.03	5.91	5.81	5.36	5.07	4.87
9	**5.12**	**4.26**	**3.86**	**3.63**	**3.48**	**3.37**	**3.29**	**3.23**	**3.18**	**3.14**	**2.94**	**2.80**	**2.71**
	10.56	8.02	6.99	6.42	6.06	5.80	5.61	5.47	5.35	5.26	4.81	4.52	4.32
10	**4.96**	**4.10**	**3.71**	**3.48**	**3.33**	**3.22**	**3.14**	**3.07**	**3.02**	**2.98**	**2.77**	**2.64**	**2.54**
	10.04	7.56	6.55	5.99	5.64	5.39	5.20	5.06	4.94	4.85	4.41	4.12	3.92
11	**4.84**	**3.98**	**3.59**	**3.36**	**3.20**	**3.09**	**3.01**	**2.95**	**2.90**	**2.85**	**2.65**	**2.51**	**2.41**
	9.65	7.21	6.22	5.67	5.32	5.07	4.89	4.74	4.63	4.54	4.10	3.81	3.61
12	**4.75**	**3.88**	**3.49**	**3.26**	**3.11**	**3.00**	**2.91**	**2.85**	**2.80**	**2.75**	**2.54**	**2.40**	**2.30**
	9.33	6.93	5.95	5.41	5.06	4.82	4.64	4.50	4.39	4.30	3.86	3.57	3.37
13	**4.67**	**3.81**	**3.41**	**3.18**	**3.03**	**2.92**	**2.83**	**2.77**	**2.71**	**2.67**	**2.46**	**2.31**	**2.21**
	9.07	6.70	5.74	5.21	4.86	4.62	4.44	4.30	4.19	4.10	3.66	3.38	3.18

df	1	2	3	4	5	6	7	8	9	10	20	50	1000
14	**4.60**	**3.74**	**3.34**	**3.11**	**2.96**	**2.85**	**2.76**	**2.70**	**2.65**	**2.60**	**2.39**	**2.24**	**2.14**
	8.86	6.51	5.56	5.04	4.69	4.46	4.28	4.14	4.03	3.94	3.51	3.22	3.02
15	**4.54**	**3.68**	**3.29**	**3.06**	**2.90**	**2.79**	**2.71**	**2.64**	**2.59**	**2.54**	**2.33**	**2.18**	**2.07**
	8.68	6.36	5.42	4.89	4.56	4.32	4.14	4.00	3.89	3.80	3.37	3.08	2.88
20	**4.35**	**3.49**	**3.10**	**2.87**	**2.71**	**2.60**	**2.51**	**2.45**	**2.39**	**2.35**	**2.12**	**1.97**	**1.85**
	8.10	5.85	4.94	4.43	4.10	3.87	3.70	3.56	3.46	3.37	2.94	2.64	2.43
30	**4.17**	**3.32**	**2.92**	**2.69**	**2.53**	**2.42**	**2.33**	**2.27**	**2.21**	**2.16**	**1.93**	**1.76**	**1.63**
	7.56	5.39	4.51	4.02	3.70	3.47	3.30	3.17	3.07	2.98	2.55	2.25	2.02
40	**4.08**	**3.23**	**2.84**	**2.61**	**2.45**	**2.34**	**2.25**	**2.18**	**2.12**	**2.08**	**1.84**	**1.66**	**1.52**
	7.31	5.18	4.31	3.83	3.51	3.29	3.12	2.99	2.89	2.80	2.37	2.06	1.82
50	**4.03**	**3.18**	**2.79**	**2.56**	**2.40**	**2.29**	**2.20**	**2.13**	**2.07**	**2.03**	**1.78**	**1.60**	**1.45**
	7.17	5.06	4.20	3.72	3.41	3.19	3.02	2.89	2.78	2.70	2.27	1.95	1.70
75	**3.97**	**3.12**	**2.73**	**2.49**	**2.34**	**2.22**	**2.13**	**2.06**	**2.01**	**1.96**	**1.71**	**1.52**	**1.35**
	6.99	4.90	4.05	3.58	3.27	3.05	2.89	2.76	2.65	2.57	2.13	1.81	1.53
100	**3.94**	**3.09**	**2.70**	**2.46**	**2.31**	**2.19**	**2.10**	**2.03**	**1.97**	**1.93**	**1.68**	**1.48**	**1.30**
	6.90	4.82	3.98	3.51	3.21	2.99	2.82	2.69	2.59	2.50	2.07	1.74	1.45
1000	**3.85**	**3.00**	**2.61**	**2.38**	**2.22**	**2.11**	**2.02**	**1.95**	**1.89**	**1.84**	**1.58**	**1.36**	**1.11**
	6.66	4.63	3.80	3.34	3.04	2.82	2.66	2.53	2.43	2.34	1.90	1.54	1.16
df	1	2	3	4	5	6	7	8	9	10	20	50	1000
1	**161.45**	**199.50**	**215.71**	**224.58**	**230.16**	**233.99**	**236.77**	**238.88**	**240.54**	**241.88**	**248.01**	**251.77**	**254.19**
	4052.18	4999.50	5403.35	5624.58	5763.65	5858.99	5928.36	5981.07	6022.47	6055.85	6208.73	6302.52	6362.68
2	**18.51**	**19.00**	**19.16**	**19.25**	**19.30**	**19.33**	**19.35**	**19.37**	**19.38**	**19.40**	**19.45**	**19.48**	**19.49**
	98.50	99.00	99.17	99.25	99.30	99.33	99.36	99.37	99.39	99.40	99.45	99.48	99.50

To find whether an F value is significant you need to know both the degrees of freedom of the numerator and the degrees of freedom of the denominator. Usually these are the degrees of freedom of the model and of the residuals, respectively, but for certain hypotheses this need not be the case. Suppose for 45 subjects that we had divided them into five groups. Our model would therefore have four degrees of freedom (four dummy variables to represent the five values). The residuals would have 40 degrees of freedom. The critical values are 2.61 and 3.83 for $p = 0.05$ and $p = 0.01$, respectively.

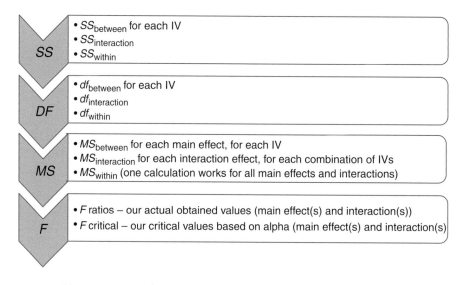

Figure 10.2   Steps to create the *F* ratio

critical *F* value then you know the probability of obtaining this value is less than what was specified by alpha. You can reject the null hypothesis and use this finding as evidence that your independent variable(s) created differences in the population.

Once we have calculated all of the critical *F* values, we are ready to begin interpreting our *F* ratio. A summary of steps from our calculations is listed in Figure 10.2.

10.8 INTERPRETING *F*

Now that we know how to calculate and make sense of our *F* values, we can test our main effects and interaction. Let's transfer all the information from our calculations into our summary table, Table 10.9, so that it is organised.

To test our first main effect we want to determine whether there are no differences in the population for weapon type ($\mu_{\text{Gun}} = \mu_{\text{Knife}}$). Let's test for this main effect first. $F(1,12)_{\text{obtained}} = 2.287 < F_{\text{critical}}(1,12) = 4.75$. Since our critical value exceeds our obtained value, we will fail to reject our null hypothesis. It appears there is not enough evidence to suggest that weapon type makes a difference. There is not a main effect of weapon type.

Our second main effect is testing whether there are no differences in the population for weapon position ($\mu_{\text{High Threat 1}} = \mu_{\text{Medium Threat 2}} = \mu_{\text{Lowest Threat 3}}$). $F(2,12)_{\text{obtained}} = 7.0259 > F(2,12)_{\text{critical}} = 3.88$. In this case, our F_{obtained} has exceeded our F_{critical} and we will reject the null hypothesis. There is a main effect of weapon position.

Table 10.9   Weapons data ANOVA summary table

Source	SS	df	MS	F	Criteria for decision
Weapon type	2.6685	1	2.6685	2.287	4.75
Weapon position	13.3956	2	8.1978	7.0259	3.88
Interaction (weapon type × weapon position)	12.5461	2	6.2731	5.3763	3.88
Within (error)	14.001	12	1.1668		
Total	45.6112	17			

Finally, we want to determine whether there is an interaction in the population between weapon type and weapon position ($\mu_{\text{weapon type}}$ does not vary by $\mu_{\text{weapon position}}$). In other words, these variables do not work together to affect perpetrator identification differently. If an interaction effect is found we will have to go back and make sense of our main effects.

There is an interaction between weapon type and weapon position, $F(2,12)_{\text{obtained}} = 5.3763 > F(2,12)_{\text{critical}} = 3.88$. For now, we will concentrate on our main effects as if there were no interaction and return to the interaction later.

10.9 INTERPRETING MAIN EFFECTS AND POST-HOC TESTS

The F tests tell us that there are differences but, because they compare all of the means for levels in an independent variable at once, they cannot tell you where the differences are coming from. Any of the following combinations between levels is possible ($\mu_1 \neq \mu_2 \neq \mu_3; \mu_1 \neq \mu_2 = \mu_3; \mu_1 = \mu_2 \neq \mu_3; \mu_1 = \mu_3 \neq \mu_2$).

When main effects are tested we are looking at only one independent variable and completely ignoring the other independent variable(s). If a main effect is detected, we use post-hoc analyses to determine which levels of the independent variable caused the difference. There are several types of post-hoc analyses that can be used, and each are associated with levels of conservativeness that are arguably too strict or too lax depending on one's perspective. Each statistical test is associated with error (type I and type II). Our α level determines the level of type I error we are willing to make. Table 10.10 gives three commonly used post-hoc tests that can be used to detect differences when a significant F value is detected, each controlling α, and thus type I error rates, differently. Of course, just like our F table we need tables to compare our critical values obtained from each comparison and the type of post-hoc analysis you decide to use will determine the type of table

Table 10.10   Example post hoc tests

Test	Conservativeness
Fisher's LSD	Least conservative; α is not adjusted so type I error rates are inflated with each comparison. For example, if α is set at 0.05 then each obtained value is compared to 0.05.
Multi-stage significance testing	Somewhat conservative; type I error rates are adjusted according to the number of comparisons for each comparison. For example, if α is set at 0.05 and there are four comparisons, then the lowest obtained p-value will be compared to 0.05/4, the next lowest would be compared to 0.05/3, and the next to 0.05/2, etc.
Bonferroni correction	Conservative; type II error rates are inflated with each comparison, adjusted $\alpha = \alpha$/divided by the number of comparisons. For example, if there are four comparisons and α is set at 0.05, then each obtained value must be compared to a critical p value of α/4 or 0.0125.

you need. Since obtaining probability values are the goal of such tests and these are available automatically with statistical software, we will forgo hand calculations of post-hoc tests and come back to them later when we discuss their use in SPSS. There are many other types of post-hoc analyses that are not discussed in this chapter.

We do not need to conduct a post-hoc analysis on our weapon type variable for two reasons. First, there was no significant main effect for weapon type. Since a non-significant F indicates that there were no significant differences that the overall model was able to detect, it would not make sense to try to detect differences in simpler analyses. This is not to say that you cannot obtain a non-significant F ratio and then go on to produce a significant difference between two or more levels in a post-hoc test. Since post-hoc tests are testing differences between only two groups at a time, it is still possible for this to happen. The second reason we do not need to conduct follow up tests for this variable is that it has only two levels. Since our weapon type consisted of only two levels, even if a significant main effect existed it would not be necessary to conduct a post-hoc analysis because we would know which group differed from which and also, simply by looking at the means, the direction of this difference. For our example, we would need to conduct a post-hoc analysis on our weapon position variable if we wanted to determine which of the three different positions were different. However, we must take our interactions into account when we interpret our main effects.

10.10 **INTERACTIONS**

Since main effects only analyse one independent variable independent of other independent variables, how do we interpret these effects when we have an interaction? In the case of a two-way ANOVA, an interaction suggests that both independent variables are affecting the dependent variable. Now what? In our case, we have an interaction that tells us that weapon type is in fact playing a role in the ability to identify a perpetrator. How can this be if our main effect for weapon type was not significant? Recall that when an interaction occurs it indicates that at least one of our independent variables is having an effect on our dependent variable, but only under certain levels or conditions of other independent variables. This being the case we can only interpret main effects in light of our interaction. In our case, since we have a non-significant effect of weapon type and we have a significant main effect of weapon position we must conclude that weapon position is affecting the ability to identify a perpetrator differently when a gun versus a knife is used.

Often the ability to conceptualise an interaction is easiest when a graph is used. A line graph is one easy way to visualise an interaction because, when an interaction exists, lines will not be parallel. Figure 10.3 illustrates a line graph of our interaction.

Notice that the difference between weapon type is greatest in the condition of least threat. Thus, it appears that when the lowest level of threat is used, the ability to identify the perpetrator is much greater when a knife is used instead of a gun.

Analysing the **simple effects** is one way of interpreting effects when an interaction is present. Simple effects provide us with an advantage over merely cautioning

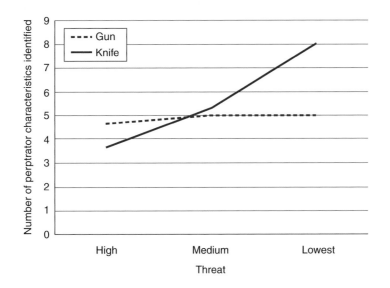

Figure 10.3　Interaction of weapon type and weapon position

readers that main effects are qualified by an interaction. They tell us the impact of one of our independent variables at just one level of another independent variable. For example, perhaps we want to know the effect of weapon position only when a knife is used. To do this we compare our cell means to see if one is significantly different from another. In our example, there are five possible simple effects we could test: (1) weapon type at high threat (4.67 = 3.67), (2) weapon type at medium threat (5 = 5.33), (3) weapon type at lowest threat (5 = 8), (4) weapon position for guns only (4.67 = 5 = 5) and (5) weapon position for knives only (3.67 = 5.33 = 8). These are demonstrated in Figure 10.4.

It is important to keep in mind that any time we run multiple statistical tests, we have a risk of error. The amount of error we are willing to accept is determined by our alpha level. Of course, when we run multiple tests each is susceptible to the amount of error we specified. Thus, with each test we run, our chance of error compounds. Like post-hoc tests, tests for simple effects are usually not *a priori*. We conduct them after we discover an interaction. If an interaction didn't exist, there would be no reason to conduct simple effect analyses, reporting the main effects would be sufficient. However, unlike post-hoc tests, we are not controlling for error with each test we conduct. Therefore, we only want to calculate simple effects between conditions that we hypothesise will play a part in our interaction, so that compounded error can be minimised. We will calculate the simple effects for all pairs. However, there appears to be less cause to test for simple effects between pairs 2 and 4 as these cell means appear similar. In order to refrain from jumping ahead and testing simple effects only for means that look really different (or developing post-hoc explanations for why they might be different in order to rationalise such a decision), one suggestion is to anticipate an interaction and develop some *a priori*

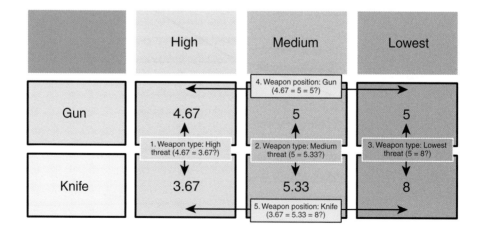

Figure 10.4   Simple effects for weapon type and weapon position

Table 10.11   Simple effects ANOVA summary chart with terms used in weapons data ANOVA

Source	SS	df	MS	F	Criteria for decision
WeaponType@HT		1			**4.75**
WeaponType@MT		1			**4.75**
WeaponType@LT		1			**4.75**
WeaponPosition@Gun		2			**3.88**
WeaponPosition@Knife		2			**3.88**
Within (Error)	**14.001**	12	**1.1668**		
Total					

hypotheses about simple effects you would find interesting and that make sense for your design should such an interaction surface.

To test for simple effects we perform F tests as we did for our main effects and interactions, only this time we ignore other effects not of immediate interest (e.g. our deviation terms = cell mean – marginal mean). Degrees of freedom and error terms remain the same so we do not have to recalculate these terms. Table 10.11 contains the values that we do not have to change. To fill in the rest of the chart all we need to calculate are our SS terms for the three simple effects of interest and use these to plug in the numbers for the rest of the chart.

$$SS_{\text{weapon type@HT}} = 3[(4.67 - 4.17)^2 + (3.67 - 4.17)^2] = 1.5$$
$$SS_{\text{weapon type@MT}} = 3[(5 - 5.17)^2 + (5.33 - 5.17)^2] = 0.1635$$
$$SS_{\text{weapon type@LT}} = 3[(5 - 6.5)^2 + (8 - 6.5)^2] = 13.5$$
$$SS_{\text{weapon position@gun}} = 3[(4.67 - 4.89)^2 + (5 - 4.89)^2 + (5 - 4.89)^2] = 0.2178$$
$$SS_{\text{weapon position@knife}} = 3[3.67 - 5.66)^2 + (5.33 - 5.66) + (8 - 5.66)^2] = 28.63$$

Once we have our SS for each of simple effects, we can use these and our remaining dfs to calculate the rest of the terms. The completed terms can be found in Table 10.12.

Looking at our simple effects, we have to re-evaluate our interpretation of our main effects. Initially, if we looked at our main effects only, we would have concluded that weapon position has an effect on perpetrator identity, while weapon type has no effect. However, the interaction indicates that weapon type does have an effect under low levels of threat. In addition, weapon position does not seem to have an effect when a gun is used.

Table 10.12   ANOVA summary table of simple effects for weapons data

Source	SS	df	MS	F	Criteria for decision
WeaponType@HT	1.5	1	1.5	1.29	4.75
WeaponType@MT	0.1635	1	0.1635	0.14	4.75
WeaponType@LT	13.5	1	13.5	11.57	4.75
WeaponPosition@Gun	0.2178	2	0.2178	0.19	3.88
WeaponPosition@Knife	28.63	2	14.31	12.26	3.88
Within (Error)	14.001	12	1.1668		
Total					

From our simple effects analyses it appears that weapon position affects perpetrator identification but only when a knife is used $F(2,12)_{observed} = 12.26 > F(2,12)_{critical} = 3.88$. When a gun was used, weapon position did not appear to have an affect $F(2,12)_{observed} = 0.19 < F(2,12)_{critical} = 3.88$. Weapon type does not appear to influence perpetrator identification under high threat levels $F(1,12)_{observed} = 1.29 < F(1,12)_{critical} = 4.75$ nor under medium threat levels $F(1,12)_{observed} = 0.14 < 4.75$. However, weapon type does influence perpetrator identification under low threat levels $F(1,12)_{observed} = 11.57 > F(1,12)_{critical} = 4.75$. More specifically, with low threat levels, a gun affects perpetrator identification more negatively than a knife.

10.11 EFFECT SIZES

Thus far our significance testing has only told us how likely it is that our findings are due to chance. Does a smaller p value then mean that our effect is more meaningful? Not necessarily. We can have significant findings but this could be for reasons other than the magnitude of the effect of our independent variable. In fact, sample size alone can have an impact on significance testing. If you have a really large sample size, you most likely will find a significant effect. Effect sizes tell us how strong our findings are, or how detectable they would be to an observer. In essence, they answer the question: How large an impact did our independent variable exert upon our dependent variable? It is good practice to report effect sizes so that a practical interpretation can be made.

Generally, effect sizes are only calculated and reported on 'significant' effects. However, effect sizes are calculated for each test in our examples for demonstration purposes.

An effect size that can be calculated for two groups is Cohen's d.

$$d = \frac{\text{mean difference}}{\text{sample } sd} = \frac{M_1 - M_2}{s}$$

Actually, d uses the population sd but most people (and statistical software packages) calculate the d with the sample sd formula above, so that is what is shown here.

Cohen's d is appropriate when examining the effect size for the mean difference of two groups. For other tests, like our ANOVA model, we have to find a measure we can use when we have three or more groups.

Two of the most commonly used effect sizes for F tests are eta^2 (η^2) and omega^2 (ω^2). Both of these measures give us an estimation of the amount of variance accounted for by our model. However, each is calculated differently and is chosen based on different circumstances.

The formula for η^2 is given below. This is the most commonly reported effect size for a factorial ANOVA. The formula is a bit simpler than the one used for ω^2. However, η^2 is considered a biased estimator because when sample means are used, sampling error exists but is not accounted for by this measure. For example, the reason we are allowed to estimate the population standard deviation (σ) by the sample standard deviation (s) is because we adjusted by dividing our sum of deviations squared by $N - 1$ instead of N. By doing this, we are able to estimate the standard deviation in the population even though we only have a standard deviation from a sample. Adjustments of this sort are not made in the η^2 formula so that we can estimate the population. Therefore, ω^2 is sometimes used instead.

$$\eta^2 = (SS_{total} - SS_{error})/SS_{total}$$

where η^2 is the value for our overall model; a measure to tell us how much our variables and interactions account for the total variance in our model.

$$\eta^2_{(\text{weapon focus data})} = (45.6112 - 14.001) / 45.6112 = 0.69$$

Partial eta^2 (η^2_p) uses the same formula but is calculated for main effects and interactions. This is the effect size that you will be reporting most often.

$$\eta^2_p = SS_{between}/(SS_{between} + SS_{total})$$

$$\eta^2_{p\,(\text{weapon type})} = 2.6685 / (2.6685 + 14.001) = 0.16$$

$$\eta^2_{p\,(\text{weapon position})} = 16.3956 / (16.3956 + 14.001) = 0.54$$

$$\eta^2_{p\,(\text{weapon type} \times \text{weapon position})} = 12.5461 / (12.5461 + 14.001) = 0.47$$

Omega^2 is often considered a better estimate of effect size and a less biased estimate than η^2. Why then is η^2 used more often? The calculations for this effect size are unruly, as can be seen from the formula below, which gives us an estimate of ω^2 for one factor only (factor A in the example below). To obtain ω^2 for other factors or interactions, the denominator terms remain the same for each calculation; simply replace the numerator with the appropriate denominator term. Howell (2010) describes the theory behind this formula as well as a more detailed description of this formula. However, the main reason η^2 is used more often is that ω^2 can only be used when sample sizes are equal, which is rarely the case for between-subject designs. There are other alternatives to either η^2 or ω^2 (e.g. ε^2) that are not discussed in this section.

$$\omega_A^2 = \frac{\dfrac{(a-1)(MS_A - MS_{within})}{\eta ab}}{\dfrac{(a-1)(MS_A - MS_{within})}{nab} + \dfrac{(b-1)(MS_B - MS_{within})}{nab} + \dfrac{(a-1)(b-1)(MS_{interaction} - MS_{within})}{nab} + (MS_{within})}$$

where MS_A = mean square for factor A; MS_B = mean square for factor B; a = the number of levels in factor A; b = the number of levels in factor B; and n = the number of participants in each condition.

$$\omega_{weapon\ type}^2 = \frac{\dfrac{(2-1)(2.6685-1.1668)}{(3)(2)(3)}}{\dfrac{(2-1)(2.6685-1.1668)}{(3)(2)(3)} + \dfrac{(3-1)(8.1978-1.1668)}{(3)(2)(3)} + \dfrac{(2-1)(3-1)(6.2731-1.1668)}{(3)(2)(3)} + (1.1668)}$$
$$= 0.0834 / (0.0834 + 0.7812 + 0.5674 + 1.1668) = 0.03$$

$$\omega_{weapon\ position}^2 = \frac{\dfrac{(3-1)(8.1978-1.1668)}{(3)(2)(3)}}{\dfrac{(2-1)(2.6685-1.1668)}{(3)(2)(3)} + \dfrac{(3-1)(8.1978-1.1668)}{(3)(2)(3)} + \dfrac{(2-1)(3-1)(6.2731-1.1668)}{(3)(2)(3)} + (1.1668)}$$
$$= 0.7812 / (0.0834 + 0.7812 + 0.5674 + 1.1668) = 0.30$$

$$\omega_{weapon\ type \times weapon\ position}^2 = \frac{\dfrac{(2-1)(3-1)(6.2731-1.1668)}{(3)(2)(3)}}{\dfrac{(2-1)(2.6685-1.1668)}{(3)(2)(3)} + \dfrac{(3-1)(8.1978-1.1668)}{(3)(2)(3)} + \dfrac{(2-1)(3-1)(6.2731-1.1668)}{(3)(2)(3)} + (1.1668)}$$
$$= 0.5674 / (0.0834 + 0.7812 + 0.5674 + 1.1668) = 0.22$$

Just as we have a measure of partial effect for η^2 we also have a partial effect measure for ω^2. To obtain a partial effect measure for ω^2, simply remove the additional effects that are not of interest from the denominator.

$$\omega^2_{pA} = \frac{\dfrac{(a-1)(MS_A - MS_{within})}{nab}}{\dfrac{(a-1)(MS_A - MS_{within}) + MS_{within}}{nab}}$$

$$\omega^2_{p\ weapon\ type} = \frac{\dfrac{(2-1)(2.6685 - 1.1668)}{(3)(2)(3)}}{\dfrac{(2-1)(2.6685 - 1.1668) + 1.1668}{(3)(2)(3)}}$$
$$= 0.0834 / (0.0834 + 1.1668) = 0.067$$

$$\omega^2_{p\ weapon\ position} = \frac{\dfrac{(3-1)(8.1978 - 1.1668)}{(3)(2)(3)}}{\dfrac{(3-1)(8.1978 - 1.1668) + 1.1668}{(3)(2)(3)}}$$
$$= 0.7812 / (0.7812 + 1.1668) = 0.401$$

$$\omega^2_{p\ weapon\ type\ \times\ weapon\ position} = \frac{\dfrac{(2-1)(3-1)(6.2731 - 1.1668)}{(3)(2)(3)}}{\dfrac{(2-1)(3-1)(6.2731 - 1.1668) + 1.1668}{(3)(2)(3)}}$$
$$= 0.5674 / (0.5674 + 1.1668) = 0.327$$

So how big an effect size is meaningful? Well, that depends. Depending on the variables of interest, a small effect might be considered meaningful in one circumstance but inconsequential in another. For example, for a health researcher, finding a small effect of a new drug therapy might be worth a tremendous investment if it improves health, even if only by a little. However, for an industrial/organisational psychologist exploring marketing or sales tactics a major investment may not be justified if it only increases sales by a very small margin. Nonetheless, general guidelines are often used by researchers to determine standardised categories for small, medium and large effects. Some of these guidelines can be found in Table 10.13. It is always important to keep in mind the context and implications of your research to determine generalisations that can be made, including those based on your effect sizes.

Table 10.13   Guidelines for effect sizes

Effect size	Small	Medium	Large
d	0.2	0.5	0.8
$\eta^2/\ \eta_p^2/\ \omega^2/\ \omega_p^2$	0.01	0.06	0.14

10.12 **SPSS**

Statistical software performs all the above calculations for us easily and organises the output into nice summaries. However, we did not waste our time with performing these calculations by hand. Walking through hand calculations helps to illustrate the concepts and underlying logic of an analysis. SPSS is currently the most commonly used software program in psychology. We will use SPSS output in this section to see how we can obtain the necessary information that we obtained above through hand calculations. Since SPSS uses precise calculations and we rounded to the nearest hundred thousandth in our calculations, our output may differ slightly.

First input the data into SPSS from Table 10.4. You should have three columns (weapon type, 1(gun) or 2(knife); weapon position, 1(high threat), 2(medium threat) and 3(lowest threat); and identify: 1–10 (subjects ability to identify the perpetrator).

Once data are entered go to Analyse → General Linear Model → Univariate. Drag your variable 'identify' to the dependent variable column. Drag your variables 'weapon type' and 'weapon position' to the *Fixed Factor(s)* box. Click on *Plots*. Drag your 'weapon position' variable to the horizontal axis box and 'weapon type' to the separate lines box, then click on *add* followed by *continue*. Click on *Post Hoc tests*. Under the post-hoc menu drag the variable 'weapon position' to the *Post Hoc Tests for:* box. Under equal variances assumed click *LSD* and *Bonferroni*. Then click *continue*. Drag all three variables from *Factors and Factor Interactions* to the *Display Means for:* box; notice that under the mean display box there is another option to obtain post-hoc tests though the selection here is more limited. Then under *display* click on *Descriptive statistics, Estimates of effect size,* and *Homogeneity plots*. Then click *continue*. We will not identify all of the output we produced in this section, just some of the main tables.

Our first item of business would be to check our assumptions. As mentioned, this is something we normally do when exploring our data and we will not walk through all assumptions here. However, in our output we find a table labeled 'Levene's Test of Equality of Error Variances' (see Figure 10.5). This table allows us to test our homogeneity of variance assumption. Levene's test is a hypothesis test, and with all hypothesis tests our null hypothesis assumes that there are no differences. Therefore, our null hypothesis for Levene's test is that there are no differences in variance in the population (i.e. $\sigma^2_1 = \sigma^2_2 = \sigma^2_3$). If our p value exceeds our specified criteria then we can conclude there are in fact no differences. However, as mentioned, ANOVA is fairly reliable even when violations of this assumption have occurred, especially if sample size among groups has remained equal. Thus, even if a significant Levene's test occurs, this does not mean that ANOVA is no longer an option.

The output produces a nice summary table like the one we created above, with a few exceptions. See Figure 10.6 for the output produced for our between subjects test. In place of a critical F value, the associated p value is already given. When this value is less than the alpha level, set *a priori*, we reject the associated null hypothesis. The rows for 'Corrected Model', 'Intercept' and 'Corrected Total' can be ignored for our purposes. The values in the rest of the table may be slightly different (with the exception of our df column) due to rounding that is necessary in hand calculations. Our effect size, η^2_p, is included in our summary table as well.

Dependent Variable: Identify

F	df1	df2	Sig.
1.648	5	12	.221

Tests the null hypothesis that the error variance of the dependent variable is equal across groups.

a. Design:
Intercept+WeaponType+Weapon
Position+WeaponType * WeaponPosition

Figure 10.5   Levene's test of equality of error variances

Dependent Variable: Identify

Source	Type III Sum of Squares	df	Mean Square	F	Sig.	Partial Eta Squared
Corrected Model	31.611a	5	6.322	5.419	.008	.693
Intercept	501.389	1	501.389	429.762	.000	.973
WeaponType	2.722	1	2.722	2.333	.153	.163
WeaponPosition	16.444	2	8.222	7.048	.009	.540
WeaponType * WeaponPosition	12.444	2	6.222	5.333	.022	.471
Error	14.000	12	1.167			
Total	547.000	18				
Corrected Total	45.611	17				

a. R Squared = .693 (Adjusted R Squared = .565)

Figure 10.6   Tests of between-subjects effects

10.13 **MAIN EFFECTS**

As can be seen, the results of our three hypothesis tests are the same. If $\alpha = 0.05$ remains as our set criteria, we have a significant main effect for weapon position ($p = 0.009$) but not for weapon type ($p = 0.153$). We also see our interaction effect ($p = 0.022$). Post-hoc tests were produced as well and can be found in Figure 10.7.

Here we can see which conditions within our weapon position factor differ by comparing our significance values. Notice the more conservative nature of the Bonferroni correction as compared to our LSD comparisons. This distinction is most evident when looking at the differences between medium and least threat levels as this value approaches significance using the LSD measure but is well over our 0.05 criteria when using the Bonferroni correction. However, we still have to consider our interaction. SPSS provided us with a graphical representation of this output which can be found in Figure 10.8..

Unfortunately, simple effects are not part of automatic output with many software programs. However, syntax is available to conduct such analyses (see Field, 2009).

10.14 **WRITING UP RESULTS**

When you write up your results, you want your reader to be able to determine what tests were conducted, the results of these tests and the practical interpretation of these results. Were your results consistent with your hypotheses? Why do you think they were/were not consistent? Below is a brief write up for our example using our statistical output. Simple effect values are taken from our hand calculations since these are not included in our output.

We were interested in determining whether weapon type or different levels of threats measured by weapon position, would produce changes in the weapon focus effect. A 2×3 ANOVA was conducted with weapon type consisting of two levels (gun vs. knife) and weapon position consisting of three levels (high threat, pointed at someone; medium threat, in hand but not directed at anyone; and lowest threat: visible but not in hand). The number of perpetrator features (out of ten possible features) that participants were able to correctly identify served as the dependent variable. Lower numbers on this scale indicated an increased weapon focus effect. There was no main effect of weapon type, $F(1,12) = 2.33$, $p = 0.15$. There was, however, an effect of weapon position, $F(2,12) = 7.03$, $p = 0.009$, $\eta_p^2 = 0.54$. Post-hoc tests using a Bonferroni correction revealed that the weapon position presenting the highest threat ($M = 4.17$; $sd = 0.98$) produced more incorrect identifications of the perpetrator than the weapon position presenting the least threat ($M = 6.5$; $sd = 1.87$), $p = 0.008$. Differences between high and medium threat levels and medium and low threat levels were not found. However, the main effect of weapon position was

Dependent Variable: Identify

	(I) WeaponPosition	(J) WeaponPosition	Mean Difference (I-J)	Std. Error	Sig.	95% Confidence Interval	
						Lower Bound	Upper Bound
LSD	high threat	medium threat	-1.0000	.62361	.135	-2.3587	.3587
		least threat	-2.3333*	.62361	.003	-3.6921	-.9746
	medium threat	high threat	1.0000	.62361	.135	-.3587	2.3587
		least threat	-1.3333	.62361	.054	-2.6921	.0254
	least threat	high threat	2.3333*	.62361	.003	.9746	3.6921
		medium threat	1.3333	.62361	.054	-.0254	2.6921
Bonferroni	high threat	medium threat	-1.0000	.62361	.404	-2.7333	.7333
		least threat	-2.3333*	.62361	.008	-4.0666	-.6000
	medium threat	high threat	1.0000	.62361	.404	-.7333	2.7333
		least threat	-1.3333	.62361	.161	-3.0666	.4000
	least threat	high threat	2.3333*	.62361	.008	.6000	4.0666
		medium threat	1.3333	.62361	.161	-.4000	3.0666

Based on observed means.

*. The mean difference is significant at the .05 level.

Figure 10.7 Multiple comparisons

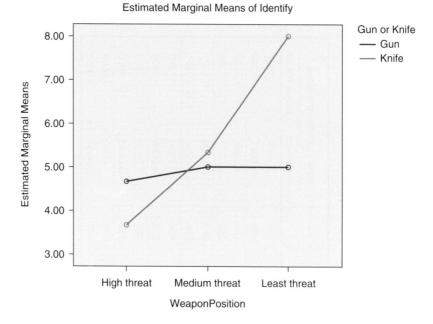

Figure 10.8   Weapon type/weapon position interaction

qualified by a weapon type × weapon position interaction, $F(2, 12) = 5.33$, $p = 0.02$; $\eta_p^2 = 47$. Simple effects revealed that weapon position had an effect when knives were used, $F(2,12) = 12.28$, $p < 0.05$, but not when guns were used. This suggests that a gun is viewed as consistently threatening regardless of position, while the perceived threat of a knife varies depending upon its position. Also, under the lowest level of threat, perpetrator identification ability was lower when a gun ($M = 5.00$; $sd = 1.00$) versus a knife ($M = 8.00$; $sd = 1.87$) was used, $F(1,12) = 11.57$, $p < 0.01$. It is probable then, that guns were viewed as more threatening than knives when they were not in the hand of the perpetrator, thus enhancing the weapons focus effect.

10.15 EXERCISES

Suppose you are an industrial/organisational psychologist hired by a company who wants to figure out how to best deter employees from pursuing the establishment of a union in their place of employment. Three presentation themes were used by the company to dissuade employees:

fear (loss of employment), guilt (disloyalty to company and co-workers), and bribery (personal gain if union not established). Employees were split up into thirds, and each third was presented with one of the tactics. It is expected that seniority will play a role in the decision so employees are divided into three groups based on seniority (less than 1 year; 1–5 years; and 5+ years. You then record how likely (on a 1–10 scale) each employee reports they would support the formation of a union; a lower number indicates that a particular tactic was more effective.

1   What type of design is this (i.e. between, within, mixed)? What are the factors? How many levels are there in each of the factors?
2   Suppose you find a main effect of tactical style but no main effect for seniority; however, you find a significant interaction. Can you say that seniority does not play a role in our effect? Why or why not?
3   In light of the interaction, you decide to conduct simple effect analyses. How many simple effects is it possible to test in this design?

10.16 DISCUSSION QUESTIONS

1   When ANOVA assumptions are violated, this does not necessarily mean we cannot conduct an ANOVA. Why can we still sometimes use an ANOVA in these circumstances? What are our alternatives if we feel our assumptions have been violated to the extent that ANOVA is no longer appropriate?
2   Small, medium and large effect sizes are determined somewhat arbitrarily. Discuss a situation where a researcher may consider a small effect to have considerable practical significance.
3   Why is it important to control for error when conducting post-hoc analyses? Discuss when it might be appropriate to use a more conservative test.
4   Why may you not always want to test for all possible simple effects in a design when conducting simple effects analyses?

10.17 FURTHER READING

Field's book *Discovering statistics using SPSS* (2009) describes both the mechanics of ANOVA and all of the options available in SPSS. Howell's text, *Statistical methods in psychology* (2010) describes the theory behind ANOVA, and many other statistics. It assumes that reader has some knowledge of statistics. Wright and London's text, *First (and second) steps in statistics* is (2009) an introduction to the most common statistics used in psychology, and assumes no previous statistics knowledge.

11

Correlation and Regression

Jeremy Miles

CONTENTS

AIMS OF THIS CHAPTER

This chapter will:

*   help you understand how a correlation represents a linear relationship between two variables;
*   teach you about the similarities and differences between correlation and regression;
*   help you be able to determine when multiple regression is appropriate, and how to interpret regression.

KEY TERMS

association	outlier
causation	Pearson correlation
ceiling effect	r
correlation	R
ecological fallacy	regression
floor effect	Spearman correlation
linearity	standardised regression
multiple R	coefficient

11.1 **INTRODUCTION**

Correlation and its grown-up brother regression are very commonly used methods in psychological research – in fact, many statistical methods that are used in psychology are actually either a form or correlation/regression, or they are based on correlation/regression. If you can understand the material in this chapter, you are a long way toward understanding almost everything you are likely to need to know about the application of statistics in psychology.

In this chapter we are going to start off by describing correlation – what it is for, what it does and how it is used. We'll then look at regression with a single predictor variable, and regression with multiple predictor variables, and we'll also look at some of the clever things that you can do with regression.

11.2 **BEGINNINGS**

To understand regression and correlation it might help to understand where they came from, and why they were developed. Francis Galton is always described as a polymath, which means that he was quite clever and knew about a lot of stuff – among other things he developed fingerprinting to identify criminals, and drew the first weather maps. He was also Charles Darwin's cousin (well, half cousin, if you want to be strict). Galton was interested in heredity (he believed that many traits were inherited, and wrote a book about this called *Hereditary Genius*, a copy of which I found in an Oxfam store once – it's not very interesting). As part of his research, he measured the heights of fathers, and the heights of their sons, and he wanted to see how closely related they were – essentially, he wanted to ask: do tall fathers have tall sons (or conversely, do tall sons have tall fathers).

We'll skip a lot of detail here, which I've been told that you're probably not going to get excited about, even if I do get excited about it (and if you want to get excited about it too, you can read the book *A Primer on Regression Artifacts* by Campbell & Kenny, 2002). We'll jump forward to a student of Galton, whose name was Karl Pearson, who also collected data on the heights of fathers and sons, and cutting a long story short, Pearson devised a measure known as the correlation – and if there's one thing that's nowadays associated with Pearson's name, it's the Pearson correlation. (Pearson did a lot of other things though – see Box 11.1.)

11.3 **CORRELATION**

11.3.1 **Representing scatterplots**

The scatterplot in Figure 11.1 shows the heights of fathers and the heights of sons (in inches) – these are Pearson's data. Each point represents a father–son pair, and

Box 11.1

Even I know that statistics is a bit of a dull subject at times, but Pearson was a very curious chap. He was born Carl Pearson, but changed the spelling to Karl, some have argued because he thought Karl Marx was a very cool guy. He almost became a philosopher (he wrote a book called *The Grammar of Science* which Albert Einstein liked), he almost became a lawyer, and was offered a job teaching German at Cambridge. Instead he became a professor of applied mathematics, and then became a professor of eugenics. As well as admiring Karl Marx, he also thought that Adolf Hitler had some sensible things to say, and that the appropriate thing to do would be for nations to go to 'war with inferior races'. Pearson had a long-running feud with Ronald Fisher (the F that you saw in Chapter 10 was named after Fisher) and the two did not speak; Fisher and Pearson both worked in the same university for a while, and each would take tea in the common room at a different time, so that they did not meet. Pearson died in 1936, so he never found out just how wrong he was about Hitler. He also declined an OBE and a knighthood, because he didn't approve of such things.

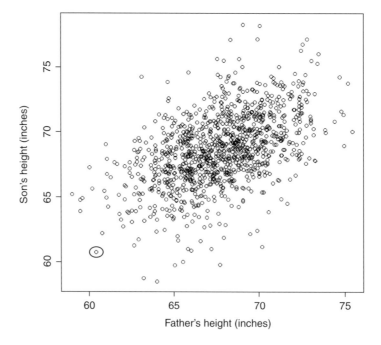

Figure 11.1   Scatterplot showing heights of sons and heights of fathers

the position of the point shows the height of both the father and the son. I've high-lighted one particular point by drawing a circle around it – both the father and the son were a little over 60 inches (that's five feet, or 1.52 m). In fact if we look at the data, the father was 60.4 inches, the son was 60.8 inches.

When we look at that scatterplot we can see that there is definitely a relationship there. Most fathers who were tall had sons who were tall, and most fathers who were short had sons who were not so tall. What we would like is a way to represent the strength of that relationship, ideally with a number. If we can describe that relationship with a number:

1   We will save a lot of space. We can present one number, instead of a whole scatterplot.
2   We can compare the strength of relationships – we can see if a son's height has a stronger or weaker relationship with his father's height or with his mother's.
3   We can test that relationship for statistical significance.

Pearson came up with a method for describing the strength of the relationship between two variables, called the correlation (for co-relation) coefficient – and often called the Pearson correlation coefficient. Pearson used the letter r to represent the correlation – notice that that is a lower case r; an upper case R is different – as we'll see later on in the chapter. (The r actually stands for regression, but that's so con-fusing that no one talks about it anymore – please remove it from your mind. I'm sorry for putting it in there.) To summarise, a correlation is a way of saying how closely points on a scatterplot fall to a straight line.

11.3.2 **The formula**

This is a book at least in part about statistics. You've got to expect to see an equa-tion or two. Frankly, it's not going to hurt you if you don't actually look at this section and jump to the next section; if you ever need to use this formula you're almost certainly going to be doing it with a computer. But if you happen to be washed up on a desert island, and need to calculate a correlation coefficient, you'll be able to do it.

There are a couple of different formulae that can be used to calculate a correlation coefficient. Here's one formula that can be used if you already know the standard deviations of the variables. The top of the equation is called the covariance, and we standardise the covariance by dividing by the product of the standard deviations of the two variables.

$$r = \frac{\left(\dfrac{\sum(x-\bar{x})(y-\bar{y})}{n-1}\right)}{\sigma_x \sigma_y}$$

And if you don't know the standard deviations either, you can use:

$$r = \left(\frac{\Sigma(x-\bar{x})(y-\bar{y})}{(N-1)} \right) \div \sqrt{\frac{\Sigma(x-\bar{x})^2}{(N-1)} \times \frac{\Sigma(y-\bar{y})^2}{(N-1)}}$$

You are probably never going to need to use these formulas, so don't worry about them too much.

11.3.3 Examples of correlation

Correlations range in size from +1.00 to –1.00. A +1.00 means that there is a perfect positive relationship, a –1.00 means that there is a perfect negative relationship. Figure 11.2a shows a perfect positive relationship – all the points lie in a perfectly straight line, from the bottom left to the top right. I made up the data to show this relationship. With real data, you will never get a correlation of +1.00 or –1.00. Figure 11.2b shows pair of variables with no correlation at all – the correlation is 0.00.

Let's look at some values for correlation coefficients that you might be more likely to see. Figure 11.2c shows a correlation of 0.70. It's pretty clear in this graph that there is a fairly strong relationship between the variables. Figure 11.2d shows a weaker correlation – 0.30. It's getting harder to see that there is a relationship just by eyeballing this graph. Figures 11.2e and 11.2f show negative relationships. Figure 11.2e shows a relationship of –0.5, Figure 11.2f shows –0.10. For Figure 11.2f it is pretty much impossible to tell that there is a relationship between the variables, because the correlation is so low.

11.3.4 Linearity, outliers and other problems

A correlation shows how close the scatterplot is to a straight line in a positive or a negative direction. But a lack of correlation should not be taken as evidence that there is no relationship between the two variables. Additionally, you should not take a correlation at face value – a large correlation does not necessarily mean that there is a relationship between two variables, because something might have gone wrong. Let's have a look at some of the things that can go wrong.

Non-linearity

If there is a relationship between two variables that is not linear, a test of correlation will not detect it. Take a look at the correlation shown in Figure 11.3a. There clearly is a relationship between the two variables – as x increases, y increases, until x gets

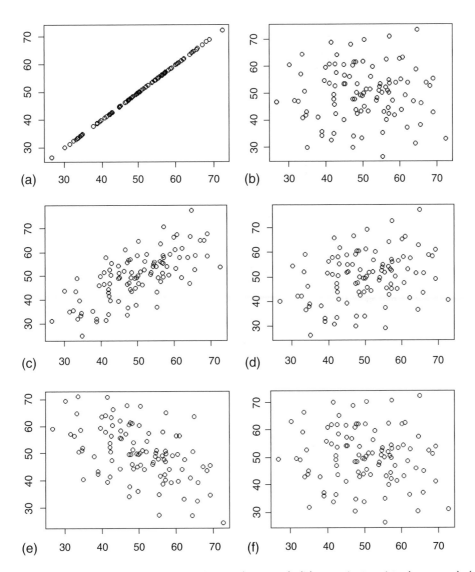

Figure 11.2 (a) Perfect positive correlation (r = 1.00); (b) no relationship (r = 0.00); (c) strong positive relationship (r = 0.70); (d) weaker positive relationship (r = 0.30); (e) negative relationship (r = −0.50); (f) weak negative relationship (r = −0.10)

to about 6 whereupon y starts to decrease. But the correlation between these two variables is zero. If you just looked at the correlation, and did not look at the scatterplot, you would believe that the variables were not related, and you'd be wrong.

Fortunately for us, this sort of relationship is very rare in psychological research. However, more common is a less severe effect of non-linearity. As an example,

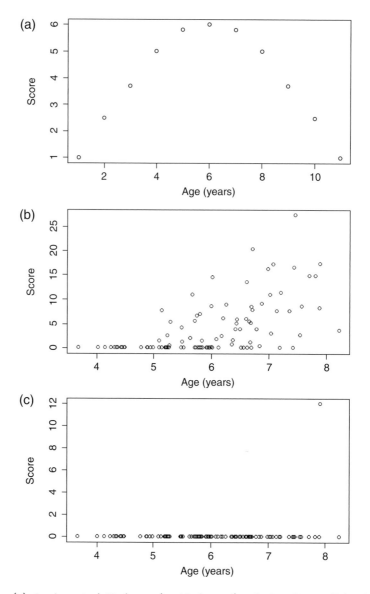

Figure 11.3 (a) An inverted U-shape (or U-shaped) relationship will lead to r = 0; (b) a floor effect occurs when some individuals are at the minimum or maximum for a test; (c) an outlier will produce a correlation (r = 0.12)

consider the relationship between reading ability and age. Up until the age of about four, children have very, very little reading ability – then the ability starts to increase rapidly.

Consider the hypothetical example shown in Figure 11.3b, showing the relationship between age and reading score on a test for a group of children. The children who are aged below five all score 0 on the test; then above age five, the scores start to increase, and older children do better.

If we calculate the correlation between the reading score and age for all children, we find that the correlation is 0.57. However, if we calculate the correlation only for those aged five or above, the correlation is 0.50 – still quite strong, but less strong. Such a relationship is known as a floor effect, and occurs when some people don't manage to get their scores off the floor – the test was too hard for younger children.

What is the lesson that we learn from this? Always draw, and look at, the scatterplot between two variables. Does it look like a straight line is a good 'fit' to the relationship, or does it look like you could do a better job with a curved line, or a line with a bend in it? If it would look better with a different sort of line, you should not necessarily trust the correlation coefficient.

Outliers

Another reason to check a scatterplot is to look for outliers. An outlier can seriously mess with your correlation. Consider Figure 11.3c. This shows a scatterplot of another set of data of reading and age – almost everyone has the same reading score, except one of the older children, who has a reading score of 23. The correlation here is $r = 0.20$; this is plainly not a good representation of this relationship. Outliers usually produce a spurious correlation; that is, they make the correlation between the variables larger than it should be.

11.3.5 **Size of correlations**

How large is a large correlation? How small is a small correlation? There are two ways to answer this question. The first way is to say, 'It depends'. It depends on what you are doing. If you measured a group of people's weight on one day, and then measured it again the next day, you would expect a very high correlation – maybe 0.95. If you measured someone's intelligence using a well-validated intelligence test a few weeks apart, you might expect a correlation of 0.90 – very high, but not quite so high. If you found a correlation of $r = 0.6$, you would say that that was low. Deary *et al.* (2000) gave a group of 101 individuals an intelligence test 66 years (to the day!) after they had first taken the test at age 11, and found a correlation of 0.63 between the two sets of scores – I think that people were surprised how high this value was. Laor *et al.* (1997) found a correlation of $r = 0.075$ between a woman's weight before she became pregnant, and the blood pressure of her child when the child was aged 17. That's a pretty low correlation, but it's still interesting. If Deary *et al.*, had found a correlation that low, they probably would have thought that they'd made a mistake.

Shih *et al.* (2010) carried out a study of survivors of trauma in Los Angeles (and thanks to Grant Marshall for letting me use the data) who had been admitted to hospital. The researchers measured posttraumatic stress disorder (PTSD) symptoms in people as soon as they could after they were admitted to the hospital, and then measured PTSD symptoms again six months later. Using their data, I found a correlation of $r = 0.55$ for PTSD measured at these two times. That's about what we would expect from a similar measure at two time points, but something which isn't very stable – a lot of people improve when they have PTSD. The scatterplot is shown in Figure 11.4. (Notice the ceiling effect, caused by some people having no PTSD symptoms at six months.)

Another way to think about a correlation coefficient comes from Mischel (1968). He wrote (disparagingly) about the results of attempts to find correlations between measures of personality and behavior, and said that such correlations rarely exceeded 0.3 – he thought this wasn't good enough (for reasons we'll discuss later). So if you find a correlation greater than 0.3 for a measure of behaviour and a measure of personality, you've done pretty well.

One final way of thinking about correlations comes from Cohen (1968) who gave us a shorthand way of saying that a correlation of 0.1 is small, 0.3 is medium and 0.5 is large. Although this is a useful rule of thumb, you should be careful not to take it out of context – a correlation of 0.5 under some circumstances would be very low; say for a measure of personality or intelligence administered on consecutive days.

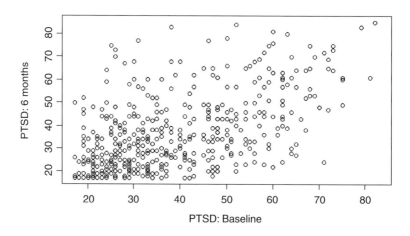

Figure 11.4 Scatterplot of the relationship between PTSD symptoms at baseline and PTSD symptoms at 6 months

At other times, a correlation of 0.3 would be impressively large – say for the correlation of a mother's weight and her child's blood pressure.

11.3.6 **Statistical significance and correlation**

In Chapter 10, you looked at analysis of variance. The test statistic for analysis of variance is F. F isn't very informative – it's just used to find the probability value associated with your hypothesis test. No one asks anyone what F value they found in their research – F is an inferential statistic; it doesn't describe, or tell you, anything. The same is true of χ^2, or t or of any other test statistic.

A correlation does tell you about the size – we've just seen that you can (usually) say that if your correlation is 0.3, you have a medium sized correlation. However, a correlation is also a test statistic; you can use a correlation to test the null hypothesis that your population correlation is zero.

If you want to know how that is done, read Box 11.2. You will not have a poorer life if you do not read the box, and jump over it. If you have a computer to work out your correlation coefficient, it will almost certainly also give the p value.

Box 11.2 Calculating a test statistic for a correlation

Let's say that we have collected our data, and found, with our sample size of 100, that we have a correlation of $r = 0.30$. We want to test the null hypothesis that the correlation in the population is equal to zero.

Test statistics, like F or t or χ^2 are not very meaningful. But one thing we like about them is that they have a distribution that we know about, so we can find the p-values associated with a null hypothesis. Correlations don't have nice distributions that we know about, but if we do a transformation, it turns out that they do have a nice distribution. In fact, we can transform a correlation so that it has a normal distribution.

The transformation is called the Fisher transformation – it's named after Fisher, the same person that F is named after. (Fisher did a lot of work on applications of ANOVA, and some people think that he named the F distribution after himself – he didn't, the distribution was named the F distribution by George Snedecor, and if you read some really old statistics books[1] you might find it referred to as Snedecor's F distribution.)

The formula for the Fisher transformation of the correlation is:

$$z = 0.5 \times \ln\left(\frac{1+r}{1-r}\right)$$

where z' is the Fisher transformed, normally distributed correlation, r is the original correlation and ln is the natural logarithm. (If you know what a natural logarithm is,

Box 11.2   (Continued)

then you get a gold star for concentrating hard in maths lessons at school. If you don't know, there's a button on your calculator that says ln on it. Press that button, you get the natural logarithm.) Almost any computer program that you are using to analyse your data has a function that will do it for you. In Excel, for example the transformation is called Fisher(). Let's plug our numbers in:

$$z = 0.5 \times \ln\left(\frac{1 \quad 0.3}{1 - 0.3}\right) = 0.3095$$

Next, we want to get the standard error of that test statistic. The standard error of z' is given by:

$$SE = \frac{1}{\sqrt{N - 3}}$$

Where N is the number of people.

$$SE = \frac{1}{\sqrt{100 - 3}} = 0.101$$

We've got a statistic and a standard error. We divide one by the other to get a t-statistic.

$$t = \frac{z}{SE} = \frac{0.3095}{0.101} = \mathbf{3.048}$$

It would be nice if I had an interesting story about why the t-statistic is called t. But I don't. I will tell you that the t-statistic was developed by William Sealy Gosset, who wrote his paper on it under the pseudonym A. Student. For this reason, the t-statistic is sometimes called Student's t. When I *was* a student and learned about Student's t, I wondered if this was some simplified version of t that was given to students, like the simplified books you get when you learn a foreign language. I wanted the lecturer's t, or even the professor's t, not the simple student's t.

Now we have a t-statistic we can look up, or calculate, the probability of a value as high, or higher, than the value that we have arising in our sample, given that the null hypothesis is true – we usually call this the p-value, because that's much shorter. First, we need to know the df of the distribution – that's just $N–2$, so we have 98 df.

I find that the p-value associated with a t-value of 3.048 with 98 df is 0.003, indicating that my result is statistically significant as it is less than 0.05.

Some people might have realized that we have a standard error, and therefore we can calculate the 95% confidence intervals of z', and from that back-transform to get the confidence intervals of the correlation coefficient. If you are one of those people, you might be cleverer than the rest of us, but we have more fun. OK?

---

1 Because that's exactly the sort of thing that I like to do at the weekend.

If you didn't read Box 11.2, I explained how to calculate the probability value associated with a correlation. The people who did read that section worked out that the probability of a correlation of 0.3 (or higher) occurring in our data if the null hypothesis (that the correlation in the population is zero) is true is 0.002. The people who didn't read it are going to look at their computer screens, where the *p*-value is usually given right next to the value of the correlation.

11.3.7 Assumptions

We need to make certain assumptions about our data in order for a Pearson correlation to be a good representation of the relationship between two variables. (We'll talk about some other correlations in a minute or two, which make fewer assumptions.)

Normal distribution

The most important assumption in correlation is that of a normal distribution. In Figure 11.3c we saw the effect of an outlier on the correlation coefficient. However, we must assume not just that each variable is normally distributed; we must assume a bivariate normal distribution. A bivariate normal distribution occurs when we can take all the points in any vertical or horizontal 'slice' of the scatterplot and find that they are still approximately normally distributed. Let me explain that a bit more.

Look at the scatterplot in Figure 11.5a. This shows the relationship between two variables (which I have helpfully called *x* and *y*), which are correlated 0.8. I have drawn a grey box on that scatterplot. Wherever I move the box, up or down, the values of *x* are still going to be (approximately) normally distributed.

Now let's look at another example. I've got another two variables – x_1 and y_1 this time. They are both approximately normally distributed – Figure 11.5b shows a boxplot of the two variables, and they appear to be approximately normally distributed. However, Figure 11.5b shows a scatterplot of two normally distributed variables, which are not bivariate normally distributed. Look at the grey box again; if I place the box there, there is not a normal distribution of the points in that box – there is clearly an outlier. Thus, univariate normality is *necessary* for bivariate normality, but it is not *sufficient* for bivariate normality.

Interval scale

First, we must assume that the data are measured on an interval or ratio scale, sometimes called a measurement scale or a continuous scale. We assume that we have a continuous scale, but it's very rare in psychology to actually have a truly 'interval' scale. We looked at PTSD and depression earlier. The depression scale has a score ranging from 0 to 24. For a scale to be truly 'interval' we should be able to

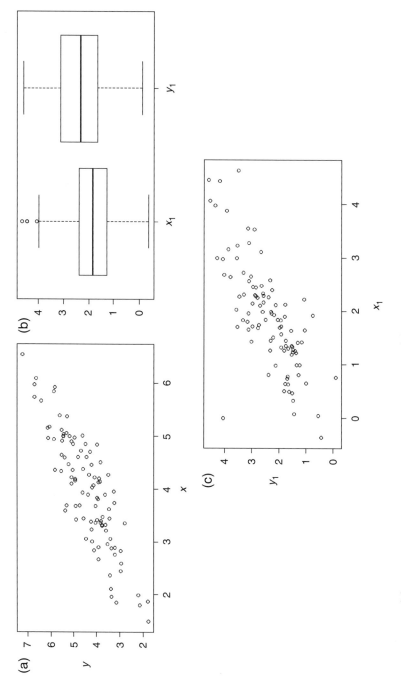

Figure 11.5 (a) Scatterplot showing bivariate normality; (b) boxplot showing that x and y are both approximately normally distributed; (c) scatterplot showing an outlier

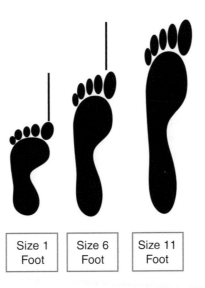

Figure 11.6   Three feet – the difference between them is 5 points

say that the same change in value represents the same change in the underlying variable, regardless of whereabouts on the scale you are. Gosh, that was a long sentence. I'll explain it with an example.

My children[1] have size 1 feet. My wife has size 6 feet. The difference between size 1 and size 6 is 5 shoe sizes. If I were to take a stick, and cut it so that my children's foot size plus the stick was the same length as my wife's foot, I could say that the stick was 5 shoe sizes long. My foot is 5 shoe sizes larger than my wife's foot, and I would find that the length of my wife's foot, plus the stick was the same length as my foot. Foot sizes are therefore measured on a continuous scale – an interval scale (Figure 11.6).

So what does that mean for depression? If person A scores 0 on a measure of depression, and person B scores 8 on a measure of depression, we could say that B has 8 more 'points' of depression than A. And then person C comes along. They score 16 on measure of depression, so do they have 8 more points on that measure than person B? Does that mean that the difference between person A and B is the same as the difference between person B and C? It's rather hard to say. Hence, we don't really have an interval scale. But are we going to let this stop us from using a correlation? No, we're not.

As long as you have a distribution that looks something like a normal distribution, you can pretty safely use a Pearson correlation. If you have Likert-scaled data,

1 They are twins. That's why they have the same size feet.

I would be pretty happy using correlations if these had five points, and only slightly uneasy if they had four points (although some people disagree with that.)

11.3.8 **Some other kinds of correlation**

So far, we have been discussing the Pearson correlation – this is a parametric correlation. There is one other important kind of correlation that we need to mention, and several less important kinds.

Spearman correlation

The Spearman correlation was developed by Charles Spearman, a psychologist who worked on things like intelligence (and had a large role in the development of factor analysis, see Chapter 12). It is a non-parametric alternative to the Pearson correlation; instead of performing a correlation calculation on the raw data, the calculation is done on the ranked data. This has the advantage that we do not need to make the assumption of interval data, or of normality – outliers do not trouble us as much if we are using a Spearman correlation. Hence the Spearman correlation just tells us how closely correlated the ranks of the variables are. The Spearman correlation is not widely used. (As a test, I searched for the term 'correlation' in the *British Journal of Health Psychology* in 2010, and found 25 articles that had used a correlation analysis at least once. Then I checked these 25 articles to see how many had used a Spearman correlation, and found only 3 – and most of these articles used more Pearson correlations than Spearman correlations.)

Other correlations

There are some other kinds of correlations that you might come across on occasion. You are very unlikely to want to use them, so we'll discuss them only briefly.

In the old days, if you didn't have a computer, doing statistics was hard.[2] Because statistics were hard, people worked out shortcuts, and the point-biserial and phi correlations are two of these shortcuts. If one of your variables was dichotomous – that is, it could only take on two values, then we can use the point-biserial correlation formula; if both of your variables are dichotomous, you can use the phi-correlation formula. These are simpler formulas. That's good if you have to do your analysis without a calculator. You have a computer, and your computer does not care (very much) whether it takes one thousandth of a second, or one five-hundredth of a second to do the analysis. Nowadays, you just ask for a Pearson correlation, and they're the same thing. Sometimes people get very upset because they can't find a

---

2 I know you think it's hard now, but really, pretend you don't have a computer, or even a calculator, and then try it.

computer program that can do a point-biserial correlation for them. That's a little bit like worrying how you will get from Manchester to London, because there aren't enough stores on the motorway that sell horse food for your horse.

Polychoric and tetrachoric correlations only tend to be used in latent variable models with categorical data. They are usually used when you have either dichotomous data or Likert-scaled data. These are pretty complex procedures, and so we won't worry about them any more here.

11.3.9 Causality and correlation

One of the biggest issues around correlation is that of causality. If we find a correlation between two variables, does that tell us that one of those variables was the cause of the other variable? The answer is no, not on its own. For example, on days (and in places) when more ice cream is sold, more people get bitten by sharks. These two variables are correlated.

The first possibility is that eating ice cream causes people to be bitten by sharks. Perhaps people who have recently eaten ice cream taste better to sharks. Sweeter and creamier. This seems unlikely.

The second possibility is that when there are sharks about, people eat more ice cream. 'I was going to go swimming but there's a shark in the water, so I won't, I'll have an ice cream instead.' This doesn't seem likely to be the case either.

The third possibility is that something else is causing both of the variables. What factors increase shark attacks, and also increase ice cream consumption? The weather. On hot days, people go swimming more. It's pretty hard to get bitten by a shark if you're not swimming, and more people go swimming in July than in December. (You can check this if you feel curious – just find the 'list of fatal unprovoked shark attacks in the United States' page on Wikipedia. Everyone killed by a shark in the 2000s in the US was killed between April and September.)

So the rule is, if two variables correlate, don't jump to the conclusion that one variable is causing the other – always try to think of the three possibilities.

Variable A causes Variable B.
Variable B causes Variable A.
Variable C (something we don't necessarily know about) causes A *and* B.

Let's look at some more examples. I was recently looking at statistics on dog ownership and house burglaries in California (in the year 2003). You won't be surprised to find out that there was a correlation between owning a dog and people trying to steal your stuff from your house. You might be surprised to find out that the correlation was positive. People who own a dog are *more* likely to have their house broken into. And this correlation was much stronger for people who were poorer – for people living below the federal poverty level, of those who had a dog, 19% said that their home had been broken into; for those who did not have a dog, 12% said that their home had been broken into. Let's think about the three possibilities: Could having a dog increase the likelihood of your home being broken into? Maybe. It could be that people with a dog leave their door open, to let the dog out during the day. Could having your home broken into increase the chances of getting a dog? Possibly – it might make you feel safer. But most people did not report that their home had been broken into – to find this result, we would have to find that almost everyone who had had their home broken into got a dog as a result.

Third, could there be some other variable that is causing people to be more likely to own a dog *and* to be more likely to be burglarised? Could it be that people who live in flats or apartments are burglarised less (because it's hard to break in a window, if the window is on the fifth floor), and people who live in those places are also less likely to get a dog (because when the dog wants to do its business in the night, it's a whole lot less convenient). We don't know, with the data that we have.

Let's look at some more examples. Some research has found that children who sleep with the light on when they are young are more likely to become short-sighted (nearsighted, myopic) when they are older. You might interpret this as a causal relationship – leaving the light on at night has an effect on children's eyes, that manifests itself as needing glasses later on. Stone *et al.* (2004) showed that this is not the case. It's a third variable, causing both the light to be left on, and the later shortsightedness. (Want to guess what, before you read on?) It's the parents – parents who are short sighted tend to leave the light on in their children's room, because the parents need it to see well. (Treading on a Lego brick in the night that you did not see is surprisingly painful.) Parents who have poor eyesight pass their genes on to their children, who then also have poor eyesight (and also will leave the light on in *their* children's room).

Have you ever slept with your shoes on? If you did, I would imagine that in the morning you had a headache. This correlation is not because of some sort of link between the condition of your feet and your head. It's because people who sleep with their shoes on tend to do so because they are so drunk they forgot to take them off. People who were drunk last night usually have a headache this morning.

Finally, and more seriously, there was a study of hormone replacement therapy (HRT). Studies had examined the relationship between women taking HRT and rates of heart disease. It appeared that women who took HRT also had lower rates of heart disease. However, this was a spurious correlation – women who took HRT in the studies also tended to be more affluent, and to be more interested in health issues, hence they ate more healthily, exercised more, smoked and drank less, and so on. It turned out that HRT actually increased the chances of their dying of heart disease – but their other healthy behaviours covered it up (Lawlor *et al.*, 2004).

So what can we say about **correlation** and **causation**? It's important to remember that correlation does not equal causation – always think critically about why a cor-relation has arisen. But it's also important to remember that causation *does* mean that there is correlation. If one variable causes another, there will be correlation between them.[3] Don't always dismiss causation out of hand. People have 'correlation is not causation' drummed into them so hard, that they sometimes overlook this. For example, if we find a positive correlation between age and how much broccoli people eat, we might be tempted to say, 'Ah, but correlation doesn't equal causation'. But then think – could eating broccoli make people grow older? Probably not. Nothing makes people grow older, except time. Could a third variable cause both broccoli eating and aging? No. Nothing makes people get older, except time. We can probably pretty safely conclude that older people eat more broccoli, because they are older.[4]

Tufte (2003) suggests: '[C]orrelation is not causation, but it sure is a hint'.

Randall Munroe, author of the web comic XKCD, puts it as in Figure 11.7.

Figure 11.7   From xkcd.com/552: the hidden message[1] says: 'Correlation doesn't imply causation, but it does waggle its eyebrows suggestively and gesture furtively while mouthing "look over there"'. (I have a t-shirt with this comic strip on it. You can have one too, from http://store.xkcd.com/.)

1 You knew that all XKCD comic strips have a hidden message, didn't you?

---

3 Actually this isn't necessarily the case, because sometimes a third variable will intervene. This is a little complex, which is why it's in a footnote. There's a causal relationship between the price of ice cream and the amount of ice cream that is sold – the higher the price, the less people buy. However, some ice cream sellers might realise that on a hot day or a very busy day they can charge more for their ice cream. Therefore they raise the price only when sales were going to be high. If they did this carefully, the correlation between the price of ice cream and sales of ice cream would be zero. But this doesn't mean that there is not a causal relationship.

4 It's also possible that the people who did not eat broccoli died. Because broccoli is a very healthy food. But perhaps they ate other healthy food with their broccoli.

11.3.10 **Associative and causative hypotheses**

Sometimes we are interested in correlation because we want to investigate a causal relationship and are interested in what it tells us about our psychological theory. Sometimes we don't care why there is a causal relationship.

Let's look at an example. We might be interested in the kind of person who has a pet, and buys food (or treats, or whatever) for their pet. People who spend more on pets might be more honest people – perhaps the fact that they spend more money on their pets means that they are a friendly, honest sort of person. Or maybe having a pet, which provides a companion who is always there and always prepared to listen to you, makes you a nicer person. We might investigate the correlation between pet ownership and mental health, and we might have a theory that could explain the direction of causation. If we are a bank, we are not very interested in whether people are nice and friendly and have psychological health. We are interested in whether or not they pay back their credit card debt. It turns out that people who use their credit cards in pet shops are much, much less likely to default on their debts than people who do not. The causal relationship is interesting from a theoretical perspective, but the fact that there is an association is interesting from a practical (to the bank) perspective.

One more example – if someone steals a credit card, they will often go to a gas (petrol) station where they can pay at the pump first – that way they can see if the credit card works, without being seen. If it works, they then might go to a jewelry store, to buy something small and expensive. If you buy gas and then try to buy jewelry, don't be surprised if your credit card doesn't work.

11.3.11 **The ecological fallacy**

A fallacy is an incorrect belief that comes about from incorrect reasoning. The ecological fallacy is a mistake that people sometimes make when interpreting correlations amongst groups of people – they then assume that what is true of the groups is true of the individuals in those groups. For example, engineering students read a lot more books with equations in them than psychology students read. And psychology students are a lot cooler than engineering students. We have found a negative correlation at the group level between the number of books you read with equations in them, and the coolness factor. Does that mean that psychology students who read more books with equations in them are less cool? No, not necessarily. If we thought that, we might have committed the ecological fallacy. The fact that it's true of the group does not mean it's true of the individuals. In fact, this book has a few equations in it. Are you reading it in a public place, like the library or the bus stop? Are people giving you admiring glances, suggesting you are a little bit cool? There you have it.

Another example of the ecological fallacy that is a very common mistake is about who votes for which party in elections. At the state level, richer states tend to vote Democrat – for example, California, Connecticut and New York all tend to elect Democrats more than Republicans. This leads many people to believe that rich people tend to vote for Democrats. They don't. Rich people tend to vote for Republicans – it's a fallacy that what is true at the state level (more money = votes for Democrats) is true at the individual level (more money = votes for Republicans). If this sort of thing interests you (please stop sniggering at the back), there is a book, and it's not a very long book, by Andrew Gelman and colleagues, called *Red State, Blue State*, which is all about this sort of issue.

11.4 REGRESSION

11.4.1 What is regression for?

Regression is the grown-up brother of correlation. (Although historically, regression came first.) Regression and correlation are actually very closely related, and you can find the same result with both of them.

Correlation tells you how closely two variables are related. That's fine, as far as it goes. But it doesn't tell you what you expect on one variable, given a value on the other variable. Sometimes we don't want to know that – and on those occasions, we can stick with correlation, but sometimes we do want to know what score we might expect on the dependent variable.

Additionally, in correlation, we just have two variables – we can call them x and y, or *variable 1* and *variable 2*, but it doesn't make any difference which is which. In regression, the two variables are not equivalent any more – we need to have an outcome variable – that's the variable that we predict (also called a dependent variable, and often referred to as y), and a predictor variable – that's the variable that we are using to predict the outcome (also called the independent variable, and usually referred to as x).[5] We say that we regress y on x, or that we regress the *outcome* on the *predictor*.

For example, I might tell you that there is a positive, and high, correlation between the hours students study and the grade that they achieve. 'OK', you say, 'I've been invited to a party tonight. I could go to the party, or I could study for three hours. What effect do you think this will have on the grade for my essay?' We have a predictor (hours worked) and an outcome (grade).

---

5 Although they are often called the dependent and independent variable, that's not a good name. Whether or not the independent variable is *really* independent is not something that our statistical tests can tell us.

If I only know the correlation between studies and grade, then I don't know the answer. I can't predict how much worse (or possibly better) your grade is going to be, if you go to the party. And that's not very useful for you, because you want to know the actual value.

Let's look at a real life example. Again, we'll use the data from Shih *et al.* This time we'll look at depression. Depression was assessed at baseline and six months later with a scale called the PHQ-8. A score of over 11 on the PHQ-8 suggests that the person may have major depression, a score of over 5 suggests a person may have milder depression. The correlation between depression at baseline and depression at six months was 0.46 ($p < 0.001$) and the scatterplot is shown in Figure 11.8.

The first thing to notice is that at baseline, very few people score zero on the measure of depression. This isn't surprising; these people were injured sufficiently badly to be hospitalised. They are not going to be in a good mood. Six months later, there are a lot of people who are scoring zero on the depression measure. If we examine the mean score at each time point, we find that this drops from 7.95 at baseline to 7.41 six months later. So, given a person's level of depression at baseline, how depressed do we expect them to be six months later? The correlation doesn't tell us that, and that's what we really want to know.

What we need to do is to put a line of best fit onto the chart, and then we could read off the value on the *x*-axis (depression at baseline) and see where the average

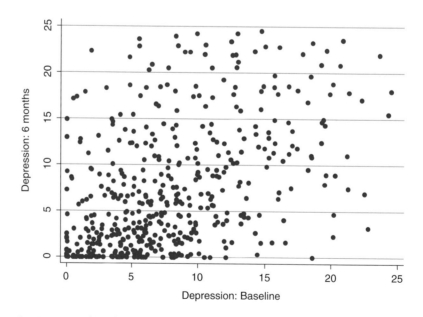

Figure 11.8   A scatterplot of Depression 6 months later with depression when hospitalized

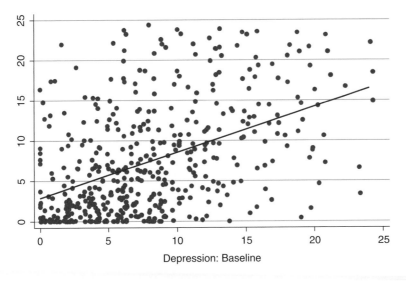

Figure 11.9   Scatterplot with line of best fit

person with that score would be expected to be on the *y*-axis (depression at six months). We've done that in Figure 11.9, and we can use that line to predict where someone will be in the future, given some starting point. To make things a little clearer, I've drawn the graph again in Figure 11.10, just showing the line of best fit.

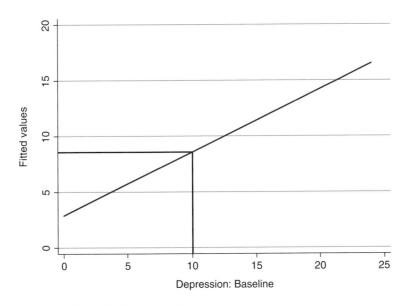

Figure 11.10   Line of best fit for depression

Let's say we want to know what depression score we expect a person to have in six months time, given that their current depression score is 10. We can draw a line straight up from 10; for example, I've drawn a line going up from the 10 on the x-axis (baseline depression) until it hits the line of best fit, and then going left to the y-axis (depression at six months). It seems that the average person who has a depression score of 10 will have a depression score of around 8 in six month's time.

11.4.2 Using the equation of a straight line

Using the graph is a little inaccurate. Instead we might like to use an equation. We're going to do another one of those bits with some maths in it. If you concentrated hard at school, you might know this already. If you have forgotten all the maths you learned, it's not hard, and we'll go gently. This is one of the maths bits you do need to read.

If we want to use an equation to get someone's predicted score, we need to know where the line is on the graph. It's a straight line, which makes life easier. To draw the line, we need to know how steep it is, that's called the slope or the gradient. The gradient of a hill is the amount you move up, when you move along 1 unit on the x-axis. If you move 1 metre along the ground, and you go up 20 centimetres (0.2 metres), that means you need to go 5 metres horizontally to rise 1 metre vertically. That slope would be 1 in 5, or 20% if it were a hill (and that would be a very steep hill for cars, but a beginner's slope for skiers). In statistics, we would describe that as a slope of 0.2 – you move along the ground 1, and you go up 0.2. We need a letter to represent this value – we'll use b.

Second, we need to know how high the line is. Hang on, the line slopes, so it's at lots of heights. We need to pick a position for the height – that is, we need to pick a number on the x-axis, where we will measure the height of the line – if everyone agrees to pick the same number, we'll all agree. It doesn't matter which number we pick, as long as we all agree. The number that statisticians have agreed to use is zero, so we give the height of the line, when x (in our case, depression at zero) is equal to zero.[6]

The height of the line is called the y-intercept, or just the intercept, because it's the position where the line of best fit intercepts (or hits) the y-axis. This value is

---

6 As you study statistical methods more, you will find lots of times when we could pick any number we want, and we all need to agree on it. Generally, if we are going to have to add stuff to the number, we choose, then we choose zero. Because adding zero to a number makes our sums easier. And if we're going to have to multiply something by a number that we choose, then we'll choose 1.

also sometimes called the constant, for reasons we don't need to worry about just now; and sometimes people refer to it by the letter a.

OK, so let's take a look at our line of best fit. First, what is the height? If I move 1 unit along the x-axis, how many points do I go up? It's a little hard to see from the graph, but I will tell you that the answer is 0.57. So $b = 0.57$.

Second, what is the height of the y-axis where the line of best fit hits it (assuming we've drawn the y-axis where $x = 0$)? Again, it's difficult to see, but I will tell you that the answer is 2.89.

We want to know the predicted score for depression at six months (y) for an individual with a certain level of depression at baseline (x). Because we are talking about a predicted level of depression, we don't want to call that value y – that would suggest we knew what it was. Instead, we put a hat on the y so it looks like this – $\hat{y}$ – and we call it 'y-hat'. For an individual y-hat can be written as $\hat{y}_i$ where the subscripted i means it's for the ith person.

If a person has a score of zero for depression at baseline, then we know what their predicted score is at six months – it's the value of the intercept, or the constant. Therefore:

$$\hat{y}_i = a$$

(We put a subscript i on the $\hat{y}$ because that's the value for one person, but everyone has the same value of a, so that doesn't get a subscript.)

But what if they have a different score at baseline? If they score 1, then we know that their predicted increase will be 1 unit of the slope – so we predict that their score will be the slope – 0.57. If they score 2 at baseline, then their predicted score will be the y-intercept, plus two times the slope. We can therefore write:

$$\hat{y}_i = a + bx_i$$

Where x means their level of depression at baseline, a is the y-intercept, and b is the slope.

Now we can plug any number into the value for depression at baseline (x_i) and find a predicted value for depression at six months ($\hat{y}_i$). For example, we can calculate the predicted value for a person who has a score of 10 at baseline:

$$\hat{y}_i = a + bx_i$$
$$\hat{y}_i = 2.89 + b \times 10$$
$$\hat{y}_i = 2.89 + 0.57 \times 10$$
$$\hat{y}_i = 2.89 + 5.7 = 8.59$$

When we (or I) looked at the graph, I estimated that it was 8, so I was close, but not *that* close.[7]

11.4.3 Standard errors and statistical significance

We can calculate the standard error of a slope, and use that standard error to calculate confidence intervals and statistical significance. Even though reading books with more equations in makes you into a cooler person, I'm not going to show you all of the equations, for two reasons. First, they're pretty hard. Second, you don't really need to know them – I can pretty much guarantee that you will *never* use these equations in your life.

Just as we can calculate a standard error of a mean or a correlation, we can calculate the standard error of a regression slope. We know that if we use depression at baseline to predict depression at six months, we have a slope of $b = 0.57$. The computer also tells us that the 95% *confidence intervals*[8] are 0.47 to 0.67. In 95% of studies, the 95% confidence intervals will contain the slope value. (Remember that that is not the same as saying that we are 95% sure that the true value lies within the confidence intervals.)

We can draw a graph showing the confidence intervals of the slope; there's an example in Figure 11.11. We are showing that the line of best fit probably lies somewhere within the grey area.

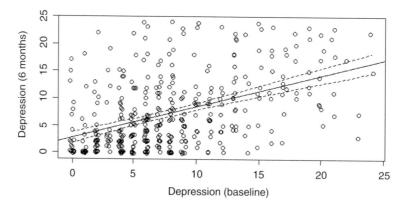

Figure 11.11 Scatterplot with line of best fit (solid line) and 95% confidence limits (dashed lines) of line of best fit shown

---

7 I could have just gone back and changed it, and you'd have been none the wiser. But I'm not that kind of person.

8 We can calculate any % confidence interval that we like, but 95% is by far the most common.

The computer also calculates a *t*-value associated with the slope and uses that to calculate a probability value. In our case, the *t*-value is 11.17, and the probability value is <0.001, indicating that the probability of getting a slope this high (or higher) if the null hypothesis is that the slope is zero, is very small. (Remember again that that is not the same as the probability of the null hypothesis being true.)

Errors and residuals

We give a predicted score for each person, but most people don't get their predicted score – some are too high, and some are too low. The differences between the depression score for someone at six months, and their predicted depression score at six months are called the *residuals*. The residual is what's left over, so after we have put in our line of best fit, we can calculate the residual – the difference between the actual depression score, and the depression score we thought that they would have. For example, the first person in the dataset has a score of 2 for depression at baseline, and a score of 10 for depression at six months. We would predict that a person with a score of 2 at baseline would score:

$$\hat{y} = a + bx$$
$$\hat{y} = 2.89 + 0.57 \times 2$$
$$\hat{y} = 2.89 + 1.14 = 4.03$$

Their actual score of 10 is 5.97 higher than their predicted score. This difference is called an error (*e*, for short). (Note that in statistics, error doesn't mean 'wrong' – it means to wander or stray from the predicted value.) For this individual, we could write:

$$10 = 2.89 + 0.57 \times 2 + 5.97$$

Or more generally, we could write:

$$y = a + bx + e$$

The residuals are interesting, because they tell us about how well we have explained the outcome variable. The smaller the total residuals, the more of the outcome variable we have explained, and the better we have predicted the outcome variable. We can test how well we have explained the residuals with the *F* statistic. The *F* statistic for our model is 124.77, with 1, 476 *df*, which gives a *p*-value <0.001.

If you are some sort of mathematical wizard, you will have noticed that the *t*-statistic for the slope was 11.17, and that the *F* statistic for the prediction was

124.77. You will also have noticed[9] (if you are a mathematical genius) that 11.17 × 11.17 = 124.77. So F is equal to t^2. If you are doing a regression that's anything like this one, it will always be the case that $F = t^2$. It's also true that the p-value associated with F will be equal to the p-value associated with t. F tests whether or not our predictor is better than chance; t tests whether our slope is different from zero. A zero slope would indicate chance prediction, so these are the same test. Hold on, because they won't be the same test later on.

11.4.4 Standardised regression lines

There is a problem with regression lines, and that is that we don't always understand the units of measurement, or that the units of measurement might change. Our depression scale was scored out of 24. But there are lots of other measures of depression out there, and many of them are scored on different scales. So how do we know what a certain gradient means?

One way to make sure that everyone understands how to interpret the gradient is to standardise the slopes. So we don't say: 'When a person scores 1 point higher on a measure of depression at baseline, we expect that they will score 0.57 units higher on a measure of depression at six months'. Instead we say: 'When a person scores 1 standard deviation higher on a measure of depression at baseline, we expect that their score at six months will be *beta* standard deviations higher'. We call this value beta, to distinguish it from our slope value b – we also call this value the *standardised slope*.

The computer tells us the value of the standardised slope for depression at six months regressed on depression at baseline is 0.456. Let's calculate the correlation between these two variables as well. If we do that, we'll find it is 0.456. It's the same number! It's the same number because a correlation and a standardised slope are just two different names for the same thing. To summarise, we can standardise a regression line to improve its interpretability. This is called a standardised slope, but it's also called a correlation.

11.4.5 Calculating the regression line

This is one of those sections that you can skip if you want to. I'm going to describe how to calculate the line of best fit. I'm not going to provide very much explanation, but some of it will become clear later on, or for more explication, the Further Reading will help.

---

9 Really, no one does. If you did, please send me an email to tell me.

We know that a standardised slope is a correlation, and we know how to calculate the correlation (it's in the formula near the beginning of the chapter). So if we know the standardised slope, all we need to do is unstandardise it, and we'll have the slope. And to do that, we multiply by the standard deviation of y (σ_y) and divide by the standard deviation of x (σ_x). So:

$$b = \frac{r \times \sigma_y}{\sigma_x}$$

Then we can calculate the constant, using:

$$a = \bar{y} - b \times \bar{x}$$

Where $\bar{y}$ is the mean of y, and $\bar{x}$ is the mean of x.

11.4.6 **Example**

It's time to recap what we have learned so far with an example. Let's look at the STARS data, and examine the relationship between age and PTSD at baseline (Figure 11.12). From the scatterplot it appears that there were more younger people than older people in the sample, but not such a skew that we should worry. It also appears that if there is a relationship, it is weak – there is little or no tendency for there to be a difference in the level of PTSD symptoms of younger or older respondents.

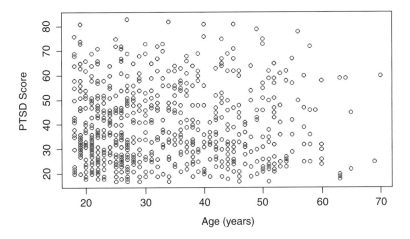

Figure 11.12 Scatterplot showing relationship between age and PTSD at baseline

The regression of PTSD score on age gave a slope of 0.007, showing that, on average, PTSD score increases only by 0.007 points for each year of age. The confidence intervals were –0.09, 0.10, and the p-value was 0.892 indicating that we cannot reject the null hypothesis that there is no relationship between these two variables. The standardised coefficient (correlation) was 0.005, indicating a very small relationship.

11.5 MULTIPLE REGRESSION

The great advantage of regression analysis is that it can be extended into multiple regression. Multiple regression is a very widely used statistical technique, and is the basis for many other kinds of statistical analysis. Analysis of variance (covered in Chapter 10) can be thought of as multiple regression, and latent variable models (Chapter 12) are very closely related to multiple regression. Multiple regression is a complex procedure, and we will not go into very much depth here. Rather, I will explain what it is for, why it is useful, and why you should want to know more.

11.5.1 What does multiple regression do?

Multiple regression allows us to evaluate the effects of multiple predictors, at the same time. It allows you to test the effects of one variable *controlling*, or *holding constant*, the effects of another variable. Let's talk about that some more. In a laboratory experiment, we control for variables by holding them constant – we make sure that all things that we think might have an effect are kept the same; for example, we try to keep the noise levels the same, ensuring that some people don't get tested in a noisy environment while others are tested in a quiet environment. We try to make sure that everyone understands the instructions – that way they will all try to do the same thing.

In research outside of a laboratory, we cannot control for additional variables. For example, in the STARS study, people were very different ages, had different kinds of injuries, had different severity of injuries, and the causes of these injuries were different. We cannot control for these factors by ensuring that they are held constant. Instead, we can control for them statistically.

11.5.2 *R* and multiple *R*

When we do regression with one predictor, we obtain a slope and a standardised slope. The standardised slope is also called the correlation. An additional part of the output that we get is called multiple R, and we also calculate the square of multiple R – called R-squared (or R^2). R is the correlation between the predictor and the outcome, when we only have one predictor, and R^2 is the square of this correlation.

When we have more than one predictor, we obtain multiple standardised slopes, but we still only get one value for R, or R-squared. This value is called the *multiple correlation* – it tells us how much all of the predictors correlate with the outcome variable. We can also think of R^2 as the proportion of variance in the outcome measures which is accounted for by the predictor variables.

11.5.3 Multiple regression example: PTSD and depression

Let's look at an example. We are interested in examining the relationship between depression and PTSD over time. PTSD and depression at baseline are likely to be correlated (and they are $-r = 0.73$, $p < 0.001$).

If we then look at the relationship between PTSD at baseline and depression at six months, we find: $b = 0.20$, 95% CI $= (0.16, 0.23)$, $p < 0.001$, beta $= 0.45$. (Remember that beta is the standardised slope – it's the correlation.)

So the people who had higher levels of PTSD at baseline are more depressed at six months. But that's not a surprise – the people who had more PTSD at baseline are also more depressed at baseline.

Let's also look at it the other way around, and see how depression at baseline is associated with PTSD at six months. We find a similar result, $b = 1.35$, 95% CI $= (1.11, 1.61)$, $p < 0.001$, beta $= 0.44$. So the people who were depressed at baseline have PTSD at six months. That's not a surprise, because the people who were depressed at baseline also had PTSD at baseline.

What we would like to know is how well PTSD at baseline predicts depression at six months, controlling for depression at baseline. And how well depression at baseline predicts PTSD at six months, controlling for PTSD at six months.

To do this, we use multiple regression. This will tell us the slope that best fits the relationship between each of the predictor variables, controlling for all of the other predictor variables. Beta is the standardised slope; when we only had one predictor, beta was equivalent to the correlation. When we have multiple predictors, beta is the correlation controlling for the other variables – that is, the correlation between each variable and the outcome, if everyone had the same value for the other predictor variables.

For depression at six months, we enter two predictors: PTSD at baseline, and depression at baseline. The results are shown in Table 11.1. This table shows that PTSD at baseline is a statistically significant predictor of depression at six months, controlling for baseline depression. That is, if everyone had the same level of depression at baseline, those with higher levels of PTSD would be more depressed at six months. Similarly, if everyone had the same level for PTSD at baseline, those who were more depressed at baseline would be more depressed at six months.

Table 11.1   Predicting depression at 6 months

Predictor	B	95% CIs	p	Beta
PTSD (base)	0.11	0.06, 0.16	<0.001	0.25
Depression (base)	0.34	0.19, 0.48	<0.001	0.27

Table11.2   Predicting PTSD at 6 months

Predictor	B	95% CIs	p	Beta
PTSD (base)	0.53	0.41, 0.66	<0.001	0.49
Depression (base)	0.22	−0.13, 0.58	0.208	0.07

Next we look at the prediction of PTSD at six months, shown in Table 11.2. Here we find that PTSD at baseline is a significant predictor of PTSD at six months – that is, those who have higher levels of PTSD at baseline have higher levels of PTSD at six months, and that this would be true if everyone had the same level of depression. However, the effect of depression is no longer statistically significant – that is, if everyone had the same level of PTSD at baseline, then depression at baseline no longer predicts PTSD at six months.

Let's think about what this result tells us. This means that if you are depressed at baseline, you will probably be depressed at six months, regardless of the level of PTSD symptoms. And if you have PTSD at baseline, you will be probably be more depressed at six months, regardless of how depressed you were at baseline. This makes sense, because having PTSD symptoms is unpleasant. PTSD symptoms involve flashbacks to the event, dreams and nightmares about the event, and feeling constantly on watch and aroused, in case the event happens again. If that is happening to you, it is not surprising that you would become depressed.

Looking at PTSD at six months, those who have PTSD at baseline are more likely to have PTSD symptoms at six months. This isn't surprsing – PTSD symptoms are persistent. However, what is interesting is that, controlling for PTSD symptoms, depression is not a predictor of PTSD. Any relationship that we found between depression at baseline and PTSD at six months would be spurious – it would have arisen because of the correlation between PTSD at baseline and depression at baseline.

This result should not really surprise us – it is easy to see how experiencing symptoms of PTSD could lead one to become depressed. It is harder to see how experiencing symptoms of depression could lead one to have PTSD.

11.6 **EXERCISES**

1 Two researchers carry out a study to investigate the correlation between two variables. The first finds a correlation of $r = 0.50$, $p = 0.03$. The second finds a correlation of $r = 0.01$, $p < 0.001$. The first researcher argues that their results are 'better', because they have a larger correlation. The second argues that their results are 'better', because they have a smaller p-value. What explains why one has a smaller p-value when the other has a larger correlation? Who is right, and which result (if any) is 'better'?

2 Match the pairs of variables and correlations in Figure 11.13 with the following:

(1) $r = -0.2$; (2) $r = -0.05$; (3) $r = 0.52$; (4) $r = 0.73$.

3 Most of the passengers who were on the *Titanic* drowned when the ship struck an iceberg and sank. However, of those who survived, many went on to live longer than the average person. Perhaps this correlation is explained by something about surviving the *Titanic* giving them a 'will to survive'. Can you think of another explanation?

   (Hint #1: Survivors were not randomly selected. If you've seen the movie, you might recall that first class passengers were much more likely to survive – in fact 60% of first class passengers survived, compared with 24% of third class passengers. Does that help?)

   (Hint #2: First class tickets on the *Titanic* were *very* expensive.[10] This meant that first class passengers had to be rich. Do rich people live longer or shorter lives than poorer people?)

4 Using the STARS dataset, I regressed depression at six months on optimism at baseline. I found:

Predictor	B	95% CIs	p	Beta
Optimism (base)	−2.11	−3.06, 1.15	<0.001	−0.20

---

10 The cost of a first class parlour suite on the *Titanic* was £870 – roughly equivalent to £64,000 in 2011. The workers who built the ship earned around £2 per week.

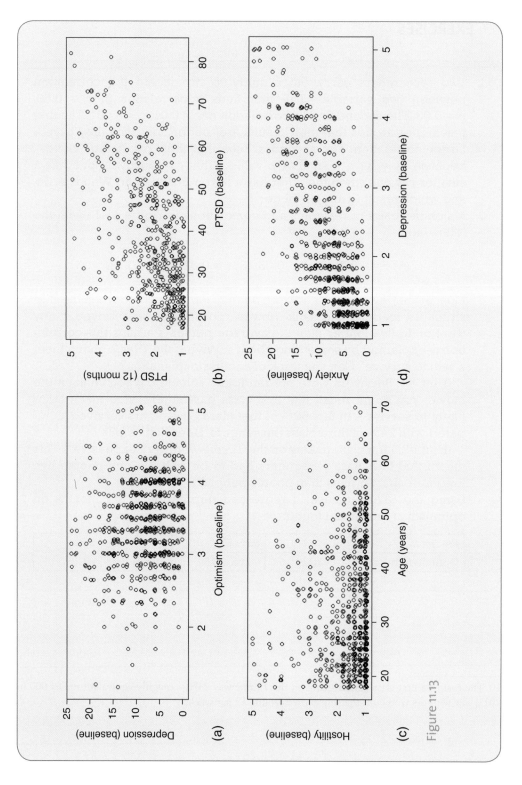

Figure 11.13

Showing that people who are more optimistic at baseline are less depressed at six months. I then repeated the procedure, with optimism *and* depression at baseline predicting depression at time 1. I found:

Predictor	B	95% CIs	p	Beta
Optimism (base)	−1.22	−2.10, −0.35	0.006	−0.12
Depression (base)	0.54	0.44, 0.64	<0.001	0.43

The regression coefficient drops from −2.11 to −1.22 when I controlled for depression. Why do you think this is? The regression coefficient is still statistically significant, even when controlling for depression. Can you interpret this result?

11.7 DISCUSSION QUESTIONS

1   Review the differences between, and similarities of, correlation and regression analyses. Discuss a situation where a correlation analysis would be appropriate, and a situation where a regression analysis would be required.

2   Regression can be used when it is not possible to carry out experimental research. For example, in the area of crime, using multiple regression some researchers have made claims using regression that more gun ownership leads to less crime, that the death penalty has no effect on crime rates and that longer prison sentences reduce crime. What dangers do you think there are in such analyses?

11.8 FURTHER READING

Cohen *et al.* (2002) is pretty much the definitive book on multiple regression and correlation for psychologists. Really, if you read this book, it's unlikely you'll need to read anything else, ever. It's a little hard going in places for beginners. A couple of more gentle introductions are Allison (1998) and Miles and Shevlin (2000). Allison (1998) has a question and answer format, which makes it very readable – and it's likely you'll be able to find your questions in there, for example, the sections are called: 'What is multiple regression', 'What is multiple regression good for', and so on. I have a soft spot for Miles and Shevlin (2000), for obvious reasons. It's positioned somewhere between the Cohen *et al.* Allison *et al.* in terms of the level of difficulty. There are several books in the Sage Quantitative Applications in the Social Sciences Series (or, as most people call them, the 'Little Green Books'). The little green books are all short, and focus on a particular issue.

12

Exploratory Factor Analysis

Daniel B. Wright and Daniella K. Villalba

CONTENTS

AIMS OF THIS CHAPTER

This chapter aims to:

1 explain what a latent variable is and why exploratory factor analysis (EFA) is used.
2 show how to interpret computer output for these techniques.
3 help you learn about extensions to EFA.

KEY TERMS

exploratory factor analysis
latent variables
manifest variables

maximum likelihood
rotation

12.1 **INTRODUCTION**

In 1904 Charles Spearman published one of the most important papers in the history of psychology. This landmark paper made separate contributions to methodology, cognition and statistics. The methodological contribution was to introduce correlational psychology to complement the dominant experimental approaches of the day of Ebbinghaus, Fenchner, and so on. Spearman said the correlational psychology approach was necessary to shed 'real light upon the human soul, unlock the eternal antinomy of Free Will, [and] ... reveal the inward nature of Time and Space' (1904, p. 203). The contribution to cognition was a description of the notion of general intelligence, or *g*. The statistical contribution was to show a way in which to estimate this general intelligence variable even though it was not directly measured. While his method built upon earlier work by people such as Galton and Pearson, Spearman's procedure is generally regarded as the beginning of latent variable modeling. Spearman's *g* is a latent variable because it is not directly observed. This contribution is the focus of this chapter. Estimating unobserved or latent variables is critical in all areas of psychology (but particularly in psychometrics, see Chapter 7). We often measure several observed or manifest variables in order to tap into some construct which is not directly observed.

Researchers use latent variable models when they believe there are just a small number of hidden variables that cause the associations among the observed variables. In the section 12.2 we present these relationships with diagrams and show how these diagrams can be translated into equations. We describe some of the general issues that are important for understanding latent variable models. Detailed mathematics of latent variable models is beyond the scope of this book (but covered in most multivariate statistics books aimed at psychologists and we provide a primer for matrices in an appendix), but thanks to computers and statistical packages these models can be calculated by anyone with good conceptual knowledge of latent variables. In section 12.3 we show examples of latent variable models and how to interpret the output from a couple of popular statistics programs. In section 12.4, we mention two ways to extend the basic latent variable model. We end with a summary and some recommendations.

The focus of this chapter is on one type of latent variable model called exploratory factor analysis, often abbreviated as EFA. Within EFA the latent variables are called factors. Other latent variable models and an alternative to EFA called principal components analysis (or PCA) are briefly discussed at the end of the chapter.

12.2 **WHAT IS A LATENT VARIABLE?**

Latent means hidden, but still exerting some effect. For example, we research something called 'social avoidance' (and its role in the eternal antinomy of free will).

Warning 1
The observed variables need to be correlated among themselves. After doing exploratory data analysis (EDA, Chapter 8), look at the pairwise correlations (Chapter 11), and create scatter plots. If the correlations are all small (i.e. less than about 0.3 in magnitude) then it does not make sense to hypothesise that a single latent variable, or a small set of latent variables, is influencing the observed variables.

Warning 2
There is a little more mathematics in this chapter than in most of the other chapters. That is inevitable given the subject matter.

People who suffer from social avoidance try to avoid social situations. When forced to be in social situations they do not engage with other people as much as those who are less socially avoidant. At one end of the scale would be hermits and at the other end would be the social butterflies. You can think where different people, for example, Theodore Kaczynski (the Unabomber) and Britney Spears (a mouseketeer), might be on this scale. Or think whether people who play team sports tend to be less social avoidant than those playing individual sports. At the next party you are at (going to a party makes you less social avoidant than Kaczynski) try observing behaviours that you think might be consistent with either high social avoidance (e.g. doing the dishes alone in the kitchen, drinking in the corner) or low social avoidance (e.g. handing out your phone number to everyone, talking when no one is listening). The theory we use states that this unobserved construct, social avoidance, *causes* people to behave in ways that we can observe.

Psychologists often ask people for their responses on pen-and-paper questionnaires (Chapter 6). Suppose we asked people to respond to the questions in Table 12.1. For each of these we expect that having a lot of social avoidance will lead people to circle higher numbers. None of these directly measure social avoidance, but we expect a socially avoidant person to be more likely to sit by a lake in Greenland, watching TV and waiting for mom to call, than going clubbing.

12.2.1 Latent variables in diagrams and equations

Figure 12.1 shows how we imagine the relationship between social avoidance and these responses. It is convention to show latent variables with ellipses and observed

Table 12.1   Sample questions the answers to which should be influenced by whether somebody is or is not socially avoidant

If I could move anywhere, it would be:						
1	2	3	4	5	6	7
Inside a South Beach club						A tent in northern Greenland

When I watch football, I like to:						
1	2	3	4	5	6	7
Go early to the stadium and enjoy the crowd				Watch on my 63" screen with my own tortilla chips		

My idea of a perfect Saturday afternoon is:						
1	2	3	4	5	6	7
Going to a massive rave					Sitting by a quiet lake	

The statement that best describes my use of a cell/mobile phone is:						
1	2	3	4	5	6	7
I txt left-handed while driving					I have it so my mom can call	

variables with rectangles. In this example, social avoidance is a latent variable and the responses for each of the behaviours are observed variables. There is an arrow going from social avoidance to each of the observed variables. According to this model, responses to each of these questions are influenced by the latent variable 'social avoidance'. There are also individual circles to the right of each behaviour with an arrow going to each of the observed behaviours. These are called the item-specific errors (also called item-unique errors), but they are better thought of as just idiosyncratic variation for that question. For example, a social butterfly might really like tortilla chips and live far from the stadium, so might opt to watch football on TV rather than go to the game. This is an example of item-specific error. Often researchers do not draw these item-specific error variables in their diagrams, but it is worth remembering that each observed variable has its own error term.

Responses to each observed variable are affected by the social avoidance latent variable and an item-specific error. Let's use the following notation: *Greenland$_i$* to refer to the first observed variable, *SocAvoid$_i$* to refer to the social avoidance latent variable, and $e1_i$ to be the item-specific error variable for the first question. Notice how we have included the subscript i on each of these to show that each individual person can have different values on these. We can write this as:

$$Greenland_i = \alpha1\ SocAvoid_i + e1_i$$

where $\alpha1$ (alpha one) is the strength of the influence of the latent variable on the observed variable, also referred to as a **loading**. This equation is similar to the regression equations in Chapter 11, except there is no intercept. This is because the mechanics of solving latent variable models re-scales the variables (if you'd like, imagine $Greenland_i$ has been standardised to have a mean of 0 and a standard deviation of 1). The scaling of the variables also means that $\alpha1$ is between -1 and 1 and can be interpreted in a similar way to Pearson's correlation r between the observed variable and the latent variable (for this simple model). Similar equations can be used for the remaining observed variables:

$$Football_i = \alpha2\ SocAvoid_i + e2_i$$
$$Lake_i = \alpha3\ SocAvoid_i + e3_i$$
$$Phone_i = \alpha4\ SocAvoid_i + e4_i$$

Complex statistical techniques provide estimates for the alphas.

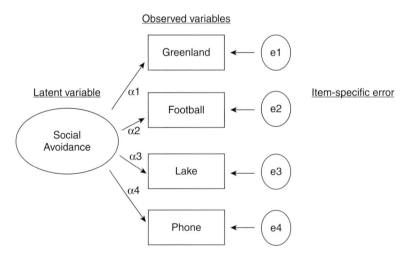

Figure 12.1 **A causal diagram showing one latent variable affecting the responses for four observed variables, which are also each influenced by its own item-specific error term**

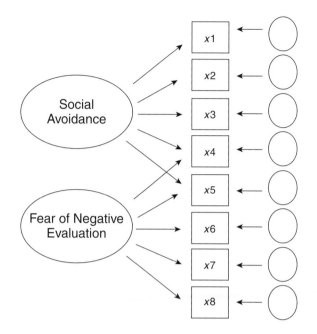

Figure 12.2 **A two-latent-variable model which shows 'Social Avoidance' affecting responses to observed variables *x*1 to *x*5, and 'Fear of Negative Evaluation' affecting responses to *x*4 to *x*8**

Human behaviour is complex and is governed by more than just one underlying latent variable. Social avoidance is usually thought of as one of the two components of social anxiety. The other component is a fear of negative evaluation. Suppose we asked a sample of people whether in the previous week they had done each of eight behaviours that clinicians describe as typical for social anxiety. It might be that social avoidance increases the chances of some behaviours (*x*1, *x*2, *x*3 in Figure 12.2), fear of negative evaluation increases the chances of others (*x*6, *x*7, *x*8), and both factors are predictive of other behaviours (*x*4, *x*5).

Figure 12.2 can be translated into a system of equations.

$$x1_i = \alpha21\ SocAvoid_i + \qquad\qquad e1_i$$
$$x2_i = \alpha21\ SocAvoid_i + \qquad\qquad e2_i$$
$$x3_i = \alpha31\ SocAvoid_i + \qquad\qquad e3_i$$
$$x4_i = \alpha41\ SocAvoid_i + \alpha42\ Fear_i + e4_i$$
$$x5_i = \alpha51\ SocAvoid_i + \alpha52\ Fear_i + e5_i$$
$$x6_i = \qquad\qquad\qquad\quad \alpha62\ Fear_i + e6_i$$
$$x7_i = \qquad\qquad\qquad\quad \alpha72\ Fear_i + e7_i$$
$$x8_i = \qquad\qquad\qquad\quad \alpha82\ Fear_i + e8_i$$

$$\text{Loadings} = \text{L} = \boldsymbol{\alpha} = \begin{bmatrix} \alpha 11 & \alpha 12 \\ \alpha 21 & \alpha 22 \\ \alpha 31 & \alpha 32 \\ \alpha 41 & \alpha 42 \\ \alpha 51 & \alpha 52 \\ \alpha 61 & \alpha 62 \\ \alpha 71 & \alpha 72 \\ \alpha 81 & \alpha 82 \end{bmatrix} \quad \text{or like} \quad \overset{\textit{SA} \quad \textit{FNE}}{\begin{bmatrix} \alpha 11 & \\ \alpha 21 & \\ \alpha 31 & \\ \alpha 41 & \alpha 42 \\ \alpha 51 & \alpha 52 \\ & \alpha 62 \\ & \alpha 72 \\ & \alpha 82 \end{bmatrix}}$$

Most computer programs output the α values in tables like that shown above.

This is called the **α** or loadings matrix (see appendix for discussion of matrices). The $\alpha 31$, for example, corresponds to the arrow in Figure 12.2 connecting the third observed variable with the first latent variable. We have written this table in two ways. In the first all the α values are written, even small ones (we have placed these in grey; most computer packages do not do this). In the second we have just left out α values that are small. Many computer programs allow the option not to print small α values. In terms of the diagram, it means that there is not an arrow connecting that latent variable to that behaviour.

We have added the labels *SA*, for social avoidance, and *FNE*, for fear of negative evaluation, above the columns in the previous equation. We looked at which variables loaded on the same construct. We saw the first five all loaded on the same construct and our theory suggests this could be social avoidance. The final five all load together so we felt this could be fear of negative evaluation. The naming of these factors is subjective, and is discussed in more detail later. If we assume the first factor is social avoidance and the second is fear of negative evaluation, then we can say, for example, that social avoidance does not influence the likelihood of doing behaviour #6 because $\alpha 61$ is small. There is a bit of circularity.

1 We defined the first factor 'social avoidance' because of the variables that load and do not load on it.
2 Then we say 'social avoidance' does not relate to one of the variables that we had used to inform how we defined it.

Care is needed when interpreting the relationship between individual observed variables and the psychological meaning of factors.

Estimating α values

There are several different methods for estimating the α values. Tabachnick and Fidell (2007) discuss seven different methods available in the packages SAS and SPSS/PASW. The package CEFA, discussed on the chapter's web page, offers eight. The method used in our examples is called maximum likelihood, but all the methods have their purposes (and usually give similar results). It is often worthwhile trying a few methods and seeing if you get similar results.

Four principles of science and statistics

1 Scientists strive for simple theories. This is called Occam's Razor, or the law of parsimony.
2 Scientists strive for theories that account for a lot of the variation in their data.
3 Analyses should reveal exciting new findings that would not be available by looking at the data without the analyses.
4 Scientists strive for theories that tell a good story (Abelson, 1995).

12.2.2 Deciding the number of latent variables

Scientists like simple theories (Principle #1 above) and like theories that account for a lot of their data (Principle #2 above). Unfortunately, there is usually a trade-off between the simplicity of the theory and how much of the data is accounted for. One measure of simplicity is the number of latent variables used to account for the data. The more latent variables there are, the more complex the model is. There are a few ways to estimate how well the model accounts for the data, but the most common way is to see how much of the variation in the data is accounted for by the model. The statistical packages calculate something called the *communality* for each of the observed variables.[1] This is the sum of the squared α values for that variable, even the small ones which do not warrant arrows in Figures 12.1 and 12.2. The communality for question #1 would be:

$$c1 = \alpha 11^2 + \alpha 12^2$$

---

1 Some packages print the *uniqueness* of a variable which is 1 minus the commonality.

This value will usually be between 0 and 1.[2] The communalities of all the observed variables can be added together to create the total variance accounted for by all the latent variables. This is the amount of the variation in the original variables accounted for by the latent variables in units of *eigenvalues*. The word 'eigenvalues' relates to the mathematics of factor analysis. An eigenvalue is a unit of measurement for the proportion of variation accounted for by the latent variables. If this total is divided by the number of observed variables you get the proportion of the total variation accounted for. Like metres and yards are both units of measurement of length, an eigenvalue is like using a ruler with different numbers. If there are 20 observed variables, then 1 eigenvalue of variation corresponds to one-twentieth or 5% of the total variation. All that it is necessary to know here is that one eigenvalue is the same as the average variation in each observed variable.

Principles #1 and #2 from Box 12.4 often compete. To examine this trade-off between simplicity and how much of the observed data is accounted for, researchers plot the two together. For factor analysis this means plotting the number of latent variables (complexity) on the *x*-axis and the proportion of variation accounted for on the *y*-axis. Researchers usually plot how much additional variation is accounted for each time a latent variable is added to the model. This is called a scree plot. In geological terms the scree is the rubble that is at the bottom of a steep mountain. It is touching the mountain but is just loose rubble. Cattell (1966) used this metaphor to describe where the statistical model starts accounting for random variation (i.e. the loose rubble). You want the model to account for the mountain, not the loose rubble. He said to choose the model with the most latent variables that is not attempting to account for the loose rubble. This is a great metaphor. Metaphors are a powerful tool both to help construct models in science and to help explain them to others. Figure 12.3 shows a scree plot superimposed onto its geological namesake. There appear to be two latent variables that are accounting for the structure. Some people use a biological metaphor and say to choose the model at the *elbow* in the line.

Some statistical packages will print a dotted horizontal line at the level equivalent to one eigenvalue. This is called the Kaiser (1960) criterion (sometimes labeled Kaiser–Guttman). Kaiser (1960) argued that if adding an additional latent variable contributes less than one eigenvalue then it may not be worth including. Textbooks disagree whether the cutoff should be exactly one eigenvalue, or slightly more or less.

Another way to compare models is with a significance test. Several of the computer programs will print a χ^2 value for how far off the model is from the observed values. This is like the residual sum of squares in ANOVA, but a χ^2 value is produced (if the computer prints more than one χ^2 value, use the one labeled 'likelihood ratio $\chi^{2\prime}$). Two models can be compared if one is nested within the other, meaning

---

2 Occasionally you do get communalities outside of this range. This usually means there is a problem, like some particularly high correlations. If some variables are correlated above 0.8 or so, try either removing one of the variables or calculating the mean of them and using the mean of these rather than both of the original variables.

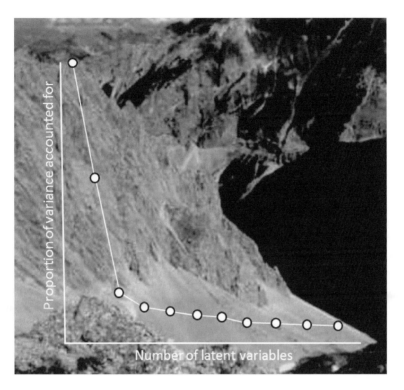

Figure 12.3   A scree plot from exploratory factor analysis plotted on top of a geological scree (in Austria, from Nova Development Corporation, 2004). The scree plot appears to show two latent variables (i.e. two factors) are appropriate

that the two are the same except that one of them has something extra. Here the extra would be that it allows an extra latent variable. The difference between the two χ^2 values is a measure of how much more variation is accounted for by the more complex model. The more complex model will almost always account for more of the data. Significance testing helps us to explore whether the additional variation accounted for is greater than chance. The difference can be looked up on a χ^2 table. The degrees of freedom are equal to the number of extra parameters estimated. If the only difference is the inclusion of one extra latent variable, there will be $k - 1$ more degrees of freedom where k is the number of observed variables. This is because a loading is calculated for each observed variable for the new latent variable. The difference is not k degrees of freedom because of the constraint placed on the loading values that the sum of their squared values is one. We will show an example of this in the second section of this chapter.

Finally, it is worth seeing how similar the correlation matrix implied by the model is to the observed correlation matrix. EFA works just on the correlation matrix so this is an important way to see, overall, if the model works, and also to see if there are any particular correlations that the model fails to predict. The method to calculate the implied correlation is to multiply the loadings which connect paths between the items. For example, items 4 and 5 in Figure 12.2 each have arrows connecting them from both latent variables. The correlation due to the first factor is $\alpha 41$ multiplied by $\alpha 51$ and due to the second factor is $\alpha 42$ multiplied by $\alpha 52$. Their sum is:

$$\alpha 41 \cdot \alpha 51 + \alpha 42 \cdot \alpha 52$$

For some complex models it is necessary to trace all the arrows for every possible implied correlation. Fortunately, the loadings matrix can be multiplied by its transpose (the matrix is flipped on its side; see appendix) to create the implied correlations. One thing to note is that this can be done with all the loadings or just those above a certain amount. In the first example we show both methods. When you get the implied correlation matrix, it is useful to subtract it from the observed correlation matrix. This will help you to locate which correlations the model is not able to reproduce well.

Some people believe that there is debate about which *single* method should be used to decide how many latent variables to have. In reality, no (respectable) researcher would use only one method. It is worth trying a few. Overall, while the scree plot is very subjective, we find it the most useful.

12.2.3 **Rotation**

Once you have decided how many latent variables to have, then you have to decide what they are. If there is only one latent variable, then look at the loadings and try to come up with a name that summarises all the observed variables which have high loadings. When you have a single latent variable you do not use rotation!

Suppose that you decide that there are two latent variables. The initial solution that the computer outputs gives the loadings, the αs, and this allows you to plot each of the observed variables. These are called the unrotated loadings. Here is what they might look like for 10 observed variables:

$$unrotated\,loadings = \begin{bmatrix} -.75 & -.42 \\ -.29 & -.22 \\ -.01 & .05 \\ .32 & .11 \\ .78 & .43 \\ .44 & -.59 \\ .09 & -.30 \\ .09 & -.01 \\ -.20 & .33 \\ -.35 & .62 \end{bmatrix} = \begin{bmatrix} -.75 & -.42 \\ -.29 & -.22 \\ -.01 & .05 \\ .32 & .11 \\ .78 & .43 \\ .44 & -.59 \\ .09 & -.30 \\ .09 & -.01 \\ -.20 & .33 \\ -.35 & .62 \end{bmatrix}$$

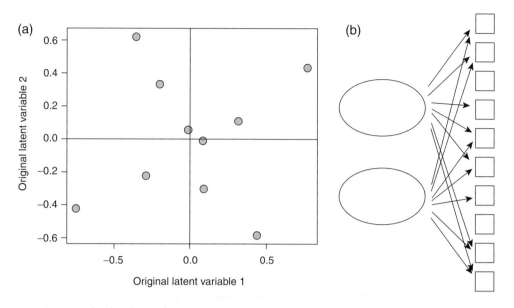

Figure 12.4 The loadings for an unrotated two-factor model represented in a scatter plot (a) and a path diagram (b). There are 14 paths shown in the path diagram (not including the item-specific errors, not shown here)

We wrote these twice. The first matrix shows loadings less than 0.20 in magnitude in grey. Figure 12.4a shows a scatter plot of the variables. Figure 12.4b shows this in a causal diagram. If we tried to describe these latent variables it would be difficult. The first latent variable is positively related to observed variables 4, 5 and 6, and negatively related to variables 1, 2, 9 and 10. The second latent variable is positively related to variables 5, 9 and 10, and is negatively related to variables 1, 2, 6 and 7. This is complex. Ideally you would want your latent variables not to relate to a lot of the same variables. Here, variables 1, 2, 5, 6, 9 and 10 all are influenced by both latent variables. It would be difficult to tell a good story with this solution.

When you conduct a factor analysis, the computer helps you to decide how many latent variables are necessary. It allows you to draw a plot like Figure 12.4a. However, its choice of where to put the axes is somewhat arbitrary. If you rotate the axes around by rotating this book, this does not affect the number of latent variables, the total amount of variation accounted for by the model or the communalities of any of the observed variables. Therefore, the data (or the axes) can be rotated to see if a solution can be found that is easier to explain. This sounds like cheating, but it is not.

Why would we want to do rotation? The answer is that it can help us to better understand the loadings. Recall from Chapter 7 that one goal of creating a good psychometric test is having items that load on one and only one construct. Consider the point in the lower-left hand side of the left panel of Figure 12.4. It has large negative values for both its *x* value (–0.75) and its *y* value (–0.42). We would prefer measures which have large values (positive or negative) on only one of the variables. This makes them better indicators of that latent variable.

Looking at Figure 12.5a we can think what the values would be like if we used different axes. We can rotate the axes until most of the observed variables load highly on only one of the latent variables, but not on the other. Ideally each behaviour would load on one and only one latent variable. In practice, observed variables will likely have at least a small loading on every latent variable, but if the loadings are below about 0.2 we usually treat them as if the latent variable does not influence that observed variable. We could guess what rotation will make variables tend to load on only one factor, but clever statisticians have developed several methods to choose how much to rotate the points. And clever computer scientists have written these methods into statistics packages. There are two main types of rotation: orthogonal (uncorrelated) and non-orthogonal (correlated). Orthogonal methods are more common and the resulting variables are more easily included in other procedures. Tabachnick and Fidell (2007) describe ten different methods available in some statistical packages (and there are more). We will consider only the most used method, called *varimax*. It tries to make each factor either load highly on an observed variable or not load on it at all. If we did this with the above data the computer would tell us that a rotation of 25.91° was what the statistician's clever function recommends.

To rotate the data 25.91° we use the following *rotation matrix* (see any trigonometry book for cosine and sine, abbreviated cos and sin, and see the appendix for how to multiply matrices):

$$\begin{bmatrix} \cos 25.91° & -\sin 25.91° \\ \sin 25.91° & \cos 25.91° \end{bmatrix} = \begin{bmatrix} .90 & -.44 \\ .44 & .90 \end{bmatrix}.$$

To calculate the degree of rotation from the numbers you need to use the inverse sine (the arc-sine) or the inverse cosine (the arc-cosine) functions ($\pi \approx 3.14$):

$$\text{arc-cosine}(0.90) \times 180/\pi = \text{arc-sine}(0.44) \times 180/\pi \approx 26°$$
$$\text{(approx. because of roundings)}$$

Mathematically, the rotation is done by multiplying the unrotated loadings by the rotation matrix (small loadings, less than .2 in magnitude, in grey, in final matrix):

$$
\begin{array}{cccc}
\text{unrotated} & \text{varimax} & \text{rotated} & \text{rotated} \\
\text{loadings} & \text{rotation} & \text{loadings} & \text{loadings}
\end{array}
$$

$$
\begin{bmatrix}
-.75 & -.42 \\
-.29 & -.22 \\
-.01 & .05 \\
.32 & .11 \\
.78 & .43 \\
.44 & -.59 \\
.09 & -.30 \\
.09 & -.01 \\
-.20 & .33 \\
-.35 & .62
\end{bmatrix}
\begin{bmatrix}
.90 & -.44 \\
.44 & .90
\end{bmatrix}
=
\begin{bmatrix}
-.86 & -.05 \\
-.35 & -.08 \\
.01 & .05 \\
.34 & -.04 \\
.89 & .04 \\
.14 & -.72 \\
-.05 & -.31 \\
.07 & -.05 \\
-.03 & .39 \\
-.04 & .71
\end{bmatrix}
=
\begin{bmatrix}
-.86 & .05 \\
-.35 & -.08 \\
.01 & .05 \\
.34 & -.04 \\
.89 & .04 \\
.14 & -.72 \\
-.05 & -.31 \\
.07 & -.05 \\
-.03 & .39 \\
.04 & .71
\end{bmatrix}
$$

Figure 12.5b shows the rotated version of Figure 12.4b. There were 14 arrows connecting latent variables to observed variables (not counting the item-specific error latent variables) in Figure 12.4b. There are only eight in Figure 12.5b. Further, now none of the observed variables are influenced by both of the latent variables. The theory suggested from Figure 12.5b is simpler than the theory suggested by Figure 12.4b. Latent variable 1 influences responses to observed variables 1, 2, 4 and 5, while latent variable 2 influences responses to observed variables 6, 7, 9 and 10.

The main non-orthogonal rotations are *promax* and *direct oblimin*. Both of these allow you to vary how correlated the latent variables are. Non-orthogonal rotation means the *x*- and the *y*-axes are rotated different amounts. This means that the resulting factors can be difficult to use in subsequent statistical methods and the mathematics is more difficult.

When there are two latent variables it is fairly easy to conceive of rotating a two-dimensional piece of paper in order to visualise rotation in two dimensions. When there are three latent variables it is more difficult to conceptualise rotating a three-dimensional space and it is extremely difficult to conceive of rotating a four-dimensional object, but the actual algorithms used for rotation have no difficulty with it. It is best just to believe that the rotation methods work regardless of the number of dimensions.

If you have three latent variables, the rotation matrix is a 3 × 3 matrix, and so on for models with more latent variables. When there are more than a few latent variables the mathematics gets more complex and you cannot make scatter plots like in Figures 12.4a and 12.5a. But you can and should make the diagrams in Figures 12.4b and 12.5b.

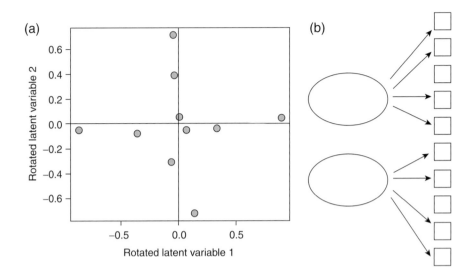

Figure 12.5 The loadings for the rotated two-factor model represented in a scatter plot (a) and a path diagram (b). There are only eight paths shown in the path diagram (not including the item-specific errors, not shown here)

Recommendation

The most common rotation method is varimax, but other methods are available with most statistics packages. It can be valuable to try several rotations and use whichever rotation makes it easiest to interpret the loadings. The purpose of rotation is to make it easier to interpret the loadings, so this is *not* cheating! If you think the latent variables are likely to be correlated, you can use the non-orthogonal rotation methods (and try different amounts of correlation). Most EFA uses orthogonal rotation.

12.2.4 Naming the latent variables

One of the most important steps in factor analysis is naming the latent variables. You need to look at the items with high loadings on each latent variable and decide a label that summarises these. Hopefully the rotation will produce a model which makes this easier. This is an important step because you will be using these labels to describe your theories. The labels will take on a life of their own. Imagine how labeling a latent variable 'anti-social personality type' will affect how you describe your theory compared with the label 'social avoidance'. It is also important that all the items that load on the factor appear related to the chosen label, and that all the items that appear related to the chosen label load on the factor.

Labeling latent variables is not something that statisticians have any special knowledge about with which to help researchers (though researchers often ask). Both knowledge about the area and thinking pragmatically about what label will be best to convey your findings are necessary for naming variables. And a bit of pazzazz doesn't hurt. One method to check the validity of your labels is to write on little slips of paper all the questions that you asked participants and write on full sheets of paper the labels that you think are correct for your latent variables. Find people with some knowledge about the area and have them place the strips of paper on top of the label that they believe is most related to the question. Further, have them place a + on the strip if high scores on the latent variable should correspond to high scores on the questions, and a − otherwise. You can then compare where participants placed the slips of paper with the loadings the computer produced (sometimes the latent variable is the opposite way around, so change the signs on all the paper strips for this exercise). You should get strips placed onto the labels which they load most highly on, and the direction of the loadings should make sense. If not, you should create different labels.

When reading journal articles that use latent variable techniques, you should consider whether the authors have used the same labels that you would have. Naming latent variables is a stage in the research process where researchers' biases are sometimes apparent.

12.2.5 Calculating latent variables

There are two reasons why people conduct latent variable analysis. The first is to understand the relationships among observed variables. The second reason is to create the latent variables, often called factor scores, and use these in other statistical procedures. There are several ways to calculate the factor scores. The most common method is the regression method. This will be shown in the second example in the next section. Do not be surprised if the latent variables have small correlations even if you use an orthogonal rotation like varimax. The correlations should be small, but they are unlikely to be exactly zero. If this bothers you, there is a method available in many packages called the Anderson–Rubin method which creates latent variables that have zero correlations. While this may seem an advantage, the simpler regression method is usually preferred (Tabachnick & Fidell, 2007). The correlations using the regression method are small enough that there will not be any problems with collinearity as described in Chapter 11.

12.3 COMPUTING EXAMPLES AND OUTPUT

Tabachnick and Fidell (2007) show how to conduct EFA and to interpret the output of EFA for SAS and SPSS, and also discuss SYSTAT. Field (2009) goes into more detail for SPSS users. These are both excellent sources. Here, we will show how to conduct and interpret EFA using the freeware R and the package SPSS. Using freeware has the advantage that anyone can use it (details for downloading R are on the chapter's web page,[3] you can also web search 'R'), but because of the popularity of SPSS it is important to understand how that program works too. We discuss a third program, CEFA (Browne *et al.*, 2009), on the web page. CEFA is a free program that specialises in factor analysis. Thus, it can do more EFA than either R or SPSS, but it can be a hassle having to use a different package than for your main analysis. One advantage it has is that it produces standard errors for the factor loadings. Thus, if an instructor or editor asks for these, CEFA is a worthwhile program to learn.

We will examine two data sets. The first is one of datasets printed in Spearman's original paper. We use it to illustrate factor analysis with a single variable. The second uses some of our own data on social anxiety to show how to approach factor analysis when you do not know how many factors are appropriate.

12.3.1 Finding *g* (general intelligence): small sample with R

R can do a large number of different procedures and is extremely flexible. The R procedure for exploratory factor analysis, called **factanal**, has fairly standard output. We will show R commands and output in **bold Courier font**. There are fewer options with this function than the EFA procedures in the other packages including SPSS.

Table 12.2 shows some data from Spearman's original 1904 paper. He had three measures of people's ability to make discriminations using psychophysics methods (pitch, light and weight) and four measures of attainment in school subjects (classics, French, English and mathematics). Spearman felt that the observed variables were all related to a general intelligence factor. There were not appropriate methods then for this model, so he created factor analysis and performed the analysis. The sample size ($n = 23$) is much smaller than is now advised for EFA, but it is used here for illustration. Table 12.3 shows the correlations among these measures.

Since Spearman collected these data there have been many modifications to the basic factor analysis and its computing ease. Factor analysis can be easily run with many statistics packages. Computing packages also make it relatively easy to screen for rogue data and perform exploratory data analytic procedures. Before running an EFA you should examine histograms of the individual variables and look at the scatter plots between all pairs of variables. If there are some correlations among the variables then you can run a factor analysis. We go through some of these

---

3 Web page: http://www2.fiu.edu/~dwright/EFA/

Table 12.2   The data from Spearman (1904, Experimental Series 3a)

Discrimination thresholds			Place in school (ranks)			
Pitch	Light	Weight	Classics	French	English	Maths
50	10	4	16	19	10	7
3	10	6	5	6	6	5
10	10	9	13	11	11	13
>60	10	9	22	23	22	22
4	12	5	1	1	1	2
2	10	10	4	2	2	1
4	10	11	12	14	13	18
20	10	11	23	22	23	23
11	10	12	8	8	15	15
11	12	11	3	5	4	4
24	14	10	7	7	7	6
5	18	7	20	15	18	16
3	18	9	10	13	14	12
5	13	13	2	3	3	3
6	13	13	11	12	12	9
7	14	11	17	18	17	13
15	19	10	21	20	21	19
11	14	13	19	21	9	21
14	13	18	18	16	8	17
15	13	28	15	10	20	10
7	19	13	9	9	16	11
4	16	16	14	17	19	20
>60	19	27	6	4	5	8

The '>60' values in the pitch column are treated as the value 60.

Table 12.3   The correlation matrix for the data in Table 12.2. There are high correlations among classics, French and English, and small correlations elsewhere

	Pitch	Light	Weight	Classics	French	English
Light	−.02					
Weight	.20	.31				
Classics	.26	.09	.02			
French	.26	.04	−.11	.94		
English	.11	.19	.10	.79	.75	
Maths	.13	.11	.09	.85	.86	.78

exploratory procedures on the chapter's web page, but not here due to space limitations.

Many packages allow factor analysis and most have similar output. The exact algorithms differ so the precise numeric output may differ, but the overall conclusions should be the same. We provide more details of all analyses on the web page. The data are stored in an object called **Speardata**. In R, to run a factor analysis looking for one factor you write: **factanal(Speardata,factors=1)**

This produces a lot of output which we will go through in sections. The first section of the output is the uniqueness scores. These are one minus the communalities. The total variation for each observed variable can be divided into the proportion accounted for by the shared factors (the communality) and the proportion not shared (the uniqueness).

Each of the original variables' variation can be divided into that unique to the variable and that shared with the latent variable(s). R prints the unique variance, called uniqueness. The high values for pitch (0.939), light (0.993) and weight (1.000) show that almost all the variation of these variables is unique to each of these variables. Very little is shared with the latent variable. The amount shared with the latent variable is the communality. These values are near zero for these three variables. The variables classics, French, English and maths all have low uniqueness values and high communalities, showing they are related to the latent variable. In sum, the uniqueness scores show that the single factor does not account for psychophysical discrimination measures (pitch, light and weight), but does account for the academic measures.

To find the communalities in R, type:

```
1-factanal(Speardata,1)$uniqueness
```

and you get (we have printed only a few of the digits):

```
pitch light weight classics french english math
0.061 0.007 0.000   0.956    0.930  0.650   0.780
```

or just subtract each uniqueness score from one by hand.

```
Uniquenesses:
  pitch light weight classics french english math
  0.939 0.993 1.000  0.044    0.070  0.350   0.220
```

The loadings show that the factor loads highly on all the academic measures, and particularly on classics and French. The blank loading, for light and weight discrimination, are less the 0.2 and the computer by default does not print these. The loading for pitch is also very low.

```
Loadings:
                Factor1
  pitch         0.247
  light
  weight
  classics      0.978
  french        0.965
  english       0.806
  math          0.883
```

> With a one factor model the square of the loadings is the communality. Thus, $0.247^2 = 0.061$, which is the communality for pitch.

The proportion of variance accounted for by the single factor is 48.3% or 3.383 eigenvalues ($3.383/7 = 0.483$).

```
                Factor1
SS loadings     3.383
Proportion Var  0.483
Test of the hypothesis that 1 factor is sufficient.
The chi square statistic is 13.01 on 14 degrees of
freedom.
The p-value is 0.526
```

This final part of the output shows that the model fits, $\chi^2(14) = 13.01$, $p = 0.526$. If this were a larger sample it would suggest that a single factor model could be appropriate.

To create the factor scores, using the regression method, type:

```
factanal(Speardata,1,scores='regression')$scores
```

which will produce the estimated g for each person. If you want to calculate the correlation matrix implied by this single latent variable model type:

```
alpha <- factanal(Speardata,1,scores='regression')
  $loadings
```

to create the loadings. Then to create the implied correlation matrix type:

```
impCORR <- alpha %*% t(alpha)
```

To make this so it has ones on the diagonal, type:

```
diag(impCORR) <- 1
```

and then type:

```
impCORR
```

to show the implied correlation matrix. To see how much this is off from the observed correlation matrix type: `cor(Speardata) - impCORR`. We do not print these matrices here, but they are on the chapter's web page. The model suggests low correlations for weight with pitch ($r = -0.003$) and weight with light ($r = -0.001$). The observed correlations were $r = 0.203$ and $r = 0.314$, respectively, so the model is poor at recreating these.

If you only want the loadings that are above some value in magnitude, say 0.20, then in the above code write:

```
alpha[abs(alpha) < .2] <- 0
```

after `alpha` is defined and repeat the steps from above. The two factor model is found with `factanal(Speardata,factors=2)` and the output is:

```
Uniquenesses:
 pitch  light weight classics  french english  math
 0.936  0.847  0.615    0.071    0.005   0.271  0.181
Loadings:
            Factor1    Factor2
pitch       0.252
light                  0.384
weight                 0.619
classics    0.961
french      0.992     -0.108
english     0.791      0.321
math        0.885      0.188
                Factor1    Factor2
SS loadings      3.387      0.687
Proportion Var   0.484      0.098
Cumulative Var   0.484      0.582
```

```
Test of the hypothesis that 2 factors are sufficient.
The chi square statistic is 4.76 on 8 degrees of freedom.
The p-value is 0.783
```

The χ^2 for the one latent variable model was 13.01 with 14 degrees of freedom. The χ^2 for the two latent variable model is 4.76 with 8 degrees of freedom. The difference in degrees of freedom (6) is the number of observed variables minus 1, here $7 - 1$. The difference between the χ^2 from this output (4.76) and that found in the output for the single latent variable model (13.01) values is 8.25. With $df = 6$ the p-value is 0.22. Thus, adding the extra latent variable does not significantly improve the fit of the model, but with the small n this is expected.

Also, the proportion of variation accounted for by the second latent variable is much less than the first (10% versus 48%) and is less than one-seventh (which is 14% and for this example is one eigenvalue). Thus, this supports (albeit with a small sample) Spearman's view of a single latent variable. To create factor scores for the two latent variable model type:

```
factanal(Speardata,2)$scores
```

If a second or third latent variable was needed, then the loadings could have been rotated. For varimax rotation, in R, write:

```
varimax(factanal(Speardata,2)$loadings)
```

Because the single latent variable model fits better than the two latent variables model, you would not need to use rotation here. The chapter's web page shows how to conduct these analyses with SPSS and CEFA, and compares the output of the three packages.

How large a sample is necessary for EFA?

As with many statistical rules of thumb the answer is complex and it depends on many things including why you are doing the EFA. Field (2009) reviewed several sources and found that samples above 300 are usually safe. With smaller samples, if a factor has several loadings above 0.6 then that factor probably has some value. With the Spearman g in the example loading highly on four variables this suggests that there is some common element to those four variables.

12.3.2 **Social anxiety: multiple factor analysis in SPSS**

We researched how easy it is (and sometimes is not) to change people's memories. It turns out that social anxiety may relate to this. We took 11 questions from a large set of items and will use these to illustrate the two factor model for 68 participants. The variables were from two scales, one purporting to measure fear of negative evaluation (items we label BFNE) and one purporting to measure social avoidance (SIAS). Therefore, we thought that there might be different latent variables which influence these items, but we were not sure. We will go step by step through this example using SPSS. The data are available on the chapter's web page along with analyses in R and CEFA. The items are labeled: BFNE_01, BFNE_05, BFNE_06, BFNE_08 and BFNE_11; and SIAS_11, SIAS_13, SIAS_14, SIAS_15, SIAS_17 and SIAS_18.

The first step would be to look at the histograms of the individual variables and scatter plots between variables (Chapter 8). Assuming all this is done and there are no strange outliers, the next step is to see if there is a correlation between the observed variables. As we have stated at the beginning of the chapter, if the observed variables are not correlated with each other then there is no need to do an EFA. Within SPSS the correlation matrix can be printed from the procedure that runs EFA or from the correlation procedure. We advise using the correlation procedure to ensure that you look at the correlations prior to conducting EFA. Details about the correlation statistic are in Chapter 11. Within SPSS go to *Analyze*, then *Correlate*, then *Bivariate* (the exact words vary among versions). Then you drag all the variables you want to correlate from the left column to the right one (labeled *Variables*). The default is Pearson's correlation. The default is to print *s for 'significant' correlations. Given the number of correlations which are all related here (because the variables are all correlated) it is unclear what any of these mean so you may want to untick the box that asks you if you want stars by the 'significant' correlations. Next, press OK. The output will look like Figure 12.6. We have changed the font to make it more easily read on a book's page and also drawn on it ourselves. With correlation matrices it is worth printing them off and looking at them! We started by drawing a line through the diagonal, because all these are 1. The correlations are the same above and below the diagonal, so we drew a squiggly line to show to ignore the ones below the diagonal. We drew lines to block off those correlations within the BFNE variables and with the SIAS variables, and a box around the correlations between these sets. Because all the questions are about social anxiety, they are all positively correlated, but it looks like the correlations within the same set are higher. We are ready to run EFA.

To conduct an EFA in SPSS go to *Analyze* then *Dimension* (or *Data*) *Reduction* and then *Factor*. Again, the exact phrases change between SPSS versions. This will open a dialogue box like Figure 12.7. Place the variables that you want to include within the EFA into the box labeled *Variables*. The tabs on the upper right

Correlations

		BFNE_01	BFNE_05	BFNE_06	BFNE_08	BFNE_11	SIAS_11	SIAS_13	SIAS_14	SIAS_15	SIAS_17	SIAS_18
BFNE_01	Correlation	1	.540**	.457**	.628**	.691**	.575**	.415**	.405**	.283*	.428**	.368**
	Sig. (2-tailed)		.000	.000	.000	.000	.000	.000	.001	.019	.000	.002
	N	68	68	68	68	68	68	68	68	68	68	68
BFNE_05	Correlation	.540**	1	.641**	.747**	.602**	.598**	.606**	.517**	.408**	.433**	.485**
	Sig. (2-tailed)	.000		.000	.000	.000	.000	.000	.000	.001	.000	.000
	N	68	68	68	68	68	68	68	68	68	68	68
BFNE_06	Correlation	.457**	.641**	1	.616**	.502**	.597**	.481**	.430**	.394**	.438**	.481**
	Sig. (2-tailed)	.000	.000		.000	.000	.000	.000	.000	.001	.000	.000
	N	68	68	68	68	68	68	68	68	68	68	68
BFNE_08	Correlation	.628**	.747**	.616**	1	.678**	.516**	.405**	.444**	.248*	.500**	.391**
	Sig. (2-tailed)	.000	.000	.000		.000	.000	.001	.000	.042	.000	.001
	N	68	68	68	68	68	68	68	68	68	68	68
BFNE_11	Correlation	.691**	.602**	.502**	.678**	1	.558**	.495**	.464**	.378**	.412**	.508**
	Sig. (2-tailed)	.000	.000	.000	.000		.000	.000	.000	.001	.000	.000
	N	68	68	68	68	68	68	68	68	68	68	68
SIAS_11	Correlation	.575**	.598**	.597**	.516**	.558**	1	.540**	.517**	.510**	.434**	.525**
	Sig. (2-tailed)	.000	.000	.000	.000	.000		.000	.000	.000	.000	.000
	N	68	68	68	68	68	68	68	68	68	68	68
SIAS_13	Correlation	.415**	.606**	.481**	.405**	.495**	.540**	1	.667**	.569**	.377**	.568**
	Sig. (2-tailed)	.000	.000	.000	.001	.000	.000		.000	.000	.002	.000
	N	68	68	68	68	68	68	68	68	68	68	68
SIAS_14	Correlation	.405**	.517**	.430**	.444**	.464**	.517**	.667**	1	.685**	.661**	.715**
	Sig. (2-tailed)	.001	.000	.000	.000	.000	.000	.000		.000	.000	.000
	N	68	68	68	68	68	68	68	68	68	68	68
SIAS_15	Correlation	.283*	.408**	.394**	.248*	.378**	.510**	.569**	.685**	1	.672**	.767**
	Sig. (2-tailed)	.019	.001	.001	.042	.001	.000	.000	.000		.000	.000
	N	68	68	68	68	68	68	68	68	68	68	68
SIAS_17	Correlation	.428**	.433**	.438**	.500**	.412**	.434**	.377**	.661**	.672**	1	.710**
	Sig. (2-tailed)	.000	.000	.000	.000	.000	.000	.002	.000	.000		.000
	N	68	68	68	68	68	68	68	68	68	68	68
SIAS_18	Correlation	.368**	.485**	.481**	.391**	.508**	.525**	.568**	.715**	.767**	.710**	1
	Sig. (2-tailed)	.002	.000	.000	.001	.000	.000	.000	.000	.000	.000	
	N	68	68	68	68	68	68	68	68	68	68	68

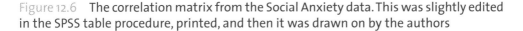

** Correlation is significant at the 0.01 level (2-tailed).
* Correlation is significant at the 0.05 level (2-tailed).

Figure 12.6 The correlation matrix from the Social Anxiety data. This was slightly edited in the SPSS table procedure, printed, and then it was drawn on by the authors

side (*Descriptives, Extraction, Rotation, Scores, Options*) of Figure 12.7 allow you to change different aspects of how the EFA is conducted and what output is reported. Field (2009) goes through the options in detail. Here we discuss just some of the options available.

The *Descriptives* tab allows you to print each variable's mean and standard deviation, and the correlation matrix, all of which you should have already examined. It also allows you to print the implied correlation matrix (labeled *Reproduced*). This is a useful option so we ticked it. The *Extraction* tab has many useful facets. First, you need to decide the method to use. We use *Maximum likelihood* so that our results are comparable with other packages. The SPSS default, at least in current versions, is to use principal components analysis, which most statisticians will be quick to point out is actually different from factor analysis. The other methods are all

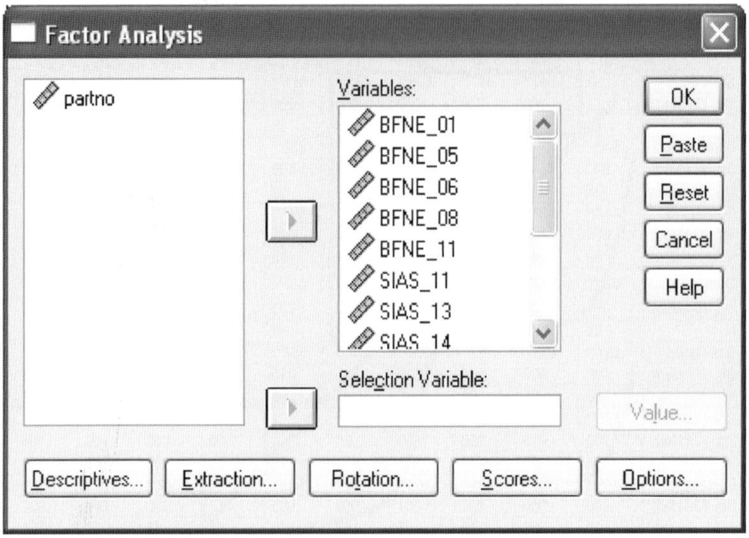

Figure 12.7 **The SPSS dialogue box for EFA. The location of the buttons and which features are included will differ between versions**

techniques that statisticians have argued can be useful in some circumstances. This tab also allows you to print a scree plot, which we always recommend. It also allows you to say how many factors you want. Usually you would decide this after you have looked at the scree plot and other output (which means you often run a series of EFAs). *Rotation* allows you to try different rotations. We ticked *varimax*. The *Scores* tab allows you save the factor scores. Regression method is the most popular. This would allow these scores to be used in other analyses. The *Options* tab allows missing values to be filled in (though we recommend using procedures specifically designed for this) and to suppress small loadings. For this example we do not use these. The complete output is shown on the chapter's web page but we will discuss some of the important parts here. The first information output is the communalities.

Communalities

Communality is the proportion of variance of each observed variable that is accounted for by the factors. Thus, for BFNE_01 the two factor solution (which is what is reported later in the output) accounts for 53.3% of the variation. A variable that shares none of its variance with any other variable has a communality of zero. If a communality is near zero the variable can be removed. If a communality is near or above one it is a sign that there may be computational difficulties.

Communalities

	Initial	Extraction
BFNE_01	.583	.533
BFNE_05	.697	.696
BFNE_06	.533	.519
BFNE_08	.744	.793
BFNE_11	.644	.608
SIAS_11	.565	.529
SIAS_13	.613	.503
SIAS_14	.677	.673
SIAS_15	.706	.808
SIAS_17	.688	.591
SIAS_18	.723	.770

Extraction method: maximum likelihood

Next SPSS outputs the variance accounted for by each factor. The output is too wide to print legibly on page, but is included on the chapter's web page. The information in the table is used to create the scree plot which is shown in Figure 12.8 (after using the

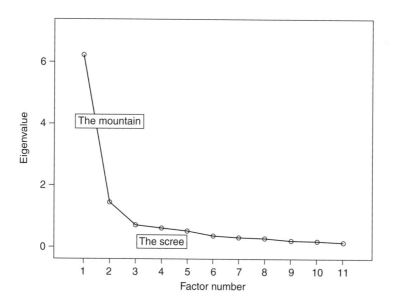

Figure 12.8   A scree plot for the social anxiety data

chart editor). The scree suggests one or two factors. Both of the first two factors have eigenvalues above 1 (6.225 and 1.453, respectively), while the eigenvalue associated with the third factor is below 1 (0.712). Because we have theoretical reasons to believe the questions are from two related but different aspects of social anxiety we would probably choose the two factor solution.

SPSS prints a χ^2 value for this two factor solution: $\chi^2(34) = 54.534$. This is most useful in comparison with other χ^2 values. The solution for the one factor model is: $\chi^2(44) = 146.261$. The reduction is statistically significant, change in $\chi^2(10) = 91.727$, $p < .001$.

Next the unrotated factor loading matrix is produced. Here we show it with the rotated matrix (though the rotated matrix is printed near the end of the output, it is useful to present it here for comparison). For the unrotated solution all the variables load on the first factor. The second factor has positive loadings for the fear of negative evaluation questions and mostly negative loadings for the social avoidance questions. For the rotated solution the fear of negative evaluation questions load mostly on the first factor and the social avoidance questions mostly on the second. The overall fit of the model does not change with rotation nor do any of the communalities (e.g. $(.634)^2 + (.361)^2 = (.696)^2 + (.219)^2 = .53$).

Factor Matrix(a)

	Factor	
	1	2
BFNE_01	.634	.361
BFNE_05	.763	.337
BFNE_06	.682	.232
BFNE_08	.714	.532
BFNE_11	.716	.309
SIAS_11	.720	.103
SIAS_13	.706	−.073
SIAS_14	.784	−.241
SIAS_15	.743	−.506
SIAS_17	.739	−.209
SIAS_18	.806	−.346

Extraction method: Maximum likelihood.
a. 2 factors extracted. 5 iterations required.

Rotated Factor Matrix(a)

	Factor	
	1	2
BFNE_01	.696	.219
BFNE_05	.767	.330
BFNE_06	.634	.342
BFNE_08	.876	.161
BFNE_11	.714	.314
SIAS_11	.565	.458
SIAS_13	.426	.567
SIAS_14	.357	.738
SIAS_15	.134	.889
SIAS_17	.350	.684
SIAS_18	.295	.826

Extraction method: Maximum likelihood.
Rotation method: Varimax with Kaiser normalization.
a. Rotation converged in 3 iterations.

SPSS prints the transformation matrix:

Factor	1	2
1	.680	.733
2	.733	−.680

Extraction Method: Maximum Likelihood.
Rotation Method: Varimax with Kaiser Normalization.

Multiplying the unrotated matrix by this rotation matrix produces the rotated factor matrix shown above (so $(0.634 \times 0.680) + (0.361 \times 0.733) = 0.696$). The data are rotated: arc-cosine(0.68) = arc-sine $(0.73) = 0.818$ in radians, which if we multiply by $180/\pi$ we get a shift of $47°$. The rotated loadings can be plotted either within SPSS or from the values above, see Figure 12.9. As can be seen the variables all still load positively on the factors. We included arrows from the origin to the mean factor loadings for the SIAS and BFNE variables. Because these arrows are not at right angles to each other it means the scores on these sets of items are correlated. This would be a situation where a non-orthogonal rotation might be used. Non-orthogonal rotations allow the factors to be correlated. As said above, these are mathematically more complex. However computationally it is relatively simple because the computer does it. You choose one of the non-orthogonal methods (in SPSS Oblimin or Promax) and how much correlation to allow (try a few values). This is explored more on the chapter's web page.

Finally, SPSS prints the correlation matrix implied by the model (shown on the web page). Here it is the two factor model. The implied matrix is the same whether the data are rotated or not. SPSS also prints the difference between the implied

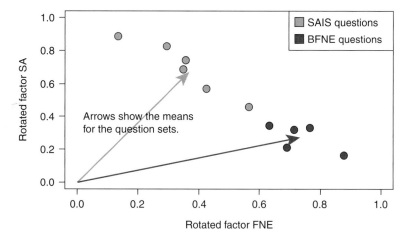

Figure 12.9 A plot of the rotated factor loadings for the social anxiety data

matrix and the sample matrix. Only 2 of the 45 correlations were off by more than 0.1, which shows that the model captures most of the associations among variables fairly well. The two slightly errant ones were that the model assumes BFNE_01 and BFNE_11 are correlated 0.57 (sample value 0.69) and that SIAS_13 and SIAS_17 are correlated 0.59 (sample value 0.38). The three factor model also has two correlations also off by more than 0.1.

In summary, this example shows running an EFA in SPSS when it is expected that a two factor model may fit. In this sense the analysis is not purely exploratory, but there are very few cases where researchers have no *a priori* beliefs about how many factors there are. Here we examine whether a two factor model fits better than other models using the scree plot, significance testing (the χ^2 tests), and how well the model reproduced the correlation matrix. Further, we looked at the rotated loadings to see if the EFA split the variables in a similar manner to our *a priori* beliefs. They did (although one of the SAIS items is close to the mean of the BFNE items so this item could be re-classified or discarded).

12.4 EXTENSIONS TO EXPLORATORY FACTOR ANALYSIS

We have talked about one type of latent variable approach: exploratory factor analysis or EFA. It is appropriate when you hypothesise that a small number of interval latent variables are responsible for variation in a larger number of observed variables, but you are unsure how they will be related. Within psychology EFA is the most used type of latent variable model. Here we briefly discuss some extensions to this model. We begin with models where you have strong *a priori* beliefs about the relationships among latent and observed variables and you want to either confirm or disconfirm your beliefs about the particular relationships.[4] Next, we describe models appropriate when either the observed or the latent variables are categorical.

12.4.1 Confirmatory methods

An alternative to exploratory factor analysis is confirmatory factor analysis, abbreviated CFA. In EFA the researcher does not specify how the latent variables are related to the observed variables. In CFA the researcher specifies these relationships. They use the diagrams with ellipses for latent variables and rectangles for observed

---

4 As noted in the last example, researchers always have beliefs about the relationship among variables. In some sense it is a matter of the degree of belief and in some cases personal preference for determining whether exploratory or confirmatory methods are used.

variables, and *they* add in the arrows, and then the computer estimates the loadings for those arrows.

EFA: Computer decides where to put the arrows.
CFA: Researcher decides where to put the arrows.
CSI: Detectives figure out who shot the arrows.

The computer also provides a measure of how good the fit is. The researcher usually runs several models and decides which models are inconsistent with the data and which ones fit well. The purpose is usually to discard bad models rather than to decide among a set of good models.

With CFA, researchers often hypothesise arrows among latent variables to show the variables are either correlated or that one is influencing another. These models are sometimes called structural equation models, or SEMs. They are mathematically more complex than EFA, and also require more care when conducting them with a statistics package. See Klem (2000), Miles and Shevlin (2003) and Thompson (2000) for introductions. The analyst has to make so many assumptions with some of these models that some methodologists argue that SEM models should be used sparingly if at all. Bartholomew and Knott (1999, p. 190) end their seminal work on latent variables with: 'When we come to models for relationships between latent variables we have reached a point where so much has to be assumed that one might justly conclude that the limits of scientific usefulness have been reached if not exceeded'.

12.4.2 **Levels of measurement of latent and observed variables**

In Chapter 2 Fife-Shaw described the levels of measurement framework to differentiate types of variables. Both the latent and observed variables could be any of these levels. The most commonly assumed levels are interval and categorical. Table 12.4 shows Bartholomew *et al.*'s (2008) classification of different latent variable models for these different levels of variables. A different name is given to each method. The methods were developed relatively independently of each other.

Table 12.4   Bartholomew *et al.*'s classification of latent variable models

		Observed variables	
		Interval	*Categorical*
Latent variables	*Interval*	Factor analysis	Item response models (Latent trait analysis)
	Categorical	Latent profile analysis	Latent class analysis

Bartholomew and Knott (1999) show how each is a special case of what they call the *general linear latent variable model.* Factor analysis was mainly developed in psychology and assumes that both the latent and observed variables are interval scales. The latent class and latent profile methods were developed mainly in sociology. Latent class analysis assumes categorical latent and observed variables. Latent profile analysis assumes interval observed variables and categorical latent variables. Latent profile analysis is rare in psychology, where other techniques (e.g. taxometric analysis, discriminant function analysis, cluster analysis) are used in these situations. Latent class models are more common than latent profile analysis, particularly in sociology.

The latent trait models, also called item response models, are common in education. The most common use of latent trait models is where you have multiple items where people either pass or fail on each item and you assume that there is one underlying latent variable (called a trait for these models rather than a factor). In fact, when students at our university take a multiple-choice exam, the feedback given to the instructor includes output from this latent trait model. The instructor could use scores on this latent trait as a measure of achievement. The output can also help the instructor to decide which questions are good and which are bad. Instructors can omit responses to bad questions from people's grades for that year and hopefully remove the offending questions from subsequent exams. Embretson and Reise (2000) have written an excellent text on these models.

Trying to decide whether your latent variables are categorical or metrical should be based largely on your theories rather than on the data. This is because often these approaches will fit both types equally well (Bartholomew, 1993). In general

Principal components analysis

A common alternative to EFA is principal components analysis, or PCA. PCA works by reducing a large number of observed variables into a smaller number of components where the components account for a large amount of the variation of the original variables. Thus, its purpose is very similar to EFA. PCA is a data reduction technique that does not make the assumption that latent variables exist. The equations for PCA are almost the opposite to those for EFA: the components are a linear combination of the observed variables (in PCA) rather than the observed variables being a linear combination of the factors (in EFA). However, both procedures work by accounting for variation among the observed variables. The solutions of the two are so similar that some statistical packages, including SPSS, simply list PCA as one way to estimate a factor analysis.

Often the two procedures are combined. A PCA is used to create a scree plot to help decide how many latent variables are needed (for technical reasons making a scree plot with PCA is more straightforward), and then an EFA is applied.

finding that a statistical model fits the data does not mean it is a good model. It is important to see how it fits compared with others. Meehl and colleagues (e.g. Waller & Meehl, 1998) have developed a set of methods to help decide whether data are more consistent with metrical or categorical latent variables, but these methods require a fairly large amount of data. Links to various sources are on the chapter's web page.

12.5 **CONCLUSION**

There seems to be something sneaky about exploratory factor analysis. How can a data analysis technique somehow allow you to measure what has not been measured? There is a South Park episode where Butters believes he has become a vampire. In part this was to elude being grounded because he believes vampires cannot be grounded. He poses the deep philosophical question to his parents: 'How can thy ground that which is ungroundable?' Similarly, how can we calculate factor scores and do any analyses with latent variables if they are un-measurable? This conundrum has meant many statisticians have been skeptical of factor analysis. Butters solved his problem by helping a group of Goths burn down a clothing shop. The way we circumvent the latent variable problem is because the question we are asking is after an assumption. First, we assume that the latent variables exist, and then we ask the computer: 'If they exist, what loadings are most consistent with the data?'. There still is a bit of hand waving, particularly when naming the latent variables, but the approach is now generally accepted within statistics. Further, it has been helpful for a hundred years of psychology. This does not mean it is right, but it does mean that it is a tool worth keeping in your statistical arsenal.

Most psychologists do not dwell on philosophical problems with statistical approaches, but ask what the approach can do for them. EFA can help (a) to reveal exciting patterns in their data, and (b) to tell a good story about their data. The EFA solution shows how the different observed variables hang together. It allows researchers to summarise their data by assuming the latent variables map onto relevant psychological constructs. Many research papers use EFA on questionnaires to to show patterns in the responses. The second main use of EFA is to create the latent variables or factor scores, and to use these in subsequent analyses. If an orthogonal rotation, like *varimax*, is used then these subsequent factors are essentially uncorrelated. This helps to provide a simple solution and avoids the collinearity problems discussed in Chapter 11.

Exploratory factor analysis has passed its hundredth birthday and is as strong as ever. The initial years were difficult because the technique had to be conducted without computers. In the past few decades advances in computing technology have led to the widespread use of many complex multivariate techniques including factor analysis. A lot of this chapter is based on the first author's student days listening to David Bartholomew's brilliance. Two things he said are most important here.

First, he started his multivariate statistics course by saying his goal was to stop us using complex multivariate procedures. He said how computing (even back then) made it too easy first to run your analyses and only then to think about what analyses you should have run. With a procedure as complex as EFA it is critical to think about what statistics you will do before doing them. His second dictum was that with many multivariate procedures the proof is in the eating. If the result of the analyses shows an illuminating pattern in the data, then that is good. For EFA this means trying a few estimation methods, a few rotations, looking at different numbers of latent variables, and finding which of the many solutions is most revealing.

12.6 EXERCISES

1 A sample of 100 people was asked to respond to eight questions. Suppose the resulting loadings for the unrotated model were:

Loadings:	Factor1	Factor2
[1,]	0.503	0.483
[2,]	-0.524	0.652
[3,]	0.760	0.205
[4,]	0.774	0.213
[5,]	-0.314	0.202
[6,]	0.603	0.415
[7,]	-0.369	0.402
[8,]	-0.504	0.473

The rotated loadings (using varimax) are:

Loadings:	Factor1	Factor2
[1,]	0.693	0.074
[2,]	-0.015	0.837
[3,]	0.727	-0.303
[4,]	0.742	-0.305
[5,]	-0.125	0.352
[6,]	0.731	-0.041
[7,]	-0.045	0.544
[8,]	-0.110	0.683

Create diagrams for both of these, using ellipses, rectangles and arrows, to show the relationships between the latent factors and the observed variables. Which diagram appears simpler? The answer may be affected by how large a loading you decide you need for drawing an arrow.

2 The rotation matrix for exercise #1 was: $\begin{bmatrix} 0.79 & -0.61 \\ 0.61 & 0.79 \end{bmatrix}$. How much were the data rotated? Describe why you would do rotation.

3 Describe the methods that you use to decide the number of factors.

4 What makes people happy? A recent movement called positive psychology examines what makes people happy. Suppose a researcher took a random sample of 1,000 people and asked them 10 attitudinal questions (called att1 to att10) and gave them a happiness questionnaire (happy). The data are saved in various formats the chapter's our web page.

    a Describe the relationships among the different attitudinal measures using correlation and EFA.

    b If you have already done multiple regression, save the factor scores from an EFA, and use these to predict happiness.

12.7 DISCUSSION QUESTIONS

1 EFA is often used to simplify how the relationships among many variables are described. Discuss why simplifying complex patterns can be helpful in science. Describe what also must be considered so that the account is not too simplified. State one interesting biographical detail about William of Ockham.

2 Suppose a researcher believed that some people are simply happy (see http://www.sohp.com/), and some are not. Could EFA be used to help the research empirically validate this belief? If so, how?

12.8 FURTHER READING

These readings are roughly in order of assumed mathematical experience (Tabachnick and Bartholomew are close in order).

Field (2009) has great descriptions of all the SPSS options available for EFA (the statistics are serious, but some of jokes you might not share with your parents). Tabachnick and Fidell (2007) gives a further survey of most of the statistical techniques psychologists learn in the first year of graduate school. Bartholomew *et al.* (2008) has a chapter on EFA but also on many of the alternatives. Aimed at first year social science graduate students, it provides the best overview of the different types of latent variable models in a manner accessible to non-statisticians. Bartholomew and Knott (1999) provides coverage aimed at applied statisticians. Mulaik (2010) is a comprehensive book on the mathematics of factor analysis, it gives a thorough and detailed review of factor analysis, and includes details of many of the controversial issues that are skirted over in introductory texts and single chapters. The book requires more mathematical knowledge than the other texts.

12.9 APPENDIX: LATENT VARIABLES IN MATRIX NOTATION

Understanding a little bit about matrices (the plural of matrix) is necessary for this chapter. The word 'matrix' sounds scary, but it is just the label mathematicians use to refer to a concept with which you are already acquainted: a table. The tables shown in the text for the α values (i.e. the loadings) are matrices. If you prefer to think 'table' when you read 'matrix' that is fine. In statistics matrices are differentiated from other objects by writing their labels in bold. Matrices have dimensions. The $\boldsymbol{\alpha}$ matrix shown towards the beginning of the chapter is tall and thin. It is 8×2 (read: 8 by 2) because there are 8 rows and 2 columns.

$$\boldsymbol{\alpha} = \overset{8 \times 2}{\begin{bmatrix} \alpha 11 & \alpha 12 \\ \alpha 21 & \alpha 22 \\ \alpha 31 & \alpha 32 \\ \alpha 41 & \alpha 42 \\ \alpha 51 & \alpha 52 \\ \alpha 61 & \alpha 62 \\ \alpha 71 & \alpha 72 \\ \alpha 81 & \alpha 82 \end{bmatrix}}.$$

In order to multiply some matrices (see later), it is necessary to transpose one of the matrices. This means that its rows become its columns and its columns become its rows. It is usually denoted with a superscripted T, although in some texts it is denoted with '. We will use T since it is easier to see.

Transposed Matrix

2×8

$$\alpha^T = \alpha' = \begin{bmatrix} \alpha11 & \alpha21 & \alpha31 & \alpha41 & \alpha51 & \alpha61 & \alpha71 & \alpha81 \\ \alpha12 & \alpha22 & \alpha32 & \alpha42 & \alpha52 & \alpha62 & \alpha72 & \alpha82 \end{bmatrix}.$$

Another matrix that you will be familiar with, even if not using the word *matrix*, is the data matrix. Let **X** be a matrix of observed data with 10 rows for the number of participants and with 8 columns for the 8 observed variables.

10×8

$$X = \begin{bmatrix} 0 & 0 & 0 & 0 & 1 & 1 & 1 & 1 \\ 1 & 1 & 1 & 0 & 0 & 1 & 1 & 1 \\ 1 & 0 & 0 & 1 & 0 & 1 & 0 & 0 \\ 0 & 0 & 0 & 0 & 0 & 0 & 0 & 0 \\ 0 & 0 & 0 & 1 & 0 & 1 & 1 & 1 \\ 0 & 1 & 0 & 1 & 0 & 1 & 1 & 1 \\ 1 & 1 & 0 & 0 & 1 & 1 & 1 & 0 \\ 0 & 0 & 0 & 1 & 0 & 1 & 1 & 1 \\ 1 & 1 & 1 & 1 & 0 & 0 & 0 & 0 \\ 0 & 0 & 1 & 0 & 0 & 0 & 1 & 0 \end{bmatrix}$$

This data matrix is a 10×8 matrix. It just has 0s and 1s. You might have a matrix like this for results in an exam where 1 means the student got the question correct and 0 means incorrect. This matrix is what you will have typed into the computer.

There is also a matrix for the latent variables or factor scores. These can be calculated in a few ways (some of which are very complicated), but they are estimated from the α values and people's values for each observed behavior. The factor matrix is usually denoted either with **F** for factors or with **Y**. For this example it will have 10 rows (for the 10 people) and 2 columns (for the 2 latent variables), so it is a 10×2 matrix.

$$\text{Factors scores} = F = Y = \begin{matrix} 10\times 2 \end{matrix} \begin{bmatrix} F11 & F12 \\ F21 & F22 \\ F31 & F32 \\ F41 & F42 \\ F51 & F52 \\ F61 & F62 \\ F71 & F72 \\ F81 & F82 \\ F91 & F92 \\ F101 & F102 \end{bmatrix}$$

We can also create a matrix out of eight item-specific error variables (the small circles in Figures 12.1 and 12.2 with *es* in them). There will be 8 columns. Each of these item variables has 10 values (for the 10 participants). We will call this 10×8 matrix E.

How to add and multiply matrices

Matrices can be added if they have the same dimensions. Adding matrices means adding the entries in each position. The resulting sum has the same dimensions as each of its addends. For example (we have written the dimensions of the matrices above the matrices, but this is normally not done), the first two matrices can be added together because they both are 2×3 matrices. The sum of them is also a 2×3 matrix.

$$\begin{matrix} 2\times 3 \end{matrix} \quad \begin{matrix} 2\times 3 \end{matrix} \quad\quad \begin{matrix} 2\times 3 \end{matrix}$$
$$\begin{bmatrix} a & b & c \\ d & e & f \end{bmatrix} + \begin{bmatrix} g & h & i \\ j & k & l \end{bmatrix} = \begin{bmatrix} a+g & b+h & c+i \\ d+j & e+k & f+l \end{bmatrix}$$

Multiplying matrices is more complex and there are a few types of matrix multiplication, but what we present is the most common. It is used for systems of equations like those used for mapping latent variables onto observed variables or for rotating factor loadings. The order of matrix multiplication is important: AB is in general not the same as BA. The dimensions of the matrices are important. A 3×2 matrix can be multiplied by a 2×4 matrix because the inner numbers (here the two 2s) are the same. If the inner numbers are not the same then they cannot be multiplied. Here is an example (with the dimensions of the matrices listed above them):

$$
\begin{array}{ccc}
3 \times 2 & 2 \times 4 & 3 \times 4 \\
\begin{bmatrix} a & b \\ c & d \\ e & f \end{bmatrix} & \begin{bmatrix} g & h & i & j \\ k & l & m & n \end{bmatrix} = & \begin{bmatrix} ag+bk & ah+bl & ai+bm & aj+bn \\ cg+dk & ch+dl & ci+dm & cj+dn \\ eg+fk & eh+fl & ei+fm & ej+fn \end{bmatrix}
\end{array}
$$

The first entry in the product ($ag + bk$) is found by multiplying the first value in the first row of the first matrix (a) by the first value in the first column of the second matrix (g), and then repeating this with all other values in this row and this column (here only 2), and adding these up. For this to work there has to be the same number of values in each row of the first matrix (i.e. the number of columns) as the number of values in each column of the second matrix (i.e. the number of rows). The resulting matrix has the same number of rows as the first matrix and the same number of columns as the second matrix.

One way to remember this is that in order to multiply two matrices, if you place their dimensions side-by-side, as above with the 3×2 and 2×4 matrices, then the inner dimension values must be the same (the 2s) and the outer dimension values become the dimensions for their product. In our example the F matrix is 10×2 so we can only multiply that by a matrix with 2 rows. The α matrix is 8×2, so we cannot estimate the product Fα. However, we can transpose the α matrix and the transposed matrix is 2×8. Once you transpose the matrix you can multiply it.

$$
\alpha^T = \begin{bmatrix} \alpha 11 & \alpha 21 & \alpha 31 & \alpha 41 & \alpha 51 & \alpha 61 & \alpha 71 & \alpha 81 \\ \alpha 12 & \alpha 22 & \alpha 32 & \alpha 42 & \alpha 52 & \alpha 62 & \alpha 72 & \alpha 82 \end{bmatrix}
$$

The model can be written out as: $X = F\alpha^T + E$. This is much shorter than trying to write out the large number of equations without using matrix notation.

In EFA you often want to calculate the correlation matrix implied by the loadings. This is:

$$\alpha\alpha^{\mathrm{T}} = \begin{bmatrix} \alpha11 & \\ \alpha21 & \\ \alpha31 & \\ \alpha41 & \alpha42 \\ \alpha51 & \alpha52 \\ & \alpha62 \\ & \alpha72 \\ & \alpha82 \end{bmatrix} \begin{bmatrix} \alpha11 & \alpha21 & \alpha31 & \alpha41 & \alpha51 & & & \\ & & & & \alpha42 & \alpha52 & \alpha62 & \alpha72 & \alpha82 \end{bmatrix}$$

$$= \begin{bmatrix} \alpha11\alpha11 & \alpha11\alpha21 & \alpha11\alpha31 & \alpha11\alpha41 & \alpha11\alpha51 & 0 & 0 & 0 \\ \alpha21\alpha11 & \alpha21\alpha21 & \alpha21\alpha31 & \alpha21\alpha41 & \alpha21\alpha51 & 0 & 0 & 0 \\ \alpha31\alpha11 & \alpha31\alpha21 & \alpha31\alpha31 & \alpha31\alpha41 & \alpha31\alpha51 & 0 & 0 & 0 \\ \alpha41\alpha11 & \alpha41\alpha21 & \alpha41\alpha31 & \alpha41\alpha41+\alpha42\alpha42 & \alpha41\alpha51+\alpha42\alpha52 & \alpha42\alpha62 & \alpha42\alpha72 & \alpha42\alpha82 \\ \alpha51\alpha11 & \alpha51\alpha21 & \alpha51\alpha31 & \alpha51\alpha41+\alpha52\alpha42 & \alpha51\alpha51+\alpha52\alpha52 & \alpha52\alpha62 & \alpha52\alpha72 & \alpha52\alpha82 \\ 0 & 0 & 0 & \alpha62\alpha42 & \alpha62\alpha52 & \alpha62\alpha52 & \alpha62\alpha72 & \alpha62\alpha82 \\ 0 & 0 & 0 & \alpha72\alpha42 & \alpha72\alpha52 & \alpha72\alpha62 & \alpha72\alpha72 & \alpha72\alpha82 \\ 0 & 0 & 0 & \alpha82\alpha42 & \alpha82\alpha52 & \alpha82\alpha62 & \alpha82\alpha72 & \alpha82\alpha82 \end{bmatrix}$$

This looks really complicated, but if you are okay with matrix algebra it is just the product of two matrices. It is easily produced in the statistics packages as shown in the text and on the chapter's web page.

This has been a brief introduction to matrices. Most multivariate statistics books written for psychologists have a chapter on matrix computations. Sources are given on the chapter's web page.

Part 3

Qualitative Research: Data Collection and Analysis

13

Introduction to Qualitative Methods

Virginia Eatough

CONTENTS

AIMS OF THIS CHAPTER

This chapter offers an overview of the field of qualitative research in psychology. After reading the chapter you should have some understanding of the following aspects of qualitative psychological research:

* the history and philosophical origins of qualitative research;
* characteristics of qualitative research;
* contemporary qualitative research in psychology.

KEY TERMS

epistemology	reflexivity
human sciences	relativism
meanings	social constructionism
realism	subjective experience

13.1 **INTRODUCTION**

In recent years, psychology has seen the steady development of a range of qualitative research methods. All British Psychological Society (BPS) accredited undergraduate degree programmes offer (at least some) qualitative research instruction alongside training in quantitative methods. It is also the case that the use of qualitative methods at postgraduate level and the number of journals publishing qualitative research is increasing. 2005 saw the formation of the BPS Qualitative Methods in Psychology Section, which is the largest section of the BPS at present (Madill & Gough, 2008).

This chapter aims to provide a broad-brush background to the field of qualitative research in psychology. It does not aim to convince you that qualitative methods are 'better' than quantitative ones (or vice versa). Rather it attempts to show you where qualitative research fits within psychology and its contribution to a versatile psychological 'tool-kit' (Hayes, 2000, p. 165) which assists psychologists to ask different questions about the topics they study.

For qualitative psychologists, a key interest is 'people's grasp of their world.' (Ashworth, 2008, p. 4). In other words qualitative researchers are interested in people's subjective experience as well as the resources available to them to make sense of and understand their world. This interest can lead to a focus on how people *construct* their world (including the relationships they have and the objects they encounter) through the social, cultural and linguistic practices they are born into. Alternatively, it can lead to an emphasis on how it is through our perceptions and the meanings we attribute to events that we come to understand our personal and social world. Reicher (2000) classifies these different approaches as *discursive* and *experiential* respectively. The following chapters will introduce you to specific methods which are underpinned by these different (yet overlapping) approaches to how people understand their worlds.

13.2 **SHORT HISTORY OF QUALITATIVE RESEARCH**

From its development in the late nineteenth century to the present day, psychology has endeavoured to be a natural science discipline. This means it has adopted both the methodology (logical positivism) and the methods of the natural sciences (hypothetic-deductive). Perhaps not surprisingly, the emerging discipline of psychology was dazzled by the achievements and insights of the natural sciences and sought to emulate these by adopting their methods. For example, the systematic manipulation of variables under controlled experimental conditions. Yet, from the outset, there has been a persistent and significant challenge to this conception of psychology and this section traces this challenge through the history of the discipline.

Importantly, some of the early psychologists you are probably familiar with as belonging to the experimental tradition were open and responsive to the value of understanding subjective experience as well as the need for appropriate methods to investigate it. It might surprise you to know that Wilhelm Wundt (1832–1920) who established his experimental laboratory in 1879 at the University of Leipzig, Germany, envisaged psychology as 'a hybrid discipline, representing a combination of a natural science and a human science' (Kendler, 1987, p. 27). Early psychologists such as Wundt and William James (1842–1910) were interested in the conscious mind and individual subjective experience rather than behaviour and sought to establish psychology as a science of experience. Wundt's introspectionist method trained research participants in the technique of self-observation and aimed to get close to their experience of the phenomenon being studied. His experiments were not natural science experiments and he was doubtful whether experimentation could provide the answers to all of psychology's questions (Danziger, 1990; Schneider, 1998).

The philosopher and psychologist, William James, understood experience holistically and described it metaphorically as a rhythmic stream of consciousness. To understand the richness and complexity of our experiential life required techniques which focused on concrete experiences in their entirety rather than breaking them down into discrete parts. For James, studying the particularities of concrete experiences was an essential first step for a proper understanding. Like Wundt, he used introspectionist methods as well as analysing documents such as personal letters, autobiographies and diaries. James recognised that understanding the subjective life of individuals required the fledgling discipline of psychology to be creative and flexible in how it investigated its subject matter.

Similarly, Edward B. Titchener (1867–1927) recognised the value and legitimacy of qualitative research and advocated a psychology which drew on its strengths as well as those of quantitative research; namely both *description* and *measurement*. Questions that began with 'how much?' left 'what?' and 'how?' questions unanswered. Thus, Titchener proposed experiments which had both qualitative and quantitative dimensions:

> The experiments are complementary, each sacrificing something, and each gaining something. The qualitative experiment shows us all the detail and variety of the mental life, and in so doing forbids us to pack its results into formulae; the quantitative experiment furnishes us with certain uniformities of the mental life, neatly and summarily expressed, but for that very reason must pass unnoticed many things that a qualitatively directed introspection would bring to light.
>
> Titchener, 1905, p. vi

Almost half a century later, both Solomon Asch (1907–1996) and Gordon Allport (1897–1967) echoed these voices. Asch believed that psychology's willingness to treat its subject matter (people) like the subject matter of the natural sciences (e.g. rocks) meant that most psychology paid insufficient attention to developing methods which harnessed and made use of our particularly human qualities – language and self-reflection:

> In their anxiety to be scientific, students of psychology have often imitated the latest forms of sciences with a long history, while ignoring the steps these sciences took when they were young. They have, for example, striven to emulate the quantitative exactness of natural sciences without asking whether their own subject matter is always ripe for such treatment, failing to realize that one does not advance time by moving the hands of the clock. Because physicists cannot speak with stars or electric currents, psychologists have often been hesitant to speak to their human participants.
>
> Asch, 1952/1987, pp. xiv–xv

Like James and the Gestalt theorists, Allport took a holistic stance and was a strong proponent of *idiographic* research which studies the individual person in all her/his complexity and richness. In today's terminology, people are embodied, situated and historical beings who cannot be studied in isolation from the social and material world in which they live out their lives. Also like James, Allport saw the value of using a variety of documents as important sources for acquiring knowledge about subjective life. Many more familiar names (e.g. Piaget, Mead and Kelly) could be mentioned to support the claim that, historically, a significant minority of psychologists were committed to a psychology which viewed subjective experience as worthy of study.

More recently, the 1970s saw a number of critical perspectives develop in opposition to mainstream psychological research and which proposed that qualitative methods were both more relevant and naturalistic ways to understand people. It was argued that people should be studied in their everyday social settings and a shift away from measurement and quantification was needed if psychology was to advance (Gergen, 1973; Harré & Secord, 1972). However, many of these writers were less concerned with developing alternative methods than they were with highlighting the limitations of a discipline which drew its methods almost solely from the natural sciences. A notable exception was the US psychologist Giorgi who, working from within the humanist tradition, developed the descriptive phenomenological method as a way of going beyond a theoretical critique of quantitative research (Giorgi, 1970, 2009). During the 1980s discourse analysis emerged as a specific qualitative method with its particular focus on the role of language and discourse for understanding psychological phenomena. By the 1990s psychologists interested in qualitative approaches engaged with grounded theory and the different forms of narrative analysis as well as seeing the development of new psychological research approaches such as Interpretative Phenomenological Analysis (IPA) (Smith, 1996). The contemporary picture of qualitative research 'is one of heterogeneity, with qualitative research best conceptualized as a fuzzy set.' (Madill & Gough, 2008, pp. 254–255).

Hopefully, this brief sketch has illustrated the historical thread that can be traced with respect to alternative ways of thinking about psychology's subject matter. We turn now to the philosophical origins of these different ways of thinking.

13.3 PHILOSOPHICAL ORIGINS OF QUALITATIVE RESEARCH

13.3.1 Human sciences for human kinds

Underpinning qualitative research is the belief in a human sciences tradition with its own set of methods and techniques to answer those questions which are not amenable to quantitative research perspectives. Many of the things that make us human are not receptive to measurement and objective mathematical precision. Furthermore, with respect to human beings, the universal laws that might be established are likely to be very small in number. Psychology from a human sciences perspective aims to understand human actions, human intentions and the meanings people impute to these actions and intentions in the context of their lives. To paraphrase the philosopher Wilhelm Dilthey (1976), 'No real blood flows in the knowing subject' when examined from a natural science perspective.

As human beings there are certain types of behaviour and actions which we can exert on ourselves and others. For example, we have a tendency to classify people into different groups on a wide range of characteristics such as gender, ethnicity and social class (not to mention more psychological classifications such as high/low IQ, neuroticism, levels of self-esteem, and so on). We are affected by these classifications not least because we experience ourselves in particular ways because of them. Such classifications *matter* and are meaningful for us. We interact with them in ways that natural kinds do not because they are not aware of how they are classified. This does not mean that human kinds are not real:

> Human kinds definitely are real, but it is a reality in which they themselves are deeply involved. It is a reality of which they are a part … Human psychological beings require sociocultural, biological and physical reality for their existence, but they are not entirely determined by their sociocultural, biological and physical constitution.
>
> Martin & Sugarman, 2001, p. 194

This view of people as human kinds not natural kinds (Hacking, 1995; Van Langenhove, 1995) encourages qualitative researchers to concentrate on the things that make us human – the tangled, messy and multifaceted aspects of experiences – so that research findings connect to peoples' attempts to make sense of their lives and which cannot be captured in experimentation for example. In terms of real-life relevance and applicability, one might argue that there is little in common between the frustration induced in laboratory-based aggression experiments and the intense slow burning rage felt by a woman who, whilst chopping vegetables, contemplates stabbing her husband.

13.3.2 **Epistemology, realism and relativism**

Epistemology is a philosophical term concerned with how, and what we can say we know about the world; in other words, epistemological issues deal with the nature of knowledge. Realism and relativism are epistemological perspectives and they refer to the different ways that psychologists approach these questions both intellectually and in a more practical sense in terms of the methods they use.

The differences between realism and relativism are best understood as a continuum with psychologists positioning themselves and the perspectives they subscribe to at various points along it. At one end of the continuum is naive realism whilst at the other is radical relativism. Positions in between include critical realism and less extreme forms of relativism. However, as you might imagine, there is sometimes disagreement over where particular perspectives are situated:

> The classification of epistemological perspectives into distinct positions necessarily requires a degree of simplification and homogenizing of perspectives. A label such as 'realist' or 'relativist' is unable to capture the true complexities and ambiguities that characterize the various epistemologies. Furthermore, the categorization of any particular method(ology) is itself a matter of judgment. Most approaches combine a number of features that are compatible with more than one epistemological position. In addition, most methods evolve over time and may modify their epistemological assumptions accordingly.
>
> Willig, 2001, p. 149

Furthermore, it is worth remembering that very few psychological researchers would adopt the extreme ends of the continuum, with most falling somewhere in between.

Naive realism refers to the perspective that we have unmediated access to the world: there is an uncomplicated relationship between our perceptions of the world and the world itself. Acquiring knowledge of the world is a matter of discovering what is already 'out there'. No qualitative researcher (indeed, very few quantitative researchers) is likely to commit to such an extreme form of realism.

In stark contrast, radical relativism proposes that there are multiple competing knowledges of the world and that these knowledges are socially constructed solely from available linguistic and discursive resources. Very simply, the only reality we can know is one which has arisen out of the language we use. A small but significant number of qualitative researchers support the view that our psychological and social worlds are derived from nothing more than the linguistic resources available to us.

Alternatively, critical realists adopt a more or less middling and pragmatic position. They acknowledge the existence of an objective and real world but argue that our access to it is mediated through a lens of social, cultural and historical practices which includes the linguistic and discursive practices we are born into. Thus, a critical realist position believes in an 'extra-discursive' world which consists of objects and entities which have an independent existence and which is partially accessible to us. Earlier in the chapter it was mentioned how the qualitative approaches you will be introduced to in the following chapters can be described as either *experiential* or *discursive*. In terms of the realist–relativist continuum, experiential methods are located variously between critical realism and realism whilst discursive methods line up towards the relativism pole.

13.3.3 **Phenomenology**

Phenomenology is an approach which was very influential in Continental European twentieth century philosophy but less so in the UK which arguably was dominated by analytic philosophy. As a philosophical approach it has influenced a number of qualitative psychological methods (one of the most well-known being IPA (Smith, 1996) which is the focus of Chapter 18) for which the fundamental unit of analysis is experience. Phenomenology is interested in how things *appear* to us through our conscious experience; reality is experiential and we experience the world through a practical and meaningful engagement with it.

'To the things themselves' is the rallying call of Husserl, whom many people consider to be the founding father of phenomenology. The aim of the phenomenological project is to describe and understand the 'things themselves' as they are meaningfully lived. This requires what we think we know already about the phenomenon (such as preconceptions and presuppositions) to be put aside so that it can be examined 'as it appears to our flesh-and-bone selves' (Varela, 1999, p. 267). Contemporary qualitative researchers recognise the impossibility of carrying out a piece of research in a neutral fashion, arguing that there is no 'view from nowhere'. Thus, throughout the research they strive to make themselves aware of the values and beliefs they bring to the process and reflect on how they might have influenced it.

Phenomenology aims to clarify, illuminate and elucidate the meaning of people's experiences in the context of what is often referred to as the lifeworld. The lifeworld is an important concept because it refers to the world we live in and experience – a world of mountains, colours, people, objects and sounds – rather than a world of scientific abstraction. This is the world in which we think, feel and practically engage with, both by ourselves and with other people. It is a subjectively lived world rather than the world of objective science. This does not mean that phenomenology rejects modern science but it does argue that the scientific world presupposes the experienced world:

> [Phenomenology] attempts to show that the exact, mathematical sciences take their origin from the lived world. They are founded on the lifeworld. The exact sciences are a transformation of the experience we directly have of things in the world; they push this experience to a much higher level of identification, and correlatively they transform the objects we experience into idealized, mathematical objects. It may seem that the exact sciences are discovering a new and different world, but what they are really doing, according to phenomenology, is subjecting the ordinary world to a new method. Through this method, the exact sciences merely increase the knowledge we have about the world in which we live; they provide a greater precision in our dealings with things, but they never abandon or discard the world that is their basis. Such sciences are nested within the life world; they do not enter into competition with it.
>
> Sokolowski, 2000, p. 147

Therefore, for phenomenology, there are not two worlds with one being more real than the other.

13.3.4 Hermeneutics

Hermeneutics is the established name used to describe the skills of interpretation, a practice which began with the interpretation of biblical texts. Much later, Enlightenment thinkers set about systematising this practice into a general method of understanding (Moran, 2000) whilst contemporary qualitative researchers use it to denote how understanding is a matter of interpretation. Humans are by nature 'self-interpreting beings' (Taylor, 1985) and how we ascribe meaning to an event, person or object is always filtered through an already existing experiential knowledge. This experiential knowledge is acquired through living our lives in a particular place and time and as such it is constrained by cultural context and historical specificity.

Thus, there are many ways to interpret life's happenings and how you do so is dependent, at least in part, on your particular perspective. For example, Gallagher (2004) suggests, somewhat provocatively, that science is simply one perspective one can subscribe to:

> The practice of science is itself hermeneutical. That is, scientists make interpretations, and their interpretations are biased in a very productive way by

the scientific tradition to which they belong, and the specific kinds of questions that they ask. Explanation is no less interpretation than understanding. The interpretation of quantitative data, for example, relies on certain developments in the history of science, and on qualitative judgments amongst scientists.

Gallagher, 2004, p. 164

Qualitative researchers of a hermeneutic persuasion do not subscribe to a false objectivity, rather they recognise how reality is contingent on sociocultural practices, individual psychological contexts and human agency. Psychological research (like all science) is a social and interpretive practice (Fowers, 1998) and psychologists 'are not, and cannot become, the neutral dispassionate observers that both empiricism and rationalism would have us be' (Packer & Addison, 1989, pp. 19–20)

None of this should be taken to mean that all perspectives have equal value. Rather it means that when we examine existing understandings we need to have both an open mind and a questioning stance: open to alternative ways of looking at things and willing to question the underpinnings of particular standpoints. Indeed, throughout our daily lives, several interpretations can often be applied to a single human action. Even when supplied with most (if not all) the facts of an event, several conclusions may be drawn. Imagine a group of psychologists of different persuasions who witness an aggressive interaction between two men and are asked to explain what is going on. The social psychologist is likely to focus on situational factors whereas the individual differences theorist might emphasise stable personality traits.

13.3.5 Social constructionism

Social constructionism is a body of postmodern thinking and practice which has had considerable influence on qualitative researchers in psychology. Discursive psychologists (see Chapter 20) whose epistemological underpinnings are relativist in orientation (see previously) are its strongest advocates while more experiential researchers tend to adopt a weaker version of its principles. Burr (1999) describes the main features of social constructionism as:

- a critical approach towards taken for granted knowledge and a corresponding concern with historical and cultural specificity;

- a belief that knowledge is constructed between people;

- a conviction that language has a privileged status in constructing the world.

The first feature clearly rejects the naive realist position described above, arguing that what we come to know of the world is not acquired through objective neutral

observation which uncovers the world as it really is. Importantly, social constructionism challenges us to question this knowledge for the assumptions that lie behind
it and the implications it has for how might people live their lives. For example, the
ways we classify and divide people and objects say more about the specific cultures
we live in than about any real divisions:

> Social constructionism bids us to seriously question whether the
> categories 'man' and 'woman' are simply a reflection of naturally occurring
> distinct types of human being. This may seem a bizarre idea at first, and of
> course differences in reproductive organs are present in many species.
> But we become aware of the greyness of such categories when we look at
> practices such as gender reassignment surgery and the surrounding
> debate about how to classify people as unambiguously male or female. We
> can thus begin to consider that these seemingly natural categories may be
> inevitably bound up with gender, the normative prescriptions of masculin-
> ity and femininity in a culture, so that that whole categories of personhood,
> that is all the things it means to be a man or a woman, have been built upon
> them.
>
> Burr, 2003, p. 3

Once we begin to question the nature of our knowledge about the world it is clear
that categories (e.g. what it means to be a child, a drunk, a mad person) changes over
time in response to shifting social and cultural practices.

The second feature acknowledges the intersubjective nature of knowledge. Social
constructionists argue that our knowledge of the world comes not from the world
as it really is, but arises out of our daily ongoing social interactions with one another
as well as the social practices we engage in. In other words, knowledge is co-
constructed through exchanges between people. For example, psychologists tend
to produce a different sort of knowledge from that produced by biologists or even
sociologists. This is because they are, in many ways, different communities
with different practices which are constituted out of a shared stock of concepts and
meanings.

This perspective highlights the third feature of social constructionism – the
importance of language and its constructive nature. Traditional psychology views
language as a vehicle which simply describes and reflects reality in an unproblematic manner. In contrast, social constructionists propose that it is through language,
talk and discourse that we fashion our worlds and identities. We cannot pre-date
language because it is language which brings us into being, we are born into a pre-
existing language. For the social constructionist, our emotions and desires are not
an essential part of human nature which would be there whether or not we had
language; rather it is through language that they are available to us and hence
structure our experience.

13.3.6 **Narrative**

In recent years, qualitative psychologists have shown an increasing interest in narrative and the role it plays in our lives. Narrative researchers point to how our lives are storied, meaning 'we are born into a narrative world, live our lives through narrative and afterwards are described in terms of narrative' (Murray, 2008, p. 111). This fundamental inclination for story telling allows us to impose a coherence and order on the events in our life, assume temporal continuity and define our sense of self.

Narrative theorists think about narratives in different yet overlapping ways. Gergen and Gergen (1986) state that narratives are social constructions that arise out of linguistic interactions enabling us to make sense of the world. Sarbin (1986, p. 301) ascribes a more ontological status to our narrative capacity: 'We are always enveloped in stories. The narrative for human beings is analogous to the ocean for fishes.' Thus, although Sarbin recognises the socially constructed nature of narratives, he does not simply reduce them to linguistic output but argues that the storied form of our lives is part of what makes us human.

Hermeneutics has also played an important part in the development of narrative psychological research. Qualitative researchers have drawn from the philosophical thinking of Paul Ricoeur, in particular his ideas about the relationship between time, meaning making and narratives:

> Human time … is neither the subjective time of consciousness nor the objective time of the cosmos. Rather, human time bridges the gap between phenomenological and cosmological time. Human time is the time of our life stories; a narrated time structured and articulated by the symbolic mediations of narratives.
>
> Zahavi, 2008, p. 106

Narrative theorists also stress how it is through narrative that we gain self-knowledge and come to understand ourselves. The events and happenings in our lives (especially those which are most significant and/or disruptive) are placed into a 'life story' in which we have the starring role – that of both narrator and main character. Our sense of self is constituted out of the stories of our life and it is through these stories that we come to know our self. However, our starring role is supported and enhanced by the presence and actions of others. For example, the beginning of our story is put in place for us by others and how our stories develop and move along various paths is a consequence of us being embedded in a web of relationships and shared community:

> [W]e are never more (and sometimes less) than the co-authors of our own narratives. Only in fantasy do we live what story we please. In life, as both

Aristotle and Engels noted, we are always under certain constraints. We enter upon a stage which we did not design and we find ourselves part of an action that was not of our making.

MacIntyre, 1984, p. 213

To conclude this section, it has introduced you to several related epistemological perspectives which underpin to varying degrees the specific qualitative approaches explained in the subsequent chapters.

13.4 CHARACTERISTICS OF QUALITATIVE RESEARCH

13.4.1 The 'essence' of doing qualitative research

Many qualitative researchers talk about research being a 'voyage of discovery' (Finlay & Evans, 2009), an 'adventure' (Willig, 2001). By this they mean that qualitative researchers deliberately adopt an attitude of openness towards the topics they investigate. Their focus on understanding people as embodied situated persons means that they expect to encounter unknowns and contradictions along the way. They do not seek to exclude these, rather they are to be accounted for in order to do justice to the phenomenon being investigated. This is one of the reasons why qualitative psychologists do not (typically) make predictions and test hypotheses. Open research questions are preferred in the attempt to achieve a more holistic understanding. Nonetheless, it should be remembered that no matter how open a research question is, it will inevitably exclude the exploration of some dimensions of the phenomenon one is interested in.

The act of carrying out a qualitative study is often described as a 'craft' (Miles & Huberman, 1994). This points to how qualitative research is a set of skills and techniques which are to be used flexibly and creatively. Qualitative researchers aim for a position of immersion, informed curiosity and careful receptivity to the research process. This is in contrast to their quantitative counterparts whose methods require detachment, prediction and control. Inevitably this leads to different sorts of questions being asked, and qualitative researchers argue that the more interesting questions are the ones which are not easily apparent nor which lend themselves readily to measurement:

Progress in science is won by the application of an informed imagination to a problem of genuine consequence; not by the habitual application of some formulaic mode of inquiry to a set of quasi-problems chosen chiefly because of their compatibility with the adopted method.

Robinson, 2000, p. 41

Qualitative researchers aim to remain open to uncertainty and ambiguity through-out the research process because their research designs are grounded in the reality of peoples' lives which, more often than not, are disordered, multifaceted and com-plex. This requires them to be resourceful throughout the research process as well as responsive to situations that might arise.

All of the above means that the laboratory is not a suitable context for carrying out qualitative research. The preference is for studying the topics of interest in the context in which they occur or at least in environments which are familiar to participants rather than unknown and artificial. For instance, researchers using interviews often prefer to carry these out in participants' homes or a venue of the participants' choice. Of course, naturalistic settings and an emphasis on real-worldness comes at a price; what is gained in terms of richness and relevance is at the expense of control and certainty.

Qualitative researchers are usually not very much interested in the quantity and measurement of a particular phenomenon but the qualities and features which make a phenomenon what it is. Qualitative researchers collect languaged data (Polkinghorne, 2005) rather than numerical data. It is worth noting that a considerable amount of quantitative data begins as languaged data (e.g. verbal reports) and is transformed into numbers. Qualitative data is analysed by employing various systematic tech-niques which reflect the epistemological underpinnings of a particular approach. These techniques are described in detail in subsequent chapters. Table 13.1 provides a useful summary of the main features of qualitative and quantitative research.

13.4.2 Evaluating qualitative research

Qualitative researchers, like their quantitative colleagues, are concerned with evalu-ating the quality, validity and value of their empirical work. However, given that the specifics of the two approaches are very different (see Table 13.1), it makes no sense to employ the same set of evaluative criteria. As Coyle (2008) suggests, this would be akin to evaluating the music of opera using the criteria applied to heavy metal or folk.

At present, there is some debate within the qualitative community as to which criteria are most useful and appropriate for gauging the quality of their work. For example, given the range of qualitative approaches with their different epistemo-logical and philosophical orientations, is it possible to have a single set of criteria? Even if the answer is 'only with difficulty', it is important to agree a set of criteria which act as guidelines for what constitutes best practice in qualitative research. However, a note of caution is needed:

> Simply following guidelines cannot guarantee good research; qualitative research is not simply a descriptive science but also relies on the capacity to

Table 13.1   Typical features of qualitative and quantitative research

Features	Qualitative	Quantitative
Key concepts	Experience, meaning, understanding, intersubjectivity, reflexivity	Prediction, probability, reliability, replication, operationalisation
Designs	Flexible, evolving, open, not prescriptive	Controlled, formal, predetermined
Sampling	Small, purposive selection, theoretical sampling	Representative, large, control groups, random selection
Methods	Participant observation, semi- and un-structured interviews, focus groups, diaries, documents	Experiments, surveys, structured observation and interviewing
Data	Words, interview transcripts, naturally occurring conversations, documents, media text	Numbers, measuring, counting, quantifiable coding
Tools	Research diaries, audio visual equipment, software analytic packages	Test scores, scales, psychometric measures
Data analysis	Systematic operations like coding, clustering and abstraction, iterative, inductive	Statistical, deductive, takes place at the end of data collection
Strengths	Detailed and in-depth, participant led, meaningful, high in ecological validity	Standardised procedures, fast, researcher control, possibility of large sample sizes
Limitations	Difficulty extrapolating to populations, unwieldy complex data, time consuming	Low ecological validity, participants constrained

evoke imaginative experience and reveal new meanings – and this core quality is not easily captured by check-list criteria.

Yardley, 2008, p. 239

Several sets of guidelines have been developed and published in recent years (see for example, Elliott *et al.*, 1999; Yardley, 2000, 2008) with some emphasising scientific rigour while others highlight the creativity and personal tone of most qualitative research. Others try to address both and a good example of this is the '4 R's criteria' (Finlay & Evans, 2009). These include *rigour, relevance, resonance* and *reflexivity* with researchers attending to each one differentially depending on the stage of the research as well as the aims and values of the researcher.

In brief, *rigour* assesses whether or not the research has been carried out competently and systematically. Is the write-up of the research understandable and decisions with respect to sampling, depth/breadth of analysis set out clearly? Are the interpretations suitably contextualised, justified and plausible? *Relevance* refers to what sort of contribution the research makes to the existing body of knowledge. Good research makes a difference in some way, whether that is practically or theoretically. *Resonance* addresses whether or not the findings of the research chime with and 'speak' to the reader. Much qualitative research deals with events which not only have personal significance for those taking part in the research but which resonate with many people's experiences. This criterion is related to trustworthiness of the findings (Polkinghorne, 1983). Many issues are raised under *reflexivity* so this is dealt with in a separate section below.

13.4.3 **Reflexivity**

Being a qualitative researcher means being a reflexive researcher. It involves adopting an attitude of self-awareness and active reflection throughout the research process. More specifically, it means thinking about the 'baggage' that you bring to the process and questioning how it has shaped and moulded the research. Willig (2001) talks about personal and methodological reflexivity. The former refers to how the researcher should examine her/his background, values and beliefs for how they might have influenced the research question(s) asked or the interpretation of the findings. Additionally, being personally reflexive might involve examining how the research has changed the researcher. The latter requires researchers to examine their assumptions about the nature of knowledge and how these, for example, will have led to particular questions being asked whilst others were excluded.

Engaging in the reflexive process is not something that is simply done before and at the end of the research. Indeed, you might not be aware of some assumptions until you are part way through the research. For instance, during the data analysis, you may become aware of a dormant preconception because something in the data brings it to the fore. Two practical ways of ensuring that reflexive attention is ensured throughout the research is by keeping a reflective diary and maintaining an audit trail (Shaw, 2010). The diary should be used to make personal notes of decisions made, problems encountered and how they were resolved, and more personal notes reflecting on their preconceptions and how they are having an effect on the research. The audit (or paper) trail is a complete record of the procedures carried out throughout the data analysis. A thorough and full audit trail means that an observer should be able to examine it and see how you moved from the raw data to provisional claims and interpretations to final conclusions.

13.5 MAPPING OF CONTEMPORARY QUALITATIVE RESEARCH

At the start of this chapter, I mentioned how the different qualitative approaches can be mapped onto an experiential-discursive dimension (Reicher, 2000). This is the simplest mapping and other researchers have proposed more substantive ones (Madill & Gough, 2008; Willig, 2001). Another way of illustrating the different approaches is to show how the differences lead to different sorts of research questions and different research designs. Box 13.1 provides examples of the types of research questions the approaches ask while Box 13.2 illustrates how different methodologies lead to different aims for a research study. For example, researchers committed to a phenomenological methodology will approach the research with a very different set of assumptions and concerns from those of a researcher who adopts a discursive approach.

The following chapters will describe in detail some of the qualitative methods of data collection and data analysis available to researchers. Here I will briefly map these methods to set the scene. The first four deal with the different ways qualitative researchers collect and elicit data whilst the remaining chapters describe four widely used data analysis approaches.

Box 13.1   Types of research questions

Interpretative phenomenological analysis (IPA):
What does it mean to become a parent?
What is it like to live with Parkinson's disease?
How does an athlete come to terms with a career-threatening injury?

Grounded theory:
How does a person become a member of a terrorist group?
How do people become proficient at playing a musical instrument?
What is the role of punishment in the teacher–pupil relationship?

Discourse analysis:
How do mediators construct 'conflict' in their interactions with clients?
How does racist discourse operate in the workplace?
How do women talk about and negotiate the menopause?

Content analysis:
What are the dominant themes in young children's storybooks?
What do nurses think when patients become angry?
How do newspapers report anti-social behaviour?

Box 13.2 Researching the topic of binge drinking using different qualitative approaches

IPA: The IPA researcher aims to elicit a rich detailed description of the lived experience of binge drinking for participants. Questions aim to draw out examples of specific times participants carried out binge drinking, prompting for details which keep participants focused on the concrete rather than the general. Other questions will tap into the personal meanings attached to the experience of binge drinking.

Grounded theory: The grounded theory researcher aims to understand the processes and mechanisms involved in binge drinking. Questions will focus on the specific times and contexts in which binge drinking takes place and how they manage their binge drinking over time. For example, the specific social situations that facilitate or inhibit binge drinking.

Discourse analysis: Discursive psychologists examine how people 'do binge drinking' in their talk allowing them to construct particular versions of reality and manage accountability. This includes identifying aspects of talk such as rhetoric. The Foucauldian analyst focuses on the cultural discourses (eg binge drinking is a normal part of British youth culture vs. binge drinking is a sign of a self-indulgent degenerate society) available to people, and how they take up and challenge these in their lives.

Content analysis: The content analyst collects qualitative data and analyses it by establishing common categories in the data or by converting it into quantitative data, e.g. numbers. Most commonly the content analyst will have a number of predetermined categories and they will examine the data to see how many examples of each category can be identified in the data. So, in the case of binge drinking they may use the categories 'normal behaviour' and 'helps to relax'.

Chapter 14 introduces you to observational methods. Observation is an everyday skill which is employed systematically in qualitative research. These methods can be used by themselves or alongside other types of data collection such as interviews. Often observation is used to examine how people behave in specific situations and the social roles and cultural practices which influence behaviour. However, more controlled and artificial settings can also be the focus. The role of the researcher can range from being an active participant observer to a non-participant one.

Chapter 15 describes another form of data collection, that of interviewing. Interviews are a widely used and very flexible data collection tool, and like observation they can be used with other techniques. Research interviews are a form of conversation (another everyday skill we have) which have a specific structure and purpose. The researcher must be a careful and attentive listener in order to gather knowledge about the topic they are interested in. Interviews sit on a continuum from structured through to semi-structured and finally unstructured. Often the metaphor of a traveller on a journey is used to describe the role of the interviewer.

Chapter 16 addresses the use of diaries and self-narratives as another way to elicit qualitative data. Diaries and narratives have a particular concern with identity issues and emphasise the storied nature of human life. Moreover, they are very good at capturing changes over time. Diary records are very versatile in terms of structure and what participants are required to do. For example, participants might be asked to keep a daily record of a specific aspect of behaviour such as recycling, or school teachers might be requested to keep a weekly diary for a term on how they managed classroom behaviour. Self-narratives often involve asking people to relate or write their life story; for example, asking a person for the story of how they became a priest or doctor or criminal.

Chapter 17 discusses the use of focus groups in qualitative research. They are often described as focus group interviews or group interviews and involve one or more discussions between selected participants on a topic chosen by the researcher. The topic to be discussed can be presented in a number of different ways: through a film or video, other media such as newspaper reports or advertisements, vignettes, or a set of questions. The method can be particularly useful for conducting research with children where games, role-play and drawing exercises can be used with good effect.

Chapter 18 introduces interpretative phenomenological analysis (IPA) which is an approach to data analysis grounded in phenomenology and hermeneutics. IPA adopts an explicitly idiographic stance aiming to understand in detail personal and lived experience. IPA studies typically use semi-structured interviews because researchers are interested in the real-time sense-making of individuals with respect to a particular aspect of their experience. To put it another way, IPA is concerned with the ways in which people ascribe meaning to the events in their lives. Often, IPA studies address events of change, transition and disruption. Through its hermeneutic focus IPA pays particular attention to the role of the researcher in co-creating these meanings.

Chapter 19 describes the grounded theory approach originally developed in sociology in the late 1960s. It aimed to develop new theories of social processes which were 'grounded' in the data and which emerged from a number of systematic analytic steps. So the process is one from the local and particular to the abstract and conceptual. This early formulation has now given rise to several 'versions' of grounded theory known as social constructivist (Charmaz, 2006), methodical hermeneutic (Rennie, 2000) and postmodern (Clarke, 2003). A key feature of grounded theory approaches is the use of theoretical sampling which develops theory by using new samples of data as the analysis progresses.

Chapter 20 gives an account of the two forms of discourse analysis, which are discursive psychology and Foucauldian discourse analysis. At the heart of both approaches is the view that language constructs our psychological and social reality. People are born into a specific language and have a finite range of linguistic resources with which to construct their worlds. Discursive psychology regards language as a form of social action through which, for example, people manage their accountability and negotiate their social interactions. Foucauldian discourse analysis emphasises the discursive resources available to people and how such discourses are involved in identity construction and power relations.

Chapter 21 addresses how content analysis can be used both quantitatively and qualitatively. Typically, studies with a content analysis design use language data but then convert it into numbers by identifying recurrent themes in the data. In a quantitative study the occurrence of clearly defined categories will be analysed statistically. In a qualitative study, there will be some counting of categories followed by an interpretive commentary. Often, categories are identified prior to beginning analysis but the category system can be developed after data collection.

13.6 CONCLUSION

In conclusion, qualitative research aims to understand the relations between people, objects and the world they inhabit without losing the complexity of these relations. It should not be regarded as a 'methodological deviation' (Kidder & Fine, 1997) but as a form of enquiry which makes a valuable contribution to understanding the topics of interest to psychologists.

13.7 EXERCISES

Develop a list of research questions on the topic of being single in one's thirties which reflect the various qualitative approaches discussed in the chapter.

13.8 DISCUSSION QUESTIONS

1   How do different qualitative researchers think about the nature of reality?
2   What are the key differences between qualitative and quantitative research approaches?

13.9 **FURTHER READING**

Ashworth (2008) and Van Langenhove (1995) discuss the development of qualitative research and the limitations of experimental psychology respectively. Martin and Sugarman (2001) describe the relationship between hermeneutics and psychology and Zahavi (2008) discusses subjectivity and the self, including ideas about the experiential and narrative self. For those who want to read more about social constructionism and the turn to language, then Burr's (2003) text *Social constructionism* (2003) provides an excellent introduction. Finlay & Gough (2003) offer an accessible and practical guide to issues of reflexivity and reflexive practice.

14

Observational Methods

Rudi Dallos

CONTENTS

AIMS OF THIS CHAPTER

This chapter attempts to offer an overview of observational methods. It starts with a description of four core features of observational research and considers these within related theoretical frameworks. It then goes on to outline, with examples from a variety of psychological research, some details of how different types of observational research are designed and conducted. The intention is to enable readers to understand and have insight into the design of observational research and some techniques of doing observation and ways of coding different types of observational data. The chapter aims to show that observation inevitably involves an interpretative process. Therefore a guiding thread running through the chapter is the suggestion that the choice of focus of the observation, the observational methods employed, and the nature of the subsequent analysis are guided by the researcher's theoretical and personal lenses. Participant observational research is discussed as exemplifying aspects of an interpretative approach to observation. The chapter concludes with a consideration of issues of validity and reliability in relation to observational research.

KEY TERMS

analytic induction
audit trail
coding schemes
complete observer
complete participant
going native
inter-rater reliability
investigative journalism

observer as participant
paralinguistic
participant as observer
participant observer
self-reflection
time event analysis
time-sampling

14.1 **INTRODUCTION**

Why might we choose to engage in observational research? Salmon (2003) argues that we should select research methods based on the questions that we want to answer and adapt, and combine or modify methods to give us the best possible ways of answering these. Our choice of research questions is in turn shaped by our research, personal and professional interests. My own work as a clinical psychologist involves the use of live observation and analysis of videos of family–therapist interactions as an integral part of the process of clinical formulation and intervention (Dallos & Draper, 2005).

Arguably all clinicians and applied psychologists employ observations as part of their daily practice which are used 'locally' to guide day-to-day practice but also contribute to a larger body of evidence and theory (Rustin, 2002). In addition practitioners may engage in more formal observational studies to develop understanding or to test particular concepts. Observational research is in a sense ubiquitous and it may be helpful to recognise its importance in generating initial research ideas as well as its contribution to more formal research endeavours. Observational research and approaches have also been used extensively in clinical contexts such as social work; to assess 'risk' and 'deficit', for example, in 'parenting abilities'. Since the stakes can be very high in the use of observational material in such contexts it is all the more important to recognise and reveal some of the assumptions that are made. 'Seeing is believing' may involve an automatic, unconscious set of interpretations which may conceal that we have already made decisions about what to look for and what it means.

More broadly, observation is an essential human activity in that from birth we need to observe and attend to our environment to help ensure our safety and survival, and later in our lives to select friends and intimate partners. The popular interest in texts on non-verbal behaviour (Argyle, 1972; Morris, 2002; Beattie, 2003) and reality television programmes also suggests that observation is of great fascination for many people and indicates that observational skills are fundamental to human activity and not just the province of psychologists. This also suggests that we need to adopt an approach to observational research which recognises that psychological observation, unlike observation in the physical sciences, involves us making inferences about persons who are similarly engaged in making observations themselves, about the aims, intentions and interest of the researcher.

14.2 **WHAT IS OBSERVATIONAL RESEARCH?**

Observational research has been a research method in its own right as well as being integrated into other forms of research methods. A variety of research methods, such as interview studies, focus groups, experimental studies and clinical case

Box 14.1	Dimensions of observational research

Theory testing	←→	Exploratory
Experimental	←→	Naturalistic
Structured	←→	Unstructured
Non-participant	←→	Participant

studies may include observational data. For example, observation may indicate participants' emotional states or how their actions are connected to aspects and changes in the social setting. Observation may reveal what people do, how they do it and how this is influenced by and in turn influences the social setting within which their actions take place.

Observational studies can broadly be conceptualised in terms of four core dimensions. Each of these dimensions can be seen as involving interpretative processes on behalf of the observer and those observed. Though the extent of this interpretation may vary, nevertheless we are invariably assigning meaning to what we observe, for example in selecting what phenomenon we choose to observe/ignore and to which aspects of the phenomenon we choose to direct our attention (Box 14.1).

14.2.1 Theory testing–exploratory

First, observational studies can be conceptualised in terms of the extent to which the intention is to test existing theory by examining what people do in various situations and circumstances. For example, early social psychological studies explored the broad theoretical proposition (based on the evidence of acts of abuse and torture committed by concentration camp guards) that people display conformity when instructed to do so by apparent figures of authority (obeying orders). Observation of participants' behaviour in the famous studies on authority and obedience (Milgram, 1983) were seen to offer confirmation of this proposition. It was observed that participants in the studies could be persuaded to apply apparently lethal dosages of electric shock to supposedly volunteer experimental 'subjects' when requested to do so and reassured by 'scientist' authority figures. Importantly, studies such as these revealed not just what people would do in certain situations but also observational indications of how people were feeling in terms of their non-verbal behaviour (such as hesitations), aspects of speech (such as changes in voice tone and stuttering), and what features of the situation were influential (such as the experimenter's white coat as a 'badge of authority').

In contrast, observation can be employed in a more descriptive way to explore different situations. This can be as a form of 'reconnaissance' – exploratory observation to generate ideas which can be researched more formally when some potential key features have been identified. As with other forms of exploratory research, such as interpretative interview studies, the aims may be to develop understanding in an inductive way to generate from the ground up possible conceptual explanations and models (Strauss & Corbin, 1998; see Chapter 19). A good example of such research was conducted by Marsh *et al.* (1978) in their exploratory observations of the behaviour of fans at football matches.

14.2.2 Experimental–naturalistic

This dimension connects with a contrast between observation conducted under experimental conditions and that which is more naturalistic. Experimental conditions typically impose various types of control in order to facilitate the development of causal explanations. This might involve observing people subjected to similar experiences. An interesting example is the *Strange Situation* (Ainsworth *et al.*, 1978) employed in studies of mother–infant attachment. This consists of a standardised procedure involving several separations between mothers and their infants and related observations of specific aspects of their behaviour, such as signs of distress and patterns of comforting on reunion, which are the key measures.

Observation has also been widely used to describe behaviours in 'natural' situations which are contrasted with situations, such as laboratory studies, which are seen as 'artificial' or not a part of 'real-life' situations. Naturalistic studies have varied in the extent to which they employ pre-determined categories, or attempt to test theories as opposed to starting with a more non-specific 'let's have a look' approach. Examples include observing the play activities of children in school playgrounds (Robson, 2002), psychiatric institutions (Goffman, 1961) and the functioning of families in their own home setting (Vetere & Gale, 1987). The latter study involved the researchers 'living in' with families over a period of several months to observe their actions, for example in various sub-groupings such as individuals, couples, parents and children.

There are a wide variety of types of observational research and the distinction between experimental/artificial and naturalistic is not a straightforward one. For example, it has been argued that even in experimental situations long-term relationships, such as in couples, families and work groups, will settle into and display their well-established patterns. In effect the 'naturalness' of the relationship can extend into whatever situation they are in. However, an important research question is whether a group such as a family changes its dynamics according to different contexts; at home, shopping, in the therapy unit, at a parents evening at school, and so on. It can also be possible to gain various forms of natural control of variables in naturalistic situations; for example, observing tasks which have a repetitive structure, such as committee meetings or where certain events (e.g. greetings and farewells at airports or railway stations) occur. Advocates of naturalistic research argue that behaviour is context specific and observation must involve close attention to the parameters of different situations, including cultural definitions. For example, there are important cultural variations in what are regarded as appropriate as opposed to inappropriate ways of behaving in different situations, such as shops, weddings, parties and with family members. Simply observing behaviour without an understanding of these contextual meanings might only offer a very partial understanding of the phenomenon we wish to explore.

14.2.3 Structured–unstructured

Structured observational studies frequently employ pre-determined coding of particular types of behaviour. Sometimes these are larger meaningful units, such as an interactional episode, or type of actions, such as showing solidarity, hostility or more minute aspects of behaviour such as expressions, movements, and so on. A widely used form of structured observation comes from studies of group decision-making processes which employ a taxonomy of different types of communications (Bales, 1950; Ellis, 1993). Observers are trained in the use of these systems and code how different members of a group contribute to the group decision-making process; for example, in terms of *task* as opposed to *socio-emotional* oriented actions, or how the pattern of such communications alters as the group dynamics develop over time.

It is also possible to approach observational research without clearly developed structures for observing events. At the extreme this has included ethnographic studies where the coding schemes are developed as the research progresses (Hammersley & Atkinson, 1995; Gomm *et al.*, 2000). Related to this is the idea that the researcher, though starting with an unstructured approach, can in collaboration with participants decide what are the important features events, actions or sequences that should be recorded.

14.2.4 Non-participant–participant

Observational research varies in terms of the role adopted by the researcher in the situation being observed. Junker (1972) described the social roles of the participant observer along a continuum, ranging from the complete observer, the observer as participant, the participant as observer, to at the other extreme, the complete participant, sometimes referred to as going native (see Box 14.2). At one extreme, the researcher tries to remain detached and objective and, at the other extreme, actively takes part in the setting. The participant observer working in naturalistic settings may find herself moving in and out of these roles, along the continuum of relative

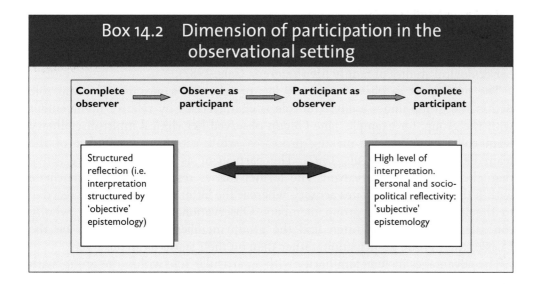

Box 14.2   Dimension of participation in the observational setting

| Complete observer | → | Observer as participant | → | Participant as observer | → | Complete participant |

Structured reflection (i.e. interpretation structured by 'objective' epistemology)

⬅ ➡

High level of interpretation. Personal and socio-political reflectivity: 'subjective' epistemology

involvement, even though she might emphasise one of these positions (see Vetere & Gale, 1987).

The complete observer role is characterised by detachment from the group under study, with no direct contact with group members during the observational work. This is approximated in some clinical work, when activity is viewed from behind a one-way screen, observations of mother–infant interactions or in a field setting, with non-declared observation, such as Michael Argyle's (1972) work observing rituals of greeting and farewell at major international airports. It is possible to use pre-prepared coding schemes, and to subject them to intra-coder and inter-coder reliability studies. Another example can be found in viewing videotapes of clinical work. There are no risks of observational reactivity, but the observer is never *in* the situation, with no opportunity to share in the experiential world of the participants.

The observer as participant joins the group with the expressed intention to observe. Their role as observer is characterised by relative detachment from the group under study, with their objective and empathic positioning emphasised. Advantages include access to a wide range of material, even private information if it becomes known that the observer can maintain anonymity for the group members. The observer is in many ways freer to ask questions in this role, unrestrained by the role demands of participation. Disadvantages of this role can include constraints of confidentiality when reporting, and a sense of marginality since the observer is only partly a part of the world of the group members. The observer needs to be mindful of the need to maintain a degree of even-handedness or neutrality relative to internal alliances and factions within the group. This can be an emotionally demanding task, particularly if the observational study separates the observer from their own social group and sources of social support and affirmation of personal identity. An example of this role can be found in the work of Vetere, in her ecological studies of family life (Vetere & Gale, 1987).

The participant as observer already has or takes on a meaningful social role within the group under study. The role is characterised by relative involvement with the group; for example, Jane Gilgun observed her clinical multi-disciplinary team colleagues' decision-making processes, while acting as a member of the team herself (Gilgun *et al.*, 1992). The participant as observer is more active than the observer as participant. The former carries responsibility to participate within the group and initiates activity, whereas the latter tends to be more reactive to the initiatives of the group members. Observational activity is not wholly concealed, but observers often find the group members evaluate them on the basis of their group participation, rather than on their status as an observer.

The advantages include familiarity with a particular role within the group, with increased understanding of group processes from this more subjective and sympathetic position. There is relative freedom to observe within the group, although observational activity may be constrained by the demands of the particular role adopted within the group. Disadvantages include limited access to some private information, with more time and energy spent participating than observing! Another example can be found in the classic work of Whyte (1943) which looked at life on the streets in Italian slums in the USA.

The complete participant is totally involved with the group of persons under study, and conceals their observational activity from the group. This allows the observer to act as a member of an 'in-group', perhaps sharing private information that would not have been disclosed to an identifiable observer. The advantage is that the observer develops an intimate acquaintance with a particular social role, and has more access to the thoughts, feelings and intentions of the participants. However, there are disadvantages; for example, ethically, our codes of conduct disallow observation without the consent of the participants, and we could be open to accusations of spying. Alongside this is the problem for the observer of subsuming their own identity in order to join the group. Managing relationships in the groups, such as alliances, can draw the researcher into being deceptive about how they are feeling and thinking. In turn, opportunities for observation outside the 'in-group' may be limited. Such studies have considerable overlaps with investigative journalism and there have been powerful investigations; for example, exploring racist attitudes in the police force. A classic piece of research is the study by Rosenhan (1973) consisting of researchers 'faking' mental illness in order to be admitted to a psychiatric institution and subsequently observing the behaviour of staff in the unit and reflecting on their own experiences. A more contemporary attempt at replication of these studies has also been conducted (Slater, 2004).

14.3 LEVELS OF OBSERVATION: BEHAVIOUR AND TALK

Researchers contemplating observational research frequently start with questions of behaviour, what people do, their actions, movements, expressions and gestures. But apart from young infants and those with severe learning disabilities or speech impairment, people's actions are usually accompanied by talk. In most situations then we will have a choice to make about whether we in some way separate out the talk from the behaviour or attempt a form of analysis which combines the two. The question applies the other way around as well; much current qualitative research is concerned with analysis of interview material or various forms of text from talk. But talk is accompanied by behaviour and shows many important paralinguistic features, such as the rate of talk, tone, hesitations, pitch, voice tremor, laughter and tears. Hence observational research can be an important accompaniment to interview and other forms of language-based research. It can also be argued (Dallos & Vetere, 2005) that in clinical research and practice such combination of verbal and observational research is essential.

The issues can perhaps be usefully considered from a perspective which emphasises human interaction in terms of communication. This offers a broader framework and acknowledges that the content of speech, its paralinguistic features (laughter, stutters, hesitations, changes in voice tone and rate, etc.) and non-verbal behaviours can be considered within a wider framework of communication. Interestingly, one of the most influential of the early communicational models of group interaction – the Bales Taxonomy (Bales, 1950) – considered the content of speech and the non-verbal features to be distinct, separable and consecutive. In contrast, Watzlawick *et al.* (1967) regarded these features to be simultaneous and as co-occurring in any piece of communication. Within this framework, research employing speech, such as interviews, necessarily involves an observational research component to examine these other features that invariably influence the meaning of what is being said.

Box 14.3 summarises the potential types of data involved in observational research. We can distinguish between observation of individual pieces of behaviour and actions to sequences of joint behaviours. As we move from relatively objective pieces of behaviour to more complex patterns, the level of interpretation in assigning behaviour to particular categories becomes greater. However, the analysis of behaviours, even small relatively uncontested pieces of behaviour remains a complex interpretative activity. For example, a fleeting look or gesture may be extremely meaningful in an interaction.

Observational research has been employed in areas where we have to rely on observation because language is absent; for example, with young infants we cannot use methods such as interviews to ask them about what they are doing and their intentions. There are a wide range of fascinating studies; for example, Brazelton and Cramer's (1991) observational studies of mother–infant interactions which revealed

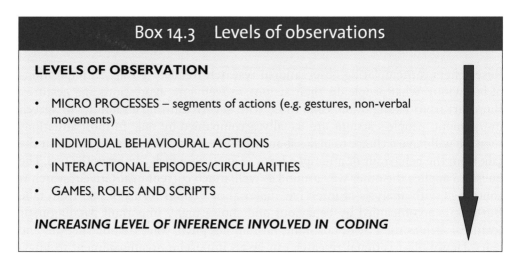

that attunement, synchronicity of actions, mutual gaze at objects and patterns of smiling develop early in infancy. There have also been studies of children's interactions in school settings; for example, play indicating patterns of friendship and gender differences (Robson, 2002).

14.4 OBSERVATION AND THEORETICAL LENSES

All observation can be seen to take place through theoretical lenses. In psychodynamic theory all behaviours and actions that can be seen are regarded as manifestations of dynamic inner processes. For example, they represent attempts to meet basic needs and reveal fundamental internal conflicts, particularly relating to needs to satisfy sexual urges, express hostility and ensure safety. Importantly, when a psychologist from a psychodynamic standpoint undertakes observational research he or she is looking for evidence, such as behavioural indications of such internal struggles. We direct our attention to particular behaviours as opposed to others, and some behaviours (for example, laughing or blushing) may be seen as particularly significant in revealing sexual desires. Observation from a behavioural perspective, in contrast, involves an emphasis on behaviour in terms of frequency, intensity and the context in terms of stimuli that may have evoked the behaviour, and contingencies, such as rewards or punishments, that appear to increase or decrease the likelihood of the behaviour occurring again. So, added to the behaviour itself is its location in time and its association in relation to other events. This includes looking for patterns over time. Developmental psychologists have looked for and observed differences in how much infants look at different combinations of visual materials, suggesting that infants have a predisposition for patterns or schemas that look like faces. In this way observation of behaviour is employed to provide evidence about potential mental states, such as interest and attention. Communicational family therapy approaches (Dallos & Draper, 2005; Watzlawick, 1964; Watzawick *et al.*, 1967) look for patterns of inter-connected actions in families in terms of behaviour but also in terms of patterns of communication, such as who talks most, interruptions and manner of talking. Early research also inspired exploration of the links between communication patterns, such as incongruities and development of different types of psychological problems (Bateson, 1972; Dallos & Draper, 2005).

The theoretical perspectives underpinning the observational research guides what we choose to look for, what we attend to as opposed to what we ignore, and also what meaning we assign to what we have observed. Observation, like any form of psychological research, has to be at least partly reductionist. We cannot observe absolutely everything because reality is too complex. The point of psychological theory is to make the observation and analysis manageable but at the same time a core issue is that we do not want to ignore what may be potentially important. As psychology has developed, there have been different positions on what is important to observe, and the relatively recent inclusion of constructivism and constructionism psychology emphasises the need to include a recognition that people, the objects of our observations, are themselves involved in observing and interpreting their own and others' actions.

In Box 14.1, it was suggested that all varieties of observation involve an interpretative component. This is in contrast to a more widely accepted view that exploratory, naturalistic, participant and unstructured approaches to observation fall into a broadly qualitative, and therefore interpretative, approach; whereas theory testing, experimental, non-participant and structured approaches fall into a quantitative, and therefore more objective, less interpretative, approach. Though this can be a convenient way of organising a discussion of observational methods, it can be argued that all of the methods can be viewed within an interpretative framework, since what we choose to observe and what sense or meaning we give to our observations involves interpretation. In observation, which is non-participant, experimental and employs quantitative measures, it is still the case that interpretation is involved in where the researcher directs his or her gaze, what behaviours are not regarded as important and what interpretations are given to the data that are gathered.

14.5 DECIDING ON WHAT TO OBSERVE – CODING SCHEMES

A starting point for any observational study is a consideration of what we will be observing. As discussed earlier this choice will fall on a continuum of being driven explicitly by attempts to test theory as opposed to a more open, exploratory, 'let's have a look' approach. The schemes that observational researchers employ are called coding schemes. These may vary from the use of categories which are highly structured and involve quantification to those which employ broad and flexible categories. Even with the use of the former the underlying research questions can be broad and exploratory. For example, the research question might be about whether there is any observational evidence of discernible differences in how co-operatively as opposed to competitively boys and girls interact in a school playground.

An example of such a study, referred to earlier, was by Ainsworth *et al.* (1978) which employed detailed exploratory observations of infant–parent interactions. The detailed observations employed two structured and quantifiable dimensions in order to generate a number of dimensions, such as the responses from the mother which indicated 'sensitivity/attunement' and those concerned with 'control/co-operation' towards the infant, both of which were seen as central to the child's healthy development. This body of research has also had widespread application as an observational diagnostic tool to assess parenting capacity and in particular to assess 'risk' that some parents may pose to their child (Crittenden, 2008).

In turn the responses of the child were studied in terms of the extent to which they displayed particular patterns of action (attachment patterns) towards their parents. This employed a structured experimental paradigm – the Strange Situation – which is a standardised situation in which infants are subjected to periods of brief separation from their mothers and also to brief interactions with a stranger. These sequences are videotaped and subsequently analysed with different observers trained in the coding scheme (trained to be 'reliable') independently analysing the interactions, and subsequently coming to agreed codings in terms of patterns defined as secure, avoidant, anxious/ambivalent or extreme/disorganised. Initially these studies employed live observation and note-taking but this has been developed and elaborated with the availability of sophisticated video-recording facilities. The fine-grained analysis made available by video recording has resulted in increasing differentiation of the attachment behaviours, and the patterns becoming elaborated to a wider range of classifications, extending the underlying theory (Crittenden, 1998).

More generally, Robson (2002) suggests a broad set of guidelines for developing coding schemes:

1. Non-verbal behaviours: bodily movements not associated with language, such as gestures, expressions and rate of movement.
2. Spatial behaviours: for example, proximity and the extent to which individuals move towards or away from one another.
3. Extra-linguistic behaviours: this includes speaking rate, loudness, and interruptions.
4. Linguistic behaviours: for example, the content of talk and features of it, such as detail and coherence.

Here we can see that, for example, the question of cooperative behaviour can be coded initially in terms of actions which are predominantly behaviours, through to more complex aspects such as the form and content of speech. The different levels can be seen as complementing each other and differences and incongruities between them as offering points for further consideration. For example, it may be interesting that boys and girls differ in the level of insight and awareness they have about their own and each other's behaviour in a situation or in what aspects they choose to talk about.

The coding scheme that is employed will depend on the research questions guiding it. In some cases there may already be an available coding scheme. If the research is specifically driven by a particular theoretical approach, such as attachment theory, then it may be felt necessary to employ the existing observational system in order that findings are compatible and comparable to the existing research literature. However, there will be many occasions where either there is no available existing system, or, where one does exist, modifications need to be made to it for the specific purposes of the research. Broadly speaking, coding systems can be seen to contain a range of issues that need to be taken into account:

- Objective–subjective: the extent to which it is possible to think about the data as objective; for example, counting specific instances of a behaviour as opposed to necessarily requiring some subjective interpretation from the observer (e.g. that an action indicates 'criticism' or 'hostility').

- Focused–unfocused: a consideration of the extent to which the observation will have clear parameters about what we look for and what to exclude from the observation; for example, in some observational studies of group decision making the individual actions of the participants was the focus but other possibilities, such as patterns of interactions between the participants or the impact of the setting was not included.

- Explicit–implicit: coding systems may vary in terms of how clearly they define what behaviours and actions are to be included in a category.

- Non-context-dependent: the definition of the category may shift with different contexts; for example, in research on communication in couples the meaning of any specific communication may be defined by the context of the previous one (e.g. previous communication could indicate that it was a neutral statement or a sarcastic negative jibe (see Box 14.4)).

- Exhaustive–specific: this is the extent to which coding attempts to cover all events as opposed to being more specific in its aims. In some cases attempts to be exhaustive may involve a large residual category (e.g. in attachment research this came to be the 'disorganised' category).

14.5.1 Coding sequences of behaviour

Frequently in observational studies the interest is in exploring sequences of behaviour and how they shift and change over time. This can include observing events and using various counting schemes to record how frequently and when an event has occurred. For example, in a behavioural analysis we may want to code examples of smiling by a member of staff towards residents in a unit. The event coding will count each instance of smiling and then also count the behaviours that follow, to see whether there is a change in the frequency of the behaviours following the smiling to suggest that these are functioning as a reward. Another form of analysis over time might be concerned with changes in states; for example, in emotions from happy to sad, angry, and so on.

Time is a key element in such recording and may be employed as a marker or map to check when the events occur. An example of a coding system that is informed by theory and is also an open coding system is the work of Gottman (1982) on relationships in couples. This also employed standardised observational scenarios, in this case asking couples to engage in certain types of interactions such as a discussion of areas of conflict. Gottman combined his observations with direct physiological measurements to assess levels of stress and arousal. The research attempted to explore whether couples who are dissatisfied with their relationship display more patterns of reciprocal emotional negative reactions. His analysis includes observing sequences of verbal and non-verbal behaviours and the identification of episodes of reciprocal negative reactions (see Boxes 14.4 and 14.5).

In this brief example, the coding system in Box 14.5 is mapping the emotional valence of the conversational turns in Box 14.4. We can then examine how the relationship unfolds over time. It is possible to see that the husband's first positive (P) greeting appears to be met with a negative (N) from his wife. This is followed by another (P) response from the husband in turn responded to by a neutral (X) response from his wife: 'I forgot'. (We might need to observe the non-verbal tone

Box 14.4   Observing talk and actions in relationships

H:	You'll never guess who I saw today. Frank Dugan
W:	So, *big deal,* you saw Frank Dugan
H:	Don't you remember I had that argument with him last week?
W:	I forgot
H:	Yeah.
W:	So, I'm sorry I forgot, all right?
H:	So it is a big deal to see him.
W:	So, what do you want me to do, jump up and down?
H:	Well, how was *your* day, honey?
W:	Oh brother, here we go again.
H:	(pause) You don't have to look at me that way.
W:	So what d'ya want me to, do, put a paper bag over my head?

From: Gottman (1982), p.114

Box 14.5	Time event analysis							
Husband	P		P		N		N		N
Wife		N		X		N		N	
Time (sec):	0	5	10	15	20	25	30	35	40

P	Positive emotional action
N	Negative emotional action
X	Neutral

of this communication though to be able to judge whether it was neutral or, if said in a sarcastic tone, was also negative (N).) From this point on they appear to move towards a mutually escalating negative pattern.

In the above example of **time event analysis** the events are coded within time scales of 5 seconds. An alternative is to record the exact time that events occur. For longer periods of observation one method is to employ time-sampling so that, for example, an observation of 5 minutes is carried out every hour. It is important to clarify whether such sampling distorts the observation. For example, some important events may occur very infrequently and be completely missed or occur regularly in the periods between the time samples.

Of course, the data from such sequence analysis can be compared, for example, with the observer's impressions of events from a more narrative observation and the participants' own insights.

14.6 INTERPRETATIVE ORIENTATION TO OBSERVATION

In the rest of the chapter we can look further at approaches where the focus of observational research is a concern to gain a picture of the underlying meanings that actions hold for the participants. This orientation can be seen to be based on constructivist and constructionist approaches to research (Kelly, 1955; Smith, 2003; Strauss & Corbin, 1998). The point of observation then becomes to observe what people are doing and importantly to try to understand why they are behaving as they are. Central to this process is an acknowledgement that this involves a reflexive, interpretative process. It has been argued that observational research in psychology has been guided by notions of science drawn from the physical sciences, especially Newtonian ideas of certainty and predictability. However, even in the inanimate world of physics these have been questioned by theories of 'relativity' which argue that we must take into account the position of the observer and the principle of uncertainty which has argued that the very process of observation transforms what we are observing (Davies, 2004):

> Using Einstein's own homespun example of playing table tennis on a moving train, the answer to the question 'How fast was the ball travelling after you hit it?' has a multitude of answers between which one cannot chose until the question 'Relative to what?' is answered. By analogy, abundant empirical evidence exists to show that the same is true for psychological measurement.
>
> Davies, 2004, p. 692

The questions of relativity become infinitely more complex when we enter into the field of observation of human action.

Observation can be seen as an active process in that what we look for is actively guided by the theoretical lens that we bring to the research. This fits with the second theme in Box 14.6. In this, observational research is seen as a construction rather than representation of reality. We create or impose meanings on what we observe; first, in that there is bound to be an element of selection in what we look for; and second, in how we then analyse our data. The observation can also try to explicitly test theory or alternatively to hold theory in 'parentheses' – to keep it in the background so that theory develops from the data rather being imposed on it. Related to this is the important issue that the observer is invariably bringing his or her assumptions to the process of observation. Even if we attempt to keep our formal theory in the background it is very difficult to remove all our personal assumptions and experiences in order to eliminate 'bias'. Instead, we can recognise and utilise our own assumptions and make these visible in the analysis by revealing our critical reflections on our interpretative processes (Stedmon & Dallos, 2009). Finally, we need to acknowledge the powerful influence of language, and the cultural assumptions that language contains, and which are liable to colour our observations. Our observational data will usually be transformed into language and this process, as well as our interpretations, will in turn be influenced by culturally shared discourses.

Box 14.6   Observation as interpretation

- Observation as active vs. passive process
- Construction vs. representation of reality
- Theory held in parentheses
- Relativity of observing position acknowledged
- Role of language in interpretation and focus

In addition these discourses shape the beliefs and actions of the people we are observing, so that in order to understand their behaviour we need to take this into account.

14.7 PARTICIPANT OBSERVATION RESEARCH

Earlier the distinction was drawn between participant and non-participant research. Participant research can consist of the researcher as a 'complete participant' who is completely immersed and part of the situation being observed, and a less extreme form of immersion – the 'participant as observer'. Such participant observational methods exemplify many features of what has been called an interpretative approach to observation. They recognise that the observation involves a subjective process on the part of the observer in that he or she utilises their own experience, thoughts, feelings and actions in the situation as important sources of data. The approach also emphasises that interpretation is a vital component of the gathering of the data and subsequent analysis. Furthermore, often the research adopts an exploratory approach whereby though there will be some guiding questions or propositions these are seen to evolve during the process of the research study.

Robson (2002) helpfully suggests that the process of conducting participant observation can be seen as involving an orientation to gathering data which involves a form of analytic induction. He argues that the researcher can helpfully adopt an active approach in which she, rather than becoming bogged down in a sea of details, can proceed more on the basis of 'progressive hypothesising'. This can be seen to consist of a number of steps:

1 Putting forward a rough definition of the phenomenon of interest. This is supported in turn by developing an initial hypothetical explanation of the phenomenon.
2 Studying a situation in the light of the hypothesis, to determine whether or not the hypothesis fits.
3 Checking whether the hypothesis fits the evidence. If it does not then either the hypothesis must be reformulated, or the phenomenon to be explained must be redefined so that the phenomenon is excluded.
4 This is repeated with a second situation. Confidence in your hypothesis increases with the number of situations fitting the evidence. Each negative one requires either a redefinition or reformulation.

This ensures an active and recursive loop between formulation of the phenomenon being observed and the process of gathering data.

Some preliminary reconnaissance can be helpful; for example, to assist the researcher in finding ways of joining the group, family, organisation or whatever social setting is the focus of the study. This can help the researcher avoid making errors, such as appearing to differ with people's opinions or routines, or requiring so much guidance and information as to become a burden on the members. Usually we gain access by contact and forming a relationship with one or more members of a group, and who these members are, can be an important issue whether they are representative of the group, their relationships to the other members, and so on. Often a way in is to have a pre-existing relationship with one or more members of a group or setting. The process of immersion can also be complex; for example, initially we might become closer to some members of a setting than others and sometimes, without being aware of doing so, communicate some level of approval or disapproval for what we observe to be going on. For the complete participant this is a highly complex issue since to fully participate does mean to become actively and emotionally engaged, otherwise we might be seen as 'uptight', 'snooty', 'distant' or 'uncaring' about what happens. Where more emphasis is placed on the observer part of the role, research can become easier but at the cost perhaps of losing some of the experiential data about what it feels like to be engaged in the group's processes.

The observer needs to invest energy into maintaining the observational roles, possibly at some personal cost, and to negotiate a planned withdrawal from the group under study. If the observer has spent significant time with the group they may have developed a sense of commitment it and may wish to keep in touch subsequently. Research supervision is helpful in identifying responsibilities to the group under study and the less helpful breaches of roles and overstepping of responsibilities within the group.

14.7.1 Collecting data

The process of gathering information in participant observation research can be seen as analogous to good investigative journalism. An important difference with research is that we will go beyond the description to develop a set of explanatory concepts and connections to psychological theory. For participant observation research this involves a recursive movement between gathering objective and subjective information. As well as collecting details of who is doing what, where and with whom, we need to gather data about what they might be feeling and thinking, judged by what they say and their behaviours. Alongside this we need to gather information about our own reflections, how we feel and think about what we are seeing going on around us.

We can identify a variety of types of data that we may use as a start to observation (see Box 14.7). Initially the emphasis is on description, how things are done rather than questions of why events occur. In practice it is very difficult to separate these and the observer has to work hard to keep a wide focus and not rush to causal

Box 14.7	Basic elements of descriptive observation
Space	layout of the physical setting; rooms, outdoor spaces, etc.
Actors	the names and relevant details of the people involved
Activities	the various activities of the actors
Objects	physical elements, furniture, etc.
Acts	specific individual actions
Events	particular occasions, e.g. meetings
Time	the sequence of events
Goals	what actors are attempting to accomplish
Feelings	emotions in particular contexts

formulations. Especially in participant observation the researcher is also likely to become involved in conversations in which participants may well offer their ideas about the reasons behind people's actions and what they think is going on. Moving down this list it is possible to see that the level of inference required from the observer increases, especially in terms of ideas about what the goals and feelings of the participants might be.

It is also important to recognise the variety of processes that may shape the data that we gather:

- *Selective attention* – invariably we will focus more on some aspects of the situation we are observing than others. Our attention is guided by our interests and our preconceptions but selective attention is also due to the basic fact that our capacity is limited and we cannot attend to and take in everything. However, we need to strike a balance in participant observation between focusing our attention and staying open to potentially important information. As a simple example we need to be in a position where we can see people's faces or pay attention to what the non-speaking participants may be doing.

- *Selective memory and forgetting* – events fade in memory rapidly and we are likely to remember events in terms of our well-established interests and beliefs which may distort events. It helps therefore if we write up observational notes quickly and use cues and memory prompts; sometimes these can be shorthand for particular episodes or visual cues. These can serve as associative prompts to help us recall and fill out details when we write up full notes following the observation.

- *Selective encoding* – in relation to selective attention and memory we may engage in selectively recording events. Often this can also involve a tendency, often implicit, to form interpretations from our initial observations.

Although this is an inevitable psychological process, as argued earlier, it is important to stay open to multiple interpretations so that we do not exclude data or narrow our gaze prematurely. As a common example, we are likely to note unusual or different events such as confrontations, but ignore periods of agreement or cooperative action and, importantly, how this is achieved.

14.7.2 **Recording**

Sometimes researchers take audio or video recordings of their participant observation sessions. In some situations this is relatively straightforward; for example, in the practice of family therapy the sessions are routinely recorded. Hence, it is a simple matter to subsequently analysis videotapes at leisure and even for the researcher, who may have been part of the session, to reflect on his or her feelings and actions during the process. It is also possible to engage in a collaborative analysis and recording by watching the tape together with members of the family (see also structured process recall (Elliot, 1986)).

However, there will be many situations where video and audio recording is not feasible and recording of information may be more complex. For example, where the researcher is fully a participant, there may be pressure to engage in some form of deception so that the process of recording is hidden. An option here is to regularly remove oneself from the situation and engage in some note-taking; for example, by retreating to the toilet or leaving the room for a drink. However, even short durations place huge demands on the researcher's memory. Important details are quickly forgotten and selective processes may mean that some important features are overlooked. If possible, on the spot note-taking is preferable but this is more feasible if the researcher's role as observer is recognised by the group. The question arises though that the group processes may have been altered by the participants' awareness of the presence of the researcher.

Another variation on data gathering can be time-sampling, where recording is conducted at particular intervals. This can also be conducted with video recording so that the camera is timed to go off at certain periods during the day. The sampling may be driven by theoretical considerations, such as wanting to observe events at particular parts of the day, such as when people meet in the morning, in committee meetings, break times and endings. Or, it may be intended to gain a picture of how events and activities vary over the day to offer an overall profile of activities.

Box 14.8 illustrates the range of different recording methods for participant observation. Points 5, 6 and 7 in particular relate to attempts to gather levels of meaning in the observation. Self-reflection can provide important information about how it felt to be in the situation, including the emotional atmosphere and communication patterns. However, if this recording follows the observation after some time, the observer's immediate responses may become smoothed out or

Box 14.8   Types of data recording

1 Video recording
2 Intermittent recording – breaks from the observation to write-up what was observed
3 Continuous – partly hidden or open note-taking
4 Time sampling – notes taken at regular periods
5 Self-reflection following or during the observation
6 Talking with participants
7 Gathering observations from participants following the observation

interpreted within her framework, so that important features experienced at the time become minimised or forgotten. Talking with participants is similarly important in order to gain understandings of their intentions and feelings. However, it can also help focus on events, or some important details that the observer may have missed. Again the timing is important since retrospective accounts may be filtered by the participant's beliefs and defences so that important actions may be ignored, forgotten or their significance minimised.

14.8 VALIDITY

There are broadly two approaches to the issues of validity. Researchers adopting the more structured, theory testing experimental paradigm employ traditional measures of validity and reliability. For such research therefore, coding schemes must be reliable. This typically involves questions of inter-rater reliability based on agreement between different observers using the system to independently code a situation. Frequently, this involves a period of training in the use of the system to build observational skills with the method. Reliability can also be offered by observations over time. For example, repetitions of an attachment observation to check if the same classification is derived. The observational scheme can in some circumstances be divided up to offer intra-coding reliability by comparing one part of the coding scheme against another. Various measures exist for calculating reliability effects; for example, inter-rater agreement can be calculated as a percentage agreement and disagreement in assignation to categories. This can be further analysed statistically employing statistical measures of agreement such as Cohen's Kappa (Cohen, 1988; Robson, 2002). There are various 'threats to validity' such as reactivity effects in how the observer's presence may influence the results. In addition there can be an 'observer drift' in that the observers may come to use certain categories more than others, or in that they come to see what they expect, or alternatively there may be a shift through a learning effect, so that there is a greater differentiation between observations later in the research.

In inductive, exploratory orientations to observation there are different questions regarding validity and reliability (Creswell & Miller, 2000). These resemble the general questions for qualitative research in which it is recognised that the generation and analysis of data invariably involves an interpretative process. Some important features for increasing validity are to offer an **audit trail** – a clear and visible account of the process of the observational research. This will include personal reflections on the impact of the situation on the observer, and details of the analysis of the data. Included in this may be prior knowledge and experience that the observer brings to the study. Interpretative orientations to observational studies can also incorporate inter-observer analysis. It is possible to have several participant observers in a setting or, with the use of videotapes, to conduct independent analyses which can then be compared. The research also needs to make clear and visible how it moves from collection of the data to the subsequent analysis of the data. Like textual analyses (see Smith, 2003) this can include material to support the analysis, which might be segments of field notes, sections of videotape, use of drawings, descriptions of sequences of action, transcripts of group conversations with annotations indicating non-verbal and paralinguistic features, pieces of visual material showing the positions and movements of participants, and so on. There can also be use of member validation so that the observation is supported by accounts from the participants. Where videotapes are available this can be done directly with a collaborative analysis of sequences. Finally, as with other forms of research, validity can be enhanced by employing other sources of data or methods of research (triangulation). Observations can be complemented by an interview study, case notes or questionnaires.

14.9 CONCLUSION

Observational research has a long history in psychological research. It has been suggested that it is possible to see observational research as a ubiquitous activity that is a necessary component of other forms of research. It can be extremely useful in generating ideas for psychological research but is also important in its own right for exploring a wide range of important phenomena. It raises a fundamental question of validity for much psychological research; for example, in exposing the possible contradictions between what people say they do (e.g. in surveys and interviews) and how they can be observed to actually behave in various situations. Importantly, it has been suggested that all forms of observational research involve an interpretative component. This is exemplified by what we choose to look for, what categories we decide to employ and how we make sense of our data. It has been argued in this chapter that whether our ways of collecting data employ relatively objective structured observational methods, or use of self in participant observation, at the end of the day an interpretative component is involved. Hence this chapter argues for an interpretative stance towards observational research which encourages a more flexible approach, suggesting that exploratory observation is necessary to build valid structural forms of observation, and that both necessarily involve processes of interpretation and reflection.

14.10 EXERCISES

1 Consider an area of observation which is of interest to you, for example how conflicts arise and are resolved. You might explore this by looking at a recording of a piece of a TV programme or a piece of a DVD of a film. Use the categories in Boxes 14.3 and 14.7 to assist you in designing a structured observational format for exploring this phenomenon and try this out for yourself. If you have the opportunity ask a friend or fellow student to undertake the observation independently and compare notes.

2 Identify an area from your life, for example at university, leisure activities or at home where you might be able to conduct a participant observation. Look at the dimensions in Box 14.3 to consider which type of participant observation might be possible and the potential value, constraints and limitations of each. Conduct a period of such observation and reflect on your notes afterwards and the experience of conducting the observation.

14.11 DISCUSSION QUESTIONS

1 What are the major problems you encounter when using observational research?
2 What do you see as the major advantages of using observational research?
3 Find an example of a published study that uses observational research in an experimental design and discuss whether the study has any theoretical or methodological limitations.
4 What are the main reasons why you might choose a complete observer as opposed to a complete participant research design?
5 How could you enhance the validity of participant observational research design?

6   What are some of the relative contributions to research offered by different levels of observation (Box 14.3)?

14.12 FURTHER READING

Barker et al. (2002) is an excellent general introduction to research methods in clinical situations with good accessible overviews of observational methods. Dallos and Vetere (2005) gives an overview of research methods, including observational approaches, especially in the context of smaller scale, clinically oriented studies. Sapsford and Jupp (1996) is an extremely accessible and useful textbook prepared for Open University undergraduate and postgraduate courses (see especially the chapter by P. Foster, Observational Research, pp. 57–93). Robson (2002) is an extremely readable general text which weaves together both qualitative and quantitative approaches in the context of conducting flexible and applicable research. A very clear and useful overview is offered of observational approaches.

15
Interviewing

Glynis M. Breakwell

CONTENTS

AIMS OF THIS CHAPTER

This chapter will introduce the reader to the design, conduct, analysis and reporting of interviewing used as a research method. It will discuss the issues to consider when selecting samples of participants to be interviewed, structuring data for interpretation, and using computer-assisted data collection. Factors affecting the validity and reliability of information collected through interviewing will be examined. Some common pitfalls which need to be avoided when using interviewing will be highlighted.

KEY TERMS

acquiescence bias
differential drop-out
inter-rater reliability
interview protocol
interview schedule
interviewer effects

fully structured interviews
partially structured
  interviews
researcher effects
sorting exercise

15.1 **INTRODUCTION**

Interviewing is an essential part of many types of social research. This chapter describes how interviewing is done in a research context. The skills needed are similar to those required when interviewing is used in other contexts such as selection or appraisal procedures but there are differences. Research interviews require a very systematic approach to data collection, analysis and description that allows you to maximise the chances of achieving meaningful, valid and reliable conclusions.

Interviews can be used at any stage in the research process. They can be used in the initial phases to identify areas or issues for more detailed exploration. They can be used as part of the piloting and validation of other instruments. They can be used as the main vehicle of data collection. They can be used once findings have been compiled to check whether your interpretations of other types of data make sense to the participants who were involved.

The interview is an almost infinitely flexible tool for research. It can encompass other techniques; for instance, as part of an interview, a self-completion questionnaire can be administered or psychophysiological measurements can be taken. Also it can be placed alongside other data elicitation procedures (e.g. it can be used in tandem with ethnography or participant observation – see Chapter 14 on Observation).

Interviewing is a research tool in that it is not tied to any one theory, epistemological orientation (whether constructivist or positivist) or philosophical tradition. Researchers from virtually all approaches will use interviewing at some time. This may be because interviews are the vehicle for deploying many more specific data collection methods. It is also because interviews are flexible in format and function. They can be configured to generate many types of information and, perhaps more importantly, the data they generate can be interpreted and represented in a myriad different ways. The section in this chapter on reporting interview data emphasises the variety that exists in the approaches to interview data. It is also evident in other chapters in this book (e.g., Chapter 16 on Diary and Narrative Methods, Chapter 17 on Focus Groups, Chapter 18 on interpretative phenomenological analysis (IPA) and Chapter 20 on Discourse Analysis) that interviewing is the basic building block of far more specific and elaborate methods.

In the context of this ubiquitousness of interviewing and the variety of its forms, you may be wondering: What is the distinctive feature of this method? Quintessentially, the distinctive feature of this method is that it involves a direct interaction or exchange, usually verbal, between the researcher and the participant or participants who are researched. The interaction does not need to be face-to-face, though often it is. It does not need to be one-to-one, though often it is. It does not need to be verbal (i.e. involving words), though almost invariably it is. It does not need to be vocal, though regularly it is.

It should be acknowledged that interview questions do not have to be addressed to one person at a time. It is possible to conduct group interviews. Chapter 17 addresses some of these issues with regard to focus groups and the peculiarities of group interviewing consequently will not be considered here.

It is important to note that no method of collecting information is free of pitfalls. This chapter will present both the strengths and the weaknesses of the interview method. When all the problems surrounding question construction, the biases introduced by the researcher and the interviewee, and the inadequacies of the available media of communication and recording mechanisms are taken into account, the method still has much to recommend it. Like any method, it has to be used with care and in the full knowledge of its limitations.

15.2 THE INTERVIEW STRUCTURE

Chapter 1 emphasised the significance of adequate specification of your research questions. Having specified the research questions, you need to translate them into a form that can be used with your interviewees. This translation process is often troublesome, because the way that the research question can be operationalised in a series of questions posed to a sample is severely limited by the complexity of the research question and level of the capacities and extent of cooperation of the respondents. The nature of the research questions will also determine the selection of participants (see Box 15.1).

15.2.1 The introduction

Interviewees will require an introduction to the interview. The participants should be given information appropriate for them to be able to give their informed consent to their participation. However, the researcher must ensure that the context of this introduction does not compromise the validity of the participants' subsequent answers to questions. For instance, it is not good practice to explain to a participant the hypothesis or proposition you hope to examine in the research. So, for example, if you are proposing that there is no strong relationship between environmentally concerned attitudes and environmentally concerned patterns of behaviour it would not be appropriate to explain this to a participant prior to asking a series of questions on environmental attitudes and behaviour. The fact that the participants have been informed of your proposition or hypothesis may mean that they provide answers that they would not otherwise have provided. Sometimes cover stories are used to frame the research so that hypotheses are not manifest.

Introductions and explanations should be designed to encourage participation and confidence in the interview but should not reveal the central research agenda.

Box 15.1   Selection of participants

There are no simple absolute rules that determine the appropriate selection of participants for interview studies. Such studies are very diverse (ranging from the single case study to surveys conducted by telephone involving thousands of interviewees). The size of the sample should be determined by the extent to which the research question demands responses from a number of people who could be said to be representative of a specific population. The diversity within that population will then determine what constitutes a representative sample. It is the research issue that you wish to study. There is no problem with the use of small, highly targeted samples that possess the characteristics you believe salient to your research question. However, you should remember that the smaller the sample and the more narrowly defined their target characteristics, the less it is possible to generalise your results beyond that specific sample.

Ideally, sample size should not be determined by resource considerations. Often, however, it is. Samples are constrained by the time available for the research, the money available to do it, the availability of willing participants, and so on. These are factors that affect all research approaches.

It is often supposed that sample size is traded off against the amount of data collected from each individual. It is suggested that small samples lend themselves to more in-depth interviewing. This is, of course, merely a practical outcome of resource constraints, not a logical necessity.

THE ISSUE OF REFUSAL

Sometimes people refuse to be interviewed. It is important to record how many refuse and any details you know about them. If it is possible, you should find out from them why they do not want to participate. This information should be included in your final report of your study.

There are two main ways of handling refusals.

- You can substitute other people into the sample in a second round of approaches to potential participants on the assumption that they share with those who refuse the target characteristics for the research. This results in achieving effectively a quota sample. This approach maintains the integrity of the sample size but does not eliminate the possibility that those who refused would have offered very different information during the interview. Thus the details of refusal must be reported.
- You can proceed with a reduced sample size and seek to analyse differences between the participants and 'refusers' on baseline characteristics, then assess whether variability in the interview sample on any characteristics on which they differed from the refusers is associated with variability in responses during the interviews. With large samples this can be an illuminating approach.

For example, the interviewer can explain the general area of the research ('this is a study of environmental attitudes and behaviour'). The interviewer could also explain that it is important for the participant to give honest and full answers. The interviewer might explain why the individual was chosen for interview, but again, only in general terms.

15.2.2 The form of questions and responses

In its entirety, the series of questions asked in an interview is usually called the interview schedule.

Interviews use many question-and-answer formats which range from the totally structured to the totally unstructured. Structure can be imposed either through the fixed nature of the questions and their sequence or through the fixed (i.e. constrained) nature of the answers allowed. The most structured interviews involve constraint of both questions and answers. In these, the researcher is usually examining highly specified hypotheses or propositions. Few actual interviews fall at either of the poles of this continuum between fixed and absent structure.

Fully structured interviews involve a fixed set of questions which the researcher asks in a fixed order. Commonly, respondents are asked to choose an answer from a fixed series of options given by the researcher. The options may include options given in any format (e.g. rating scales, sorting exercises or multiple-choice alternatives). This type of interview structure yields information which is easily quantified, ensures comparability and consistency of questions and response elements across respondents, and makes certain that the necessary topics are included. It is often used when large numbers of participants are required in a study to address the research question. However, like all pre-structured data elicitation techniques it leaves little room for unanticipated discoveries. People often feel constrained because they are not free to give the information that they feel is important. You may miss very salient issues in this way.

In partially structured interviews, the researcher has a number of topics to cover but the precise questions and their order is not fixed; they are allowed to develop as a result of the exchange with the respondent. Open-ended answers allow the interviewees to say as little or as much as they choose. Comparability across respondents is sacrificed for the sake of individual relevance. It would be wrong, however, to think that the flexibility of the unstructured interview of necessity permits a deeper analysis than the structured interview. In both cases, the richness of the data is determined by the appreciation that the researcher has of the topic and the extent to which the research question is properly addressed.

Analysis of partially structured interviews can be done in many ways. Many researchers who use partially structured interviews use no quantification. They believe that by immersing themselves in the data they can understand the key themes which emerge. These they believe can be illustrated through taking direct quotes from transcripts and linking these in a coherent description of the themes. Ideally, the quotes allow the interviewees to speak for themselves, telling their own story. The researcher acts as the editor only in so far as quotes must be chosen. Some of the qualitative approaches are described in other chapters in this book, notably in the chapters on IPA, discourse analysis and grounded theory – Chapters 18, 19 and 20, respectively.

The analysis of partially structured interviews is not inevitably purely qualitative. Post-hoc content analysis of responses will provide categorical data which is open to quantification (Chapter 21 contains a description of how to conduct a content analysis). There are now sophisticated software packages which, given the word-processed transcript of an interview, will count the incidence of certain phrases or words for you, taking some of the pain out of content analysis. This issue of analysis of interview data is explored further in section 15.8 and Box 15.4.

Whether you use structured or less structured interviews there are a number of guidelines to follow in formulating questions and in asking them (see Box 15.2). Avoiding these traps in formulating the questions may seem relatively easy. However, a surprising number of experienced researchers fall into them.

Box 15.2   Question formats that should not be used

Questions should not:

1   Be double-barrelled. (Example: Do you think whaling and seal culling should be banned? A 'No' answer could mean no to either whaling or seal culling or both.)

2   Introduce an assumption before going on to pose the question. (Example: Do you think that the terrible cruelty of whaling has been adequately reported in the press? This question assumes that whaling is seen to be cruel by the respondent. The assumption may or may not be true and makes interpretation of any response indeterminate.)

3   Include complex or jargon words. (Example: Do you think you are eco-conscious? This might be inadvisable unless you checked that the respondent shared your definition of eco-consciousness.)

4   Be leading. (Example: I suppose you know what eco-consciousness is? Some people might say no to the question in that form but the pressure is on them to say yes.)

5   Include double negatives. (Example: Do you think now that not many people would not understand the term eco-consciousness? Could you be sure what a no response meant?)

6   Act as catchalls. (Example: Tell me everything you know about the Green movement and how it has influenced you. After the silence which the question is likely to engender, it is unlikely you will get anything useful without a series of further prompt questions.)

15.2.3 **The sequence of questions**

There is a further set of problems which also need to be tackled. An interview schedule needs to be looked at in its entirety. Getting the individual questions right is vital but they also have to be ordered appropriately. A good interview schedule has a rhythm to it which takes the respondent through what appears to be a set of issues which are sensibly related. Interviews should not jump, without explanation, from one topic to another. Even if it is not the complete rationale for the research, the respondent has been given some notion of why the questions are being asked and must feel that the sequence of questions makes sense. If the schedule fails to do this, respondents can become confused, suspicious and, sometimes, belligerent. Necessary jumps between topics can be covered by short but apparently reasonable explanations. For instance, often at the end of an interview it is necessary to get data that will allow socio-economic status to be assessed. Respondents sometimes fail to see why this is relevant to the views they have just been offering you. The switch to questions about their occupational status or educational qualifications can be made if you use a link explanation such as: 'As a matter of routine we collect information on what jobs our interviewees do, I hope you do not mind me asking you …'. If the respondent then queries the relevance of the questions, it can be helpful just to add: 'Occasionally, we find differences between the views of people who have different jobs.' The key thing in constructing link explanations is that they should not suggest what you expect people to say in answer to the next set of questions.

15.2.4 **Concluding the interview**

When designing the interview, you should also include clear guidelines on how to conclude the interview. Some debriefing, which involves a more comprehensive explanation for the questions asked or the way the research will be used, may be needed. Often respondents want the interviewer to tell them immediately what their answers reveal about them. The interviewer has to be ready with a response which is non-committal and not likely to cause offence. It is best to anticipate this request for immediate analysis by stating at the end that you cannot say anything about individuals or that the findings will take a long time to produce. Whatever strategy you choose to adopt at the end of the interview, it is good practice to be consistent across respondents. Sometimes interviews trigger highly emotional responses in interviewees. This obviously depends on the subject matter of the interview but it is always useful to have decided how to deal with interviewees who become upset as a result of your interview. Usually, having clear referral routes to experts in the area of concern is preferable. You might even provide information about such experts to all interviewees as a matter of course if you anticipate any possibility of distress being initiated by the interview. There are many arenas where research will have the potential to trigger a negative reaction. For instance, if you are interviewing people about their experience of bereavement or of illness or of being the victim of a crime or of bullying (the list is endless), they can get upset. It is a responsibility of the researcher to have thought about how to deal with the reaction of the interviewee. Where possible, the researcher should have identified counselling or support avenues in advance so that if a problem emerges help can be offered. It is, of course, important that the researcher does not cross into the territory of offering advice or counselling themselves. Even if qualified to offer advice in the area, researchers should avoid conflating research with therapy or counselling or advice-giving.

15.3 PILOTING THE INTERVIEW

Since there are so many problems in getting the individual questions, the order in which they are asked and the links between them absolutely right, interview schedules need to be piloted. In the same way that you would pilot a questionnaire (see Chapter 6), an interview schedule must be tested and refined. There is no required routine for piloting an interview schedule. The following stages are, however, frequently used:

Stage 1

Test whether your explanation for the interview is understood by a small sample drawn from the same population as people you intend to interview. Normally, understanding in this context is ascertained by having this pilot sample explain the interview back to you in their own words. They can also be asked to tell you about any doubts or queries they might have about the interview. Getting the explanation for the interview right is fundamentally important. Not only will it influence the data you get from the people you manage to interview, it is very likely to have a big impact upon whether people are willing to be interviewed at all. The most successful explanations are those which emphasise the significance of the research, the significance of the particular individual's participation in it, the confidentiality of all data, and the possibility of withdrawing from the interview if at any point the person wishes to do so. At the pilot stage, you may wish to try alternative types of explanation in order to test if they will influence willingness to participate or, indeed, responses given during the interview itself.

Stage 2

Use the same pilot sample to test comprehension of particular questions which you know have not been used with this population before or which you feel are difficult (e.g. possibly ambiguous, lacking relevance, involving too advanced vocabulary, etc.).

Stage 3

Amend introduction and questions in the light of stages 1 and 2. Surprisingly, researchers often go through the motions of piloting and then ignore what they find. This is a form of intellectual arrogance and research hypocrisy. There is no point in doing the pilot work if you do not respond to the information it gives you and then check by further piloting that your changes were the right ones.

Stage 4

With a new subsample, test the revised explanation and all questions for comprehension. This should be a complete run through of the entire interview schedule. It is still possible to make changes at this point. It is better to fine-tune the questions in the course of the pilot work at this stage than to get into a never-ending cycle of re-sampling in order to test out small refinements of the schedule.

Stage 5

With a new subsample, use the interview schedule to establish whether the answers you are getting are the ones which interest you. This stage moves away from testing comprehension to being genuine data collection. Nevertheless, even if the schedule is working as you wished, the data from this stage should not be collapsed with data later collected from the main sample since this would change the sample structure (obviously, this warning only matters if your sample structure is important to you – see Box 15.1). Assuming that the schedule is performing as you expected, it is possible at this point to proceed to the main study.

Properly conducted pilot work pays off: it minimises the chances of finding midway through the study that a vital issue has been ignored or that certain parts of the participant group cannot understand batches of questions. Of course, to be maximally useful, the pilot work must be conducted on a subsample which is thoroughly representative of the sample you will ultimately use. Rigour in choosing the subsample for pilot work is important and often missing. It should be noted that piloting is just as important for unstructured interviews as it is for structured interviews. The unstructured interview, despite not having a fixed list of question in a fixed order, must be informed by a thorough appreciation of which routes of questioning are likely to be productive, what sorts of questions make sense, and so on. It is impossible for the researcher to achieve that understanding without preliminary pilot work. In the absence of good piloting, unstructured interviews can all too easily lose sight of the main research issue they were addressing. Chapter 18 gives an excellent description of the way piloting should be done when small numbers of participants are involved in relatively unstructured and in-depth interviews.

15.4 **CONDUCTING THE INTERVIEW**

Piloting should result in an interview protocol that can be used with ease. Yet the conduct of the interviews must also be very systematic as you move into the main formal part of the study.

While there are traps lurking for you when you formulate questions, there are also traps waiting for you when you ask them. In order to avoid them, there are a few golden rules that should be followed. First, be thoroughly familiar with the interview schedule before you start. Second, ask all questions of all respondents, even if you think you know what some of them will say. Give all respondents an equal hearing. Some approaches do not impose this requirement, for instance IPA (see Chapter 18) does not. If you do decide to vary the questions asked across interviewees, it is important to reflect on the implications for the sense that you can make of the information they offer – particularly in making any comparisons across interviewees. Third, know what each question is meant to tap and, if you are failing to get relevant material, probe further. Probes (e.g. non-committal encouragements to extend answers using eye contact, glance, repetition of the answer, gentle queries like 'I'm confused here') should be non-directive. Prompts (which suggest possible answers to the interviewee) should only be used if they are deployed consistently to all. In pursuing a point it is important not to seek or give unrelated or irrelevant information. It is essential to avoid offering advice or counselling as part of a research interview unless this has been explicitly agreed in advance. If the interviewee does become upset or aroused the researcher should ensure that this is acknowledged and normally should not leave until the interviewee is calmed or other support arranged. The researcher handling sensitive subject matter should be sure to have information ready which will tell the interviewee where advice can be found. Fourth, whatever technique for recording that you use, be consistent in recording answers (see Box 15.3 on recording techniques). Fifth, an answer in a face-to-face interview has both verbal and non-verbal components. It is sometimes useful to encode non-verbal aspects of the answers even when visual recording is not used. They can change the underlying message substantially. Bull (2004) illustrates the value of analysing both verbal and non-verbal components of interviews in his insightful exploration of equivocation by politicians in media interviews.

15.5 **MEDIUM OF THE INTERVIEW**

Interviews do not have to be face-to-face. Increasingly, researchers are using telephone interviewing. Telephone interviewing seems to yield similar data to face-to-face interviews, though perhaps inevitably not so rich since non-vocal data cannot be captured. Telephone interviewing is cheaper and faster than other methods.

Box 15.3   Recording techniques

Where interviews are recorded (audio or video) it is possible to transcribe the tapes and use these transcriptions as the basis for analysis. Usually, it is easier to content analyse from the transcripts since moving backwards and forwards in the text is easier than doing so from the tapes. The transcripts can include systematic records of the non-verbal communication involved (Auerbach & Silverstein, 2003; Rich & Patashnick, 2002). Transcription is a slow and expensive business and it may be necessary to be selective about which elements of the interviews you choose to get transcribed fully (it usually takes about 7 hours to transcribe 1 hour of speech). Selection can be driven by theoretical concerns. Initial selections can always be revised later. The tapes should always be available as the complete and permanent record, they can always be re-examined.

Semi- or unstructured interviews require careful consideration of the way in which interviewees' responses to questions will be recorded. Note: any methods of recording should only be used with the explicit permission of the interviewee. There are three prime recording methods:

- note-taking during or immediately after the interview;
- audio-recording of the interview;
- audio-visual recording of the interview.

PROS	CONS
Note-taking can be selective and facilitate quick analysis if pre-structuring of response categories has been done (e.g. following piloting). Note-taking is low cost.	Note-taking is partial and can lose significant information from the interview. It can reinforce interviewer biases.
Audio-recording provides a comprehensive (but not visual) record.	The audio-record must be translated to a written record to some degree. Complete transcription of tapes is time-consuming and costly. If total transcription is not conducted, then partial transcription is open to some of the same criticisms of researcher bias as note-taking. Total transcription is now regarded as good practice.
Audio-visual recording equipment is now low cost and unobtrusive in the interview context.	Audio-visual recordings require very complex transcription to capture and analyse the visual elements of the interviewees' responses (Bull, 2004) and analysts have yet to develop shared systems for reporting and interpreting the visual components of the interview. Few interviews are structured to take advantage of the extra data generated in the visual medium. There is no commonly shared system for codifying visual interview data.

Since interviewers can be all located in one place using a bank of telephones, it is easier to monitor their performance and to assess problems with the interview schedule. The telephone interview does have its drawbacks. It is difficult to predetermine who in a household will answer your call. Women in the UK are apparently more likely to pick up the phone at most times of the day than men, and this results in telephone interview samples containing more women unless steps are taken to ensure gender equality in the sample. 'Cold calling' for interviews (i.e. without any prior warning or agreement) is likely to mean that the interviewee is pulled away from some other activity to answer your questions. When this happens, it is difficult to ascertain whether the context (for instance, what they were doing immediately previously) is important in determining their responses. People are unwilling to talk on the telephone for very long periods. A maximum of 15 minutes has been suggested for the standard interview. Anything longer needs to be timetabled in advance. Answers to open-ended questions also seem to be truncated on the telephone. People are faster in their responses and silences seem to be avoided. Complex questions (or those with a large number of response options) prove more difficult to understand on the telephone and this means that question structuring needs to be tailored for the telephone administration specifically. Response rates achieved by telephone contacts vary according to subject matter of the interview and by nationality (Reuband & Blasius, 1996). They are said to be worse for evening and weekend calls (perhaps because people who are at home are busier at these times). The effect of gender of interviewer on the telephone might be expected to interact with the subject of the interview in determining response rates achieved from telephone contacts. For instance, Hutchinson and Wegge (1992) found no interviewer-gender effects on sample demographic characteristics but they did find that male participants provided different information on their political views when interviewed on the telephone by a female. Caution should be applied when summarising the effects on information collected that might emerge as a result of the medium of the interview. Thus far there has been no comprehensive empirical examination of the effects of the medium of the interview. Now that the vast majority of households in industrial societies have telephones, one of the problems that used to militate against the use of telephone interviewing, namely the exclusion of lower income households from the sampling frame, has been removed. On balance the scales weighing the pros and cons of telephone interviewing seem nowadays to be tipping increasingly in its favour – particularly for short, well-structured interview schedules.

With the increasing availability of online electronic access through the Internet, researchers have sought to move beyond telephone interviewing to web or email interviewing. Indeed, the web is already regularly used for surveys involving questionnaires (see Chapter 6). It seems fair to say that currently both telephone and web-based media methods are less amenable to exploratory, extended, semi- or unstructured interviews. They are primarily advantageous if the researcher requires large, geographically disparate samples.

Computer-assisted administration of interview schedules is also now frequently used. Computer-assisted telephone interviewing (CATI) involves the interviewer being linked to a computer which cues the questions to be asked and allows answers to be immediately coded and input directly. Some researchers have taken this one step further and have replaced the interviewer with an automated interactive voice response (IVR) system. Corkrey and Parkinson (2002) showed that the use of IVR systems could improve self-report of sensitive behaviours (e.g. consumption of alcohol or marijuana) because they induce greater perceived confidentiality. They also found that there were no differences in response rates between CATI and IVR.

Computer-assisted self-interviews (CASI) and computer-assisted personal interviews (CAPI) are also often used. CASI entails the interviewee providing responses directly to the questions delivered on screen by the computer. CAPI involves the researcher relaying the questions from the computer to the interviewee and the answers back to the computer. These approaches are likely to become increasingly available as communications technologies grow more sophisticated. Two things in particular should be remembered when using them. First, they represent a mechanism for collecting information, they require the researcher to do all the background specification of the research question, sampling, question structuring, and so on that are required for non-computerised data capture. Second, the medium of data collection may interact with the nature of the subject matter and with the characteristics of the sample studied and this should not be ignored, it should be examined.

15.6 **INTERVIEWING CHILDREN**

There are some categories of people who are particularly difficult to interview effectively. These include children and the very elderly. There are a number of hazards to watch out for especially when dealing with children. Some of them clearly apply when dealing with other respondents who may feel themselves to be in a less knowledgeable or powerful position relative to the researcher (e.g. in cross-cultural exchanges). There are also ethical questions that must be addressed when dealing with participants who may not fully understand the process in which they are asked to engage (see Chapter 1).

Young children are often unwilling to assert themselves or to contradict an adult. They will, therefore, answer questions in a way they think you want them answered. Of course, teenagers may relish contradicting adults which results in a totally opposite bias in information derived from interviews. Either way, it is important to guard against giving the interviewee clues about what you expect them to say. They have to be encouraged to disclose their own opinion. This can be achieved by reassuring them that you are really only interested in what they think and that there are no right or wrong answers. Any approach which looks like a test should be avoided since this will either silence them or release a store of responses which they think people like you (e.g. age, class, ethnicity, etc.) would like to hear. There is a strong acquiescence bias in children: children tend to say 'yes', irrespective of the question or what they think about it (Wilson & Powell, 2003). Questions should be posed so that they are not open to a yes/no response. For instance, 'Did you want to do that?' would become, 'How did you feel about doing that?'.

Besides the acquiescence bias which is most marked when they are eager to please, children exhibit a preference for 'don't know' responses. Children say 'don't know' for a variety of reasons: they aren't interested in answering; they don't understand the question either conceptually or in its vocabulary; they think you expect them not to know; they do not wish to admit what they know; they are too shy to say more; they don't know how to explain what they know; and, they really do not know. Consequently, 'don't know' is a response which needs cautious treatment. It is sensible never to base a conclusion on 'don't knows', especially the conclusion that children actually 'don't know'.

Children may be relatively easily distracted. They pay attention to unpredictable aspects of the interview situation or the questions. They can become fascinated by your pen, the lorry loading outside the window or an itch in their nose. Besides being disconcerting to the interviewer, it can result in time-wasting and irrelevant information. To retain their attention, an interview must be full of different topics and changes of pace, with verbal questions giving way to visual materials (e.g. cartoons or objects) and responses perhaps being in the form of some physical activity (e.g. the child illustrates what she did in the situation you are talking about or draws a picture which depicts her feelings). Cappello (2005) describes the use of photographs in interviews with children. Nigro and Wolpow (2004) examine the use of props in interviews. Lewis and Porter (2004) describe how to interview children with learning disabilities using varied tools for engagement. A quiet location, not overlooked, and free of strong emotional connotations (e.g. not the head teacher's office where the child was recently severely reprimanded) can improve concentration. However, it would be foolishly optimistic to expect to get more than 15 minutes worth of good answers from young children even in optimal conditions. Therefore, it is important to keep the interview short.

Young children, like any novice to a linguistic community, tend to interpret questions literally. Metaphors, similes and analogies should all be excluded from questioning. Any phrasing of the question which relies upon an underlying set of assumptions about cultural or social mores must be carefully checked so as to ensure that children of the age group actually understand these assumptions. Essentially, any question such as, 'When do you think your sister has been as good as gold?', tells you as much about what the child knows of the aphorism as what she thinks about her sister's activity.

Children have quite different priorities to those of adults. They may not understand that the implicit rule of the interview is that one person asks questions and the other person answers. They may wish to ask as well as answer questions. Particularly, they are likely to be curious about you, whether you are new, why you are there, all sorts of personal details. Responding to these questions briefly, without showing any exasperation is the best tactic. For children who get into the infinite regress of 'Why?' questions, the best strategy is to distract them with a new topic.

Very often children explain what other people do in terms of their own feelings or characteristics. They find it difficult to see the world through another person's eyes (what is called taking the role of the other). This is one aspect of childhood egocentricity (something which returns in another form in some very elderly people). It means that it is important that you check when accepting an answer that the child is actually focusing upon the right subject. For instance, you might ask a child 'Why did your mother shout at you last night?'. The child might say 'She was sad'. It would be necessary to check whether the sadness mentioned referred to the feelings of the mother or the feelings that the child experienced.

Children, and other categories of people who have some vocabulary deficits, may hesitate in answering questions. The pauses which ensue introduce a pressure upon the researcher to jump in to offer suitable words. In essence, this means that the researcher answers for the respondent. This is a temptation which must be resisted.

Some groups of people, and children and the elderly are amongst these, are often interviewed in an institutional setting (for instance, the school or hospital). This entails taking them away from the normal activities of the institution, interviewing them, and then returning them. Once back, they are liable to talk about the interview with others in the institution who will subsequently be interviewed. This introduces the possibility of a feedback loop with early interviewees acting as informants for later interviewees. There is a very real prospect for the gossip about the interview to result in rumour and to a distorted expectation of what the interview entails. The later interviewees may develop a distorted picture of what you are doing. This needs to be controlled. You can ask later interviewees what they have heard and what they expect and then clarify any misconceptions. The possibility of feedback between interviewees is not peculiar to institutional settings; it can happen elsewhere. It is a possibility to which the researcher should always be alert.

It can be especially difficult to keep accurate records of what an interviewee is saying if you are reliant upon note-taking when the responses are perhaps self-contradictory and the interviewee requires coaxing. The note-taking is also disruptive since a child interviewee may lose interest in the moments it takes you to get your notes in order. It is best to have someone else record the interaction or, if possible, use audio or video taping.

The chief hazards in interviewing children, among other difficult types of people, can be summarised as: the tendency to say 'yes'; the tendency to say 'don't know'; susceptibility to distraction; literal-mindedness; different priorities; egocentricity; the urge to prompt; feedback loops; and recording problems.

15.7 **VALIDITY AND RELIABILITY OF INTERVIEW DATA**

There is no evidence to suggest that in any generic manner interviewing as a data elicitation technique yields data which are less valid or reliable than other methods. There are artefacts intrinsic to the interview method which affect the validity and reliability of the data it produces but these tend to be common to many methods.

Like any self-report method, the interview approach relies upon respondents being able and willing to give accurate and complete answers to questions posed no matter what their format. Yet respondents may be motivated to lie. They may dislike or distrust the researcher. They may wish to sabotage the research. They may be too embarrassed to tell the truth. Even if they wish to cooperate, they may be unable to answer accurately because they cannot remember the details requested or because they do not understand the question.

You can overcome some of these difficulties by constructing a systematic set of questions which at the same time as helping the respondent to remember or to understand will provide evidence of consistency (or not) across responses. Having a pattern of questions which allows for internal consistency checking offers you one way of assessing the validity of the data. If a respondent is inconsistent in the pattern of answers, you may wish to extend the questioning to achieve clarification or you may choose to exclude that data from the analysis. Of course, consistency of response does not guarantee accuracy but inconsistency certainly entails some inaccuracy. The other way to establish the validity of interview data is by complementing it with other types of data. You might use observation, diary techniques or experimental procedures in addition to the interview. Collecting such ancillary data may not be necessary for the entire sample. To assure you that the interview is effective it may be sufficient to take additional evidence from only a subsample of respondents.

There is a common belief in the research community that the validity of data collected in interviews improves if you can talk to the participant repeatedly. It is thought that interviewing someone on several occasions increases openness and honesty. Of course, since only people who have a positive attitude towards the research are likely to agree to be interviewed repeatedly it is possible that the apparent power of repeated interviewing to induce frankness is an artefact of the sample bias which develops in any panel study because of differential drop-out.

Like any method where the researcher is an overt participant in the data collection process, interviewing involves 'researcher effects' (elsewhere labelled experimenter effects). In an interview the characteristics of the researcher (e.g. demeanour, accent, dress, gender, age, power, and so on) will influence the respondents' willingness to participate and the nature of their answers. Various effects have been catalogued in the past and not all of these will still apply today: people have been shown to engage in more self-disclosure to an interviewer who they think is similar to themselves; people of both sexes and of all ages have been shown to be more likely to be willing to talk to a middle-aged woman rather than a man of any age about sexual matters; people have been shown to be more likely to comply with requests for information from someone who speaks with a received pronunciation accent rather than a regional accent, and so on. The specifics of these biases will doubtless change over time. Also, it is evident from the research which has focused on interviewer effects that the characteristics of the interviewer interact with the subject matter of the interview to determine how the interviewee will respond. An interviewer characteristic which is not salient in one interview will become important in another. For instance, the fact that the interviewer and interviewee are of different religious backgrounds may be unimportant when the topic of the interview concerns responses to traffic noise, the religious differences may encroach if the topic was responses to the conflict in a province torn apart by religious rivalry.

Such interviewer effects cannot be eliminated but steps can be taken to control for them. One way to do this entails having the same interviewer conduct all interviews. This serves to hold the stimulus provided by the interviewer constant. This will not wipe out the possibility that the same interviewer has different effects with different interviewees as a result of some complex interaction between the interviewer's characteristics and those of the interviewees. In any case, using a single interviewer may be impractical in any large-scale study. Another way to tackle the problem is to use many interviewers and randomly allocate them to respondents. This allows you to eradicate any strong effects of any one interviewer. It also allows you to analyse the extent of interviewer differences. The interview data collected by each interviewer are compared with those collected by others. Any systematic differences can be identified, attributed to some characteristic of the interviewer, and, if sensible, some weighting procedure can be used to moderate the data. This approach is obviously only practicable if the sample size is large. Sometimes, interviewer effects are countered in a different way which uses matching procedures. For instance, if interviewer gender is thought to be the biggest potential bias, the research director might use a pool of interviewers who were all female or all male. Alternatively, in such a situation, interviewer gender might be matched to interviewee gender. The matching approach can only be used if you know which interviewer characteristics are likely to have a significant effect upon the interviewees.

Interviewer effects do not simply occur because the respondent reacts to some attribute of the interviewer. It is also possible that they occur because the interviewer reacts to some characteristic of the respondent and this influences how questions are asked or how responses are recorded. Since the interviewer may be completely unaware that this is happening, controlling it is notoriously difficult. Clearly, following the guidelines described above, which emphasise consistency in question presentation, will reduce the problem, but in unstructured interviews the effect can be considerable. In large samples, with large numbers of interviewers and assuming the bias is randomly distributed relative to the research question, the effect could become unimportant statistically. It is where the bias introduced by the interviewer is pertinent to the research issue or where the interviewer conducts large parts of the study that the problem is significant. Good initial training of the interviewers will serve to heighten their awareness of their own prejudices, etc., that are relevant to the research topic. This may reduce the likelihood that they will be completely oblivious to biases which they are introducing. Therefore, it makes sense, when using a team of interviewers, to include a procedure for debriefing the interviewers. This would include a component which allowed them to express any doubts that they had about their conduct of particular interviews in a systematic manner (perhaps as a written comment required after each interview). Where any doubt is expressed by the interviewer, that interview or set of interviews could be compared with data from interviews with other similar individuals in the sample to explore if there are apparent inconsistencies. This process might result in some interviews being excluded from subsequent analysis. Some epistemological approaches (reflected in Chapters 18, 19 and 20) would also argue that the researcher must always analyse in a reflexive manner their own position with regard to the research topic and participants. They are expected to report their position fully and frankly (as far as they can ever be aware of it). Such traditions suggest that attempts to control for researcher effects are bound to fail. The effects need to be acknowledged and this becomes part of the conclusions of the research.

The best way to exclude interviewer bias from the recording of responses (as opposed to eliciting responses) is to use some mechanical method for recording them. Audio taping is cheap and easy. Video taping captures the fuller range of information (e.g. non-verbal communication). Either way, the record is permanent and open to verification by other researchers. There is no good evidence to show that audiotaping constrains what respondents are willing to say. Even video recording has now apparently lost its power to intrude, as many people now have access to the technology.

15.8 ANALYSING INTERVIEW DATA

People using interviews as a research tool often find that they collect an enormous amount of information and then do not know how to interpret it. The problem is obviously less acute if you use fully structured interview schedules since then the response variety is constrained. In a structured interview the data are usually already framed ready for analysis. With unstructured or partially structured interviews, there are detailed guidelines in other chapters of this book (notably those on IPA, Grounded Theory, Discourse Analysis and Content Analysis – Chapters 18, 19, 20 and 21, respectively) which could focus your activity.

Whichever method you use, allow your research questions to act as a prism through which you view the data collected. This can be illustrated here using the content analysis approach. Content analysis (described in detail in Chapter 21) can be used to reduce the data to a manageable scale and it can be supplemented with systematic quotations from the interviews to illustrate conclusions. There will be problems in deciding what categories to use in the content analysis. You are trying to generate slices of meaningful information and knowing where to cut into the flow of information is tricky. It may be necessary to try out several cutting positions before you find one which reveals relevant results for your research question. Also, remember that some of the best researchers rely on spotting what is omitted from what the respondent says in order to draw conclusions. It is sensible to stand back occasionally from the attempt to impose order (which is essentially what a content analysis does) and search for the disorderly elements, the discord which shows important differences. Look for themes which you expected to find but which are surprisingly absent. This may guide you to a new perspective. Sometimes people fail to say what they treat as common knowledge or very obvious. Many of the most central understandings in a community are unspoken because they are taken for granted. If you are driven by a simplistic approach to your content analysis you will misinterpret these apparent absences (see Box 15.4 for principles of structuring content analysis).

Second, your analysis should be open to verification as far as possible. You should provide a description of the data on which you base your conclusions which is good enough for someone else to repeat what you have done and check your conclusions. It is advisable to include estimates of inter-rater reliability (Chapter 21) to establish that your interpretations of the data are not idiosyncratic. In the interests of verification, you should always keep raw data for a significant period after you publish or report on it. Nowadays, digitised data recording makes this relatively simple.

'Authenticate interpretations' is a dictum which has helped many researchers. Taking the conclusions back to the interviewees (or some subset of them) to check whether they make sense has become frequent. There are, of course, difficulties in knowing what to do when the interviewees do not agree with your conclusions.

Box 15.4 Principles of structuring data content analysis

PRE-INTERVIEW

You can set up prior to the interview a content analysis category system that allows responses to be coded. A priori category systems for content analysis tend to be more useful if the questions used are highly structured (even if open-ended responses are allowed). A priori systems are more likely to be feasible where an area of research is relatively mature and other researchers have provided substantial prior data on the topic. This allows new researchers to anticipate the form and content of interviewee responses and this generates relevant a priori category systems. Even without substantial earlier research in an area, it is possible to decide prior to the interviews what information will be valuable for your research question and choose to record and analyse only that.

Box 15.4   (Continued)

POST-INTERVIEW

There are many approaches to post-interview data interpretation and all require some form of data structuring. However, conceptually there are four broad types of approach to structuring data post-interview: categorical, thematic, network and holistic

Categorical	Looks at the content of the interview responses, establishing 'units', 'categories' or 'elements' that are salient in the responses from a repeated examination of the interviews' contents. This approach has been computerised and computer assisted qualitative data analysis software (CAQDAS) is now available (e.g. QSR*NVIVO software, Bringer *et al.*, 2004). Typed transcripts can be electronically interrogated to determine when and where the elements occur and patterns across interviewees. These elements, once established, can be cross-tabulated with any other sample characteristic, allowing many forms of analysis.
Thematic	Repeatedly examines interviews for quite complex, elaborated statements, not easily open to conversion into simple elements or categories. These can be regarded as themes emerging from what respondents say. Each usually involves a number of different elements (that might be evident from the categorical content analysis) that are habitually or frequently linked together. This technique is often used with information from focus groups (Wilkinson, 2004).
Network	This form of data structure content analysis is concerned with the linkages between constellations of elements or between themes. It results in descriptions of patterns across the interviewee's overall responses. These linkages are often depicted in terms of hierarchies or clusters with sub-clusters within them. So for instance, the interviewee may attest to a particular value, the behaviour implications of holding that value may form a sub-cluster, the attitudinal association may form another sub-cluster. This approach is illustrated in the laddering technique (Miles & Rowe, 2004) and in cognitive mapping methods (Farsides, 2004).
Holistic	This approach seeks to summarise in a coherent way the overall content, meaning and implications of the interviewee's responses. It can be seen to operate in some forms of narrative analysis where the researcher is primarily trying to describe in its entirety the story which the interviewee has told during the interview. Chapter 16 examines this approach further.

Who is right and at what level becomes an interesting issue. It is not necessarily the researcher who is wrong.

Following these guidelines will help you to produce a relevant and focused analysis of the interview material. If there is a single thing to remember when using interviewing, it is that it is a data elicitation technique which can deliver the broadest possible variety of data types. The analysis you choose must match the measurement level of the data you collect and be sensitive to your sample structure but there is usually more than one way to examine the data. Try multiple techniques in the analysis. See whether they lead you to the same conclusions. Stop the analysis only when you are satisfied that you understand the data fully.

15.9 REPORTING INTERVIEW RESEARCH

Box 15.5 summarises the key elements that should be included in the formal report of a piece of research using interviews. It should be evident that reporting of an

---

Box 15.5 Key elements in a report of research using interviewing

The report format used will depend upon the theoretical orientation of the research and the place (journal article/book/monograph, etc.) where it will be published. However, good practice typically requires certain key elements:

1 Clear statement of the research question/reason for the study and its objectives.
2 Characteristics of the sample: number, relevant socio-demographic background (e.g. age, gender, educational status), etc.
3 Details of how the sample was located and invited to participate.
4 Level of refusal to participate (with reasons if available).
5 Description of the context in which interviews took place (e.g. location, date, time of day, etc.) with details of variation across interviews which might be pertinent to analyses.
6 Details of the interviewer(s) involved (if more than one including how they were trained to achieve a common approach to the interview).
7 Details of the interview protocol and schedule.
8 Details of the response recording methods.
9 Details of the data analysis techniques used.
10 Specification of any data analysis verification (e.g. inter-rater reliabilities, independent audit).
11 Summary of the main findings (the style will depend on approach to data analysis but will often be enhanced by illustrative verbatim quotations from the interviewees).
12 Description of how the raw data is being stored and accessibility for other analysts.
13 Discussion of the implications of the findings for the research question originally posed.
14 Consideration of the methodological weaknesses (including any researcher effects identified) and the strengths of the study design and analysis.
15 Conclusions for future research in the area.

interview study shares many characteristics with reports required by other methods. The most important requirement for any research report is that it should be accurate and comprehensive. The guidelines in Box 15.5 act as a template for achieving this.

15.10 CONCLUSION

This chapter introduced the reader to the design, conduct, analysis and reporting of interviewing used as a research method. It discussed the issues to consider when selecting samples of participants to be interviewed, structuring data for interpretation and using computer-assisted data collection. Factors affecting the validity and reliability of information collected through interviewing were examined. Some common pitfalls which need to be avoided when using interviewing were highlighted.

15.11 EXERCISES

1 Record a TV broadcast where a well known presenter conducts an interview with a senior political or business figure. List how many times and in what ways the presenter fails to comply with the good practice principles for interviewing listed in Box 15.2.
2 Construct an interview schedule that you would use with a child where your research question was: Do children know when their parents are arguing? Assume the age range you are dealing with is 4–7 year olds. Identify what problems you have considered in deciding to use the schedule that you construct.

15.12 DISCUSSION QUESTIONS

1 What are the major problems you encounter when using interviewing?
2 What do you see as the major advantages of using interviewing?
3 Find an example of a published study that uses interviewing in an experimental design and discuss whether the study has any theoretical or methodological limitations.
4 How could you substantiate the validity of conclusions drawn from a single case interview study?
5 How far should you use unscripted follow up questions in an interview that is semi-structured?

15.13 **FURTHER READING**

Arkovitz *et al.* (2008) introduce what is now a very popular clinical use of interviewing technique. Motivational interviewing is a client-centred, directive therapeutic style to enhance readiness for change by helping clients explore and resolve ambivalence. An evolution of Rogers's person-centred counselling approach, it elicits the client's own motivations for change. Cognitive interviewing Beatty and Willis (2007) was developed as a method of maximising the accuracy of factual information gained from witnesses (particularly in criminal cases). It has now emerged as one of the more prominent methods for identifying and correcting problems with survey questions. In this context, cognitive interviewing is the administration of draft survey questions while collecting additional verbal information about the survey responses, which is used to evaluate the quality of the response or to help determine whether the question is generating the information that its author intends. Beatty and Willis review the range of current cognitive interviewing practices, focusing on three considerations: (1) what are the dominant paradigms of cognitive interviewing – what is produced under each, and what are their apparent advantages; (2) what key decisions about cognitive interview study design need to be made once the general approach is selected (e.g. who should be interviewed, how many interviews should be conducted, and how should probes be selected), and what bases exist for making these decisions; and (3) how cognitive interviewing data should be evaluated, and what standards of evidence exist for making questionnaire design decisions based on study findings. In considering these issues, they highlight where standards for best practice are not clearly defined, and suggest broad areas worthy of additional methodological research. Fielding (2003) is a comprehensive guide to the ways in which interviewing can be used in research. It is a good guide to the common errors of interpreting interview data and good on the recent developments in computer software for analysing interview data. Fielding and Thomas (2008) provides a further examination of the value of qualitative interviews. Rubin and Rubin (2005) emphasise a qualitative approach to interview analysis. It treats the interview as an extended conversation and examines the credibility of the process. It is a good guide to generating transcripts and to coding data. It is also particularly good on preparing follow up questions. Wengraf (2007) is especially useful as a detailed account of the use of narrative methods in interviewing.

16

Diary and Narrative Methods

Glynis M. Breakwell

CONTENTS

AIMS OF THIS CHAPTER

This chapter will introduce two data elicitation methods that both rely upon the research participant producing self-records: diaries and narratives. The term 'self-record' is used to denote that the participants are producing their own record of themselves. Often this is a record not just of and by themselves but for themselves, and in this sense is more than what is normally associated with the term self-report as there is an inevitability about the existence of an audience in addition to the self. The chapter will illustrate how and when diaries and narratives may be used, examining their strengths and weaknesses. Techniques for analysing data generated from the two methods will be outlined.

KEY TERMS

archetypal narratives	self-record
co-construction	self-selection of material
narrative	thematic analysis
over-reporting	under-reporting
sample maintenance	

16.1 **INTRODUCTION**

Many research methods in psychology use some form of self-reporting. Questionnaires and interviews rely on the research participant reporting verbally, textually or pictographically something of what they think, feel or do. The self-recording methods can be regarded as a sub-set of the self-report genre. Self-recording specifically entails the participant describing – and sometimes explaining – aspects of their own lives and often of their personal history. Self-recording is a particularly useful tool in exploring identity structure and processes. It is also used for gaining detailed access to the events in an individual's everyday life.

There are two popular methods for self-recording: the diary and the narrative. These are described in turn below. It should be noted that since diaries and narratives are simply data collection techniques they can be used as part of any type of research design. Both techniques have been used in experimental and quasi-experimental research designs as well as in single-case studies, large-scale surveys and ethnographies.

16.2 **WHAT ARE DIARY TECHNIQUES?**

The diary record is one of the oldest methods used by psychologists. Neugebauer in 1929 constructed a model of three phases of emotional and volitional development (capacity for joy and happiness, delicacy of feelings and capacity for perseverance) based on a diary record of the growth of her son. Any data collection strategy which entails getting respondents to provide information linked to a temporal framework is essentially a diary technique. The record of information in relation to the passage of time is referred to as the diary. In fact, this record may be unlike anything that would be recognised as a traditional diary purchased in a stationery shop and would not necessarily involve a *daily* record of events: the frequency of entries differs according to the research purpose. Diaries can involve various media (most obviously verbal or written records but also photographic or video images). Nowadays, researchers might use multimedia diary records. The diary techniques allow the medium of the record to be chosen so as to best suit the topic and the type of respondent studied. One study, for example, used the original idea of a *postcard* diary for tracking health care utilisation (Reuben *et al.*, 1995). In this study, participants sent the researcher a postcard with a description of their health care uptake on the day they used it. This meant that the respondents did not have to maintain the physical diary record themselves and meant that the researcher had real time data to analyse. Electronic diary collection is sometimes used to ease the burden for participants who may be experiencing pain or discomfort (Peters *et al.*, 2000).

The reports required can differ substantially in the amount of structure imposed by the researcher and the flexibility permitted the diarist. Some demand very detailed accounts of one type of behaviour. For instance, consumer researchers may wish to know how often certain groups of people purchase eco-labelled products. They can find out something about this by asking samples from those groups to keeping shopping diaries in which they simply have to tick against a checklist what they purchase on a daily or weekly basis. In such diaries, entries are carefully pre-structured. If, however, the object was broadly to understand more about eco-friendly behaviour, the researcher might ask each individual to describe in the diary what he or she thought they had done during that period which had some bearing on environmental conservation.

The time period over which the diary is drawn can vary widely from a few hours to several years and this is echoed in variability in the periodicity of entries, which can range from every few minutes to every few months.

Diary studies can use reports which are specially elicited or can be analyses of spontaneously generated records of information over time. So, for instance, a researcher attempting to identify the way military leaders make decisions under stress may ask a sample of such leaders to produce diaries during an operation specifically for the study or may consider it more useful to analyse the published diaries of senior army commanders. The value of historical diary material has recently been more accepted by psychologists, some of whom now argue that this is one route to test claims that psychological processes are socio-culturally and temporally specific. However, comparing diary accounts generated in different historical periods is obviously fraught with difficulties, since the writers will reflect in some way the literary mores of their era and these may obscure the possibly more specific differences between writers. It will always be uncertain whether there were changes in psychological processes over time, changes in the norms of self-report over time, or differences between the specific writers chosen.

There is, of course, a problem that arises when using published material. Publication usually entails some form of editorial control that may change the substance of the diary. Also, diaries written for publication may have different emphases from those written for private purposes. Anticipation of publication may result in the elimination or addition of some forms of information. Diaries produced for a research study may be subject to some of the same self-censorship. Researchers have considered this possibility and it is examined in the section on the pros and cons of diary methods later in this chapter. Diaries produced initially neither for publication nor a research study might be a particularly valuable source of data. There is, however, no recent published research that has used such private spontaneous self-records listed in even the most comprehensive abstract databases.

It should be noted that requesting a research participant to produce a diary record can be used as an intervention in itself. The requirement to produce the diary can be the manipulation that the researcher is introducing in the study. This is based upon the recognition that the act of recording that the behaviour has occurred can change the subsequent likelihood of the behaviour. For example, Kiernan *et al.*

(1999) found that the driving behaviour of older drivers could be improved when they were asked to self-monitor their driving behaviour using a driving diary.

16.3 WHAT SORTS OF DATA ARE SUITABLE FOR DIARIES?

Diary techniques can be used with virtually any type of data. The breadth of subject matter is as large as the imagination of the researcher. They may entail reports of actions, thoughts or feelings as well as accounts of physical or social context. An interesting example of unusual subject matter for a diary comes from the work of Freud on the interpretation of dreams. He compiled records of his own dreams by writing down what he remembered of them as soon as he awoke each morning. Dream researchers still use this method. More conventional early uses of diaries tended to concentrate on such issues as consumer buying patterns, household work activities or TV viewing patterns. However their usage has spread to a much greater range of psychological issues. Some examples drawn from the psychological literature utilised the technique to study social interaction (Nezlek, 1991), cognitive therapy (Campbell, 1992), illness behaviour (Dworkin & Wilson, 1993), mood or emotional states (King & Wilson, 1992), stressful events and HIV/AIDS (Coxon, 1994).

In addition, diaries are now often used in combination with other psychological methods, such as questionnaires (see Chapter 6) or interviewing (see Chapter 15) or psychometric testing (see Chapter 7), to provide a more rounded picture, or as part of the process of triangulation. This diverse list is by no means comprehensive, but clearly illustrates how ubiquitous the diary technique has become. Diary records are a good way to access responses to diverse social experiences (i.e. ones where there are likely to be big differences between individuals or big differences for one individual across time, such that anticipating the nature of the events might prove difficult and make more structured elicitation methods – like checklists – less viable). However, if the breadth of the diary method can be linked to other more limited techniques, the researcher may enhance the effectiveness of both approaches. Lundh and Sperling (2002), for instance, used diary records to study the relationship between social anxiety and socially distressing events. Their study is an interesting exemplar in that they paired the diary record of socially distressing events with a standardised questionnaire assessment of social anxiety. Linking methods in this way can be very valuable.

Sometimes, diary records are compared with other sources of information about the same behaviour. For instance, Wolke *et al.* (1994) compared maternal responses to the Crying Pattern Questionnaire (CPQ) with a 7-day 24-hour systematic diary record by parents of crying behaviour of their infants. They found moderate to good convergence between maternal reports in the CPQ and the diary. Similarly, Libman *et al.* (2000) compared a sleep questionnaire with a sleep diary. Frequently, these comparison studies are conducted to validate the questionnaire rather than validate the diary record. In fact, of course, to assume the greater veracity of the diary record may be an error. Rather than on an *a priori* basis treating one method as more likely to yield accurate recording, it may be more useful to explore the discrepancies in the records generated by different methods. For instance, researchers concerned with sexually transmitted diseases are seeking valid records of sexual behaviour and there has been much debate about the relative merits of diary and questionnaire recording (Coxon, 1999). In the absence of any absolute evidence that diary records are more or less valid it is important to acknowledge their possible limitations and to use them as far as possible in conjunction with other methods that will reveal the range of discrepancies in self-records.

We might assume that the diary technique would be restricted to a single individual making self-reports about some aspect of themselves or their life. However, this is not necessarily the case. Numerous studies involve respondents completing diaries on themselves and others (in studies of social interaction for example), or pairs of respondents completing diaries about the same events (husband and wife for instance) (Dunn *et al.*, 1993). There is no rule that the self-record has to be individualised. It can be a negotiated construction with the investigator prompting the participant or it can be collaborative with other research participants who can challenge or corroborate or improve the self-description. However, to the extent that others are significantly involved, the method moves closer to other forms of data elicitation described in this book – such as the interview, the focus group or the capture of discourse.

16.4 THE PROS AND CONS OF THE DIARY APPROACH

Since diary techniques have no simple uniform guise, it is not easy to draw up simple lists of the pros and cons associated with them as a research method when exploring psychological processes. Some forms of diary technique have some types of advantages and disadvantage; other forms have different costs and benefits. It is, however, possible to give general indications of the strengths and weaknesses of this approach to data collection.

The diary approach can be used to great effect because respondents are typically familiar with the notion of what a diary is. When you ask someone if they will keep a diary of activities of a specific kind every day over a fortnight, the person understands the task. You may need to refine that understanding through careful instruction, but you have the advantage of the respondent having some initial appreciation of what you want. This may be very helpful if you are dealing with individuals who are especially anxious, suspicious or ignorant about psychological assessments. Having said this, one should bear in mind that when we recruit a sample for any type of psychological study, the characteristics of the volunteers may differ from those of the non-volunteers. There is some evidence that even when using essentially non-threatening diaries, those who volunteer are likely to be more stable and have less anxious personalities than those who do not (Waite *et al.*, 1998).

The diary approach can be particularly useful, and cost-effective, when you want data from the same person over a considerable period of time and/or very frequently. Given appropriate instructions, respondents can be generating information, often for long periods, without the need for the researcher to be in contact. They can be given the diary to complete and only re-contacted at the end of the study. It should be noted, though, that respondents who are not in regular contact with the researcher may cease to complete the diary in the prescribed manner and may just stop participating in the research.

Of course, the greatest advantage of the diary approach is that it yields information which is temporally ordered. It tells you the sequence of events, giving you the profile of action, feelings or thoughts across time. There are other ways of doing this but they tend to involve greater intervention by the researcher and consequently higher potential interference with the sequence under consideration. This makes the diary method a valuable tool when first formally exploring an area of psychological processes. The method can be used to open areas of investigation and to identify the broad parameters of the issues involved that may need later be explored in greater detail with more intrusive techniques.

Diaries are often used in order to access so-called 'intimate' information (e.g. as indicated above, about sexual behaviour), in the belief that iterative self-reporting, mostly without any interpersonal interaction, will engender self-revelation and honesty. Whether this assumption is valid or not has not been fully established; however, it seems likely that respondents may be prone to under-reporting events/behaviour they believe may be disapproved of, and conversely over-reporting things they think people will approve of. In some cases this common social desirability bias can be allowed for and factored into the interpretation of data. It also remains the case that the range and variety of personal information elicited in a diary can be very great and this suggests that social desirability and conformity effects are not eliminating diversity in individual responses.

Diaries can be used to map the variety of human experiences salient in a domain. In doing this, it is sometimes useful to use spontaneously generated diaries. Just because a diary was not produced specifically for your research does not mean that it is not useful to your research. There are essentially two types of spontaneously generated diaries as mentioned earlier: those produced for private consumption and those produced for public consumption through publication. There is some evidence that women are more likely to keep private diaries than men but this is hard to prove. It has been suggested that the act of diary keeping may be interpreted as a self-initiated coping strategy for life's hassles, involving reflection and aiding in the management of emotions.

Both types of diary can be useful for the psychological researcher. They differ significantly in two ways: their accessibility and their probable veracity. The accessibility difference is evident. Getting hold of diaries which have not been produced for publication can be difficult for obvious reasons: you are unlikely to know of their existence and, even if you do, you are unlikely to get permission to use them. The veracity difference is more contentious. Diarists writing for public consumption are subject to a variety of pressures which may lead to misrepresentation of events or their sequencing. In the simplest terms, diarists who seek publication of their diaries are unlikely to wish to represent themselves negatively. They will wish, most probably, to justify or excuse themselves. Questions concerning their accessibility and veracity obviously limit the real usefulness of spontaneously generated diaries for psychological researchers. They will, nevertheless, remain attractive sources of information because they provide access to a range of people who might never ordinarily agree or be able to participate in a psychological study (for instance, the rich, the powerful, the isolated, the dead).

The debate concerning the usefulness of diaries from different historical periods to provide evidence of changes of psychological significance over time will doubtless continue and is unlikely to be reconcilable. Irrespective of their capacity to provide evidence of changes in underlying psychological processes, the diaries of different eras can provide important clues about the social priorities and attitudinal structures of different historical periods. Comparative analysis of such diaries could be interesting but it would need to be undertaken with great care. Comparing the diary of a wealthy upper middle class Victorian well-educated wife and mother in her thirties living in a London suburb after the early death of her first husband with that of a similarly wealthy upper middle class twenty-first century well-educated wife and mother in her thirties living in a London suburb after the early death of her first husband might yield some useful insights into the historical differences. However, the significant practical task lies in matching for characteristics other than period before coming to conclusions about the effect of period.

The advantages of the diary approach can be summarised therefore in a few key words: familiarity; cost-effective sampling of information; sequencing data; intimacy; exploration; spontaneity; access to unusual participants; and historicity. The potential disadvantages of the diary approach can be ameliorated and are not inevitable. They should nevertheless be summarised before examining the ways to overcome them. Most importantly, control over the data elicited is always difficult to achieve. Clearly, if you use spontaneously generated diaries you have no real control over what data are provided. These diaries inevitably involve self-selection of material by the diarist. Even if you use diaries which you request, your level of control is suspect. You can, of course, ask for specific categories of information. However, getting people to remember to make entries at the right time about the right things can be difficult, even when they have good will towards the research and every intention of complying with your instructions.

One of the possible advantages of the diary technique is that it can represent contemporaneous reporting of events or experiences. One of the possible disadvantages is that the diary may be constructed retrospectively. With spontaneous diaries, this retrospective construction could be a considerable time after the actual events took place. Even with research-initiated diaries there may be some temptation to leave the task for a while and then catch up later. Any doubt about whether the record is contemporaneous is a weakness in the data.

The diary technique is plagued by a further lack of control. Diary studies suffer significant problems with dropout: respondents do not continue to provide information throughout the designated period. This problem of sample maintenance often can be exacerbated by poor initial recruitment into the study. Completing a diary (especially over any lengthy period) can be seen as onerous and will result in people being unwilling to join the study in the first place. This combined with subsequent potentially high dropout rates is likely to mean that the sample is highly biased by the end of the study. This suggests that any research question that requires a good representative sample would be difficult to address using a diary method.

There is another sampling issue that affects the value of diaries. The individual asked to generate the diary must be capable of reflecting upon themselves (minimally upon their behaviour but probably also upon their thoughts and feelings) and recording their conclusions in the manner required in the study. This means that the method cannot be used with people who are incapable of such self-reflection. This may mean that the method cannot be used effectively with young children, or indeed with some older people or people with certain illnesses. There is also the problem of ascertaining whether a potential participant is capable of the required self-reflection or not. It may not be immediately obvious that someone is not capable of the self-recording task involved. This suggests that before embarking on a study using diary methods, it is important to assess the participant pool to determine not just their willingness but also their ability to do the task required.

Another disadvantage of the diary approach harks back to the issue of veracity. Getting the respondent to tell you the truth may be difficult but, more importantly, you may never be able to ascertain whether they did or not. It may be necessary, if you are very concerned with verifiability of data, to use other methods alongside the diary approach. As indicated earlier, a number of such studies have been conducted to establish the validity of diary data by comparing them with such methods as checklists, interviews, questionnaires, observation and mechanical recording methods. By and large the results have been encouragingly positive, although reporting biases have been shown to occur in some cases, as mentioned earlier.

Like any intrusive research technique, the diary when initiated by the researcher may produce data affected by 'reactance'. The very fact of having to produce the diary may alter the behaviour, thoughts, feelings, and so on, that are recorded. An example of this effect comes from Freud's dream diaries. As he got into the habit of recording the dreams, he found that he 'dreamed more often' (i.e. tended to wake at a point in the sleep cycle when he was more likely to recall his dreams). The extent of reactance is essentially not assessable and may vary over time throughout the period of the research, thus influencing results in a non-constant fashion. It is clear, however, that if we require individuals to make large numbers of entries, or write extensively about events, then the action 'diary filling in' becomes a significant element of everyday behaviour. While in general we look for psychological methods that have low reactance, occasionally the process of conducting the study can be deliberately planned so as to have positive effects. At least one such study involving the diary technique has used this approach. In this case, the research was concerned with the management of information systems development, and it was found that the act of filling in the diaries supported reflection and changed work habits by the respondents.

The disadvantages of diary techniques can be summarised in a few key words: control of content; achieving contemporary recording; dropout; poor recruitment; demands on participant ability; veracity and verifiability; and reactance.

16.5 GETTING THE BEST OUT OF DIARY TECHNIQUES

The advantages of the diary approach can, obviously, be enhanced and the disadvantages minimised by careful construction of the research. In the case of diaries initiated by the researcher there are certain key guidelines to follow.

First, it is important to choose the right recording medium for your type of respondents. Respondents lacking the necessary level of literacy should not be asked to produce written diaries (this might include the young, the ill-educated, and anyone who for physical reasons – for example, poor eyesight – might find the task impossible). Alternative recording forms such as audio-taping or video-taping should be considered.

Second, respondents should be given very comprehensive and comprehensible instructions on how to complete the diary. Pilot work should be used to establish that the instructions are understandable. These instructions should emphasise the importance of accuracy and offer assurances of confidentiality and anonymity where appropriate. They should be explicit that the researcher has no brief to evaluate the appropriateness or otherwise of the behaviour, thought or feelings described in the diary. They should indicate that entries need to be made regularly at the times specified and explain that entries made retrospectively, relying on memory, are subject to distortions which detract from the value of the information. The possibility of reactance should be described to the respondents in simple terms so that they are on guard against it.

Third, the diary format should be straightforward and uncluttered. With written diaries, the print quality of the booklet is important as a cue to the professionalism of the research. Wood layout is vital for the written diary. Respondents have to be given enough room to provide their answers. Box 16.1 is an example of a diary layout which might be used in a piece of research designed to establish how unemployed men spend their time. The format imposes a clear structure on the record, indicating which types of activity should be reported and what the unit of report is to be (i.e. length of time).

Fourth, no matter how clear the diary format and instructions are, there will be respondents who fail to understand. It helps to give respondents an example of a completed entry to the diary so that they can see what they are supposed to be doing. Also, part of the procedure for diary administration, whenever possible, should include talking the respondent through the diary. This will allow you to cue and target appropriate recording. As a general rule, therefore, diary placement would normally involve personal contact by a member of the research team, rather than sending diaries by post.

Fifth, problems with sample maintenance are reduced if you can ensure relatively frequent contact with respondents. This is particularly important in the early stages of a diary study. There will inevitably be queries about category definitions

---

Box 16.1   Example of a diary page

MONDAY

Please enter today's date here:

Please enter in the table below how much time (in minutes) you spent in the 24 hours between 12 midnight Sunday and 12 midnight Monday doing each of things listed.

	Number of minutes
Sleeping	
Physical exercise (e.g. walking, football)	
Doing housework (e.g. cooking, cleaning)	
Looking for a job	
Watching TV	
In the pub	
House maintenance (e.g. painting, repairs)	
Gardening	
Shopping	
Leisure Activity	

(what, for example, in Box 16.1, constitutes a 'leisure activity'?), questions about the boundaries between various activities, the level of detail required and so on. It may be useful to provide respondents with a telephone number, so that they can contact you to resolve such queries fairly quickly. If this is not done then they may abandon the recording because they are uncertain about what to record, or perhaps even worse, make their own decisions about what should be recorded and thus provide large numbers of entries that are useless for your analysis.

An occasional postcard (e.g. birthday or Christmas cards) or telephone call for long-term diary studies has been shown to improve sample retention. Requiring diaries to have frequent entries also seems to improve sample maintenance. Material incentives (such as small payments) tend to have a good effect upon retention. Along these lines, researchers have used lotteries to encourage both joining and remaining in studies. The prospect of winning something has been shown to incite initial interest but, once the outcome of the lottery is known, some researchers have found large-scale dropout. One answer seems to be to operate with repeated lotteries but this practice is now less effective as the general public have become sensitised to the technique.

Sixth, in order to maximise initial response rates and to retain the sample subsequently, it has been shown that it is best to start with relatively brief diaries. If you need to collect lengthy diaries, it seems to be most effective to introduce the respondent to the process by first using a short diary. They can be transferred from the short to the long version more easily than persuading them to start from scratch on a lengthy diary.

Finally, various ingenious techniques have been used to ensure that people remember to make entries when they are supposed to do so. It is now not uncommon to give respondents electronic paging devices and ask them to make their entries when the devices bleep. Alternatively, researchers may enlist the help of other members of the family to remind the respondent at meal times. Some studies have used computer-assisted diaries (Baumann *et al.*, 1996), while others have used electronic devices for a time-use diary (Kalfs & Willem, 1998).

16.6 **WHAT ARE NARRATIVE TECHNIQUES?**

The concept of narrative has come to play an important role in a variety of disciplines – literary theory, linguistics, historiography, psychotherapy, ethnology, philosophy, and, psychology. What is a narrative? As used in psychology, a narrative, at the most simplistic level, is a story or an account that the individual tells about themselves, currently or in the past, or about events or people that they have experienced. It is diary-like in that they may recount events in a time sequence but narratives are not required to do so (though sometimes they do; McAdams, 1999). A narrative may have a disjointed temporal frame. It can vary in the extent to which it includes not just descriptions of the subject matter (such as events, feelings, thoughts) but also explanations or interpretations of that subject matter. A narrative record can allow the participant full reflexivity: to describe, explain and evaluate their own explanation.

Narrative techniques have now been used in many types of psychological research. For instance, Ussher and Mooney-Somers (2000) studied the life narratives of young self-styled 'lesbian Avengers' that operated as an inner city gang; Dickinson and Poole (2000) examined eye witness narratives of particular crimes; and Ewing (2000) conducted a cross-cultural comparison of dream narratives to explore the role of cultural myths in dream memory. Narrative techniques are used a lot with children (e.g. Ely *et al.*, 1998).

The use of the capture of self-narratives to study identity has gathered momentum in recent years (following the theoretical work of Ricoeur (see Ezzy, 1998) and Bakhtin (see Bell & Gardiner, 1998)). It has been tied to a way of seeing the self or identity as a work of memory that relies upon narratives to achieve coherence over time and social relevance and understandability (Beike *et al.*, 2004; Singer, 2004; Teichert, 2004). Renegotiation or restructuring of narratives is thus seen to allow development of the identity.

As a source of data, narrative records can be very complex. They can have many layers of information. The method allows the researcher to ask the participant to talk about long periods of their life and the relationships between what they did or what happened to them over these different times. The method has enormous potential to explore complicated research questions. By the same token, it is easy to become so immersed in the richness of the narratives that the research question is not addressed (see the advice on focusing upon answerable research questions in Chapter 1).

Box 16.2 provides a narrative record constructed solely for the purpose of illustrating the type of structure a narrative record often has. This narrative clearly has no simple linear structure. There is no start–middle–end sequence such as might be found in a formal story. The narrative record builds a picture of the experience but through fragments of information. Some elements of that information seem to hang unresolved (e.g. the planes that fired on the tank) and are not integrated in the account. The narrator jumps backwards and forwards in time. There is reference to a broader range of experience that informs the narrator's interpretation of the events (i.e. the family connections and the 'old man'). Amidst all of this, a theme emerges: the overwhelming importance of being tired during this experience.

The narrative in Box 16.2 illustrates some of the common characteristics of a narrative record that is collected about a recent experience or about an experience that the participant has not recorded often before. It has a rawness or lack of resolution typical of initial narrative records collected just after an event. There seems to be a tendency for the refinement of the narrative if there is iterative retelling. This results in narratives that have a more traditional story-like structure, that

---

Box 16.2   Illustrative narrative record

From a soldier asked to talk about his part in an invasion army:

> I was in the lead tank and we had been going for 54hrs straight, barely a break. I had never been on any operation like his one before. No exercise prepares you for it. The smoke was bad but the sand was worse. We got into a minefield. That was after we had taken some prisoners further down the road. They had just given up, not a fight. Well, the minefield was just suddenly all round us. Then these planes appeared from nowhere, firing at us. I had been scared for days. First, waiting for the call and then for the go. All the time expecting a NBC [nuclear, biological or chemical] attack. My family has a tradition of soldiering and I had been told what to expect. In the minefield, I just knew we had to go East. The co-ordinates we got from command were telling us to go North. My old man had always said ignore your instincts at your peril but ignore your commander and you've had it. Later, after we had been going another 20–30hrs, it might have been different. Then, we were totally done in.

---

incorporate more acknowledgement of socially acceptable or expected descriptors, and that provide more opportunity for self-justification. Schuetz (1998) showed that narratives introduced more defensive and favourable self-descriptions as their authors' self-esteem needs were increased. In effect, Schuetz described a process where narratives were refined and reshaped to exaggerate certain aspects of the experience of the self and to minimise other aspects in such a way as to redirect attention to the more positive and distract from the negative. The transformation of the narrative record over time and for particular self-presentational purposes is probably to be expected. The narrative record may be a form of self-defence.

16.7 ELICITING THE NARRATIVE

Narrative collection can be located within a wide range of research vehicles (the interview, the postal request, the focus group, etc.). Narratives, like diaries, can be captured in many media: text, verbal, visual (Ziller, 2000, used photo-self-narratives), and performative (Brockmeier & Carbaugh, 2001, asked participants to act out their narrative). Use of alternative media can broaden the participant pool for research beyond the literate. Visual media are a particularly flexible mechanism for self-record. However, interpretation of such visual narrative records is especially difficult (Minami, 2000).

Like diaries, narrative records can be spontaneously generated (e.g. in autobiographies or in the accounts people produce of momentous events in which they have participated – like scaling a mountain or single-handedly sailing across the sea). Such narratives can be used in psychological research but they carry the same advantages and disadvantages as spontaneously generated diary material.

Approaches to eliciting narratives specifically to address a particular research question differ greatly. However, the same guidelines that apply to getting the best out of diary techniques can be applied when using narrative techniques. Choose the medium for recording the narrative that suits the participant pool and the subject matter. Participants should be given clear instructions about the nature of the task. The same instructions should be used with all participants. The subject matter for the narrative should be clearly stated. The nature of the subject matter will differ. Box 16.3 describes various categories of subject matter. Specification of the subject matter should be closely tied to the research question. If production of the narrative involves the participant in more than one session, measures must be taken to ensure continuing commitment to the study.

Narratives as rich individual records can be used in single-case studies. They can also be co-constructed (Ellis, 1998; Gergen, 1998) by two or more people. The co-construction of a narrative can be used in various ways. The process of constructing the narrative itself can be the object of the research. This would entail careful recording of how the narrative was produced (the role of all participants, the contributions made at what points, the nature of any debate or disagreement, the changes imposed on initial drafts of the narrative, etc.). Of course, the outcome of this process may be the sole object of the research. If so it can be subjected to the same

Box 16.3 Narrative subject matter categories

Typically, requests for narrative records fall into three categories or types:

1 Narratives about a specified time period (and this can be very short, e.g. a day in the life of, or can be very long, e.g. the school years)
2 Narratives about a particular type of event (and these can be any sort of event, for instance deaths in the family, sporting successes, the first kiss)
3 Narratives about certain relationships (and these can be from the fleeting – the encounter on the train with a stranger – to the very long term – with parents)

Within these categories, the researcher may well be expecting to elicit information on particular thoughts or emotions characteristic of the individual. Sometimes, the researcher will ask directly for a narrative about individual feelings or thoughts and this could be said to be a fourth category of narrative. However, such narratives are usually tied to one of the other three categories.

analyses as any other narrative record. Usually, with a co-constructed narrative the researcher will want to understand the relative contributions of all the participants to the narrative.

16.8 ANALYSING DIARY AND NARRATIVE RECORDS

Since the forms of data yielded from diary or narrative studies vary widely, many analytic approaches are possible. It is possible to use any or all of the methods that are described in Chapters 18–21 of this book (i.e. interpretative phenomenological analysis , grounded theory, discourse analysis and content analysis).

The decision that you take concerning the amount of structure which you impose upon the record will affect all subsequent analysis decisions. If you leave the diarist or narrator free to choose what is recorded you are virtually sure to need to conduct some form of content analysis before doing any further data processing. The procedures involved in content analysis are described in Chapter 21 and have been mentioned in the chapter on interviewing. Having done some form of content analysis, you can subject the data to either a qualitative or a quantitative description.

Content analysis, when tied to simple quantification, is most likely to result in a matrix which tells you how many people report each category of behaviour or event and how often these occurred. This may be all you need to do but that is unlikely. A major feature of a diary technique is that it gives you data which are ordered over time. To take advantage of this you need to use analyses which allow you to map sequences or patterns in the data across time.

One way to do this with non-parametric data is to use an analysis which identifies whether within the sample there are groups of respondents whose sequences of entries are similar to each other and different from the patterns of other groups. So for instance in a sample of 25 men completing diaries for the first 3 months of a period of unemployment, there might be 10 who spend most of their time in job searching for the first month, house maintenance for the second and watching TV for the third. Another 10 might focus on housework in month 1, job searching in month 2 and TV watching in month 3. The remaining 5 might concentrate on TV watching in month 1, job searching in month 2 and TV watching again in month 3. The analysis would show the range of profiles that exist in the sample. It would also show whether the distribution of individuals across the profiles is not statistically significant and might be expected by chance. Profiles exemplified by either more or less of the sample than would be expected by chance are worth exploring further since these may be indicative of 'types' or 'anti-types' of response. The task of the psychologist would then be to explain the origin of these 'types'. One statistical technique which will allow you to identify these profiles is called configural frequency analysis (e.g. von Eye, 1990). There are, of course, many other mechanisms for structuring qualitative data (see e.g. Chapter 15).

When you use highly structured entry formats in a diary the range of analytic approaches available is very broad. There is no reason why the diary should not include standard questions with response categories such as those used in a questionnaire. In this case, you would be able to use all of the techniques described in Chapter 6.

Research using a single-case design will sometimes mean that the analysis of a narrative record entails the detailed exploration of material generated by one participant. The same underlying principles of content and thematic analysis can be used. For instance, Josselson (2009) reports a study of the narrative of one person over time to explore how memories are reframed and reconstituted. Anyone interested in the range of evidence that can be gathered from single cases using the narrative approach should start with an article by Josselson and Lieblich (2009) which presents a long-term series of narrative studies.

More often, narrative records are subjected to cross-individual analysis. For instance, van der Molen (2000) examined the narratives of six cancer patients who provided accounts of their illness and conducted a thematic analysis, looking for commonalities of theme or emphasis across their narratives. She showed all six shared a belief that they had been given or had available to them too little information concerning their disease. A thematic analysis will emphasise both commonalities and differences between participants concerning the dominant themes. It is important when analysing narrative records to capture both the similarities and the differences between people.

Understanding the meaning of a narrative is not without difficulties. Narratives depend upon shared understandings of symbols and icons for their interpretation. The researcher that is not part of the community of shared meanings may not 'receive' the full implications of the narrative. For instance, Banks (2004) looked at the identity narratives of US people who retired to Mexico and showed these narratives to be very complex with apparently contradictory stories about their host culture being presented simultaneously. The host population was characterised as happy, friendly, helpful, polite and enterprising, but also as untrustworthy, inaccessible, lazy and incompetent. Banks argued that the apparent inconsistencies served an important identity purpose for the retiree expatriates, showing them to be culturally tolerant and pragmatically adaptable. To make and support this argument, Banks needed to understand the broader value system and cultural stereotypes of those creating the narratives.

Some argue that there are archetypal narratives (McAdams, 2004) that we all have access to and can use as appropriate to reflect our own condition when called upon to describe and explain ourselves. McAdams refers to the 'redemptive self' narrative manifest in the US in life stories that characteristically focus upon the transformation of personal suffering into positive-affective life scenes that serve to redeem and justify one's life. Narratives of national identity appear to be particularly high in impact upon individual autobiographical narratives (Feldman, 2001).

Other researchers have also shown the importance of archetypal narratives, not through their adoption but through their vehement rejection. For instance, May (2004) found that lone mothers in Finland constructed a counter-normative account of their status, focusing upon the value of their independence. Analysis of the narrative record must acknowledge the existence of these archetypal or stereotypical narratives where they can be shown to exist, in so far as they provide an interpretive frame for the content of the individual narrative. The problem for the researcher lies in establishing that they actually do exist.

The approach to the analysis of narrative research has been affected by the implications of the 'recovered memory' debates. Recovered memories refer to those memories of early life events (normally traumatic) remembered during psychotherapy or hypnotic trance. There has been extensive argument about the possibility that these are false memories, reconstructed as a result of the therapeutic intervention. The significance of these phenomena for narrative research cannot be ignored, particularly as they might affect the interpretation of narrative identity data. Singer (1997) argues that the phenomenon may provide some clues as to the way that narrative identity is constructed and suggests that the relation of narrative identity to objective truth is unspecifiable. Rather more importantly, the phenomenon suggests that, as a method, use of the narrative record should be concerned only with the narrative itself, not in some simplistic way with the assumed underlying truth that it represents. Narrative can thus be analysed for its structure, even its purpose, but not sensibly for its relationship to historical facts (except in so far as these can be ascertained independently of the narrative). The significance of the phenomenon for diary techniques is less debated in the literature but could be argued to be parallel.

The work of Ken and Mary Gergen has emphasised the broader importance of studying narratives. Their analysis is less concerned with the content of specific narratives but with the functions that the processes of creating narratives serve in social life (Gergen & Gergen, 2010). They argue that narratives are the basis for making experience meaningful and, as a consequence, they can be used to support efforts to engender social change. Gergen and Gergen (2006) extend this suggestion to examine how evoking and challenging and juxtaposing narratives that are used in conflict situations can be the basis for resolving conflict. This is fascinating work and the journal where it is published (*Narrative Inquiry*) can be used as a good source for other material on narratives and their analysis.

In choosing analytic approaches to any self-record technique the vital thing to remember is that you are using them merely as tools that will give you answers to the questions you posed at the start of the research. Amid the flood of data that a diary or narrative technique can generate, it is easy to lose sight of your original objectives for the research. You can get lost in the minutiae of the specific life stories. The process of analysis should be one which allows you to see genuine patterns within these data. Thus it is vital to choose analytic tools which give you relevant answers and which are appropriate for the type of data you have.

16.9 **CONCLUSION**

The two self-record approaches described here are diary and narrative methods. The chapter illustrates how and when these two methods may be used, examining their strengths and weaknesses. Techniques for analysing data generated from these two methods have been outlined. It should be clear that the diary technique and the narrative technique are potentially extremely useful as means of collecting psychological and behavioural data. As with other methods they have both advantages and disadvantages. Before embarking on a diary study you should ask yourself: 'Do I *really need* to collect data on a continuous basis over time?'. Before using either diary or narrative techniques you must have a very clear idea of your research objectives. The reason for this was mentioned earlier. Diaries and narratives can be a very rich source of data, and unless we have a clear view of the purpose of the study, the volume of data generated can overwhelm the unwary researcher. Finally, do not be seduced by the apparent simplicity of these techniques. The quality of the data will be directly related to the quality of the data elicitation design and execution. Above all, know how you intend to analyse the data before you collect it.

16.10 **EXERCISES**

1 Keep a dream diary for a week. Decide how to structure the recording of your recollections of your dreams. Decide when to make the record (e.g. immediately upon waking). Record any change in the pattern of your sleep and waking cycles during the recording period. You will need to decide how to code your recollections of your dreams and you may wish to consult Chapter 21 to see how content analysis is conducted. Do some background literature review on how attempting to record dreams affects sleep patterns and the pattern of dream recall over time.

2 Design a study that would collect narratives from women of two generations (20–40-year-olds and 60–70-year-olds) concerning their beliefs about food – how it should be prepared and how it should be consumed. Think about how you would collect the narratives, would they be retrospective across a lifetime or just contemporaneous? Would you want to have individuals generate the narratives or would you want to have women brought together in groups to produce joint narratives? How would you analyse and report your results?

16.11 **DISCUSSION QUESTIONS**

1 What do you consider to be the strengths and weaknesses of the diary method?
2 What do you think are the limitations of narrative analysis?
3 Are there ways of negating the biases that enter the narrative approach due to differences in linguistic competence across narrators?
4 Can diary methods be used effectively in large-scale survey research?
5 How would you use new technologies for recording narratives in innovative ways?

16.12 **FURTHER READING**

Any of the articles referred to in the text would be a useful additional source of understanding about these two techniques. However, of particular value would be: on diary methods, Coxon, 1999; Lundh and Sperling, 2002; on narrative methods, McAdams, 2004; Singer and Singer, 2004.

In addition Burck (2005) gives a good practical consideration of the relationships between grounded theory, discourse analysis and narrative analysis. Floresch *et al.* apply methods from thematic, grounded theory and narrative analytic techniques to the same qualitative data to illustrate how they provide different interpretive meanings. Findings from each are blended to produce an integrated conceptual framework for understanding adolescent experience of psychiatric medication. This is a rare example of researchers juxtaposing different qualitative approaches. It is something which we should do more often. Herman and Vervaeck provide a comprehensive introduction to the use of narrative analysis in a wide variety of contexts. Morone *et al.* (2008) is a good example of the creative use of diary methods associated with a grounded theory approach. It was designed to identify the effects of mindfulness meditation on older adults with chronic low back pain. It found several themes reflecting the beneficial effects of mindfulness meditation on pain, attention, sleep, and achieving well-being. Pace (2008) presents an interesting new application of narrative analysis: marketing and consumer behaviour studies often apply narrative analysis to understand consumption. The consumer is a source of both introspective narratives and stories. YouTube is a relatively new context in which subjects tell stories to an audience through self-made videos and re-edited TV programs. After defining the pros and cons of different approaches to the study of YouTube, this paper presents narrative analysis as a possible means of understanding YouTube. Webster and Mertova (2007) is particularly useful in examining how narrative analysis can allow the examination of critical life events.

17

Focus Groups

Lynne Millward

CONTENTS

AIMS OF THIS CHAPTER

The aim of this chapter is to introduce the focus group method as a legitimate psychological tool. From this general overview, readers will be able to decide whether to use focus groups as their primary means of gathering evidence, as a tool to complement other methods of data collection within a multi-method framework, or as a focus of study in its own right. Readers will also be guided on how to manage a focus group study (including design and implementation); and on how to handle the data appropriate to the particular nature of the evidence being sought.

KEY TERMS

focus group content	focus group process
focus group facilitator	focusing stimuli
focus group interview	topic guide

17.1 **INTRODUCTION**

17.1.1 **What is a focus group?**

The focus group is a discussion-based interview that produces verbal data generated via group interaction. Focus groups aim to build conversation among participants rather than conversation between the interviewer (or focus group facilitator) and individual participants, which would be akin to doing a 'round robin' exercise (Clark, 2009). It is the 'interaction element' that is important to understanding how focus groups can be used to generate a very different type of evidence than is possible from a one-to-one interview (Morgan, 2010; Box 17.1). Verbal data is a qualitative form of evidence and will be of analytic interest in the form of individual participant contributions and/or dialogue occurring between individuals (Halkier, 2010). The 'focus' of a group discussion can be anything, from the concrete (e.g. images, objects) to the abstract (e.g. shared activities, critical events and experiences). To ensure that the discussion occurs in a focused way, it is managed by an external moderator or interviewer who is able to regulate the group dynamic.

17.1.2 **Historical origins of the focus group method**

While the study of focus group processes has a rich and substantial research history, the focus group method challenges the predominant focus of psychology on intra-psychic individual processes and behaviours (i.e. mechanisms inside the individual's brain and mind that can explain behaviour). Although psychology is much more 'open' to the use of diverse methodologies now, over ten years into the millennium, than it was at the start of the twenty-first century, there is still some reticence about the use of focus groups as a legitimate psychological tool.

The earliest known *scientific* use of the focus group method can be traced to the work of Bogardus (1926), testing his social distance model with groups of schoolboys. However, a more formal articulation of the method is attributable to Merton and Kendall (1946) from their research into the social effects of mass communication otherwise known as 'wartime propaganda'. Ironically the evolution of focus groups as a viable research tool is less rooted in this sociological tradition than in what Berg (1995) has called the 'vulgar world of marketing'.

For decades, marketing research relied on focus groups as the quickest and most cost-efficient means of obtaining consumer-relevant information. Essentially, the focus group method largely evolved as a 'quick and dirty' means of generating a lot of data quickly rather than as a sophisticated research tool.

In 1988, Morgan (p. 75) noted that 'the contribution of focus groups to social science research … is more potential than real'. In the ten years after that, there was an exponential rise in the number of published works legitimising the focus group

Box 17.1 What focus group evidence may look like

The following excerpt is taken from Halkier (2010, p. 81) to illustrate the nature of interactive data. The focus group comprises women from Denmark all of whom had been participating in a project on 'Cooking in Medicalised Society' looking in particular at the role of a particular magazine in their cooking practices.

Connie: Yes and then there is the thing that IF it REALLY shall be delicious…[pause]
Birte whispering: Then you must make it YOURSELF], then you must make it yourself.
Birte: Yep.
Connie: You know, your…and your jam.
Ellen: Yes.
Anja: Do you really think so? You know, you can get something that's delicious… you know honestly…
Connie [interrupts]: Yeah, you can sort of, but…
Anja: Some of that Meyer's something…
Connie: Well now, I am not exactly sitting and saying what I DO in real life.
[all participants laugh]

This excerpt arises from an exercise where a 30-year-old women had been invited to sort food into piles one suitable for guests and one not suitable for guests. Connie sets up a norm that food suitable for guests is homemade, confirmed by Birte and Ellen. However, Anja disagrees with this criterion noting that delicious things suitable for guests can also be bought. Connie concedes and then differentiates between what is ideal and what happens in practice. In this way she excuses herself from being judged as someone who poses unrealistic expectations on the group; and some consensus is achieved.

 Morgan (2010) notes that dialogue in focus groups that shifts from being moderator directed to being participant owned occurs when participants are sparked (what Wilkinson, 1998 p. 337 has termed 'electrified') by a topic and then between themselves proceed to 'extend, elaborate and embroider' (Wilkinson, 1998 p. 337).

method (e.g. Barbour & Kitzinger, 1998; Greenbaum, 1998; Krueger, 1994; Morgan & Krueger, 1997). By the turn of the century, within psychology alone, the method gained a substantial foothold as a means of distinctively 'qualitative research' (Breakwell, 2004; Silverman, 2004; Smith, 2003; Wilkinson, 2003, 2004b). In the decade between 1995 and 2004, the rise in use of the focus group method (either for primary or secondary data gathering) was substantial, with 2,367 papers extracted from PsychInfo, compared with only 138 publications between 1985 and 1994, and a mere 7 recorded between 1975 and 1984. In September 2010, the total number of papers extracted from PsychInfo to date either using, or investigating the focus group method, rose to a remarkable 13,191. Indeed, the focus group method has achieved what Morgan (2008) describes as 'well recognized' status in qualitative research. The method is seen to be especially popular within applied psychology, and in the last decade or so the uptake of the focus group method in health psychology is particularly noteworthy. There is also an interesting rise in the use of focus groups in research involving children and young people (e.g. Clark, 2009).

While the full potential of focus groups as a distinctively psychological tool is beginning to be realised, this is still much more often said than done (Morgan, 2010). This chapter highlights further some of this relatively untapped potential, demonstrating, I hope, how focus groups can not only enhance the ability of psychologists to answer their research questions but also, more importantly, generate questions from new angles and perspectives.

17.1.3 The use of focus groups to address PROCESS (i.e. how, why) as well as CONTENT (i.e. what) questions

In the words of Wilkinson (1998, p. 182), the focus group method is 'distinctive not for its mode of analysis, but rather for its data-collection procedures, and for the nature of the data so collected'. To this end, some additional practical issues will also be addressed, including the use of Internet forums and telephone facilities to generate discussion across participants distributed in both space and time, and also issues of analysis arising from the use of focus groups as interactive forums. It will be argued that the future of focus group research in psychology depends not only on the quality and rigour of its use (Krueger, 1993) but also in appreciating how focus groups can furnish 'tiny glimpses of the world' (Hollander, 2004, p. 605) one might not normally be able to see (Halkier, 2010).

By skillfully managing the group dynamic, it is possible to cultivate 'natural' conversation and discussion (through 'synergy, snowballing, stimulation and spontaneity') as a focus of investigation in its own right (Catterall & MacClaran, 1997; Jovchelovitch, 2000; Linell, 2001). For example, Kitzinger (1994) describes a major shift she witnessed in her research on illness explanations from personal and self-blaming (e.g. 'I should have been stronger') to structural/systemic (e.g. 'If we all felt confused a leaflet would have helped us deal with it better') as a function of a focus group dynamic. She concludes, from this and other similar findings, that people's attitudes are 'not necessarily neatly encapsulated in reasoned responses to direct questions' (1995, p. 108); they are more likely in fact to be constructed through discussion and interaction (see also Morgan, 2010; Wilkinson, 1998). In other words, focus groups have a relatively untapped potential to explore answers to 'how' and 'why' (i.e. process) questions as well as 'what' (i.e. content) (e.g. Munday, 2006).

17.2 **THE APPROPRIATENESS OF THE FOCUS GROUP METHOD**

Used alone or in combination with other methods, the conventional aim of focus groups is to capture *content* in the form of understandings, perspectives, stories, discourses and experiences 'not otherwise meaningfully expressed by numbers' (Berg, 1995, p. 3; see also Hoepfl,1997). In the last few five years or so, the role played by interaction in the production of content has also been emphasised within the analytic frame on focus groups (Morgan, 2010). Either way, focus groups are not suitable to the formal testing of hypotheses although they can be used for hypothesis formulation and/or construct development.

The focus group can be used either as a primary means of data collection or as a supplement to a multi-method approach depending on how it fits into the overall research plan (Lambert & Loiselle, 2007). The overall research plan will also involve a particular set of epistemological assumptions (e.g. essentialist, social construction-ist – see section 17.3). Secondary, more practical uses of the focus group (e.g. for decision-making, intervention, collective empowerment and social change), for obtaining some end other than research (e.g. attitude change, problem-solving) do not fall strictly within a research remit. For a fine example of agenda based use of focus groups, readers could usefully consult published work by Eggins *et al.*, (2008).

In practice, the focus group method is most commonly used for the following:

- To develop and/or test constructs as a first step in developing a questionnaire; for instance, Anatchkova and Bjorner (2010) explored fluctuations in role participation across the life span with eight focus groups as the basis for developing an 'item bank' for questionnaire development.

- To check the validity of conceptual models; for instance, Stanton *et al.* (1993) used the framework of 'protection motivation theory' to frame a group discussion looking at how adolescents protect themselves from sexual risk.

- To supplement other more traditional methods (Box 17.2); for instance, Winborne and Dardaine (1993) used the focus group to generate additional, more open-ended conversation among teachers about survey results on 'at risk' children in an educational setting. Wutich *et al.* (2010) provide an interesting comparison of focus group and questionnaire responses with regards to 'water decision makers in a desert city'. They demonstrate the complementary nature of each method for producing a more complete picture of the decision-making scenario under investigation.

- To invite a uniquely different perspective on an issue; for instance, Michell (1998) found that focus groups produced a completely different sort of evidence

> ## Box 17.2 Focus groups within a multi-method approach
>
> Recently, Lambert and Losielle (2007) used focus groups to complement interview findings on decision making and information seeking in cancer patients. They illustrated how:
>
> - focus group evidence informed their exploration of individual accounts;
> - individual accounts enabled some in-depth refinement of initial focus group findings where patients honed in mainly on issues common to everyone present;
> - multi-methods enabled some convergence across findings to be identified across focus group and interview data, for example, on the kinds of information that patients need in order to make an optimal decision; and
> - multi-methods enabled both individual and contextual factors to be captured in relation to decision making practices; for instance, focus group discussions emphasised contextual influences on decision making such as the role of professionals through sharing experiences, whilst individual interviews looked closely at decision making processes.
>
> However, Lambert and Loiselle (2007) cautioned that combining data from different methods poses an integration challenge that cannot be taken lightly. They used a grounded theory approach (see Chapter 19) and advocate the use of visual data matrices to help map out the findings obtained by each method across themes (see section 17.9).

on peer group structures than was possible using other methods. Likewise Michell and West (1996) found unexpectedly that teenagers in their study came across as more self-regulated than anticipated, being actively involved in the decision to smoke or not (rather than easily coerced or bullied into smoking by peers).

- To generate conversation worthy of analysis in its own right; for instance, Lunt (1996) used the focus group to study tensions in discourses on 'savings' (e.g. between discourses on cash and credit, between budgeting and borrowing, between necessity and luxury, and between prudence and pleasure), linking these tensions to discourses on social and economic change.

It is clear that focus groups can offer evidence from an alternative and equally valid perspective on a topic than is possible using more traditional methods (see also Bloor *et al.*, 2001, for other examples). There is an especially fast growing interest in using focus groups to produce conversation that can be studied in itself. Exploration of this kind is consistent with a post-modern turn on the use of focus groups to analyse discourse (e.g. Halkier, 2010; Lunt, 1996; Myers, 2000), conversation (Halkier, 2010), processes of social construction (e.g. Linell, 2001), narratives (e.g. Anatchova & Bjorner, 2010) and positionings (Halkier, 2010).

17.3 WHAT TYPE OF EVIDENCE DO FOCUS GROUPS PRODUCE?

17.3.1 The essentialist position

Conventional uses of the focus group fit squarely into an 'essentialist' framework, which is an approach to research that assumes that there is 'truth' to be found and that some methods are better than others at getting closer to it. The advantage of focus groups is that, when managed well, they can produce a broader as well as more in-depth understanding of an issue or topic, because the *interaction process* stimulates memories, discussion, debate and disclosure in a way that is less likely in a one-to-one interview (Wilkinson, 2003).

The emphasis within the essentialist framework is on content (i.e. thoughts, feelings, beliefs, values, knowledge, ideas, and so on) and on being skilled enough to moderate the interaction process to optimise both the *quantity* and *quality* of the content produced by the focus group discussion (Krueger & Casey, 2000). Accordingly, all the usual guidelines on how to conduct a focus group study are underwritten by a requirement to harness the group process to *maximise disclosure and minimise the likelihood that the truth will be 'clouded'* by problems of inhibition (i.e. silence) and self-presentation (manifest, for example, in exaggeration or invention) arising from dysfunctional group dynamics (e.g. groupthink/conformity, status dynamics and polarisation) (Catterall & Maclaran, 1997; Morgan, 1997). In Hollander's (2004) words, even if there is a 'truth' to be told, 'people may choose not to tell it'.

Debates centre on whether groups comprised of participants who all have something in common (so-called 'homogenous groups') facilitate the disclosure of 'truth' more than groups comprised of divergent individuals with no obviously shared interests or experiences, and whether members who already know each other produce better-quality data than a group of strangers (e.g. Wellings *et al.*, 2000) (see below for a more detailed discussion of 'sampling issues' connected with focus group research). It is clear, however, that what the focus group cannot do is measure attitudes in the conventional sense of a survey (Wilkinson, 2003).

17.3.2 The social constructionist position

Hollander (2004) points out that focus groups are actually *very limited in their potential for understanding individual thoughts, feelings and experiences* but are excellent for 'analysing processes of social interaction'. Given that the former is the most common use of focus groups (Wilkinson, 1998), it is important to appreciate that no matter how skilled or experienced the moderator, they cannot and do not provide a 'transparent window on reality' (Frith & Kitzinger, 1998, p. 304). On the contrary, it can be argued that the 'reality' represented by focus groups is collaboratively produced through a process of context-specific meaning making (Wilkinson, 2003). Of particular interest here is not so much the 'reality' itself (or the meanings created by the discussion process) but the way this reality is 'constructed, defended and modified' (Wilkinson, 2003), particularly if group members are empowered to guide the direction and flow of the discussion (Glitz, 1998).

From this so-called 'social constructionist' position, the focus group is much more than a tool for accessing cognitions and meanings – it is 'by definition an exercise in group dynamics and the conduct of the group, as well as the interpretation of results obtained, must be understood within the context of group interaction' (Stewart & Shamdasani, 1990, p. 7).

Formally stated, then, two interrelated forms of evidence can be produced from focus group discussions: the group process (the way in which people interact and communicate with each other) and the content around which the group process is organised (the focal stimulus and the meanings arising from it). Analysis wise, the group process can be understood on two different levels: the intra-personal (i.e. the thoughts, feelings, attitudes and values of the individual) and the intra-group (i.e. how people communicate and interact with each other within the group).

With regard to the 'content' of the discussion, one advantage of using the group as opposed to the individual as the medium of investigation is its 'isomorphism to the process of opinion formation and propagation in everyday life' in so far as 'opinions about a variety of issues are generally determined not by individual information gathering and deliberation but through communication with others' (Albrecht *et al.*, 1993, p. 54).

From this perspective, focus groups are communication events in which the interplay of the personal and the social can be systematically explored. Gervais (1993), for instance, used focus groups (among other qualitative methods) involving Shetlanders to look closely at their processes of social representation in the wake of an oil spill. Each focus group comprised a natural social unit (a family, a crew of fishermen, fish farmers, local council members and a group who had got together after the spill to act on behalf of the community). Evidence revealed the evolution of a collective rhetoric which maintained community integrity by minimising the impact of the crisis despite it being experienced `like a death in the family' (engendered by the intimate relationship that Shetlanders have with their land). The rhetoric was derived from Shetlanders' representations of their identity as 'resilient' and of the archipelago as 'the Old Rock'. The focus groups thus provided the ideal forum in which the collective mobilisation of community resources and traditions could be captured and analysed in the face of crisis.

On the issue of 'process', one way of investigating how meanings are produced in context is to look at what happens when people are confronted with active disagreement and are provoked into analysing their views more intensely than during the individual interview. Jarrett (1993), for instance, describes how, in her study involving low-income black Americans, participants tended to 'perform for each other'; a climate was established in which they were encouraged to discuss things with greater licence than they would otherwise. The reality created was tempered by peer pressure to 'tell it like it is' whenever idealism prevailed. In this way group pressure inhibited people from providing misleading information. This example illustrates how attempts to resolve differences provide leverage on the basis of which participants build comprehensive accounts to explain their various experiences, beliefs, attitudes, feelings, values and behaviours. The challenges that group members can level at each other (e.g. pointing out discrepancies between what is said and assumptions made) during a member-'empowered' focus group discussion may not be the kind that are possible or even ethical for a researcher (Hyden & Bulow, 2003). Such an example highlights the potential of this method to provide unique insights into 'the complex and varying processes through which group norms and meanings are shaped, elaborated and applied' (Bloor *et al.*, 2001, p. 17).

There is a growing and increasingly apparent tension between the essentialist and social constructionist perspectives on focus group research. Until recently, few researchers had taken up the potential within focus group contexts to examinine communication processes *per se* and the impact of these on the way meanings are constructed *in situ*. However, examples are beginning to emerge in a shift towards investigating these processes in focus group discussions comprising naturally occurring groups (e.g. Lunt & Livingstone, 1996), including work groups consistent with an emerging interest in 'organisational ethnography' involving the investigation of natural cultural processes (e.g. Steyaert & Bouwen, 2004).

One rare early example of this potential for focus groups to investigate meaning making is provided by Delli-Carpini and Williams (1994) who examined the relationship between television and the formation of public opinion. The focus group was seen as a vehicle (a 'conversational metaphor') for examining the way opinions are formed via discourse generated by television. This conversational metaphor for examining the influence of the media contrasts radically with the idea that the media work like a 'hypodermic' syringe, 'injecting' people with opinions.

17.4 THE FOCAL STIMULI

The 'focusing' component of focus group research refers to the boundaries of the discussion in relation to a particular stimulus object, event or situation. Originally the stimulus object was a form of mass media communication (e.g. a film or a pamphlet). In marketing, the focus of research might be people's reactions to a particular advertising campaign or consumer product. In the social sciences, the stimulus might be a scenario (e.g. a sexual encounter as a way of accessing attitudes towards safer sex; O'Brien, 1993), a concrete event (e.g. driving and young people's risk taking; Basch, 1987), or even a concept (e.g. household crowding and its effects on psychological well-being; Fuller *et al.*, 1993). The range of possible stimuli is in fact quite broad, extending to the use of projective techniques, role-play scenarios, word association exercises, sentence completion and fantasy themes, which have proved especially effective in producing discussion among children (Bagnoli & Clark, 2010; see also section 17.11.2). There is also a growing interest in using PhotoVoice techniques in focus group contexts (Box 17.3).

One suggestion put forward by Stanton *et al.* (1993) is to use 'theory' as the focusing vehicle especially if the topic or issue is complex and/or potentially sensitive (personally or politically). As an example of this, Hilder (1997) used Schein's model of organisational culture to focus employee discussion. Culture is a topic that employees might not have thought much about before, and even if they had, they may not easily be able to comment on it without being provided with some kind of discussion context. Using theory, however, as a focusing device, the researcher is faced with a dilemma. If the discussion is framed using constructs from a model, there is an obvious risk of driving the content of the conversation. 'Advance organisers' like this can inhibit other avenues of discussion that might otherwise come up, risking loss of useful information. On the other hand, participants may not know where to start or what to say, and may end up talking endlessly about quite superficial aspects of the topic or using the focus group to 'offload'. Since some

---

Box 17.3　The use of PhotoVoice in focus group contexts

The use of visual images to help people think critically about their lives and experiences is not new (e.g. Freire, 1970). PhotoVoice is however a particular photographic technique in which participants use a camera to record their real life experiences and then bring them to a discussion forum (see for example, Gosselink & Myllykangas, 2007 Gotschi *et al.*, 2009). Cooper and Yarborough (2010) illustrate the use of PhotoVoice in what they call a 'tell me – show me' method to gather insight into health conditions in rural Guatemala. In phase one, participants engaged in a more traditional focus group discussion and then took photos of their experiences. In phase two, the same participants viewed and responded to each other's photos. Cooper and Yarborough (2010, p. 651) conclude that 'photographs can be viewed as tools to enrich and extend existing interview methodologies by providing information that cannot always be obtained through direct analysis.'

kind of 'focus' is necessary and limitless time is not available, it may be more sensible, Hilder (1997) says, to scene-set to hopefully gain quality input on the preferred topic within an agreed time-span.

In general, research objectives guided by theory are not likely to be exactly the same as the aims presented to participants and which are used to frame the discussion process. In research reported by Stanton *et al.* (1993) it is unlikely that the participants were told that the focus group was designed to 'explore developmental, socio-historical and cultural concepts' influencing sexual behaviour! Rather, participants will be informed more concretely that the aim is to find out what they think or how they feel about particular sexual behaviors. Likewise, for an investigation of 'processes' the aim of the focus group will be the research objective translated into a set of practical questions or issues for exploration. For instance, a study into the effects of certain contextual factors (e.g. gender) on both the process and the content of discussion may employ a topic of conversation that is most likely to throw up gender issues (e.g. experiences of violence) (Hollander, 2004). The onus is then on the researcher to translate this into an aim that will both focus and facilitate group discussion around this issue in anticipation of being able to witness gender differences in both process and content (e.g. 'the aim of the discussion is to find out what your feelings are about …'). Where focus groups are guided purely by practical rather than substantive concerns (e.g. to find out what clients think about the quality of a particular hospital service), the aims are likely to be more transparent. The question of what to tell participants about the research aims is likely to become particularly important in a sensitive organisational context. Participants may become suspicious and likely to withhold information or to say only what they feel is expected of them, if they perceive that they are not being properly informed. Participants may suspect a 'hidden agenda' and will need to be reassured that this is not so. Gaining participation in defining the nature and scope of the 'focus' for discussion is one way of achieving a sense of group ownership which can help to open people up to further discussion (Hilder, 1997).

17.5 FOCUS GROUP DESIGN AND PLANNING

Morgan (2008) reiterates the valuable point he made back in 1993, that there is no 'one right way to do focus groups'; on the contrary, a pragmatic approach built on a clear understanding of the goals and outcomes of the research is fundamental to the design and planning stage. Clarity of goals also depends on the epistemological approach, which will in turn also impact on the style of moderation most suited to getting the evidence you need. Morgan (2008) addresses the option of running repeated focus groups over a duration of time, rather than necessarily always using them as one off sessions.

17.5.1 **Sampling and recruitment of participants**

It is not the intention of focus group studies to produce conclusions that can be generalised beyond the context in which they are conducted, so random sampling is not necessary. Nonetheless, it is important to be systematic when deciding on group composition. The sample should be chosen to reflect those segments of the population who will provide the most meaningful information in relation to the project objectives. Participants should have something to say about the topic of interest or something to demonstrate when using focus groups to understand processes. Recruitment strategies have important consequences for the degree of cooperation and commitment generated amongst respondents. The time and energy invested in meeting with 'local' people and making personal contact with potential participants at the outset can help build group rapport.

Focus group researchers disagree on whether it is necessary to use screening procedures during the recruitment process. One argument in favour of screening says that differences in participant background and/or lifestyle might inhibit the flow of discussion due to lack of common ground. Others argue to the contrary that if all participants were to share virtually identical backgrounds the discussion would be flat and unproductive. The general rule of thumb is that group members should have at least some common characteristics (e.g. same socio-economic class, same age group) to facilitate disclosure because of the rapport it creates among people who are otherwise unknown to each other (Box 17.4)

Another argument in support of screening is based on the principle of reactivity. Ordinarily, the reactivity arising from the screening process is seen as a liability: participants are given the opportunity to familiarise themselves with the research issues and may therefore enter the focus group situation with prejudice and bias. Alternatively, the reactivity created by screening procedures may give people the time to mull over the topic in advance, but this can enhance rather than undermine the validity of the content generated by the discussion. The issue of bias, however, is only problematic if the aim is to get 'closer to the truth' of something.

If, on the other hand, the aim of the focus group is to investigate the interrelationship between various contextual factors (e.g., gender, socio-economic status, extent of acquaintance, topic context, and so on), interaction and discussion processes, as well as the content of what is discussed, the question of bias is irrelevant. The important consideration in this respect is to be aware of all relevant 'contextual factors' including moderator characteristics and preconceptions. From this perspective there is no absolute truth to be accessed: 'what' is said is entirely relative and must be appropriately contextualised (Hollander, 2004). For instance, in a discussion about experiences of violence, men in predominantly male focus groups downplay their victimisation stories and exaggerate their role as perpetrators; women do the opposite. Hollander (2004) put this down to norms of masculinity becoming salient in predominantly male groups (i.e. where men are motivated to strategically

Box 17.4   Sampling criteria

Knodel (1993) advises on running separate focus group sessions with homogenous but contrasting subgroups against certain sampling criteria. Criteria are selected on substantive grounds and involve the subdivision of groups in ways that furnish potentially contrasting views and experiences on the topic of investigation. For example, the sample may comprise females who are subdivided by role criteria – e.g. 'housewife and mother' and 'career woman' – in an investigation of social representations of women in connection with female identity. Other examples of sampling criteria might be socio-economic class, language and culture. Socio-demographic differences within a focus group could create power dynamics that inhibit full discussion, as could cultural barriers. Facilitating a mixed language group will also pose a challenge to even the most skilled moderator (Clark, 2009). There is nonetheless a limit to the number of sampling criteria that can be applied to any one study. Knodel suggests that 'breaking' up the sample into subgroups should be kept to a minimum, otherwise both the sampling and the analysis process will become unwieldy and also very costly. At the very least, one focus group will need to be conducted for each combination of sampling criteria. Clark (2009) provides an example of how they divided up their focus group sample in a study of high risk youth. The research team decided to use school as a key criterion because of longstanding rivalry between the two schools attended by the youths in question. Sex was also another criteria, but the research team decided instead to use a skilled facilitator to work with mixed-sex groups to create richer discussion.

One caveat to the use of criteria for sub-sampling is that having something in common is by no means a guarantee of increased disclosure and in some cases may inhibit it – e.g. males disclosing experiences of fear in a study of violence are less likely in all-male groups (Hollander, 2004; Wellings et al., 2000).

present themselves with strength and bravado in relation to their male peers), especially in groups where 'what one says' in the group discussion could have ramifications for maintaining valid masculine identities back in the real world. In other words, if participants know each other, what they say may have longer-term consequences. The issue here is not so much 'what' was found (which was different to data obtained from surveys) but why, and what self-presentational purposes are being served (Michell, 1998). Ultimately the decision rests on determining the composition of the group which will maximise the probability of obtaining the most theoretically relevant information. There is mounting evidence that males and females interact differently in mixed-sex as opposed to same-sex groups, and this has prompted some to suggest that focus group sessions should be homogenous in terms of gender (Stewart & Shamdasani, 1990). However, this assumes a focus on content only rather than process (Hollander, 2004). Some would argue that the dynamics of gender in a focus group context is interesting in itself. Social scientists argue that there are many occasions when participants not only have something in common but also a shared history. Not only can a shared history facilitate openness by offering validation via the sharing of experience but it may in itself be of interest to the investigation (Frith, 2000). There are many examples of focus groups being successfully conducted with naturally occurring communities of people (e.g. Gervais, 1993; Taylor *et al.*, 1991). Taylor *et al.* (1991), for instance, used 'natural' focus groups to examine the psychosocial impact of solid waste facilities within exposed communities.

One crucial consideration in reflecting on the relevance of culture to the above discussion, is the issue of whether the idea of participating in a focus group is contrary to some cultural norms (Halcomb *et al.*, 2007). Willgerodt (2003) for example, notes the discomfort of the Chinese with the 'norms' of the focus group method whilst Strickland (1999) found that participants in North West India, embraced the discursive nature of the method. On the other hand, focus groups have played and can continue to play an important role in helping to voice the perspectives of culturally and linguistically diverse participants (Halcomb *et al.*, 2007). Clearly the onus is much on the skill of the moderator to capture diversity in the most appropriate way in the focus group forum.

17.5.2 **Sample size**

Sample size (not group size, note) varies widely from as small as 21 (e.g. occupational therapy practitioners in Llewelyn, 1991) to one rare exception of 744 (e.g. parents, adolescents and educators in Croft & Sorrentino, 1991). The number of focus group sessions conducted will be a function of both sample and group size. Some researchers have noted that the data generated after about 10 sessions are largely redundant. The decision rests on the type of evidence required and from whom, as well as considerations of cost in terms of time and resources.

17.5.3 **Group size**

A systematic review of recent focus group research in psychology yields an average of nine participants per session as conventional, with a range of six to twelve. This conclusion is consistent with the figures quoted in the focus group methods literature, although some would advocate between six and eight participants as ideal (Albrecht *et al.*, 1993; see also Wilkinson, 2003). There are several reasons why it is advisable to keep groups as small as possible whilst still being able to elicit the breadth of responses required. Large groups are unwieldy to manage, allow free-riding and can be apt to fragment as subgroups form. Also it may be hard to obtain a clear recording of the session: people talk at different volumes and at different distances so the discussion may be difficult if not impossible to track. It is common practice to over-recruit for each session by 20 per cent since it is inevitable that not all of those recruited will actually turn up. The group size on the day will therefore vary.

17.5.4 Location, setting and length of session

The issue of location assumes that the focus group will involve a number of co-located people engaged in face-to-face conversation. However, there is a move towards considering ways in which to engage people in focus group discussion through Internet and telephone forums, removing the need to think about location and setting (see section 17.11.1). For the conventional co-located group members choice of location will need to balance the needs of the research with those of participants. It should set the tone of the research as professional and, where possible, be on neutral ground. However, there are times when the sample will be hard to reach unless the research is conducted on home territory (e.g. a hospital), or it may be of particular interest to frame the research in a particular context.

Two prime considerations for participants are convenience and comfort. The location should be easy to reach and the research schedule should not pose any difficulties for them (e.g. child care and transportation problems). Once in place, the conditions of the room itself should be conducive to a smooth-flowing discussion and basically comfortable (e.g. an appropriate ambience of informality, availability of refreshments, nearby toilets, suitable seating and table arrangements). It is also usual to supply name tags. Most focus group researchers agree that between 1 and 2 hours is the standard duration for each session involving adults, and a maximum of 1 hour for sessions involving children.

17.6 FOCUS GROUP IMPLEMENTATION

At its most basic level, the successful implementation of a focus group study depends on two key factors: preparation and good people skills (Greenbaum, 2000; Wilkinson, 2003). The exact nature of the preparation and the skill involved will, however, depend on epistemological stance, perhaps even more so than the question(s) being asked. Broadly speaking, an investigation of content will necessitate a very different kind of preparation and moderation (e.g. active process facilitation) than an investigation of processes of meaning construction and negotiation in a natural group (e.g. strategic retraction from both group content and process). In the content-oriented scenario, the aim is to maximise disclosure by actively engaging all participants in the discussion, minimising group biases and status dynamics. The discussion will perhaps be guided in this instance by a fairly strict topic guide (see below), the intention being to elicit and record as many individual utterances as possible.

In the more process-oriented investigation, the idea is to create a situation where participants direct their conversations towards each other in as natural way as possible (Hollander, 2004) group members are effectively *empowered* to direct the flow and direction of the dialogue that ensues (Wilkinson, 1998). Here the focus of interest is the 'interaction process'.

17.6.1 Facilitator style and skills

From the above it is clear that the style and skills of the facilitator are fundamental to the effectiveness of the focus group. In some instances also the moderator must be someone with whom the participants can identify so as to be able to gain their trust and commitment (e.g. members of low-income ethnic minority groups). In practice people will talk surprisingly freely about a wide variety of personal topics so long as the climate is permissive and non-critical. From an essentialist perspective, the best moderator guides the proceedings in an unobtrusive and subtle way, intervening only to the extent of maintaining a productive group. For example, one or two of the more dominant group members may be engaged in a heated exchange at the expense of others in the group who are obviously experiencing some discomfort. In this case the moderator needs to take active steps to defuse the situation, refocus the group and balance out the discussion process (Box 17.5).

If the interest of the study is the content of the discussion, there are three additional criteria for ensuring that 'focus' is maintained: specificity, range and depth.

- Specificity: this is about the extent to which minute detail is sought in people's responses and reactions to the stimulus object or event. It is the moderator's task to elicit meanings and differential responses.

- Range of coverage: this is about the skill of the moderator in actively facilitating transition from one area of a discussion to another.

- Depth: this is about the personal context of the response or reaction elicited by the stimulus. Eliciting in-depth responses involves expanding on responses beyond limited reports of 'positive' or 'negative', 'pleasant' or 'unpleasant' reactions. The moderator's task is to diagnose the level at which participants are talking to each other (i.e. ranging from superficial description to detailed elaboration) and where necessary to deepen it.

All these criteria can be met by the moderator who is skilled in listening and questioning techniques. There are some instances where group members may themselves *spontaneously* take responsibility for the flow as well as the content of the discussion. This would occur when, say, someone in the group tries to reorient a

Box 17.5   Style of group facilitation

There are two basic styles of group facilitation most appropriate to the implementation of a focus group depending on whether the study has an essentialist or a social constructionist focus. An essentialist approach will involve the facilitator taking control over *what* is discussed as well as *how* it is discussed. A social constructionist focus will by contrast focus only on the skillful facilitation of the group dynamic but not so much the topic of discussion.

When the focus is more on the group dynamic the aim is to maximise involvement and interaction. Interaction is facilitated by ensuring that the discussion is productive (i.e. all the relevant issues are covered and in sufficient depth). Only the issues to be focused on are determined in advance. However, there will be occasions when the research objectives are revised based on the results of the focus group discussions. In this case the facilitator should mainly allow the participants to determine the agenda. A pose of 'incomplete understanding' but not ignorance (which will appear insincere) is recommended; the facilitator makes it clear that s/he is there to learn from the participants. In some cases, it may be necessary for the facilitator to completely stand back and allow the group to manage both what is discussed and how. Initially this will require that the facilitator empowers the participants to take progressively more responsibility for the group dynamics as well as the topic of the discussion. This kind of focus group will provide the opportunity to see how participants naturally organise their discussions of certain issues. The climate is then also ripe for the discussion of controversial or sensitive topics that would otherwise threaten rapport if the researcher introduced them. The main disadvantage for the essentialist stance is the complete absence of standardisation, thus rendering it difficult to compare findings across different focus groups within the same research project. If the focus is on what is discussed rather than how, without prompting, some topics may never come up. Hence, the facilitator will need to stick more to a script of topic areas and questions to ensure that everything is covered.

discussion that has gone off track or who frequently asks others for clarification. From a social constructionist perspective this will be a phenomenon of interest in its own right. Jarrett (1993) describes how the low-income African-American women in her study challenged each other's 'idealised accounts' (e.g. as strong women who have to manage errant husbands, disobedient children and meddlesome mothers) of their housewife role. The extent to which self-management of this kind occurs depends on the climate established by the moderator at the very outset. Overall, the smaller the degree of external control, the smaller the opportunity for moderator influence (e.g. unwittingly leading participants into a particular area of discussion that provides validation for previous work), thereby increasing the external validity of the information derived (Box 17.5).

17.6.2 **Topic guide**

A topic guide is necessary only if content is the focus of the study. The guide should nonetheless only be suggestive, giving the moderator latitude to improvise fruitful questions and pursue unanticipated lines of inquiry. The guide should not be used in the form of a questionnaire or interviewing straitjacket. Reliance on fixed questions may undermine the ability of the moderator to listen analytically to the content of the discussion, thereby overlooking the implications of what is said. Sometimes the feelings being expressed in people's comments are cloaked in abstractions and rationalisations. The moderator might develop a hunch about the nature of the undercurrent and raise it in the form of tentative questions, creating a climate in which people are encouraged to articulate their feelings. To ward against using the guide as a script, some have advocated that the issues to be covered are instead committed to memory. The number of issues raised will depend on the extent to which the group identifies with the topic as a whole and the type of thinking they are required to engage in (e.g. highly sensitive topics may lead quickly to emotional fatigue). It may be advisable to pre-test the 'tone' of the discussion to collect clues about the appropriateness of the focus group method for how easily or openly a topic is discussed and the range of emotions elicited.

17.6.3 **Listening and questioning skills**

Whatever the epistemological stance, the listening and questioning style of the facilitator is key to determining the nature of the discussion. This will be reflected in the sequence of questions as well as how the questions are worded. Overall, question wording should facilitate openness. For instance, rather than direct people to say either 'yes' or 'no' without elaboration ('Are you happy with …?'), a question should invite a disclosure and elaboration (e.g. 'What are your thoughts about …'). Consistent use of open or probing questions helps create a climate of attentiveness and listening where people feel able to respond in any way they like (Box 17.6).

Questions need to be strategically and sensitively used by a facilitator when initiating transitions in the discussion, perhaps cued by something said or alluded to by a respondent or by a more strategic desire to revisit an issue that was side-stepped, superficially discussed or not mentioned at all. However, cues for transition originating from the respondents help maintain the flow of the discussion, whereas the more stylised kind of moderator-initiated moves can interrupt the flow if not managed carefully. Other requirements for moderator intervention may arise from 'difficulties' with particular people (Box 17.6).

Silence is also a powerful way of getting people to talk, allowing them time to think about and formulate a response. Moderators should not be tempted to fill every single void with a question, and certainly, within a framework of interest in the process of interaction, silence in terms of what is not being said and why is a relational issue and thus an important form of data in itself (Michell, 1998).

Box 17.6   Managing group dynamics

Focus group discussions can sometimes become imbalanced, being dominated by one or two members. If the intention is to engage everyone on a fairly equal basis without inhibition, the 'domination' by certain participants is likely to be problematic to the aims of the investigation. If on the other hand, the aim is to investigate language and interaction, this picture of domination may tell us something important. For example, it might tell us about information status differentials or it may reveal some power dynamics. Lakoff (1990, p. 45) says that the first person to speak at length in a discussion can set the tone and direction of the conversation, legitimising some topics as the focus of conversation over others. This is 'difficult' for a discussion in which the intention is to increase the breadth and depth of discussion about a range of preplanned topics, but a rich source of data for those interested in looking at group dynamics. On the other hand, the facilitator will need to be mindful of the ethics of allowing someone not only to inhibit the contributions of others but also potentially to upset them. The group facilitator may need to intervene if other group members are becoming visibly disengaged or distressed by the 'dominating' participant.

Skilled use of questions in particular requires double hearing or the ability to read between the lines of a discussion in order to 'ferret' out what is only implied (e.g. in linguistic derivatives) rather than relying totally on what is made explicit. By explicating the implied (e.g. tentatively playing it back to respondents in the form of a clarifying question), it is rendered legitimate (e.g. it is acceptable to talk about this) and respondents may then feel able to elaborate.

17.7 RECORDING THE DATA

Focus groups generate data in the form of transcripts produced from audio tape supplemented by a few general field notes to minimise the burden of having to simultaneously observe, listen and facilitate. It is crucial to first obtain the informed consent of the participants and to give assurances of confidentiality. Note that the larger the group the less easy it is to get a clear recording using one tape recorder alone, so it is important to carefully plan and trial the logistics of recording.

17.8 TRANSCRIPTION

Transcription is a primarily mechanical task. Its time-consuming and laborious nature, however, has often led researchers to analyse the content directly from the tape, which entails transcribing only the most illustrative comments. Since the purpose of a focus group is to gain insight into how respondents' represent a particular issue as a whole and on a collective rather than an individual basis, it is important to capture the entire character of the discussion, warts and all. Any form of short-circuiting of the transcription process or selective editing is therefore undesirable, particularly insofar as the interactive process is integral to the way that particular content is produced (e.g. Hopkins, 2007).

17.9 **ANALYSIS OF FOCUS GROUP DATA**

It is clear, as Wilkinson (2003, p. 203) succinctly puts it, that there is 'no single canonical – or even preferred – way of analysing (focus group) data'. The practicalities are, she recognises, that focus group data are 'voluminous, relatively unstructured and not easily analysed'. The form of analysis, moreover, will depend fundamentally on whether it is the 'content' or the 'interaction process' (i.e. group dynamic) that is the 'data' of interest. From an essentialist perspective in which 'content' is foremost, some form of content analysis will be the most appropriate approach to use. By contrast, a discourse analytic approach will be more appropriate to a social constructionist epistemology because it takes into consideration both the content of discussion and the interaction process.

This discussion of content analysis as it is used to analyse transcription data is equally applicable to other types of data that can be reduced to textual form (e.g. discourses and historical materials) (see Chapter 21). Content analysis comprises both a mechanical and an interpretative component (Krippendorf, 1980). The mechanical aspect involves physically organising and subdividing the data into categories, while the interpretative component involves determining what categories, are meaningful in terms of the questions being asked. The mechanical and interpretative are inextricably linked in a cycling back and forth between the transcripts and the more conceptual process of developing meaningful coding schemes. Two methods of interpretation applicable to the analysis of focus group material, are interpretative phenomenological analysis (IPA) and discourse analysis.

Interpretative phenomenological analysis is a form of qualitative analysis which explicitly acknowledges that the process of analysing experiences and the meaning of these experiences will necessarily involve 'interpretation' on the part of the researcher (Smith and Osborn, 2008 see Chapter 18). As a fundamentally idiographic approach to investigation and analysis, IPA is concerned with the exploration of *intrapersonal* rather than group experiences. This has prompted some researchers to maintain that using focus groups in 'phenomenological' research is an oxymoron (e.g., Bradbury-Jones *et al.*, 2009). However, there may be instances where people find it easier to talk openly about their personal perceptions and experiences in a context in which these experiences can be shared with similar others.

Alternatively, there may be good practical reasons why focus group interviews are being used to explore individual experiences – including cost and time considerations. In such instances, the *individual perceptions and experiences* will need to be parsed out from the group discussion (and to an extent this will only be possible if the facilitator has engaged each and every individual at an experiential level in the discussion process) (Bradbury & Jones *et al.*, 2009).

By contrast, discourse analysis is based on the epistemological assumption that what people say is a form of purposive social action which has a function to serve in a particular interactional context (see Chapter 20). In this instance, the focus group is the interactional context in which statements are made. Discourse analysis is an especially useful way of looking at both content and interaction within a social constructionist framework. Wilkinson (2003, p. 202) illustrates this by using a data extract from a discussion between two pub landladies where they collaboratively produce ideas about the role of their profession in 'causing' breast cancer. However, only a very small proportion of focus group data can be handled using discourse analysis; it does not furnish the researcher with the potential to summarise the data in any general way.

Another means of qualitative analysis more pertinent to the capturing of shared experiences is furnished by techniques associated with grounded theory. Grounded theory's theoretical background is in sociology, underpinned by the assumption that meanings are made sense of in social interaction (see Chapter 19). Grounded theory should be used when the researcher wants to explore complex issues or processes and create a theory. It involves the progressive identification and integration of categories of meaning from textual data. Researchers often look for negative cases – instances that do not fit with the identified categories – to ensure they have understood the full intricacy of the data

Analysing interaction *per se* is a more recent development but is core to the qualitative research agenda (Barbour, 2007; Lyons & Coyle, 2007), although there is no consensus yet on how to do this (Linell, 2001). Leboux Poland and Daudelin (2006, p. 2092) provide one practical template for addressing questions like, 'What types of interactions occur among participants (e.g. limited, empathic, negative, constructive, etc)?', 'To what extend do these interactions reflect broader social contexts (e.g. gender, age, status, authority etc)?' and 'Who do participants represent when they meet (e.g. own experience, particular role or group membership)?'.

By contrast to this thematic approach to looking at processes (as well as content), others have offered frameworks for a finer-grained approach to 'interaction analysis'. For instance, Rothwell (2010) developed an interaction coding system she calls EGCCS (Emotional Group Culture Categorisation System). Using this template, she shows how adolescents used joking as a mechanism to deflect the discussion away from the issue of quitting smoking. Exploring this further she shows how peer interaction in the focus group put pressure on participants to continue smoking. Rothwell illustrates how the interactions captured in the focus group discussion may replicate those occurring in everyday life. Her research offers rare insight into the social and interpersonal difficulties adolescents may face among their peers if they wish to stop smoking.

17.10 FEEDBACK OF RESULTS/FINDINGS

Feedback to participants or an organisation raises a dilemma for the researcher. It is unusual for access to be granted within a company without some expectation of feedback. However, some of the information arising out of the focus group may not be what the sponsor wants to hear and may even be personally compromising. One also has to consider that what people have talked about in the group may be not what they would wish to pass on, and not pleasant to receive. The decision as to how much, if any, of the information and analysis to discuss with the company sponsor has to be an individual one. Clearly no attributable information should be given; the confidentiality agreed with the group members must be absolute. However, if the focus groups are part of a potentially long-term relationship between you, the researcher and the company, then the relationship with the sponsor is also an important one. Thus, while diplomacy in the analysis given may be appropriate, there is little point in hiding non-attributable information which will form part of the longer-term study (Hilder, 1997). On a more positive note, the focus group environment is particularly conducive to 'freedom of speech' within the constraints of the research agenda and skill of the moderator (Lezuanm, 2007).

17.11 FUTURE DEVELOPMENTS IN FOCUS GROUP RESEARCH

17.11.1 The 'e-focus group'

Advances in technology and the 'globalisation' of real-time communication have seriously opened up the scope for running focus groups across cultural, spatial and temporal boundaries to be run either using 'online' forums (Greenbaum, 1998; Markham, 2004) or conference calling (Frazier *et al.*, 2010). With regards to online forums, as Markham (2004, p. 95) puts it: '[A]s a communication medium, a global network of connection, and a scene of social construction, the internet provides new tools for conducting research and new means for understanding the way social realities get constructed and reproduced through discussion behaviours'. In particular, the opportunity via an online medium to 'witness and analyze the structure of talk, the negotiation of meaning and identity, the development of relationships and communities' (Markham, 2004, p. 97) is one that researchers are beginning to capitalise on in the pursuit of the study of collective sense-making. Two types of online global focus group are being used: real-time focus groups who log on to the network at a

Box 17.7   Global focus groups

The concept of 'global focus groups' opens up a whole realm of research possibilities, but also brings with it potential logistical problems and issues of 'virtual' facilitation. Kenny (2005) used a computer program called WebCT© to facilitate on-line engagement and interaction among a group of nurses brought together (from any location at any time) to explore certain nursing issues. She describes the experience as positive, enabling her to 'collect richly detailed research data' (2005, p. 417). Whether the unmanaged and ongoing aspects of on-line discussion groups which are somewhat akin to the practice of 'Twittering' (Dorsey, 2006) mean that they can no longer be called focus groups is yet to be contemplated. Such groups may be better used for practical (e.g. information sharing) rather than research ends, such as reported by Low and Dugmore (2009) whose e-mail focus groups were beneficial to teamwork among mental health professionals distributed in time and space across the service. One problem with the real-time discussions is ensuring that everyone knows what time to sign on and that the timings are coordinated exactly across time zones (see Greenbaum, 1998, for more on this).

set time for a set period to discuss a topic or issue, and ongoing focus groups whose members sign on and off whenever they wish, and contribute whenever convenient and/or appropriate (Box 17.7).

In the real-time version a focus group is run in the traditional fashion with a facilitator keeping the discussion on track, probing wherever necessary, and so on. In the ongoing version a discussion is not easily managed or facilitated, the group itself being responsible for determining the shape and direction of the dialogue that ensues. An example of this type of online focus group is reported by Low and Dugmore (2009) in a study on FOCUS e-mail discussion. Real-time 'virtual' focus groups are staged, while ongoing focus groups are not and exist irrespective of whether all their members are signed on at any one time.

Some like Greenbaum (2000) have argued that computer-mediated focus groups are not sound alternatives to the conventional face-to-face forum because of what can get lost in the process. Specifically, he says that discussion can be inhibited because of the absence of social context cues. For instance, there is some evidence that online groups produce less discussion (in terms of words contributed) than face-to-face groups (Hiltz *et al.*, 1987). Reid and Reid (2005) have also compared online and face-to-face focus groups against a broader range of criteria (i.e. number of ideas contributed), process (e.g. interaction processes, self-disclosures, uninhibited behaviours), and satisfaction measures. Across the same amount of time, online groups contributed less than face-to-face groups. There were no differences, however, across groups in equality of contribution and no differences in process dynamics. And contrary to expectation, online participants did not feel less inhibited about contributing. On the other hand, face-to-face participants experienced their discussion as more satisfying than online participants. However, after controlling for number of words contributed, the online group were more productive of ideas. Reid and Reid (2005) concluded that online focus groups can be sound alternatives to face-to-face groups insofar as the dynamics do not substantially differ, and may in some instances be advantageous in producing better quality content.

On the use of telephone conferencing to run focus groups, there is little evidence to draw on with regard to their viability relative to face-to-face forums. With this rationale, Frazier *et al.* (2010) compared four telephone with five face-to-face focus groups controlling all but the forum, for understanding employment experiences after a gynaecologic cancer diagnosis. They found no differences in terms of the content produced using thematic analysis; but interestingly, they did find that telephone participants disclosed more emotionally sensitive experiences. Frazier *et al.* suggest that telephone participation facilitated deeper disclosures because of visual anonymity.

Overall, what little we do know about the workings of online, telephone and face-to-face groups, suggests that it is important to think through the potential advantages and disadvantages of each forum before deciding on whether there is a risk of trading content for logistical convenience or whether, in fact, the absence of social cues may facilitate discussion of sensitive issues. In the end, the decision will ride much on what is being discussed and by whom. Reid and Reid (2005) were using focus groups to capture general attitudes towards marriage and body image, whilst Frazier *et al.* (2010) were engaging participants in a much more personal and emotionally sensitive topic.

The issue of comparability across online and face-to-face groups is not so relevant for research conducted in a more social constructionist vein. In principle a focus group can be managed equally well across online, telephone and face-to-face forums, because contextual and interactional variations are integral to understanding content (Halkier, 2010).

17.11.2 Using focus groups with children and young people

There has been a surge of interest in using focus groups for research on children and young people (e.g. Olsen *et al.*, 2008; Pfefferbaum *et al.*, 2008). This interest is mainly derived from the potential of focus groups to generate discussion about semi-public issues, content that might otherwise be difficult to obtain from children and young people in one-to-one interviews. Clark (2009) cites the following example of how asking 12-year-olds in a one-to-one interview to talk about how to prevent bicycle injuries is likely to produce the 'right answers' like obeying traffic signs and wearing a helmet. However, in a focus group it is possible to facilitate debate about whether there may be situations in which 12-year-olds might not feel they 'need' to wear a helmet, which is much more informative about actual bicycle attitudes and habits. Clark, however, cautions against the risk of focus groups lapsing into round-robin exercises in which each child contributes something in turn. This can occur when facilitators are not skilled in managing group dynamics and/or where they may be prone to lapsing into a 'teacher-like' classroom style.

On the other hand, children are unlikely to feel comfortable participating in a controversial debate, and in fact, may not be developmentally 'ready' to contribute to discussions of this kind. Clark recommends using 'youthful' facilitators to help gain rapport with children and adolescents, but they will need to have the requisite skill to manage genuine discussion. Bagnoli and Clark (2010) emphasise the critical importance of rapport as a prerequisite to the engagement of young people in any type of research, in combination with the introduction of some 'colour'; for example, by introducing some activity as a stimulus to discussion rather than just 'sitting and talking to an adult' (p. 111). This is consistent with the call by Hopkins (2007) for more creativity generally in the use of focus groups in qualitative research.

17.12 CONCLUSION

This chapter has described and explained the potential of the focus group method to generate both content and process data depending on which epistemological approach is used to underwrite the choice of method. Design and implementation of a focus group study is discussed according to which of these two foci of investigation – if not both – is of primary research interest. Accordingly, various analytic approaches are also introduced including basic content analysis, as well as the application of more sophisticated qualitative approaches underpinned by a particular analytic approach such as discursive analysis, interpretative phenomenological analysis and grounded theory. Innovative uses of the focus group online as well as to investigate active sense-making processes in context are noted.

17.13 EXERCISES

1 Design a focus group study to investigate mothers' ways of managing what and how much their children eat. What epistemology will you assume and why? Who will you sample and why? What questions will you ask? How will you manage the data?

2 Run a focus group comprising at least four students to discuss the transition from A-level to university. Identify the key themes arising.

17.14 **DISCUSSION QUESTIONS**

1   What is the difference between the use of focus groups in psychology and the use of focus groups in marketing contexts?
2   Why would a psychologist want to use focus group discussions as opposed to separate one-to-one interviews?
3   What are the challenges face by the person who facilitates the focus group discussion and how might these be addressed?
4   Find an example of two published studies, one that uses focus groups in an 'essentialist' way and one that uses focus groups in a 'social constructionist' way. What are the key differences in focus group design, implementation and analysis?
5   What are the challenges faced in analysing focus group data as opposed to data from single interviews?

17.15 **FURTHER READING**

There is a burgeoning literature on the focus group method. A classic in terms of handbooks on the focus group method is Greenbaum (1998), which introduces the idea of 'global focus groups' and also examines the relevance of technological advances for the focus group method; others are Bloor *et al.* (2001); Edmunds (1999); and in particular Morgan *et al.* (1998), which comprises a set of six books each devoted to a particular aspect of the focus group method, from design and planning through to implementation and analysis.

Greenbaum (2000) is a must for advances in uses of the focus group method for different types of purposes. Krueger and Casey (2000) specifically address problems likely to be encountered during focus group research, providing a down-to-earth set of guidelines on how to optimise the potential of the focus group method. Other recommended books include Stewart and Shamdasani (1990), which has now acquired the status of a theoretical classic on the focus group method. For a distinctively psychological perspective on focus groups and, in particular, on how to handle the data analysis, Wilkinson's (1998, 2003, 2004b) work is an inescapable must, to help funnel people to respond on a more concrete and specific level if necessary while maintaining openness. Halkier's (2010) paper on focus groups as social enactments is a major contribution to understanding how to apply well-established methods of analysing interaction to focus groups. Finally, Morgan's (2010) reflections on how to 'use' interaction in focus group analysis is essential reading for all focus group followers.

18

Interpretative Phenomenological Analysis

Jonathan A. Smith and Virginia Eatough

CONTENTS

This chapter will outline interpretative phenomenological analysis's theoretical orientation and the sorts of research questions it is suitable for. This will be followed by a description of suitable methods of data collection for interpretative phenomenological analysis (IPA), in particular the semi-structured interview. A set of guidelines for the stages of analysis will be described in detail using examples and we will offer some suggestions for how to write up an IPA study. Finally we will consider the issue of quality in IPA research.

KEY TERMS

cool cognition	idiographic
double hermeneutic	inductive
hermeneutics	phenomenology
homogenous sample	semi-structured interviews
hot cognition	

INTRODUCTION

At the heart of interpretative phenomenological analysis (IPA) is the notion of people as 'self-interpreting beings' (Taylor, 1985). By this we mean that individuals are actively engaged in interpreting the events, objects and people in their lives, and this interpretative activity is captured by the phrase 'sense making'. Thus the central concern for IPA is the analysis of how individuals make sense of their lived experiences. It aims to provide a detailed exploration of these personal lived experiences as well as a close examination of how participants make sense of them. The main currency for an IPA study is the meanings particular experiences, states, events and objects have for participants.

Phenomenology and hermeneutic inquiry form the dual epistemological underpinnings of IPA. Phenomenology is concerned with attending to the way things appear to us in experience; how, as individuals, we perceive and talk about objects and events. This is in contrast to an attempt either to produce an objective statement of the object/event in itself or to examine the object/event in terms of pre-existing conceptual and scientific criteria. Husserl was the first to write programmatically for this agenda for phenomenological philosophy. Heidegger took the project on and emphasised the material nature of human experience which always takes place within a situated context in the world and, in addition, requires an interpretative component to be understood. Following Heidegger, IPA's aim is achieved through interpretative activity on the part of the researcher. This is a familiar and human activity carried out empirically and systematically. Thus IPA is, on the one hand, attempting to understand what it is like to stand in the shoes of the participant whilst recognising, on the other hand, that this is never completely possible. IPA emphasises that research is a dynamic process with an active role for the researcher in that process.

Access to the participant's experience depends on, and is complicated by, the researcher's own conceptions and these processes are necessary in order to make sense of that other personal world through a process of interpretative activity. This is described as a double hermeneutic or dual interpretation process in which 'the participants are trying to make sense of their world; the researcher is trying to make sense of the participants trying to make sense of their world' (Smith & Osborn, 2008, p. 53). 'Reality' as it appears to and is made meaningful for the individual is what is of interest to the IPA researcher, and she/he recognises her/his dynamic role in making sense of that reality.

It is possible to think of this double hermeneutic in another way as one which combines both an empathic and critical hermeneutics (Ricouer, 1970). Thus, consistent with its phenomenological origins, IPA aims to understand what an experience, an event, an object is like from the point of view of the person. Yet at the same time IPA can assume distance from the participant, asking interested and critical questions of their accounts; for example, what is the person trying to achieve here? Is something leaking out here that wasn't intended? Do I have a sense of something going on here that maybe the person themselves is less aware of? Both modes of interpretation can be part of sustained qualitative inquiry and IPA studies will often contain elements of each. Permitting both aspects of inquiry is likely to lead to a richer analysis and do greater justice to the totality of the person's lifeworld. In sum, IPA synthesises ideas from phenomenology and hermeneutics resulting in a method which is descriptive because it is concerned with how things appear and letting things speak for themselves, and interpretative because it recognises there is no such thing as an uninterpreted phenomenon. For more on the theoretical underpinnings of IPA, see Smith *et al.* (2009) . For more on phenomenology, see Moran (2000); for hermeneutics, see Palmer (1969).

18.2 IPA AND PSYCHOLOGY

IPA locates itself firmly within the discipline of psychology, seeing opportunities for a useful dialogue between the various traditions, which can contribute to the debate as to what constitutes a viable mode of inquiry for psychology. First, IPA's emphasis on sense making by both participant and researcher means that cognition can be usefully seen as a central analytic concern and this suggests a compelling theoretical alliance with the dominant cognitive paradigm in contemporary psychology. IPA shares with cognitive psychology and social cognition a concern with unravelling the relationship between what people think (cognition), say (account) and do (behaviour). However, notwithstanding this shared concern, IPA differs when it comes to deciding the appropriate methodology for such questions. Cognitive psychology continues to be committed to quantitative and experimental methodology whilst IPA employs in-depth qualitative analysis. Thus IPA shares with Bruner (1990) a vision of cognitive psychology as a science of meaning and meaning-making rather than a science of information processing. See Smith (1996) for more on this.

IPA is one of several closely related approaches to phenomenological psychology (Smith, 2004). These approaches share a commitment to the exploration of personal lived experience but have different emphases or suggested techniques to engage in this project. For example, Giorgi (Giorgi & Giorgi 2008) has developed a method for conducting empirical phenomenological inquiry which aims to ascertain the underlying essential structure of psychological experience. Ashworth (2008) is particularly interested in identifying the elements of the 'lifeworld' in participants' accounts: selfhood, sociality, embodiment, temporality, spatiality, project, discourse. However, he stresses that these fragments are no more than the 'perspectives or analytical moments of a larger whole which is the situated embodiment of the human individual' (Ashworth, 2003, p. 151).

A particular characteristic of IPA is its commitment to an idiographic, case study level of analysis. In contrast to the nomothetic principles underlying most psychological empirical work, IPA is resolutely idiographic, focusing on the particular rather than the universal (Smith *et al.*, 1995b). In nomothetic studies, analysis works at the level of groups and populations and the researcher can only make probabilistic claims about individuals; for example there is an 85 per cent chance that person X will respond in this way. In idiographic studies, it is possible to make specific statements about those individuals because analyses are derived from the examination of individual case studies. For IPA, these two ways of acquiring knowledge do not require an either/or stance. Rather, it argues for (a) the intensive examination of the individual in her/his own right as an intrinsic part of psychology's remit, and (b) that the logical route to universal laws and structures moves step by step from an idiographic starting point (Harré, 1979).

Thus for IPA the analysis always begins with a detailed reading of the single case. One can then write that case up as a case study or can move to an equally attentive analysis of the second case, and so on. Supposing that the analysis is of a group of individuals, a good IPA study will at all times allow itself to be parsed in two different ways – it should be possible to learn something about both the important generic themes in the analysis but also something about the narrative lifeworld of the particular participants who have told their stories. It is the case that even among qualitative methodologies, IPA is unusual in having this idiographic commitment.

Qualitative research is characterised by epistemological diversity, and recently, researchers have begun to reflect on the ways in which the various approaches converge and diverge. Reicher (2000) distinguishes between *experiential* research (a focus on understanding, representing and making sense of peoples' ways of thinking, motivations, actions, and so on) and *discursive* research (a focus on the ways in which language constructs peoples' worlds). At the simplest level, one might say that IPA clearly fits in the former category, while discourse analysis (see Chapter 20) clearly fits in the latter. Yet, IPA recognises the importance of language in influencing how individuals make sense of lived experiences and then in turn researchers make sense of participants' sense making. However IPA would disagree with a claim that language is the sole or primary constructor of reality. See Eatough and Smith (2008) for more discussion of this.

18.3 SUITABLE RESEARCH QUESTIONS FOR IPA

Not only does interpretative phenomenological analysis (IPA) study people idiographically, it emphasises the strength of an open inductive approach to data collection and analysis, what has been referred to as 'big Q' research (Kidder & Fine, 1987). Qualitative research rejects hypotheses in favour of open-ended questions, and which for IPA aim to generate (at the minimum) rich and detailed descriptions of the phenomenon under investigation. IPA's concern with the in-depth exploration of the participants' lived experiences and with how they are making sense of those experiences helps define the type of question which is suitable for an IPA study. Below are some examples of the sorts of questions that might guide an IPA project:

- How do people make the decision whether or not to have a genetic test?

- What does jealousy feel like?

- How do people view voluntary childlessness?

- How does redundancy affect the individual's sense of self?

- How do parents manage the challenge of living with an autistic child?

Thus, IPA studies are more often than not concerned with big issues, issues of significant consequence for the participant either on an ongoing basis or at a critical juncture in her/his life. These issues are frequently transformative, often they are about identity and a sense of self, because thorough, in-depth, holistic analyses of individual accounts of important experiences or events almost always affect self and identity. Research questions can be specific and well defined ('How does a person decide whether to have a genetic test or not?') or much broader ranging ('How does bringing up a child influence a parent's anger expression?'). IPA's concern with the participant's sense making generates questions which can tap into hot cognition – those issues in a person's life which are burning, emotive and dilemmatic or those involving cool cognition – involving longer-term reflection across the life course. The common thread running throughout IPA studies and the questions they pursue is the meticulous exploration of the lived experience of the participant.

18.4 HOW MANY PARTICIPANTS?

Usually, IPA studies have small sample sizes. The main concern is to do justice to each participant's account (case) and detailed case-by-case analysis is time consuming. This means that, early on, careful choices have to be made: 'Do I want to give an exhaustive and nuanced account about a particular participant's experiences or do I want to say something more general about a group or specific population?' How these questions are answered determines the subsequent methodology and research design. Importantly, not least because of time limitations with most research, it is rarely possible to do both. Having a larger sample size simply because that is more common in psychological studies means that one can end up in the trap of being swamped with data with the end result being a superficial qualitative analysis.

So how many participants should one include? There is no *right* answer to this question. In part it depends on:

- one's commitment to the case study level of analysis;
- the richness of the individual cases;
- how one wants to compare/contrast cases;
- the pragmatic restrictions one is working under.

Published IPA studies include sample sizes of 1, 4, 9, 15 and more. There seems to have been some convergence in British clinical psychology doctoral programmes that six to eight is an appropriate number for an IPA study (Turpin *et al.*, 1997). This gives enough cases to examine similarities and differences between participants but not so many that one is snowed under by the amount of data generated. With respect to undergraduates wanting to use IPA, we would argue that three to four participants are sufficient. This is primarily because IPA should be about depth before breadth. In our experience, three good interviews give an undergraduate enough material to produce a detailed and nuanced analysis of the participants' experience. At this level, with larger numbers, the danger is that the amount of data will be overwhelming and the resulting analysis superficial. The PhD is, of course, a more complex beast which can take many different shapes so it is difficult to give a useful number for participants in this case. It is important that a certain figure does not become reified. In certain situations, a case can be made for $n = 1$; at other times, a detailed examination of convergences and divergences in three cases would be the best way to proceed. Other projects will require larger numbers. See Brocki and Weardon (2006) and Reid *et al.* (2005) for more on this.

Recently, we have been arguing and demonstrating the case for a sample size of one (Bramley & Eatough, 2005; Eatough & Smith, 2006; Rhodes and Smith, 2010; Smith, 2004). Psychology has largely passed over the single person case study (Radley & Chamberlain, 2001; Smith, 1993; Yin, 2003) and we would argue that often it is the logical choice for a psychological understanding of the subjective and richly patterned lived experiences of the person. Of course, if one is submitting work for a degree, then the decision to carry out a single person case study should be carefully thought through. A high level of commitment and some confidence is required to sustain an exclusive focus on one person, and one needs to be cautious in the selection of the case scrutinized. And it remains the case that some examiners will be uncomfortable with a case study approach. Nevertheless, phd students including a case study as one study in the thesis can discover the merit of staying with an absorbing, complex case and attempting to do justice to it in its own right.

There are two key advantages of carrying out a single person case study. First, a great deal is learnt about that particular person and their lived experiences of the phenomenon under investigation. It is also possible to focus on connections between different aspects of the participant's account. The study of the individual can also illuminate and affirm 'the centrality of certain general themes in the lives of all particular individuals' (Evans, 1993, p. 8), bringing the researcher closer to note-worthy aspects of the general by connecting the individual unique life with a common humanity.

Typically, IPA researchers aim for a fairly homogenous sample. Very simply, it is not helpful to think in terms of random or representative sampling if one is interviewing, for example, six participants. Rather, through purposive sampling IPA studies aim to find a more closely defined group for whom the research question will have relevance and personal significance. How the specificity of a sample is defined can depend on a number of factors; the subject matter to be investigated may define the boundaries of the relevant sample (e.g. if the topic is rare). Alternatively, if the topic is more common the sample may be made up of individuals with similar demographic/socio-economic status profiles.

In this respect, the IPA researcher is emulating the social anthropologist who carries out ethnographic research in one particular community. The anthropologist provides detailed descriptions and commentary about that particular culture but does not profess to say something about all cultures. Over time, later studies can investigate other groups and generalisation becomes possible through a steady accumulation of similar cases (Hammersley, 1992; Smith *et al.*, 1995b). Researchers can also think in terms of theoretical rather than empirical generalisability. Theoretical propositions can be refined and modified through comparison with other cases, other conceptual claims in the extant literature, and the personal and professional experience of the researcher/reader. The IPA study is then evaluated in terms of the insights it gives concerning the topic under investigation.

However, it must be remembered that a pragmatic approach to these issues is essential. Inevitably, the research sample selects itself in the sense that potential participants are or should be free agents who choose to participate or not. So it is not unusual to have to adapt or redraw the criteria for inclusion if it transpires that not enough of the originally defined group agrees to take part in the study.

18.5 **DATA COLLECTION METHODS**

IPA studies require a flexible method of data collection, one which gives experience a central place whilst recognising the multiple influences on any experience: its historical and cultural situatedness, including language and social norms and practices. The vast majority of IPA studies have been conducted on data obtained from face-to-face semi-structured interviews, and this method of data collection might be considered the exemplary one for IPA. Chapter 15 provides an overview of the interview in psychological research, and in this section we simply try to give the reader a flavour from the perspective of the IPA researcher. As discussed above, IPA attends to the experiential world of the participant attempting to understand it from the perspective of that person. Thus, as suggested by Kvale (1996), an appropriate metaphor for an IPA study is that of the researcher as a traveler who:

> wanders along with the local inhabitants, asks questions that lead the subjects to tell their own stories of their lived world, and converses with them in the original Latin meaning of conversation as 'wandering together with'.
>
> Kvale (1996) p. 4

At the same time, the interpretative focus of IPA means that the researcher adopts a critical and probing stance towards the meaningful worlds offered by the participants. This dual focus requires the semi-structured interview for the IPA study to be participant led in the fullest sense yet guided by the researcher; and for the researcher to be empathic but also, where necessary, questioning. Both are needed to produce meaningful and useful theoretical and conceptual accounts of the phenomenon under investigation.

Interviewing is one of the most powerful and widely used tools of the qualitative researcher, and the advantage of the semi-structured format for IPA is that the researcher is, in real-time, in a position to follow up interesting, important and even unexpected issues that emerge during the interview. However, it is important not to be exclusionary about this because rich verbal accounts can be collected by other means. For example, participants can be asked to write autobiographical or other personal accounts or to keep diaries over a designated time period (Smith, 1999). See Chapter 16 for more on these types of methods.

Semi-structured interviewing lies on a continuum from unstructured to structured, but just what researchers mean by these terms can vary considerably. The IPA researcher develops a set of questions which address the topic of interest but these are used to guide rather than dictate the course of the interview. If the participant opens up a novel and interesting area of inquiry then this should be pursued. The researcher using a semi-structured format treats people as experiential experts on the topic under investigation (Smith & Osborn, 2008). The aim is to facilitate the giving and making of an account in a sensitive and empathic manner, recognising that the interview constitutes a human-to-human relationship (Fontana & Frey, 2000). Box 18.1 presents some illustrative interview questions from a project of the authors on women's experiences of anger and aggression (see Eatough & Smith, 2006, for more details).

Here the interviewer starts with a very general question and hopes that this will be sufficient to enable the participant to talk about the topic. Individuals tell their stories with varying degrees of ease, not least because they do not always view them

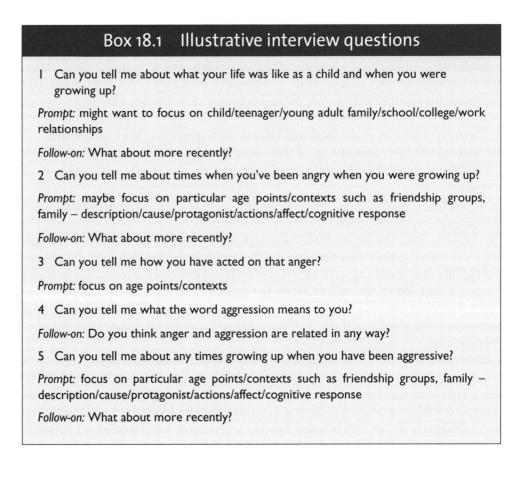

Box 18.1   Illustrative interview questions

I Can you tell me about what your life was like as a child and when you were growing up?

Prompt: might want to focus on child/teenager/young adult family/school/college/work relationships

Follow-on: What about more recently?

2 Can you tell me about times when you've been angry when you were growing up?

Prompt: maybe focus on particular age points/contexts such as friendship groups, family – description/cause/protagonist/actions/affect/cognitive response

Follow-on: What about more recently?

3 Can you tell me how you have acted on that anger?

Prompt: focus on age points/contexts

4 Can you tell me what the word aggression means to you?

Follow-on: Do you think anger and aggression are related in any way?

5 Can you tell me about any times growing up when you have been aggressive?

Prompt: focus on particular age points/contexts such as friendship groups, family – description/cause/protagonist/actions/affect/cognitive response

Follow-on: What about more recently?

as interesting to an outsider. Starting at the outset with questions about anger and aggression episodes, and nothing else, might have narrowed down the topic too prescriptively too early, telling us little about how such events influence and shape the totality of their experiences. Also by starting too quickly with a potentially sensitive topic, it might have made the participant uncomfortable and reluctant to talk. We hoped therefore that the more open question would enable both the participant and researcher to relax into the interview and to begin establishing trust and rapport. However, it is important to realise that there are no fixed rules about these decisions – they must be made in the context of the particular topic being discussed and the particular type of person being interviewed.

Questions 2 and 5 are more specific and are there to help the conversation where a participant needs more assistance in moving from the general to the more particular. Typically, a successful interview will include both specific and general questions and will move between the two types fairly seamlessly. Constructing an interview schedule takes time and thought and will usually require a couple of drafts. Having constructed it, our suggestion is that you learn it by heart so that at the interview it acts as a mental prompt, if needed, not something to which you are constantly referring.

The interviewer does not have to follow the sequence on the schedule, nor does every question have to be asked, or asked in exactly the same way of each participant. Thus the interviewer may decide that it would be appropriate to ask a question earlier than it appears on the schedule because it follows on from something the participant has just said. Similarly, how a question is phrased, and how explicit it is, will partly depend on how the interviewer feels the participant is responding.

For IPA, the interview may well move away from the questions on the schedule. It is quite possible that the interview may enter an area that had not been anticipated by the researcher but which is extremely pertinent to, and enlightening about, the project's overall question. Indeed these novel avenues are often the most valuable, precisely because they have come unprompted from the participant and, therefore, are likely to be of especial importance for her/him. On the other hand, of course, the researcher needs to ensure that the interview does not move too far away from the agreed topic. In essence, you are aiming for a conversational and participant led style of interviewing that allows the participant's perceptions of and stories about the topic to come to the fore.

For IPA it is necessary to audio record and transcribe the whole interview, including what is said by the interviewer. Leave a wide enough margin on both sides of the transcript to make your analytic comments. However, for IPA one does not need the more detailed prosodic features of the interview which are required in conversation analysis (Drew, 2008). Transcription of the tapes is a lengthy process, depending on the clarity of the recording and one's typing proficiency. As a rough guide, allow seven hours of transcription time per hour of interview for the type of transcript required for IPA.

18.6 STAGES OF ANALYSIS

Before we take you through the various analytic stages, it is worth pointing out that the novice qualitative researcher should feel positive about dealing with the data. At the outset it is sometimes difficult to imagine that you will be able to make sense of the many pages of interview material. However, if you are careful, systematic and *take your time* with each analytic stage, you will begin to develop confidence.

It is useful to think in terms of totally *immersing* yourself in the data, as far as is possible stepping into the participants' shoes. You are aiming to give evidence of the participants' sense making with respect to the topic under investigation, and at the same time document your own sense making as the researcher. The latter involves looking at the data through a psychological lens, making sense of it by applying psychological concepts and theories.

IPA is not a prescriptive approach; rather, it provides a set of flexible guidelines which can be adapted by individual researchers in light of their research aims. This is particularly true when it comes to the analysis. This section describes the analytic steps we went through in the anger and aggression study in order to help the reader see how the analysis unfolds but this should not be treated as a recipe, the only way of doing IPA, rather as an illustration of one way of doing it. The study is an idiographic in-depth case study which examines one woman's lived experiences of anger and aggression, how she made sense of her emotions and behaviour, and the contexts in which they happened. The interviews were carried out by the second author.

In brief, the analytic stages were:

- several close, detailed readings of the data were made, to obtain a holistic perspective so that future interpretations stayed grounded within the participant's account;

- initial themes were identified and organised into clusters and checked against the data;

- themes were then refined and condensed, and examined for connections between them;

- a narrative account of the interplay between the interpretative activity of the researcher and the participants' account of their experience in their own words was produced.

Here we describe these stages in more detail and give a worked example. Also see Smith *et al.* (2009) and Smith and Osborn (2008) for other detailed treatments of this process. First, during transcription, the interviewer kept a record of initial thoughts, comments, and so on. It was felt they might be useful to return to and check against later interpretations during the analysis. Then the first transcript was read several times and one margin used to make notes on anything that appeared significant and of interest (Box 18.2). With each reading, the researcher should expect to feel more 'wrapped up' in the data, becoming more responsive to what is being said. Box 18.2 demonstrates this stage of analysis for a small section of the interview with Marilyn (name changed).

The next stage involved returning to the transcript afresh and using the other margin to transform initial notes and ideas into more specific themes or phrases, which calls upon psychological concepts and abstractions (Box 18.3). Caution is essential at this point so that the connection between the participant's own words and the researcher's interpretations is not lost. These early stages of analysis require the researcher to be thorough and painstaking.

Box 18.2　First stage of analysis

V: Can you tell me about your life from as far back as you can remember?	
M: I think the first memory, memory that I have is when I was 6. I can't remember anything before that. It was when my mum and dad divorced. I remember the argument, picturing the argument and my dad hitting my mum, erm, then my mum walked out with me and my brother. And we went to live with my auntie for a short while and then we moved in with my stepfather's parents for a long while and erm, in between that time, while they were splitting up type of thing, I was admitted into hospital for tonsillitis, I had my tonsils removed. And erm, it's quite vague really I can't remember a lot about my childhood previous to that and it's quite vague after that until my teens. Erm, I remember my mum was always with my brother, he was always you know the lad and my mum used to be like, say that I used to look like my dad and she didn't like me dad so I always thought she didn't like me. What can I remember before, after that. Erm.	*First significant memory* *Divorce* *Physical aggression* *Separation from father* *Temporary home* *Second temporary home* *Hospitalization – separation* *Vague memories of childhood* *Mother-brother connection* *Negative comparison to father* *Mother's dislike of father* *Perception of mother's dislike of her*
V: Do you remember it being happy?	
M: I think 10 onwards or perhaps just a bit before 10, er I hated, I wasn't very happy at all, not at all but I think a lot of that was between me and my mum and erm but I think I was a happy child or seemed to everybody else I was a happy child but I wasn't, I think deep down. Erm.	*Feels hatred – unspecified* *Unhappiness* *Unhappiness attributed to mother* *Happy child/unhappy child*
V: So can you tell me about your relationship with your mother, it might be easier to talk about your relationship with your mum as a child.	
M: yeah, erm, I mean like I said she was always my brother. I mean my brother could never do anything wrong but I think that was because she was in two minds whether he was my stepfather's. She, I think she'd been having an affair with him and I think she might have thought he was my stepfather's and not my real dad's. She used to always compare me to my dad in my ways and my looks and my actions and that and it just wasn't, I mean there was never any affection.	*Mother–brother connection* *Brother perfect in mother's eyes* *Different father from Marilyn* *Comparison to father*

Box 18.2 (Continued)

I mean I can't remember ever her putting her arm around me and kissing me. Erm, my stepdad he used to but my mum never. My dad was very loving, I remember that, he really was.	*Perceived lack of affection* *No memories of physical closeness* *Father loving/Mother not loving*
V: Not even as a teenager? Did it improve at all at any time?	
M: Got worse as a teenager because I started on my own now, on me own and she wanted me to be there for her in a pretty pink dress with lovely pigtails and I was too big for that (laughs). And she used to think more of my cousin who was a dainty, she was the same age as me, there were two weeks between us but she was small, she was petite you know, prettier looking and I think she was more with her, she was how can I say it, she showed her more emotion than she did me. Well, I mean, I've lost myself now.	*Deteriorating situation with Mother* *Separateness poss. Independence* *Self perception – overweight* *Mother's preference for cousin* *Physical comparison with cousin* *Negative comparison – size* *Negative comparison – prettiness* *Mother–cousin connection* *Mother showed more emotion for cousin*

The next stage consists of further refining the data by establishing connections between the preliminary themes and clustering them appropriately. Ordinarily one would compile themes for the whole transcript before looking for connections and clusters. In Box 18.4 we have shown how this works for a small piece of text so the reader can see how it is done. The clusters are given a descriptive label which conveys the conceptual nature of the themes therein. To help with this, maybe 'imagine a magnet with some of the themes pulling others in and helping to make sense of them'. (Smith and Osborn, 2008, p. 70). At this point, some of the themes may be dropped; either because they do not fit well with the emerging structure or because they have a weak evidential base.

In the worked example given here, there is a strong interrelationship between the clusters. In order to emphasise these connections, rather than considering each cluster as a separate superordinate theme, we have regarded them as a set of subthemes nested within a single superordinate theme we have named 'Disconnection from Mother.'

More typically, each superordinate theme stands more separately. A final table might comprise of a number of superordinate themes. When working with more

Box 18.3   Turning initial notes into themes

	V: Can you tell me about your life from as far back as you can remember?
	M: I think the first memory, memory that I have is when I was 6. I can't remember anything before that. It was when my mum and dad divorced. I remember the argument,
Father absent	picturing the argument and my dad hitting my mum, erm,
Lack of stability (home life)	then my mum walked out with me and my brother. And we went to live with my auntie for a short while and then we moved in with my stepfather's parents for a long while and erm, in between that time, while they were splitting up
Family absent	type of thing, I was admitted into hospital for tonsillitis, I had my tonsils removed. And erm, it's quite vague really I can't remember a lot about my childhood previous to that and it's quite vague after that until my teens. Erm, I
Mother–brother bond	remember my mum was always with my brother, he was always you know the lad and my mum used to be like, say that I used to look like my dad and she didn't like me dad
Marilyn–father connection	so I always thought she didn't like me. What can I remember before, after that. Erm.
	V: Do you remember it being happy?
	M: I think 10 onwards or perhaps just a bit before 10, er I hated, I wasn't very happy at all, not at all but I think a lot
Unhappiness	of that was between me and my mum and erm but I think I
Unhappiness attributed to mother	was a happy child or seemed to everybody else I was a happy child but I wasn't, I think deep down. Erm.
Happy child/unhappy child	
	V: So can you tell me about your relationship with your mother, it might be easier to talk about your relationship with your mum as a child.
	M: yeah, erm, I mean like I said she was always my
Brother perfect in mother's eyes	brother. I mean my brother could never do anything wrong but I think that was because she was in two minds whether he was my stepfather's. She, I think she'd been having an affair with him and I think she might have thought he was my stepfather's and not my real dad's. She used to
Negative comparison to father	always compare me to my dad in my ways and my looks and my actions and that and it just wasn't, I mean there
Perceived lack of affection	was never any affection. I mean I can't remember ever her
Lack of physical closeness	putting her arm around me and kissing me. Erm, my stepdad he used to but my mum never. My dad was very
Father loving/Mother not loving	loving, I remember that, he really was.

Box 18.3 (Continued)

	V: Not even as a teenager? Did it improve at all at any time?
Alienation from mother	**M:** Got worse as a teenager because I started on my own now, on me own and she wanted me to be there for her in a pretty pink dress with lovely pigtails and I was too big for that (laughs). And she used to think more of my cousin
Mother's preference for cousin	who was a dainty, she was the same age as me, there were two weeks between us but she was small, she was petite
Negative self–other physical comparison	you know, prettier looking and I think she was more with her, she was how can I say it, she showed her more
Mother–cousin bond	emotion than she did me. Well, I mean, I've lost myself now.

Box 18.4 Clustering of themes

SUPERORDINATE THEME: 'DISCONNECTION FROM MOTHER'

Mother's connection with other	*Mother's rejection*
Mother's preference for cousin	Alienation from mother
Brother perfect in mother's eyes	Perceived lack of affection
Mother–brother bond	Lack of physical closeness
Mother–cousin bond	Father loving/mother not loving
Instability	*Unhappiness*
Father absent	Unhappiness
Family absent	Unhappiness attributed to mother
Lack of stability (home life)	Happy child/unhappy child
Negative comparisons	
Negative comparison to father	
Negative self–other physical comparison	
Marilyn–father connection	

material, a brief illustrative data extract is usually presented alongside each theme. It is also useful to add identifying information such as interview and page number.

For the researcher, the final superordinate themes are the outcome of an iterative process in which she/he has moved back and forth between the various analytic stages ensuring that the integrity of what the participant said has been preserved as far as possible. If the researcher has been successful, it should be possible for someone else to track the analytic journey from the raw data through to the end table. As we have done with this study, a single participant's transcript(s) can be written up as a case study. If your study has several participants then you need to repeat the stages presented above for each case. After this, one examines the individual tables of themes in order to elicit themes which transcend the individual cases. One needs to be disciplined to discern repeating patterns but also acknowledge new issues emerging as one works through the transcripts. Thus, one is aiming to respect convergences and divergences in the data – recognising ways in which accounts from participants are similar but also different.

On a practical note, researchers adopt various strategies to organise and condense the themes. For example, clustering the themes can be done on a computer by 'cutting and pasting'. Alternatively, write each theme on a piece of paper and use a large space (e.g. floor or wall) to place them into clusters. This has the advantage of giving a bird's eye view and makes it easy to move themes around. The final table of themes forms the basis and structure of the write up of the analysis.

18.7 WRITING UP AN IPA STUDY

Analysis continues into the formal process of writing up a narrative account of the interplay between the interpretative activity of the researcher and the participant's account of her experience in her own words. The aim is to provide a close textual *reading* of the participant's account, moving between description and different levels of interpretation; at all times clearly differentiating between them.

This section briefly illustrates how writing up the analysis involves moving between description and low-level interpretation of the data to a more highly nuanced, interpretative and theoretical level. This quality of moving between levels reflects the multifaceted nature of psychological process and gives qualitative psychology its imaginative force (Smith, 2004). A first-level description may involve producing a rich full description of the topic under investigation; for example, how anger is experienced by the participant:

> Marilyn's experience of anger is intense and complex. Her rage is felt bodily through the sensation of a hot, red face. Simultaneously, she has a felt sense of being changed by the anger.

Enough data should be presented for the reader to assess the usefulness of the interpretations. IPA's iterative process means that the interpretative levels acquire more depth as the researcher moves beyond a description of the phenomenon to interrogating the participant's sense making. For example, Marilyn attempts to make sense of her anger and aggression by making causal attributions: 'I think a lot of it is hormonal, my aggression and things like that.'

Here, the researcher can demonstrate a hermeneutics centered in empathy and meaning recollection (Smith, 2004) and more or less accept what the participant says at face value. However, the researcher can engage more critically and ask questions of the accounts which the participant might be unwilling/unable to do. At this level, the empathic reading is likely to come first and may then be qualified by a more critical and speculative reflection.

Interpreting the data at a more subtle and conceptual level involves the researcher building an alternative coherent narrative from the messy sense making of the participant – a messiness which is only revealed when the researcher moves beyond accepting what is said at face value. For example, in the worked example Marilyn says 'My mum was always *with* my brother'. At its simplest level, this can be seen as indicating Marilyn's belief that her brother was her mother's favourite. However, the researcher might want to critically reflect on Marilyn's use of the word *with* and offer a tentative reading that mother and brother have a shared identity that excludes Marilyn and places her outside. To strengthen this interpretation, the researcher can look for examples elsewhere in the data. At a later point, Marilyn says 'I mean like I said she was *always my brother.*' This corroborates the shared identity reading and at the same time pushes the interpretation further: the identification between mother and brother appears to be experienced by Marilyn as not simply shared but merged.

Finally, two broad presentation strategies are possible. In the first, the 'results' section contains the narrative account of the analysis with the researcher's descriptions and interpretations interspersed with verbatim extracts from the transcripts, and the separate 'discussion' examines that analysis in light of the extant literature. A second strategy is to discuss the links to the literature as one presents each superordinate theme in a single 'results and discussion' section. Box 18.5 shows a very short piece from the final write-up of the anger and aggression study. In this case we used the former writing strategy.

18.8 **QUALITY IN IPA**

Doing good IPA takes time. Like most qualitative approaches IPA requires a range of skills which can be thought of as combining a need for careful, systematic, rigorous procedure alongside a requirement for creativity and boldness. Novices not surprisingly find this hard to achieve. Training in qualitative research in psychology

Box 18.5   Writing up an IPA study – a brief illustration

"Below, Marilyn offers an explanation as to why her mother preferred her brother [ ]:

> Like I said she was always my brother [sic]. I mean my brother could never do anything wrong but I think that was because she was in two minds whether he was my stepfather's. She, I think she'd been having an affair with him and I think she might have thought he was my stepfather's and not my real dad's. She used to always compare me to my dad in my ways and my looks and my actions and that and it just wasn't, but I mean there was never any affection. I mean I can't remember ever her putting her arm around me and kissing me [ ].

Not only does this extract illuminate the complicated nature of the family nexus, it is a potent display of how Marilyn experiences the relationships. The opening sentence, 'I mean like I said she was always my brother' carries tremendous symbolic force; her mother and brother do not simply have a close bond, rather they have psychologically merged for Marilyn into 'one' person. Similarly, Marilyn and her father have become 'one', and it is a 'one' that is hated by her mother. From Marilyn's perspective, there is a clear division between herself and her father who looked and behaved the same (the old family); and her mother, brother and stepfather (the new family). The affection Marilyn received from her father and stepfather was not enough to compensate for her mother's lack of it." (Eatough and Smith, 2006, p. 128)

is still relatively new and underdeveloped and students will typically therefore approach it with a mindset developed from much fuller training in quantitative methodology. At this early stage in the development of qualitative psychology, we think it important that students have a go at doing it, with the risk that the early attempts may not be especially strong. As qualitative psychology matures, as more examples of good practice are available and training becomes fuller, we expect the general level of student work to become stronger, deeper and richer.

There is now a substantial corpus of work using IPA. Recently one of the authors (Jonathan) has conducted a review of this work (Smith 2011a,b) starting with a description of the main areas of study and then employing a guide to assess the quality of one major area of research – that of the experience of illness. The first instantiation of the guide was developed by both of the authors but was modified and developed during the evaluation exercise. The two review papers demonstrate key qualities of good IPA:

1   Well evidenced, supporting claims made with sufficient extracts from the participants' accounts.
2   Data presented should be strong.

3 As interviewing is still the dominant method of data collection in IPA, this crucially depends on the interviewing skills of the researcher.

4 Finally, the IPA write up should present a detailed interpretative commentary of the extracts presented, cumulatively working towards a nuanced analysis of the participants' experience, and pointing to both convergence and divergence therein.

The two review papers illustrate the criteria employed in the evaluation, report the results and offer summaries of those papers rated good in the evaluation. Newcomers to the approach can usefully look at the two review papers to help them see how to conduct good IPA.

18.9 CONCLUSION

This chapter has aimed to provide readers with a clear exposition of the theoretical underpinnings of IPA, as well as explaining the practicalities of carrying out an IPA project. IPA is committed to understanding phenomena from the perspective of the individual's lived experiences but recognises that this in an interpretative process. It attempts to be scientific in being systematic in its procedures but also involves the application of creative personal skills as part of the endeavour of understanding the participants' experiences. We hope these dual aspects of the approach are both clear to, and resonate with, the reader.

18.10 EXERCISES

1 Use the guidance offered in this chapter to construct a short interview schedule with three questions (and prompts) on the experience of listening to music. Discuss the schedule with a friend to try to ascertain how well it works and modify the schedule in the light of the discussion.

2 Find a published paper employing IPA and conduct a critical evaluation of it in the light of what you have read in this chapter. What are the good things about it and what are its weaker points?

18.11 DISCUSSION QUESTIONS

1 What type of experience is IPA most suitable for exploring?

2 Discuss the arguments for and against a sample size of three participants in an IPA study.

3   Think of a research question for which IPA is not appropriate and explicate why this is.
4   Exemplify what is meant by the double hermeneutic in IPA.
5   How do you think IPA might develop in the future?

18.12 FURTHER READING

There is now a full length text on IPA (Smith *et al.*, 2009). This is the best place to go if you are considering conducting a study using IPA or want to know more about it. The book outlines the theoretical foundations of IPA, gives detailed guidance to conducting IPA research and offers extended examples of work from the authors' own research studies. For other writing on the theoretical basis for IPA, see Smith (1996, 2004) and Eatough and Smith (2008). For another detailed description of how to do IPA, see Smith and Osborn (2008). There is extensive coverage of IPA in Lyons and Coyle (2007) and discussion of various aspects of the method can be found in Brocki and Wearden (2006) and Reid *et al.* (2005). There are now many studies using IPA. Here are just a few suggestions for following up. Eatough and Smith (2006) present a case study from the womens' anger and aggression study. Chapman (2002) discusses the social and ethical implications of changing medical technologies. French *et al.* (2005) show how a group of men with heart problems attempt to make sense of the cause for their condition. Golsworthy and Coyle's (1999) paper is concerned with how older adults come to terms with the death of their partners. There is an IPA website which gives lots of useful information. http://www.psyc.bbk.ac.uk/ipa/.

19

Grounded Theory

Karen Henwood and Nick Pidgeon

CONTENTS

AIMS OF THIS CHAPTER

This chapter describes the intellectual background to and methodological strategies of grounded theory, a core approach to qualitative data analysis used within psychology and the social sciences today. We describe how this differs from traditional hypothetico-deductive research, and in particular the flexible and iterative nature of 'emergent design' alongside the core commitments of theoretical sampling and constant comparison. A number of specific data analysis strategies are outlined, including: open coding, memo writing, category refinement and building conceptual models. The chapter concludes with a discussion of writing and evaluating grounded theory studies.

KEY TERMS

axial coding	reflexivity
disciplinary knowledge	relabelling categories
emergent design	splitting categories
focused coding	theoretical agnosticism
indexing system	theoretical memos
integrating categories	theoretical sampling
interpretative thematic analysis	theoretical saturation
member validation	theoretical sensitivity
open coding	theory-building

19.1 **INTRODUCTION**

The idea that understanding, explaining and theorising should be well grounded in the processes and products of empirical inquiry is now well established within social, psychological, health and clinical research. The methodology of qualitative research and analysis which has come to be labelled 'grounded theory' explicitly codifies the ways in which theoretical accounts can be generated through the close and detailed inspection and analysis of qualitative data, in ways that hold a clear relevance to real-world problems and phenomena.

The term 'grounded theory' itself has two interrelated meanings in the literature. First, it refers to a type of theory; specifically, one can talk of a grounded theory when this has been generated from (hence is grounded in) a close inspection and analysis of a corpus of complex qualitative data. Second, it refers to a method of analysis; specifically, the commitments and procedures for data analysis first advo-cated by the sociologists Glaser and Strauss (1967) for achieving this goal, and developed in subsequent years by researchers from a range of social sciences disci-plines, particularly in the health and practitioner domains. One of the major reasons why grounded theory has gained contemporary widespread appeal is that it is often read as describing a generic set of techniques for conducting and gaining credibility for qualitative inquiry, through theory-building from qualitative data. In particular, we view grounded theory as exemplifying some of the core 'strategies' of qualita-tive inquiry that involve the creative interplay of theory and method during the integrated processes of social research.

Conceptually, grounded theory has an especially long-standing association with the pragmatist and symbolic interaction philosophical traditions which emerged in America in the 1920s and 1930s (see Blumer, 1969). These served to frame several generations of researchers' theorising, questions and inquiries, especially within social psychology and micro-sociology. The symbolic interaction tradition holds an important historical place in the development of qualitative research practice as it is today, providing an early and coherent alternative to quantitative approaches that measured essential properties of events, objects and people's perceptions of them. Symbolic interactionism presented a case for studies that both explored the activities and interactions involved in the production of meaning, and used these as a platform to illuminate people's complex social worlds.

When grounded theory first emerged on the scene in mainstream UK psychology in the early 1990s, the main focus of methodological discussions was upon how it offered a different approach to quantitative research, and especially the challenge it posed to orthodoxy in the form of the experimental method and quantitative research (Henwood & Pidgeon, 1992). Historically, psychology has privileged the use of experiments, measurement and statistical methods. But in so doing psycho-logical researchers have been denied the opportunities that could be offered to them by a wide variety of naturalistic, real-world and qualitative enquiry methods.

Accordingly, grounded theory offers much-needed resources to psychologists wishing to develop their methodological skills in a number of areas: handling and analysis of large volumes of ill-structured qualitative data; conceptual development and theory generation; and interpretative thematic analysis of the meanings of qualitative data. These remain equally relevant today, but do have to be viewed in relation to the availability of a far greater range of qualitative methodologies across the social sciences. There has been a rapid expansion in psychologists' familiarity with and proficiency in using qualitative approaches and methods, among them content and thematic analysis, grounded theory, case studies, ethnographic/fieldwork methods, individual interviews and focus groups, participatory and action research, and specialist methods for the analysis of talk and text (such as discourse analysis, narrative analysis and semiotics) as well as use of analysis tools (such as computer-assisted qualitative data analysis software (CAQDAS) packages).

Among the types of projects and questions addressed by grounded theorists are the following.

1   The meaningful patterns and processes of action, interaction and identity within many different time, space and culturally bounded settings, organisations and other kinds of 'social worlds' – including those of health and illness, adults and children, and public and private spheres.
2   The interpretative analysis of peoples' subjective meanings. These might include actors', participants', patients' and professionals' understandings, phenomenological points of view or perspectives – to characterise either detailed 'structures of experience' or taken-for-granted, routine or skilled knowledge and practices. Linking grounded theory and phenomenology in this way usefully reflects the current situation in health and clinical psychology, and some other health care studies, where interpretative approaches are often used to investigate people's lived experiences and 'lifeworlds'.
3   The complexity, fluidity and multiplicity of meanings and accounts as they relate to social contexts and settings, in order to bring the micro-social, symbolically, textually or discursively organised character of roles, identities, cultures and power relations into view. Grounded theorists often use detailed case studies here, since these provide a resource for the holistic analysis of processes in specific settings.

It is important to note, however, that grounded theory studies have always been part of a broad qualitative and interpretative inquiry tradition. Grounded theory is sometimes inappropriately portrayed, in psychology at least, as being solely associated with the collection and analysis of interview data. Nothing could be further from the truth. Although interviews are indeed the main material of analysis in a range of phenomenologically based studies, the analytic strategies which we go on to describe have been used with a variety of source materials, as illustrated in Box 19.1.

> # Box 19.1   Materials typically analysed using grounded theory
>
> Transcripts from one-to-one interviews
> Transcripts from focus groups
> Researcher's notes of interviews or focus groups
> Observational field notes (perhaps of an organisation or other social setting)
> Documentary sources (such as inquiry reports, printed media, historical records)
> Secondary interaction or verbal data (television programmes, political speeches)
> Accounts of other research studies
> Multiple data sources (from any of the above)

19.2 EMERGENT DESIGN, FLEXIBILITY AND ITERATION

As noted earlier, although grounded theory indicates a property of a conceptual system (strictly an outcome of research), the term has over time become associated with the methodological strategies used to achieve that outcome (a set of processes). The core flow of work in a grounded theory study is shown in Figure 19.1. In overall terms the analyst typically works from an initial topic or research question(s), to data gathering, through initial treatment of unstructured materials (using the varied analytic operations shown), possibly more data gathering and analysis, and on to a set of theoretical categories, interpretations, models and written accounts of theory. This flow is accompanied by a gradual development of the conceptual focus away from local descriptions inherent in the data towards more ordered and analytic (i.e. theoretical) concepts and categories.

Some writings on the topic, often in order to contrast grounded theory with the traditional hypothetico-deductive method common to experimental psychology, describe the general approach as one of classical induction. Certainly the original writings by Glaser and Strauss give this impression. However, a risk here is that grounded theory might then be followed as if it were a prescriptive method – a standardised procedure for guaranteeing 'true' representations of the psychosocial world. Philosophically speaking, theory cannot 'emerge' from or reflect data in any simple manner. Interpretation and analysis are always conducted within some pre-existing conceptual framework brought to the task by the data analyst.

In this respect grounded theory shares some elements with more constructivist interpretative approaches (Charmaz, 2006) such as discourse analysis (see Chapter 20). This way of thinking about grounded theory also captures more nearly the essential characteristics of its combination of systematic rigour in analysis with the essentially creative and dynamic character of the interpretative research process. For this reason we prefer to use the term 'generation' of theory, rather than discovery, as it more accurately describes both the epistemological and practical realities of the approach. In particular, rather than theory being discovered or emerging from a purely inductive process, grounded theory always involves a constant two-way process, a back and forth or 'flip-flop' between raw data and the researcher's emerging conceptualisation of that data.

In actual practice, the core processes of generating grounded theory exhibit both linear and iterative qualities. Figure 19.1 illustrates the interrelationships between the core stages, with the flow of intellectual work, in very broad terms, a linear one. The analyst works from an initial topic or research questions towards more ordered

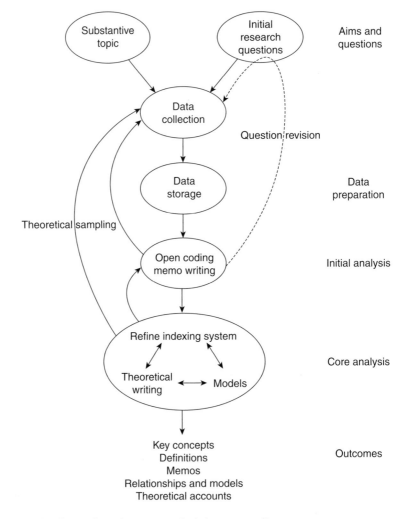

Figure 19.1　The flow of work in grounded theory studies.
Source: Pidgeon and Henwood (2004, p. 631)

analytic (theoretical) concepts and categories. However, in its detailed execution the flow of work is also flexible and iterative, reflecting the ongoing 'flip-flop' between data and conceptualisation. This also means that research design decisions, such as sampling, which aspects of the data to concentrate upon, even the very research question itself, are likely to be emergent (i.e. modified as the analysis proceeds) rather than fixed indelibly in advance.

Hence, Figure 19.1 indicates pathways through which the researcher will move from later back to earlier operations as necessary, and as the analysis proceeds. For example, the research question itself, which may only be tacitly understood at the outset of the enquiry, is often sharpened and refined – sometimes changed entirely – by the process of data analysis. In a similar way, a recategorisation of codes can follow the development of the emerging theoretical analysis, or a realisation by the analyst that initial terms and concepts used do not in fact fit the data in the ways originally assumed. And data analysis may prompt a new round of data collection, in order to check out emerging ideas or to extend the richness and scope of the sample and theory.

It is the intertwining of data gathering and analysis in classical accounts of grounded theory methodology that most clearly distinguishes the approach from the principles and practices of experimental method. Clearly, in the experimental model, if data are being gathered to specifically test prior hypotheses it would be anathema to change the data to fit the hypotheses, since this would undermine the logic of that mode of enquiry. However, in grounded theory the mode of enquiry is quite different. The researcher seeks to work creatively but systematically with rich, relevant and possibly wide-ranging sources of data, so as to generate understandings and explanations of the phenomena under investigation that are most plausible and credible in the circumstances.

19.3 THE ORIGIN POINT AND USE OF THE PRIOR LITERATURE

Figure 19.1 depicts what is, in some ways, an unremarkable design dilemma: envisaging a set of clearly planned choices while simultaneously acknowledging that, because grounded theory research has a contingent and unfolding character (emergent design) in the search for appropriate theory, some of those decisions at least are likely to change. It is important to recognise that all research projects inevitably have to start from somewhere, and that this will involve developing some form of guide, plan or protocol of how the study is designed at the outset. This maximises the researcher's chances of being able to arrive at a successful set of results, interpretations or conclusions. Our own experience of teaching grounded theory to students is that new researchers often struggle to put into practice the ideal (which they readily and enthusiastically glean from the classic writings on the topic) that they should approach fieldwork without any prior preconceptions. In our view this does not mean that the prior literature should be ignored when designing and beginning to analyse a grounded theory study (as discussed below).

It would be fair to say that many writings in the grounded theory tradition are less than helpful on, and in some instances muddle, the issues surrounding study origin and (at least initial) research design. Many studies that report adopting a grounded theory methodology are indeed often prompted by quite general research interests at the outset. Initial research goals might be: to identify actors' perspectives on a topic; to investigate social processes or phenomena of interest within their local contexts and settings; to devise explanatory schemes relevant to locally situated, real-world problems; or explore an underresearched topic where a clear gap in existing knowledge exists. The suggestion that questions must be developed early on to guide the subsequent course of an investigation brings grounded theory more closely into line with other accounts of qualitative research design and widely read resource books on qualitative methods (Willig, 2001). All of these caution against the dangers of too-loose initial research designs, so as to avoid researchers becoming personally overwhelmed by too much data and studies becoming conceptually diffuse. New researchers, in particular, may be unable to focus sufficiently to provide insights, accounts or explanations of important or relevant issues (or commence effective data gathering) if they do not make explicit what interests them about their chosen topic area, and state these interests as tentative research questions fairly early on in their investigations.

Giving at least some priority to question formation in study design goes beyond the practical issue of asking manageable and answerable questions, but also begins to delimit the conceptual scope of subsequent analysis. By thinking ahead to what is likely to be relevant in a particular topic and investigation, researchers will also be able to deploy their background or disciplinary knowledge so as to refine their research questions, avoid merely repeating studies that have been done before, move knowledge and theorising about a problem or issue forward, and build into projects the capacity to benefit fully from the exercise of theoretical sensitivity. Whether this then forecloses upon possible creative insights about the data is a point of issue in the methodological literature on grounded theory.

Embedding projects in background and disciplinary knowledge in order to formulate not just workable but maximally useful research questions early on when designing a study brings the role of the theoretical literature into view. The principle that people new to grounded theory often read into descriptions of the approach – of completely setting aside the literature at the start of the project so as to maintain sensitivity to relevance in the data – is displaced by a more discriminating strategy of using the literature early on in specific ways. We would recommend here using the theoretical literature prior to entering the study to promote clarity in thinking about concepts and possible theory development. Others have advocated an early skimming of the literature to provide a partial framework of local concepts that identify a few main features of the situations that will be studied (actors, roles, organisational goals, etc.). This position reflects an awareness that researchers, far from approaching analysis as a *tabula rasa*, sometimes can use a first pass at the existing literature (necessary even if the objective is to address a significant gap in that literature), alongside their own existing theoretical sensitivities, to support what might otherwise remain a tacit orientation towards the investigative process. The special counsel that applies within grounded theory is to avoid being tied to particular theoretical positions and key studies in the literature in ways that overly direct ways of looking, and stymie the interactive process of engagement with the empirical world being studied. Theoretical agnosticism is a better watchword than theoretical ignorance to sum up the ways of using the literature at the early stages of the flow of work in grounded theory.

19.4 THEORETICAL SAMPLING

Theoretical sampling is the process of data collection for generating theory whereby the analyst jointly collects, codes, and analyses his [sic] data and decides what data to collect next and where to find them, in order to develop his theory as it emerges. This process of data collection is controlled by the emerging theory.

Glaser and Strauss, 1967, p. 45

Grounded theory shares with much qualitative research the use of non-probability sampling and, in particular, the use of theoretical sampling. In this respect the aim of sampling is not guided by the overriding need to ensure precisely comparable experimental groups, as in experimental studies, or to generate a demographically representative subset of the population, as in much survey research. Rather, theoretical sampling involves specifying new samples of data as the analysis proceeds, in order to elaborate and build up emerging insights and theory. Typically, one might recognise a clear gap in the initial sample (perhaps a group of individuals with clearly contrasting views to those studied already, or a different context in which the phenomenon of interest might be manifest) which needs to be filled to achieve theoretical closure. For example, in an environmental psychology study of the meanings and values that woodlands and trees hold for people in Wales, the current authors initially convened five community focus groups (Henwood & Pidgeon, 2001). As we wished to access a broad spectrum of beliefs and values amongst the local community where the study was being conducted (Bangor, North Wales) the overall sample of groups was designed to include a mix of genders, ages and socio-economic groups. In effect, this represented a stratified purposive sample. However, once initial coding and memo writing for this set of data had commenced (see also section 19.7) it became clear that individuals' perceptions of their local environment were dependent upon not only the physical nature and extent of woodlands experienced in their locality, but also an area's social geography (e.g. with respect to the extent to which Welsh was spoken in the area) as well as whether participants had been born in the area or not. None of these criteria had featured in our sampling decisions at the outset of the study. Accordingly, we decided to extend the study by sampling from four further socially and geographically distinct areas of Wales, giving particular consideration also to explicitly including groups of locally born and incomer residents in the new focus groups.

As this example suggests, subsequent stages of data collection are controlled by the emerging account. This process continues until nothing new is being said about the concepts and ways of theorising being explored (the analysis reaches 'theoretical saturation'). Theoretical sampling is central to the successful prosecution of an iterative data–theory interaction, and hence the generation of theory. There is now a wealth of guidance upon the types of sample that might be selected on theoretical grounds. Box 19.2 lists some of the most important examples for grounded theorists, many of which would be useful for psychologically based projects.

Many grounded theorists would claim that one can only identify truly 'extreme', 'typical', 'sensitive' or 'subgroup' cases through the process of at least some initial data analysis and conceptualisation. Similarly, 'maximum variation' is bound up with the principle of theoretical saturation: only through some initial comparative data analysis can the researcher judge whether maximum theoretical variation (or saturation) has been achieved, or alternatively whether new cases need to be sampled to build further theoretical density.

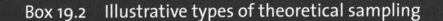

Box 19.2   Illustrative types of theoretical sampling

1   Extreme or deviant cases (which may prove to be troublesome, counter to, or enlightening in relation to emerging theory)
2   Theory-based selection (elaborates and examines an important theoretical construct)
3   Typical cases (highlights what is average or 'normal', and avoids claims that theory is grounded in atypical cases)
4   Maximum variation sampling (to encompass the range of variations, or extremes, that emerge in relation to different conditions)
5   Critical cases (which permit maximum application of findings to other cases)
6   Politically important or sensitive cases (as a focus for drawing attention to the findings or study, perhaps for policy purposes)
7   Confirming and disconfirming cases (elaborating initial analysis, seeking exceptions, looking for variation)
8   Stratified purposeful sampling (illustrates subgroups, facilitates group comparisons)
9   Rich response sampling (to provide the richest or most explanatory data sources)

However, the question can also be raised: what guides sampling before the initial emergence of theory begins to prompt theoretical sampling? Here one can argue that initial data collection does not differ from later selection in the need to be guided by relevance and appropriateness. But this needs to be balanced against the very real danger of becoming prematurely locked into a (possibly costly) data collection strategy that does not ultimately yield dense conceptualisation. In pragmatic terms, in grounded theory studies it is often appropriate to commence data collection with a small number of 'rich response' cases or sources, such as a key 'gatekeeper' with the most experience of the topic. In other instances, initial sampling can be prompted by a first pass at the available literature (albeit disciplined by theoretical agnosticism, and the need to develop a theoretical sampling strategy as data analysis proceeds). In practice, then, research using grounded theory commences inquiry from a number of starting points.

An important final consideration, as shown in Box 19.1, is that grounded theorists treat any relevant medium or combination of media as data. In this respect theoretical sampling can be viewed more generically as the activity that treats 'everything as data'. If the goal is to maximise the possibilities of being able to make conceptual comparisons and developing theorising through emergent fit, then the researcher must be constantly alert to any data resource that might achieve this.

19.5 STORAGE: THE RESEARCH RECORD

For grounded theory work to proceed, the data must first be assembled in some form of permanent record that allows ready access during analysis. When working from documentary or archival data sources, photocopies have traditionally formed this permanent record (leaving sufficient space in the margins for jotting the theoretical codes generated). Alternatively, with interview, observational or interactional (e.g. focus group) studies tape recordings can be treated as the record (thus preserving a range of paralinguistic features of talk). More typically, though, the full data from taped interviews or other verbal interactions are transcribed verbatim. Transcription itself is highly labour-intensive, taking a minimum of six hours per hour of tape (and significantly longer if interactional or paralinguistic features are also transcribed). However, as Chapter 15 on interviewing notes, transcription is becoming normal practice with much contemporary qualitative research.

A frequent next step in handling each discrete data set (from a single document or interview, say) is to provide it with a label (e.g. indicating date, source and topic). A second is to allocate a numerical reference to segments of the text, typically numbering pages, paragraphs or sometimes lines in the record. The level of coarseness at which this initial segmentation is conducted is, in some respects, a matter of judgement. Our own preference when working manually has always been to segment text into naturally occurring paragraph breaks or, where interaction is involved, into individual turns in talk. There is a sense in which very fine segmentation and subsequent coding (say, at the level of sentences or even individual words) runs the danger of losing sight of overall context, or the contrasts and continuities in individual or group discourses, when text segments are subsequently accessed. Also, too fine a segmentation may restrict the possibility for potentially fruitful multiple codings on a single segment. On the other hand, too large a segment (a page or above) will mean that a code's precise referent in the text may be hard to identify later. The aim here is to provide a systematic labelling system through which any particular segment of raw text can be quickly identified, accessed, compared to other segments and interrogated on the basis of subsequent coding operations. It can also help in maintaining the anonymity of participants, and so is a way of implementing one of the standard ethical practices in the conduct of qualitative research.

It is accordingly no surprise to find that today many CAQDAS packages, such as Ethnograph, HyperResearch, Atlas-TI and NVivo, are founded upon the theory generation approach, and some explicitly reference grounded theory as their source of analytic logic. Such software is invaluable where a project involves large and complex data sets, which the analyst needs to organise, sift and sort for complex comparisons and emergent relationships, or for organising the database for access by teams of researchers. In our experience CAQDAS programs greatly simplify the mechanics of open coding, although this may be outweighed by the effort to properly set up a database in ways that fully exploit a particular program's capabilities. Even more importantly, it is still the researcher who must provide the interpretative work which generates the label, and who decides which segments of data to compare. Accordingly, our general recommendation is that such software should be utilised by the beginner grounded theorist only with care.

19.6 OPEN CODING AND CONSTANT COMPARISON

The analytic steps in conducting grounded theory are given in Box 19.3. Having collected and recorded a sufficient quantity of material, the next task is to build an indexing system for the data through 'open' (or 'substantive') coding, as soon as practical after the first round of data collection. The indexing system will subsequently allow the researcher to compare and reorder the data collected as interpretations develop, traditionally by highlighting, cutting, pasting and re-sorting photocopies of documents or transcripts. In the language of CAQDAS analysis packages, the basic indexing amounts to a code and retrieve paradigm. The technique we describe here involves building an indexing system manually on file cards, using the term 'file card' interchangeably to represent both manual and virtual devices.

Open coding proceeds by means of the tentative development and labelling of concepts in the text that the researcher considers of potential relevance to the

> ## Box 19.3　Core steps of data analysis
>
> 1　Open coding to capture the detail, variation and complexity of the basic qualitative material (sometimes also referred to as substantive coding)
> 2　Constantly comparing data instances, cases and categories for conceptual similarities and differences (the method of constant comparison)
> 3　Sampling new data and cases on theoretical grounds as analysis progresses (theoretical sampling) to extend the emergent theory by checking out emerging ideas, extending richness and scope, and in particular to add qualitative variety to the core data included within the analysis
> 4　Writing theoretical memoranda to explore emerging concepts and links to existing theory
> 5　Subsequently, engaging in more focused coding (including focused, axial and theoretical coding) of selected core categories
> 6　Continuing to code, make comparisons, and sample theoretically, until the point at which no new or further relevant insights are being reached (theoretical saturation)
> 7　Further tactics to move analysis from descriptive to more theoretical levels: for example, grouping or reclassifying sets of basic categories; writing definitions of core categories; building conceptual models and data displays; linking to the existing literature; writing extended memos and more formal theory

problem being studied. To construct such a set of codes we start with the first paragraph of the transcript and ask: 'What categories, concepts or labels do I need in order to account for what is of importance to me in this paragraph?' Clearly, the facets of the data that are coded will vary depending upon the aims of the study and the theoretical sensitivities of the researcher. Even when using CAQDAS programs, it is the researcher who must provide the difficult interpretative work which generates the label.

When a label is thought of it is recorded as the header on a file card. A précis of the data of interest, together with a reference for accessing the specific transcript and paragraph, is noted on the card, with the latter filed in a central record box. This initial entry then serves as the first indicator for the concept (or category) described by the card header. Open coding continues by checking whether further potentially significant aspects of the paragraph suggest different concepts (almost certainly they will), and continues in this way with subsequent paragraphs.

At this stage, the labels used may be long-winded, ungainly or fanciful, and they may be formulated at any conceptual level that seems to be appropriate. Indeed, later success in moving the analysis from initial coding on to a greater level of abstraction will depend in part upon choosing an appropriate level of abstraction for the concepts in question. The use of highly particular terms (member categories or *in vivo* codes) that are a direct précis of the data will tie the analysis to the specific context of that interview or document. Other terms (researcher categories) may refer to more generalised theoretical ideas. A particularly difficult judgement for beginners to make here is the level of coding to be adopted: a common trap is to generate mainly member categories with few researcher categories.

When conducting open coding it is crucial that the terms should 'fit' the data well – that is, provide a recognisable description of the item, activity or discourse under consideration. As coding continues, not only will the list of concepts (and hence store of file cards) rapidly expand, but also concepts will begin to recur in subsequent paragraphs or data segments. For the purposes of subsequent analysis, it is important to recognise that the aim is not principally to record all instances of a particular concept, but to record different instances which highlight significant variations on that concept. In this way the aim of open coding is to seek similarities and diversities, using the indexing to collect together a range of indicators that point to the multiple qualitative facets of a potentially significant concept. The active flip-flop between the data and the researcher's developing conceptualisations also demands a dynamic process of changing, rechanging and adjustment of terms used where fit can be improved. For example, in a study of adult mother–daughter relationships one of the authors (Henwood, 1993) conducted 60 interviews with mother–daughter dyads. The initial coding led to the development of a long and varied, but highly unwieldy, list of instances under the label 'relational closeness'. The attributes that had been coded on the card were initially glossed as attaching global value to the relationship. However, closer reading and comparison of the individual instances indicated a much more mixed view of the emotional intensity of the relationships, ranging from a welcome but painful sense of gratitude and debt to a stance of hypersensitivity and a desire to flee from a relationship which involved 'confinement' or 'smothering'.

The exercise of coding to explore similarities and differences is basic to implementing the analytic method of constant comparison, upon which the generation of grounded theory is founded. The method of constant comparison involves continually sifting and comparing elements (basic data instances, emergent concepts, cases or theoretical propositions) throughout the lifetime of the project. By making such comparisons the researcher is sensitised to similarities and nuances of difference as a part of the cognitive exploration of the full range and complexity of the data, as well as to further cases to sample. In short, similarities and differences are central to promoting dense conceptual development. Taken together, the commitments of constant comparison and theoretical sampling define the analytic dynamic of the grounded theory process, which involves the researcher, as we have suggested, in a highly interactive and iterative process.

It is particularly important for researchers to be aware of the differences between the practices and aims of coding and analysing data in grounded theory and those of 'objective' coding methods such as content analysis. Content analysis involves arriving at definitive criteria prior to data coding and analysis of the precise categories that will be used (specifically, what they will and will not contain). Subsequently, the frequencies with which data units are coded into the categories will be tabulated or analysed statistically. It is assumed that this kind of process will make the quality of the analysis easier to judge as any inferences should be made systematically. This is different to grounded theory since, here, the researcher seeks to develop a meaningful understanding of the data by generating and refining codes and categories (or themes) in the course of data analysis, and uses various strategies to shift that understanding to a more abstract or conceptual level. While it would be possible to use the categories generated by a grounded theory study as the prior coding scheme for a subsequent content analysis study, typically knowledge is built up in a very different way.

The contrast between grounded theory and content analysis is important in highlighting the characteristic features of an interpretative qualitative approach to thematic coding and analysis (Chamberlain *et al.*, 2004). Such an approach does not assume that meanings inhere within the data or that boundaries between data segments that have been coded similarly are fixed (as is assumed in 'objective' coding methods such as content analysis). Rather, it is assumed that codes or themes that have been identified in the data contain meanings that can be analysed at multiple levels. In interpretative approaches to qualitative thematic analysis there is an important distinction to be made between manifest meanings (viz. observable meanings in the data) and latent meanings (which have to be inferred by the researcher). As latent meanings require referring to other parts of the data to discern what they signify, their analysis involves a process of 'contextualisation', a key element of interpretative practice. Analysis of latent meanings is, therefore, a different approach than content analysis, as the latter involves fixing meaning by applying a standardised coding frame to the data.

19.7 THEORETICAL MEMOS

As the list of open codes builds up, some indexed to many incidents across the data corpus, some indexed to few, the analysis begins to involve other operations with the explicit aim of taking conceptual development forward. Theoretical memos, in particular, are often stimulated by the intellectual activity of coding, and many researchers build up a separate record system (or 'memo fund') for them. Unlike categories (which have to 'fit' the data), the contents of memos are not constrained in any way and can include: hunches and insights; comments on new samples to be checked out later; deliberations about refinements of file cards; links to existing theory; and explanations of modifications to categories. Memos serve both as a means of stimulating theoretical sensitivity and creativity, and as a vehicle for making public the researcher's emerging theoretical reflections. Indeed, memoing can be at the heart of the whole theory generation process, as they provide a publicly available trace of the set of ideas about codes and their relationships as they occur to the researcher. In short, memoing leads naturally to abstraction of theory.

Memos can subsequently be used: to discuss the emerging analysis with colleagues; as a part of a 'reflexive account' charting the course of interpretation; as core material during the writing up of the research; or to make connections to the existing literature. Conducting memoing and open coding as parallel operations allows sensitivity to existing literature and theory to be combined with a commitment to grounding in data. In the environmental psychology study mentioned in section 19.4, our initial coding of the talk about woods and trees was accompanied by a series of short memos noting: first, an initial hunch that some individuals were expressing an 'insider' view of the environment; second, that such participants also at times resisted having a 'nationalist' discourse imposed on them in the group discussions; and finally, that in places there were clear contrasts between the environmental discourses of ex-city dwellers who had moved into the area from elsewhere, and those of participants who had been born as well as lived in North Wales itself (Henwood & Pidgeon, 2001). These tentative observations in the memos then led to the conclusion that an important conceptual distinction should be made between those members of the community who were locally born and those who could be classed 'incomers'. They also led us to consider the literature from rural studies in Wales, which had previously discussed and categorised such differences in terms of local identity, power and rural economic factors.

Memo writing as an activity is, of course, only one of several ways in which grounded theorists raise the conceptual level, albeit one that is likely to continue throughout the lifetime of a project (as analysis develops, the content will shift from being 'memos on data' to 'memos on memos'). Also, there is no simple distinction one can make between memo writing and the assembly of a final account. The latter (as a first draft to, say, a thesis chapter, research report or journal article) would expect to draw upon some earlier memos, but also to continue with the process of conceptual development started in these early memos. Grounded theories are always provisional and contingent, never complete.

19.8 CORE ANALYSIS I: REFINING AND SATURATING CATEGORIES

Open coding leads to categorisation through fragmentation of the data. However, over time the analysis increasingly involves other core activities (see Box 19.3 and Figure 19.1) designed to both raise the conceptual level and (re)construct an orderly theoretical account. The early phases of grounded theory (open coding and initial memoing) can be likened to stepping deeper into a maze, a place of uncertainty (and some anxiety), particularly for the new researcher. During the core analysis phase the researcher has to find suitable routes out of this maze. In this section we briefly discuss a number of strategies we have used for conceptual development.

Alongside further analytic memo writing, core analysis typically involves a refinement of the indexing system through category splitting, renaming and integration, often as a direct product of the application of constant comparison at the level of data (i.e. with respect to instances collected under a single index card or category). As described in section 19.6, in the adult mother–daughter study an initial category of 'relational closeness' was generated with many entries (Henwood, 1993). Constant comparison of the individual instances subsequently indicated a much more mixed view of the emotional intensity of the range of relationships described on the concept card. This eventually led the researcher to subdivide the concept and entries under two new codes, with the inextricable link between the two concepts resulting from this subdivision retained and coded through their respective labels 'closeness' and 'overcloseness'. This link then became a key stimulus and focus for conceptual development and reflection, in turn mediated by the writing of theoretical memos.

Operations such as splitting categories, integrating categories and relabeling categories to adjust fit are likely to occur repeatedly during the early phases of the core analysis. However, there comes a point at which the collection and coding of additional data no longer contribute further insights to a specific category or categories; that is, the researcher perceives nothing new – no more conceptual variation – as new data are coded. At this point a category may have become 'theoretically saturated', to use Glaser and Strauss's term. The researcher's task then is to try to make the analysis more explicit by summarising why all of the entries have been included under the same label. One way of commencing this process is to write a definition for the concept that explicitly states the qualities that were already recognised in an implicit manner when a new entry was classified. This is a demanding task (and is typically comparative at the level of both data and concepts), but one which can nevertheless be crucial to the analysis. It often leads to a deeper and more precise understanding of central categories.

Alongside saturation of key categories, the research process also involves category integration – typically, through clarifying the relationships between emerging categories by linking, by reclassifying under higher-level concepts, and by conducting conceptual sorting exercises on both file cards and on theoretical memos. This might eventually involve drawing up various forms of diagrammatic, network or tabular representation. Alternatively, even in this age of computer support, there may be no substitute for sorting paper memos, file cards and concepts into piles, perhaps returning several times to re-sort these, in order to develop a deeper understanding of basic classes and relationships.

Finally, it should be noted that as the indexing system grows, many cards will hold only one or very few instances. This does not necessarily mean such categories are unimportant. However, processes of 'forgetting' (about less relevant cases, instances or categories) are as much a part of the cognitive processes involved in generating grounded theory as is the explicit narrowing of focus upon a set of core or particularly well-saturated categories.

19.9 CORE ANALYSIS II: BUILDING THEORY AND MODELS

Perhaps the most critical stage of the whole analysis comes at the point of theoretical saturation, where the researcher focuses on important core categories (focused coding) and relationships between them and more formal theory. In the spirit of theory generation, maximum flexibility in theoretical coding is also desirable here. Glaser, for example, argued that one should think in terms of families of theoretical codes expressing broader social and social–psychological constructs, at differing levels of analysis. A researcher could use any family or combination of such to integrate an account from Glaser's list of 18 generic families, 3 examples of which are the 6 Cs (causes, contexts, contingencies, consequences, covariation, conditions), process families (stages, phases, progressions, passages) and identity families (self-concept, social worth, identity loss).

Integrating elements of generic social science concepts with those more directly derived from the data is often achieved using models. The simplest of models are skeletal organising schemata that mainly serve to catalogue the features of codings and categories, and are more implicit in suggesting relationships between them. Many qualitative studies (within and beyond grounded theory) report their findings in this way, and so the usefulness of this simple representational device must not be understated. Models can also depict, explain or otherwise account for time-event sequences, patterns of action and interaction, or 'processes' of (for example) transition and change, typically by assuming some variant of a representational theory of meaning. Visual displays of the relationships and conceptualisations specified in a model are frequently used as devices to immediately convey its particular kind of analytic message (e.g. flow charts, concept maps, matrices, typologies, taxonomies and other sorts of ordering and pattern template diagrams). For example, in a study of the human and organisational preconditions to major industrial accidents and disasters that uses time as one of its central dimensions, Turner and Pidgeon (1997) develop the core analytic category of the 'disaster incubation period'. Here a series of seemingly unrelated events and human errors combine over time to produce an unnoticed unsafe situation. They illustrate this idea through event sequence diagrams which allow the contributory causes and their interactions to be concisely displayed in visual form for any specific case study accident, while at the same time clearly illustrating the processual nature of the higher-level theory.

A further classic example of grounded theory research resulting in an explanatory model is Kathy Charmaz's study of how people with serious chronic illness struggle to have valued lives and selves (Charmaz, 1990, 2000). The study revealed two interrelated issues for studying identities in this context: the role of 'preferred identities' and the development of 'identity hierarchies'. Preferred identity refers to an individual's choice of identities through outlining plans and assessing choices. They symbolise assumptions, goals, hopes, desires and plans for a future that can no longer be realised. The model specifies four different types of preferred identity, and how they also constitute particular levels in an identity hierarchy reflecting relative difficulty in achieving specific objectives and aspirations. Specifically, a 'super-normal identity' refers to an identity demanding extraordinary achievement; a 'restored self' to a reconstruction of previous identities before the illness; a 'contingent' self to a hypothetically possible but uncertain identity because of possible illness progression; and a 'salvaged' self to a retained past identity based on a valued activity or attribute while becoming physically dependent. The explanatory value of the model lies in its portrayal of people's experiences of chronic illness as often resulting in a reduction of identity goals, and aiming for a lower level in the identity hierarchy where the illness becomes more debilitating. Living with chronic illness, by this model, means shifting identity goals and aiming for a more or less preferred identity depending upon difficulties primed by the illness.

One important means to (re)assemble substantive codes, developed by Strauss and Corbin (1990), involves an intermediate process called axial coding. This is both a heuristic analytic device and a theoretical commitment, in that it is closely aligned with a concern for how socio-structural conditions inform interaction and meaning. In essence, they recommend the exhaustive coding of the intersecting properties of core conceptual categories along important dimensions or axes. They also describe axial coding along multi-space typologies, whose axes are defined by the dimensions to important concepts, and the way in which axial coding can be fruitfully used to link socio-structural conditions with contexts and consequences, as well as to elaborate emergent hypotheses.

Our own view is that axial coding is only one among many potential pathways to theoretical development (and, indeed, not all psychology projects will be centrally concerned with underlying socio-structural causes of behaviour and meanings), and like any other path is unlikely to guarantee a straightforward or simple route. The most appropriate way of displaying or modelling information, ideas, concepts, processes and events needs to be found for the particular project and the stage it has reached, for its targeted audience, and to reflect the researcher's varied interests in describing, explaining and understanding aspects of the human and social world.

19.10 WRITING AND EVALUATING GROUNDED THEORY STUDIES

One final, interlinked set of considerations remains outstanding. How is the quality of research likely to be judged and by whom? How is it possible to foster informed

---

Box 19.4   Writing up grounded theory studies

At the outset of the account elucidate the context of the research.

State how sampling decisions were initially made. Did they change over time as the analysis developed?

Document the process of analysis in as transparent a way as possible.

Fully describe and/or define key categories.

What negative examples are there that do not fit the emergent theory?

Try to reflect the complexity of the account (however messy this might seem).

Use diagrammatic, network or tabulated representations to summarise linkages and key concepts.

Document whether respondent validation was attempted, and to what effect.

Document the analytic and personal commitments of the researcher (reflexivity).

---

appreciation and criticism of its credibility, quality or validity? What strategies are best used when presenting study outcomes or findings? While pertinent from the outset, these considerations tend to gain primacy as a project moves towards completion. This is also an important consideration when writing up a grounded theory study. Considerations to be taken into account when doing this are given in Box 19.4.

Some guidance on these issues can be found in the dedicated grounded theory literature, where they appear as integral to the task of building conceptual schemes and explanatory models out of the core grounded theory operations. Typically notions of 'credibility', 'plausibility' or 'trustworthiness' of qualitative analyses (as viewed both by researchers and readers) are used within their narratives of the ways in which grounded theory projects are brought to a close, and why discovery methods are as important in social inquiry as verificationist ones (rather than being a mere prerequisite to subsequent, more rigorous testing). At the point of theoretical saturation, at which point systematic efforts at coding data and constantly making conceptual comparisons no longer produce new insights, and when a high level of conceptual density and integration has been reached, enquirers will deem it appropriate to disseminate their work based on a belief that the account will both fit (provide a recognisable description) and work (be of use to other researchers and practitioners). The terms fit and work, as coined by Glaser and Strauss, signal such plausibility and credibility: conveying a strong analytic logic, its underpinnings in the systematic use of data, and a meaningful picture that can be grasped by people (because its theorisations remain grounded in the actions, interactions, symbolism, commonsense knowledge and human experience making up actual social worlds).

Proposed sets of criteria for use in the evaluation of qualitative studies more generally now exist in a number of disciplines, each with slightly different emphases. Tensions still remain in some guidelines. It is not uncommon in some disciplines, for example, for users of grounded theory to interpret the proposal to eliminate 'researcher bias' as signalling the need for researchers to demonstrate credibility of coding schemes by having senior researchers check junior researchers' codes for their 'accuracy', or by calculating inter-rater reliability scores. However, this quantitative technique lacks consistency with the approach of grounded theory and other similar forms of qualitative enquiry that use coding and categorising where quality concerns are met by demonstrating links between data and conceptualisation and, ultimately, the conceptual clarity of categories. As important as it may be to demonstrate credibility of categories and codes, this needs to be done without losing sight of the principle that they should capture the subtlety and complexity of contextual and/or experiential meanings. In some studies, where the stated goal of a study involves illuminating participants' phenomenological experiences and worlds, very tightly formulated conceptualisation may be read as overwriting participants' meanings with externally imposed frameworks in overly controlling ways. The technique of member validation commonly exists in lists of quality criteria for qualitative studies. Demonstrating that the categories derived from the research process are recognisable and acceptable to study participants represents a 'validity' criterion, however, only when there are grounds for believing that participants have special insights into the social worlds and issues under study. More typically, such commentaries work best if they are also treated as additional data.

Two further techniques – external auditing and triangulation – are often also deemed to overlap with quality concerns within grounded theory. External auditing can be appropriate where projects attach special importance to the transparency of the definitions of categories or systems of meaning, for example, in multi-site studies, or in multi- or interprofessional working teams. It is feasible to use triangulation in studies using multiple sources of observations and data, and it can be conceptualised so that practising it is consistent with 'subtle realism' and even constructivist theories of meaning. It is possible to set aside the traditional navigational metaphor (where multiple measurements are taken because a single one would not determine an object's unique position in a dimensional space) and see triangulation as a way of opening up different facets of complex phenomena to view.

When seeking to build in a concern for research quality in a grounded theory study, it is above all important to bear in mind the key tenets of the approach. Openness of inquiry is one such issue, as is the aim of studying the research subject in its full complexity and *in situ*. Taking into account and documenting, as far as possible, the role of multiple perspectives of both the researcher and researched (sometimes referred to as **reflexivity**) is another. Putting these sorts of principles into practice offers its own kind of precision in much of contemporary qualitative inquiry, but especially that which is based on grounded theory.

19.11 **CONCLUSION**

The grounded theory approach provides a set of rigorous and creative strategies and methods for the analysis of diverse kinds of unwieldy, initially unstructured qualitative data. In this chapter we have emphasised how its logic of enquiry is markedly different from the hypothetico-deductive tradition that remains pervasive within many areas of psychology, and which underpins the majority of teaching of undergraduate and postgraduate research methods. We recognise that some writers about grounded theory take a different view, explicating closer parallels with the logic and strategies of quantitative research. More typically, when grounded theory is embraced in psychology, it is as a means of taking forward the interpretative thematic analysis of meanings. As such, it tends to be linked with key concepts that signal the important characteristics of interpretative approaches to qualitative research. Intense intellectual work is involved in grounded theory studies, along with a good deal of uncertainty which has to be channelled productively throughout the research process. The products of such efforts can also have high impact when they meet the applied aims of using the approach: intelligibility to research users and interested readers, and relevance to the important practical and policy problems at hand.

19.12 **EXERCISES**

1 Select a newspaper or magazine which regularly publishes detailed obituaries of famous people. Use theoretical sampling to select between 10 and 15 different obituaries of a similar length – with the objective of selecting a range of issues (i.e. what the people were or did to make them worthy of an obituary), occupations (e.g. scientist, politician, artist, businesspersons etc.) and equal numbers of men and women. Starting with the first obituary, begin to construct a set of category labels grounded in the text which describe (a) what was important in the person's life and (b) the qualities by which the person is described (dedicated, inspirational, high social standing, etc.). Do this for successive obituaries, noting on coding cards both where a concept or idea used in an earlier obituary recurs as well as developing different cards whenever a completely new idea is presented.
2 When all of the obituaries used in Exercise 1 have been coded, write a short (no more than 20 lines) paragraph on what the data as a whole says about (a) 'what makes a life meaningful' and (b) 'the personal and social qualities of people as found in obituaries'. If writing these two

paragraphs leads you to consider changing any of the original set of category labels note this on a memo card, with the reasons why.

3 Gender theorists over the past 30 years have criticised the ways that men and women are often portrayed by society (in books, newspapers, TV, etc.). In particular such theorists have pointed out that the roles, occupations and behaviours traditionally associated with men are often portrayed as the main norm for evaluating everybody's conduct, leading to a hierarchy of value. Use the obituaries and codes developed in Exercises 1 and 2 to carefully compare the different ideas about men and women found in these data. Write a short theoretical memo exploring whether the hierarchy of value proposition does, or does not, hold true in your obituaries.

19.13 DISCUSSION QUESTIONS

1 How does the approach of grounded theory differ, in philosophical terms, from more quantitative types of psychological research?

2 Think of a type or source of qualitative data suitable to analyse using grounded theory to address a broad research question. What different types of sample might you construct for your study (give examples, and reasons for the types of sample selected)?

3 What is the value of describing a piece of data using a 'researcher' rather than a 'member' category, and what are the potential dangers of doing this?

4 Under what circumstances would a segment of qualitative data be assigned to two or more categories/codes?

5 Why is it important for the analyst to be able to change codes and categories as a grounded theory analysis proceeds?

6 Writing memos is often the first stage in conducting a more theoretically informed account of the data. At what stages of the analysis can memo writing occur, and how do we use references to the prior literature in memos (try to write your own example of a memo)?

7 Why is constantly comparing data, codes and cases so important to the grounded theory approach?

8 What is the value of using diagrams and charts (however preliminary or rough) for describing an emerging (or final) set of concepts/codes?

9 In what ways do grounded theory processes build rigour as well as creativity into the analysis and writing of qualitative data?

19.14 **FURTHER READING**

The original work on grounded theory by Glaser and Strauss (1967) is still worthy of a close read. Later grounded theory texts now provide useful reflections on the method. We would recommend Kathy Charmaz's book *Constructing grounded theory* (2006) as a theoretically sophisticated yet very practical guide.

Henwood and Pidgeon (1992) make the general case for using qualitative research – and grounded theory in particular – in psychology. Charmaz and Henwood (2008) provide a particularly clear account of the logic, use and emergence of grounded theory, and what can be learned by comparing across different social science and clinical disciplines. Henwood (2006) provides specialist guidance in the context of mental health research.

Strauss and Corbin (1997) give good examples of a range of grounded theory projects. Marshall and Rossman's (4th edition, 2010) text is very useful for help with research design and orienting questions. Miles and Huberman (1994) give examples of integrating and data display techniques for use when building theory.

Lincoln and Guba (1985) give a general discussion of qualitative epistemology and approaches. Blumer's (1969) text is a classic on the symbolic interactionist tradition.

Henwood and Pidgeon (2003) explore coding and memoing through a closely worked example. This student-friendly chapter also provides unique insights into theoretical sensitivity as a key issue in qualitative inquiry.

Finally, Renata Tesch's text (1990) is essential reading for anyone interested in grounded theory and computer assisted qualitative data analysis (CAQDAS).

20

Discourse Analysis

Adrian Coyle

CONTENTS

AIMS OF THIS CHAPTER

This chapter aims to provide an account of discourse analysis that examines the assumptions that underpin the approach and the practicalities of using it. The process of subjecting data to discourse analysis is illustrated through basic analyses of some brief data excerpts. Readers should emerge with an informed understanding of what discourse analysis involves, together with a critical appreciation of the approach.

KEY TERMS

action orientation
coding
critical discourse analysis
critical discursive psychology
discourses
discursive psychology
epistemology
Foucauldian discourse
    analysis

functions
ontology
positioning
reflexivity
social constructionism
texts
variability

20.1 **INTRODUCTION**

In the summer of 2010, news reports appeared concerning a furious response to a proposal to locate an Islamic cultural centre with a prayer space several blocks from the site of New York's World Trade Centre, which was destroyed in the attack in 2001. In a commentary on the heated debate surrounding this issue, the British journalist and broadcaster Charlie Brooker wrote the following:

> I've been thinking some more about the 'Ground Zero mosque' debate. Specifically, I've been thinking about the horrible brilliance of the opponents' endlessly parroted, emotionally charged phrase 'Ground Zero mosque', used to describe something which [ ] isn't at Ground Zero and isn't a mosque [ ] Nothing riles an anti-mosque demonstrator more than being called a bigot. It's a grotesque, misleading smear on a diverse group of individuals – a bit like claiming all Muslims are terrorists (which, coincidentally, the guy beside them is currently doing through a loud-hailer) [ ] I tried to invent a shorthand term to describe the sort of perpetually furious rightwing weevil who claims to be a patriot, not a bigot, then immediately muddies the water by saying lots of bigoted things. [ ] Still, a lot of people erroneously believe that saying 'I'm a patriot' automatically absolves them from any and all charges of bigotry.

In this commentary, Brooker analyses how language has been used in the debate and traces its implications. In the extract above, he notes the psychosocial effects of language, with the term 'bigot' being said to arouse anger among those who are labelled as such and the term 'patriot' serving to inoculate speakers against charges of bigotry. He suggests that people use language in ways that seem inconsistent, deflecting charges of bigotry while speaking in bigoted terms and using language against other people in a way that they resist when it is used against them. He also observes that language may not map onto the 'reality' that it might be assumed to represent ('"Ground Zero mosque", used to describe something which [ ] isn't at Ground Zero and isn't a mosque').

What Brooker is doing here is a basic form of discourse analysis. This is an approach to research that developed within psychology following the publication in 1987 of Jonathan Potter and Margaret Wetherell's classic text *Discourse and Social Psychology: Beyond Attitudes and Behaviour*. This work called for a radical reformulation of the issues that social psychology had traditionally addressed. Social psychologists have long worked with language and text in the form of spoken responses within interview settings and written responses to questionnaire items. The question then arises as to what status should be given to this material. It is generally assumed that language is a neutral, transparent medium, describing events or revealing underlying psychological processes in a more or less direct, unproblematic way. Psychologists recognise that people may distort reality in their use of language to present themselves in favourable ways or because of memory biases. Yet it is assumed that these can be eradicated or at least minimised by refining the ways in which data are generated and collected.

Discourse analysis adopted a very different understanding of the nature of language, one that was influenced by schools of thought within philosophy, sociology and linguistics. This can make it difficult to provide an accessible introduction to the approach. To a psychology student schooled in traditional approaches to psychological research, discourse analysis can seem as though it involves a different language – and one that is dauntingly complex. This is one reason for opening the chapter with the quotation from Brooker. It shows that discourse analysis is not an arcane academic pursuit; versions of it can be found in newspapers, magazines and television programmes where the implications of language use for socially important matters are critically considered. However, formal discourse analysis rests upon some fundamental assumptions about language and about our social and psychological worlds. It is not possible to get very far without grasping these assumptions and so, even though it may be a rather off-putting way to begin, that is where our attention turns next. If the ideas that are put forward in the next section are hard to follow, you may find it easier to understand them when you see them applied to data in section 20.5.

20.2 DISCOURSE ANALYSIS: ASSUMPTIONS, APPROACHES AND APPLICATIONS

20.2.1 Social constructionism

Within the approach to psychology that underlies discourse analysis, language is represented not as reflecting psychological and social reality but as *constructing* it. In other words, the language that we use is not treated as if it reflects some objective truths that exist 'out there' and that can be accessed if we use the appropriate scientific methods. Instead, language in the form of discourses is seen as constituting the building blocks of 'social reality' (note that it is common practice to use inverted commas to draw attention to the constructed nature of taken-for-granted 'things'). The analysis of discourse emphasises how social reality is built up or constructed through language and it aims to gain 'a better understanding of social life and social interaction from our study of social texts' (Potter & Wetherell, 1987, p. 7).

Discourse analysis can therefore be classed as a social constructionist approach to research. In broad terms, the social constructionist perspective adopts a critical stance towards the taken-for-granted ways in which we understand the world and ourselves, such as the assumption that the categories we use to interpret the world

Box 20.1   The social construction of sexuality categories

The categories 'gay man', 'lesbian' and 'homosexual' are now a taken-for-granted part of how we talk about sexualities. It is easy to forget that defining people in terms of their preference for sexual partners of the same gender as themselves only began in the eighteenth century. Prior to this, there were terms that referred to sexual activity involving people of the same gender but these terms did not denote a particular kind of person. Furthermore, the ways in which these behaviours were socially organised, regulated and responded to varied across cultures. The term 'homosexual' was not coined until the mid-nineteenth century with the increasing medicalisation of sexuality. Terms such as 'gay man' and 'lesbian' were only adopted in the 1960s and 1970s in line with the political concerns of the gay liberation and women's movements (for detailed analyses of the social construction of 'the homosexual' up to that point, see Plummer, 1981). And with the postmodern trend within 'queer theory', concepts of 'the gay man' and 'the lesbian' have been subjected to critical scrutiny (Sedgwick, 1990; Simpson, 1996). So, from this one example, it can be seen that there is nothing fixed or inevitable about what may appear to be commonsense ways of representing the world: they are socially constructed.

correspond to 'real', 'objective' entities (Burr, 2003). These ways of understanding are seen as having been built up through social processes, especially through linguistic interactions, and so they are culturally and historically specific (see Box 20.1 for an example).

Most people will concede this to some extent when they think about situations in which we deliberately construct a purposeful version of events. For example, when applying for a job, we tend to include on the application form material that shows us in the best possible light. Anything that indicates the sorts of strengths that we want to claim will be emphasised and anything that might weaken our application will be glossed over or, if possible, omitted altogether. In that situation, we are using language to build up a particular version of ourselves that is oriented towards specific ends, that is, securing an interview and ultimately securing the job.

However, social constructionism goes much further than this, seeing *all* social categories as constructed through language, even those that appear grounded in seemingly fixed qualities. For example, it might be imagined that the sex categories male and female are biologically determined and distinguished. Yet, the existence of intersex people (people whose biological sex cannot be clearly classified as either male or female) shows that this is not the case. The way in which intersex people have been treated by medicine indicates just how much is at stake when people's bodies challenge the social construction of sex categories as an either/or binary (Kessler, 1998).

Social constructionism represents what is called the epistemology of discourse analysis. Epistemology is a philosophical term that refers to the assumptions we make about what knowledge is, how we generate knowledge, what we know, and how we know what we know. It is often discussed alongside ontology, which refers to the assumptions we make about the nature of being, existence or reality (and discussions sometimes slip between the two). All research approaches and methods are based on a set of epistemological assumptions. The emphasis on language as a constructive tool is one of the core assumptions of discourse analysis. The language user is viewed as selecting from the range of linguistic resources available to them (words, phrases, metaphors, clichés, etc) and using these resources to construct a version of events, although not necessarily in an intentional way. The person may not recognise that they are constructing something when they speak or write, but this simply highlights the extent to which the constructive use of language is a fundamental, taken-for-granted aspect of social life, one that we may not even be aware of.

It is important to grasp a major implication that follows from this social constructionist epistemology for psychologists who employ discourse analysis. Unlike most other research approaches in psychology, discourse analysis does not use people's language as a means of gaining access to the 'reality' of their psychological and social worlds. Instead, discourse analysis examines how people use language to construct versions of their worlds (including their psychology) and what is gained from these constructions.

20.2.2 Defining 'discourse'

So far, we have been referring constantly to 'discourse analysis' but have not yet defined what we mean by 'discourse'. It can be difficult to specify exactly what discourses are, because various meanings have been ascribed to the term. Drawing out the common features, discourses can be defined as sets of (written or spoken) linguistic material that have a degree of coherence in their content and organisation and that perform constructive functions in broadly defined social contexts. Different discourses can be invoked to construct any object, person, event or situation in a variety of ways. Some discourses are standard resources for sense-making in particular cultures (see Box 20.2). Incidentally, it is worth noting that, in their classic text, Potter and Wetherell (1987) preferred the term 'interpretative repertoires' rather than 'discourses' because they said the idea of 'repertoire' implies flexibility in the ways in which the linguistic components of the repertoire can be put together.

20.2.3 Different approaches to discourse analysis

Discourse analysis assumes that linguistic material has an action orientation: language is used to perform particular social actions or functions such as justifying,

Box 20.2 Liberal individualism as a culturally hegemonic discourse

One standard discourse used in many different social contexts in the Western world is the discourse of liberal individualism. Within this discourse, the public sphere is constructed as populated by autonomous individuals who have rights not to be unduly interfered with by society (Marquand, 1991).

Consider how a father might justify his decision to pay for his daughter to be educated at a private school rather than at a local state school. He might say that it is his right as a parent to do whatever he thinks necessary to obtain the best education for his daughter in order to improve her chances of success in later life and that the high quality facilities and small class sizes offered by private schools increase the likelihood of her obtaining a good education. This justification is constructed within a discourse of liberal individualism. Claims about the 'right to choose' are based upon a liberal assumption that the individual's choices should be tolerated and respected (usually provided they are legal), even if, in making those choices, the individual does not contribute to or even undermines the common good. So a friend might challenge the father by saying that, in opting out of state education, he absolves himself from the need to lobby for and contribute to improvements in his local state school, leaving this to those parents who cannot pay for private education. In such a discussion, the father who speaks from within a discourse of liberal individualism, emphasising his right to do the best for his daughter, may seem reasonable and may 'win out' because he is using a standard discourse for making sense of our actions and one that seems entirely reasonable because it is so commonplace. The term that is sometimes applied to such dominant, powerful discourses is 'hegemonic'. The friend who argues against it by stressing the importance of the collective may end up being dismissed as 'politically motivated'.

questioning and accusing. Key tasks that discourse analysts within this action-oriented approach set themselves are to identify *what* functions are being performed by the linguistic material that is being analysed and to consider *how* these functions are performed and what resources are available to perform these functions. This entails a close and careful inspection of qualitative textual data. In this process, some discourse analysts are concerned with the fine grain of talk. These writers tend to adopt and adapt the approaches of conversation analysis in their work (see Atkinson & Heritage, 1984). Generally, though, discourse analysis is more concerned with the social organisation of talk rather than with its linguistic organisation. This approach involves looking at what discourses are shared across texts and what constructions of the world the material can be seen as advocating.

Exploring this issue of different approaches further, it is worth noting that there are two main approaches to the study of discourse within British psychology, with different possible versions and combinations of these. The approach known as discursive psychology views language as a form of social action, addresses the social functions of talk and considers how these functions are achieved. It is particularly attentive to the ways by which 'factual accounts' and 'descriptions' (which might be interpreted by other research approaches as straightforward 'objective' representations of internal or external psychological and/or social realities) are made to appear as such. In more recent years, its focus has encompassed linguistic interaction in everyday settings (e.g. see Wiggins, 2004) and institutional contexts (e.g. see Hepburn & Wiggins, 2005). Discursive psychology has been most closely associated with the work of writers such as Jonathan Potter and Derek Edwards (e.g. Edwards & Potter, 1992; Potter, 1996). Work conducted within this tradition adopts a thoroughly social constructionist position. Writers do not deny that a material reality exists but they do not see it as reflected in our language use. Therefore questions about whether and how language accurately describes 'reality' are set aside.

This approach has been represented as politically limited by other practitioners who are more concerned with issues such as identity and selfhood, ideology, power relations and social change. This perspective has been termed Foucauldian discourse analysis because it is said to owe a particular debt to the work and/or commitments of the philosopher, Michel Foucault (although this claim has been contested: see Hook, 2001). This form of discourse analysis arose from the work of Ian Parker, Erica Burman and Wendy Hollway (e.g. Hollway, 1989; Parker, 1992; Burman & Parker, 1993a). Writers within Foucauldian discourse analysis see the world as having a structural reality, which they usually describe in terms of power relations; these are viewed as underpinning how we understand and talk about the world (Burr, 2003). The Foucauldian approach holds that discourses 'facilitate and limit, enable and constrain what can be said, by whom, where and when' (Willig, 2008, p. 112). Hence, dominant discourses privilege versions of social reality that accord with and reinforce existing social structures and the networks of power relations associated with them. Analysts study the availability of discursive resources within a culture and the implications that this carries for those living within that culture.

As we can see, although Foucauldian discourse analysts agree with the discursive psychology emphasis on the linguistic construction of social reality, one major difference is that they advocate a need to hold on to some idea of language representing things that have an existence independent of language. Parker (1992) has suggested that 'things' should be represented as having different statuses as objects. Some objects are said to exist independently of thought and language, that is, those that are needed for thought to occur (such as our brains and bodies) and around which thinking can be organised (such as the physical and organisational properties of the environment). Yet, we do not have direct knowledge of these objects because thinking is a constructive, interpretative process. Other objects are constructed through language but are treated in language as if they had an enduring reality.

One feature of discourse analytic research that is associated with Foucauldian discourse analysis is positioning, which comes from the work of Bronwyn Davies and Rom Harré (1990). This represents one discursive interpretation of the social psychological concept of identity. When an individual is constructed through discourse, they are accorded a particular subject position within that discourse, which brings with it a set of images, metaphors and obligations concerning the kind of response that can be made. For example, within a biomedical discourse, people who are ill are placed in the subject position of 'the patient', with its obligation to act as a passive recipient of care from those who are placed in the subject position of 'medical experts'. In their linguistic response to that positioning, the individual can accept it (and fulfil the obligations of their position) or they can resist it. Of course, the person can also position themselves within a discourse and their audience can accept or reject this positioning. Any individual may assume some positions fairly consistently within their talk while other positions are more temporary, giving rise to variability. As Davies and Harré (1999: 35) have commented, the question of 'who one is … is always an open question with a shifting answer depending upon the positions made available within one's own and others' discursive practices'.

In addition to the two approaches outlined so far, a third approach has emerged which attempts to synthesise discursive psychology and Foucauldian discourse analysis. This has been termed critical discursive psychology. The tenets of this approach have been expounded by Margaret Wetherell (1998) and it can be seen in action in her work on masculinities with Nigel Edley (e.g. Edley & Wetherell, 1999). A final approach that is worth noting is critical discourse analysis, which is more commonly encountered outside psychology. For an overview of this approach, see Fairclough and Wodak (1997).

20.2.4 Discourse analytic research questions

Although discourse analysis has been used to investigate a wide variety of research topics, it is only appropriate for the exploration of particular types of research questions. Many research questions from elsewhere in psychology are based on a logic of factors and outcomes, whereas discourse analytic research questions focus on construction, rhetoric, ideology and action.

Potter (2003) identifies four foci in discourse analytic research questions:

- How specific actions and practices are linguistically done in particular settings. For example, Kurz *et al.* (2010) examined how politicians from the major Australian political parties invoked and managed the issue of 'climate change' in parliamentary debates, public speeches, media interviews and press releases in the run-up to the 2007 general election there.

- How particular accounts of things are constructed and made to seem factual and objective or how seemingly factual accounts are challenged. For example, Wallwork and Dixon (2004) examined how fox hunting was constructed as a defining national issue in Britain in pro-hunting newspaper and magazine articles.

- Psychological practice: this involves re-framing psychological concepts in discursive terms. For example, Craven and Coyle (2007) showed how counselling psychologists moved between two different repertoires in their talk about 'psychopathology' and the use of psycho-diagnostic categories in counselling psychology practice.

- Exploitation, prejudice and ideology: this involves examining how racism, sexism, ageism, homophobia and other oppressions are expressed, justified or rendered invisible. For example, see Wetherell and Potter's (1992) extensive study of racist language and practice in New Zealand and Forbat's (2005) examination of themes of care and abuse in talk about informal care relationships.

With these critical and analytic foci, it is not surprising that discourse analysis has been taken up with enthusiasm by those who wish to give psychology a radical, political edge. Some analysts choose to focus on discourses which reproduce social relations of dominance and oppression and/or which include oppressive aspects that are often glossed over. Discourse analysis can be used to indicate that alternative discourses could be constructed in their place. Yet it is important to acknowledge that the supplanting of oppressive discourses is a complex and lengthy process and there is no way of predicting with confidence what the social implications of discursive change might be.

20.3 SAMPLING DISCOURSE

In order to conduct an analysis of discourse, texts are required in which discourses may be discerned. All spoken and written material can be conceptualised as a text and subjected to discourse analysis, in the same way that within traditional scientific paradigms, almost anything can be construed as data and analysed. There has been some debate among researchers about the most appropriate types of data for discourse analysis (see Potter & Hepburn, 2005). However, discourse analytic studies have used a range of data sources, including transcripts of 'naturally occurring talk' (i.e. talk that would have happened anyway if the researcher had not been present, such as discussions in professional meetings), articles from newspapers and magazines, transcripts of television programmes and web pages (in section 20.5.2, song lyrics are briefly analysed), and researcher-generated talk in focus groups (see Chapter 17) and individual interviews (see Chapter 15).

Within traditional approaches to sampling in psychological research, the emphasis is placed upon securing as large and representative a sample as possible. Within discourse analysis, if interview material is used as a source of data, there is no necessity to sample discourse from a large number of people. If newspaper reports of a particular event are to be used, it is not necessary to collect all reports from all newspapers on that event. The analysis stage of qualitative data is almost always more laborious and time-consuming than the analysis of structured data, so the researcher must beware of ending up with an unmanageable amount of unstructured data to sift through. What is important is to gather enough text to discern the variety of discursive forms that are commonly used when speaking or writing about the research topic. This may be possible from an analysis of relatively few interview transcripts or newspaper reports, especially where common discursive forms are under consideration. In this case, larger samples of data add to the analytic task without adding significantly to the analytic outcome. Where an analysis is purely exploratory and the analyst has little idea in advance what the analytic focus might be, larger samples of data are required.

Recordings of talk in interaction (whether 'naturally occurring' or in interviews) need to be transcribed before analysis. Accurate transcription of recordings is a lengthy process which is made even more laborious if the transcriber wishes to include every 'um' and 'uh' uttered by the speakers and to measure pauses in speech production. This sort of detailed approach is less often seen in discourse analysis than in conversation analysis, although Wooffitt (2001, p. 328) has rightly observed that 'it is a good methodological practice always to produce as detailed a transcription as possible'.

20.4 TECHNIQUES OF DISCOURSE ANALYSIS

While it is relatively easy to expound the central theoretical tenets of discourse analysis, specifying exactly how one goes about doing discourse analysis is a different matter because there is no rigid set of formal procedures. It has been contended that the key to analysing discourse is scholarship and the development of an analytic mentality rather than adherence to a rigorous methodology (Billig, 1988). The emphasis is placed upon the careful reading and interpretation of texts, with interpretations being backed by reference to linguistic evidence in the texts. The first step is said to be the suspension of belief in what is normally taken for granted in language use (Potter & Wetherell, 1987). This involves seeing linguistic practices not as simply reflecting underlying psychological and social realities but as constructing and legitimating a version of events.

However, one cannot help feeling that a more systematic methodological approach would be beneficial to those entering the field for the first time. It is all very well to suggest that to conduct discourse analysis, one needs to develop 'a sensitivity to the way in which language is used', especially to the 'inferential and interactional aspects of talk' (Widdicombe, 1993, p. 97). Yet, it is unclear exactly how this sensitivity is developed and systematised. In an attempt to provide some pointers,

Potter and Wetherell (1987) suggested a loose ten-stage approach, with two stages devoted to the analytic process: note how these stages overlap with and differ from those specified by Willig (2008) for Foucauldian discourse analysis in section 20.5.2.

The process begins with what is termed coding, which refers to the process of examining the text closely. With a large data set, it may be worth using appropriate software to help organise and code the data, such as NVivo (Lewins & Silver, 2007). If the research focus has been specified in advance, instances of the research focus are identified at this point. It is worth being as inclusive as possible and noting what appear to be borderline instances of the research focus. This makes it possible to discern less obvious but nonetheless fruitful lines of inquiry. The coding process is more complex if the research focus has not been determined in advance. In this case, it is necessary to read and reread the text, looking for recurrent discursive patterns shared by the accounts under analysis. It is at this stage that Widdicombe's (1993) notion of sensitivity to the way in which language is used is important. Impressions about which discourses are being invoked in the text are developed and reformulated in light of whether the linguistic evidence needed to support them is available. It is important that the analyst should remain open to alternative readings of the text and to the need to reject preliminary impressions that are not supported by the text.

A useful strategy for the next stage of analysis involves reading the text mindful of what its functions might be. Any text is held to have an action orientation and is oriented towards fulfilling certain functions, so the question is: 'What functions is this text fulfilling and how is it fulfilling them?' The formulation of hypotheses about the purposes and consequences of language is central to discourse analysis. However, identifying the functions of language is often not a straightforward process because these functions may not be explicit. For example, when someone asks you to do something, they may phrase it not as an order or command ('Do the washing up') but as a question to which the expected answer is 'Yes' ('Would you like to do the washing up?').

In seeking to identify discursive functions, a useful starting point is the discursive context. It can be difficult to divine function from limited sections of a text. A variety of functions may be performed and revisited throughout a text, so it is necessary to be familiar with what precedes and follows a particular extract in order to obtain clues about its functions. Although Foucauldian discourse analysts also emphasise context, they attach a specific meaning to the term. Parker and Burman (1993) have stated that the analyst needs to be aware of broader contextual concerns such as cultural trends and political and social issues to which the text alludes.

Another analytic strategy that may be helpful is to examine a text in a situated way, mindful of what version of events it may be designed to counteract. Any version of events is but one of a number of possible versions and therefore must be constructed as more persuasive than these alternative versions if it is to prevail. Sometimes alternative versions will be explicitly mentioned and counteracted in a text (e.g. in a transcript of court proceedings) but on other occasions they will be implicit. If analysts are sensitised to what these alternative versions might be, they may be well placed to analyse how the text addresses the function of legitimating the version constructed therein.

In analysing function, it is useful to become acquainted with the ways in which various features of talk and text are described in the discourse analytic and conversation analytic literatures. These features frequently perform specific rhetorical functions. Therefore, if analysts are able to identify these features, they can examine the text mindful of the functions that these features typically perform. For example, the use of terms such as 'always', 'never', 'nobody' and 'everyone' may represent what have been called 'extreme case formulations' (Pomerantz, 1986). These take whatever position is being advocated in the text to its extreme, and thereby help to make this position more persuasive. For those interested in becoming acquainted with these technical features of discourse, Potter (1996) has outlined a wide range, but the best strategy is to examine studies which have used discourse analytic and conversation analytic approaches.

According to Potter and Wetherell (1987), one means of elucidating the functions of text is through the study of variability. The fact that any discourse varies appears to be a commonsense statement. If we were analysing talk from different people about a particular phenomenon, we would expect variations related to whether individuals evaluated the phenomenon positively or negatively. However, variation also occurs *within* an individual's talk, dependent upon the purposes that discourses are fulfilling within the talk. Indeed, this was a key feature of Craven and Coyle's (2007) study of counselling psychologists' talk about 'psychopathology' and the use of psycho-diagnostic categories in counselling psychology practice (see section 20.2.4). It has been claimed that, in their search for individual consistency, mainstream approaches to psychology have sought to minimise or explain away intra-individual variation (Potter and Wetherell, 1987). Discourse analysis, in contrast, actively seeks it out. As variability arises from the different functions that the discourse may be fulfilling, the nature of the variation can provide clues to what these functions are. The process of discourse analysis therefore involves the search for both consistency (in the identification of discourses) and variability (in the analysis of discursive functions).

20.5 **WORKING WITH DATA**

These principles of discourse analysis can sound rather abstract and complex but, in this section, we see how they are translated into practice, taking two examples of different approaches using different types of data. The first example draws chiefly but not exclusively upon a basic discursive psychology approach, with some positioning also being analysed. The second example demonstrates a basic Foucauldian discourse analytic approach. These analyses are designed to demonstrate some fundamental aspects of the analytic process in simple terms: they are not meant to be comprehensive. For examples of more complete and complex analyses, the reader is referred to the journals *Discourse & Society* and the *British Journal of Social Psychology* and to the discourse analytic research articles that have already been cited.

20.5.1 Warranting strategies in querying Christian discourse on homosexuality

The data in the first example come from a study conducted by the author which examined an attempt to construct an alternative to the traditional condemnatory Christian discourse on homosexuality in a workshop for members of a predominantly lesbian and gay church. This discourse is grounded in interpretations of Biblical texts and centres around claims that same-sex sexual activity is sinful and unnatural. One denomination that has tried to counter and reinterpret this has been the Metropolitan Community Church (MCC). The majority of MCC's clergy and congregations in Europe and North America are gay or lesbian. This denomination has reinterpreted those Biblical passages that are customarily seen as referring to and condemning homosexual activity and, by extension, gay men and lesbians. The essence of the alternative discourse it offers is that the Bible contains no unequivocal prohibitions against same-sex sexual activity and that a belief in God, the authority of the Bible and homosexuality are entirely compatible. MCC has attempted to propagate its alternative discourse primarily through its congregations and publications. The following analysis draws upon a transcript of a day-long workshop provided by MCC in East London facilitated by an American, who will be referred to as 'David', who was then a senior figure in MCC's theological college in Europe. The text was obtained through recording workshop proceedings, having obtained the permission of the workshop facilitator and participants. Various factors meant that it was only possible to produce a basic transcript of the proceedings.

As there was no pre-determined analytic focus, this transcript was read and reread closely, looking for broad recurrent discursive patterns. One which was discerned was the establishment of legitimacy or warrant by the facilitator for his reinterpretation of the traditional discourse. As we have noted, the attempt to ensure that one's own version of events prevails against competing versions is a common feature of accounts. This aspect of the proceedings was therefore selected as a potentially interesting analytic focus.

The principal warranting strategies that were discerned in David's talk during the workshop involved positioning himself as an expert through expositions of his scholarship; positioning himself as a benign teacher or guide; presenting tales of his personal experiences with the traditional discourse; and working up assurances of his honesty. These were juxtaposed and interwoven to create a powerful cumulative warranting effect. Although these strategies involve positioning, it is impossible to demonstrate the cut-and-thrust of positioning (where positions are assigned, nego-tiated and accepted or rejected) because the data consist mostly of a monologue: David took questions from his audience only occasionally. In the analyses below, two of these strategies will be examined: expositions of scholarship and tales of his personal experience.

At several points during the workshop, David emphasises his Biblical scholarship, particularly his skills in Biblical languages. For example, at different points he says:

> What I'm going to say to you has very sound academic structure – founda-tion. I don't intend to overwhelm you with the academics of it which can be quite boring. I do have the academic background and the study in the origi-nal languages to support what I'm going to say.

> The Bible was written in ancient languages. The Old Testament is written in Hebrew with some Aramaic in the Book of Daniel and one of the other prophets. The New Testament is written in Greek – in koine Greek which was the common language of the people. Greek is a very complex language with balanced clauses and classic literary Greek is great fun to translate which is where I started my Greek studies. The New Testament Greek is sort of common street slang language sometimes and is great fun – the koine Greek.

The use of this strategy establishes credibility and validity specifically for the rein-terpretations of Biblical passages that he will expound later and generally for any other pronouncements that he will make (note that we make no assumptions about whether David used this strategy intentionally). If his views are regarded by his audience as informed opinions, underpinned by scholarship and expertise, they are more likely to prevail than if they are seen as uninformed speculation. However, a heavy emphasis on scholarship may risk alienating the audience if they are made to feel inadequate in comparison or if they assume that what will be said will be 'over their heads'. This possibility is counteracted by the way in which David constructs his learning. He reassures his audience that 'I don't intend to overwhelm you with the academics of it which can be quite boring.' One could draw out his positioning of his audience here by filling in the implied 'to the layperson' at the end of this utterance, which positions David as an expert, the possessor of privileged insight into the material he is about to address.

Within the second extract ('Greek is a very complex language [ ] the koine Greek'), he also creates the impression that he wears his learning lightly and points to the enjoyment he derives from it. The juxtaposition of the account of the

> ## Box 20.3　How much data to present in discourse analytic reports?
>
> Discourse analysts vary in the amount of data they present in their research reports. Some offer many brief extracts of data; others present a few relatively lengthy data extracts; others present a combination. Due to space constraints, the analyses offered here are illustrated by relatively short excerpts. If these were supposed to be complete, comprehensive analyses, this would be problematic because the brief excerpts would seem rather decontextualised: here the reader is not given a clear sense of what exactly was going on in the workshop when David produced these words. Discourse analytic researchers routinely face this problem when writing up their work for publication. There is a need to balance the desire to present a range of interpretations from the data set with the requirement to ground interpretations in textual evidence.

complexity of classic literary Greek (complete with the introduction of the quasi-technical term 'balanced clauses') and the description of it as 'great fun' further stress David's scholarship. Note how the notions of complexity and fun are accompanied by terms of emphasis ('very complex'; 'great fun'). Their presence draws attention to the possibility that these notions are carrying out important work in this extract. Whatever the public perception of classic literary Greek might be, it is unlikely that fun features significantly. While it takes a high level of intellectual capacity to become proficient in as complex a language as Greek, one would imagine that an even more rarefied level of operation would be required to find it 'fun'. Note also how the range of David's learning is stressed here. Not only is he skilled in 'classic literary Greek' but also in the 'common street slang language [ ] the koine Greek', which is again described as 'great fun'. Consider the use of the technical term 'koine Greek'. David provides a description of what this means, so one could ask what function the use of the technical term serves. It adds nothing in terms of meaning and could easily have been omitted, so it may be seen as performing an explicitly rhetorical function. This is an example of an occasion when the analyst needs to be mindful of potential alternative versions of the text. It may be that the use of the term again stresses David's expertise by giving an example of the privileged knowledge to which he has access. So we can see that in these extracts, David positions himself as an expert and subsequently reinforces that positioning.

Although David bases his warrant largely on his scholarship, he appears to belittle this scholarship at one stage. However, the way in which he elaborates his point means that he ends up emphasising his scholarly skills and further reinforcing his position as expert. He says:

At that point there came in hand [ ] a book by an Anglican clergyman called *Homosexuality and the Western Christian Tradition* by Derek Sherwin Bailey.

He wrote this as a part of the Wolfenden report and it was published as you see in 1955 and he was saying only with all the basic academic apparatus that I didn't have and with all of the scholarly qualifications the very same thing that I had discovered and I was quite bowled over by it.

This is an instance of variability in the account that David is providing of himself. We have seen how earlier he assiduously emphasised his scholarship, yet here he actively denies it. What clues does this variability provide about the function of this description? Although he underplays his 'academic apparatus' and 'scholarly qualifications', he claims that, independently, he reached the 'very same' conclusions (note the emphasising 'very') as Bailey. He exalts Bailey's standing by associating him with the Wolfenden report on which was based the 1967 law reform decriminalising consensual private sexual activity between men aged over 21 years. This interpretation is founded on an understanding of the context which David is evoking, which underlines how important it is for the analyst to be familiar with the context in which the text under analysis is located. The rhetoric in the extract implies that underlying whatever formal academic training David has is an inspired mind that enabled him to reach the same conclusions as such an intellectually esteemed figure as Bailey. His humility at this discovery is conveyed by his reaction to it ('I was quite bowled over by it'). That this reaction is expressed in folksy terms again underlines his construction of himself as an ordinary person. He is thus simultaneously positioned in quite different ways. The function these positionings serve is to reassure the audience that David possesses the formal scholarship and the creative thinking necessary for the expression of informed opinions, while downplaying any threat that this scholarship may present.

Gergen (1989, p. 74) observed that 'one may justifiably make a claim to voice on the grounds of possessing privileged [ ] experience'. David invokes this warranting strategy when he uses various powerful rhetorical devices to construct an emotive testimony of his personal involvement in the arguments that he will advance, saying:

I have a very personal stake in this material. I came out of a church which taught me that God does not love gay and lesbian people – that God condemns us out of hand and it was a very conservative church in the United States. I was married. I have three children. When my wife and I separated the minister who succeeded me at that church used the scriptures to take my children away. I mean to take their minds away convincing them that I was going to go to hell because I'm gay and I haven't seen two of my three children in twelve years and I have a very personal stake in what the Bible says.

The deeply personal emphasis within this extract acts as a counterbalance to any connotations of objectivity that the emphasis on scholarship may have created.

This extract sees David's first explicit statement of his sexual identity which may be viewed as another convention of warrant. He establishes warrant for his deconstruction of the traditional Christian discourse on homosexuality and for the need to offer an alternative discourse because he, as a gay Christian, has suffered personally and grievously at the hands of those who wield the traditional discourse. Furthermore, David's disclosure of his sexual identity positions himself alongside his audience, most of whom had earlier presented themselves as gay or lesbian. This positioning is achieved through the statement: 'I came out of a church which taught me that God does not love gay and lesbian people – that God condemns us out of hand.' The clause 'that God condemns us out of hand' restates and emphasises the point made in the clause 'that God does not love gay and lesbian people'. However, its more important function is that, in replacing 'gay and lesbian people' with 'us', David explicitly presents himself as gay and constructs a commonality of oppression between himself and his audience. The workshop participants are thereby incorporated into his personal testimony of having been oppressed by the traditional discourse, which imparts legitimacy to the need to rework it, not just for David's sake but for the sake of all present.

This analysis of a transcript of a single workshop shows how David established legitimacy or warrant for his reinterpretation of the traditional Christian discourse on homosexuality through employing certain warranting strategies. However, in this process of reinterpretation, other warranting strategies may be used in other contexts and may draw upon other linguistic resources. Hence the next step in the research would be to obtain data from other sources, such as sermons provided at MCC services where reinterpretation is being transacted (e.g. at Gay Pride services), and before other audiences. After that, the research might move beyond the MCC context and obtain data on reinterpretation endeavours in other Christian denominations and other religious traditions. Thus an increasingly detailed picture can be developed of the warranting strategies employed in challenging and reinterpreting traditional Christian discourse on homosexuality across religious contexts. The researcher *might* find that, wherever they turn, the same strategies can be discerned and so he or she may decide to halt data collection/generation. Remember what we said in section 20.3: the main consideration in sampling within discourse analysis is to gather enough text to discern the variety of discursive forms that are commonly used when speaking or writing about the research topic.

20.5.2 Female dependence and passivity in a discourse of romantic love

Earlier we noted that any spoken or written material can be conceptualised as text and subjected to discourse analysis. This includes song lyrics too, although we lose the rhythms by which the lyrics are delivered unless we use a detailed, technical form of transcription. To illustrate the concerns of Foucauldian discourse analysis, we shall briefly examine the chorus and one verse from the song that won the 2010 Eurovision Song Contest for Germany ('Satellite', sung by Lena and written by Julie Frost and John Gordon). The lyrics have been transcribed in a basic way below:

> Love oh love I gotta tell you how I feel about you
> Cause I oh I can't go a minute without your love
> Like a satellite I'm in an orbit all the way around you
> And I would fall out into the night
> Can't go a minute without your love [ ]
> Where you go I'll follow
> You set the pace we'll take it fast or slow
> I'll follow in your wake oh oh oh
> You got me you got me
> A force more powerful than gravity
> It's physics there's no escape.

Willig (2008) specifies six stages in Foucauldian discourse analysis. The first involves considering the ways in which discursive objects are constructed. In the text above, we might focus on the construction of the relationship between the female singer and (given that love songs are almost invariably based on assumed heterosexuality) the male to whom the song is addressed. Normally an analyst would highlight all explicit and implicit references to the object but in this case the whole text is relevant.

The second stage involves locating the various constructions of the object within wider discourses; the third stage considers the action orientation of the text (i.e. its functions); and the fourth stage is concerned with positioning. These three stages will be engaged with together.

The relationship between the singer and the object of the song is located within a discourse of romantic love, with some standard features of this discourse evident in the text. We see talk of overwhelmingly intense impulses and feelings ('I gotta tell you how I feel about you/Cause I oh I can't go a minute without your love') but also a sustained positioning of the singer in a wholly dependent and self-minimising relationship with the song's object. Consider the central simile: 'Like a satellite I'm in an orbit all the way around you'. The female singer is like a 'satellite' orbiting – as satellites do – around a larger, more significant body upon which the satellite is gravitationally dependent: without him, she would 'fall out into the night'. This wholly secondary, dependent position is emphasised in 'Where you go I'll follow/You set the pace we'll take it fast or slow/I'll follow in your wake oh oh oh', with the singer positioning herself as entirely passive in determining their route (perhaps through life) and pace of progress. It could even be argued that this passivity is eroticised, through the gasping 'oh oh oh'. The singer constructs herself as a possession of the song's object ('You got me you got me') and disavows any possibility of being held responsible for this by constructing the dependence in terms of a law of nature ('A force more powerful than gravity/It's physics there's no escape'). So the text is located within a wider discourse of romantic love but it also draws upon a related discourse of highly traditional gender relations involving women's dependence on and passivity in relation to men.

The fifth stage of Foucauldian discourse analysis is concerned with how discursive constructions and subject positions open up or close down possibilities for action – a distinctively Foucauldian discourse analytic concern. The sixth stage considers how taking up the subject positions in the text might shape subjective experience (thinking and feeling). However, a thorough social constructionist perspective views 'thinking' and 'feeling' as ideas generated within cultures to mediate people's dealings with each other and to enable them to engage in social life. Some discourse analysts would therefore contest the premises of this analytic stage.

Considering the data in light of these stages, here the text's context of production (or presentation) is noteworthy. This account of a woman's passivity and dependence was presented before an enormous audience across Europe and beyond in 2010 and, partially through a public vote across the continent, easily won a contest which featured 24 other songs that night. We might wonder about the acceptance of this account of gender relations that may be signalled by this emphatic win, and about the role that the song might play in culturally reinforcing this account with its normalisation of a position of female passive dependence in relations with male partners. In this, we might engage with the substantial literature which considers the negative implications of such gendered constructions for women's lives. Then we might extend the analysis by considering the lyrics of the other songs (in English) at the 2010 Eurovision Song Contest in terms of the versions of gender relations in intimate heterosexual relationships that they work up (e.g. the Albanian entry was entitled 'It's All About You'). Through invoking other research, we might consider whether the discursive patterns are specific to this context or whether they represent an instance of broader cultural and cross-cultural constructions of gender relations.

20.6 EVALUATING THE QUALITY OF DISCOURSE ANALYTIC WORK

Having engaged with two examples of discourse analysis, you may be wondering whether analysts 'put words into the mouths' of those whose talk or writing (or, in the case above, singing) is being analysed. It may seem as if we are unnecessarily complicating apparently straightforward speech acts. Yet, language use may have consequences that the speaker did not intend. For example, in their analysis of talk about community care policies, Potter and Collie (1989) pointed out how the notion of 'community care' invokes a reassuring community discourse, centred around images of neighbourliness, close ties and social support. This poses problems for those who wish to criticise community care, because, in naming it, they end up invoking these positive associations and thereby undermining their arguments. As people may not be aware that their language creates such effects, the method that is sometimes advocated for evaluating qualitative analyses, which involves asking those who produced the data to comment on the analyses, is inappropriate for discourse analysis. In relation to our analyses here, David and the writers of 'Satellite' might protest 'but I never meant that', yet this does not invalidate the analyses. The analyst elaborates the perhaps unintended consequences of the language that was used, tracing the ripples that particular constructions create in the pool of social meaning into which they are tossed.

This does not mean that analysts are free to put forward whatever interpretations they want: they have to be mindful of whether their interpretations satisfy criteria for a 'good analysis'. There has been some debate about what those criteria might be for discourse analysis and for qualitative research more generally. Discussions about the evaluation of psychological research generally focus on success in hypothesis testing and concerns about reliability and validity. It is inappropriate to evaluate discourse analytic work within such a framework because discourse analysis is located outside this tradition. Criteria such as reliability and validity are based on the assumption of 'scientific objectivity', which in turn assumes that researcher and researched are independent of each other. With discourse analysis, this cannot be the case. Analysts who demonstrate the socially constructed nature of other people's talk and writing cannot make an exception for their own talk and writing. Like the person whose language use they are analysing, analysts construct a purposeful account of their texts, drawing upon their available linguistic resources and ideological frameworks. In the analyses offered in this chapter, factors such as my training as a social psychologist and a psychologist of religion, my familiarity with existing work relevant to the research topics and my political outlooks all influenced the ideological framework which I brought to bear on the analyses – my 'speaking position'. Acknowledging this and reflecting upon it is termed **reflexivity**. It should not be seen as undermining the analysis because no one can adopt a perspectiveless, 'objective' stance to the world. Instead, it should be seen as part of a process of making research more accountable, more transparent and easier to evaluate.

This reflexivity bridges the chasm that more traditional research approaches create between researcher and researched, and makes it impossible to assess an analysis of discourse using traditional evaluative criteria. Yardley (2000) suggested four alternative criteria for the evaluation of qualitative research, namely sensitivity to context, commitment and rigour, transparency and coherence, and impact and importance. With some modifications and caveats, these criteria can assist in the evaluation of discourse analytic work. However, the method of reporting discourse analytic studies potentially provides the most useful means of evaluating them. Alongside interpretations, the analyst should try to present as much of the relevant text as possible, demonstrating how analytic conclusions were reached with reference to the text. Readers can then judge for themselves whether the interpretations are credible. They can offer alternative readings of the text so that, through debate, coherent and persuasive interpretations can be achieved.

20.7 POSSIBLE LIMITATIONS OF DISCOURSE ANALYSIS

Since it was formally introduced to social psychology, discourse analysis has made tremendous strides in terms of its theoretical and conceptual development and its influence on the discipline – and not only on social psychology. Discourse analytic work has also appeared in British journals in health psychology, counselling psychology and developmental psychology among others. However, it is not without its potential limitations and pitfalls.

One pitfall sometimes seen in the work of novice discourse analysts is the tendency to reify discourse, that is, to treat it as if it were a sort of 'thing'. It is easy to get the impression that discourses are somehow embedded in the text and that the analyst plays the role of the linguistic archaeologist, simply chipping away the surrounding linguistic material to excavate and reveal the discourses (and, in the case of interview data, often ignoring their role as interviewer in constructing the data). As Parker and Burman (1993) noted, this reifying tendency leads to discourses being represented as static and unchanging. To counteract this, they urge discourse analysts to study the fluctuations and transformations of discourses. Furthermore, the archaeological model of discourse analysis is inappropriate because any discourse analysis involves interpretation by the analyst and is constructed from the analyst's reading of the text. As has already been noted, this means that a discourse analytic report can itself be seen as a text which attempts to construct a particular version of social reality, and which can itself be subjected to discourse analysis.

One long-standing technical problem within discourse analysis is the difficulty it has had in dealing effectively with types of data that are not spoken or written. While photos and other visual images can be treated as text and examined, it is more difficult to incorporate gestures, facial expressions and analogous non-verbal data (i.e. data generated through 'naturalistic' observation or video recording – see Chapter 14) in a way that gives these data equivalent status to verbal data. For example, Hegarty (2007) examined social action that cannot be meaningfully engaged by an approach that focuses exclusively on or privileges language. As an example, he pointed to 'cruising' behaviour, that is, the non-verbal assessment and communication of sexual availability and desire between men, conducted through looking and moving within particular contexts. Behaviours in which people seem to be deliberately avoiding verbal forms of communication or where verbal communication is very much a secondary concern present challenges for a research approach such as discourse analysis, even though these behaviours may be the medium for a process of social construction.

A fundamental concern that has been expressed about discourse analysis from its early days is that it is far removed from 'real-life' issues and threatens psychologists' aspirations to influence practices and policies outside the research domain (Abraham & Hampson, 1996). If we accept that '[l]anguage (organised into *discourses*) [ ] has an immense power to shape the way that people [ ] experience and behave in the world' (Burman & Parker, 1993b, p. 1, original emphasis), discourse analysis *does* have considerable practical potential. Willig (1999) produced an edited volume entitled *Applied Discourse Analysis* which demonstrated how discourse analysis can inform social and psychological interventions on issues such as smoking, sex education and psychiatric medication. Since then, others have developed this case for the practical value of the insights produced by discourse analysis (e.g. see Hepburn & Wiggins, 2007) and have routinely oriented to the implications of discourse analytic work for practice in diverse domains (for example, see Hepburn, 2006, on how an analysis of calls to a child protection helpline was found useful by call takers).

20.8 **CONCLUSION**

This chapter has outlined the principles and practicalities of discourse analysis, illustrating the analytic process through engagements with brief excerpts of data and offering some critical reflections upon the approach. Although it is hoped that some indication has been provided of how discourse analysis might be undertaken, it is also hoped that readers have gained a clear sense of how discourse analysis cannot be treated merely as an analytic technique. Researchers who choose to use discourse analysis also choose to employ a range of assumptions about the social world (although the precise nature of these assumptions will vary according to the type of discourse analysis used) and, in exclusively discourse analytic studies, should ensure that their research questions, analyses and discussion of the implications of the research fit with these assumptions.

In conclusion, it is fair to say that, while discourse analysis is perhaps not a research approach for the faint-hearted, nonetheless it can prove very rewarding for those who can work with text in a sustained, detailed way and who relish the prospect of critically interrogating the 'taken-for-granted' of social life. Moreover, as Abell and Walton (2010) have indicated, even those who do not sign up to the whole discourse analytic enterprise can take its primary insights about language as a site where psychological life is produced and played out, and can profitably integrate these into other forms of psychological research.

20.9 **EXERCISES**

The following are exercises that invite you to try some discourse analysis so that you can learn by doing, which is really the only way of developing competence in the approach.

1 In section 20.6, we recommended that the analyst should demonstrate how analytic conclusions were reached with reference to the text in order to allow readers to judge whether the interpretations are credible. In section 20.5, did you find any interpretations of the data difficult to accept? If so, what alternative, more persuasive interpretations would you wish to offer?

2 In section 20.7, we noted that a discourse analytic report can itself be seen as a text and subjected to discourse analysis. Look at my analysis of David's language use in 20.5.1 or my analysis of the lyrics of 'Satellite' in 20.5.2 and consider how I legitimate my analyses through warranting strategies. Remember that you should look at how my use of language in my writing builds up credibility for my analyses rather than speculating about my motives.

3 In section 20.7, we observed that discourse analysis can have difficulty in dealing with data that are not verbalised or written. It is even possible that facial expressions, gestures and postures could challenge an analysis based solely on verbal data. See if you can find footage of Lena performing 'Satellite' in the 2010 Eurovision Song Contest (on youtube. com) and consider her non-verbal behaviours during that performance. In light of these, would you want to question any of the analyses offered in section 20.5.2? If so, what alternative interpretations would you wish to put forward – and why?

4 What subject positions do I take up in my analyses as I relate to my readers (see 20.2 on positioning)? What functions do these subject positions seem to be performing in the text?

20.10 **DISCUSSION QUESTIONS**

1 In light of your reading about other qualitative approaches to psychological research, what do you think are the main ways in which discourse analysis overlaps with them and differs from them?

2 Think of research questions for which discourse analysis would not be appropriate. What is it about these questions that makes them unsuitable for exploration through discourse analysis?

3   What makes for a good interpretation of data within discourse analysis? What makes for a bad interpretation?

4   What might be the main obstacles to using discourse analysis alongside other research approaches to explore a particular research question?

5   If you were using discourse analysis in a dissertation, how would you convince classmates who used other approaches that your research was as 'useful' as theirs?

20.11 FURTHER READING

Potter and Wetherell's (1987) very readable and broad-ranging seminal text remains the obvious starting point for anyone interested in discourse analysis. Potter (1996) offers a clear and comprehensive account of the history, epistemology and practicalities of discursive approaches, with many clarifying examples. For an outline of the principles of what has become known as Foucauldian discourse analysis, see Parker (1992). The volumes by Wetherell et al. (2001a, 2001b) and Potter (2007a, 2007b, 2007c) are invaluable to novice analysts as they focus on the process of analysis within different traditions and present a wide range of examples. Willig (1999) provides examples of how different versions of discourse analysis can inform interventions on a range of practical issues.

21

Content Analysis

Glynis M. Breakwell

CONTENTS

AIMS OF THIS CHAPTER

This chapter introduces the basic principles of content analysis as a research tool. It describes the decisions that have to be taken by a researcher when employing content analysis. It explains the qualitative and quantitative applications of content analysis and indicates how the method underpins the techniques, such as interviewing and narrative analysis, described elsewhere in this book. It illustrates some ways in which the results of a content analysis may be reported and depicted graphically.

KEY TERMS

content category   sociogram
data   timeline
inter-rater reliability

21.1 **INTRODUCTION**

Content analysis is the systematic observation, recording and interpretation of information and, as such, can be seen to date back to the work of the Greek philosophers concerned with the analysis of rhetoric (Brickhouse & Smith, 1995). Conceptually, content analysis is probably the most common technique used in research. It is the basic building block of other techniques. All measurement, at some level, is content analysis. At its simplest, content analysis is the systematic description of phenomena. The phenomenon could be anything. It could be a single material object, such as an article of clothing or a motorised vehicle. It could be a complex array of such objects, such as a wardrobe full of clothes or an overflowing car park. It could be one social event or a complex set of social processes, such as, on the one hand, an email exchange or, on the other, the election of the US President.

Content analysis can be applied to data, information or evidence from a broad range of contexts including: participant and non-participant observation, interviews, archives and documents within non-experimental, experimental and quasi-experimental designs. In some of the earlier chapters in this volume there has been reference to the use of content analysis (e.g. in the chapters on interviewing and narrative and diary methods). Some of the methods described in earlier chapters (e.g. discourse analysis and narrative analysis) are essentially variants of content analysis and the more you understand about content analysis, the more you can hope to become expert in these other methods.

In many respects, content analysis is the medium that links qualitative and quantitative approaches to data. All data analysis relies on the structured re-representation of the information collected. The qualitative approach does not seek to use numbers to represent that information. The quantitative approach will certainly use numbers and will often seek to determine whether the information can test a hypothesis via numerical or statistical comparisons. However, in both approaches, there is the imposition of order upon the information so that conclusions can be drawn. This imposition of order is essentially content analysis.

Content analysis is used by psychologists to examine behaviour, thoughts and feelings of both individuals and of groups. However, the generic term 'content analysis' is used to signify a vast range of actual data organising techniques. Typically, the techniques entail classifying data (the term 'data' is used in this chapter as shorthand for any information or evidence collected) into categories or themes.

The term content analysis was probably first used in modern social sciences by researchers in the 1930s who were trying to analyse the characteristics of messages in the mass media in order to understand how processes of persuasion and propaganda worked (Berelson, 1947; Berelson & Lazarsfeld, 1948). Berelson (1984) summarised the development of content analysis methods in communications research and articulated the value of breaking down a message into its defined constituent elements and quantifying the frequency with which each appeared. This represented a move to make the analysis of messages more systematic and subject to verification by other researchers. Work in this area of communications research opened up a new approach to the analysis of complex, naturally occurring data that researchers in many other areas adopted. Content analysis, using the examination of the occurrence of clearly defined elements (or categories) within the phenomenon to be studied, became a generic tool used by scholars across all disciplines.

There are now debates in the literature (e.g. Krippendorf, 2004; Neuendorf, 2002) about whether it is right to use 'content analysis' as if it encompasses qualitative approaches like rhetorical analysis, narrative analysis, discourse analysis or normative analysis. Some people like to talk about content analysis as exclusively referring to quantitative approaches to data. However, trying to impose a strict segregation between quantitative content analysis and the qualitative analysis of content is probably destined to failure. This is suggested by the fact that in January 2011 a Google search for the phrase 'qualitative content analysis' yielded 7,790,000 references and the phrase 'quantitative content analysis' yielded 8,950,000. While learning about the techniques of content analysis, it is probably worth keeping an open mind about its categorisation as qualitative or quantitative. Researchers do use the method in many ways.

21.2 STAGES IN USING CONTENT ANALYSIS

The essential steps in conducting a content analysis are:

1   Specify your research question – what do you want to know? Be as clear and comprehensive as you can in stating your question.
2   Specify the phenomena you wish to describe. This will entail clarity about who will give you data; the type of data, and the method of data collection. You may determine at this stage how you will be classifying the data during analysis. This requires you to determine the categories or themes you will use to describe the data. This would then shape the way data were collected. Pre-determining the content category system for analysis can streamline data collection in some instances, allowing you to focus only on the information relevant to the category system. Alternatively, you can decide to construct the category system after collecting the data. If you want to be open to all of the possible ways of thinking about the phenomena under investigation, this may be the best option.
3   Collect the data.
4   If you have not done so before collecting the data, specify the classification system that you will use to analyse the data.
5   Apply the classification system to the data.

6 Check the reliability of your analysis.

7 Describe your findings fully using qualitative and/or quantitative techniques for data exploration.

8 Relate your findings to your original research question and examine their implications for theory and/or practice.

9 Report your conclusions, providing a thorough description of your data collection and analysis.

Chapter 1 summarised how to formulate a research question and how to specify the phenomena that you wish to describe. That set of issues will not be addressed again here. Each of the other steps in conducting a content analysis are considered in the next sections of this chapter.

21.3 WHAT DETERMINES THE CLASSIFICATION USED?

Content analysis requires that the data are essentially grouped into meaningful units. This begs the question: what dictates what will be considered 'meaningful'? There are four main determinants of the categories or themes that are used in content analysis:

- *The nature of the question that the research is set up to address.* The category system must be driven by the research question that you are addressing. Moreover, you have to be able to justify your choice. It is not unknown for a content analysis to be robust in every sense except that it is irrelevant to the question originally posed for the research.

- *The data or the context in which it is collected.* The category system can be generated after the data are collected and after the full scope of the data is understood. The categories (or themes) may be said to emerge from the data or sometimes from the context in which the data were collected. Contextualising the content categories can make the analysis much more relevant to research participants and may make it more pertinent to the research question. However, this is not an easy option. It is sometimes difficult to justify post hoc decisions about the categories that are used. This issue is addressed further later in this chapter.

- *The past literature on the research question.* If there is existing literature on the research topic and it has used content analysis, it is valuable to examine what classification systems have been used in the past. There are two good reasons to do this assiduously. First, if you use systems that have been used previously, it will be possible for your work to contribute directly to a body of knowledge in a cumulative fashion and may mean that it has a broader, more attentive audience.

Second, if you review previous systems and find them weak or inadequate, you can improve them and further contribute to the growth of knowledge. Adopting a content analysis method is no excuse for ignoring the research that has been done in your area previously.

- *The theoretical framework that the researcher employs.* Theories limit what data will be treated as relevant or interesting. So, theory will initially shape the data that is collected. But additionally, the theory chosen will constrain the way you need to classify the data because, unless you make the data meaningful in particular ways, will not be able you to test or evidence the theoretical arguments with which you start your research. This is a form of discipline. It requires rigorous interpretation of the theory and also careful examination of the data. Some researchers would argue that theory-driven data collection and analysis is too limiting and obscures alternatives. This is an issue that is considered further later in this chapter.

Not all of these determinants will play a part in every content analysis. For instance, some researchers do not wish to have theory driving the way they structure their evidence. Others wish to have *a priori* category systems established before they collect their data.

The category itself can be very simple and can also be very complex. So, for instance, a content analysis of a conversation between two people might focus upon how often each participant smiles. The simplest category system might entail treating every facial movement that the researcher considered to be a smile as a single unit. A more elaborate category system might use facial recognition software to differentiate various degrees of smiling (ranging from the fleeting tiny movement of the lips, without changes in the skin around the eyes to a full, mouth-open, teeth-revealing, eyes-wrinkled grin). Another category system might differentiate types of smile in terms of the apparent function of the expression within the conversation (e.g. flirtatious, coy, nervous and humourous) as interpreted by the researcher or as explained by those interacting. So, the category system moves from a single concept (the smile) to a differentiated concept (several types of smile) but the complexity does not need to stop there. The classification may not be just concerned with whether a type of smile occurs and how frequently it occurs, it may also be concerned with the sequence in which different types of smile occur (either in the interaction between people or over time in the repertoire of an individual).

Often content analysis operates simultaneously at several levels. It will describe the existence of the simple low level category but it will also be set up to identify co-occurrence of categories that are then said to comprise super-ordinate categories. In the case of the smile sequences, the nervous smile followed by the coy smile followed by the flirtatious smile might be subsequently treated as a unit of analysis in its own right (and be given its own label – for instance, the attraction smile sequence).

Since a content analysis can operate at so many levels – and sometimes the researcher wants to use each level – the forms of reporting the results are very diverse. Some approaches to reporting content analysis are described below.

If you are conducting a quantitative content analysis you would need first to define the categories (at all levels) that you wish to use. You would then need to count the instances of those categories that occur in the material that you collect. Box 21.2 offers an illustration of research that does this. The website associated with this book provides material that you can use to practise how to define a category and how to apply it when counting occurrences.

21.4 HOW DO WE KNOW THAT THE CONTENT ANALYSIS IS RELIABLE?

Establishing that a content analysis is reliable is important. It is not sufficient for the researcher simply to claim that certain content categories were present in the data. Normally, the researcher will ask an independent person to go through the data (or some subsection of the data) and re-run the content analysis. The person will need to understand the category system fully (so may need to be trained and their understanding tested if the category system is complex). This person re-runs the content analysis without having any knowledge of the results gained by the researcher (i.e. they are 'blind' to the researcher's conclusions). The results from the researcher and the independent person are then compared. Typically, this is done by examining the statistical correlation of the two sets of classifications and producing an inter-rater reliability measure (the inter-rater reliability expressed either as a correlation coefficient or percentage agreement).

If the researcher's and the independent content analyses are concordant the results may be reported. If there are substantial differences between them (e.g. a correlation of less than 0.8) then the researcher must identify why the disparities exist. For instance, there may be some categories that are ill-defined. Alternatively, there may be some assumptions that the researcher is making that are not evident in the raw data. Sometimes the data are then reviewed by both persons together and an agreed categorisation achieved. Sometimes the categories require redefinition and refinement in order to make them capable of unambiguous and consensual application to the data. It is essential that the researcher ensures that the content analysis that is ultimately reported is reliable.

The greater the complexity of the category system, the greater will be the difficulty in training the independent analyst. Categories can be wide-ranging or very narrow. The nature of the category is not problematic as long as it is clear what is and what is not eligible for inclusion. Clarity in specifying the category types and system is vital. Clear definitions of what constitutes an example of the category must be given. So, for example, if your proposition in your research was that emails sent to friends contain greater emotionality, how would you go about designing a content analysis study to examine this? You might start by deciding what constitutes 'emotionality'. Try it for yourself. What exemplars would you allow to count as expressions of emotionality? Would you use as the unit of analysis single words, strings of words or perhaps the whole message? Would you be concerned with the topic of the message or would you focus upon the way the topic was written about? Would you only take naturally occurring emails or would you set up an experiment to elicit material? The answers you give to each of these questions will interact with whether you are locating the content analysis in a non-intrusive field study (e.g. using archive data) or in a quasi-experimental or experimental design. The important point to remember is that you have to take the decisions in a conscious manner. What's more, you should have a good rationale for answering them in the way that you do. So, the key is to be rigorous in your definition of your categories and to be able to defend your choice of category.

Being clear in your own mind about the definition of the categories is not enough. You must be able to communicate the definition to other researchers. Your report of your research must make it possible for others to replicate the content analysis if given the raw data. Whether you later subject the content system to a quantitative analysis or not, you still need this rigour in explicit definition of the categories. Even where the categories emerge from the data, it is necessary subsequently to provide clear descriptions of their content. It is also necessary to be able to evidence with reference to the data that these are the categories that actually did emerge. It is always valuable to think about how you would rebut a sceptic's rejection of your analysis and to include in your report the facts that would undermine that rejection.

21.5 AUTOMATED CONTENT ANALYSES

There are many software packages that are designed to allow textual data to be content analysed. They include NVivo, ATLAS.ti, CAQDAS Comparison,CDC EZ-Text, Code-a-Text, Ethnograph, HyperResearch, MAXqda and QDAMiner. There are many pattern recognition software packages that will analyse visual displays. These include Qualifers, Qualrus and Transana. Details of these software packages are readily available from the web, where properties of updated versions will be described.

All rely on category definition. Some smart systems will develop the category system for you, for instance, on the basis of frequency of occurrence of elements in the material. You do not need to tell the package what to look for; it can decide itself by applying an algorithm that basically will ask it to pick out elements that appear in the data according to certain criteria. The criteria can focus upon anything – frequency, unusualness, co-occurrence, and so on. This is a way of exploring data for emergent categories – ones that were not expected or predicted at the start of the investigation.

These can be very valuable tools – as long as you understand what they are actually doing. Mindless application of the software is not advisable. Mehl *et al.* (2010) provide a good review of automated text analysis (ATA). ATA has been defined as a set of methods that automatically extract statistically manipulable information about the presence, intensity or frequency of thematic or stylistic characteristics of textual material. It is particularly useful for online behavioural research.

Automated content analysis opens the way for some very large-scale studies. One example of such a study comes from the field of the psychology of personality. Goldberg (1993) proposed the 'lexical hypothesis', which states that the most meaningful personality attributes tend to become encoded in language as single word descriptors. In order to determine what they are, he examined dictionaries to identify all those adjectives that refer to personality. His analysis revealed five clusters of adjectives (usually now referred to as the 'Big Five'): extraversion, agreeableness, conscientiousness, emotional stability and openness to experience (sometimes called intellect or imagination). Goldberg, having done his content analysis of the dictionaries to extract all of the relevant adjectives, determined the five categories through the application of factor analysis. The interesting thing about this study is that the method is simple (though on a grand scale) but the theoretical question is very complex and very important. It is also interesting that much subsequent research has supported the Big Five proposition – though it has been elaborated and refined.

21.6 **CONTEXTUALISING THE CONTENT ANALYSIS**

Virtually the opposite of an automated content analysis is an informed content analysis. Such a content analysis can be achieved where the material collected is handed over for analysis to individuals chosen because they have some privileged knowledge of the issue being researched. For instance, it could be the participants from whom the material has been collected or it could be independent experts on the topic of the research. Sometimes this approach is adopted so that the researcher may gain new insights into the meaning of the data. Often it is used without any *a priori* attempt by the researcher to impose a category system upon the analysts. The category system that then emerges is seen to be contextualised, emanating as it does from the people closest to the data.

Using research participants to analyse their own data is fraught with problems. However, if it is used in a way that encourages reflection and perhaps allows the researcher to get a better understanding of what the participants actually meant, it can be beneficial. You will see that as soon as the method is extended in this way, it becomes similar to others that use classification by participants as the major mechanism for deriving data. Sorting or twinned comparison techniques are classic examples of classification data elicitation methods. Asking the research participant to engage in the classification of data they have previously generated is not unusual and occurs regularly in other methods. In content analysis, it affords researchers the extra value of potentially validating their own interpretation of the data.

21.7 FORMS OF DATA REPRESENTATION

Content analysis lends itself to many forms of data representation, ranging from the very simple (even for very complex category systems) to the very elaborate (even for quite simple category systems).

The format of data representation that should be used will depend on the research question and the purpose of the data presentation. It is important to remember when choosing a method of data representation that the approach used to analyse the data (e.g. a statistical test) may not be the best way to explain the data to an independent audience – this may require something more graphic or illustrative. So when thinking about content data analysis it may be useful to consider a 2 × 2 cross-tab: description versus analysis and qualitative versus quantitative methodological approaches. It is not rare for researchers who adopt a largely qualitative approach to use some quantification in their representation of their data. At the lowest level, this might entail reporting how many instances of a particular theme or category appeared in the information set collected. This is sometimes used as a basis for supporting a contention that the theme or category is of importance. Similarly, it is not rare for researchers from a quantitative approach to apply sophisticated statistical models to their data in order to calculate the statistical significance of some finding, but then choose to describe the finding in a non-numerical way – typically using diagrammatic representations. How qualitative and quantitative approaches are used in tandem will depend on the purpose of the researcher. Segregation or separation of the qualitative and the quantitative is no simple matter in the real world of research.

A qualitative content analysis typically entails reproducing the information collected selectively with commentary and/or interpretation. Normally, some count of the incidence of themes/categories is used. This may then be subjected to statistical analysis but often it is not. A quantitative content analysis will be just as selective but it will seek to impose systematic counts of the incidence of categories/themes. It will usually subject these counts to a statistical analysis.

Box 21.1 gives an example of a qualitative content analysis. Box 21.2 has an example of a study that used content analysis allied to a quantitative approach.

Box 21.1 An example of content analysis with qualitative analysis

Breakwell and Barnett (2001) interviewed senior editors and journalists working at major newspapers and asked them what factors they took into account when deciding whether and how they would report about a major hazard (e.g. a health risk, a terrorist threat or an environmental scare). Breakwell and Barnett then catalogued the range of considerations these press representatives mentioned. These included:

- whether the story would sell papers;
- the novelty of the story;
- whether they had an exclusive on the story;
- the story's relationship to their paper's editorial policies/stance;
- the entertainment value of the story;
- the quality of the information available about the story;
- the level of involvement of celebrities or significant societal figures;
- the extent to which the story would arouse strong emotions (e.g. shock, horror, fear or sympathy);
- what links the story had to other stories currently running or previously printed;
- their own reputation with regard to issues associated with the story;

Breakwell and Barnett showed that these representatives of the media applied a complex decision tree when determining how they would present a story – shaping their response to the story around a number of parameters. The researchers did not attempt to quantify their data. This was a preliminary investigation in an area where there had been little prior psychological research. The qualitative analysis provided a basic framework that was amenable to further, perhaps more quantitative analysis subsequently.

It should be said that the vast majority of content analysis studies involve some sort of quantification – if only to say that one category occurred more frequently than another or occurred more in association with one rather than another. Finding a 'pure' qualitative content analysis study is consequently not easy. However, Russell and Russell (2009) conducted a very elegant predominantly qualitative content analysis. They looked at alcohol messages in prime-time television series. They were interested in them because television programmes containing messages about alcohol are a source of information about drinking for a large number of people. They conducted content analysis of an eight-week sample of 18 prime-time TV programmes. Alcohol messages were coded based on modalities of presentation, level of plot connection and valence (positivity–negativity). Their analysis reveals that mixed messages about alcohol often coexist but the ways in which they are presented differ: whereas negative messages are tied to the plot and communicated verbally, positive messages are associated with subtle visual portrayals.

Box 21.2 An example of content analysis with a quantitative analysis

A study by Rebecca Sixsmith and Adrian Furnham (2010) explored the structure of advertisements about food that were either aimed at children or at adults. They expected to find systematic differences between the advertisements targeted at these two different consumer groups. They recorded 87 advertisements sampled from 45 hours of British television. They considered 35 to be child-focused and 52 to be adult-focused. Child-focused advertisements were mainly for convenience foods and snacks. They then examined whether each advertisement contained certain categories of information or image.

They coded each advert for the presence or absence of 14 categories of content. They confirmed the accuracy of their coding by having an independent person rate a subset (20) of the adverts for the content categories in which they were interested. They found a mean agreement rate of 96.79 per cent, suggesting they were not idiosyncratic in their assessments of the advertisements.

They then conducted separate chi^2 analyses to test the statistical significance of the difference between the child-focused and adult-focused advertisements in the presence/absence of each content category.

The advertisements that they had labelled 'child-focused' contained more claims of health benefits and scientific information; were shot in 'leisure' settings; with male characters; had cartoons; and were often fantasy-based. In contrast, significantly more 'adult-focused' advertisements contained price/value information; were shot in 'shop' settings; with female characters; and featured celebrities.

The report of this study in *Health Promotion International* is very clear and a good example of how to describe this sort of content analysis study. It would be useful to read it. Like all studies, it might be open to criticism. For instance, given the subjects of the advertisements were different for children from those for adults (i.e. more snacks and convenience foods) the difference in the content of the adverts for children could have been driven more by the nature of the thing that was being sold than by the purchase target group. Also, the initial categorisation into 'child-focused' and 'adult-focused' on an *a priori* basis might be questioned since there is no explanation given in the report. There might also be some query about the use of so many chi^2 comparisons (without some moderators to compensate for the possibility of discovering statistically significant results as an artefact of the number of tests conducted). A multivariate statistical approach might have been more appropriate. This critique is presented in order to encourage you to recognise that any study should be examined critically. This is the best way of determining exactly what you can truly conclude from a piece of research.

The web page for this chapter gives some examples from the qualitative and quantitative traditions.

Content analysis data are amenable to many forms of representation. Of course, there is the simple textual representation. There are established coding systems that predetermine the form of representation. The classic Thematic Apperception Test (TAT) is a good exemplar. The TAT was designed to allow the analyst to determine the emotional preoccupations of the participant and derived from a psychoanalytic tradition of research. The participant is presented with a fixed set of stimuli (static pictures of scenes that have potentially emotional connotations – e.g. a little boy crying) and asked to say what they think is happening in the situation depicted. What they say is coded according to a system that has evolved since and for which there are norms (by socio-demographic and psychological background). The coding system is prescribed and allows comparison of the participant with others of the same and different backgrounds. There are many coding systems that can be used when embarking on a content analysis study. It is always worthwhile checking whether one exists in the area that you want to research before embarking on your data collection. Where such an established coding system exists, there are standard ways of representing the findings – typically this involves describing the profile of the specific instance and reporting how it compares to the norms.

Of course, any category system can be subjected to simple numerical representations and there are statistical representations of varying complexity. Figurative representations are varied and can be very effective. There is an exercise at the end of this chapter that requires you to decide how best to represent a data set.

Since there are many examples of textual and statistical data representation elsewhere in this book, here we will concentrate on the figurative options for content analysis representation. There are three key figurative approaches. Each represents a different component of the content analysis findings; and all can be used with data from a single individual or with data from a number of individuals:

- connections

- scale

- change.

21.7.1 **Connections**

Figure 21.1 presents a schematic representation of the linkages between different elements in a content analysis. It could be a reflection of a qualitative analysis of a

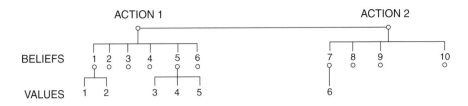

Figure 21.1 Linkages Between Elements in a Content Analysis

set of narratives elicited from a group of people who were asked to explain why they had decided to buy a car with a hybrid electric engine or one with a more common diesel engine. The elements in the category system in the content analysis comprised actions (two), beliefs (ten) and values (six). Action 1 (buying a hybrid) is linked to six beliefs (cars produce too much CO_2, hybrid cars generate less CO_2, hybrids are well-designed, hybrids are a status symbol, hybrids are economical to run and hybrids attract less tax). Two of these beliefs are in turn linked to values. The belief that cars produce too much CO_2 is linked to two values (it is important for pollution to be reduced and it is important to be personally active in improving the environment). Action 2 (buying a diesel engine car) is linked to four beliefs (diesel engines last longer, diesel engines are cost-effective, diesel engines offer greater power, diesel engines are well-proven). Only one of these beliefs is linked to a value. Believing diesel engines last longer is linked to valuing reliability.

The linkages represent co-occurrence. They do not reflect causal relationships. They do not reflect the strength of relationships. This sort of figure is a very elegant way of showing how elements fit together (and sometimes how they do not fit together). The representation in effect echoes what you would produce if you subjected more quantitative data to statistical analyses like hierarchical cluster analysis.

21.7.2 Scale

Figure 21.2 also shows connections but in addition it is designed to reflect the strength or prevalence in the data set of those connections. In this case, the figure represents the way people interact in a social setting (let's say a disco) – the elements are the individuals and the lines linking them reflect whether an individual talks to another, and the thickness of the lines reflects the length of time they spend together during the observation period. Just by briefly examining the figure it is possible to see that one individual interacts with more individuals than others and that two individuals interact with no others. The thickness of the lines shows that there are relatively few interactions that are lengthy. This sort of diagram is commonly used to map the interactions between individuals (and is called a sociogram). However, the same form of representation can be used for other types of content

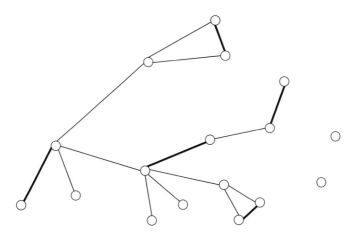

Each node is a person, the lines represent an exchange of some sort during a fixed time period. Notice, some nodes are not connected.

Figure 21.2   Graphical Representation of the strengths and patterns of linkages between elements in a content analysis

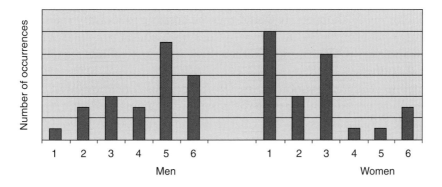

Figure 21.3   Histogram of the frequencies that stressors are mentioned

analysis material. For instance, when depicting an individual's cognitive representation of the origins of a risk, researchers will often use this approach to draw the links between one element and others in the mental model of the risk.

Figure 21.3 is a simpler way of reflecting scale in the content analysis. This is a straightforward histogram. In this example, it is reflecting the number of times men and women in the Army mention six specific stressors (i.e. sources of concern, pressure or distress) during an interview about their experiences on active service. The graph suggests that men and women are perceiving stressors differently. It appears that absolute levels of stressors do not differ but the type of stressor does.

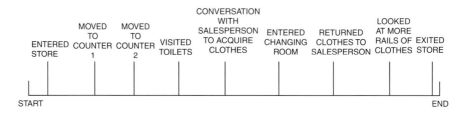

Figure 21.4   Timeline of an Event Sequence

Change

Figure 21.4 introduces an attempt to look at a sequence of events – change over time. In effect it represents a timeline. It depicts the sequence in the occurrence of a set of categories. In this example, the timeline refers to elements in an observational study that used CCTV footage shot in major retail stores to examine the behavioural repertoires of shoplifters. The timeline represents the behaviour of one shopper – who may or may not have been a shoplifter. The research would collect the timelines for many shoppers. It would then be possible to identify individuals who were caught shoplifting and to compare their behavioural timelines with those of innocent shoppers to determine whether there were any telltale signals or precursors for shoplifting.

A timeline sequence cannot be used to infer causal relationships. However, a timeline can be useful in suggesting the possibility that one element causes another. For instance, if A always occurs after B, the notion that A causes B would appear less likely.

Figure 21.5 is more complex. It represents change over time. This example reflects changes in the way experts and the lay public talk about the risk of pandemic influenza over the period of one year. It seeks to represent two dimensions of change simultaneously: an aspect of the meaning of their statements (i.e. the level of fear they express) and an aspect of the complexity of their statements (i.e. the number of constructs they use when referring to pandemic influenza). The figure shows that over time the lay public increase the complexity of their statements whereas the experts do not do so as much. The lay public are initially more fearful, but the figure also shows that both lay public and experts peak in their fearfulness in the middle of the period.

It is good to think about connections, scale and change when deciding how to represent your data. The five types of figures illustrated here are by no means the only ways in which these three dimensions can be represented. Experimenting with diagrammatic and figurative representations of your data can be very helpful in

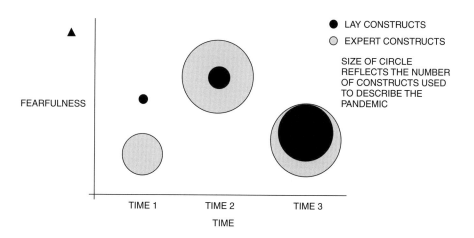

Figure 21.5   Changing Perceptions of Risk over Time

making sense of them. Sometimes you find that drawing the picture reveals things that you had not guessed. It also sometimes suggests that preconceptions you held were inappropriate. [There is an exercise on the web page for this chapter to allow you to practise representing the same data in different ways.]

Diagrams like those in Figures 21.1–21.5 are tools for understanding and describing data but they should not be used as if they allow assertions about statistical significance. They do not allow you to conclude that one pattern or set of relationships is more likely than another. If you want to make assertions about probability, you really do have to translate the data into numerical units (e.g. frequencies or ratings) and then subject them to a statistical test. For instance in Figure 21.3, the comparison of men and women in the Army, could have been accompanied by chi^2 tests of the statistical significance of the difference between the sexes in perception of each of the six stressors. The graphical representation of the data can be a precursor to the choice of a statistical test.

21.8 ETHICAL ISSUES

Like all other methods, content analysis requires that the researcher pays keen attention to the ethical issues that may be raised by the study. There are the habitual ethical concerns about the right of the researcher to gain access to particular data; the right of the research participant to maintain anonymity; and the right of the researcher to disclose findings, in whole or in part. However, in many content analysis studies there is another ethical dimension. The researcher must ensure the validity of the analysis. There must be no misrepresentation of the material, either through inappropriate or selective reproduction of information or through bias in the category selection or definition. At one level this is a matter of methodological rigour and competence but at another it is ethical. It is a matter of the need for scrupulous honesty – explicitly and implicitly.

21.9 CONCLUSION

Content analysis is an invaluable research tool. It is the basis for many other data exploration and representation techniques. When using content analysis the most important task is to determine the category system you will use to reflect your data. This chapter has presented the things that you must consider when you set out to create a category system. You will do well if you have in mind that the categories should be exclusive and exhaustive – that is, the categories should not overlap one another and they should cover all the material that you need to record in order to address your research question. You should also remember that you must be explicit in the definition of your categories. Other researchers must be able to look at your data and understand what you have done and why you have drawn the conclusions that you have.

Content analysis is an enormously flexible approach. Consequently, its results can be reported a wide variety of ways. The use of diagrams to illustrate findings is valuable and is open to imaginative innovations. As always, it is important to be absolutely clear where the boundary between reporting the data and interpreting those data actually lies. Slipping from description to inference without noting the demarcation is to be avoided at all costs.

21.10 EXERCISES

1 Record copies of text messages or emails that you send over a period of a week. Design a content category system that will allow you to examine whether the structure (i.e. emotional tone, complexity, etc.) rather than the substantive content of your texts/mails differs according to whom you are sending them. Remember – define the structural categories so that someone else could replicate your analysis.

2 Find two ways of representing diagrammatically the following information: Jack is observed to walk into a bar, order a glass of orange juice, take the drink to a table and sit down. He reads a newspaper for 10 minutes and then takes out his phone and makes a call. He speaks to someone for 3 minutes and finishes the call. He gets another drink and some peanuts. He talks to the bartender for 4 minutes. Then he returns to his seat. A young woman comes in and sits down with him. He gets

her a drink. Another man and woman come into the bar and join the original pair. They talk for 10 minutes. The women then leave the table to visit the washroom. After one minute, the men start to talk to two other women who have just come into the bar. They begin to laugh together. After 5 minutes, the two original women return from the washroom and the men abruptly cease their exchange with the other women. Note – in choosing the ways to represent this, you should specify how the two representations bring out different aspects of the information.

21.11 DISCUSSION QUESTIONS

1   What are the major problems you encounter when using content analysis?
2   What do you see as the major advantages of using content analysis?
3   Find an example of a published study that uses content analysis in an experimental design and discuss whether the study has any theoretical or methodological limitations.
4   Are there any specific characteristics of research questions that can be best addressed using content analysis?

21.12 FURTHER READING

Krippendorf (2004) provides an introduction to the history of the development and use of content analysis in the social sciences, with special emphasis upon the analysis of texts. Neuendorf (2002) presents the steps in conducting quantitative content analysis. The books explains how quantitative and qualitative content analyses can be differentiated. It argues that qualitative approaches like rhetorical analysis, narrative analysis, discourse analysis and normative analysis, are not actually content analysis, because they do not intrinsically require quantification. Mayring (2000) summarises bundles of techniques for systematic text analysis developed over 20 years in the longitudinal study of the psychosocial consequences of unemployment. Mehl *et al.* (2000) provide an introduction to the application of automatic text analysis (ATA) in online behavioural research. The term ATA is used synonymously with the terms computer content analysis, computer-assisted content analysis, computer-assisted text analysis and computerised text analysis. ATA has been defined as a set of methods that automatically extract statistically manipulable information about the presence, intensity or frequency of thematic or stylistic characteristics of textual material. The chapter focuses on ATA tools that extract quantitative information that can be subjected to statistical analysis. The chapter covers basic information that helps researchers identify how they can use ATA in their online research. It focuses on two ATA tools: Linguistic Inquiry and Word Count. Yurtal and Artut (2000) investigate Turkish children's perception of violence in school as represented through drawings and narratives. To elicit children's perception of violence, the children were asked to draw a picture of a violent incident they had heard, experienced or witnessed. The children mostly drew pictures of violent events among children but there were also pictures of violent incidents perpetrated by teachers against children. This is an example of how a topic which is difficult to research (not least because children might find it difficult to talk about) can be addressed using a very simple content analysis. Many content analyses studies now focus upon the analysis of electronically transmitted messages (not just the traditional TV and film but e-mails, tweets, social media venues, etc.). Fullwood *et al.* (2009) is a good example of the genre and concerns the content of MySpace blogs and whether it differs from the blog style found on sites specifically designed for blogging. A content analysis of MySpace blogs was conducted to investigate trends in purpose, format, and style and to compare these across sex and age categories. Most blogs were written in a positive tone, and the main motivations for blogging appeared to be writing a diary and as an emotional outlet. While there were no significant sex differences, blog purpose and style differed across age groups. Bloggers over 50 were more likely to use the blog as an emotional outlet with a negative tone. Bloggers between 18 and 29 predominantly used a semiformal language style, whereas bloggers over 30 were equally as likely to use a semiformal or a formal style. The results suggest that MySpace blogs are not dissimilar from other forms of blogging.

Part 4

Writing Up Your Research

22

What if Victor Had Used the APA Manual to Write Up His Research?

Daniel B. Wright, Jonathan A. Smith and Glynis M. Breakwell

CONTENTS

22.1 **INTRODUCTION**

You have reached the final chapter! Congratulations and thank you for getting this far. Your journey has taken you through the broad collection of methods that are popular within psychology. This should allow you to transform an interesting research question into a well-executed study and to decipher the data.

Conducting a great study is the first step, but on its own it will not get you an A on your report or get your paper published. You have to be able to communicate your study effectively to your audience. Good scientific writing is different from good novel writing and also different from what a lot of people are taught is *good writing*. Complex literary prose, wrapped around an intricate plot with sub-plots, foreshadowing of intertwined storylines that force the reader to think and to discover the novel, may be appropriate for the novelist (and for novelists with better command of writing than almost all psychologists), but it is not how to write a scientific paper.

Write simply. Write clearly. Do not replace simple words with complex words. A classic example of this is using the word 'demonstrate' when the word 'show' would work just as well. Using the word 'demonstrate' tells the reader that you are trying to use long words because you think that your professor or a reviewer will be impressed that you can press the thesaurus button on your word processer. Sometimes a complex word fits better and may be necessary, but if a simpler word fits just as well, use the simpler word. The graphical equivalent of this is pressing the 3D button on your graphics package. This shows that you want to make data appear more complex than they are. The desire to show off technological gadgetry triumphs over the desire to communicate. The key to good scientific writing is being able to explain complex concepts simply and clearly. One way to make this easier is to write in short sentences. Also, do not worry about repeating the same word or phrase. If you mean the same concept, repeat the word or phrase (otherwise the reader will think you are referring to a different concept). While we are describing scientific writing, this advice is found in any 'how-to-write' book, for example the classic Strunk and White (1999). This does not mean that it is not important to write well, but writing well means clearly communicating your ideas.

The first step in good writing is avoiding typos, spelling errors and grammatical errors. These mistakes tell the reader that you do not care enough about the paper to proofread it carefully. Thus, an important rule is:

> Proofread the paper several times yourself and
> and get friends to proofread it for you.

The graphical equivalent is using the often-poor default settings from graphics packages to display your findings. If you do not appear to care about your paper, it is unlikely that readers will care.

Being able to write scientific reports well is a useful skill whether you plan to be a scientist or not. It will help you to read about science, and the skills can transfer when you are writing for other purposes. It is important to think about your audience when you write.

22.2 THE APA MANUAL: A CRITICAL APPRAISAL

There are some general writing guidelines that are applicable to all sciences (e.g. Gibaldi, 2003; Miller, 2004). Because of the size of the discipline of psychology, we have our own guidelines which incorporate aspects of the general guidelines. The best known of the psychology guidelines is the *Publication Manual of the American Psychological Association* (American Psychological Association, 2009, see www. apastyle.org). This began as a seven-page document, but over the decades has turned into hundreds of pages. Some parts are about specific technical details like how large the margins should be and how to report statistical analyses. Other parts are about style, like avoiding sexist language and the difference between the words *affect* and *effect*. The APA Manual and various offshoots have had a huge influence not just on all psychology journals, but on scientific writing in general. Because of the efforts put in by the APA, this manual has influenced guidelines from other disciplines and is among the top-selling books on Amazon. There are many courses (particularly in the US) where the manual is the text for the course. There is an excellent online tutorial at: www.apastyle.org/learn/tutorials/basics-tutorial.aspx.

In the UK the British Psychological Society has also produced guidelines (British Psychological Society, 2004). In large part they follow the APA manual, with some exceptions for British English. They are available at: bps.org.uk/document-download-area/document-download$.cfm?file_uuid=1B29ADB1-7E96-C67F-D51D3ADFC581A906&ext=pdf. While the BPS document is shorter than the APA Manual, because the BPS journals say to use the APA Manual and also to look at the BPS document, the result is like having to read both the APA Manual and BPS Style Guide.

The notion of having style dictated has critics. In fact, the APA Manual is both feared and disliked! The APA Manual has become its own industry and many writers feel that being told how to write takes away the wonderful freedom that is creative writing. This is partly to do with the evolution of the Manual from being written by editors of the journals who were interesting in the dissemination of science to being produced by a committee interested in writing. While agreeing that the committee-Manual has overstepped its role (and we give an example below), we believe that in general it gives good advice for clear writing. The *fear* factor is because students get marks deducted when breaking one of the APA style rules. As a student you can do two things. First, think of *getting* marks when you follow APA guidelines, and second, just do it! For example, if you know that you need to write out the journal name, volume, pages, and so on, in the reference section to get full marks, just do it!

If you feel strongly that your literary skills are being held back by the APA, talk to your professor and explain why your approach is clearer than the APA guidelines. If your professor agrees that your reasons are justified and convincing, then you might be able to use your style. Of course, 'I didn't feel like following the APA Manual' and 'The *what* Manual?' are unlikely to be acceptable justifications.

A good example of an author challenging APA dogma is Roediger (2004), whose final conclusion was that a new manual without some of the APA Manual's 'silliness' (his word) should be produced. For the first 100 years of the discipline the people who took part in psychology experiments and filled out questionnaires were usually referred to as 'subjects'. In the 1980s the APA Manual decreed that this description was inappropriate and that these people should be referred to as 'participants'. In April 2004, Roddy Roediger was writing as the President of what is now called the Association for Psychological Science. He had previously been a Chair of the Council of Editors of the APA, and is a great psychologist and writer. Despite these accolades, Professor Roediger has a problem. He has a phobia of the word 'participant'. He is a member of *Sufferers of Participant Phobia* and *Participant Phobia Syndrome Survivors* (neither of these are in the DSM … yet). When a copy-editor tried to make him use the p-word, he argued on the basis of these psychological conditions. He described how using the p-word was damaging for people with his condition. He had first tried convincing the copy-editor that he should be able to use 'subjects' based on logic and arguments about freedom of speech, but knew that these reasons would not sway the APA machine. While Roediger's comment was entertaining and humorous (while still cutting), others including members of the very powerful National Institutes of Health (NIH) in the US were more direct, stating the change to 'participant' was 'motivated by political correctness, not truth' (Resnik & Bond, 2007). Perhaps because of high-profile criticism, the APA has retreated and now states that the word 'subjects' is appropriate.

22.3 THE APA MANUAL: SOME BAREBONES

The BPS and APA websites, and what your instructor says, are the definitive guides to how you should construct your assignments. There are several books on how to use APA style and numerous websites. We will not reiterate details here, both because there are excellent resources and because, as shown above, the guidelines can change, so it is worth going to the primary sources for up-to-date information. The APA site (www.apastyle.org) has a wealth of information and links. One of the most useful resources is their webpage of sample papers: http://supp.apa.org/style/PM6E-Corrected-Sample-Papers.pdf. This shows how to organise different types of scientific papers. Another useful resource is an online tutorial which we require you to use for one of the exercises.

Here we just cover some general issues for the basic single study paper. We chose this type of paper because it is the mostly likely type that you will be conducting. And remember, no matter what we say, if your instructor tells you to do something, do that! Often the people marking assignments have particular rules. For example, at many universities assignments have to be submitted in a format that allows them to be analysed using plagiarism software (and if you submit an APA formatted paper in this way it will look as if part is plagiarised because each individual reference should be written exactly like it is in other papers).

22.3.1 Some general issues

Page numbers should be in the upper right hand corner of each page. Use a clear font (the APA recommends Times New Roman for text, and Arial for figures) that is large enough to be seen (at least 11 or 12 point). Double-spacing is part of APA and BPS guidelines, so ask your instructor beforehand if you want to try to save trees using single spacing. Margins should be at least an inch (markers get upset if they do not have space to write their comments).

APA has rules for the titles of different sections according to what 'level' the section is. This is confusing, so in general we recommend looking at sample papers. The levels are:

LEVEL ONE HEADINGS
Level Two Headings
Level three headings
Level four headings
Level five headings

What constitutes each of the different levels depends on what type of paper you have. Here we discuss them with reference to a single study paper, but see the APA resources for other types and further clarifications.

Title page

Choose a title that is clear and describes your study. If you want to come up with a clever/cute title, be very sure that it matches what you have done. Also put your name on the title page, unless instructed otherwise (for some assignments you may just put your student number so that marking is *blind*). In addition, you need a 'running head' which is a brief description of the paper. An 'Author note' is also included which gives an address for correspondence and any other pertinent information (for journal articles this includes funding and any conflicts of interest). For an assignment this might be expressing thanks to your roommate for helping prepare materials or proofreading, or to the teaching assistant for statistical advice.

Abstract

Page 2 is the abstract. This is a brief summary of the study. Different journals have different length restrictions (most have a maximum of 125–250 words). A list of up to five keywords that are used to index the paper in bibliographic sources is also included on the abstract page.

The main text

Begin with the introduction. This starts on a new page with the paper's title at the top. This should explain what your research question is, why it is important, and why you are examining it in the way that you do. It should have a concise summary of some existing work in the area - making reference to important research that has been done and how your study links to, develops from or is different from what has been done before.

Next is the methods section. For a single-study paper this requires a Level 1 heading, so the word Method is capitalised, in bold and centred. The methods section is often subdivided into sections for Participants/Subjects, Design, Materials and Procedure. These are Level 2 headings, so left-justified and bold. Each of these may have Level 3 headings for further sub-sections. This is particularly common in personality research where the authors wish to describe each of several personality measures. This is the most straightforward section to write. You document in sufficient detail exactly what you did, in the order you did it in, so that the reader is in a position to clearly understand your research design and how your results were ascertained.

Results, bold and centred, is the next section. The important point of the results is to explain the findings clearly to readers who may not be very experienced with the techniques described in this book. Often people write sentences that can only be understood by someone with a PhD in statistics. Quantitative studies usually have quite short sections presenting basic numerical and statistical analyses which are then interpreted and explained in the discussion section. The results section of a qualitative report is different. It is often the longest section and comprises a narrative where the researcher outlines what has been found. Findings are often supported with extracts from participants and the section may well include an interpretation of these extracts.

An important point of the results, and the entire report, is to accurately and honestly describe what was done. It can be tempting to only report information consistent with your original hypotheses or even to alter information. We have seen students do this with assignments, which is baffling. Having your data 'turn out' a certain way is unlikely to affect your grade. Why risk the academic penalties which include being thrown out?

The final level 1 heading of the main text is the Discussion. Do not just restate the findings. As the name implies, you should discuss what you found and say why your findings are important. This should include connecting your work to the extant literature. How does what you have done help illuminate some prior work? And second, how does some existing work help make sense of what you have found?

References

The reference section begins with a new page with the word 'References' centred at the top. You need to include all the articles, books, chapters, etc., that you have cited, and do not include any that you have not cited. There are particular ways to cite sources. The sample papers from the web page listed above show current APA rules. Incorrect references almost always result in loss of grades on assignments. So, do them correctly.

Footnotes

After the references, there is a page for footnotes. You should use footnotes sparingly if at all. If you do not have any footnotes in the text, then you do not need to worry about this page. If you do use them, then have a superscript number in the text, like this[4] and then have the footnotes listed with their numbers on the footnotes page. Do not put the footnotes at the bottom of the page unless your professor tells you that is okay (some will allow this because it saves paper and is easier to read).

Tables and figures

Tables and then figures are next. Each table and figure should be on its own page. With tables, use no vertical lines and as few horizontal lines as possible. With figures, make them as simple as possible. Tufte (2001) is a wonderful reference for presenting tabular and graphical information.

Appendices

Appendices are not often used in journal articles, but are very common in theses and lab reports. Your professor will probably want you to include any questionnaires used in an appendix. You might be required to include your data, consent forms, statistical calculations, sample extracts from the transcript, and so on, in appendices.

22.4 SUBMITTING TO A JOURNAL

You have completed your project. It is a well-designed and conducted study because you read this book so carefully (and listened to your professors, and are hard-working, and are bright, and you missed that party to proofread it, etc.). You walk into your supervisor's office. She tilts her glasses, stares at you, and says: 'We should try to publish this'. This is great. Your supervisor feels the study is so important that it should become part of the permanent record of psychology research. If published, it allows psychologists from all over the world to learn about your study! That is really cool. But, it is not easy.

There are several useful guides for preparing papers for publication. The APA resources mentioned above are valuable. Most journals give instructions for how they want articles. These are usually printed on the inside cover of printed issues of the journal and also on the journal's web page. For APA journals, see http://apa.org/pubs/authors/instructions.aspx. Most journals also publish editorials where the editor says the types of articles that are likely to get published in the journal. Another valuable resource is Sternberg and Sternberg's (2011) *The Psychologist's Companion*. For a brief guide on writing from our friend with *Participant Phobia*, see Roediger (2007). The following is a list of some of the things which we have found important when judging if a paper is likely to be accepted or not.

22.4.1 Choose an appropriate journal

When an article is rejected it is often because it does not fit well with the journal. Also, journals vary a lot in how likely they are to reject a paper. Some journals reject 90 per cent of papers, while others accept most of those submitted. Journals which reject most papers tend to be read by more people (and the papers tend to be better).

22.4.2 Avoid the paper sounding like an essay

Long literature reviews show your professor that you know the area. Good job. They are also appropriate for review papers, but not for empirical papers. For empirical papers, give enough background so the reader knows why your study is important and why you conducted it in the manner you did, but you do not need to show that you know everything about the area (this will be assumed). Readers want to know what you did (the Methods section), what you found (the Results section), and why this is important (the Discussion section).

22.4.3 **Proofread again and again**

If reviewers think that the authors are careless in their writing and proofreading, they are likely to think the authors are also careless in how they conducted the study and how they analysed the data. Did you catch the problem with the 'important rule' at the start of this chapter?

22.4.4 **Sound excited**

If you sound unexcited by your study, the readers will be unexcited too.

22.4.5 **Do not sound too excited**

Do not go over the top and pretend the findings from a single study will change the world (most do not). Most often science progresses slowly. Your study is likely to have pushed the frontiers of science slightly forward or filled in some missing part. This is important, so sound excited, but if you did not cure cancer, end war, and so on, keep your conclusion in perspective.

Additionally, avoid absolutes. You should not say: 'No one has ever looked at X' for two reasons. First, are you sure? Do you feel that confident that your literature search was exhaustive? What about that poster at a conference in Bulgaria last week (which you were not at)? Second, the editor will choose some of the most knowledgeable people about this topic on the planet to review the paper. They are chosen because the editor thinks they have relevant knowledge. This likely means that they have done research that is in some way relevant to X. Your statement may anger them, and angered reviewers seldom write nice things.

22.4.6 **Detailed cover letters**

Treat all correspondence with the editor with the same care as you do the manuscript. The review and publication process is detailed below. One aspect of it is resubmitting a paper after taking into account the reviewers' and editor's comments. The cover letter should detail how you addressed every comment. In the letter be kind about the reviewers because they will likely see the letter. If an editor or a reviewer thinks that you have not addressed one of the comments, if you are lucky they will send it back and give you a second opportunity to address the comment. Another response is rejecting the paper stating that the authors were given the opportunity to change the paper with respect to this comment, did not, and

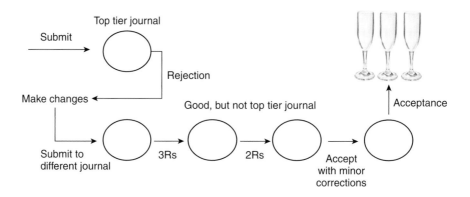

Figure 22.1 A schematic diagram of a typical review process. The paper is rejected from one journal, the "Top tier journal" at the top of the figure, submitted to a second journal, and then through the revise-and-resubmit cycle is eventually accepted (and toasted with champagne)

therefore have lost that opportunity. This may sound mean, but reviewers are unpaid and their time should not be wasted.

The final question is what happens when you submit a paper. Figure 22.1 shows a typical sequence. You send the paper to a top tier journal, they send it to several reviewers who after a few months submit useful but critical comments. The editor writes a polite letter but 'rejects' it. You read the letter carefully, and it is clear it is what is called a 'straight reject' where they are not inviting or suggesting that you re-submit the paper there. Assuming you do not think any of the criticisms make the paper unpublishable, you change the manuscript according to the wishes of the editor and reviewers (assuming that you agree with their comments, but these are the expert reviewers so their views are valuable). You choose another journal. Usually the second journal has a higher acceptance rate than the first; the second journal is not quite as good as the first journal. Importantly, there is a good chance that some of the same reviewers as for the first journal may be chosen by the second journal, so it is worth addressing all the reviewers' concerns.

Four months pass, and you get a letter from the editor that also says 'reject'. This time, however, the phrase is something like: 'I am rejecting the paper, but I think careful consideration of the reviewers' comments, particularly the points about X, Y and Z, will improve the paper greatly. The journal would be willing to consider a paper along these lines.' This is a 3Rs letter: Reject, Revise and Re-submit. The editor has rejected the paper, but left the door slightly ajar. You make the changes and write the detailed cover letter thanking the editor and the reviewers for their insightful comments. You say how you addressed all of their comments (or explain why you did not address some, but be careful, these are experts who do not like people disagreeing with them). You re-submit. The editor sends it to some of the original reviewers and one new one.

Another three months has passed and you get a 2Rs letter. This is revise and re-submit. Sometimes editors differentiate major and minor corrections. Major corrections mean the editor is still unsure whether the paper can be re-written so that it is publishable. Minor corrections mean the editor thinks it will be publishable if you make the specified changes. You make the changes and write another detailed letter. The editor reads the new resubmission, sees that you addressed everything, and 'accepts with minor revisions'. The editor wants you to change some wording and use proper APA format for a table. You read the letter, yell, go to the pub, wake up, take aspirin, make the changes, allow you and your co-authors one more proofread, and then submit. Your cover letter is shorter this time, and the editor 'accepts' two days later. This is over a year from when you first submitted to the paper. It takes that long.

Next, you get the copy-edited proofs, where somebody skilled in technical writing has gone through it, and/or the page proofs, which look like the final journal version. You go through these to triple check everything. If you miss any detail here, like an odd number in a table, you are stuck with the error for the rest of your life (and after-life if you believe in that). Then the paper is published. The time between the paper being accepted and it being published is called the publication lag. This can vary from about three months to well over a year. Often a paper is published three or more years after the study was conducted.

22.5 CONCLUSION

It is difficult to overstress the importance of good dissemination skills. Consider the research of Victor Frankenstein. He was able to reanimate the dead, a truly stupendous scientific breakthrough, but rather than write up his findings in the appropriate format for scientific journals, he let Adam run amok in the town producing a hostile reaction, and ruining his chances of getting tenure.

This does not mean that you have to memorise every facet of the APA Manual to prevent the townspeople from chasing you around the streets at night with pitchforks and torches. None of us are APA Manual experts (that sounds like something that should be in the DSM with Roediger's syndromes) and none of us has ever been chased around the streets by crowds with pitchforks and torches. What you need to be able to do is think about how to convey, most clearly and concisely, the difficult scientific concepts that went into your research project. Clarity is the key. To help you in this endeavour, many journal and scientific committees have produced documents which should guide you towards clear writing. The best known of these is the APA Manual, and it is over-prescriptive and daunting. However, if you just follow the instructions this will be less daunting.

22.6 **EXERCISES AND DISCUSSION QUESTIONS**

1 Summarise in 100 words the tutorial on: http://www.apastyle.org/learn/tutorials/basics-tutorial.aspx.

Calculate the 'readability' score for your summary. Make sure your readability score is above 70 (if using the Flesch Reading Ease equation, or less than 6 if using the Flesch–Kincaid Grade level score).

Many word processing packages calculate 'readability' for you (e.g. for Word, search 'readability' on the Microsoft page). If not, here is how they are calculated (this is from the Microsoft webpage).

Flesch Reading Ease (100-point scale with high scores being more readable) is:

$$206.835 - (1.015 \times ASL) - (84.6 \times ASW)$$

where ASL = average sentence length (the number of words divided by the number of sentences) and ASW = average number of syllables per word (the number of syllables divided by the number of words).

An alternative statistic is the Flesch–Kincaid Grade level. A score of 6 means that a sixth grader should be able to understand the text. In the US a sixth grader is about 11–12 years old. The statistic is:

$$(0.39 \times ASL) + (11.8 \times ASW) - 15.59$$

where ASL and ASW are the same as above.

2 Trade your summaries from exercise 1 with a classmate. Proofread your classmate's summary and make changes to improve the clarity. Has the 'readability' changed?

3 Find two journals in the area of psychology in which you are most interested. Are there differences in the types of articles that these journals tend to publish? Which journal do you think is a harder journal to get a paper accepted at, and why?

Glossary

Acquiescence bias: A tendency to agree with any question regardless of its content.

Action orientation: The assumption that language is used to perform particular social actions or functions.

Alpha level: The probability of making a type I error when H_0 is true.

Alternative hypothesis: Not the null hypothesis. It is usually that there are differences among groups or that there are relationships among variables.

Analysis of variance (ANOVA): A statistical technique that tests whether means differ among a conditions and/or variables. It is widely used in psychology experiments.

Analytic induction: A form of "progressive hypothesising" that involves adapting and reformulating of hypotheses in the light of evidence provided by observing the phenomenon of interest.

Approximate value: When measuring a continuous variable you record a single figure but this represents an interval on the measurement scale rather than a single value. It is therefore always an approximation of the true value.

Archetypal narratives: Narratives that we all have access to that reflect our condition when asked to explain ourselves.

Association: means that two variables are related. Knowing something about a score on one variable tells you something about the likely score on the other variable.

Audit trail: Useful in increasing the validity of research. An interpretative tool in which the observer contributes to the research via personal reflection on the situation. A detailed account of how the data were analysed is also provided.

Axial coding: Exhaustive coding of intersecting properties of core conceptual categories.

Back translation: In cross-cultural research, translating your questionnaire into another language and having it translated back into English by another person to see if the meaning of the questions has been retained.

Between-groups design: An experimental design in which each condition in the experiment is performed by a different group of participants. Also known as a between-subjects design.

Between groups variance: Also known as treatment variance, is the variability among means between the groups we are comparing.

Between-subjects design: See between-groups design.

Blind testing: An experimental procedure in which the participants remain unaware of which condition they are in, in order to prevent their expectations from affecting their responses.

Bogus pipeline: A suggestion to respondents that you have an independent way of knowing whether their answers are truthful even when you have not.

Box plot: A graphical depiction of the five-number summary.

Carry-over effects: Occur when exposure to one IV before another, affects the response to the subsequent IV.

Categorical responses: Responses that fall into distinct categories, e.g. male/female.

Causation: This occurs when one variable (or the underlying cause of that variable) is directly responsible for changes in another variable.

Ceiling effect: A ceiling effect occurs when a measure does not have sufficient sensitivity at the high end, and many people score maximum. For example, a test which is too easy to separate the 'A' students from the 'B' students is not a good test.

Cells: The values, for any statistic, for some combination of variables. Cells in a contingency table are often frequencies.

Census: A complete enumeration of the population, information is collected on all units.

Central limit theorem: The theorem which states that the sampling distribution of random variables with finite mean and variance will be approximately normally distributed as the sample size become very large.

Chi-square: Both a common statistical test for examining associations among categorical variables, and a statistical distribution that is used for many statistical tests.

Classical Test Theory (CTT): Underlies the construction of most psychometric tests that have ever existed.

Closed-ended formats: Questions where only a number of predetermined responses are allowed.

Clustering: A sampling procedure in which sample units are drawn in a series of stages, such as pupils being sampled from a first-stage sample of schools.

Co-construction: A narrative account of an event that is constructed by two or more people.

Coding: The initial stage in discourse analysis, involving a close examination of text.

Coding errors: Mistakes made by the researcher in turning people's answers into numerical data for analysis.

Coding schemes: A systematic method of categorising behaviours.

Cohort effects: Differences between groups in a study produced by variables other than the independent variable that is of interest to the experimenter. For example, a study on age differences needs to take account of the fact that 'young' and 'old' do not differ solely on chronological age, but also in many other ways (they have lived in different historical periods, had different cultural experiences, etc.).

Communalities: The proportion of variability in the observed variables accounted for by the factors.

Compensatory rivalry: This occurs when the control group learns about the treatment and develops a competitive attitude towards the treatment group which can equalise later performance across the groups and therefore increased the chance of NOT seeing a treatment effect when there is one.

Complete observer: The observer is detached from the observed group and has no direct contact with the participants during data collection.

Complete participant: The observer becomes immersed within the observed group and conceals their identity, thus engaging with members of the group on a more intimate, personal level.

Complex sample design: A random sample design which gives units in the population different selection probabilities.

Computer Adaptive Testing (CAT): Choosing the questions to ask based on responses to previous questions. Allows the test to measure the construct as accurately as traditional methods using fewer questions.

Confidence interval: A numerical range, or band within which we can say that, at some level of confidence (e.g. 95%), the true value in the population will be found. For example, we might say that we are 95% confident that the average minutes of exercise taken by people in Great Britain on a weekday is between 25 and 35 minutes.

Confounding variables: Variables producing effects that might interact with the experimenter's manipulations of an independent variable. Confounding variables can make it difficult to interpret the results of a study, because it is often impossible to know to what extent the observed results have arisen from the effects of the confounding variables, as opposed to the experimenter's manipulations of the independent variable(s).

Contamination effects: These occur when the treatment and control groups influence each other or interact in some unintended way such that the independent variable is no long what it was intended to be.

Content category: Is the unit used to identify distinct elements in a data array.

Continuous variables: Variables where there are an infinite number of possible values that fall between any two observed values. Continuous variables can be divided up into an infinite number of fractional parts.

Cool cognition: Longer term reflection looking back at on one's life course.

Correlation: A correlation measures the linear relationship between two variables. The most common correlation, Pearson's product moment correlation, is denoted r.

Counter-balancing: A means of avoiding order effects in a repeated-measures design, by ensuring that as many participants are tested in one order as are tested in the opposite order. For example if you have two conditions, A and B, then half of the participants do them in the order 'A then B' and the rest do them in the order 'B then A' (See also **Latin Squares**).

Critical discursive analysis: An approach to the study of discourse that focuses on identifying social and political domination in text and talk.

Critical discursive psychology: An approach to the study of discourse that integrates discursive psychology and Foucauldian discourse analysis to produce data-grounded analyses which are attentive to socio-political issues.

Cross-sectional design: A between-groups design that involves using different groups of participants to represent different points in development (e.g. different ages).

Data: At its simplest is information structured to address a research question essentially it is any information or evidence collected.

Degrees of freedom: The number of scores we are working with that are free to vary before our statistic is fully determined.

Dependent variable (DV): A variable that is measured by a researcher, in order to assess the effects of the researcher's manipulations of an **independent variable**. Examples include reaction time, number of errors, number correct, rating scales.

Descriptive statistics: Tell you about characteristics of your sample.

Differential attrition: See differential mortality.

Differential Drop-out: See differential mortality.

Differential item functioning: The extent to which test items are measuring the same construct in different populations.

Differential mortality: A threat to the validity of a study produced by the loss of participants from one or more groups during the course of the research. The participants who remain may differ in important ways from those who leave (e.g. in motivation, enthusiasm, etc.) and these factors may contribute in unknown ways to any perceived differences between the groups in the study.

Disciplinary knowledge: Knowledge of what has been carried out in terms of former research may be used when formulating a research programme.

Discourses: Sets of coherent linguistic material that construct social 'objects'.

Discrete variables: Variables that can have only discrete, whole number values.

Discursive psychology: A detailed approach to the study of discourse that views language as a form of social action, addresses the social functions of talk and considers how these functions are achieved.

Disproportionate stratification: A sampling procedure where the proportion sampled within each population sub-group (or stratum) is disproportionate to its size in the population.

Double-blind testing: An experimental procedure in which the participants and the experimenter interacting with them remain unaware of which condition the participants are in. This is done to avoid the data being affected by either the participants' or experimenter's expectations.

Double hermeneutic: Both researcher and participant are engaged in interpretative activity; the researcher is interpreting the account of the participant's interpretation of their experience.

Dummy variable coding: When a variable is assigned 1 for the presence of some characteristic and 0 for its absence. If there was a three category variable (e.g., favourite food: pizza, chocolate, broccoli) it could be re-coded into two dummy variables for pizza (1 if pizza, 0 otherwise) and chocolate (1 if chocolate, 0 otherwise).

Ecological fallacy: This is a fallacy that because there is a relationship between two measures when people are assessed in groups, must also apply for individuals within those groups.

Ecological validity: The extent to which research findings can be generalised to real-world settings.

Effect sizes: Measures that allow us to determine the strength of our findings.

Eigenvalue: A mathematical term used in calculating several advanced statistics procedures. For the purposes in this book it is a unit of measurement for how much variation is accounted for by the latent variables.

Emergent design: The process of data analysis may change according to the characteristics of the data. Therefore, there are no hard and fast rules.

Epistemology: A philosophical concept which refers to the assumptions we make about what knowledge is, how we generate knowledge, what we know, and how we know what we know.

Epsem: A sampling strategy in which each population unit is given an equal probability of selection into the sample.

Equivalence: Is the extent to which an assessment is free from gender, ethnic or other forms of bias.

Evaluation apprehension: Participants' performance may be affected by their anxieties about how well they are performing, and what the experimenter thinks of them as a result.

Exhaustiveness: For categorical variables it is the idea that the category system should have enough categories so that all the observations can fit into a category.

Experiment: A systematic procedure for testing an hypothesis about some aspect of the world. The experimenter manipulates one or more independent variables (IVs), and measures the effects of these manipulations on one or more dependent variables (DVs). For example, an experimenter might examine the effects of manipulations of the IV 'alcohol consumption' by testing a group of participants twice, once when they are drunk and again when they are sober. These effects could be measured in terms of the DV 'ability to walk along a straight line' (measured in terms of number of deviations from the line). In true experiments, as opposed to quasi-experiments, manipulations of the IV are entirely under the experimenter's control. This is normally achieved by randomly allocating participants to experience one condition ('level') of the IV or another.

Experimenter effects: Influences on the outcome of a study, produced by the experimenter's expectations of what the results will be.

Exploratory data analysis (EDA): The process of looking for patterns in your data.

External validity: The degree to which the conclusions in your experiment would hold for other people/animals/cases in other places and at other times.

F ratio: The ratio produced by our $MS_{between}$ variance divided by our MS_{within} variance.

Factor scores: The values for each participant for the hypothesised factors. These can be created with all EFA software.

Factors: Within ANOVA and experimental design, the independent variables in the design. Within latent variable models, the latent variables are often called factors.

Falsifiability: The idea that a hypothesis or theory can only be regarded as scientific if it is formulated in such a way that it would be in principle possible to show that it was wrong (false).

Filter questions: Questions that direct the respondent to different sub-sections of the questionnaire; for example, 'Are you male or female? If you are female now go to section X which asks about pregnancy.'

Five-number summary: Provides the researcher with five numbers that divide the sample scores into four approximately equal sized groups.

Floor effect: A floor effect occurs when a test is not sufficiently sensitive at the lower end. For example, a test which is unable to distinguish between the failing students and the 'C' students.

Flynn effect: The year by year increase of about 0.35 IQ points per annum in IQ test scores that has been ongoing for the past century.

Focus group content: The substantive themes arising from the discussion.

Focus group facilitator: The person(s) who manages the discussion process.

Focus group interview: A type of semi-structured interview conducted in a group setting with a clear topic focus.

Focus group process: The dynamics of the group discussion.

Focused coding: Developing a more detailed coding system as the research develops.

Focusing stimuli: The topic, image or object that is the focusing device in relation to which the interview is guided.

Foucauldian discourse analysis: An approach to the study of discourse that is concerned with issues of identity and selfhood, ideology, power relations and social change.

Fully structured interviews: An interview where the questions have been predetermined prior to its start.

Functions: What a text is doing – for example, persuading, justifying, questioning or accusing.

Going native: The observer becomes an integral part of the data-collection process, involving themselves in the process of observation by engaging with the observed group.

Hawthorne effect: Changes to participants' performance, produced by their awareness that their behaviour is being measured.

Hermeneutics: The theory and practice of interpretation.

Histogram: A sample's distribution for a single variable.

History effects: These are factors that lead to an experimental effect which is not attributable to the treatment (or independent variable) but is due to some other event.

Homogenous sample: A sample purposively selected so that participants share key characteristics defined for that study.

Hot cognition: The process of trying to make sense of issues in one's life which are current, important and emotive.

Human sciences: A perspective which encourages the systematic study of human existence in all its complexity. Methods appropriate for understanding human phenomena should be used rather than methods appropriated from the natural sciences.

Hypothetico-deductive method: The cyclical process of making predictions or hypotheses that are subjected to some form of empirical test. Deductions are made about the theory that generated the hypotheses based on the results of this test. This generates further predictions from the theory which are then subjected to tests and further deductions are made. If, over time, the theory has not been falsified our confidence in it increases. If at any point the test evidence does not support the theory it is either rejected or revised.

Idiographic: An approach to research which begins with detailed examination of particular cases. The process of analysis means that as one moves to a more general claim for a group of participants, it is still possible to retrieve an analysis of the individuals in the study.

Implied correlation matrix: The matrix that the model is able to recreate. This should be close to the observed correlation matrix, otherwise the model does not fit the data well.

Independent variable (IV): A variable that is systematically manipulated by an experimenter, in order to produce measurable effects on a dependent variable. For example, a researcher who is interested in treating phobias might manipulate the independent variable of 'phobia treatment' by comparing different groups of participants, each of which received a different treatment for their phobia. These different conditions are referred to as different *levels* of the IV.

Indexing system: A method of coding data that involves devising categories initially and adapting them as the research progresses.

Inductive: An approach to research which starts with an open research question rather than attempting to test a pre-defined hypothesis. Analysis works bottom up from the data as opposed to top down from the researcher's theoretical conceptions.

Inferential statistics: Take information from your sample and allow you to make inferences about the population.

Instrumentation effects: The reliability of the instrument may change in calibration (if using a measuring device) or from change in human ability to measure differences (due to fatigue, experience, etc.).

Integrating categories: Categories that represent some similarity may be integrated.

Inter-rater reliability: This method of reliability testing requires that two or more independent observers agree with their assessments of certain behaviours.

Interactions: The effects two or more factors have in combination on the dependent variables.

Internal validity: The degree to which we can accurately claim that the independent variable produced the observed effect and that the effect on dependent variable was only due to variation in the independent variable(s).

Interpretative thematic analysis: Analysing data by means of interpretation and the use of a thematic approach (looking for key themes in the data).

Interrupted time series: A study of the same people across three or more occasions where the treatment intervention 'interrupts' an otherwise seamless time series of observations.

Interview Protocol: Is the description of the entire process in setting up and executing the interview.

Interview schedule: The series of questions asked at an interview.

Interviewer effects: Where the characteristics of the interviewer and the subject matter influence the responses.

Investigative journalism: The detailed mainly descriptive recording of a set of events.

Item Response Theory (IRT): Plots the probability of answering an item in a particular way against an underlying latent trait.

Item-specific errors: The errors assumed to apply separately to each variable. They are the *e*s in circles added to some path/causal diagrams.

John Henry effect: Refers to the fact that if participants are aware that they are in a control condition and feel resentful of this, they may work harder in order to compensate. For example, if some children in a school received extra training in reading but others didn't, the parents of the latter might put more effort into teaching their children to read, in order to overcome their perceived disadvantage.

Latent variables: Variables which are not directly measured, but assumed to exist. In exploratory factor analysis they are usually called factors.

Latin Squares design: Used to take account of possible order effects in repeated-measures designs that involve a number of conditions. Essentially, they ensure that each possible sequence of conditions occurs in the study. For example, if you have three conditions (A, B and C) then the possible orders are ABC, BCA, CAB, CBA, ACB and BAC. Equal numbers of participants are tested in each of these orders.

Levels: The conditions within an independent variable.

Linearity: Linearity is the extent to which the relationship between two variables falls on a straight line.

Loading: Denoted with the Greek letter α or the letter L, shows the strength between the latent variable and the observed variable.

Longitudinal design: A repeated-measures design that is often used in developmental research. A group of participants is tested repeatedly over time (e.g. at different ages).

Main effects: The effects each factor has on the dependent variable, alone and in isolation from other independent variables.

Manifest: Observed variables are those which are directly measured.

Mann–Whitney U test: can be used for assessing whether two independent samples are significantly different from one another when sample is not normally distributed.

Marginal means: Row and column means that correspond to each level of your factors.

Matched-pair *t*-test: The test appropriate when you are comparing the mean the difference between scores on two variables when all subjects are measured on both variables. One of the assumptions is that the differences are normally distributed.

Matched-pairs design: An experimental design in which participants are carefully matched on variables that might be relevant to the research (such as age, socioeconomic status, intelligence, etc.) Matching may increase the experiment's sensitivity (its ability to detect differences between the various conditions in the study) by reducing variability in the data introduced by the fact that the participants in the different conditions are dissimilar to each other in many respects.

Maturational effects: Changes in performance that would have occurred anyway due to the passage of time rather than exposure to any treatment or manipulation.

Mean squares: The terms for variance in ANOVA.

Mean: The sum of all the values divided by the number of values.

Meanings: How people understand events in their own and other people's lives by imputing meaning to them.

Measurement: The assigning of numbers to objects according to a set of rules to indicate either a quality or quantity.

Member validation: Categories derived from the research process are recognisable to study participants.

Mixed design: An experimental design which combines within-subjects and repeated-measures independent variables (e.g. the effects of sex and alcohol on memory performance could be investigated with a mixed design. Sex is an independent-measures IV, while alcohol could be a repeated-measures IV, with everyone tested twice – once while sober and once while drunk.) Mixed design can have other meanings dependent on the context in which it is used.

Multifactorial design: An experimental design in which the effects of more than one independent variable are investigated within the same study. Multifactorial designs permit investigators to study how variables might interact with each other.

Multiple R: Multiple R (note upper case R) is a measure of how well a set of predictor variables is able to predict the scores on an outcome variable.

Multiple response items: Questions with categorical responses where more than one response is allowed.

Multiple time-series design: An extended series of data collection points are used with both a treatment group and the non-equivalent control group.

Mutual exclusivity: For categorical variables, this is the idea that each observation (person, case, score) cannot fall into more than one category.

Narrative: An individual's account of their experience.

Non-attitudes: Responses given to attitude questions that do not reflect a real attitude toward the target object.

Non-parametric tests: A phrase sometimes used to refer to tests that do not make assumptions about the distribution of variables. Distribution-free tests is the preferred phrase here. Non-parametric (and semi-parametric) are phrases also used for some more advanced statistical procedures.

Non-response bias: The difference between the true value in the population and a survey estimate, which arises due to differences on the variable in question between the responding and the non-responding units.

Null hypothesis: The hypothesis that is usually being tested. It is usually something like there are no differences among group or there is no association between two variables.

Observer as participant: Refers to the aspects of talk and features such observations as the rate, pitch, voice tremor and tone of speech.

Ontology: The assumptions we make about the nature of being, existence or reality.

Open coding: A system of coding data building upon the available evidence and key issues that emerge as the data collection process develops.

Open-ended formats: Questions that people can answer in any way they wish – usually free in text format.

Operational definition: A means of defining a phenomenon in terms of the methods used to measure it. For example, 'aggression' is notoriously difficult to define precisely, but an operational definition for research purposes might be 'punching, kicking or biting'. If these behaviours are observed, then 'aggression' is deemed to have occurred.

Order effects: In a repeated-measures design, these are systematic effects on participants' performance that would be produced if everyone did the conditions in the same fixed order. If the order of conditions is kept constant, variables such as practice and fatigue have the potential to affect the conditions in a systematic fashion, and hence become confounding variables.

Outlier: An outlier is a case with an unusual value or set of values. It is unusual to be 8 feet tall – such a person would therefore be an outlier. It is not unusual to be 6 feet tall, unless that person was 5 years old. Hence being 6 feet tall is not sufficient to be an outlier, but being that tall at that age is sufficient.

Over-reporting: Participants over-emphasise behaviours or beliefs they feel may be approved of.

p-value: The observed p-value is the probability of observing an effect as large as observed, or larger, assuming that the null hypothesis is true and that the assumptions are all meet. The critical p-value is the value that the observed p-value needs to be less than in order for the user to reject the null hypothesis.

Paralinguistic: This refers to aspects of language and communication which are not related to the specific semantic content of the words employed. Examples are; laughter, giggles, intakes of breath, sighs, sudden increase or decrease in volume and speed of speech. These can indicate the emotions of the speaker, their lack of interest, and relational positions, such as mockery or sympathy towards the receiver/s of the communication.

Partially structured interviews: Where questions are partially determined prior to the interview start, however the questions will be allowed to vary in order to respond to answers in situ.

Participant as observer: The observer participates within the activities of the observed group and adopts a meaningful role within the group.

Participant observer: The researcher is actively involved in the situation which is being observed and is making a significant contribution to any activity taking part. There may be attempts made to conceal their identity as a researcher in order to maintain their status as an active participant.

Pearson correlation: The most common correlation measure. It was developed by Karl Pearson and its full name is the Pearson product moment correlation.

Phenomenology: The philosophical approach concerned with the meaning of lived experience. It attempts as far as possible to capture experience in its own terms rather than according to pre-existing conceptual and scientific criteria.

Placebo effect: In psychology, this refers to an effect on behaviour which is produced by participants believing that they have received an effective treatment, when in fact they have not. (Traditionally a 'placebo' is a pharmacologically inactive substance that mimics the effects of a real drug, due to the recipients believing that they have taken the latter).

Population: The group you want to make statements or inferences about.

Positioning: A discursive interpretation of the concept of identity.

Post-hoc analyses: Tests conducted following an analysis to determine the sources of significant effects. It is common practice to require a lower p value for declaring that an effect has been detected.

Post-test only/control group design: An experimental design in which participants are allocated randomly to different conditions; given different treatments (different levels of an independent variable); and then tested in some way, in the expectation that the different treatments will have affected their behaviour in some way (as reflected by their scores on the dependent variable that has been chosen by the experimenter). At a minimum, this design would consist of an experimental condition (in which some treatment is administered) and a control condition (in which this treatment is withheld). Random allocation of participants to the different conditions is assumed to ensure that the conditions do not differ systematically in any respect, other than in terms of the experimenter's manipulations of the independent variable.

Power: The probability of detecting an effect of a particular size when it is true. Power increases with sample size and when the researcher is only trying to detect if a large effect exists.

Pre-test/post-test control group design: Subjects are allocated to groups and are measured both before some manipulation and after the manipulation. The results are often analysed with an Analysis of Covariance (ANCOVA).

Precision: A term used to denote the width of a confidence interval. An estimator with a narrower confidence interval is a more precise estimator.

Probability distribution: Functions which describe the probability of a random variable taking particular values.

Proportionate stratification: A sampling procedure where the proportion sampled within each population sub-group (or stratum) is proportionate to its size in the population.

Psychometrics: The science of psychological assessment.

Pygmalion effect: Changes in children's academic performance produced by teachers' expectations about how well those children are likely to perform.

Quasi-experiment: A study where participants are not randomly allocated into conditions. For example, comparing extroversion between psychologists and biologists would be a quasi-experiment because the subjects would not be randomly allocated into conditions.

Quota sampling: A non-random sampling technique which aims to achieve representativeness by matching the sample to the population on known population characteristics.

r: The lower case r is used as a symbol for correlation.

R: Upper case R is usually used to refer to the multiple correlation. R is also the name of the popular statistics language.

Randomisation: A method of ensuring that the only systematic difference between the conditions in an experiment is the one that is introduced by the experimenter. In a **between-groups** experimental design, participants should be allocated randomly to the different groups of the study. In a **within-subjects** experimental design, participants should be allocated randomly to the different orders in which the conditions are performed.

Ranking scales: People are asked to place a number of things or attributes in an order.

Rating scales: Response scales that imply more or less of some characteristic; for example, 'Not important at all' through to 'Extremely important'.

Reactivity: A threat to the validity of a study arising from the fact that participants' behaviour may be affected by their awareness that they are taking part in a study.

Real limits: For continuous variables, each score corresponds to an interval on the measurement scale. The boundaries that separate these intervals are called *real limits*.

Realism: An epistemological perspective which claims that there is a straightforward relationship between people's perceptions of the world and the world itself. The two main types are naïve realism and critical realism.

Reflexivity: The process by which researchers' acknowledge and reflect upon the different ways they might influence the research process, including their personal beliefs and values as well as their assumptions about knowledge. This term can also refer to the way in which the outcome of a qualitative analysis might itself be analysed using the same analytic approach.

Regression: Within statistics this is used to refer to use one or more variables to predict one or more variables. Most statistical procedures can be described as some kind of regression.

Regression to the mean: Refers to the phenomenon that a variable that is extreme on its first measurement will tend to be closer to the center of the distribution on a later measurement.

Relabeling categories: Re-defining specific categories in terms of their labels.

Relativism: An epistemological perspective which claims that there are multiple competing realities of the world which are constructed from linguistic and discursive resources.

Reliability: Within psychometrics this has the technical definition of how much the assessment is free from error. Within methods more broadly this can refer to how reproducible/replicable the study's results are.

Repeated measures design: An experimental design in which each participant takes part in more than one condition of the study.

Replication: Repeating experiments or studies in order to increase our confidence that the deductions made the first time the study was done are justified.

Researcher effects: The impact of the researcher, often unintentional upon the data gathered.

Response rate: For a random sample, the proportion of the total issued sample that provided an interview. The response rate can be used as an indicator of potential non-response bias in the sample.

Rotation: Used to make the loadings from an exploratory factor analysis easier to interpret. *Varimax* is the most common orthogonal rotation.

Sample: A sub-set of units drawn from a population, according to a formalised set of procedures.

Sample maintenance: Participants may drop out or fail to provide information during the research process. It is important that samples are maintained.

Sample selection bias: A bias where the sample studied is not representative of the intended population (usually through some systematic process; e.g. prior interest in the topic of the study).

Sampling distribution: The distribution of possible values of a statistic under repeated sampling from a population.

Sampling frame: A list of population units from which a sample can be drawn.

Sampling without replacement: When a population unit is selected for inclusion in a sample, it is excluded from subsequent draws from the sampling frame.

Satisficing: Responses, usually quickly made, that the respondent thinks are 'good enough' to get through the survey quickly but may not reflect carefully considered positions.

Scree plot: A line graph of additional variation accounted for with the number of latent variables. It is useful for decide how many latent variables are needed. The scree plot is often made using a procedure called principal components analysis, which is described at the end of this chapter.

Selection–maturation interaction: An interaction between a maturational effect and a selection bias such that, for example, a group of children may show more improvement than a group of adults, but this could be because their brains are developing faster relative to their age.

Self-record: A general term used to describe any record that a participant keeps of their activities.

Self-reflection: Involves recording the observer's response to being an integral part of the observational sequence.

Self-selection of material: The diarist may decide which information to include in their diary. The researcher has little control over this issue.

Semi-structured interviews: The researcher develops a set of questions which address the topic of interest but these are used to guide rather than dictate the course of the interview. If the participant goes into a novel and interesting area, this should be pursued.

Simple effects: The effects of one IV at just one level of another IV on the outcome measure.

Simple random sample: A random sampling technique in which every unit in the population is given an equal probability of selection.

Social constructionism: A perspective that sees psychological, social and other categories as constituted and maintained through social processes, particularly language.

Sociogram: The description, typically graphical, of the relationships between individuals or between groups, in a defined social network.

Solomon four-group design: An experimental design in which participants are allocated randomly to different groups, given different treatments (different levels of an independent variable), and then tested in some way, in the expectation that the different treatments will have affected their behaviour in some way (as reflected by their scores on the dependent variable that has been chosen by the experimenter). Half of the groups are pre-tested, to ensure that random allocation has been effective in eliminating initial systematic differences between the groups. The remaining groups are not pre-tested: by comparing these groups to the pre-tested ones, it is possible to determine whether pre-testing has, in itself, affected the groups.

Sorting exercise: A task requiring the respondent to group stimuli (i.e. any material relevant in the research) into categories or clusters.

Spearman correlation: The Spearman correlation is a method of calculating the correlation coefficient that is used for ranked data, a distribution free test.

Splitting categories: Creating sub-categories from the existing pre-defined categories.

Standard deviation: A measure of how spread out a variable or a distribution is.

Standard error: The standard deviation of a sampling distribution.

Standardisation: The setting of standards whereby a test score can be interpreted.

Standardised regression coefficient: This is the regression coefficient that is expressed in standard deviation units, rather than the original units of the variables. When there is one predictor, the standardised regression coefficient is the (Pearson) correlation.

Statistical inference: The procedures by which we are able to make statements about the quantitative characteristics of populations from information collected from samples.

Subject or participant mortality: The loss of participant to a study that required participants to engage with the study on multiple occasions.

Subjective experience: Experience understood from the perspective of the person who lives that experience.

Sums of squares: The sums of squared deviations that fall about the mean.

Survey mode: The method by which questionnaires are administered to respondents, such as Computer Assisted Personal Interview (CAPI), Computer Assisted Telephone Interview (CATI), or web self-completion.

Systematic random sampling: A sampling procedure with specific rules for assigning probabilities for being selected into the sample.

t-test: A test to compare the means, either of two variables for one group of people or of one variable for two groups of people. For the first of these it is assumed the distribution for each group is Normal. For the second it is assumed that the difference in values in Normally distributed.

Testing effects: The finding that later performance on a test is enhanced if participants are familiar with the test instrument itself and can recall being exposed to it before.

Texts: Any sort of spoken or written materials.

Thematic analysis: This method of analysis requires the researcher to establish themes that occur within the data. By structuring the data in this way, the researcher is able to emphasise the commonalities and differences between participants.

Theoretical agnosticism: To be open-minded about past research when referring to it as a guide to future research.

Theoretical memos: Observations regarding the data collection process. These observations are made by the researcher and may involve comments regarding the data collection process or any theoretical issues that may emerge as the research develops.

Theoretical sampling: Involves specifying new samples of data as the analysis proceeds.

Theoretical sensitivity: To be aware of what has been discovered in past research to move a stage further in the research process.

Theoretical saturation: The point reached when the addition of any extra data contributes no further insights to the analysis.

Theory-building: Building a theory from the data.

Time event analysis: The recording of coded events that occur within specific, pre-determined time scales. Also, recording the exact time that events occur over an extended period of observation.

Time-sampling: Involves recording events that occur at specific times or particular intervals within the period of observation.

Timeline: The temporal pattern of events.

Topic guide: The minimal structure of the interview in terms of the key substantive topics to be covered.

Type I error: Rejecting a true null hypothesis.

Type II error: Failing to reject a false null hypothesis.

Unbiased estimator: A statistic which, when applied to sample data of sufficient size, converges on the true population value.

Under-reporting: Participants fail to report beliefs or behaviours the feel may be disapproved of.

Vague quantifier: A term such as 'often' or 'regularly' which implies a quantity but there is some uncertainty about whether respondents will interpret the term in the same way. For example, does 'regularly' mean daily, weekly or on once every year?

Validity: The extent to which an assessment measures what it is purported to measure. There are a number of kinds of validity discussed in the literature.

Variability: The observation that talk or writing on any topic will vary not just across different speakers or writers but within the same speaker or writer.

Weighting: A statistical adjustment applied to sample data to correct for unequal probability of selection from the population.

Within-groups variance: Also known as error variance, is the variability among scores within each group that comes from a source other than our independent variable(s).

Within-subjects design: See repeated-measures design.

References

Abell, J., & Walton, C. (2010). Imagine: towards an integrated and applied social psychology. *British Journal of Social Psychology, 49*, 685–690.

Abelson, R. P. (1995). *Statistics as principled argument*. Mahwah, NJ: Erlbaum.

Abraham, C., & Hampson, S. E. (1996). A social cognition approach to health psychology: philosophical and methodological issues. *Psychology and Health, 11*, 223–241.

Adams, E. W. (1966). On the nature and purpose of measurement. *Synthese, 16*, 125–129.

Afkhami, R., Higgins, V., & de Kort, S. (2009). Ethnicity: Introductory User Guide. Economic and Social Data Service Government. Retrieved from http://www. esds. ac. uk/government/docs/ethnicityintro. pdf.

Ainsworth, M. D. S., Blehar, R. M. C, Waters, E., & Wall, S. (1978). *Patterns of attachment: A psychological study of the strange situation*. Hillsdale, NJ: Erlbaum.

Albrecht, T. L., Johnson, G. M., & Walther, J. B. (1993). Understanding communication processes in focus groups. In D. L. Morgan (Ed.), *Successful focus groups: Advancing the state of the art*. London: Sage.

Allison, P. (1998). *Multiple regression: a primer*. Newbury Park, CA: Pine Forge Press.

American Psychological Association (2009). *Publication manual of the American Psychological Association* (6th edn.). Washington DC: American Psychological Association. Retrieved from http://apastyle. org/

American Psychological Association. American Psychological Association Ethics Code. Retrieved from www. apa. org/ethics/code

Anatchkova, M. D., & Bjorner, J. B. (2010). Health and role functioning: the use of focus groups in the development of an item bank. *Quality of Life Research, 19*, 111–123.

Arkowitz, H., Westra, H.A., & Miller, W.R. (2008). *Motivational interviewing in the treatment of psychological problems*. New York: Guilford Press.

Argyle, M. (1972). *The psychology of interpersonal behaviour*. Harmondsworth: Penguin.

Asch, S. E. (1987). *Social psychology*. New York: Oxford University Press. (Original work published 1952).

Ashworth, P. (2003). An approach to phenomenological psychology: The contingencies of the lifeworld. *Journal of Phenomenological Psychology, 34*, 145–156.

Ashworth, P. (2008). Conceptual foundations of qualitative psychology. In J. A. Smith (Ed.), *Qualitative psychology. A practical guide to research methods* (pp. 4–25). London: Sage.

Atkinson, J., & Heritage, J. (Eds) (1984). *Structures of social action: Studies in conversation analysis*. Cambridge: Cambridge University Press.

Auerbach, C., & Silverstein, L. (2003). *Qualitative data: an introduction to coding and analysis*. New York: New York University Press.

Bagnoli, A., & Clark, A. (2010). Focus groups with young people: a participatory approach to research planning. *Journal of Youth Studies*, 13, 101–119.

Bales, R. F. (1950). *Interaction process analysis: A method for the study of small groups*. Cambridge, MA: Addison-Wesley.

Bandura, A., Ross, D., & Ross, S. A. (1961). Transmission of aggression through imitation of aggressive models. *Journal of Abnormal and Social Psychology, 63*, 575–582.

Bandura, A., Ross, D., & Ross, S. A. (1963). Imitation of film-mediated aggressive models. *Journal of Abnormal and Social Psychology, 66*, 3–11.

Banks, S. P. (2004). Identity narratives by American and Canadian retirees in Mexico. *Journal of Cross-Cultural Gerontology, 19*(4), 361–381.

Barbour, R. S. (2007). *Doing focus groups*. Sage: London.

Barbour, R. S., & Kitzinger, J. (Eds) (1998). *Developing focus group research: Politics, theory and practice*. London: Sage.

Barker, C., Pistrang, N. & Elliott, R. (2002) *Research methods in clinical psychology* (2nd edn.). Chichester: Wiley.

Barrett, M. (2006). Practical and ethical issues in planning research. In G. M. Breakwell, S. Hammond, C. Fife-Schaw, & J. A. Smith (Eds), *Research methods in psychology* (3rd edn., pp. 24–49). London: Sage.

Bartholomew, D. J. (1993). Estimating relationships between latent variables. *Sankhyā, 55*, 409–419.

Bartholomew, D. J., & Knott, M. (1999). *Latent variable models and factor analysis (Kendall's Library of Statistics 7)*. London: Arnold.

Bartholomew, D. J., Steele, F., Moustaki, I., & Galbraith, J. I. (2008). *Analysis of multivariate social science data* (2nd edn.). Boca Raton, FL: Chapman & Hall/CRC.

Basch, C. E. (1987). Focus group interview: An underutilized research technique for improving theory and practice in health education. *Health Education Quarterly, 14*, 411–448.

Bateson, G. (1972). *Steps to an ecology of mind*. New York: Ballantine.

Baumann, U., Laireiter, A. R., & Krebs, A. (1996). Computer-assisted interaction diary on social networks, social support, and interpersonal strain. In J. Fahrenberg & M. Myrtek (Eds) *Ambulatory assessment: Computer assisted psychological and psychophysiological methods in monitoring and field studies*. Göttingen: Hogrefe and Huber.

Bausell, R. B., Lao, L., Bergman, S., Lee, W. L., & Berman, B. M. (2005). Is acupuncture analgesia an expectancy effect? Preliminary evidence based on participants' perceived assignments in two placebo-controlled trials. *Evaluation and the Health Professions, 28*(1), 9–26.

Beattie, G. (2003). *The new psychology of body language*. London: Routledge.

Beike, D. R., Lampinen, J. M., & Behrend, D. A. (Eds) (2004). *The self and memory*. New York: Psychology Press.

Bell, M. M., & Gardiner, M. (Eds) (1998). *Bakhtin and the human sciences: No last words*. London: Sage.

Bellisle, F., Dalix, A. M., & De Castro, J. M. (1999). Eating patterns in French subjects studied by the 'weekly food diary' method. *Appetite, 32*(1), 46–52.

Berelson, B. (1947). Detecting collaboration in propaganda. *Public Opinion Quarterly, 11*(2), 244–253.

Berelson, B. (1984). *Content analysis in communications research*. New York: Hafner.

Berelson, B., & Lazarsfeld, P. F. (1948). *The analysis of communication content* (not in print, available in microfilm, SI).

Berg, B. (1995). *Qualitative research methods for the social sciences* (2nd edn.). Boston: Allyn & Bacon.

Berry (1993). *Multiple regression in practice*. Thousand Oaks, CA: Sage.

Beatty, P.C., & Willis, G.B. (2007). Research synthesis: the practice of cognitive interviewing. *Public Opinion Quarterly, 71*(2): 287–311.

Billig, M. (1988). Methodology and scholarship in understanding ideological explanation. In C. Antaki (Ed.), *Analysing everyday explanation: A casebook of methods*. London: Sage.

Blalock, H. M., Jr. (1988). *Social statistics* (rev. 2nd edn.). Singapore: McGraw-Hill.

Bloor, M., Frankland, J., Thomas, M., & Robson, K. (2001). *Focus groups in social research*. London: Sage.

Blumer, H. (1969). *Symbolic interactionism*. Englewood Cliffs, NJ: Prentice Hall.

Bogardus, E. (1926). The group interview. *Journal of Applied Sociology, 10,* 372–382.

Borsboom, D. (2006). When does measurement invariance matter? *Medical Care, 44*(11), S3, S176–S180.

Boulton, M. (Ed.) (1994). *Challenge and innovation: Advances in social research on HIV/AIDS*. Brighton: Falmer Press.

Bradbury-Jones, C., Sambrook, S., & Irvine, F. (2009). The phenomenological focus group: An oxymoron? *Journal of Advanced Nursing, 65,* 663–671.

Bramley, N., & Eatough, V. (2005). An idiographic case study of the experience of living with Parkinson's disease using interpretative phenomenological analysis. *Psychology & Health, 20,* 223–235.

Brazelton, T. B., & Cramer, B. G. (1991). *The earliest relationship: Parents, infants and the drama of early attachment*. London: Karnac Books.

Breakwell, G. M. (1994). The echo of power: An integrative framework for social psychological theorizing. *The Psychologist, 7*(2): 65–72.

Breakwell, G. M., & Barnett, J. (2001). *The impact of social amplification upon risk communication* (Research report 322/2001). Sudbury: HSE Books. (Summarised in G. M. Breakwell (2007) *The psychology of risk* (pp. 156–165). Cambridge: Cambridge University Press.

Breakwell, G. M., & Canter, D. V. (1993). *Empirical approaches to social representations*. Oxford: Oxford University Press.

Breakwell, G. M., & Rose, D. (2006). Theory, method and design. In G. M. Breakwell, S. Hammond, C. Fife-Schaw & J. A. Smith (Eds), *Research methods in psychology* (3rd edn., pp. 2–23). London: Sage.

Brickhouse, T. C., & Smith, N. D. (1995). *Plato's Socrates*. New York: Oxford University Press.

Bringer, J., Johnston, L., & Brackenridge, C. (2004). Maximising transparency in a doctoral thesis: the complexities of writing about the use of QSR*NVIVO within a grounded theory study. *Qualitative Research, 4*(2), 247–265.

British Psychological Society (2004). *Style guide*. Leicester: British Psychological Society. Retrieved from http://bps. org. uk/document-download-area/document-download$. cfm?file_uuid=1B29ADB1–7E96-C67F-D51D3ADFC581A906&ext=pdf

British Psychological Society (2009). British Psychological Society Ethics Code. Retrieved from www. bps. org. uk/the-society/code-of-conduct

Brocki, J., & Wearden, A. (2006). A critical evaluation of interpretative phenomenological analysis in health psychology. *Psychology & Health, 21,* 87–108.

Brockmeier, J., & Carbaugh, D. (Eds) (2001). *Narrative and identity: Studies in autobiography, self and culture*. Amsterdam: John Benjamins.

Brooker, C. (2010, August 30). Somewhere there's an evil Don Draper coining buzzwords for blowhards., and he's damn good at his job. *The Guardian*, G2, p. 9.

Brown, T. A. (2006). *Confirmatory factor analysis for applied researchers*. London: The Guilford Press.

Browne, M. W., Cudeck, R., Tateneni, K., & Mels, G. (2009). *CEFA: Comprehensive exploratory factor analysis* (version 3. 03). Retrieved from http://faculty.psy.ohio-state.edu/browne/software.php

Bruner, J. (1990). *Acts of meaning*. Cambridge, MA: Harvard University Press.

Burck, C. (2005). Comparing qualitative research methodologies for systemic research: the use of grounded theory, discourse analysis and narrative analysis. *Journal of Family Therapy*, 27(3), 237–262.

Bull, P. (2004). The analysis of equivocation in political interviews. In G. M. Breakwell (Ed.) *Doing social psychology research*. Oxford: Blackwell.

Burman, E., & Parker, I. (Eds) (1993a). *Discourse analytic research: Repertoires and readings of texts in action*. London: Routledge.

Burman, E., & Parker, I. (1993b). Introduction – discourse analysis: the turn to the text. In E. Burman & I. Parker (Eds) *Discourse analytic research: Repertoires and readings of texts in action*. London: Routledge.

Burr, V. (1999). The extra-discursive in social constructionism. In D. J. Nightingale & J. Cromby (Eds), *Social constructionist psychology. A critical analysis of theory and practice* (pp. 113–126). Buckingham: Open University Press.

Burr, V. (2003). *Social constructionism*. London: Routledge.

Campbell, J. M. (1992). Treating depression in well older adults: Use of diaries in cognitive therapy. *Issues in Mental Health Nursing*, 13(1), 19–29.

Campbell, D. T., & Fiske, D. W. (1959). Convergent and discriminant validation by the multitrait-multimethod matrix. *Psychological Bulletin*, 56, 81–105.

Campbell, D. T., & Stanley, J. C. (1966). *Experimental and quasi-experimental designs for research*. Chicago: Rand McNally.

Cappello, M. (2005). *Field methods*. Thousand Oaks, CA: Sage.

Carlucci, M. E., Kieckhaefer, J. M., Schwartz, S. L., Villalba, D. K., & Wright, D. B. (2011). The South Beach study: Bystanders' memories are more malleable. *Applied Cognitive Psychology*, 25, 562–66.

Cattell, R. B. (1966). The scree test for the number of factors. *Multivariate Behavioral Research*, 1, 245–276.

Cattell, R. B. (1981). *Personality and learning theory*, Vols I and II. Berlin: Springer.

Catterall, M., & Maclaran, P. (1997). Focus group data and qualitative analysis. *Sociological Research Online*, 2(1) (http://www. socresonline. org. uk/2/1/6. html).

Chalmers, R. F. (1999). *What is this thing called science? An assessment of the nature and status of science and its methods* (3rd edn.). Maidenhead: Open University Press.

Chamberlain, P., Camic, P., & Yardley, L. (2004). Qualitative analysis of experience: Grounded theory and case studies. In D. Marks & L. Yardley (Eds), *Research methods for clinical and health psychology*. London: Sage.

Chapman, E. (2002). The social and ethical implications of changing medical technologies: The views of people living with genetic conditions. *Journal of Health Psychology*, 7, 195–206.

Charmaz, K. (1990). Discovering chronic illness: Using grounded theory. *Social Science and Medicine*, 30, 1161–1172.

Charmaz, K. (2000). Grounded theory: Objectivist and subjectivist methods. In N. Denzin & Y. Lincoln (Eds) *Handbook of qualitative research* (2nd edn., pp. 509–535). London and Thousand Oaks, CA: Sage.

Charmaz, K. (2006). *Constructing grounded theory: A practical guide through qualitative analysis.* London: Sage.

Charmaz, K., & Henwood, K. L. (2008). Grounded theory. In C. Willig and W. Stainton-Rogers (Eds), *The Sage handbook of qualitative research in psychology* (pp. 240–259). London and Thousand Oaks: Sage.

Clark, L. (2009). Focus group research with children and youth. *Journal for Specialists in Pediatric Nursing, 14,* 152–154.

Clarke, A. E. (2003). Situational analyses: Grounded theory mapping after the postmodern turn. *Symbolic Interaction, 26,* 553–576.

Cohen, J. (1988). *Statistical power analyses for the behavioural sciences* (2nd edn.). Hillsdale, NJ: Erlbaum.

Cohen, J. (1992). A power primer. *Psychological Bulletin, 112,* 155–59.

Cohen, J., Cohen, P., Aiken, L., & West, S. (2002). *Applied multiple regression/correlation analysis for the behavioral sciences.* Hillsdale, NJ: Erlbaum.

Conner, M., Fitter, M., & Fletcher, W. (1999). Stress and snacking: A diary of daily hassles and between meal-snacking. *Psychology and Health, 14*(1), 51–63.

Conrad, P. (1987). The experience of illness: Recent and new directions. *Research in the Sociology of Health Care, 6,* 1–31.

Converse, P. E. (1964). The nature of belief systems in mass publics. In *Ideology and discontent.* New York: Free Press.

Cook, T. D., & Campbell, D. T. (1979). *Quasi-experimentation: Design and analysis issues for field settings.* Chicago: Rand McNally.

Cooper, C. M., & Yarborough, S. P. (2010). Tell me – show me: Using combined focus group and photo-voice to gain understanding of health issues in rural Guatemala. *Qualitative Health Research, 20,* 644–653.

Corkrey, R., & Parkinson, L. (2002). A comparison of 4 computer-based telephone interviewing methods: Getting answers to sensitive questions. *Behavioural Research Methods Instruments and Computers, 34*(3), 354–363.

Costa, P. T. Jr., & McCrae, R. R. (1992). *NEO PI-R professional manual.* Odessa, FL: Psychological Assessment Resources.

Coxon, A. P. M. (1999). Parallel accounts? Discrepancies between self-report (diary) and recall (questionnaire) measures of the same sexual behaviour. *AIDS Care, 11*(2), 221–234.

Coyle, A. (2008). Introduction to qualitative psychological research. In E. Lyons & A. Coyle (Eds), *Analysing qualitative data in psychology.* London: Sage.

Craven, M., & Coyle, A. (2007). Counselling psychologists' talk about 'psychopathology' and diagnostic categories: A reflective account of a discourse analytic study. In E. Lyons & A. Coyle (Eds), *Analysing qualitative data in psychology.* London: Sage.

Creswell, J. W., & Miller, D. L. (2000). Determining validity in qualitative inquiry. *Theory into Practice, 39*(3), 124–131.

Crittenden, P. (1998). Truth, error, omission, distortion, and deception: An application of attachment theory to the assessment and treatment of psychological disorder. In S. M. Clany Dollinger & L. F. DiLalla (Eds), *Assessment and intervention issues across the life span.* London: Erlbaum.

Crittenden, P. (2008). *Raising parents: Attachment, parenting and child safety.* Cullompton: Willem.

Croft, C. A., & Sorrentino, M. C. (1991). Physician interaction with families on issues of AIDS: What parents and youth indicate they desire. *Journal of Health Behavior, Education and Promotion, 15*(6), 13–22.

Dale, A., Gilbert, G. N., & Arber, S. (1985). Integrating women into class theory, *Sociology, 19*, 384–409.

Dallos, R., & Draper, R. (2005). *An introduction to family therapy* (2nd edn.). Maidenhead: McGraw-Hill/Open University Press.

Dallos, R., & Vetere, A. (2005). *Researching psychotherapy and counselling.* Bletchley: McGraw-Hill.

Dallos, R. & Vetere, A. (2005). *Research methods in psychotherapy and counselling.* Maidenhead: McGraw-Hill/Open University Press.

Danziger, K. (1990). *Constructing the subject: Historical origins of psychological research.* Cambridge: Cambridge University Press.

Davies, B., & Harré, R. (1990). Positioning: the discursive production of selves. *Journal for the Theory of Social Behaviour, 20*, 43–63.

Davies, B., & Harré , R. (1999). Positioning and personhood. In R. Harré & L. van Langenhove (Eds), *Positioning theory.* Oxford: Blackwell.

Davies, J. B. (2004). Bring on the physics revolution. *Psychologist, 17*(12), 692–693.

Davison, M. L., & Sharma, A. R. (1990). Parametric statistics and levels of measurement: factorial designs and multiple regression, *Psychological Bulletin, 107*, 394–400.

De Leuw, E., & Hox, J. (2001). Trends in household survey nonresponse: A longitudinal and international comparison. In R. Groves, D. Dillman, J. Eltinge & R. Little (Eds), *Survey nonresponse.* New York: Wiley.

Deary, I. J., Whalley, L. J., Lemmon, H., Crawford, J. R., & Starr, J. M. (2000). The stability of individual differences in mental ability from childhood to old age: Follow-up of the 1932 Scottish mental survey. *Intelligence, 28*(1), 49–55.

Deffenbacher, K. A., Bornstein, B. H., Penrod, S. D., & McGorty, E. K. (2004). A meta-analytic review of the effects of high stress on eyewitness memory. *Law and Human Behavior, 28*(6), 687–706.

Delli-Carpini, M., & Williams, B. A. (1994). Methods, metaphors and media research: The uses of TV in political conversation. *Communication Research, 21*(6), 782–812.

Dickinson, J. J., & Poole, D. A. (2000). Efficient coding of eyewitness narratives: A comparison of syntactic unit and word count procedures. *Behavior Research Methods, Instruments and Computers, 32*(4), 537–545.

Dilthey, W. (1976). *Wilhem Dilthey: Selected writings.* Cambridge: Cambridge University Press (Edited and translated by H. P. Rickman).

Dorsey, J. (2006). Retrieved from http://en. wikipedia. org/wiki/Twitter, 13 March, 2011.

Draper, S. (2009). The Hawthorne, Pygmalion, placebo and other effects of expectation: Some notes. Retrieved from http://www.psy.gla.ac.uk/~steve/hawth.html.

Drew, P. (2008). Conversation analysis. In J. A. Smith (Ed.), *Qualitative psychology. A practical guide to research methods* (2nd edn., pp. 133–159). London: Sage.

Duchaine, B. C., & Weidenfeld, A. (2003). An evaluation of two commonly used tests of unfamiliar face recognition. *Neuropsychologia, 41*(6), 713–720.

Dunn, N. J., Seilhamer, R. A., Jacob, T., & Whalen, M. (1993). Comparison of restrospective and current reports of alcoholics and their spouses on drinking behaviour. *Addictive Behaviours, 17*, 543–555.

Dworkin, S. F., & Wilson, L. (1993). Measurement of illness behaviour: Review of concepts and common measures. In P. M. Conn (Ed.), *Paradigms for the study of behavior.* New York: Academic Press.

Eatough, V., & Smith, J. A. (2006). 'I feel like a scrambled egg in my head': An idiographic case study of meaning making and anger using interpretative phenomenological analysis. *Psychology and Psychotherapy, 79*, 115–135.

Eatough, V., & Smith, J. A. (2008). Interpretative phenomenological analysis. In C. Willig and W Stainton Rogers (Eds), *Handbook of qualitatitive psychology* (pp. 179–194). London: Sage.

Edgeworth, F. Y. (1888). The mathematical theory of banking. *Journal of the Royal Statistical Society, 51*(1), 113–127.

Edley, N., & Wetherell, M. (1999). Imagined futures: Young men's talk about fatherhood and domestic life. *British Journal of Social Psychology, 38,* 181–194.

Edwards, D., & Potter, J. (1992). *Discursive psychology.* London: Sage.

Eggins, R. A., O'Brien, A. T., Reynolds, K. J., Haslam, S. A., & Crocker, A. S. (2008). Refocusing the focus group: AIRing as a basis for effective workplace planning. *British Journal of Management, 19,* 277–293.

Elliott, R. (1986). Interpersonal Process Recall (IPR) as a process research method. In L. Greenberg & W. Pinsof (Eds), *The psychotherapeutic process.* New York: Guilford Press.

Elliott, R., Fischer, C., & Rennie, D. (1999). Evolving guidelines for publication of qualitative research studies in psychology and related fields. *British Journal of Clinical Psychology, 38,* 215–229.

Ellis, D. G. (1993). *Small group decision making.* New York: McGraw-Hill.

Ellis, C. (1998). Exploring loss through autoethnographic inquiry: Autoethnographic stories, co-constructed narratives, and interactive interviews. In J. Harvey (Ed.), *Perspectives on loss: A sourcebook* (pp. 49–61). Philadelphia: Brunner/Mazel.

Ely, R., Melzi, G., Hadge, L., & McCabe, A. (1998). Being brave, being nice: Themes of agency and communion in children's narratives. *Journal of Personality, 66*(2), 257–284.

Embretson, S. E., & Reise, S. P. (2000). *Item response theory for psychologists.* Mahwah, NJ: Erlbaum.

Evans, M. (1993). Reading lives: How the personal might be social. *Sociology, 27,* 5–13.

Evans, R. I., Rozelle, R. M., Mittelmark, M. B., Hansen, W. B., Bane, A. L., & Havis, J. (1978). Deterring the onset of smoking in children: Knowledge of immediate physiological effects and coping with peer pressure, media pressure and parent modelling, *Journal of Applied Social Psychology, 8*(2), 126–135.

Ewing, K. P. (2000). Dream as symptom, dream as myth: A cross-cultural perspective on dream narratives. *Sleep and Hypnosis, 2*(4), 152–159.

Ezzy, D. (1998). Theorizing narrative identity: Symbolic interactionism and hermeneutics. *Sociological Quarterly, 39*(2), 239–252.

Fairclough, N., & Wodak, R. (1997). Critical discourse analysis. In T. A. van Dijk (Ed.), *Discourse as social interaction: A multidisciplinary introduction.* London: Sage.

Farsides, T. (2004). Cognitive mapping: generating theories of psychological phenomena from verbal accounts and presenting them diagrammatically. In G. M. Breakwell (Ed.) *Doing social psychology research.* Oxford: Blackwell .

Faul, F., Erdfelder, E., Lang, A. G., & Buchner, A. (2007). G*Power 3: A flexible statistical power analysis program for the social, behavioral, and biomedical sciences. *Behavior Research Methods, 39*(2), 175–191.

Feldman, C. F. (2001). Narratives of national identity as group narratives: patterns of interpretive cognition. In D. Carbaugh & J. Brockmeier (Eds), *Narrative and identity: Studies in autobiography, self and culture* (pp. 129–144). Amsterdam: John Benjamins.

Field, A. (2009). *Discovering statistics using SPSS* (3rd edn.). London: Sage.

Field, A. P. (2005). Sir Ronald Aylmer Fisher. In B. S. Everitt & D. C. Howell (Eds), *Encyclopedia of statistics in behavioral science* (Volume 2, pp. 658–659). Chichester: Wiley.

Field, A. & Hole, G. (2003). *How to design and report experiments.* London: Sage.

Fielding, N. (2003). *Interviewing.* London: Sage.

Fielding, N., & Thomas, H. (2008). Qualitative interviewing. In: N. Gilbert (Ed.) *Researching social life*. London: Sage.

Fielding, N., Lee, R. M., & Blank, G. (2008). *The handbook of online research methods*. London: Sage.

Finlay, L., & Evans, K. (2009). *Relational-centred research for psychotherapists*. Chichester: Wiley-Blackwell.

Finlay, L., & Gough, B. (2003). *Reflexivity*. London: Blackwell Science.

Floersch, J., Longhofer, J.L., Kranke, D., & Townsend, L. (2010) Integrating thematic, grounded theory and narrative analysis: a case study of adolescent psychotropic treatment. *Qualitative Social Work*, 9(3), 407–425.

Flynn, J. (2009). *What is intelligence? Beyond the Flynn effect*. Cambridge: Cambridge University Press.

Flynn, J. R. (1984). The mean IQ of Americans: Massive gains 1932 to 1978. *Psychological Bulletin, 95*, 29–51.

Flynn, J. R. (1987). Massive IQ gains in 14 nations: what IQ tests really measure. *Psychological Bulletin, 101*, 171–191.

Fontana, A., & Fry, J. H. (2000). The interview: From structured questions to negotiated text. In N. K. Denzin & Y. S. Lincoln (Eds), *Handbook of qualitative research* (2nd edn., pp. 645–672). Thousand Oaks, CA: Sage.

Forbat, L. (2005). *Talking about care: Two sides to the story*. Bristol: Policy Press.

Fowers, B. J. (1998). Psychology and the good marriage: Social theory as practice. *American Behavioral Scientist, 41*, 516–541.

Fox, J. (1991) *Regression diagnostics*. Thousand Oaks, CA: Sage.

Frazier, N., Wood, B., & Yarnal, B. D. (2010). Stakeholder perspectives on land-use strategies for adapting to climate change enhanced coastal hazards, Sarasota, Florida. *Applied Geography, 30*(4), 506–517.

Freire, P. (1970). *Pedagogy of the oppressed*. New York: Continuum.

French, D. P., Maissi, E., & Marteau, T. M. (2005). The purpose of attributing cause: Beliefs about the causes of myocardial infarction. *Social Science & Medicine, 60*, 1411–1421.

Frith, H. (2000). Focusing on sex: Using focus groups in sex research. *Sexualities, 3*, 275–297.

Fuller, T. D., Edwards, J. N., Vorakitphokatom, S., & Sermsri, S. (1993). Using focus groups to adapt survey instruments to new populations: Experience from a developing country. In D. L. Morgan (Ed.), *Successful focus groups: Advancing the state of the art*. London: Sage.

Fullwood, C., Sheehan, N., & Nicholls, W. (2009). Blog function revisited: A content analysis of MySpace blogs. *CyberPsychology & Behavior, 12*(6), 685–689.

Gage, N. L. (1963). *Handbook of research on teaching*. Chicago: Rand McNally.

Gallagher, S. (2004). Hermeneutics and the cognitive sciences. *Journal of Consciousness Studies, 11*(10–11), 162–174.

Galton, F. (1907). Vox Populi. *Nature, 75*, 450–51.

Gardner, H. (1983). *Frames of mind: The theory of multiple intelligences*. New York: Basic Books.

Gaskell, G., Wright, D., & O'Muircheartaigh, C. (1993a). Reliability of surveys, *The Psychologist, 6*, 500–503.

Gaskell, G. D., Wright, D. B., & O'Muircheartaigh, C. A. (1993b). Measuring scientific interest: The effect of knowledge questions on interest ratings. *Journal for the Public Understanding of Science, 2*, 39–57.

Gergen, K. J. (1973). Social psychology as history. *Journal of Personality and Social Psychology, 26*, 309–320.

Gergen, K. J. (1989). Warranting voice and the elaboration of the self. In J. Shotter & K. J. Gergen (Eds), *Texts of identity*. London: Sage.

Gergen, K. J. (1998). From control to co-construction: New narratives for the social sciences. *Psychological Inquiry, 9*(2), 101–103.

Gergen, K. J. & Gergen, M. M. (1986). Narrative form and the construction of psychological science. In T. Sarbin (Ed.), *Narrative psychology: The storied nature of human conduct* (pp. 22–44). New York: Praeger.

Gergen, K. J., & Gergen, M. M. (2010). Scanning the landscape of narrative inquiry. *Social and Personality Psychology Compass, 4*(9), 728–735.

Gergen, M. M., & Gergen, K. J. (2006). Narratives in action. *Narrative Inquiry, 16*(1), 112–121.

Gervais, M.-C. (1993). How communities cope with environmental crises: The case of the Shetland oil spill. Paper presented at the BPS Social Psychology Section Annual Conference, Jesus College, Oxford, September.

Gibaldi, J. (2003). *MLA handbook for writers of research papers* (6th edn.). New York: Modern Language Association of America. Retrieved from http://www. mla. org/.

Gilgun, J. F., Daly, K., & Handel, G. (1992). *Qualitative methods in family research*. London: Sage.

Gillham, W. (2008). *Developing a questionnaire* (2nd edn.). London: Continuum International Publishing Group.

Giorgi, A. (1970). *Psychology as a human science*. New York: Harper Row.

Giorgi, A. (2009). *The descriptive phenomenological method in psychology: A modified Husserlian approach*. Pittsburgh: Duquesne University Press.

Giorgi, A., & Giorgi, B. (2008). Phenomenology. In J. A. Smith (Ed.), *Qualitative psychology. A practical guide to research methods* (2nd edn., pp. 26–52). London: Sage.

Glaser, B., & Strauss, A. (1967). *The discovery of grounded theory*. New York: Aldine.

Glitz, B. (1998). *Focus groups for libraries and librarians*. New York: Forbes Custom Publishing.

Goffman, E. (1961). *Asylums*. Chicago: Aldine.

Goldberg, D. (1972). *The detection of psychiatric illness by questionnaire*. London: Oxford University Press.

Goldberg, L. R. (1993). The structure of phenotypic personality traits. *American Psychologist, 48*(1), 26–34.

Golden, C. J., Hammeke, T. A., & Purisch, A. D. (1978). Diagnostic validity of a standardized neuropsychological battery derived from Luria's neuropsychological tests. *Journal of Consulting and Clinical Psychology, 46*, 1258–1265.

Golsworthy, R., & Coyle, A. (1999). Spiritual beliefs and the search for meaning among older adults following partner loss. *Mortality, 4*, 21–40.

Gomm, R., Hammersley, M., & Foster, P. (2000). Case study and generalization. In R. Gomm, M. Hattersley & P. Foster (Eds), *Case study method*. London: Sage.

Gosselink, C. A., & Myllykangas, S. A. (2007). The leisure experiences of older U.S. women living with HIV/AIDS. *Health Care for Women International, 28*, 3–20.

Gotschi, E., Delve, R., & Freyer, B. (2009). Participatory photography as a qualitative approach to obtain insights into farmer groups. *Field Methods, 21*(3), 290–308.

Gottman, J. M. (1982). Emotional responsiveness in marital communications. *Journal of Communications*, Summer, 108–120.

Greenbaum, T. L. (1998). *The handbook for focus group research*. London: Sage.

Greenbaum, T. L. (2000). *Moderating focus groups: A practical guide for group facilitation*. Thousand Oaks, CA: Sage.

Groves, R., Fowler, F., Couper, M., Lepkowski, J., Singer, E., & Tourangeau, R. (2004). *Survey methodology*. Hoboken, NJ: Wiley.

Guttman, L. (1944). A basis for scaling qualitative data. *American Sociological Review, 9,* 139–150.

Hacking, I. (1995). The looping effect of human kinds. In D. Sperber, D. Premack & A. J. Premack (Eds), *Causal cognition: A multi-disciplinary approach* (pp. 351–383). Oxford: Clarendon.

Haladyna, T. M., & Roid, G. H. (1983). A comparison of two approaches to criterion referenced test construction. *Journal of Educational Measurement, 20,* 271–282.

Halkier, B. (2010). Focus groups as social enactments: Integrating interaction and content in the analysis of focus group data. *Qualitative Research, 10*(1), 71–89.

Hammersley, M. (1992). *What's wrong with ethnography? Methodological explorations.* London: Routledge.

Hammersley, M., & Atkinson, P. (1995). *Ethnography: Principles in practice* (2nd edn.). London: Routledge.

Harré, R. (1979). *Social being.* Oxford: Basil Blackwell.

Harré, R., & Secord, P. F. (1972). *The explanation of social behaviour.* Oxford: Basil Blackwell.

Harris, P. (2008). *Designing and reporting experiments in psychology* (3rd edn.). Milton Keynes: OUP.

Hayes, N. (2000). *Doing psychological research. Gathering and analysing data.* Buckingham: Open University Press.

Hegarty, P. (2007). What comes after discourse analysis for LGBTQ psychology? In V. Clarke & E. Peel (Eds), *Out in psychology: Lesbian, gay, bisexual, trans and queer perspectives.* Chichester: John Wiley.

Henkel, R. E. (1975). Part–whole correlations and the treatment of ordinal and quasi-interval data as interval data. *Pacific Sociological Review, 18,* 3–26.

Henwood, K. L. (1993). Women and later life: The discursive construction of identities within family relationships. *Journal of Ageing Studies, 7,* 303–319.

Henwood, K. L. (2006). Grounded theory in mental health and related research. In M. Slade & S. Priebe (Eds), *Choosing methods in mental health research century* (pp. 68–84). London: Brunner Routledge .

Henwood, K. L., & Pidgeon, N. (1992). Qualitative research and psychological theorising. *British Journal of Psychology, 83,* 97–111.

Henwood, K. L., & Pidgeon, N. F. (2001). Talk about woods and trees: Threat of urbanisation, stability and biodiversity. *Journal of Environmental Psychology, 21,* 125–147.

Henwood, K. L., & Pidgeon, N. F. (2003). Grounded theory in psychological research. In P. Camic, L. Yardley & J. Rhodes (Eds), *Qualitative research in psychology* (pp. 131–155). Washington DC: American Psychological Association Press.

Hepburn, A. (2006). Getting closer at a distance: Theory and the contingencies of practice. *Theory & Psychology, 16,* 325–342.

Hepburn, A., & Wiggins, S. (2005). Size matters: Constructing accountable bodies in NSPCC helpline interaction. *Discourse & Society, 16,* 625–645.

Hepburn, A., & Wiggins, S. (Eds) (2007). *Discursive research in practice: New approaches to psychology and interaction.* Cambridge: Cambridge University Press.

Herman, L. & Vervaeck, B. (2005). *Handbook of narrative analysis.* Nebraska: University of Nebraska Press.

Hilder, J. (1997). Notes on the use of focus groups in organizational settings. Unpublished manuscript, Social Psychology European Research Institute, University of Surrey.

Hoepfl, M. (1997). Choosing qualitative research: A primer for technology education researchers. *Journal of Technology Education, 9* (http://www. borg. lib. vt. edu/JTE/jte-v9n1/hoeofl. html).

Hole, G. J. (2007). *The psychology of driving.* Mahwah, NJ: Erlbaum.

Holland, P. W., Dorans, N. J., & Peterson, N. S. (2007). Equating test scores. In C. R. Rao (Ed.), *Handbook of statistics*, 26. North Holland: Elsevier.

Hollander, J. A. (2004). The social context of focus groups. *Journal of Contemporary Ethnography*, 33, 602–637.

Hollway, W. (1989). *Subjectivity and method in psychology: Gender, meaning and science*. London: Sage.

Hook, D. (2001). Discourse, knowledge, materiality, history: Foucault and discourse analysis. *Theory & Psychology*, 11, 521–547.

Hope, L., & Wright, D. (2007). Beyond unusual? Examining the role of attention in the weapon focus effect. *Applied Cognitive Psychology*, 21, 951–961.

Hopkins, P. E. (2007). Thinking critically and creatively about focus groups. *Area*, 39, 528–535.

Howell, D. C. (2010). *Statistical methods in psychology* (7th edn.). Pacific Grove, CA: Duxbury.

Hui, C. H., & Triandis, H. C. (1989). Effects of culture and response format on extreme response style. *Journal of Cross-Cultural Psychology*, 20, 296–309.

Hutchinson, K., & Wegge, D. (1991). The effects of interviewer gender upon response in telephone survey research. *Journal of Social Behaviour and Personality*, 6(3), 575–584.

Hyden, L.-C., & Bulow, P. H. (2003). Who's Talking: Drawing conclusions from focus groups – some methodological considerations. *International Journal of Social Research Methodology*, 6, 305–321.

Jaccard, J. (1998). *Interaction effects in factorial analysis of variance*. Newbury Park, CA: Sage.

Jaccard, J., & Jacoby, J. (2010). *Theory construction and model-building skills: A practical guide for social scientists*. New York: Guilford Press.

Jackson, D. N. (1977). *Jackson vocational interest survey manual*. Ontario: Research Psychologists Press.

Jarrett, R. L. (1993). Focus group interviewing with low-income minority populations. In D. L. Morgan (Ed.), *Successful focus groups: Advancing the state of the art*. Newbury Park, CA: Sage.

Josselson, R. (2009). The present of the past: Dialogues with memory over time. *Journal of Personality*, 77(3), 647–668.

Josselson, R., & Lieblich, A. (2009). Reflections on the narrative study of lives. *Narrative Inquiry*, 19(1), 183–198.

Jovchelovitch, S. (2000). Corruption flows in our blood: Mixture and impurity in representations of public life in Brazil. In M. Chaib & B. Orfali (Eds), *Social representations and communicative processes*. Jönköping: Jönköping University Press.

Junker, B. H. (1972). *Fieldwork: An introduction to the social sciences*. Chicago: University of Chicago Press.

Kaiser, H. F. (1960). The application of electronic computers to factor analysis. *Educational and Psychological Measurement*, 20, 141–151.

Karlsen, C. F. (1987). *The devil in the shape of a woman: Witchcraft in colonial New England*. New York: Vintage Books.

Kashima, Y. (2000). Maintaining cultural stereotypes in the serial reproduction of narratives. *Personality and Social Psychology Bulletin*, 26(5), 594–604.

Kelly, G. A. (1955). *The psychology of personal constructs, vols. 1 and 2*. New York: Norton.

Kendler, H. H. (1987). *Historical foundations of modern psychology*. Pacific Grove, CA: Brooks/Cole.

Kenny, A. J. (2005). Interaction in cyberspace: An online focus group. *Journal of Advanced Nursing*, 49, 414–422.

Kessler, S. J. (1998). *Lessons from the intersexed*. New Brunswick, NJ: Rutgers University Press.

Kidder, L., & Fine, M. (1997). Qualitative methods on psychology: A radical tradition. In D. R. Fox & I. Prilletensky (Eds), *Critical psychology: An introduction* (pp. 34–50). Thousand Oaks, CA: Sage.

Kiernan, B. D., Cox, D. J., Kovatchev, B. P., Kiernan, B. S., & Giuliano, A. J. (1999). Improving driving performance of senior drivers through self-monitoring with a driving diary. *Physical and Occupational Therapy in Geriatrics, 16*(1–2), 55–64.

King, R. M., & Wilson, G. V. (1992). Use of a diary technique to investigate psychosomatic relations in atopic dermatitis. *Journal of Psychosomatic Research, 35*, 697–706.

King, G., Keohane, R. O., & Verba, S. (1994). *Designing social enquiry: Scientific inference in qualitative research*. Princeton, NJ: Princeton University Press.

Kitzinger, J. (1994). The method of focus group interviews: The importance of interaction between research participants. *Sociology of Health and Illness, 16*(1), 103–121.

Klem, L. (2000). Structural equation modeling. In L. G. Grimm & P. R. Yarnold (Eds), *Reading and understanding more multivariate statistics* (pp. 227–260). Washington, DC: American Psychological Association.

Knodel, J. (1993). The design and analysis of focus group studies: A practical approach. In D. L. Morgan (Ed.), *Successful focus groups: Advancing the state of the art*. London: Sage.

Krippendorf, K. (1980). *Content analysis: An introduction to its methodology* (1st edn.). Beverly Hills, CA: Sage.

Krippendorf, K. (2004). *Content analysis: An introduction to its methodology* (2nd edn.). Thousand Oaks, CA: Sage.

Krippendorff, K. (2004). Measuring the rehability of qualitative text analysis data. *Quality and Quantity, 38*(6), 787–800.

Krosnick, J. A., Holbrook, A. L., Berent, M. K., Carson, R. T., Haneman, W. M. *et al.* (2002). The impact of 'no opinion' response options on data quality. *Public Opinion Quarterly, 66*, 371–403.

Krosnick, J. A., & Schuman, H. (1988). Attitude intensity, importance, and certainty and susceptibility to response effects. *Journal of Personality and Social Psychology, 54*, 940–952.

Krueger, R. A. (1993). Quality control in focus group research. In D. L. Morgan (Ed.), *Successful focus groups: Advancing the state of the art*. London: Sage.

Krueger, R. A. (1994). *Focus groups: A practical guide for applied research* (2nd edn.). London: Sage.

Krueger, R. A., & Casey, M. (2000). *Focus groups: A practical guide for applied research* (3rd edn.). Newbury Park, CA: Sage.

Kurz, T., Augoustinos, M., & Crabb, S. (2010). Contesting the 'national interest' and maintaining 'our lifestyle': a discursive analysis of political rhetoric around climate change. *British Journal of Social Psychology, 49*, 601–625.

Kvale, S. (1996). *Interviews: An introduction to qualitative research interviewing*. London: Sage.

Labovitz, S. (1975). Comment on Henkel's paper: The interplay between measurement and statistics, *Pacific Sociological Review, 18*, 27–35.

Lakoff, G. (1990). *Women, fire and dangerous things*. Chicago: University of Chicago Press.

Lambert, S. D., & Loiselle, C. G. (2008). Health information-seeking behavior. *Qualitative Health Research, 17*, 1006–1019.

Laor, A., Stevenson, D. K., Shemer, J., Gale, R., & Seldman, D. S. (1997). Size at birth, maternal nutritional status in pregnancy, and blood pressure at age 17: population based analysis. *British Medical Journal, 315*, 449.

Lawlor, D. A., Davey Smith, G., & Ebrahim, S. (2004). Commentary: The hormone replacement-coronary heart disease conundrum: Is this the death of observational epidemiology? *International Journal of Epidemiology, 33,* 464–467.

Legg, C., Puri, A., & Thomas, N. (2000). Dietary restraint and self-reported meal sizes: Diary studies with differentially informed consent. *Appetite, 34*(3), 235–243.

Lehoux, P., Poland, B., & Daudelin, G. (2006). Focus group research and 'the patient's view. *Social Science and Medicine, 63,* 2091–2104.

Lewins, A., & Silver, C. (2007). *Using software in qualitative research: A step-by-step guide.* London: Sage.

Lewis, A., & Porter, J. (2004). Interviewing children and young people with learning difficulties. *British Journal of Learning Disability, 32*(4), 191–197.

Libman, E., Fichten, C. S., Bailes, S., & Amsel, R. (2000). Sleep questionnaire versus sleep diary: Which measure is better? *International Journal of Rehabilitation and Health, 5*(3), 205–209.

Lilienfeld, S. O. (2007). Psychological treatments that cause harm. *Perspectives on Psychological Science, 2*(1), 53–70.

Lincoln, Y., & Guba, E. (1985). *Naturalistic inquiry.* Beverly Hills, CA: Sage.

Linell, P. (2001). A dialogical conception of focus groups and social representations. In U. Sötterlund Larson (Ed.), *Sociocultural theory and methods: An anthology.* Department of Nursing, University of Trollhöttan/Uddevalla.

Llewellyn, G. (1991). Adults with an intellectual disability: Australian practitioners' perspectives. *Occupational Therapy Journal of Research, 11,* 323–335.

Low, J., & Dugmore, O. (2009). What can the FOCUS e-mail discussion group tell us about the issues facing CAMH professionals? *Child and Adolescent Mental Health, 14,* 76–80.

Luce, R. D., Krantz, D. H., Suppes, P., & Tversky, A. (1990). *Foundations of measurement, volume 3: Representation, axiomatisation and invariance.* New York: Academic Press.

Luce, R. D., & Tukey, J. W. (1964). Simultaneous conjoint measurement: A new type of fundamental measurement. *Journal of Mathematical Psychology, 1,* 1–27.

Lundh, L. G., & Sperling, M. (2002). Social anxiety and the post-event processing of socially distressing events. *Cognitive Behaviour Therapy, 31*(3), 129–134.

Lunt, P. (1996). Discourse of savings. *Journal of Economic Psychology, 17,* 677–690.

Lunt, P., & Livingstone, S. (1996). Focus groups in common and media research. *Journal of Communication, 42,* 78–87.

Lynn, P., Beerten, R., Laiho, J., & Martin, J. (2001). *Recommended standard final outcome categories and standard definitions of response rate for social surveys* (Working Papers of the Institute for Social and Economic Research 2001–23). University of Essex, Colchester.

Lyons, E., & Coyle, A. (Eds) (2007). *Analysing qualitative data in psychology.* London: Sage.

MacIntyre, A. (1984). *After virtue.* Notre Dame: University of Notre Dame Press.

Madill, A., & Gough, B. (2008). Qualitative research and its place in psychological science. *Psychological Methods, 13,* 254–271.

Markham, A. N. (2004). Internet communication as a tool for research. In D. Silverman (Ed.), *Qualitative research: Theory, method and practice* (pp. 95–124). London: Sage.

Marquand, D. (1991). Civic republicans and liberal individualists: The case of Britain. *Archives Européennes de Sociologie, 32,* 329–344.

Marsh, P., Rosser, E., & Harre, R. (1978). *The rules of disorder.* London: Routledge and Kegan Paul.

Marshall, C., & Rossman, G. B. (2010). *Designing qualitative research* (4th edn.). London: Sage.

Martin, J., & Sugarman, J. (2001). Interpreting human kinds. *Theory & Psychology, 11,* 193–207.

May, V. (2004). Narrative identity and the re-conceptualization of lone motherhood. *Narrative Inquiry, 14*(1), 169–189.

Mayring, P. (2000). Qualitative content analysis. *Forum: Qualitative Social Research,* 1(2), Art. 20.

McAdams, D. P. (1999). Personal narratives and the life story. In O. P. John & L. A. Pervin (Eds), *Handbook of personality: Theory and research* (2nd edn., pp. 478–500). New York: Guilford Press.

McAdams, D. P. (2004). The redemptive self: Narrative identity in America today. In J. M. Lampinen & R. Beike (Eds), *The self and memory* (pp. 95–115). New York: Psychology Press.

Mehl, M. R., Gill, A. J., & Gosling, S. D. (2010). Automatic text analysis. In J. A. Johnson (Ed.), *Advanced methods for conducting online behavioural research* (pp. 109–127). Washington, DC: American Psychological Association.

Merton, R. K., & Kendall, P. L. (1946). The focused interview. *American Journal of Sociology, 51,* 541–557.

Michell, L. (1998). Combining focus groups and interviews: Telling how it is: Telling how it feels. In R. Barbour & J. Kitzinger (Eds), *Developing focus group research* (pp. 36–46). London: Sage.

Michell, J. (2000). Normal science, pathological science and psychometrics. *Theory and Psychology, 10*(5), 639–667.

Michell, L., & West, P. (1996). Peer pressure to smoke: The meaning depends on the method. *Health Education Research, 11*(1), 39–49.

Miles, M. B., & Huberman, A. M. (1994). *Qualitative data analysis* (2nd edn.). London: Sage.

Miles, S., & Rowe, G. (2004). The laddering technique. In G. M. Breakwell (Ed.) *Doing social psychology research*. Oxford: Blackwell.

Miles, J., & Shevlin, M. (2000). *Applying regression and correlation*. London: Sage.

Miles, J., & Shevlin, M. (2003). Structural equation modelling: Navigating spaghetti junction. *The Psychologist, 16,* 639–641.

Milgram, S. (1983). *Obedience to authority: An experimental view*. New York: Harper/Collins.

Mill, J. S. (1882). *A system of logic, ratiocinative and inductive: Being a connected view of the principles of evidence and the methods of scientific investigation* (8th edn.). New York: Harper and Brothers. Available online from: http://www.archive.org/details/systemofratiocin00milluoft.

Miller, J. E. (2004). *The Chicago guide to writing about numbers*. Chicago: University Of Chicago Press. Retrieved from http://www.press.uchicago.edu/ucp/books/book/chicago/C/bo3636131.html

Minami, M. (2000). The relationship between narrative identity and culture. *Narrative Inquiry, 10*(1), 75–80.

Minium, E. W., King, B. M., & Bear, G. (1993). *Statistical reasoning in psychology and education*. New York: Wiley.

Mischel, W. (1968). *Personality and assessment*. New York: Wiley.

Moran, D. (2000). *Introduction to phenomenology*. London: Routledge.

Morgan, D. (2010). Reconsidering the role of interaction in analyzing and reporting focus group data. *Qualitative Health Research, 20,* 718–722.

Morgan, D. L. (1988) *Focus groups as qualitative research*. Newbury Park, CA: Sage.

Morgan, D. L. (1997). *Focus groups as qualitative research* (2nd edn.). Thousand Oaks, CA: Sage.

Morgan, D. L., & Krueger, R. A. (1997). *Focus group kit*. London: Sage.

Morone, N., Lynch, C.L., Greco C.M., Tindle, H.A., & Weiner D.K. (2008). 'I felt like a new person.' the effects of mindfulness meditation on older adults with chronic pain: qualitative narrative analysis of diary entries. *Journal of Pain*, 9(9), 841–848.

Morris, D. (2002). *Peoplewatching: Desmond Morris guide to body language*. London: Vintage.

Moser, C. A., & Kalton, G. (1971). *Survey methods in social investigation*. London: Heinemann.

Mulaik, S.A. (2010). *Foundations of factor analysis* (2nd edn.). Boca Raton, FL: Chapman & Hall/CRC.

Munday, J. (2006). Identity in focus: The use of focus groups to study the construction of collective identity. *Sociology*, *40*, 89–105.

Murray, M. (2008). Narrative psychology. In J. A. Smith (Ed.), *Qualitative psychology. A practical guide to research methods* (pp. 111–132). London: Sage.

Myers, G. (2000). Becoming a group: Face and sociability in moderated discussions. In S. Sarangi & M. Coulthard (Eds), *Discourse and social life* (pp. 121–137). Harlow: Pearson.

Neuendorf, K. A. (2002). *The content analysis guidebook*. Thousand Oaks, CA: Sage.

Neugebauer, H. (1929). The emotional and volitional life of my son in his early childhood/Das Gefuehls und Willensleben Meines Sohnes in Seiner Fruehen Kindheit. *Zeitschrift Fuer Angewandte Psychologie*, *34*, 275–310.

Nezlek, J. B. (1991). Self-report diaries in the study of social interaction. *Contemporary Social Psychology*, *14*(4), 205-210.

Nigro, G., & Wolpow, S. (2004). Interviewing young children with props. *Applied Cognitive Psychology*, *18*(5), 549–565.

Nova Development Corporation (2004). *Art explosion: 800,000 premium quality graphics* CD-Rom.

O'Brien, K. (1993). Improving survey questionnaires through focus groups. In D. L. Morgan (Ed.), *Successful focus groups: Advancing the state of the art*. London: Sage.

Olsen, C. K., Kutner, L. A., & Warner, D. E. (2008). The role of violent video game content in adolescent development: Boys' perspectives. *Journal of Adolescent Research*, *23*, 55–75.

Oppenheim, A. N. (1992). *Questionnaire design, interviewing and attitude measurement*. London: Printer Publishers.

Pace, S. (2008). YouTube – an opportunity for consumer narrative analysis? *Qualitative Market Research*, 11(2), 213–226.

Packer, M. J., & Addison, R. B. (1989). Introduction. In M. J. Packer & R. B. Addison (Eds), *Entering the circle: Hermeneutic investigation in psychology* (pp. 13–36). Albany, NY: SUNY Press.

Palmer, R. (1969). *Hermeneutics*. Evanston, IL: Northwestern University Press.

Parker, I. (1992). *Discourse dynamics: Critical analysis for social and individual psychology*. London: Routledge.

Parker, I., & Burman, E. (1993). Against discursive imperialism, empiricism and constructionism: Thirty-two problems with discourse analysis. In E. Burman & I. Parker (Eds), *Discourse analytic research: Repertoires and readings of texts in action*. London: Routledge.

Penfield, R. D., & Camilli, G. (2007). Differential item functioning and item bias. In C. R. Rao (Ed.) *Handbook of statistics*, 26. Elsevier: North Holland.

Peters, M. L., Sorbi, M. J., Kruise, D. A., Kerssens, J. J., Verhaak, P. F. M., & Bensing, J. M. (2000). Electronic diary assessment of pain, disability and psychological adaptation in patients differing in duration of pain. *Pain*, *84*(2–3), 181–192.

Pfefferbaum, B., Houston, J., Wyche, K., Van Horn, R., Reyes, G., Slaughter, J., & North, C. (2008). Children displaced by Hurricane Katrina: A focus group study. *Journal of Loss and Trauma*, *13*, 303–318.

Pfungst, O. (1911/1965). *Clever Hans (the horse of Mr. Von Osten)*. New York: Holt, Rinehart and Winston (reprint of 1911 original).

Pickel, K. L. (1998). Unusualness and threat as possible causes of 'weapon focus'. *Memory, 6(3)*, 277–295.

Pidgeon, N. F., & Henwood, K. L. (2004). Grounded theory. In M. Hardy & A. Bryman (Eds), *Handbook of data analysis* (pp. 625–648). London: Sage.

Plummer, K. (Ed.) (1981). *The making of the modern homosexual*. London: Hutchinson.

Polkinghorne, D. E. (1983). *Methodology for the human sciences*. Albany, NY: SUNY Press.

Polkinghorne, D. E. (2005). Language and meaning: Data collection in qualitative research. *Journal of Counseling Psychology, 52*, 137–145.

Pomerantz, A. M. (1986). Extreme case formulations: a new way of legitimating claims. *Human Studies, 9*, 219–230.

Popper, K. (1963). *Conjectures and refutations*. London: Routledge & Kegan Paul.

Potter, J. (1996). *Representing reality: Discourse, rhetoric and social construction*. London: Sage.

Potter, J. (2003). Discourse analysis. In M. Hardy & A. Bryman (Eds), *Handbook of data analysis*. London: Sage.

Potter, J. (Ed.) (2007a). *Discourse and psychology: Volume I Theory and method*. London: Sage.

Potter, J. (Ed.) (2007b). *Discourse and psychology: Volume II Discourse and social psychology*. London: Sage

Potter, J. (Ed.) (2007c). *Discourse and psychology: Volume III Discursive psychology*. London: Sage.

Potter, J., & Hepburn, A. (2005). Qualitative interviews in psychology: Problems and possibilities. *Qualitative Research in Psychology, 2*, 38–55.

Potter, J., & Wetherell, M. (1987). *Discourse and social psychology: Beyond attitudes and behaviour*. London: Sage.

Powell, G. E., & Adams, M. (1993). *Introduction to research on placement*. Paper presented at the Clinical Psychology Forum, 12–16 March, British Psychological Society.

Radley, A., & Chamberlain, K. (2001). Health psychology and the study of the case: From method to analytic concern. *Social Science and Medicine, 3*, 321–332.

Rasch, G. (1980). *Probabilistic models for intelligence and attainment testing*. Chicago: University of Chicago Press.

Ray, P., & Page, A. C. (2002). A single session of hypnosis and eye movement desensitisation and reprocessing (EMDR) in the treatment of chronic pain. *Australian Journal of Clinical and Experimental Hypnosis, 30(2)*, 170–178.

Reese, R. A. (2005). Boxplots. *Significance, 2*, 134–135.

Reese, R. A. (2007). Bah! Bar charts. *Significance, 4*, 41–44.

Reicher, S. (2000). Against methodolatry: Some comments on Elliott, Fischer, and Rennie. *British Journal of Clinical Psychology, 39*, 1–6.

Reid, D. J., & Reid, F. J. M. (2005). Online focus groups: An in-depth comparison of computer-mediated and conventional focus group discussion. *International Journal of Market Research, 47*, 131–162.

Reid, K., Flowers, P., & Larkin, M. (2005). Exploring lived experience: An introduction to interpretative phenomenological analysis. *The Psychologist, 18*, 20–23.

Reitan, R. M. (1955). An investigation of the validity of Halstead's measures of biological intelligence. *Archives of Neurology and Psychiatry, 73*, 28–35.

Rennie, D. L. (2000). Grounded theory methodology as methodical hermeneutics: Reconciling realism and relativism. *Theory & Psychology, 10*, 481–502.

Resnik, D., & Bond, C. (2007, May). Use of 'subjects' should not be subjective. *Observer*. Online version used, retrieved from http://www. psychologicalscience. org/index. php/uncategorized/ use-of-subjects-should-not-be-subjective. html.

Reuband, K., & Blasius, J. (1996). Face-to-face-, telephone- and mail questionnaires: Response rates and pattern in a large city study. *Kolner Zeitschrift fur Soziologie und Sozialpsychologie, 48*(2), 296–318.

Reuben, D. B., Wong, R. C., Walsh, K. E. & Hays, R. D. (1995). Feasibility and accuracy of a post-card diary system for tracking healthcare utilization of community-dwelling older persons. *Journal of the American Geriatrics Society, 43*, 550–552.

Rhodes, J., & Smith, J. A. (2010). 'The top of my head came off': An interpretative phenomenological analysis of the experience of depression. *Counselling Psychology Quarterly, 23*, 399–409.

Rich, M., & Patashnick, J. (2002). Narrative research with audio-visual data: VIA and NVIVO. *International Journal of Social Research Method, Theory and Practice, 5*(3), 245–261.

Ricoeur, P. (1970). *Freud and philosophy*. New Haven: Yale University Press.

Robinson, D. N. (2000). Paradigms and 'the myth of framework': How science progresses. *Theory & Psychology, 10*, 39–47.

Robson, C. (2002). *Real world research*. Oxford: Blackwell.

Robson, C. (2011). *Real world research* (3rd edn.). Oxford: Blackwell.

Rodriguez, N., & Ryave, A. (2002). *Systematic self-observation*. London: Sage.

Roediger, H. L. III (2007). Twelve tips for authors. *Observer*. Online version used, retrieved from http://www. psychologicalscience. org/index. php/uncategorized/twelve-tips-for-authors. html.

Roediger, R. (2004, April). What should they be called? *Observer*. Online version used, retrieved from http://www. psychologicalscience. org/observer/getArticle. cfm?id=1549.

Roethlisberger, F. J., & Dickson, W. J. (1939). *Management and the worker*. Cambridge, MA: Harvard University Press.

Roid, G. H. (1986). Computer technology in testing. In B. S. Plake & J. C. Witt (Eds), *The future of testing* (pp. 29–69). Hillsdale, NJ: Erlbaum.

Ronald, A., Happé, F., & Plomin, R. (2005). The genetic relationship between individual differences in social and nonsocial behaviours characteristic of autism. *Developmental Science, 8*, 444–458.

Rosenhan, D. L. (1973). On being sane in insane places. *Science, 179*, 250–268.

Rosenthal, R. (1966). *Experimenter effects in behavioral research*. New York: Appleton Century Crofts.

Rosenthal, R., & Jacobson, L. (1992). *Pygmalion in the classroom: Teacher expectation and pupils' intellectual development*. Irvington: New York.

Rothwell, E. (2010). Analyzing focus group data: content and interaction. *Journal for Specialists in Pediatric Nursing, 15*, 176–180.

Rubin, H.J., & Rubin, I.S. (2005). *Qualitative interviewing: the art of hearing data* (2nd edn.). London: Sage.

Rust, J. and Golombok, S. (2009). *Modern psychometrics: the science of psychological assessment* (3rd edn.). London: Routledge.

Russell, C. A., & Russell, D. W. (2009). Alcohol messages in prime-time television series. *Journal of Consumer Affairs, 43*(1), 108–128 (Box 1 example).

Rustin, M. (2002). Research, evidence and psychotherapy In C. Mace, S. Morley & B. Roberts (Eds), *Evidence in the psychological therapies*. Hove: Brunner-Routledge.

Salmon, P. (2003). How do we recognise good research? *The Psychologist, 16*(1), 24–27.

Sapsford. R. & Jupp, V. (Eds) (1996). *Data collection & analysis*. London: Sage.

Sarbin, T. (Ed.) (1986). *Narrative psychology: The storied nature of human conduct*. New York: Praeger.

Schneider, K. J. (1998). Toward a science of the heart: Romanticism and the revival of psychology. *American Psychologist, 53,* 277–289.

Schuetz, A. (1998). Autobiographical narratives of good and bad deeds: Defensive and favorable self-description moderated by trait self-esteem. *Journal of Social and Clinical Psychology, 17*(4), 466–475.

Schuman, H., & Presser, S. (1996 [1981]). *Questions and answers in attitude surveys: Experiments on question form, writing and context.* London: Academic Press.

Sedgwick, E. (1990). *The epistemology of the closet.* London: Penguin.

Shadish, W., Cook,T., & Campbell, D. (2002). *Experimental and quasi-experimental designs for generalized causal inference.* Boston: Houghton Miflin.

Shaw, R. (2010). Interpretative phenomenological analysis. In M. A. Forrester (Ed.), *Doing qualitative research in psychology. A practical guide* (pp. 177–201). London: Sage.

Sherliker, L., & Steptoe, A. (2000). Coping with new treatment of cancer: A feasibility study of daily diary measures. *Patient Education and Counseling, 40*(1), 11–19.

Shih, R. A., Schell, T. L., Hambarsoomian, K., Belzberg, H., & Marshall, G. N. (2010). Prevalence of posttraumatic stress disorder and major depression after trauma center hospitalization. *Journal of Trauma, 69*(6), 1560–1566.

Sieverding, M., Decker, S., & Zimmermann, F. (2010). Information about low participation in cancer screening demotivates other people. *Psychological Science, 21*(7), 941–943.

Silverman, D. (Ed.) (2004). *Qualitative research: Theory, method and practice.* London: Sage.

Simpson, M. (Ed.) (1996). *Anti-gay.* London: Freedom Editions.

Singer, J. A. (1997). How recovered memory debates reduce the richness of human identity. *Psychological Inquiry, 8*(4), 325–329.

Singer, J. A. (2004). Narrative identity and meaning making across the adult lifespan: An introduction. *Journal of Personality, 72*(3), 437–460.

Sixsmith, R., & Furnham, A. (2010). A content analysis of British food advertisements aimed at children and adults. *Health Promotion International, 25*(1), 24–32.

Skinner, C., Holt, D., & Smith, T. (1989). *Analysis of complex surveys.* New York: Wiley.

Slater, L. (2004). *Opening Skinner's box: Great psychological experiments of the twentieth century.* New York: W. W. Norton.

Smith, J. A. (1993). The case study. In R. Bayne & P. Nicolson (Eds), *Counselling and Psychology for Health Professionals* (pp. 249–265). London: Chapman & Hall.

Smith, J. A. (1996). Beyond the divide between cognition and discourse: Using interpretative phenomenological analysis in health psychology. *Psychology & Health, 11,* 261–271.

Smith, J. A. (1999). Towards a relational self: Social engagement during pregnancy and psychological preparation for motherhood. *British Journal of Social Psychology, 38,* 409–426.

Smith, J. A. (2003). *Qualitative psychology: A practical guide to methods.* London: Sage.

Smith, J. A. (2004). Reflecting on the development of interpretative phenomenological analysis and its contribution to qualitative research in psychology. *Qualitative Research in Psychology, 1,* 39–54.

Smith, J. A. (2011a). Evaluating the contribution of interpretative phenomenological analysis. *Health Psychology Review, 5,* 9–27.

Smith, J. A. (2011b). Evaluating the contribution of interpretative phenomenological analysis: a reply to the commentaries and further development of criteria. *Health Psychology Review, 5,* 55–61.

Smith, J. A., & Osborn, M. (2008). Interpretative phenomenological analysis. In J. A. Smith (Ed.), *Qualitative psychology. A practical guide to research methods* (2nd edn., pp. 53–80). London: Sage.

Smith, J. A., Flowers, P., & Larkin, M. (2009). *Interpretative Phenomenological Analysis.* London: Sage.

Smith, J. A., Harré, R., & Van Langenhove, L. (1995a). *Rethinking methods in psychology.* London: Sage.

Smith, J. A., Harré, R., & Van Langenhove, L. (1995b). Idiography and the case study. In J. A. Smith, R. Harré & L. Van Langenhove (Eds), *Rethinking psychology* pp. 59–69. London: Sage.

Sokoloswki, R. (2000). *Introduction to phenomenology.* Cambridge: Cambridge University Press.

Spearman, C. (1904). 'General intelligence,' objectively determined and measured. *American Journal of Psychology, 15,* 201–293. Retrieved from http://psychclassics.asu.edu/Spearman/.

Spencer, L., Faulkner, A., & Keegan, J. (1988). *Talking about sex.* London: Social and Community Planning Research.

Stanton, B., Black, M., Laljee, L., & Ricardo, I. (1993). Perceptions of sexual behavior among urban early adolescents: translating theory through focus groups. *Journal of Early Adolescence, 13*(1), 44–66.

Steblay, N. M. (1992). A meta-analytic review of the weapon focus effect. *Law and Human Behavior, 16,* 413–424.

Stedmon, J., & Dallos, R. (2009). *Reflective practice in psychotherapy and counselling.* Maidenhead: Open University Press.

Steptoe, A., & Wardle, J. (1999). Mood and drinking: A naturalistic diary study of alcohol, coffee and tea. *Psychopharmacology, 141*(3), 315–321.

Sternberg, R. J. (1990). *Wisdom: Its nature, origins, and development.* Cambridge, MA: MIT Press.

Sternberg, R. J., & Sternberg, K. (2010). *The psychologist's companion: A guide to writing scientific papers for students and researchers.* New York: Cambridge University Press.

Stevens, S. S. (1946). On the theory of scales of measurement. *Science, 103,* 677–680.

Stewart, D. W., & Shamdasani, P. N. (1990). *Focus groups: Theory and practice.* Newbury Park, CA: Sage.

Steyaert, C., & Bouwen, R. (2004). Group methods of organizational analysis. In C. Cassell & G. Simon (Eds), *Essential guide to 1ualitative methods in organizational research* pp. 140–153. London: Sage.

Stine, W. W. (1989). Meaningful inference: the role of measurement in statistics. *Psychological Bulletin, 105,* 147–155.

Stone, R. A., Maguire, M. G., & Quinn, G. E. (2000). Myopia and ambient night-time lighting. *Nature, 404*(6774), 144.

Strauss, A., & Corbin, J. (1990). *Basics of qualitative research.* London: Sage.

Strauss, A., & Corbin, J. (Eds) (1997). *Grounded theory in practice.* London: Sage.

Strauss, A., & Corbin, J. (1998). *Basics of qualitative research: Techniques and procedures for developing grounded theory* (2nd edn.). Newbury Park, CA: Sage.

Strunk, W. Jr., & White, E. B. (1999). *The elements of style* (4th edn.). Boston: Allyn & Bacon.

Sudman, S., & Bradburn, N. M. (1982). *Asking questions: A practical guide to questionnaire design.* San Francisco: Jossey-Bass.

Tabachnick, B. G., & Fidell, L. S. (2007). *Using multivariate statistics* (5th edn.). Boston: Allyn & Bacon.

Taylor, C. (1985). Self-interpreting animals. In *Philosophical papers: Vol 1. Human agency and language* (pp. 45–76). Cambridge: Cambridge University Press.

Taylor, S. M., Elliot, S., Eyles, J., Frank, J. *et al.* (1991). Psychosocial impacts in populations exposed to solid waste facilities. *Social Science and Medicine, 33,* 441–447.

Teichert, D. (2004). Narrative, identity and the self. *Journal of Consciousness Studies, 11*(10–11), 175–191.

Tesch, R. (1990). *Qualitative research: Analysis types and software tools.* New York: Falmer Press.

Testa, M., Fillmore, M. T., Norris, J., Abbey, A., Curtin, J. J., Kenneth, E. *et al.* (2006). Understanding alcohol expectancy effects: revisiting the placebo condition. *Alcoholism: Clinical And Experimental Research, 30*(2), 339–348.

Thompson, B. (2000). Ten commandments of structural equation modeling. In L. G. Grimm & P. R. Yarnold (Eds), *Reading and understanding more multivariate statistics* (pp. 261–283). Washington, DC: American Psychological Association.

Thompson, B. (2004). *Exploratory and confirmatory factor analysis: Understanding concepts and applications.* Washington, DC: American Psychological Association.

Titchener, E. B. (1905). *Experimental psychology: A manual of laboratory practice. Vol. 2, Qualitative experiments, part 1, Student's Manual.* New York: MacMillan.

Todman, J., & Dugard, P. (2001). *Single-case and small-n experimental designs.* Mahwah, NJ: Erlbaum.

Townsend, J. T., & Ashby, F. G. (1984). Measurement scales and statistics: The misconception misconceived. *Psychological Bulletin, 96,* 394–401.

Tufte, E. R. (2001). *The visual display of quantitative information* (2nd edn.). Cheshire, CT: Graphics Press. Retrieved from http://www. edwardtufte. com/tufte/.

Tufte, E. R. (2003). *The cognitive style of PowerPoint.* Cheshire, CT: Graphics Press.

Tukey, J. W. (1977). *Exploratory data analysis.* Reading, MA: Addison-Wesley.

Turner, B. A., & Pidgeon, N. F. (1997). *Man made disasters* (2nd edn.). Oxford: Butterworth-Heineman.

Turpin, G., Barley, V., Beail, N., Scaife, J., Smith, J. A., & Walsh, S. (1997). Standards for research projects and theses involving qualitative methods: Suggested guidelines for trainees and courses. *Clinical Psychology Forum, 108,* 3–7.

Urbina, S. (2004). *Essentials of psychological testing.* Hoboken, NJ: John Wiley and Sons.

Ussher, J. M., & Mooney-Somers, J. (2000). Negotiating desire and sexual subjectivity: Narratives of young lesbian avengers. *Sexualities, 3*(2), 183–200.

Van der Molen, B. (2000). Relating information needs to the cancer experience. 2. Themes from six cancer narratives. *European Journal of Cancer Care, 9*(1), 48–54.

Van Langenhove, L. (1995). The theoretical foundations of experimental psychology and its alternatives. In J. A. Smith, R. Harré & L. Van Langenhove (Eds), *Rethinking psychology* (pp. 10–23). London: Sage.

Varela, F. J. (1999). The specious present: A neurophenomenology of time consciousness. In J. Petitot, F. J. Varela, B. Pacoud & J. M. Roy (Eds), *Naturalizing phenomenology: Issues in contemporary phenomenology and cognitive science* (pp. 266–316). Stanford, CA: Stanford University Press.

Vetere, A., & Gale, T. (1987). *Ecological studies of family life.* Chichester: Wiley.

Villalba, D. K., & Wright, D. B. (under review). Informational influences on co-witness memory.

von Eye, A. (1990). *Introduction to configural frequency analysis.* Cambridge: Cambridge University Press.

Wainer, H. (1984). How to display data badly. *American Statistician, 38,* 137–147.

Waller, N. G., & Meehl, P. E. (1998). *Multivariate taxometric procedures: Distinguishing types from continua.* Thousand Oaks, CA: Sage.

Wallwork, J., & Dixon, J. A. (2004). Foxes, green fields and Britishness: On the rhetorical construction of place and national identity. *British Journal of Social Psychology, 43,* 21–39.

Wand, M. P. (1997). Data-based choice of histogram bin width. *American Statistician, 51,* 59–64.

Warnock, M. (1987). *Memory.* London: Faber and Faber.

Watzlawick, P. (1964). *An anthology of human communication.* Palo Alto, CA: Science and Behaviour Books.

Watzlawick, P., Beavin, J., & Jackson, D. (1967). *Pragmatics of human communication.* New York: Norton.

Waite, B. M., Claffey, R., & Hillibrand, M. (1998). Differences between volunteers and non-volunteers in a high demand self-recording study. *Psychological Reports, 83*(1), 199–210.

Webster, L., & Mertova, P. (2007). *Using narrative inquiry as a research method.* Routledge: Oxford.

Wellings, K., Branigan, P., & Mitchell, K. (2000). Discomfort, discord and discontinuity as data: Using focus groups to research sensitive topics. *Culture, Health and Sexuality, 2,* 255–267.

Wengraf, T. (2001). *Qualitative research interviewing biographic narrative and semi-structured methods.* London: Sage.

Westfall, R. S. (1983). *Never at rest: A biography of Isaac Newton.* Cambridge: Cambridge University Press.

Wetherell, M. (1998). Positioning and interpretative repertoires: Conversation analysis and post-structuralism in dialogue. *Discourse & Society, 9,* 387–412.

Wetherell, M., & Potter, J. (1992). *Mapping the language of racism: Discourse and the legitimation of exploitation.* Hemel Hempstead: Harvester Wheatsheaf.

Wetherell, M., Taylor, S., & Yates, S. J. (Eds) (2001a). *Discourse theory and practice: A reader.* London: Sage/Open University Press.

Wetherell, M., Taylor, S., & Yates, S. J. (Eds) (2001b). *Discourse as data: A guide for analysis.* London: Sage/Open University Press.

Whyte, W. F. (1943). *Street corner society: The social structure of an Italian slum.* Chicago: University of Chicago Press.

Wiggins, S. (2004). Good for 'you': Generic and individual healthy eating advice in family mealtimes. *Journal of Health Psychology, 9,* 535–548.

Wilkinson, L., & The Task Force on Statistical Inference, APA Board of Scientific Affairs (1999). Statistical methods in psychology journals: Guidelines and explanations. *American Psychologist, 54,* 594–604.

Wilkinson, S. (1998). Focus group methodology: A review. *International Journal of Social Research Methodology, 1,* 181–203.

Wilkinson, S. (2003). Focus groups. In J. A. Smith (Ed.), *Qualitative psychology: A practical guide to research methods* (pp. 184–204). London: Sage.

Wilkinson, S. (2004a). Focus groups. In G. M. Breakwell (Ed.) *Doing social psychology research.* Oxford: Blackwell.

Wilkinson, S. (2004b). Focus group research. In D. Silverman (Ed.), *Qualitative research: Theory, method and practice* (pp. 177–199). London: Sage.

Willig, C. (Ed.) (1999). *Applied discourse analysis: Social and psychological interventions.* Buckingham: Open University Press.

Willig, C. (2001). *Introducing qualitative research in psychology. Adventures in theory and method.* Buckingham: Open University Press.

Willig, C. (2008). *Introducing qualitative research in psychology: Adventures in theory and method* (2nd edn.). Maidenhead: McGraw-Hill/Open University Press.

Wilson, C., & Powell, M. (2003). A guide to interviewing children. *Applied Cognitive Psychology, 17*(2), 249.

Wilson, G. D., & Patterson, J. R. (1968). A new measure of Conservatism. *British Journal of Social and Clinical Psychology, 7*, 264–290.

Winborne, D. G., & Dardaine, R. P. (1993). Affective education for 'at risk' students – the new urban principles. *Urban Review, 15*(2), 139–150.

Wolke, D., Meyer, R., & Gray, P. (1994). Validity of the crying pattern questionnaire in a sample of excessively crying babies. *Journal of Reproductive and Infant Psychology, 12*(2), 105–114.

Wooffitt, R. (2001). Analysing factual accounts. In N. Gilbert (Ed.), *Researching social life* (2nd edn.). London: Sage.

Wright, D. B. (1997). *Understanding statistics: An introduction for the social sciences.* London: Sage.

Wright, D. B., Horry, R., & Skagerberg, E. M. (2009). Functions for traditional and multilevel approaches to signal detection theory. *Behavior Research Methods, 41*, 257–267.

Wright, D. B., & London, K. (2009). *First (and second) steps in statistics* (2nd ed). London: Sage.

Wutich, A., Lant, T., White, D, Larson, K., & Gartin, M. (2010). Comparing focus group and individual responses on sensitive topics: A study of water decision-makers in a desert city. *Field Methods, 22*, 88–110.

Yardley, L. (2000). Dilemmas in qualitative health research. *Psychology & Health, 15*, 215–228.

Yardley, L. (2008). Demonstrating validity in qualitative psychology. In J. A. Smith (Ed.), *Qualitative psychology. A practical guide to research methods* (pp. 235–251). London: Sage.

Yin, R. K. (2003). *Case study research: Design and methods* (3rd edn.). Thousand Oaks, CA: Sage.

Yurtal, F., & Artut, K. (2010). An investigation of school violence through Turkish children's drawings. *Journal of Interpersonal Violence, 25*(1), 50–62.

Zahavi, D. (2008). *Subjectivity and selfhood. Investigating the first-person perspective.* Cambridge, MA: MIT Press.

Ziller, R. C. (2000). Self-counselling through re-authored photo self narratives. *Counselling Psychology Quarterly, 13*(3), 265–278.

Index

INTRODUCTORY NOTE

References such as "178–9" indicate (not necessarily continuous) discussion of a topic across a range of pages. Wherever possible in the case of topics with many references, these have either been divided into sub-topics or only the most significant discussions of the topic are listed. Because the entire work is about 'research methods' and 'psychology' the use of these terms (and certain others which occur constantly throughout the book) as entry points has been restricted. Information will be found under the corresponding detailed topics.